American Pop

American Pop

Popular Culture Decade by Decade

VOLUME 1
1900–1929

Edited by Bob Batchelor

GREENWOOD PRESS
Westport, Connecticut • London

Library of Congress Cataloging-in-Publication Data

American pop : popular culture decade by decade / Bob Batchelor, set editor.
    p. cm.
    Includes bibliographical references and index.
    ISBN 978–0–313–34410–7 (set : alk. paper)—ISBN 978–0–313–36412–9 (v. 1 : alk. paper)—
ISBN 978–0–313–36414–3 (v. 2 : alk. paper)—ISBN 978–0–313–36416–7 (v. 3 : alk. paper)—
ISBN 978–0–313–36418–1 (v. 4 : alk. paper) 1. Popular culture—United States.
2. United States—Civilization.   3. National characteristics, American.   I. Batchelor, Bob.
  E169.1.A4475 2009
  973—dc22   2008036699

British Library Cataloguing in Publication Data is available.

Library of Congress Catalog Card Number: 2008036699
ISBN: 978–0–313–34410–7 (set)
        978–0–313–36412–9 (vol 1)
        978–0–313–36414–3 (vol 2)
        978–0–313–36416–7 (vol 3)
        978–0–313–36418–1 (vol 4)

First published in 2009

Greenwood Press, 88 Post Road West, Westport, CT 06881
An imprint of Greenwood Publishing Group, Inc.
www.greenwood.com

Printed in the United States of America

The paper used in this book complies with the
Permanent Paper Standard issued by the National
Information Standards Organization (Z39.48–1984).

10 9 8 7 6 5 4 3 2 1

Contents

8/09

1910s

1920s

Foreword: Popular Culture's Roots Run Deep

Ray B. Browne

Ray and Pat Browne Popular Culture Library
Bowling Green State University, Bowling Green, Ohio

Although *American Pop* focuses on popular culture as it developed in the twentieth century, it is critical that readers understand that most of these topics did not spring to life without roots running deep into the nation's past. In today's fast-paced, computer-dominated society, it is easy to forget history and innovation because so much of American idealism is based on looking toward the bright future. We are a nation obsessed with the idea that better days are on the horizon.

What one discovers when examining the development of culture over the course of the twentieth century is that each innovation builds off a predecessor. America has always had a popular culture, although what that means might change with each new technological breakthrough, national craze, or demographic shift. And, while defining culture is not an easy task, it can be seen as a kind of living entity. Similar to a growing garden, culture is the gatherings of community beliefs and behaviors, which depends on its roots for sustenance. As the plants grow both individually and collectively, they develop and influence the surrounding societies.

People in Colonial America, for example, had their cultural roots deeply implanted from the cultures of the lands from which they emigrated, but every people or group of individuals must harmonize the old with the new in order to justify one's culture. The unifying themes that emerged from the development of a new national culture enabled people to make sense of the world and their relationship to it. American colonists, therefore, adjusted to the old-world cultures of the people who were already settling the nation, while at the same time creating a new popular culture based on their lives as members of the new country.

The harmonization of the new with the old might be called *folk-pop* or *pop-folk* because the result led to a new everyday culture. This evolution is a neverending process in which the new is blended with the old and a new is born. Human nature demands cultural and individual cooperation for safety and advancement, which it achieves in various ways. Inventions and discoveries, for example, are not as helpful in shaping cultures as are innovation and dissemination of those inventions and discoveries. Culture must speak to its constituencies in their vernacular before it can be understood and fully appreciated. Cultures both lead and follow cultural politics, policies, and social movements.

The fields of entertainment from which the colonists could draw were rich: traveling acrobats, jugglers, circuses of various kinds, animal shows, "magic lantern" shows, group or individual singers, Black "Olios" (one-act specialities), drinking houses, card games, and other group activities.

In the conventional forms of culture development certain figures stand tall. Benjamin Franklin, after his move to Philadelphia, contributed in various ways through his writings in *Poor Richard's Almanac* (1732–1757) and others. He stated that his highest admiration was for "the people of this province...chiefly industrious farmers, artificers [skilled craftsmen] or men in trade [who] are fond of freedom." Inventor of the lightning rod and the Franklin Stove, and many more technological and cultural innovations, no one did more to advance popular culture in these early days than Franklin. In the twenty-first century, one finds similar figures who are much revered for their ability to create. Steve Jobs, Apple founder and executive, is a modern day Franklin in many respects, inventing products that transform popular culture, while at the same time, cementing his place in that history.

Less comprehensive but far more inflammatory were the political contributions of Thomas Paine (1737–1809). On January 10, 1776, he published *Common Sense* and sold it for a few cents so that everybody could own a copy. In a few months no fewer than 500,000 copies had been sold. Another of his great contributions was *The American Crisis,* which opens with the fiery words, "These are the times that try men's souls." Paine intuited and valued the power of the popular culture and wrote his works as if by a common citizen for other common citizens. Today's Thomas Paines may be the countless citizen journalists, primarily Internet-based, blogging, posting, and carrying out the kind of agenda Paine advocated. The writer turned to pamphlets as a method of keeping down price, just as today's bloggers use inexpensive tools to reach audiences nationwide.

Another powerful voice in popular culture was Harriet Beecher Stowe. Through *Uncle Tom's Cabin* (1852) Stowe alerted the public to the evils of slavery (with the help of the Almighty, in her words). After the enormous success of the work, the author claimed that God had dictated the book, with her merely writing down His words. Regardless of these claims, for the next 50 years the work was performed on stages worldwide more frequently than any other play in English (with the possible exception of Shakespeare's collected works).

A little more than a century later, racism still plagued the nation, but instead of being represented by a novel, two charismatic leaders took center stage. Dr. Martin Luther King Jr. and Malcolm X stood at opposite poles in the fight for equality, King preaching nonviolence, while Malcolm advocated "by any means necessary." As powerful as these leaders were, however, they became icons after their assassinations. As a result, their images transcend who they were as leaders, attaining a kind of immortality as popular culture figures.

Colonists loved professional plays. The first such presentation in America was "Ye Beare and Ye Cubbin Accomac County" staged in Virginia in 1665. The first theater in the Colonies was built in Williamsburg, Virginia, sometime between 1716 and 1718. *Romeo and Juliet* may have been presented in New York City in 1730 and *Richard III* in 1750, in addition to Williamsburg a year later. In 1752 the Charleston, South Carolina, theater presented 58 different offerings, including Shakespeare. Fourteen of Shakespeare's plays were staged 150 times in pre-Revolutionary Virginia, and from the 1850s to the Civil War Shakespeare was performed in all the major cities and several small ones.

For the second half of the nineteenth century one of the distributors of popular culture was widespread black-faced minstrelsy—thousands of such dramatics were presented on stage by whites with faces blackened by charcoal. No one can identify exactly when and why the first Negro minstrel show became so popular. Some authorities suggest that African Americans seem to be natural-born entertainers. Others are firm in their belief that the minstrel show flourished because blacks saw it as a means of social equality with whites who otherwise held them in slavery.

Minstrelsy was in its heyday from 1830 to 1870. So-called songsters, cheap songbooks running from 20 to some 50 pages and selling for 10–50 cents, were the main distributors of minstrel pieces, as well as songs from other sources. During the popularity of the minstrel show there were more than 100 shows running and some 2,000 songsters distributing at least 20,000 songs. Not all minstrel shows were black-on-white. Some were black-on-black, after black actors realized that white shows were exploiting them and they could in fact create their own shows. Minstrel shows were later eclipsed by vaudeville.

From these beginnings, one can trace the origins of Tin Pan Alley, which helped launch ragtime and jazz. In addition, the songsters and minstrel shows initiated a kind of crossover success that became the gold standard in the music business. "Crossing over," or scoring hit records in different genres, would come to define many of the industry's biggest stars from Elvis Presley and Johnny Cash to Chuck Berry and Little Richard.

The most enduring form of popular culture is the printed page, even though some observers feel that books, magazines, and newspapers are doomed in the Internet age. Books in particular, though, carry a special place in peoples' hearts, not only as tools for learning but as objects of affection. Many readers simply like to hold a book in their hands and feel the pages glide through their fingers. Even the most ardent techie does not get the same emotional lift from reading text on a screen, whether a laptop or hand-held device.

The most influential literary form breaching the gap between the nineteenth and twentieth centuries has been the detective story. This form of literature has from its beginning satisfied deep interests of large groups. From the earliest times, people have wanted answers to the mysteries of life that keeps us continually looking back at history. Our fascination with the archaeological and anthropological past, for example, leads many to believe in monsters such as Big-Foot (Sasquatch) and the Loch Ness Monster. Many small towns and local villages have similar folktales of creatures frequenting dark mountains, forests, and deep lakes. Today, this love affair with fear and the unknown drives much of the current film and television industries. From the low budget sensation *The Blair Witch Project* to big budget movies filled with blood and gore, people thrive on their imaginations resulting from a collective indoctrination to fear.

These prehistoric beings supposedly living among us also help keep alive the mysteries and manifestations of the past, delivering some kind of answer in the form of explanations and comforting conclusions. Histories and mysteries need what scholar Russel Nye called a "hook" to keep readers on the edge of their curiosity. But mysteries search more deeply into human existence and help explain us to ourselves. Einstein was certainly right when he said, "The most beautiful thing we can experience is the mysterious. It is the source of all true art and science." The enticement of the mysterious is a never fading light in the darkness of life's many anxieties.

Literary interest in horror developed in Europe in Mary Shelley's *Frankenstein* (1818) and pushed ahead vigorously in the *Memoirs* of Francois Eugene Vidocq, a reformed French thief who joined the police force and electrified Europe with publication of his underground activities in 1829. Edgar Allan Poe (1809–1849) caught the imagination of Americans beginning with *Murders in the Rue Morgue* (1841). Film scholars see Poe's writing inspiring the American film noir movement in the 1940s, 1950s, and 1960s.

The coals ignited by the interest in mystery and drama glowed especially in the publication of the adventures of Sherlock Holmes and Dr. Watson in 1887. Many Americans tried their pens at the art. Mark Twain published several works in the type, for instance, but found little success. But the door into the riches of mysteries had been opened to authors and readers of the twenty-first century. Mystery, having metamorphosed through the broadened titles of "Crime Fiction" and lately "Novels of Suspense," is the most popular form of fiction today, and is being used by historians for the true human emotions and actions contained in them. Historians a century or more from now may find themselves doing the same with the novels of Stephen King or James Patterson, novelists who sell millions of books, yet are taken less seriously by the cultural elite because they do so well.

One of the results of popular culture's interest in the make-believe and distortion of the minstrel show was the literary hoax, which flourished in such works as Poe's "Balloon Hoax," published in the *New York Sun* on April 13, 1844, an account of eight men crossing the Atlantic in a large balloon held up by coal gas. Others include Mark Twain's "The Petrified Man" (one of several by him), in which a character is discovered with his thumb on his nose in the timeless insulting gesture—the credulous public does not recognize the joke.

Other real-life hoaxes cropped up on every street corner. P.T. Barnum (1810–1891), famous for working under the philosophy that there's a sucker born every minute, opened his American Museum of Freaks in New York City, exhibiting all kinds of freaks and captivating the public especially with his Cardiff Giant, a plaster duplicate of the discovery on a farm outside Cardiff, New York. It was 10 feet long and weighed 3,000 pounds and had been proven a hoax, but still fascinated the public. The hoax, literary or physical, fed the American dreams of freedom and expansion and was an example of the American dream of personal fulfillment.

Another stalk growing from the same root included the works of the so-called Southwest humorists, who carried on in their stories and language the literature of the hoax. David Ross Locke (Petroleum V. Nasby), Henry Wheeler Show (Josh Billings), and George Washington and his Sut Lovingood stories created exaggerated physical and linguistic caricatures of their fellow citizens in a world they expected and hoped would be recognized as hoaxes. Instead of laughable hoaxes, however, they created a world of reality that is carried over in American popular culture today. The stereotype of the illiterate Southerner has a central role in the twenty-first century, particularly in television sit-coms and movies. The standup routines of Jeff Foxworthy and Larry the Cable Guy are built around the premise of the South being strangely (although often lovingly) different than the rest of the nation.

Another popular form of literature developed out of the idea of the hoax—graphic caricature and literature. Although the caricature had been common from the earliest days of America, the so-called common caricature known as the comic strip narrative, developed by the Swiss cartoonist Rodolphe Topfer in 1846, was probably introduced into America in the *San Francisco Examiner* on February 16, 1896, as "The Yellow Kid." Since then most newspapers have run their series of comic pages in the United States and abroad—especially in Japan, where they are read by all members of a family under the name *anime*. They are likewise pervasive in American (and world) culture, especially in animation, movies, and advertising, particularly when used to pitch products to children and young people.

Because of our growing knowledge of and interest in archaeology and anthropology, our interest in the 6,000 or so languages spoken worldwide, and the suspicion that humanity may be doomed to future space travel and colonization, more works are developing in comics and movies of the extreme past and the imaginative future. Such comic strips and books, now called graphic novels, to a certain extent feed on the hoax works of the nineteenth century and intellectually are not rocket science, as we freely admit.

Many of the ideas and artwork in today's comic books are useful in understanding modern popular culture and its influence. For example, graphic novels have been published for both political parties in the 2008 presidential campaigns. Furthermore, many of the ideas and artwork are highly suggestive to the genuine rocket scientist, and the art work is highly prized for its newness of ideas and execution of detail by comic book aficionados. One original picture of Mickey Mouse, for example, recently sold for $700,000. Many comic book fans live in a world of their own making, but to a certain extent in America's broad, rich, and complicated popular culture, each area is something of an island of culture all its own, justifying its existence.

Just as English poet William Wordsworth said that the child is father to the man, so a culture in one form and one power or another is always a product and variant of its predecessors. It grows and alters or breaks down the restrictions of its sometimes elite, sometimes popular predecessors as the force of the new development becomes overwhelming and suggestive. Sometimes the popular culture grows and sometimes fades, but, although it may diminish in use and memory, it seldom disappears. Popular culture is like animated wall murals and graffiti that permanently etches a record of the lifeblood of a culture of the moment.

The cornucopia of twentieth-century present and developing American popular culture has resulted from the free flow of opportunity provided by its predecessors. So it was up to the last century. The garden of popular culture seemed to the culture traditionalist a patch of weeds overwhelming the flowers. But a new culture in the process of finding and developing itself was not crowded. The new cultures were driven by the changing dynamic of a new people in a new land with opportunities for all men and women to live by and in the cultures they both desired and found satisfactory. Suggestions and opportunities will continue to be found and developed.

The power of the twentieth century continues to develop in the twenty-first as the richest and most energetic culture so far produced continues to flourish—sometimes to the bewilderment and consternation of the citizenry, but always irresistibly, Americans and non-Americans—as long as human nature insists that it wants or needs something new, improved, or just different and finds it in America. Popular culture is the voice of a worldwide, but especially American, growing insistence on democracy in all aspects of life, and the voices of the people—especially in America—will continue to flourish, be creative, and heard.

From the beginning, American popular culture, given a virgin land in which to grow, has developed fully and rapidly. Its influence has been especially forceful domestically and globally in the twentieth century as a result of its growth in the preceding century in the arts and extended cultures. American popular culture impacts the cultures of the world everyday, creating and resolving tensions that are labeled "Created and Made in America." In the popular cultural world in all its manifestations the most influential label on world life at the present is and in the future will be "Lived in America."

Preface

American Pop: Popular Culture Decade by Decade provides a survey of popular culture across America from 1900 to the present and presents the heart and soul of America, acting as a unifying bridge across time and bringing together generations of diverse backgrounds. Whether looking at the bright lights of the Jazz Age in the 1920s, the rock 'n' roll and lifestyle revolutions of the 1960s and 1970s, or the thriving social networking Web sites of today, each period in America's cultural history develops its own unique take on the qualities that define our lives. *American Pop* is a four-volume set that examines the trends and events across decades and eras by shedding light on the experiences of Americans young and old, rich and poor, along with the influences of arts, entertainment, sports, and other cultural forces.

Based partly on Greenwood's "American Popular Culture through History" series, this four-volume set is designed to give students and general readers a broad and inter-disciplinary overview of the numerous aspects of popular culture. Each of the topical chapters stands alone as a testament to the individual decade, yet taken together, they offer an integrated history and allow readers to make connections among each of the decades. Of course, this organization also encourages readers to compare the sometimes striking differences among decades.

WHAT'S INCLUDED IN *AMERICAN POP*

The volumes in this set cover the following chronological periods.

- Volume 1, 1900–1929
- Volume 2, 1930–1959
- Volume 3, 1960–1989
- Volume 4, 1990–Present

Each volume, in turn, covers the popular culture of the decades through chapters focused on specific areas of popular culture, including:

An Overview of the Decade	Fashion
Advertising	Food
Architecture	Music
Books, Newspapers, Magazines, and Comics	Sports and Leisure
	Travel
Entertainment	Visual Arts

In addition, each group of chapters is preceded by a timeline of events for the decade, which gives extra oversight and context to the study of the period.

Sidebars and Other Features

Within many of the chapters, the text is supplemented by sidebars that feature the significant, fascinating, troubling, or just plain weird people, trends, books, movies, radio and television programs, advertisements, places, and events of the decade. In addition sidebars provide lists of new words and phrases for the decade; new foods introduced during the decade; and "How Others See Us," information on how people outside of the United States adopted, reacted to, or disdained American popular culture. The chapters are enhanced with photos and illustrations from the period. Each volume closes with a Resource Guide, providing selected books, articles, Web sites, and videos for further research.

The appendices feature "The Cost of Products"—which spans from 1900 to the present and shows the prices of selected items from food to clothing to furniture—and a list of potential classroom resources of activities and assignments for teachers to use in a school setting. A carefully selected general bibliography for the set, covering popular culture resources of a general or sizeable nature, rounds out the final volume. A comprehensive index offers access to the entire set.

ACKNOWLEDGMENTS

American Pop is an audacious project that pulls together more than one million words about popular culture in the twentieth and twenty-first centuries. A series like this one owes a large debt to many wonderful authors, researchers, writers, and editors. First and foremost, my deepest gratitude goes out to Ray B. Browne, the series editor of the original "American Popular Culture through History" books. Like so many other popular culture scholars over the past several decades, I owe Ray more than I could ever hope to repay.

I would also like to thank all of the authors who poured their collective hearts into the series: David Blanke, Kathleen Drowne, Patrick Huber, William H. Young, Nancy K. Young, Robert Sickels, Edward J. Rielly, Kelly Boyer Sagert, Scott Stoddart, and Marc Oxoby. Their work provides the backbone of this collection. Several excellent writers contributed to the more than 300 sidebars that appear throughout this set: Mary Kay Linge, Ken Zachmann, Martha Whitt, Micah L. Issitt, Josef Benson, Cindy Williams, Joy Austin, Angelica Benjamin, Peter Lazazzaro, Jillian Mann, Vanessa Martinez, Jessica Schultz, Jessica Seriano, and Brie Tomaszewski.

Not even Superman could edit a collection like *American Pop* without a superstar team of editors. I have been lucky to benefit from the wisdom and leadership skills of

Kristi Ward and Anne Thompson throughout the project. *American Pop* would not exist without their enthusiasm, hard work, and dedication. Thanks also to Cindy Williams for her original editing of the project. She is wonderful.

My great honor in editing *American Pop* has been picking up where Ray left off. I have had the pleasure of writing three books in the series, so all told, I have spent more than five years of my life with this series. My sincere thanks go to my parents, Jon and Linda Bowen, and my brother Bill Coyle for their support. As always, my wife, Kathy, has lived this collection with me. I appreciate her sense of humor, sound advice, and thoughtfulness. My whole heart belongs to our daughter Kassie. Her smile, hugs, and kisses were always awesome diversions from writing and editing.

Bob Batchelor
University of South Florida
Tampa, Florida

Introduction

In the early decades of the twentieth century, popular culture in the United States transformed as its focal point shifted from its traditional European roots to a uniquely American perspective. The nation stood at a critical crossroads. On one hand, the United States grew rapidly into a military and economic superpower, which forced an even more intimate relationship with the rest of the world. The country's cultural development, however, had to catch up by breaking from its fascination with Europe, instead emphasizing its "Americanness"—a popular culture distinct and unique from that of the Old World.

The newfound focus on American culture from American sources enabled the country to culturally stand on its own. From naturalist literature and homegrown jazz music to architecture that pointed skyward and the development of sports distinct from Europe, the United States created its own culture in the first three decades of the new era. The changes were profound and long-lasting, essentially laying the groundwork for what would later be described as "the American Century."

Popular culture stood at the heart of the nation's development in the early twentieth century. Despite being difficult to define because of its nebulous nature, popular culture served as a type of unifying system. Using popular culture as a guidepost, people navigated among one another, using its symbols, representations, and ideas to make sense of the world. While the large-scale influences on people's lives were often difficult to understand or interpret, popular culture provided something of a common language—critical in a time when immigration led a population explosion. From 1900 to 1929, these signposts ranged from discussions of social criticism in movies by Charlie Chaplain or D. W. Griffith to the Jazz Age tales of author F. Scott Fitzgerald. They were serial radio programs and Model T Fords and everything in between.

In addition to forming a uniquely American culture, the power of popular culture enabled society to begin the long journey toward overcoming barriers such as race, class, wealth, education, and profession. Of course, this trek did not take place without pain and struggle—the evil forces of hatred and bigotry ran deep in the nation's historical roots. And, at the same time, the gap between wealthy individuals and the rest of the nation grew exponentially. All this led to a volatility that, while not unprecedented, wondered far astray from what most people assumed to be the American Dream.

This entanglement of the American Dream and popular culture became deeply knotted in the national psyche. The steadfast belief in the power of this idea enabled people to trudge on, even during times of cataclysmic change, such as World War I, and emerge from such an epic event ready to take on the new day. This feeling in itself is wholly American—continually assessing the past for lessons and guideposts, while simultaneously peering into the future for glimpses of what may be soon to come.

So, what was popular culture in this early twentieth-century period? On the surface, the combination of technological innovations, a strong economy, military and international might, and strong leadership across a number of fields propelled America's cultural growth like a shot from a cannon.

Through the lens of popular culture, the American people found a way to interpret themselves and the world around them. Sometimes, this meant that people willingly allowed themselves to be blinded to reality. A fascination with the latest motion pictures, radio, or celebrity gossip, made it easier to put off thoughts of war, economic disparity, and melancholy. At other times, however, popular culture educated and infused a sense of unity in people that did not really previously exist. As a result, popular culture—literally the study of what influences people as they conduct their daily lives—regularly served as a force for reinterpreting and changing the world. Or, it could be used to mask reality in favor of a Hollywood dream-factory version of life that emphasized happy endings and rainbows.

The challenge in analyzing American popular culture in the early twentieth century or any other timeframe is finding a technique to simultaneously capture the broadness of the field, while at the same time limiting the survey to keep it manageable. One way to achieve this balance is to look at an era thematically. Breaking popular culture into broad categories enables an integrated perspective to bubble to the surface, yet still enabling the nuances of each individual event to shine.

By examining popular culture within categories of leaders, money, innovation, and culture, an overview of the issues driving everyday America from 1900 to 1929 will emerge. From a broad perspective, these forces transform society almost the same way wind changes local or regional weather—most of the time invisibly, yet powerfully, but in other instances with force and intensity. Therefore, while popular culture is ever-shifting, the often undetected forces of technology, economics, political systems, and culture are working their magic on the system. All the roots of popular culture trace back to these forces.

One must acknowledge, however, that the choice to divide a field as broad as popular culture into these subcategories is deliberate. During the era under examination, for example, change took place regardless of whether one realized that a broader series of technological innovations were transforming the nation. A historical perspective makes it much easier to recognize these forces driving change, which may or may not have been discernable at the time.

Many instances of pop culture transformation, in fact, blur the lines between these topics. At what point, for instance, does the automobile move from a technological wonder developed through the force of will of a great leader to become a cultural topic? Did the car become Americana when Henry Ford dropped the price of the Model T to make it affordable to middle-class citizens or when the car became a central focus of movies and literature?

At its essence, however, popular culture is about context. It may be difficult, if not impossible, to statistically measure the impact of Theodore Roosevelt on the cultural development of the 1900s, but understanding his leadership does provide the framework for grasping the broader meaning of culture during his tenure as an iconic political leader.

The ability to examine the actions of the government or a particular leader or group of leaders is arguably the most positive aspect of popular culture. Rooted in free speech, the rise of mass media enabled Americans to criticize their leaders and institutions, thus opening new opportunities for collective education and information. For example, advertising, films, literature, and songs that examined the "new woman" in the 1910s led a more intelligent view of women's rights and the suffrage movement.

As millions of Americans interacted with mass media, whether watching the same movies or listening to radio programs, a common language developed that opened lines of communications between disparate groups. The downside to this unintended focus on mass communications, some argued, was that a growing fascination with pop culture actually diverted attention from important challenges the nation faced, ultimately serving as a kind of placebo. Therefore, popular culture enabled people to feel good about the world around them without really forcing them to directly confront critical issues.

LEADERS

Placing an individual leader at the head of a movement is a standard way to examine historical periods, such as "The Age of Roosevelt" or "The Babe Ruth Era" in the early twentieth century. Often these designations are warranted, particularly when the development of a truly American popular culture seemingly occurred foisted up on the back of an individual leader who symbolized wider transformations taking place. President Roosevelt, for example, served as one of these early trendsetters, dominating political and cultural life in the United States for more than a decade. Later, in the 1920s, New York Yankees slugger Babe Ruth changed the way the public viewed athletes, becoming a national cultural icon.

Although towering figures receive the limelight, more often it is a confluence of different forces that enable an iconic individual to dominate an age. In the 1920s, for example, Americans began their longstanding love affair with sports like never before. A closer look at the reasons behind the change reveals a complex series of factors that more or less pushed people toward sports figures that went beyond the charisma of individual athletes, such as baseball's Ruth or boxing champion Jack Dempsey. These compelling figures certainly deserve the spotlight, however, the context runs deeper.

In the 1920s, for instance, greater numbers of people across class divisions enjoyed increasing amounts of leisure time. For members of the middle and working classes, a significant drop in working hours (from about 60 hours weekly to 45) transformed free time. At the same time, wages increased. Families took vacations more often. The combination of greater free time and more disposable income funneled money into the blossoming entertainment complex. Between 1919 and 1929, American spending on recreation and leisure almost doubled to reach $4 billion a year. The nation would not eclipse this figure again until after World War II. The combination of middle class prosperity and family leisure time, as a result, deserves as much credit for the burgeoning fixation on celebrity culture as do the era's towering figures.

MONEY

Early in the 1900s, Senator Albert J. Beveridge of Indiana looked out over the nation and declared American prosperity a divine right. In his eyes, God granted America preeminence as His "chosen people" who would "lead in the regeneration of the world." Within the boundaries of this global stewardship, Beveridge claimed, the divine mission "holds for us all the profit, all the glory, all the happiness possible to man. We are trustees of the world's progress, guardians of its righteous peace." Mixing profit, prosperity, and progress, Beveridge spoke to the keystones of American exceptionalism.

Although it is impossible to ignore the bombastic egotism in Beveridge's statements, this kind of sentiment took root in the American populace. People believed in the blossoming power of the United States to right the wrongs of Old World Europe. For countless millions of immigrants streaming into the country at the time, America represented a fresh beginning and a chance to live a better life. Equating progress and economic prosperity painted a vivid picture of the opportunity America held for its people. His remarks reached an audience of fervent believers in the power of the young nation to thrive and prosper.

As a result, it is in this early period of the twentieth century that the idea of an American Dream solidified. Subsequently, for much of the timeframe covered in this volume, the nation rode a steady wave of optimism prompted in large part by its economic power. People believed in the American Dream and continued to, even during the darkest days of World War I and the Great Depression.

Few monuments spoke more directly to America's obsession with money and technology than its booming corporate skyscrapers. Business headquarters like the Woolworth Building in New York City emerged as bold expressions of the nation's power and influence in the early years of the new century. President Woodrow Wilson, a savvy observer of American culture, dubbed the Woolworth Building the "Cathedral of Commerce."

Frank Woolworth used his own cash to finance the Gothic-inspired Woolworth Building (designed by famed architect Cass Gilbert), a 57-story symbol of the nation's capitalist success. Ironically, the skyscraper was paid for from profits derived from Woolworth's chain of five-and-dime discount stores that catered to working class folks.

At the same time, New York City grew into the skyscraper capitol of the world, emphasizing the city's importance in global finance and power as architects paid homage to the city vertically. From 1900 to the early 1930s, one or more new skyscrapers appeared in New York City each year. Designers responded by continually pushing the envelope a bit further in their yearning to maximize space above city streets.

Tall buildings had a sweeping impact on the psyche of the nation. On the most mundane level, tall buildings merely served as advertisements for their owners. In many respects, however, the appearance of skyscrapers marked a rite of passage for cities across the nation. Soon, a downtown area had to have a signature skyscraper or several to make its case for being a real city. They reflected the power of the United States and the modern technological age.

Yet, skyscrapers also catered to romanticism. Looking at beautiful buildings that confronted the limits of height and imagination caused excitement and invoked feelings of awe. Places such as Chicago's Tribune Tower and New York's Chrysler Building served as more than mere office complexes. Tourists flocked to them as destinations. They became landmarks and part of the city's identity. People took pride in the architecture of *their* cities, while the most famous tall buildings served as backdrops for films and novels, as well as songs and skits. Skyscrapers represented America's economic power, defined its cities, and, in some senses, what it meant to be an American.

INNOVATION

In American vernacular, innovation is usually equated with technological progress. What begins as a focus on mechanical evolution, however, soon take on both cultural and economic consequences. The shift from quirky idea or seemingly divine inspiration to booming business or corporate powerhouse happens in a flash, whether it is Thomas Edison's invention and development of the telephone or Milton S. Hershey's manufacturing and marketing of the first American-made chocolate bars.

The early decades of the twentieth century witnessed a flood of new technologies that transformed life culturally, economically, and technologically. For example, the combination of Henry Ford's assembly line with the scientific management studies of Frank and Lillian Gilbreth turned the idea of automated manufacturing on its ear. Developed late in the nineteenth century, the automobile improved quickly over the next three decades. The transformation from gimmick to American cultural touchstone occurred in this era. The ripple effects of Ford's ingenuity were felt for decades across all aspects of American society and arguably into the next century as well.

Looking into the future, Ford declared that he would "democratize the automobile." The fusion of scientific management and piecemeal assembly line production enabled Ford to revolutionize the automobile industry. Between 1908 and 1925 more than 15 million Model T Fords rolled off the assembly line. The democratization took hold as Ford's emphasis on volume sales permitted him to slash the cost of the car, from $950 in 1909 to just $290 in 1925. Other manufacturers benefited from the national car craze initiated by Ford. By 1929 annual automobile production reached 5.3 million in the United States, a figure that would not be surpassed for 20 years.

In Jazz Age America, young socialites and urban hipsters viewed cars as a trendy accessory. Behind the wheel, they could escape the prying eyes of their elders and melt into the romanticism snazzy cars represented. The image of the automobile fell into the hands of brilliant marketing strategists and sophisticated advertisers who offered seduction as a selling feature. Offering new, improved models each year, the manufacturers appealed to the fickle nature of the newly wealthy and gave advertisers selling points. The automobile companies spent millions of dollars on magazine and newspaper ads.

The downside of innovation also became apparent rather quickly. In the case of automobiles, the vicious cycle of increased sales meant more congestion. Local, state, and federal governmental agencies had to build roads to accommodate all the new drivers. Reckless driving, accidents, and fatalities necessitated larger police forces and changed the way hospitals operated. Early drivers were notoriously bad. About 33,000 people died in automobile accidents in 1930, the majority pedestrians hit by vehicles.

Urban dwellers faced a seemingly endless amount of congestion, noise, and pollution at the hands of automobiles. Cars also changed rural America, introducing pollution and litter, while prompting advertisers to construct giant billboards to sell wares to those out for a leisurely Sunday drive. The era saw an increase in suburban living as middle class professionals opted out of city congestion for the bucolic lifestyle offered a short drive away. In 1923, the nation's first suburban shopping center opened in Kansas City, Missouri, called Country Club Plaza. Soon, similar plazas dotted the countryside, catering to the needs of families in the suburbs.

Revolutionary changes took place as the automobile came to occupy a central role in American popular culture. The national love affair with cars took hold quickly and developed into a defining feature of how Americans viewed themselves. Within three short decades, the automobile moved from technological wizardry to cultural icon—the kind of evolution that one witnesses over and over again in popular culture. Cars moved from invention to innovation to industry to iconic status seemingly overnight.

CULTURE

People in the twenty-first century believe that time moves faster based on the speed of the Internet, perhaps never considering the consequences of early innovations on society. The development of mass media during the early twentieth century decades, for example, played a significant role in altering the pace of life. Most visitors from 50 years earlier would have found life in the early twentieth century altogether too frenzied and chaotic. This early period is one that permanently changed the speed at which society operated.

People not only moved faster via automobiles and trains crisscrossing the nation, but the very notion of sound changed as commercial radio infiltrated one's life. During the Jazz Age, popular music broadcasts served as the core radio programming, generally broadcasting live performances in-studio or at offsite locations, such as concert halls and hotel ballrooms.

Similar to what took place in many other industries, as the booming radio business opened new avenues for companies to make money, corporations formed to gain a competitive advantage over smaller entities. The National Broadcasting Company (NBC) formed in 1926, while a year later Columbia Broadcasting Systems (CBS) joined the fray. The networks featured corporate-sponsored programming, such as *The Palmolive Hour* and *The Voice of Firestone*. By 1930, 51 million listeners tuned in each night to listen to the radio. The nation's major corporations saw the power in reaching mass audiences and partnered with the radio networks to appeal to potential consumers.

The business industry also had a stake in the development of radio. It did not take long for music producers to realize the power of sound. People responded to great songs and performers by purchasing the phonograph recording and/or accompanying sheet music. The union of media, culture, and commerce established the framework for how the entertainment industry worked.

By the late 1920s, more than 100 million moviegoers viewed films each week. In response, Tin Pan Alley publishing firms produced songs for motion pictures. People flocked to see the first talking movie, *The Jazz Singer* (1927), giving further impetus to integrating music and film. For the next step in the evolution, producers made lavish, big-budget musicals that appealed to people's love of sound and motion together. Metro-Golwyn-Mayer's *The Broadway Melody* (1929) won the Academy Award for Best Picture, the first musical to achieve the honor.

Music played a central role in people's lives. The union of radio, movies, and records proved how vital sound had become. Record sales alone skyrocketed in the 1920s, topping 110 million disks (78 rpm, selling for 35–75 cents), up 400 percent from the 1914 figure. Soon, singers and band leaders churning out hit records became brand names themselves. Paul Whiteman and His Orchestra filled the top spot among dance bands in the 1920s, while veteran vaudeville singer, dancer, and showman Al Jolson became a national celebrity, dubbing himself "the World's Greatest Entertainer." After charting a dozen Number One hits in the decade, Jolson transitioned into one of Hollywood's biggest attractions, starring in both *The Jazz Singer* and *The Singing Fool* (1929).

In his 1905 presidential inaugural address, Theodore Roosevelt commented on "modern life," explaining that it was "both complex and intense." Furthermore, he said, "the tremendous changes wrought by the extraordinary industrial development of the last half century are felt in every fiber of our social and political being." While the president stood in awe as he looked back over the recent past, he would have been even more shocked at the transformations that stood poised on the horizon. By the time the era under consideration ended, the nation survived world war and industrial revolution, while confronting a teetering global economy.

In the first three decades of the twentieth century, America grew into an economic and military superpower. The hope and sparkle of the 1900–1929 era ended, however, when the stock market crashed in late October 1929. The economic disaster that set off the Great Depression ensured that the next several decades would be somewhat darker, but ironically rather optimistic.

What did not change, however, despite wars, economic troubles, political intrigue, and fundamental changes in demographics, was the force of popular culture—whether that meant guiding the nation, mirroring its mental condition, or charging off into the future. As a defining icon of the early twentieth century, Roosevelt advocated boldness, tackling challenges as they arose, and combating them (hand-to-hand, if necessary) as a means of strengthening the nation.

In the face of rapid change, the American people remained steadfastly optimistic, looking ahead with a fervor that was nearly palpable. The Great Depression would dampen that outlook to some degree, but the people themselves believed wholeheartedly in the American dream. They pictured a future filled with technological and scientific wonder. They had high hopes for the future, which sustained them through difficult times. The United States stood as an ideal and popular culture helped people understand and make sense of that idea.

1900s

Timeline

of Popular Culture Events, 1900s

1900

The Automobile Club of America sponsors the first automobile show in Madison Square Garden.

Sister Carrie is published by Theodore Dreiser.

The International Ladies' Garment Workers Union (ILGWU) is founded.

The first Davis Cup tennis match pits the United States against Great Britain.

Kodak introduces the $1.00 Brownie Box Camera.

The College Entrance Examination Board is established by representatives from 13 colleges and preparatory schools.

"A Bird in a Gilded Cage," written by Arthur J. Lamb and Harry Von Tilzer, becomes a hit song.

1901

General Electric develops the first corporate research laboratory.

United States Steel is formed and is the nation's first billion-dollar corporation.

The United States declares the war in the Philippines is over.

President William McKinley is shot by anarchist Leon Czolgosz, and the president dies nine days later on September 14. Vice President Theodore Roosevelt takes oath of office to become president on September 14.

President Theodore Roosevelt causes a national controversy when he dines with black leader Booker T. Washington at the White House.

1902

Owen Wister publishes *The Virginian*.

Dr. Charles Wardell Stiles discovers hookworm, a parasite affecting countless poor whites in the South.

Michigan defeats Stanford 49–0 in the first Tournament of Roses Association football game.

Congress authorizes the building of a canal across Panama.

1903

May 23–July 26: Dr. Horatio Nelson Jackson and Sewall K. Crocker complete the first cross-country automobile trip.

The Boston Red Sox defeat the Pittsburgh Pirates in the inaugural baseball World Series.

The 23-story, steel-framed Fuller Building is completed in New York City; because of its unique shape, it becomes known as the Flatiron Building.

The Great Train Robbery, directed by Edwin S. Porter, is the nation's first action movie.

1904

The first organized automobile race, dubbed the Vanderbilt Cup race after William K. Vanderbilt, a wealthy auto enthusiast, takes place on Long Island.

The first Olympic Games held in the United States take place as part of the St. Louis World's Fair.

The first segment of the New York City subway, from the Brooklyn Bridge to 145th Street, opens.

Theodore Roosevelt elected as the twenty-sixth president of the United States.

1905

First nickelodeon (nickel theater) opens in Pittsburgh.

The radical labor union the Industrial Workers of the World (IWW) is established in Chicago as a reaction against the conservative policies of the American Federation of Labor (AFL).

May G. Sutton becomes the first U.S. player to win a Wimbledon singles title.

The Rotary Club, the first business-oriented services organization, is founded in Chicago.

1906

Upton Sinclair publishes *The Jungle,* a novel that reveals impure food-processing standards in Chicago.

Theodore Roosevelt wins the Nobel Peace Prize for his efforts in negotiating a settlement to the war between Japan and Russia.

A race riot erupts in Atlanta, leaving 21 people dead (18 blacks), and the city is placed under martial law.

Devil's Tower in Wyoming is declared the first national monument by Theodore Roosevelt.

1907

As a result of the Immigration Act of 1907, Japanese laborers are excluded from immigrating to the continental United States by presidential order.

Ziegfeld's Follies opens on Broadway.

The *Lusitania,* the world's largest steamship, sets a new speed record, crossing the Atlantic from Ireland to New York in five days.

1908

Henry Ford introduces the first Model T, which sells for $850.

New York City passes the Sullivan Ordinance, which bans women from smoking cigarettes in public.

The first airplane fatality occurs when Lieutenant Thomas W. Selfridge dies in the crash of a plane piloted by Orville Wright, who is also seriously injured.

The first blood transfusion is performed in New Jersey by Doctors E. Zeh Hawkes and Edward Wharton Sprague.

The electric razor is introduced.

William Howard Taft is elected the twenty-seventh president of the United States.

1909

George Bellows paints *Both Members of the Club.*

The Federal Bureau of Investigation (FBI) is established.

Football is banned from the New York City public schools due to injuries and death rate.

Alice Huyler Ramsey is the first woman to drive across the United States—from New York to San Francisco.

Scribner's pays former president Theodore Roosevelt $500,000 for an account of his hunting trip to Africa.

Frederick Cook and Robert E. Peary both claim to have reached the North Pole first. The suspense grips the nation, but experts determine Peary is the winner.

Seventy-year-old Edward P. Weston walks from New York to San Francisco in 107 days, 7 hours.

Overview

of the 1900s

*Age of Innocence (coined by Edith
    Wharton in the late 1910s)*
Progressive Era
The Peaceful Decade

NICKNAMES FOR DECADE, 1900–1909

GOVERNMENT

At the 1901 Pan American Exposition in Buffalo, New York, the United States showed off its technological prowess with the spectacular Electric Tower, which rose 375 feet and illuminated the night air. Surrounded by fountains and magnificent gardens, the Electric Tower symbolized the realization of American military, economic, and industrial power. The Exposition, designed to link together North and South America, ultimately showed visitors that the United States dictated matters in the Western Hemisphere.

President William McKinley and his wife visited the Pan American Exposition on September 5. The President delivered a speech applauding the industrial growth demonstrated at the fair and discussed reciprocal commercial relations between North and South America. The next day, McKinley stood in the Temple of Music, greeting and shaking hands with hundreds of well-wishers. One young workman, whose hand was bandaged, approached McKinley. The workman, anarchist Leon Czolgosz, had concealed a .32-caliber revolver in his bandage and shot the president twice in the stomach at close range.[1]

Immediately, a dozen or more men jumped on the assassin while he tried to fire off more shots.[2] McKinley seemed to recover over the next week while staying in Buffalo. Late in the second week, however, gangrene set in from the gunshot wounds to his stomach, and he died on September 14. His vice president, Theodore Roosevelt, took the oath of office in the house where McKinley lay dead. Over the next several days, businesses suspended operations, telegraphs and cable messages took a five-minute pause of silence in his honor, and for 10 minutes, every railway in the nation stood still. Czolgosz was indicted and executed in the electric chair in late October, less than two months after the attack.

To some, McKinley's death showed a seedy underbelly existed in the United States that threatened the serene view many people held. Divisions ran deep along class, ethnic, and racial lines, and this would flare up countless times throughout the decade.

Theodore Roosevelt

Theodore Roosevelt embodied the best and the worst of the 1900s. A hero of the Spanish-American War, an adventurer, and a public intellectual, he captured the public's imagination long before he ascended to the presidency after McKinley's assassination. On one hand, he was a hero to American citizens. On the other hand, he preached, cajoled, and basically demanded support on numerous moral crusades, and charged forward with nearly reckless abandon. His foreign policy, which centered on extreme nationalism, had little regard for local populations.

Roosevelt became a folk hero at a time when the people truly believed in the righteousness of the United States. He fervently believed in the might of the young country, the sanctity of democratic ideals, and America's deserved place at the forefront among the world's powers. He built a strong alliance with the middle class, embodying their hopes and aspirations, while turning a blind eye to extremists from both ends of the political spectrum. Although he would use both to his advantage, Roosevelt was no friend to organized labor or to big business conglomerates.

Roosevelt's concepts of morality and efficiency were not just ideals; they were core beliefs. Instead of viewing Roosevelt simply as a member of the Republican Party, he should be viewed as a conservative activist political leader, despite how foreign that may sound to modern ears. The Progressive movement played an important role in Roosevelt's conception of conservatism. He sought

Swift & Co.'s Packing House in Chicago, 1906. The publication of Upton Sinclair's *The Jungle* in 1906 brought national attention to the food industry, which led to the passage of the 1906 Pure Food and Drug Act and the Meat Inspection Act. Prints & Photographs Division, Library of Congress.

stability and order through change that he managed, which was another reason he distrusted extreme factions of different reform movements. For example, Roosevelt could simultaneously embrace the idea of reform in the meatpacking industry after reading Upton Sinclair's exposé of it in *The Jungle* (1906), but at the same time admonished the author for the socialist overtones in the book, which the president believed muted the importance of the work.

Invoking the spirit of Abraham Lincoln, Roosevelt established the model of how an activist president should act, especially in foreign affairs and in regulating business interests. Building the Panama Canal, negotiating peace between Japan and Russia, and annexing strategic islands in the Pacific proved that the United States could play a major role on the world stage. Fighting monopolies, establishing consumer protection laws, and intervening in disputes between business and labor paved the way for the presidents who followed.

Politics in the Progressive Era

In 1904, Roosevelt declared in his fourth annual message to Congress that the growth of the United States as a world power required the enlargement of the national government.

Roosevelt's counsel to expand government influence cautiously, while retaining a system of controls similar to those in place at private companies, in many ways sums up the ideology of the Progressive movement at the turn of the century. The Progressives, a loosely knit group of reformers, were primarily middle-class, urban idealists who believed that many Americans were missing out on the economic, social, and cultural opportunities presented by the new century. Given the tremendous changes people experienced as a result of the massive influx of immigrants, the changing industrial order, involvement in foreign affairs, and huge urban growth, the average person needed to believe that someone or something was working on his or her behalf.

Although the Progressives never had the kind of cohesive national organization that could affect wholesale change, they still fought against big business and for increased government intervention in the economy and social realm. Essentially, the Progressives wanted to formalize and professionalize bureaucratic institutions to ensure that government worked for the public interest.

Primarily urban reformers, Progressive leaders, including many mayors and governors, envisioned the enemy to be the alliance between business leaders and political bosses. Their first targets were the state and local bosses who had a stranglehold on government. The Tammany Hall machine, which ran New York City government, symbolized the power and arrogance of the boss system, but corruption left few towns or cities unscathed. Reformers also battled against franchises for local utilities, such as water and sewage, gas, electricity, and public transportation, awarded to the highest bidder, usually a corrupt private company. Not surprisingly, the graft worked its way into local law enforcement circles, saloons, prostitution rings, and among civil servants.

The power of the political machines grew to such an extent that reformers fought back by attempting to pass more than 1,500 amendments to state constitutions between 1900 and 1920. Among the many reforms that passed during these years were the referendum, the recall, the primary system, women's suffrage, and popular election of U.S. senators. Recalls were especially effective in city movements.

While a large number of Progressives concentrated on political reform, others specialized in humanitarian relief. Settlement houses, a kind of community center for the poor run by middle-class workers, multiplied in the 1900s. These were based on Hull House in Chicago, reformer Jane Addams's pioneering effort at helping immigrants acclimatize to American life. Other reformers fought for improved child welfare, elementary and secondary education, and worker safety. Progressives were instrumental in passing many child labor and workman's compensation laws during the decade.[3]

President Roosevelt encouraged Progressive reformers to battle for stricter child labor and safety laws in factories. However, as a conservative, he believed that women should stay at home, exerting themselves as housewives, and that men should be the primary breadwinners so that children would grow up healthy.

Many laws were passed, such as the 1906 Pure Food and Drug Act, the Meat Inspection Act, and the Hepburn Act of 1906, which regulated railroad rates and strengthened the Interstate Commerce Commission—and yet, extreme factions in the nation grew stronger. In 1910, Wisconsin elected Socialist Party member Victor Berger to Congress, and the next several years witnessed the election of 73 Socialist mayors and 1,200 officials in 340 cities and towns.[4] Most of the real leadership of the Progressive Era happened on the local and state level, where individual efforts equated to real results.[5]

Progressivism comprised so many different aspects and initiatives that historians have found it difficult to define. Most Progressive leaders, including Roosevelt, wanted a gradual evolution of government, not the kind of revolution advocated by socialists, anarchists, and other groups who were viewed as extreme in the 1900s. An example of this thinking is the selective regulation of corporate monopolies. Roosevelt staked his claim as a trust-buster, but could have gone much further in breaking up illegal industrial combinations. J. P. Morgan and John D. Rockefeller, who headed corporate monopolies, viewed the president's actions with disdain, but regarded him as more of a nuisance than an actual threat.

As for control, Progressive leaders envisioned a government that placed control over things they believed needed to be restricted. Thus, conservatives hoped for control over immigration, which they viewed as detrimental because of long-held racist viewpoints and the fear that mass immigration would somehow debase the nation. Reformers on the front lines wanted controls placed over housing standards, public health initiatives, and welfare. Progressives hoped that government would swoop in when necessary to eradicate what they saw as societal evils, but at the same time understand when involvement was too much. The Progressives believed the answer lay with strong leaders, such as Roosevelt, La Follette, and mayors such as Cleveland's Tom L. Johnson and Toledo's Samuel M. Jones.

Diplomacy: Carrying a Big Stick

The United States not only showed off its military readiness in the 1900s, but also pushed its

Hundreds of men gather for the 1901 Florida State Democratic Convention. At the turn of the century politics was an all-male affair. Courtesy of the Florida State Archives.

way into foreign markets in search for new selling avenues. American political leaders realized that they would benefit from a healthy dose of economic and diplomatic stability overseas.

The victory in the Spanish-American War (1898) catapulted the United States to a more central role and convinced its citizens that an activist foreign policy was in the nation's best interests. The victory also symbolized the melding of diplomatic and economic initiatives, since the United States intervened in part to protect American sugar and tobacco interests in Cuba. The difficulty in overcoming the public's reticence regarding diplomatic maneuverings can be seen in the final count of the vote to ratify the Treaty of Paris with Spain in late 1898, which ended the war. Although the United States gained the Philippines, Puerto Rico, and Guam in exchange for $20 million, the final Senate vote was 57 to 27, only two votes more than the two-thirds necessary for ratification. The Philippines rebelled against U.S. occupation, and it took three years to squelch the rebellion. The United States quickly learned that it was harder to govern a territory than to acquire it.

In East Asia, the primary goal was to keep an interest in the region and not allow the European powers or Japan to intervene and divide the spoils among themselves. Secretary of State John Hay outlined an Open Door policy in 1899 and 1900, which would allow the Western powers to enter

China peacefully. Basically, the United States hoped to avoid military operations in China and settle disputes amicably. The policy aspired to take advantage of perceived economic markets in China.

Soon, Japan and Russia went to war over China, Manchuria, Korea, and other interests in the Far East. Although Japan emerged with a stunning victory over Russia, both sides overextended themselves and were ready for peace in 1905. Roosevelt negotiated the Treaty of Portsmouth, which ended the war on September 5, 1905. Serving as negotiator gave Roosevelt a bit more swagger on the international stage, but it hardly made up for America's lack of power in China. Hay's successor as secretary of state, Elihu Root, reinforced the Open Door policy in 1908.

While U.S. actions in the Far East were essentially a carryover from the McKinley days, the country's actions in the Western Hemisphere were stamped by Roosevelt's brand of cowboy bravado: "Speak Softly and Carry a Big Stick."

Toward this end, Roosevelt promoted a program to increase vastly the size of the navy by building at least two battleships per year. In a display of power, Roosevelt sent a fleet of 16 battleships and 12,000 men around the world from December 1907 to February 1909. The message was clear and aimed directly at Germany and Japan: America would fight to protect its interests.

As excavation began on a canal across the Isthmus of Panama (see Travel of the 1900s), the United States decided that it should ensure that their Latin American neighbors were, in Roosevelt's words, "stable, orderly, and prosperous." However, if a nation stepped out of line, it may "force the United States, however reluctantly, in flagrant cases of such wrongdoing or impotence, to the exercise of an international police power."[6] This sanction, dubbed the Roosevelt Corollary to the Monroe Doctrine, ensured that the United States would intervene whenever it saw fit to preserve an orderly system.

THE ECONOMY

The Rise of Big Business

Many of American history's most prominent businessmen, including financiers John D. Rockefeller and J. P. Morgan, steel magnate Andrew

Carnegie, and automobile manufacturer Henry Ford, dominated industry in the 1900s. These men set the tone for the way in which business leaders conducted themselves in the era. They could be merciless in dealing with competitors or small businesses that stood in their way, but frequently they acted in the nation's best interests; for example, Morgan intervened in the financial crisis of 1907, saving Wall Street.

The decade gave rise to moguls and dominant corporations, and it also changed the prevailing social order. The corporation enabled a new white-collar, managerial class to emerge, which reshaped the relationship between labor and capital. The rise of big business changed the way people looked at education as a career-building institution, put farmers at the mercy of fluctuating world markets, and impacted government at all levels.

John D. Rockefeller and J. P. Morgan changed the way people viewed big business. Neither man had much use for the age-old idea of business competition, so they set out to eliminate it by building what they called trusts, which Rockefeller believed were necessary and safe. Those trusts were in fact monopolies. The financiers felt that corporate combinations provided stability to the economy. Smaller concerns would be sacrificed for the good of the national economy.

From 1895 to 1904, more than 2,000 companies were consolidated into large enterprises, which wielded a great deal of power. For example, the United States Steel Corporation, America's first billion-dollar corporation, consisted of 213 different manufacturing concerns, included 41 mines, and owned more than 1,000 miles of railroad track and 112 ore ships. All told, this company accounted for 60 percent of the nation's steelmaking output and 43 percent of the pig-iron capacity. These large business consolidations occurred for many reasons, but the primary reason was to dampen price wars and allow one company to determine rates.[7]

Many small businesses also thrived during this period, especially in the manufacturing industries that did not require intricate production processes or advanced marketing skills, including lumber, publishing, and clothing manufacturing. Whenever big business saw no real benefit from taking over a small business, it allowed the small business to continue. Small owners could protect themselves to some degree by obtaining patents over their manufacturing processes.

Rockefeller and the Modern Corporation

John D. Rockefeller grew up in upstate New York, but made Cleveland, Ohio, his adopted hometown. As a young man, Rockefeller built a mini-empire in oil refining. In 1870, Rockefeller rolled all of his interests into the newly founded Standard Oil Company and headquartered the company in Cleveland, the nation's principal refining center. After his early attempt to form a cartel failed, Rockefeller spent from 1872 to 1879 buying up competing refineries. Noted for his fairness, he paid honest prices for the companies as he gobbled them up. Refineries that did not sell out soon found that they could not compete with Rockefeller's machine.

Along the way, Rockefeller squeezed every cent out of the process by maximizing efficiencies, but he did not micromanage his empire. He trusted his lieutenants to work hard, and his fair treatment of

---

THE BIRTH OF PAPER TOWELS

Philadelphia-based Scott Paper capitalized on the demand for improved hygiene by manufacturing and selling assorted brands of toilet paper. In the early 1900s, the company essentially invented the market for toilet paper. Later in the decade, Scott Paper introduced the world's first paper towels, first called Sani-Towels, but later renamed Scott Towels. Again, Scott Paper used advertising to convince the public that it needed these products.

The first paper towels were actually made by accident, when one of Scott's mills made a tissue that was too thick to use as toilet paper. Company founder Arthur Scott had heard about a Philadelphia schoolteacher who cut up copy paper for her students to use to wipe their hands, instead of using a communal cloth towel, which spread germs. Scott realized a use for his thick, absorbent tissue, and the paper towel was born.

workers was markedly different from that of the industrial leaders in railroads, steel, and coal. By the late 1870s, Rockefeller controlled from 90 to 95 percent of the nation's refining power.

The hegemony Rockefeller established in the refinery industry carried over into feeder business segments such as big railroads and the kerosene market. His command over the railroads forced them to pay him kickbacks on Standard's shipments and even on his competitors' shipments.

Gradually, public opinion turned against Rockefeller. Editorial cartoons appeared showing Rockefeller and Standard Oil as a giant octopus, with its tentacles spread out around the world. Rockefeller became the richest man in the world, but disgruntled competitors filed lawsuits. In Pennsylvania, they filed an indictment against Standard Oil executives for criminal conspiracy. The latter forced Rockefeller to abolish the system of rebates and other shady practices. To combat the loss of competitive advantage, Rockefeller created the Standard Oil Trust, which centered the collective power of the subsidiaries into one overarching company directed by nine trustees.

The formation of the trust was a short-lived victory. The federal and state governments were moving against monopolies, bolstered by the Sherman Anti-Trust Act, which outlawed monopolistic combinations in restraint of trade. They brought suit against Standard Oil. The attorney general of Ohio won a case against Rockefeller, and the trust was dissolved in 1892. Rockefeller used the corporate-friendly laws of New Jersey to reorganize Standard. He increased the capital of the company from $10 million to $110 million and turned New Jersey Standard into the corporate headquarters for the new Standard Oil empire. In 1900, Standard Oil profits reached $56 million, but climbed to $83 million by 1906.

Again, several states and the federal government brought suits against the oil giant. The company endured a $29 million fine in 1907, but could not withstand the U.S. Supreme Court decision in 1911 that required New Jersey Standard to divest itself of all subsidiaries.

By 1913, Rockefeller's fortune reached $900 million. He devoted much of his life from the 1890s onward to philanthropic activities. He endowed the University of Chicago in 1892 and established a foundation to give money to education and health organizations around the world. The breakup of Standard Oil actually increased Rockefeller's wealth, since he gained shares in numerous oil-related industries.

Morgan: America's Financier

The mid-1900s were prosperous times for American businessmen. They borrowed money at an alarming rate to gobble up stocks. When a failed takeover bid at United Copper Company happened in the fall of 1907, two brokerage houses collapsed, and worried financiers started pulling money from their banks. Money and credit dried up, and even large institutions, such as the New York Stock Exchange, had trouble funding daily operations. The government at that time had no real authority to step into the crisis. As a matter of fact, only one man could save the day—J. P. Morgan.

Born into a Hartford, Connecticut banking family in 1837, Morgan built an empire which included vast railroad holdings and just about every other American industry. Morgan instilled fear in those around him; even his business associates and partners feared him. For much of the nation, especially the West and South, Morgan represented the money and power of the Eastern establishment.

When British investors began removing their money from the American market in 1893, President Grover Cleveland realized a crisis was brewing. The nation's treasury supply of gold dwindled down below $50 million, about half the amount that officials considered the bare minimum. In the midst of possible financial chaos, Cleveland reached out to Morgan. Morgan quickly organized a group of investors to buy $50 million in government bonds, with an option on an additional $50 million.

The president suggested a public sale of bonds, but both he and Morgan knew that the United States and Europe would stop the financial bloodletting only if Morgan stepped in. They struck a deal, and the crisis was averted. Estimates suggest that Morgan made anywhere from $250,000 to $16 million by rescuing the treasury. Morgan felt it was fair, even though he was criticized by government officials for "profiteering," since the financier restored the credit of the federal government. Less than a decade later, Morgan bought out venerable industrialist Andrew Carnegie and formed the world's largest company, United States Steel, with a market capitalization of $1.4 billion.

Theodore Roosevelt realized he could gain publicity and support by taking on the big corporate monopolies of the day. In 1902, he went after Northern Securities, a railroad trust controlled by Morgan. Morgan personally visited the president, attempting to work out their differences diplomatically, but Roosevelt rebuked the great financier and warned that others would be in jeopardy if they did not obey the law. Roosevelt took great pride in standing up to Morgan, but before long the businessman would be called on, yet again, to save the nation financially in 1907.

The prosecution of Rockefeller's Standard Oil Company on antitrust violations and increased regulation in the railroad industry put pressure on companies to find money to cover their exposure on Wall Street. A study revealed that 8,090 companies with liabilities of $116 million went bankrupt during the first nine months of 1907. The collapse of F. Augustus Heinze's attempt to take over the United Copper Company Trust caused a widespread panic on Wall Street, cutting cash reserves to a dangerous level. Morgan, who was attending an Episcopal Church convention in Richmond, Virginia, did not return to New York. He believed that if the public saw him rushing back to New York, it would cause a deeper panic.[8]

Once again, as during the Cleveland administration, no government agency existed that could step in to provide safeguards for the economy. In the past, when banking crises erupted, reformers called for greater governmental control, but the uproar always subsided when the tumult ended. As the 1907 panic unfolded, Morgan returned to New York and assembled an ad hoc financial team to combat the downturn. It included Rockefeller, James Stillman of the National City Bank, George F. Baker of the First National Bank, railroad titan Edward Harriman, and an assortment of banking and finance experts.

After closing the Knickerbocker Trust Company, a venerable bank in the heart of New York's financial district on October 21, 1907, Morgan grappled with a solution to the panic. No simple solution existed, as it had in 1895. Morgan gave the Trust Company of America a $2.5 million loan to keep it going. He disliked the financial trusts, but he knew that if more of them went under, it would make stabilizing the economy more difficult. Morgan organized a group of banks to loan money to the trust and buoyed the public's spirits to a degree. After Morgan's display of strength, the national government deposited $25 million in select New York City banks to help out the troubled trusts and banks.[9]

Over the next several days, several more banks crumbled, and the New York Stock Exchange (NYSE) suffered from depleting credit. NYSE President Ransom H. Thomas personally visited Morgan and told him that he did not have the funds to stay open. Realizing this would be a fatal blow to public confidence, Morgan called the leaders of the city's most powerful banks and persuaded them, in 10 minutes, to ante up $25 million. The move brought about a round of applause on the trading floor and kudos from the *Wall Street Journal*.

When New York City threatened to go into default, Morgan again acted quickly to raise the millions of dollars it took to pay the city's employees. Over the following weekend, Morgan decided to organize all the remaining trust companies, and forced the presidents of the trusts to band together to give the others a $25 million loan. By November 6, 1907, the panic had ended. The federal government issued low-interest bonds and gave the proceeds to the various banks.

In May 1908, Congress passed a currency law that guarded against money shortages by allowing banks to issue money secured by the federal government. The bill also created the National Monetary Commission, but the crowning achievement was the development of the Federal Reserve System, led by the Federal Reserve Board, in 1913. The board, known as the Fed, monitors the availability of capital to banks, and gives the country a blanket of security that Morgan provided in the 1900s. Under the provisions of the Federal Reserve Act, money could be delivered quickly to local banks in times of crisis to avoid future panics.

LABOR AND THE WORKPLACE

The issues gripping working life in the 1900s exposed the very heart of Progressivism—the fight between private power and public welfare. At a basic level, organized labor challenged many basic assumptions Americans held dear: the rights of private property holders, the sanctity of business, and the power of democratic institutions. When labor organized, business viewed it as a threat. Socialists and other radicals in the labor movement were a minority of the total membership, but their activism prompted businesses to be ruthless in its attempts to stop unionization.

Like most other areas of life, workplaces were changing. Factories became larger and a new type of middle management focused on efficiency, stability, and solidifying its own power over workers. By 1900, more than 1,000 factories had more than 500 workers; only a handful of factories this size had existed in the 1870s. Swift & Co., a meatpacking company, employed 23,000 workers in 1903, up from 1,600 in 1886. The use of new technology centered on making manufacturing more efficient, regardless of how the pace impacted workers. With a steady supply of immigrant labor, managers could replace anyone who could not keep pace or complained.

Unions became more cohesive in the 1900s. Between 1897 and 1903, membership in the American Federation of Labor (AFL) jumped from 400,000 to almost three million. Perhaps more important, labor withstood the counterattacks made by big business and the periodic economic downturns that gave employers more of an upper hand, such as the panic of 1907.

Labor relations were relatively quiet until 1903, but the rest of the decade witnessed a virtual war between unions and employers. From 1903 to 1905, a battle raged in the mining fields of Colorado. The governor there declared martial law and sent the militia to thwart a strike by the Western Federation of Miners, whose workers demanded the right to organize and to be represented by the union. Fights broke out on the streets of Chicago in 1905, and the decade culminated in the bombing of the Los Angeles Times building.

The rise of a new managerial class that emphasized efficiency and focused on production numbers affected workers' lives, but on the shop floor workers still fought to retain control. Foremen still held great influence, often determining who was hired and fired, setting pay rates, and ultimately, establishing production levels. Workers fought against management's directives to raise production levels and control personnel. Workers were willing to fight because working conditions were dangerous, workdays were long, job security did not exist for most workers, and the pay was abysmally low.

For all its technological superiority, the United States still had one of the highest workplace accident rates in the world. For example, from 1907 to 1910, in one Pittsburgh steel mill, 3,723 new immigrant workers were injured or killed. From the clothing manufacturers of New York City to the textile mills of the South, workers toiled under unsafe conditions for pay that barely met the poverty line.

The Rise of the Wobblies

Violence was the Progressives' worst nightmare—they wanted orderly change, and labor was not willing to play along. In 1905, a group of 200 radical labor activists met in Chicago and formed the Industrial Workers of the World (IWW), nicknamed the "Wobblies." The IWW was committed to empowering all workers, especially the non-skilled laborers excluded from the American Federation of Labor (AFL). Believing that the nation's most exploited and poorest workers deserved a voice, the Wobblies called for "One Big Union" that would challenge the capitalist system first in the United States and later worldwide.[10]

The Wobblies' rise to national prominence can be understood only within the context of the vast changes taking place in America in the early twentieth century. The influx of immigrants transformed society and provided the workforce that was coveted by corporations. Poverty was a way of life, however, for most working-class families. The IWW was overwhelmingly leftist and called for the ultimate overthrow of capitalism worldwide. Immediately feared by most and despised by AFL leader Samuel Gompers, the Wobblies challenged the status quo and fought for the rights of America's working poor. The Wobblies planned to do what no union had tried before: unite blacks, immigrants, and assembly line workers into one powerful force.

IWW leaders included Big Bill Haywood, head of the Western Federation of Miners, Mary "Mother" Jones, a longtime union advocate, and Eugene Debs, the leader of the Socialist Party. The Wobblies began organizing strikes around the nation as a prelude to a general worldwide strike among the working class. Initially, the ranks of the IWW were filled with Western miners under Haywood's control. These individuals became increasingly militant when they were marginalized by the AFL. Traveling hobo-like by train, IWW organizers fanned out across the nation. Wobbly songwriters, such as Joe Hill, immortalized the union through humorous folk songs. The simple call for an inclusive union representing all workers took hold. IWW membership approached 150,000, although only 5,000 to 10,000 were full-time members.[11]

The Wobblies mixed Marxism and Darwinism with American ideals to produce a unique brand of radicalism. They led strikes that often turned bloody; newspapers, the courts, and the police attacked them; and "goon squads" were formed to protect the interests of corporations. The Wobblies battled for free speech and higher wages across the nation. It seemed that violence and mayhem followed them everywhere, and the Wobblies became the scourge of middle-class America.

As the Wobbly "menace" became more influential, American leaders took action to limit the union's power. World War I provided the diversion the government needed to crush the IWW once and for all.

The lasting importance of the IWW was bringing unskilled workers into labor's mainstream. After the demise of the Wobblies, the AFL gradually became more inclusive and political. The Congress of Industrial Organizations (CIO), founded in 1935 by another mining leader, John L. Lewis, successfully organized unskilled workers. In 1955, the AFL and CIO merged to form the AFL-CIO, America's leading trade union throughout the second half of the century.

LIVING CONDITIONS

Life and Death

The United States was a harsh place to live in the 1900s. According to most estimates, more than two African Americans were lynched each week between 1889 and 1903. Union men died in state-sanctioned acts of brutality, such as those carried out by the Pennsylvania State Constabulary of 1905 involving a mounted police force called the "Cossacks" and by company-sponsored thugs breaking up a strike by the Teamsters in Chicago the same year.

Disease and unsafe living conditions in overcrowded cities took many lives, predominantly those of immigrants. Bathrooms, often shared among multiple families or open to the streets, led to a germ-ridden society with high mortality rates. Pittsburgh had the highest mortality rate for typhoid in the world with 1.2 deaths per 1,000 people between 1902 and 1908.[12] Disease was a major cause of death, but if fire broke out, no real escape existed for most apartment dwellers. More than 250 people died in apartment fires in Manhattan between 1902 and 1909.[13]

Infectious diseases were the leading cause of death throughout the early twentieth century. Yellow fever, cholera, and smallpox thrived in the crowded metropolises, while people constantly fought influenza, pneumonia, measles, and tuberculosis. In the South, hookworm and malaria were frequent causes of death among the poor. Of all these diseases, however, tuberculosis was the most deadly prior to 1915. In addition to the lives it took, it had a profound impact on society. Colorado and California attracted those suffering from the disease because of their abundance of clean air and sunshine, and legislators passed laws requiring teachers, nurses, and public health officials to submit to regular tuberculosis tests. Even the "dipper," a crude tin water fountain popular in public areas, was removed and replaced by glass-lined water coolers and paper cups.[14]

Mary Mallon, or "Typhoid Mary" as she was better known, was the first carrier of typhoid to be identified in the United States. An immigrant from Northern Ireland, Mallon worked as a cook for many wealthy families in New York City over a seven-year span. As a carrier, Mallon never caught the disease herself, but she spread the disease from household to household. At least three deaths and 53 cases of typhoid can be directly attributed to Typhoid Mary. Some observers believe she may also have been responsible for an outbreak in Ithaca, New York, in 1903, which led to 1,400 cases. Mallon entered a hospital in the Bronx in 1907 and was held there until 1910. She dropped out of sight, but reappeared four years later, and was quarantined for life at Riverside Hospital in New York. She died there in 1938.

In the 1900s, the front pages of daily newspapers across the nation, including the *New York Times,* blared with gruesome accounts of suicides, double suicides, and murder-suicides. Perhaps much of this fascination with suicide can be credited to the sensational nature of the press, but it also speaks to the way in which people viewed death in the 1900s. People dealt with a number of calamities, from financial ruin to terminal illness, by ending their lives. Another answer may lie in the wave of neurasthenia, or "American nervousness," which swept the nation in the 1900s. This disease, reportedly caused by the agitation and stress of modern life, could have driven many people to act out their rage, especially given the number of husband and wife murder-suicides that occurred. According to journalist Mark Sullivan, the suicide rate was 11.5 per 100,000 in 1900, which compares with the murder rate of 2.1 per 100,000 citizens. (By contrast, *The 2008 Statistical Abstract,* published by the U.S. Census Bureau, reports that the suicide rate in 2004 for the general population was 10.9 per 100,000 and the homicide rate was 5.5 per 100,000 citizens.) In comparison, cancer had a death rate of 63; tuberculosis reached 201.9 per 100,000.[15]

Even the nation's literature contained characters that decided to kill themselves, rather than continue confronting a frustrating world. Beginning with Kate Chopin's *The Awakening* (1899), authors dealt with the angst of the modern world by having their characters kill themselves. Other authors that used suicide in their work included Stephen Crane, Jack London, Theodore Dreiser, Frank Norris, Willa Cather, and Edith Wharton. Their characters, from Wharton's look at upper-class life, to the seedy worlds of Dreiser and Norris, are unable to overcome the stresses of their age, including social status, financial well-being, and marital happiness.[16]

Disaster

Some of the decade's disasters can be attributed to a new way of life which clashed with the old; for example, trains and cars smashing into horse-drawn carriages and hitting pedestrians. In Berkeley, California, at the turn of the century, people had a terrible time with trains. Since the main line traveled directly through the center of town, trains frequently hit horses, cows, milk wagons, people, and other trains. People found it difficult to judge the speed of steam trains and electric street cars as they passed over the tracks, even though the liners were only moving at 15 miles per hour.

One of the first cataclysmic events of the decade occurred on the island city of Galveston, Texas, on September 7, 1900. On Labor Day weekend, as Galveston filled with tourists and revelers, a hurricane approached the region. Gale force winds reaching 102 miles per hour and rain smashed into the city, and a storm surge carried away the bridges that linked Galveston with the mainland. Soon, telegraph poles and homes were ripped from the ground and tossed in the air like matchboxes. Tidal waves repeatedly washed over the city and, at one point, the sea rose four feet in four seconds. At dawn, a thousand people wandered the city naked and in a daze; the storm had ripped the clothes from their bodies. In one strip four blocks wide and three miles long, every single house and building had been destroyed. Nothing remained but fallen timber and dead bodies.[17]

In the end, more than 6,000 people died in Galveston. More than 5,000 others were injured in the hurricane, and 10,000 were left homeless. The 32,000 survivors had no food, shelter, clothing, light, or power. The number of dead bodies overwhelmed gravediggers, and every available man was put on duty to bury the victims.[18]

As news of the destruction of Galveston blared across the front pages of newspapers across the country, relief poured in. Millions of Americans contributed to the effort. In just over a month, more than $1.5 million had been raised to help the survivors. Newspaper magnate William Randolph Hearst, who led the charity effort in New

York, organized fund-raising events featuring Broadway stars. The money raised was used to build a hospital and given to other relief efforts.

Built in the 1880s in Southwest Florida, the city of Arcadia quickly grew to more than 1,000 residents and became the center of the state's cattle industry. Like most swelling cities at the turn of the century, Arcadia's downtown area was a mix of cypress and pine-framed buildings that housed numerous stores and offices. Builders could not keep up with the influx of people or businesses to the city, and as a result, residents had to go without many basic services, such as a public water system and firefighting equipment.

On November 30, 1905, the people of Arcadia celebrated Thanksgiving. It was an unseasonably hot day, forcing many residents indoors to avoid the hot sun. That night, for reasons that were never determined, a fire broke out in downtown Arcadia. Brisk winds propelled the fire. Witnesses recalled that the fire made an unbearable noise and produced thick, heavy smoke that blanketed the town.[19]

Men and women formed bucket brigades to fight the fire. At daybreak, little remained except ruins and piles of ash. Only three brick buildings in downtown Arcadia were saved; most prominent was the town's new brick bank. In total, 43 buildings were destroyed in "the big fire," as the people of Arcadia have called it ever since. The estimated loss reached $250,000, and only about 25 percent of it was covered by insurance.

Arcadia officials and citizens banded together to rebuild the city. They wanted it to be a model for others of its size. One of the first ordinances they passed was a law requiring all buildings in the business center to be built with brick, stone, or concrete. Next, streets were graded and paved,

Devastation from the San Francisco earthquake, 1906. Prints & Photographs Division, Library of Congress.

View of street in San Francisco, California, in the aftermath of the earthquake a man patrols with a rifle, 1906. Prints & Photographs Division, Library of Congress.

trees were planted, and water and electric plants were built. Arcadia was not going to take any more chances with fire.

In the morning hours of April 18, 1906, an earthquake shook Northern California on a 200-mile stretch along the San Andreas Fault. The tremor lasted for 40 seconds, then stopped for 10 seconds, then resumed for another 25 seconds. A series of smaller tremors then struck periodically. In San Francisco, the earthquake buckled streets, which producing great cracks. It broke water pipes, tossed buildings into the air, and set off fires that raged across the city's hilly streets. The walls of City Hall fell in, the Valencia Hotel caved in and caught fire, gas mains broke, and telecommunications lines fell—the city was in ruins.[20]

The earthquake was intense, but the resulting fires raged on for several days after, covering 500 blocks and 2,800 acres, completely destroying the financial district and 60 percent of the homes in the city. Winds propelled fires across the city, and witnesses reported that the flames stretched a mile high on the night of April 6. The loss of property reached an estimated $350 to $500 million. Despite all this, the people of the city rallied. Jack London reported that he saw "no hysteria, no disorder" and "no shouting or yelling."[21]

Pictures taken after the earthquake and in the following days support London's assertions. The people who gaze out from these photographs look confused but orderly. Most of the women are properly dressed, wearing the day's big, floppy hats, and the men are all wearing ties and bowlers—this decorum despite the fact that thousands of people were sleeping outside and taking all their meals from soup kitchens. The nation once again contributed heavily to the relief efforts, sending medical supplies, food, and doctors and nurses. President Roosevelt asked Congress for $2.5 million to help in the rebuilding of the region.

Advertising

of the 1900s

In the 1900s, industrialism and consumerism converged to form a culture of consumption in the United States and elsewhere. Advertising emerged as the most pervasive technique for promoting the budding consumer culture. The advertising industry was as innovative and clever in developing new ways to get people to buy things as the manufacturing industry was in creating modern production practices.

In its earliest form, advertising meant simply placing announcements in newspapers and magazines. However, as the medium evolved and the avenues for reaching the public expanded, advertising quickly appeared everywhere. Signs appeared on billboards, in store windows, on the outside of buildings, and on public transportation. They urged people to validate their self-worth through the products they purchased.

Advertising became embedded in people's daily consciousness thanks to the constant bombardment of advertising messages. As a result, class and social status even more clearly marked the difference between the "haves" and the "have-nots" in American culture. Blatant displays of newly acquired wealth permeated the land, especially in the urban centers, where the rich congregated and tried to outdo one another through displays of wealth.

The rich, however, were not the only ones to prosper in the new century. Americans purchased increasing numbers of machine-made goods because the rising middle class acquired more disposable income than in past generations. The upward mobility of the middle class was guaranteed by the millions of immigrants, who moved to the United States and took their place in factories and other points of production, virtually pushing those ahead of them up the social ladder. The immigrants themselves formed another buying class targeted by advertisers.

Advertising helped bring the immigrants to America in the first place. Agents working for the railroads and businesses that needed a steady flow of labor took out ads and handed out leaflets that urged Europeans to migrate to the United States. In 1904, steerage prices dropped, which allowed Europeans to board ships bound for America and be there a month later for as little as $10. Usually guaranteed a job upon arrival in the United States, they worked the fare off quickly.[1]

As the quantity of consumer goods increased, the outlets to purchase them expanded as well. Urban department stores, chain retail stores, and mail-order catalogs granted people greater access to goods they felt they needed. Advertisers embraced the idea of progress and used it to sell goods. In the 1900s, science, technology, and health care were consistent themes in advertising campaigns.

The creation of a modern consumer culture required introducing new products in innovative ways, which persuaded people to buy them. In many respects, advertisers needed to establish new domestic habits, which people would pick up and practice daily. For instance, advertisers had to convince people to buy boxed crackers wrapped in wax paper instead of crackers scooped out of a big, open-air crate at the general store. Advertisers linked packaging and product presentation to an emerging lifestyle, which focused on saving time and improving the quality of life.

As the United States transformed from a rural country of small towns and villages into a nation of bustling cities, advertising played a critical role in defining the new urban way of life. The idea of convenience, whether at work or in one's own kitchen, meant installing electric lighting and gas and electric stoves, and buying foods that cut down on preparation time.

These ideas became realities; for example, Colgate & Company taught consumers about the benefits of brushing one's teeth. Colgate booklets, such as *ABC of the Teeth,* produced by advertising agencies, were distributed at county fairs and other places where people congregated. The process had two goals: to inform people about performing basic dental hygiene on a daily basis, and to sell Colgate toothpaste.[2]

The same forces combined to deliver similar ideas about shaving and other areas of personal grooming. The Gillette razor, in advertisements featuring company founder King Gillette himself, convinced male consumers that they needed to shave daily and that his product was the ultimate tool for the purpose. Gillette's "shaving lessons" ads made his product popular, even though the typical Gillette razor cost $5, a luxury when industrial workers usually earned between $10 and $15 a week.[3]

Even a pure luxury item, like the newly invented line of Kodak cameras, could be incorporated into everyday life. Through an aggressive ad campaign that targeted both upper-class and middle-class audiences, the Eastman Kodak Company made taking pictures a normal part of life. Next, Kodak convinced the public that photography was so easy that a child could do it and introduced the Brownie line, an inexpensive camera which fit in

"The Kodak Girl," who advertised Kodak cameras, approximately 1909. Prints & Photographs Division, Library of Congress.

ADVERTISING SLOGANS OF THE 1900s

Uneeda Biscuit boy/"Lest you forget it, we say it yet, Uneeda biscuit." National Biscuit Company, late 1890s/early 1900s*

"King of Bottled Beers," Budweiser, 1900s

"Don't experiment. Buy a Ford," Ford Motor Company, 1904

"Ask the man who owns one," Packard Motor Company, 1900s

"Delicious and Refreshing," Coca-Cola, 1904

"Good to the last drop," Maxwell House, 1907*

"His master's voice," RCA Victor Talking Machine, 1901*

"The milk from contented cows," Carnation Milk, 1907

*Among *Advertising Age's* 100 Best Ads of 20th Century. http://adage.com/century/

one's pocket. Kodak also successfully promoted major holidays, primarily Christmas, as important picture-taking opportunities.

MERCHANDISING

With companies manufacturing more consumer goods and more shoppers willing to buy them, retail outlets flourished. At the same time, mail-order catalog companies used improvements in transportation, packaging, and the national postal service to expand their services.

Packaging itself was transformed. Cans, bottles, and other devices were designed to be both practical and appealing. Wax-sealed cartons kept many foods, such as breakfast cereals and snacks, fresh for longer periods. Other innovations included sealed glass jars and bottles, cans, tins, and metal tubes. Outside wrappers changed as advertisers realized that designing packages that appealed to customers visually and stood out against the competition on store shelves developed brand recognition. Brand identification and loyalty drove sales, especially as shoppers (primarily women) had more time to hunt for the best price at many different stores.[4]

Mass merchandisers worked to change America's shopping experience and, in the process, solidified the unwritten rules that still govern the process to this day. For example, retailers now set the price of goods. The haggling for the best price, a common practice in nineteenth-century America, ended—no one argued with Macy's or Marshall Field's over prices. The new pricing policy enabled the department stores and chains to hire large numbers of low-paid, young salespeople. Workers were just another form of overhead to the owners. To cover their wages, rent, electricity, shipping, and other costs, the goal became to move merchandise as quickly as possible. Selling quickly required that shoppers be able to find what they needed as fast as possible. The retailers solved this dilemma by setting up stores with different departments that catered to one's needs. A man who wanted suits could now go directly to that area and find what he desired. Placing goods in departments gave management the ability to track what items sold the best and also how individual employees performed.

Mass merchandisers also realized the importance of giving shoppers a place where people would want to spend time. Luring people into the cities to shop, especially middle-class suburban women, was a key element in forming the consumer culture. On the other hand, large catalog retailers fulfilled the needs of people in rural areas. People who wanted to stay at home were catered to by such stores as Philadelphia's John Wanamaker's department store, which took telephone orders around the clock beginning in 1907.

At the end of the 1800s, department stores offered a wider array of services to draw people to the stores and keep them there longer. At first, they built soda fountains and lunchrooms for patrons. Gradually they added other conveniences, such as post offices, women's parlors, and child-care facilities. One common way to describe the largest department stores at the turn of the century was to liken them to palaces. Not only did department stores offer just about any product under the sun, they also offered lectures, live music performances, beauty shops, and even libraries to help people in their quest for personal improvement—a favorite theme in the 1900s.[5]

In 1902, both Marshall Field's (in Chicago) and Macy's (in New York) built cavernous new stores with more than a million square feet of floor space. In the process, they became important employers. Marshall Field's had 10,000 employees and estimated that 250,000 customers passed through its doors during the holiday seasons. Thousands of smaller department stores instituted similar ideas, just scaled down to a manageable level. They all used advertising specialists and filled local newspapers with ads emphasizing price and quality. To get slow-moving goods off the shelf, retailers offered deep discounts on the merchandise, thus beginning the phenomenon of clearance sales and bargain shopping.[6]

Chain stores, which stood between the small mom-and-pop general stores and the large department stores, became the next development in mass merchandising. Chain stores began when local entrepreneurs expanded their businesses, while at the same time adopting the economies of scale—low prices, low profit margins, and high volume—which characterized bigger stores. Moving from the local market to the regional and

A typical advertisement of the early 1900s for a still-familiar product. Waiter holding a bottle of Budweiser beer on a tray, approximately 1908. Prints & Photographs Division, Library of Congress.

national required detailed central management and an emphasis on low prices. Chains had to offer something different to make people want to switch their shopping routines. Usually the differentiation came in the form of less expensive goods and a wider variety of products. Two of the more recognizable names, Woolworth's and J. C. Penney's, reached great heights in the following decades, with Woolworth's hitting the 600 store mark in 1913 and Penney's opening 300 stores by 1920.[7]

The first mail-order firm, Montgomery Ward, catered to the needs of the Grange, the nation's leading farmers' organization, when it began operation in 1872. Two decades later, the Montgomery Ward catalog listed 24,000 items. Customers paid cash on delivery and paid only if they were satisfied with what they received. Richard Sears began his business by selling watches in 1886. The company grew quickly. Just before the turn of the century, the Sears catalog contained nearly 800 pages. By 1900, it was the nation's largest mail-order company.[8]

Sears revolutionized the mail-order business by expanding its operations into manufacturing and bringing its auxiliary services, including transportation, mail sorting, and billing procedures, into modern times. In 1906, Sears moved into a 40-acre plant, with buildings connected by underground tunnels, railroad tracks, and wiring. The Sears empire grew to include ownership or partial ownership of 16 manufacturing facilities. Workers labored around the clock to fulfill the Sears goal of providing "nearly everything in merchandise." On a daily basis, more than 2,000 Sears employees processed 900 sacks of mail, while the express companies, railroads, post office, and telegraph company all operated branches on the complex. To run the operations, Sears owned its own printing plant and controlled the second largest power plant in Chicago, right after the Edison Company itself.[9]

The success of Sears depended heavily on advertising because the Sears Catalog is actually one long ad for both the products and the company itself. Sears established innovative methods of selling goods. The company created card indexes showing all the goods ever bought by every single customer. Also contained on the card were details about address changes, preferences, and family information. Sears used the card index to further segment its customer base. According to one historian, America's largest mail-order firm collected files on four to six million people.[10]

Arguably, no product has used advertising better in its history than Coca-Cola. Asa Candler bought the rights to the product in 1888 after the death of its inventor, John S. Pemberton, an Atlanta chemist. By most accounts, Candler wasn't sure what to make of the drink. Originally conceived as a possible headache remedy, the company's advertising was ambiguous on the issue into the 1890s. At one point, it alternated between portraying Coke as a "nerve and brain tonic" and a "remarkable therapeutic agent."[11]

Despite the rumors that Coke actually contained trace quantities of cocaine and that the company pumped it full of excessive amounts of caffeine, it caught on as a fountain drink, then as a bottled drink. By 1909, the company had more than 375 bottling plants. Heavy advertising for the soft drink began in 1902. Several years later, the company installed an animated sign on the Penn railroad tracks between Philadelphia and New York. In 1909, a blimp with the Coca-Cola script lettering flew over Washington, D.C. At that time, the Associated Advertising Clubs of America reported that Coke was "the best advertised article in America."[12]

ADVERTISING AGENCIES

Over the course of the decade, advertising agencies evolved into entities quite similar to today's firms, though on a much smaller scale. Large agencies hired copywriters who specialized in the text and slogans contained within an advertisement. Artists and designers took over the look and feel of the ad, which in earlier times had been left to the whim of the printer. The position of account executive, a role entailing focus on the bottom line and the return on investment, gained importance as a middle ground between the creative types at the agency and the clients.

Over time, advertising agencies took control over complete campaigns and developed into highly professional firms to keep control over the process. Clients demanded coordination, a necessity considering the number of new products introduced by companies. Advertising agencies commanded synchronization between the strategic planners, copywriters, designers, media placement experts, and clients.

Early advertising agencies employed a trial-by-fire mentality. The leaders tried to lay the ground rules for the budding industry and debated over the place of advertising in the twentieth-century world. At various intervals, art took precedent over text and slogans; at other times, the copywriter's message held sway. One of the earliest uses of advertising was preparing slogans to adorn streetcars. Realizing the power of pictures early on, and as the use of colorful illustrations spread, advertising companies hired gallery artists to work on accounts. Famous artists, including N. C. Wyeth and Norman Rockwell, were among the many who lent their talents to advertising campaigns.

With little of the outside stimuli provided by today's multimedia gadgets, advertising ditties

An article on women photographers from the highly influential *Ladies Home Journal,* November 1901, p. 13. Prints & Photographs Division, Library of Congress.

stuck in people's minds. One copywriter prepared weekly slogans for the streetcars in 80 cities. Others used the slogans to tell linked stories, so the public clamored for the next week's installment. The most popular advertising ditties were carried over to toys, plays, political cartoons, and other marketing avenues.[13]

While slogans caught the public's imagination, seeing familiar characters over and over again in advertising media gave consumers a warm feeling about the company and its products. Technological innovations in printing contributed to the use of characters and art in advertising campaigns. At the turn of the century, printers were able to produce varying shades of light and dark tones and print in color. In 1900, four-color front and back covers and one or two-color interior ads became standard in the magazine industry.

THE AGE OF *LADIES' HOME JOURNAL*

One of the earliest and best examples of the symbiosis between advertising agencies and magazines can be found in the phenomenal success of the *Ladies' Home Journal.* In 1883, publisher Cyrus H. K. Curtis created a new magazine by expanding a column titled "Women and the Home," written by his wife, Louisa Knapp, in one of his existing magazines. The popularity of the column rested on Knapp's no-nonsense approach to middle-class women's duties in the modern family. Contributions might include a melodramatic short story, several topical essays on items ranging from health to cosmetics, hints and tips on running a well-organized home, or a brief and often humorous analysis of current events from the perspective of "the ladies." A "typical" reader might examine two or three essays, scan a few others, and generally browse the pages in her spare time, looking for items of interest. Significantly, the spread of visual (rather than verbal) advertisements suited this glancing reading style very well. From the outset, Curtis intended the new publication to appeal to both subscribers and to the advertisers who wanted access to this vital group of active consumers. The strategy proved wildly successful. Claiming 270,000 subscribers in 1886, the number expanded to more than 400,000 only three years later, 800,000 by 1900, and more than one million—the first magazine to do so—by 1903.

Statistics for *Ladies' Home Journal* taken from Theodore Peterson, *Magazines in the Twentieth Century* (Urbana: University of Illinois Press, 1964); Salme Hrju Steinberg, *Reformer in the Marketplace: Edward D. Bok and the* Ladies' Home Journal (Baton Rouge: Louisiana State University Press, 1979); and John Tebbel and Mary Ellen Zuckerman, *The Magazine in America: 1741–1990* (New York: Oxford University Press, 1991).

Uneeda Biscuit

The National Biscuit Company, then known as NBC, produced and marketed a cracker in a distinctive package, sealed in a wax paper lining (dubbed the "In-Er-Seal") to keep the crackers fresh. This method of selling crackers was totally different from the traditional way of letting customers take their own from open barrels, with no concern for sanitation or freshness.

NBC leader Adolphus W. Green insisted on the low price of five cents a box for his crackers so everyone could afford them—which meant an extremely low profit margin. The company would have to sell tremendous numbers of crackers to make money, so advertising was a critical concern. Looking for a likable name and symbol for the cracker, NBC turned to the N. W. Ayer and Son advertising agency in New York. The agency recommended "Uneeda" (pronounced "You Need A") and created the biscuit slicker boy, a young child posed in a hat and raincoat, and the phrase, "Lest you forget, we say it yet, Uneeda biscuit."[14]

After winning the client's approval, Ayer launched the first multimillion dollar ad campaign in 1899. The success of the slicker boy fueled NBC's other products, including Fig Newtons, Barnum's Animal Crackers, and Oysterettes crackers. Almost immediately, NBC saw a return on the advertising expenditure. In 1900, it sold 10 million boxes of Uneeda crackers a month, and in 1907 alone, NBC made $4 million in profits. After Green's death in 1917, Uneeda fell to the wayside, but NBC's ideas regarding sanitation, packaging, and a finely orchestrated national campaign were ahead of its time.[15]

William Wrigley

During his lifetime, William Wrigley Jr. was widely regarded as "the world's greatest salesman," transforming a small soap business into the top chewing gum manufacturer in the world. Relying heavily on various forms of advertising, Wrigley pushed the William Wrigley Jr. Company to the top, making his name virtually synonymous with chewing gum.

In 1891, after working in his father's soap business for 20 years, Wrigley moved to Chicago at age 29 with his wife, Ada, and their young daughter to go into business for himself. He planned to sell soap in Chicago for his father's company and offer baking powder as a premium. For the rest of his business life, Wrigley advocated giving a bonus with each purchase.

Wrigley arrived in Chicago with $32 in his pocket, but he was able to secure a $5,000 loan from an uncle on the condition that his cousin serve as Wrigley's business partner. Wrigley soon saw that customers were more interested in the baking powder than his soap, so he quickly switched to the baking powder business.

Looking for another premium to offer, Wrigley turned to chewing gum. He gave away two packages of chewing gum with each baking soda purchase, and again the premium was more popular than the product. In 1892, Wrigley Chewing Gum offered its first two brands: Lotta Gum and Vassar. Gradually he phased out baking powder and concentrated on chewing gum.[16]

In the late 1800s, there were at least a dozen companies pushing their wares, and in 1899 the six largest merged to form a chewing gum trust.

Although a newcomer to the industry, Wrigley was offered a place in the monopoly, but he refused. The young businessman plowed ahead, often teetering on the verge of bankruptcy.

Wrigley realized the power of advertising early in his career. Much of the company's budget focused on selling the product through advertisements and gimmicks. He expanded his premium offers, giving away items ranging from lamps and razors to cookbooks and fishing tackle. Wrigley even published premium catalogs to help customers choose what they wanted.

Wrigley used every form of advertising at his disposal. In his company's ads, Wrigley repeatedly told people about the benefits of the product. He bought space in newspapers, magazines, and even outdoor posters. In 1893 and 1894, Wrigley introduced Juicy Fruit and Wrigley's Spearmint

A very large Wrigley ad appears on a building in Martinez, California, ca. 1900. Entrepreneur William Wrigley made the most of advertising by using newspapers, magazines, outdoor posters, and even oversized paintings on buildings. Courtesy of the Contra Costa County Historical Society.

flavors. Wrigley designed the logo on the Spearmint package and decided that the company would concentrate on popularizing spearmint, which no other company had been able to do.

The public did not accept Wrigley's Spearmint immediately, but Wrigley pushed it relentlessly. In 1907, a depression year, Wrigley was able to buy over $1.5 million worth of advertising in cash-strapped New York for $284,000. The gamble paid off when sales jumped dramatically. Company revenue topped $1.3 million in 1909, and a year later, Wrigley's Spearmint was the top-selling gum in the United States.

Wrigley soon became the largest chewing gum manufacturer in the world. He bought the Zero Company in 1911, which had been making Wrigley's gum since 1892. From that point forward, the newly named William Wrigley Jr. Company manufactured its own products.

Albert Lasker

Albert Lasker propelled advertising through frequently murky waters in the 1900s. Working for the Chicago advertising firm of Lord & Thomas, Lasker controlled his workers with artificial deadlines that were ahead of schedule, the constant threat of firings, and a colossal ego. Unlike most men with his authority, Lasker stayed out of the public eye, wielding power behind the lines.

Beginning his career at Lord & Thomas as an office boy, sweeping up after the principals and cleaning spittoons, he later became a salesman in the Midwest. His success there, bringing in $50,000 in new business after just a few months, sent him down the path to prominence. By 1902, Lasker was the firm's star salesman. Two years later, after Lord retired, he bought 25 percent of the firm. At the age of 24, Lasker became a partner. Lasker's innovations included a card system that allowed the agency to determine which outlets (newspapers, magazines, etc.) were most successful for their clients. The results gave Lasker hard data, which impressed clients and resulted in higher budgets for campaigns.[17]

Lasker was also revolutionary in his thinking about writers. He liked advertising copy to resemble news pieces. Lasker paid writers extremely well,

but if they did not produce, he was quick to fire them. The firm's revenues went from $800,000 in 1898 to $3 million in 1905, and then to $6 million seven years later.[18] In 1912, Lasker bought out his partners and ran the largest advertising agency in the world.

MAKING ADVERTISING PROGRESSIVE

The reform movement sweeping America in the 1900s looked at the advertising industry with a wary eye. Patent medicines, cure-alls, wonder pills, and health devices were all targeted by critics of advertising. The movement began when the influential editor of the *Ladies' Home Journal,* Edward W. Bok, began to crusade against unsubstantiated claims in medical advertising in the early 1890s. Other magazines joined Bok's crusade. The effort culminated in a muckraking article, which appeared in *Collier's* in 1904 that included a chemical breakdown of the ingredients of several advertised products. Later available as a book entitled *The Great American Fraud* (1906) compiled by Samuel Hopkins Adams, the articles proved that such supposed "remedies" contained no secret ingredient and, as a matter of fact, contained many additives that were either addictive or unhealthy. Even more frightening in the eyes of reformers were the chemical additives put into foods to extend shelf life. Scientists developing these preservatives worried more about effectiveness than the long-term consequences of consumption on customers.[19]

Spurred by Bok's efforts, along with Upton Sinclair's muckraking novel *The Jungle,* which investigated the grotesque conditions of Chicago's meatpacking plants, the consumer movement led to government regulation. In 1906, strong federal laws such as the Meat Inspection Act and the Pure Food and Drug Act forced companies to change the way they manufactured goods. Laws required businesses to list ingredients on food containers, medicine bottles, and pill holders. Advertising also had to adhere to the new rules. (See Food of the 1900s.)

Henry J. Heinz, born in Pittsburgh, founded the H. J. Heinz Company in 1888. Heinz used advertising to build brand recognition. The famous slogan "57 Varieties," describing Heinz's pickles, was actually a made-up number that sounded good to consumers and Heinz. At the turn of the century, the company already produced close to 200 products. For product distribution, Heinz used brightly painted wagons and freight cars painted bright yellow and decorated with the Heinz pickle emblem. The Heinz Company participated in world's fairs, markets, and expositions. At the World's Columbian Exposition in Chicago (1893), Heinz had the largest space designated for a food manufacturer. The company hired girls to hand out samples and mementos, such as a green pickle labeled "Heinz," which could be worn as a charm. Officials had to enforce crowd regulation for fear that the floor would cave in around the Heinz booth.[20]

Heinz established the Crystal Palace by the Sea on the Heinz Ocean Pier in Atlantic City. Visitors walked under an arch to a glass-encased Sun Parlor, which had comfortable furnishings and a full kitchen where hot and cold Heinz products were demonstrated. Next, adventurous guests could walk 900 feet out on the pier to the Glass Pavilion, which had a 70-foot-tall electric sign that read, "57." The pavilion contained an art gallery, lecture hall, and display of all the products manufactured by Heinz. In Pittsburgh, Heinz used his industrial complex as a living museum, where visitors could witness the cleanly scrubbed "Heinz girls" working in spotless surroundings. By 1900, more than 20,000 people visited the plant a year.[21]

Heinz became one of the first industrial firms to hire women—mostly German, Polish, and Italian immigrants from Pittsburgh. The women wore clean uniforms to impress the many visitors passing through the complex, and they were spotless themselves, a far cry from the unsanitary sweatshop conditions other immigrant women faced in the 1900s. Like many firms of the period and throughout the early part of the century, Heinz watched over the moral and physical welfare of workers. They were given cultural and recreational facilities for outside activities, and the company paid each worker's medical and dental bills. Other companies—Ford was a notable

example—employed cultural and sociological means to control workers and to attempt in many ways to "Americanize" them, especially if the company relied heavily on an immigrant workforce.

Heinz was an authoritarian and did not allow unions in his plants, but he also realized that a great company could not cheat its customers and still be considered an outstanding business. Consequently, Heinz took a public stance against the preservatives and additives used and supported by many of his colleagues.

Advertising played a fundamental role in bringing the issue of sanitation standards, both at home and in business, greatly improving the health and welfare of citizens in the early twentieth century. Schools, organizations, boards of health, and concerned citizens groups all combined to focus on education, and used advertising to do so.

Metropolitan Insurance joined the fight for sanitation through advertising campaigns directed at the immigrants who bought insurance policies at the firm. The company sent agents into immigrants' homes to extol the virtues of cleanliness (at a time when a "clean" person bathed once a week on average). Agents handed out pamphlets that explained how diseases were transferred. Metropolitan then installed disposable drinking cups on many railroad lines and gave away fly swatters with the message, "Clean Homes, Pure Food, Clean Milk, No Flies, and No Mosquitoes."[22]

In this health-conscious framework, many entrepreneurs, including those at Scott Paper, produced goods that helped fight disease. In 1908, Hugh Moore used disposable drinking cups, but the idea did not catch on until health activists published a study proving the dangers of using publicly shared drinking containers. Moore then promoted the cups heavily through advertising. One ad, which incorporated the tagline "Spare the Children," showed a diseased man drinking from a public basin, while a young girl waited in line behind him. Advertisements like these seem heavy-handed, but they were effective, and Moore's Dixie Cups became the most famous, best-selling disposable cups in history.

Architecture

of the 1900s

American architects in the 1900s were more than simply builders or designers; they considered themselves artists. As such, architects faced many of the same challenges experienced by artists in other disciplines, such as overcoming European influences, dealing with modernity, and finding their way in an age dominated by industrialism and machinery. For the period's greatest architects, like Louis Sullivan and his protégé Frank Lloyd Wright, the answer was to find an essentially American soul and allow that spirit to personify their work.

Since the discipline combined artistic value with science, engineering, and technological innovations, architecture served the needs of growing corporations. If businesses could add revenue-generating floor space by building skyward, they could maximize the potential of each parcel of land they purchased. This became especially important in such growing cities as Chicago, New York, and San Francisco.

In the late 1800s, American architects built large, imposing buildings that celebrated the increasing wealth and might of the nation. Because they used a variety of styles from the past (Gothic, Romanesque, Renaissance, and Baroque), there was little uniformity. Sometimes several styles made it into the design of a single building. As time advanced, however, architects adopted specific styles to meet the needs of the growing nation.

Building materials had advanced throughout the nineteenth century, which allowed designers in the 1900s to be more adventurous and daring in their work. Architects used standardized sizes of prefabricated lumber (called "balloon framing" for its lightness in comparison to older structures) to build wooden skeletons for housing, offices, and other buildings. The success of the wooden balloon frame, although highly susceptible to fire, led architects and engineers to consider other sources of structural framing.

Building tall structures was not the only innovative design work taking place at the turn of the century. Architects were crafting a new America, represented by its tall buildings and magnificent structures on one hand, and homes and factories on the other.

SKYSCRAPERS

The skyscraper was one of the most impressive tributes to the twentieth century. These structures celebrated modern technology, materials, and innovation.

The development of iron and steel as structural materials fueled the idea of the tall building in the early nineteenth century. Steel allowed architects to move skyward with a minimum of bulk, thus enabling larger windows and more flexible interior spaces. Before the development of a safe passenger elevator in 1857, the traditional limit for buildings had been five stories.

Many of the early advances in skyscrapers can be attributed to the devastating fire that wiped out most of Chicago in 1871. City planners and architects turned to fireproof iron and steel instead of wood and masonry. Modern business also demanded large working spaces. Because of these factors, along with high real estate costs, the skyscraper took shape in Chicago.

The men behind the rebuilding of Chicago were Boston financiers. They urged Chicago architects to build tall buildings to maximize profits, and encouraged designers to keep the structures simple by eliminating nonessential ornamentation. The resulting approach, renowned for its minimalism, became known as the Chicago Style. Louis Sullivan, in particular, realized the necessity of recognizing height, not just magnitude, in structures. Sullivan viewed himself as a poet first and an artist second. Sullivan immortalized his ideology when he coined the phrase "form follows function" in an 1896 essay written for *Lippincott's* magazine.

Sullivan soared to the top of the profession in the late 1800s, building great structures in Chicago, along with the Prudential Building in Buffalo in 1895. The Bayard Building (constructed between1897 and 1899), his only design in New York City, has been called a "spiritual ancestor" to the towering skyscrapers that now line the streets of the city. After his partnership with Dankmar Adler broke up, Sullivan had fewer and fewer commissions. His prickly personality and righteous attitude about his work drove away many potential clients.

Despite Sullivan's eccentricities, his reputation won him new projects. He designed what many consider his best work in the early 1900s: the Schlesinger & Mayer Store (later sold to the Carson Pirie Scott Company) in Chicago. Although not a tall building (the functions of a department store meant its form had to be somewhat blocky), Sullivan nonetheless used innovative techniques in the structural design so that the department store could remain open during the busy Christmas holiday season. Under his direction, workers put in a new foundation under the old one while customers shopped above them.

As the decade progressed, Sullivan turned to other types of buildings to express his "democratic" style of architecture. He secured commissions to design rural banks to serve primarily farming customers.

Sullivan's ideas about building tall structures served as the guide for construction over the next several decades. However, the stage moved from his beloved Chicago to the city that would become known around the world for its massive skyscrapers—New York. Fueled by what they had witnessed in Chicago, New York architects pulled out all the stops to surpass their Midwestern rivals. In the mid-1890s, New York skyscrapers already pushed past 20 stories.

Ironically, the architect who showed New York what a skyscraper could be was Chicagoan Daniel Burnham (1846–1912). Burnham joined with another famous Windy City architect, John Wellborn Root, to build a number of Chicago's most famous structures from that period: the Montauk Block (1882), the Rookery (1886), and the Rand-McNally Building (1890).

After Root's death in 1891, Burnham took over the agency. The newly renamed D. H. Burnham and Company grew into Chicago's largest firm, and then opened offices in New York and San Francisco. Burnham designed the Wannamaker department store in New York (1903), Chicago's Orchestra Hall (1904), and Union Station in Washington, D.C. (1907). Burnham also gained international renown as an urban planner. He played a major role in the redevelopment of Chicago, which resulted in Grant Park, throughout the 1900s. Burnham helped design urban plans for other cities, including one for San Francisco after the earthquake and fire of 1906.

Although Burnham achieved great fame with many projects, it was his design of the Flatiron Building (1902) that has been described as the ideal skyscraper. A joking reference to the shape, the Flatiron Building has a steel frame covered in terra cotta and stone. The building is situated on a relatively narrow triangular site at the intersection of three streets; it faces Madison Square Park. The Fuller Building (the building's official name), along with the Statue of Liberty and the Brooklyn Bridge, shortly became a major tourist attraction and adorned countless postcards.

The Flatiron looks more like an alien craft cutting through space than a 22 story office building. The head of the triangle is accentuated by a single row of windows fronting the structure. Edward Steichen, the building's most famous photographer, captured the building towering over the trees in the adjacent park in a magnificent black-and-white photograph that depicts the remarkable thinness of the structure. Steichen's photograph juxtaposes the man-made Flatiron with a slightly crooked tree in the foreground, contrasting nature with fabrication, a key theme of architects and artists in the 1900s.[1]

Burnham's structure transformed the way in which people viewed office towers. More than just a place to work and maximize space, Burnham's

Steichen's photograph of the Flatiron Building on a rainy evening, with horses and carriages in foreground, New York City. Prints & Photographs Division, Library of Congress.

design made tall buildings a source of corporate pride. Skyscrapers, in essence, defined corporate America, showed off the accumulating wealth of the nation, and helped solidify the burgeoning "corporate culture" engulfing American workers. For corporate leaders, it was not enough to have a thriving business: a skyscraper with the company's name emblazoned on it became the new corporate symbol of power.

From 1900 until the Great Depression hit in 1929, at least one new skyscraper appeared every year in New York. Tall buildings had an even more sweeping effect on the psyche of the nation. In many respects, skyscrapers marked a rite of passage for cities around the world. On the one hand, they were perpetual advertisements for their owners; on the other, skyscrapers catered to the romanticism of the masses. They reflected the power of the United States and the modern technological age.

PRIVATE BUILDINGS

Classicism and Revivals

Between the Civil War and World War I, various styles of architecture gained popularity with the changing times and were influenced by the divergent climates across the nation.

The actual infrastructure of houses changed as well. Technological innovations like electricity, central heating, and plumbing made homes more livable. Building materials like stucco and tile were used to make houses built in warm climates, such as California and Florida, more bearable. Mass customization of the construction industry also played a significant role in housing styles. As the decade wore on, necessities like doors, windows, and roofing shingles were mass-produced and could be transported around the nation. This led to a more uniform look in cities and suburbs, where building houses quickly to meet the demand was essential.

One approach, which recalled the classical forms of Europe, was spread by American architects who trained in Europe and returned to America to practice their profession. Many Americans studied at the Ecole des Beaux Arts in Paris, the foremost architectural school in the

Architecture

world. The Americans who studied there, led by Richard Morris Hunt (the first American graduate), brought its techniques and theories back to the United States. The Beaux Arts style centered on lavish ornamentation, low-pitched roofs, exaggerated stonework, masonry walls, and arched windows.[2]

The Beaux Arts influenced designers built mansions in this style, which gave an air of royalty and power to America's new industrial rich. The New York firm of McKim, Mead, and White designed the mansion Rosecliff (1902) in fashionable Newport, Rhode Island, a summer getaway for the wealthy, along with many other mansions along the East Coast. Stanford White designed Rosecliff with Louis XIV's Versailles in mind.

The firm, led by Charles Follen McKim, William Rutherford Mead, and Stanford White, developed into the leading architectural firm in the nation in the 1900s. The accomplishments achieved by the firm included Penn Station, Madison Square Garden, the Brooklyn Museum, the Boston Symphony Hall and Public Library, and Low Library at Columbia University. The firm remodeled the White House, adding additional executive offices. McKim, Mead, and White carried out traditional designs, primarily centered on Renaissance and Romanesque styles. Although modernists scorned this type of architecture, it remained popular for much of the twentieth century.[3]

Between 1880 and 1910, the château style flourished, based on sixteenth-century French chateaus that combined Gothic elements and Renaissance detailing in stone masonry. The style, adopted primarily for wealthy patrons in the United States, included steeply pitched roofs and high spires. The most famous example of the château style is George W. Vanderbilt's Biltmore estate in Asheville, North Carolina (1895). At one time, the estate, landscaped by Frederick Law Olmsted who designed New York's Central Park, was a retreat. Today open to the public, it highlights the architecture and decorative arts of the period.[4] This style also found its way into many churches, college buildings, and government buildings.

A Tudor revival grew in popularity, first among the wealthy suburbanites of New York, Chicago, and other large cities, then gradually as designers built less expensive models for average home buyers. Tudors feature tall, narrow windows, large chimneys, and Renaissance detailing on doors and windows.

The Colonial revival stood as the symbolic rebirth of early English, Dutch, Spanish, and French designs, adapted to conditions in the United States with modern materials. Different styles of Colonial dominated different regions: in California, one found Spanish and Pueblo revivals; on the East Coast, Georgian and Dutch houses were common. Later, the Colonial form underwent a slimming process, down to a single story, which resulted in the Cape Cod style.[5]

The unassuming bungalow, which had made its appearance in the late nineteenth century, continued in the 1900s, setting off a national bungalow craze, which lasted into 1930. Designers modeled bungalows after the single-story houses used by the British in India (the name comes from the Bengal province in India where regional dwellings were termed bang'la or bang'ala by the locals). In the United States, bungalows, appropriate for a warm climate, were first built in Southern California. Builders in other regions, in spite of harsh weather conditions, adopted the style for low-income and lower middle-class families. In the end, the structures were simply cheaper to build than traditional suburban middle-class homes. Because of their low cost, they began to appear in industrial neighborhoods, such as the small steel mill town of Clairton, Pennsylvania, and in large sections of Cleveland, Ohio, which sprang up around Republic Steel.[6]

Interior Design

Begun in England and accentuated at the Philadelphia Centennial Exposition of 1876, the Colonial revival in America influenced how people decorated the insides of their houses. Dubbed the Arts and Crafts movement, the philosophy hinged on a general rejection of the excesses of the Industrial Revolution and machine-made products. Looking back with nostalgia at the Colonial period, interior designers discarded wallpaper and heavy carpeting and returned to hardwood floors and simple styles of furniture. The movement turned into a crusade for simple living. In 1904, there were 25 Arts and Crafts societies in the

United States, whose purpose was to take urban dwellers back to a simpler way of life.

The women of the 1900s rejected the Victorian interiors so popular a decade before in exchange for simpler designs. A typical Victorian home was dark and cluttered with antiques, sculptures, and paintings mixed together with heavy draperies, embroidered tablecloths, and various lace curtains and doilies.

The main proponent of the style in the United States was Gustav Stickley (1858–1942), founder of *The Craftsman* (1901), a magazine trumpeting the movement. He advised that home decorating be unadorned, with paneled walls and small windows with groups of square panes. Stickley used built-in corner seats, fireplace nooks, and other cozy touches. He also advocated a sensible variety of furniture, labeled Mission style. These pieces used rough-hewn timber and no nails or glue to hold them together. Mission carpenters used oak as the standard material and finished it until it turned a golden brown. Stickley used *The Craftsman* to fuel the movement and to comment on other areas that touched his readers' lives, including art, education, politics, and urban planning.[7] The craze for natural-looking furnishings helped drive the bungalow rage, which featured exposed wood and heavy, organic fittings.

The Arts and Crafts movement was especially popular in California. A group of architects, including Joseph Worcester, Irving J. Gill, and Julia Morgan, among others, built structures that underscored practicality. They used native materials and color schemes to boost natural living. The Arts and Crafts movement influenced the nation as a whole. Sears, Roebuck and Company offered Craftsman home kits and matching Mission furniture in its mail-order catalogs. By mid-century, the company boasted that enough of its materials had been purchased to build a city containing 25,000 people.[8]

Many firms responded to the Colonial revival by designing handcrafted furniture, pottery, and glasswork. Frank Lloyd Wright used this style in his own designs. He emphasized large fireplaces where the family could gather together, exposed wooden beams in ceilings, and stained wood detailing.

For many women, as the country transitioned from a rural to an urban nation, the home ceased to be a place of production. Women, at least married women, became full-time homemakers. Single women, usually between the ages of 16 and 20, worked outside the home and accounted for nearly 60 percent of the female workforce in the early 1900s. Many women worked in the years they spent between school and marriage. Wives, however, had fewer opportunities for outside work, although these opportunities increased as the decade progressed.[9]

For women both on the farm and in the suburbs and cities, however, domestic life changed quickly. They may have rejected industrialism in decorating, but adopted the most innovative labor saving devices. Even the means for acquiring such goods became simpler. Women could turn to mail-order catalogues to fulfill just about every need: from a coffee grinder (49 cents), to a rocking chair ($2.95), to a full-sized wood-burning stove ($17.48), to a hair-waving iron (11 cents).[10]

Frank Lloyd Wright

America's greatest architectural genius was Frank Lloyd Wright (1867–1959), the son of a preacher father and a school teacher mother. During the first decade of the 1900s, Wright established much of his early reputation. After finding his mentor in Louis Sullivan, who was considered the father of modern American architecture, Wright helped the firm of Adler and Sullivan design the Wainwright Building in St. Louis, the Garrick Theatre in Chicago's Schiller Building, and many other buildings.

Wright referred to Sullivan as "Lieber Master," or beloved master, although the two men had a falling out over Wright's accepting private commissions to design houses (later in life they renewed their friendship). In 1893, Wright set up his own shop in Oak Park, Illinois, a suburb of Chicago. The first masterpiece he designed was the Winslow House (1893) in River Forest, Illinois.

Wright's Prairie-style houses reflected horizontal, rather than vertical, lines. Wright wanted his residential homes to be simple, relaxing, and promote harmony and quiet domesticity. There were

Architecture

Robie House by Frank Lloyd Wright. Designed for efficiency and in a modern design, this house, built 100 years ago, still looks contemporary in the twenty-first century. Prints & Photographs Division, Library of Congress.

no basements or attics in Wright's Prairie homes, and the wood was always stained, never painted, to emphasize the material's natural beauty. The outside of the buildings featured wide, overhanging eaves; the interiors were somewhat sparse and lit primarily with outside light.

The houses were supposed to adapt to the natural surroundings. Wright was striking out against the ornamentation and overwrought structures that dominated the American scene. In a Wright Prairie-style home, it is not uncommon to see the landscape meld with the walls and to find built-in planter boxes, meshed together perfectly with the overall rectangular design.

The Robie House (1909) in Chicago was arguably Wright's most powerful design of the decade. Fred Robie, an ideal client for Wright, wanted a modern house that emphasized ease of life. The Robie House was built with brick, stone, concrete, glass, and tile with efficient electric lighting, telephone, and burglar alarm systems. Robie, an engineer and efficiency nut, wanted his house to be free from "curvatures and doodads," which did little but collect dust.

Another of Wright's famous Prairie-style homes was built for wealthy heiress Susan Lawrence Dana in Springfield, Illinois. In the Dana House (1902), Wright rejected the idea that individual rooms had to be a series of boxes and positioned his rooms diagonally, achieving his goal of "destroying the box." The Dana House was Wright's first to be built with a two-story living room.[11]

Then, Wright moved on to the exterior, expanding the number and size of windows. He also invented a way of wrapping windows around corners, making the corners of the house look like they vanished into thin air. Next, he made the roof longer and wider, extending it 20 feet past the last masonry support.

In the Dana House and others of the 1900s, Wright made artistic changes that were both admired and advanced. Wright's roofs were angled to protect inhabitants from harsh sunlight, but still allowed it to come in during the winter. He also built central heating systems with hot water pipes, thus keeping the architectural masterpieces artistic and livable. He even took into consideration cross ventilation in the summer to cool the houses, which was especially important in the days before air conditioning.

Throughout the decade, Wright designed dozens of homes, primarily in and around Chicago and part of Wisconsin. In 1904, Wright designed his first corporate building, the Larkin Building in Buffalo, New York. The Larkin Company was a thriving national mail-order business that manufactured its own products.

The Larkin Building, in downtown Buffalo, was adjacent to train tracks on one side and busy city streets on the other. Wright decided that the building must be grand, lending an air of dignity to the otherwise drab Larkin complex, which consisted mainly of factories. The building also had to be sealed off from its environment, which is routine today, but virtually impossible in Wright's day. The list of innovations Wright achieved with the Larkin facility includes double-glazed windows to reduce noise, heat, and cold, subfloor electric light and telephone connections, the use of magnesite, a synthetic, fireproof material as durable as concrete but softer, and wall-hung toilets with ceiling-hung stall partitions. The interior of the building featured a five story atrium, topped by a huge skylight. Although some observers likened the building to a closed society or church of work, Wright designed it to be worker friendly, providing fresh air (a rarity next to the coal-burning railroad cars) and an early form of air-conditioning.

Although the edifice Wright built was demolished in 1950 and was never fully appreciated by its owners, the building holds a lofty place in the annals of architectural history.

Books

Newspapers, Magazines, and Comics of the 1900s

A transformation took place among America's up-and-coming writers in the 1900s. A unique style emerged that loosened the nation's long-standing cultural ties to Britain and Europe. Writers in the United States asserted their "Americanness" and began examining the daily life of common people.

To a large degree, writers in the period were fueled by the nation's ascendancy in global economic and military affairs and the repercussions of the United States emerging as the world's most powerful nation. Its writers began the new century with a heightened sense of authority.

American writers interpreted the upheaval occurring all around them. Some reacted bitterly, like Henry James and Henry Brook Adams. The two old friends felt out of place in the new nation at the turn of the century. Henry James, from his perch in London, called the period from the Civil War to World War I "The Age of the Mistake." In his masterpiece, *The Education of Henry Adams,* privately published in 1907, the descendent of Presidents John and John Quincy Adams portrayed himself as bumbling and searching for meaning in the new century, but ultimately finding only doubt and confusion.[1]

Others relished the opportunity to contribute to the intellectual conversations gripping the nation. Taking their cue from the political leaders of the Progressive movement, African Americans, women, and immigrants lent their voices to a literary movement that included them more than it had in the past. W.E.B. Du Bois and Booker T. Washington made significant inroads for black authors, and a number of women writers impacted the regional and national literary scene, including New England authors Sarah Orne Jewett and Mary E. Wilkins Freeman.

Mixing investigative reporting and literary nonfiction, a group of enterprising writers, angrily denounced as "muckrakers" by President Theodore Roosevelt, exploited middle-class anxiety by exposing society's ills in newspapers and magazines. Middle-class readers reacted forcefully to stories illustrating the evils of big city life or the growing power of corporations. During the reform era, the nation's politicians listened as well. Upton Sinclair's masterful novel *The Jungle* (1906), depicting the gruesome conditions in Chicago's meatpacking plants, spurred Congress to pass the Pure Food and Drug Act of 1906.

As in other periods of the nation's history, sensationalism sold. Newspaper and magazine owners and editors quickly exploited this fact. Since the public could not turn to television or radio, newspapers and magazines wielded a great deal of influence. As early as 1900, more than 5,500 periodicals were published in the United States.

They ranged from literary journals, such as the *Atlantic Monthly, Harper's Magazine,* and *The Century,* to general interest or political weeklies and monthlies, including *Cosmopolitan, The Saturday Evening Post,* and *Independent.* The circulation figures are impressive, even by modern standards. The literary magazines boasted sales in excess of 100,000 copies a month; others climbed to as high as one million. In 1900, there were 2,226 daily newspapers with a combined circulation of more than 15 million.[2]

Technological advances in print production, which permitted color to be used more frequently, enabled publishing companies to sell a new style of magazine at 10–15 cents a copy, and to direct them to specific segments of the reading population. Women, in particular, were targeted by numerous publications. Among the most successful was *Ladies' Home Journal,* founded in 1883 and edited by Edward W. Bok. The magazine's circulation surpassed one million in 1902. Bok and other savvy editors realized they could offset the cover price by accepting advertising from the companies that catered to the middle class's newfound consumer culture.

Cheap binding, faster print production, and a better understanding of mass marketing led to the birth of the bestseller. Readers in the 1900s bought sentimental, romance, and historical romance novels approximately ten times as often as the works critics considered "literature."

Although his stature has risen dramatically in the many decades since his death, Jack London became America's first millionaire author by capitalizing on the public's insatiable appetite for adventure stories. London had failed as a gold prospector in Alaska as a young man, but his tales of the Klondike, such as *The Call of the Wild* (1903) and *White Fang* (1906) made him rich and famous. London's work habits were legendary—he worked all day and night, barely breaking to eat or drink, and slept less than five hours a night, reportedly writing 1,000 words a day for 17 years.

Dime novels (so called because of their cheap price and appeal to young readers with action-packed stories), first published in the 1850s, were still extremely popular in the 1900s. Most were published weekly, with lurid covers enticing their mostly male readership. Over the years, dime novels moved beyond Westerns, and readers increasingly picked from stories about detectives, life on the railroads, sports, and the city. The new century did not hurt the popularity of the Horatio Alger stories, which sold in department stores for 19 cents. These rags-to-riches sagas featured city boys preoccupied with making good and ultimately succeeding despite problems along the way.

NOTABLE BOOKS

Lord Jim, Joseph Conrad (1900)

To Have and to Hold, Mary Johnston (1900)

The Wonderful Wizard of Oz, L. Frank Baum (1900)

Sister Carrie, Theodore Dreiser (1900)

The Simple Life, Charles Wagner (1901)

Mrs. Wiggs of the Cabbage Patch, Alice Hegen Rice (1901)

Kim, Rudyard Kipling (1901)

The Octopus, Frank Norris (1901)

The Tale of Peter Rabbit, Beatrix Potter (1902)

Up from Slavery, Booker T. Washington (1901)

The Virginian, Owen Wister (1902)

Heart of Darkness, Joseph Conrad (1902)

The Story of My Life, Helen Keller (1902)

Rebecca of Sunnybrook Farm, Kate Douglas Wiggin (1903)

The Call of the Wild, Jack London (1903)

The House of Mirth, Edith Wharton (1905)

The Education of Henry Adams, Henry Adams (1907)

The Jungle, Upton Sinclair (1906)

White Fang, Jack London (1906)

A Room with a View, E. M. Forster (1908)

Anne of Green Gables, Lucy M. Montgomery (1908)

The Trail of the Lonesome Pine, John Fox Jr. (1908)

The Circular Staircase, Mary Roberts Rinehart (1908)

Books

Books

REALISM AND NATURALISM

The United States entered the new century riding a wave of industrial and military might that solidified its status as one of the world's great powers. But with the newfound strength came an ever growing list of domestic evils, including racism, sexism, and poverty, which mocked America's pledge of equality, opportunity, and progress. These disparities made the 1900s much more than an "Age of Innocence," as novelist Edith Wharton labeled the decade.

A more fitting categorization of the 1900s would be the "Age of Contrasts." The decade witnessed a widening gap between urban and rural, black and white, and rich and poor. A battle existed between the overt optimism brought on by technology, industry, and power and the realities of everyday life for most Americans.

The carnage and agony of the Civil War still haunted people, and racial brutality was a daily reminder of the conflict. Immigrants poured into the country by the millions, and people who had been content to stay on the family farm a generation earlier flocked to the cities in search of a steady income and a better quality of life. City leaders were unprepared for the strain on infrastructure networks, and the worst sections in many cities became ghettos filled with filth and despair.

Swarming with overcrowded streets, factories, and tenements, American cities in the 1900s turned gritty. Diligent efforts made by local officials could not stem the influx of people nor keep up with the infrastructure demands placed on the swelling cities. For example, New York City grew 500 percent between 1860 and 1900, from a population of 750,000 to more than 3.5 million. Chicago topped the 2 million mark.

In these frenzied and chaotic times, American writers asserted themselves as interpreters of the changes taking place before their eyes. Because large segments of the public yearned for literary work in magazines, journals, and newspapers, they had no shortage of outlets to explore new ideas and theories.

William Dean Howells, largely ignored by today's scholars, was the era's unofficial dean of letters and led the "realist" school. This loose association of writers explored life and morality in a culture driven by big business and corporations. Realist authors focused on concrete facts and turned away from portraying genteel society, romantic excess, and utopian idealism—notions that dominated the literary scene prior to 1900. Howells and Henry James actively campaigned for the realist cause, and their works were widely read by the general public and studied by scholars.

Realism in America picked up steam at the turn of the century when society seemed threatened to some degree by the changes taking place—technological advances, never-ending streams of immigrants, and a growing reliance on urban life at the expense of the nation's farmers. The attempt to understand the rapidly changing nation proved to be a fertile ground for writers like Mark Twain, Henry James, and Howells. Realism, however, meant different things to each author. For James, realist fiction explored the inside of characters' minds, a stream of consciousness effect that attempted to reconcile a person's interaction with the outside world and one's inner sensibilities. Twain, on the other hand, concentrated on the use of authentic dialect and shunned the genteel.[3]

Realists tried to probe beneath the surface, essentially starting with facts, then using literary imagination and creativity. Realism, which took hold gradually after the horrors of the Civil War, served as a backlash against the Victorian romanticism popular throughout the nineteenth century. James and Howells, however, did not want their work to venture into violence, death, or extreme situations.

Naturalist writers, such as Frank Norris, Theodore Dreiser, and Jack London, took realism a step further by burrowing down deep into the lives of everyday people and examining characters as victims of society's unchallengeable forces, such as capitalism, poverty, and violence. For naturalists, the world was filled with immorality that distorted everyday life and destroyed republican idealism. They revealed a world that was cruel and indifferent to the plight of the downtrodden.[4]

The biggest difference between the realists and the naturalists was that naturalists were willing to expose the terrible things that happened in society when people are confronted with forces beyond their control.

William Dean Howells established his reputation as an influential editor of the *Atlantic Monthly.* In the 1900s, he served as editor of *Harper's Monthly,* where he wrote a column called "The Editor's Easy Chair." From this pulpit, Howells championed realism and earned the title of "Father of American Realism." He advocated fiction that incorporated psychology, sociology, and accurate depictions of everyday life. Howells authored more than 100 books, concentrating on the lives of characters from the upper middle class.

Howells's changing idealism acted as a philosophical bridge between the post-Civil War generation and those who came of age in the early twentieth century. At the same time that Howells served as a pillar of the literary establishment and urbane society, he also championed socialism, the labor movement, and women's rights. He marched in support of women's rights and took part in the creation of the National Association for the Advancement of Colored People (NAACP).

The other two reigning literary giants in the 1900s were Mark Twain and Henry James. Both authors adopted realism and actively served as mentors, critics, and friends to the next wave of writers following in their wake.

Although Twain is best known for his works published prior to 1900, he still cast a wide shadow over the new century. In his last decade (Twain died in 1910), he moved almost completely into promoting and selling himself and capitalizing on his reputation.

Some of Henry James's novels of the 1900s were considered among his greatest works—*The Wings of the Dove* (1902), *The Ambassadors* (1903), and *The Golden Bowl* (1904)—but he felt alienated from society and his audience. An expatriate living in London, James set foot in America only once during the decade, on a book tour in 1904 and 1905. He later published his diary from the trip as *The American Scene* in 1907. The book stands as a vivid portrait of a writer who no longer understands the changes taking place around him—either the money culture enveloping the nation or the mass immigration propelling city growth. Twentieth-century America, in James's mind, was overrun with immigrants and controlled by monopolistic corporations pushing consumption onto "the wage-earners."[5]

Frank Norris

American realism found its champion in Frank Norris, who grew up in the upper-middle class in San Francisco. Norris wished to portray life as it actually was, without the literary pretensions employed by the romantics.

After enrolling at the University of California at Berkeley and attending writing classes at Harvard, Norris joined the staff of *McClure's Magazine* in New York City. He arranged a meeting with Howells, who became a mentor to the young man.

Over the next several years, Norris wrote overtly masculine novels filled with brutish characters, including *McTeague* (1899), *Blix* (1899), and *A Man's Woman* (1900). With the publication of *McTeague,* the story of a brutal, self-taught San Francisco dentist, Norris became a full-time author and was regarded as one of the top writers of his generation.

Norris planned a trilogy, which he planned to call the "Trilogy of Wheat" and hoped would be the great American novel. The books followed the life cycle of wheat: growth in California, sale in Chicago markets, and distribution worldwide via railroad and steamship. Norris believed a novel should have a purpose, which he equated with telling the truth. With moral support from Howells, and bolstered by the sales of *McTeague* and his other early books, Norris planned a modern epic that would encompass contemporary issues. In preparation, Norris spent four months in San Francisco and the San Joaquin Valley conducting field research and collecting interviews. He decided to base the novel on the bloody battle between wheat ranchers in San Joaquin and a sheriff's posse representing the Southern Pacific Railroad. The encounter at Mussel Slough left eight men dead and forced other ranchers off their land.

After returning to New York, Norris worked at a feverish pace. By some accounts, he wrote the book in one long burst in December 1900. *The Octopus,* published in 1901, tells the story of Magnus Derrick, a wealthy rancher who tries to stand up to the power of the railroad. He tries to save the valley, but he is predestined to fail—a great man felled by the forces of evil represented by the steel tentacles of the railroad spreading across the land. While the story is dramatic, Norris introduced many of the problems plaguing farmers: foreign competition, high freight rates, railroad regulation, and worker unrest. *The Octopus,* in the spirit of the period's muckraking books, examines the dark side of capitalism.

The book cemented Norris's reputation. Howells and Jack London praised the book. Unfortunately, Norris died before completing his trilogy of wheat. He finished the next book in the series, *The Pit,* but died in San Francisco of a perforated appendix on October 25, 1902. His work expanded the definition of American realism and served as a model for a generation of writers who followed.

In an ironic twist of fate, Norris discovered his successor two years before his death while working as a reader for publishing company Doubleday, Page and Company. He received an unsolicited manuscript from Theodore Dreiser, a journalist and budding novelist. Norris claimed *Sister Carrie* (1900) was the best novel he had ever read and urged its publication, which led to a contract being offered.

Theodore Dreiser

Born into a large, poor Catholic family in Terre Haute, Indiana, in 1871, Dreiser experienced poverty on a daily basis. Prior to Theodore's birth, his father had built a thriving wool factory business, but he had no insurance and lost everything when a fire destroyed the mill. The family then bounced around various Midwestern cities searching for work. Tired of constantly moving, Dreiser left home at 16. He lived in Chicago for a time and spent a year at Indiana University. After leaving school, Dreiser held a series of menial jobs, but later returned to Chicago.

In 1892, Chicago's *Daily Globe* hired Dreiser as a reporter. In Chicago, then later at papers in Pittsburgh, Cleveland, St. Louis, Toledo, and New York City, Dreiser witnessed firsthand the brutalities that befell beggars, alcoholics, prostitutes, and the lowest members of the working poor.

Dreiser first tried writing short stories and published the first four he completed. A friend urged him to write a study of the hard, harsh realities that made up life in the city. Fulfilling that challenge

with *Sister Carrie,* Dreiser became the first American writer to fully explore the landscape of city life in fiction.

Sister Carrie chronicles urban struggle in the early twentieth century and the Darwinian ascent of Carrie Meeber, an ordinary girl who leaves Middle America to seek fame and fortune in Chicago. Her fascination with the city mirrored Dreiser's own, and he pulled pieces of the story from the experiences of his own sister, Emma, who had run away with a bartender years earlier. Tiring of factory life, where she first works, Carrie becomes the mistress of two men and manipulates each of them to her advantage. She eventually finds stardom as an actress on the Broadway stage. The tragic figure is the family man and manager of a respectable bar, George Hurstwood, who becomes a shell of his former self through his relationship with Carrie, and finally commits suicide in a cheap hotel. Dreiser's message appears to be that the relentless pursuit of money is a fool's quest and leads to tragedy; although Carrie does well for herself financially, she is not happy.

Even with Frank Norris's approval, publisher Frank Doubleday requested major revisions, deeming the book too scandalous for the reading public. Unwilling to change the book, Dreiser forced Doubleday to honor its contract by threatening a lawsuit for breach of contract. In response, the publisher printed 1,000 copies but did not promote or advertise *Sister Carrie.* Without the backing of his publishing house, Dreiser's book sold less than 500 copies.

The initial failure of *Sister Carrie,* coupled with several harsh reviews, drove Dreiser to a nervous breakdown. In 1903, he suffered from depression, insomnia, constipation, and headaches, and was unable to write. Doctors diagnosed Dreiser as a "neurasthenic," a debilitating nervous disorder thought to disturb the affluent who could not cope with the cultural, social, and economic changes characterizing the age. In an attempt to cure Dreiser, doctors submitted him to a rigorous set of exercises, followed by various drugs, diets, and homeopathy.[6]

Dreiser's brother Paul, a successful songwriter and composer, sent him to a sanitarium in White Plains, New York. Dreiser rebounded and accepted a position as an editor at Butterick's, a company that published magazines to promote dress patterns. Life as an editor afforded Dreiser the wealth and affluence he craved. In 1907, Dreiser bought one-third of a new publishing company, B. W. Dodge, and reissued *Sister Carrie* himself. The book sold more than 4,500 copies in 1907 and more than 10,000 the following year. The book received rave reviews and vaulted the author to the top of the literary mountain.

The power of *Sister Carrie* lies in Dreiser's portrait of urban life filled with sketches of the Chicago shoe factory, various saloons and hotels, and other streetscapes. Dreiser made the consumer culture gripping the nation a focal point of the book. He also recognized the influence of popular culture on the working class and how entertainment influenced their lives.

Dreiser's bottom-up look at contemporary society shocked upper and middle-class readers, but at the same time alerted them to another world.

THE READING PUBLIC

History, biography, and poetry did sell well during the 1900s, but fiction was the cornerstone of the industry. The romantic novel remained the most popular form of fiction after the Civil War and continued to hold the title.

Eager to capitalize on the market, publishing houses pumped romances out in massive quantities using the distribution systems built in the last years of the previous century. Improvements in print technology and paper production also aided the publishers. As the decade progressed, many serious authors found their way onto the bestseller lists, including Jack London and Edith Wharton. The mainstays, however, were writers who wrote about love, heroism, and the nostalgic past.

In the summer of 1901, Paul Leicester Ford sold 275,000 copies of *Janice Meredith* (1899), while Johnston's *To Have and to Hold* numbered 285,000. Even more impressive, Winston Churchill (not related to the British statesman) concentrated on historical fiction and sold more than 700,000 copies of *Richard Carvel* (1899) and *The Crisis* (1901), the romantic story of a fiery Southern heroine and a solemn Yankee hero. Other authors produced works that sold well for years, including Alice Hegen Rice's *Mrs. Wiggs*

of the Cabbage Patch and John Fox Jr.'s *The Little Shepherd of Kingdom Come* (1903). Edward Westcott's *David Harum,* published posthumously in 1898, a tale of a shrewd, heroic country banker, had sold an amazing 1.2 million copies by 1909 and was made into a movie in both 1915 and 1934, the latter starring Will Rogers.

One of the most prolific novelists of the period was Francis Marion Crawford, who produced more than 45 novels between 1882 and 1909. He wrote formulaic, though historically accurate, dramas, which gave readers a glimpse of life in India, Germany, Turkey, and other exotic locales. The public gobbled up his tales, whose characters ranged from New York debutantes to middle-class Romans.

Book publishing itself turned from a genteel profession prior to 1900 to one driven by profits, despite the outcry from many honorable older publishers who equated their professions with teaching and the ministry. Publishers feared meeting the fate of Harper's and Appleton, two of the country's oldest and most respected houses, which had to be saved from bankruptcy in 1900 by Wall Street financiers. The infusion of business-minded professionals changed the industry, enabling it to adopt new ideas, including marketing, globalization, and the widespread use of innovative technologies. In 1900, more than 600 publishers combined to produce in excess of 7,000 new books; the number reached a record in 1907 of 9,620.

The importance of marketing and sales increased dramatically. With more and more companies vying for advertising space in magazines, ad rates shot up, and estimates revealed that even small publishers spent upward of $50,000 a year on advertising. The 1900s began a trend in the book industry that continues to this day—high advertising and marketing costs cut deeply into the profits, even on best sellers.[7]

MUCKRAKERS

At the turn of the century, America entered a reform-minded period with politicians, reporters, and civic activists spearheading the charge. Driven by society's ills and a desire to expose the seedy underbelly of the new age, a group of

Books

enterprising writers began to poke into government and corporate corruption. President Roosevelt derisively labeled them "muckrakers," after a character in John Bunyan's *Pilgrim's Progress* (1678) who slandered those engaged in public work. While the president thought they went overboard and focused on the sensational, middle-class readers clamored for more. In fact, the muckrakers directly influenced the work of politicians and subsequent legislative efforts.

Like the realist fiction writers of the era, the muckrakers reacted to the changes sweeping the nation, focusing primarily on injustices in the corporate world and government. Investigative journalism came of age in the early 1900s, but it had its roots in the work done after the Civil War. The muckrakers grabbed the spotlight

when technology made magazines less expensive to publish and national illiteracy rates dropped. These influences, combined with the progressive political and social movement, made the first decade of the new century ripe for the muckrakers.

Magazines and investigative journalists fed off one another in the Progressive Era. The muckrakers fueled the growth of magazines, and at the same time were given a platform on which to present their work. Magazine prices gradually dropped to ten cents a month and a dollar for a year's subscription, which allowed the pioneering *McClure's* to jump from just over 100,000 in circulation in early 1895 to half a million in 1907.[8] Other magazines that grew through the publication of muckraking articles included *Collier's, Cosmopolitan, Everybody's,* the *Independent, Success,*

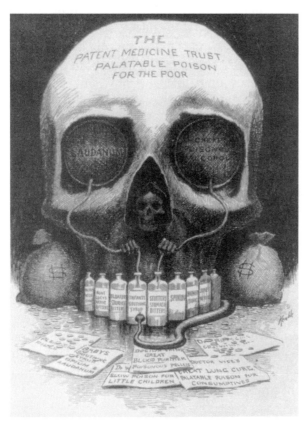

An example of muckraking journalism of the early 1900s. This cover of *Colliers* magazine, June 3, 1905, shows a cartoon by Kemble: "Death's Laboratory— The patent medicine trust," illustrating an article on problems with the phony medicines sold in such abundance during the period. Prints & Photographs Division, Library of Congress.

A poster advertising *The Jungle* by Upton Sinclair, showing a lion standing on the skull of a steer, 1906. Prints & Photographs Division, Library of Congress.

and the *American Magazine.* The January 1903 issue of *McClure's* ushered in the muckraking movement when it published an article on municipal graft written by Lincoln Steffens, a chapter from Ida Tarbell's history of Standard Oil, and an essay written by Ray Stannard Baker.

The muckraking movement ran virtually parallel to Roosevelt's presidency. Although he disliked the sensationalistic tactics employed by some writers, he respected their work. The president knew the writers and editors at the journals and sometimes invited them to White House luncheons. Many muckrakers, including Tarbell, Steffens, Baker, and Upton Sinclair became quite famous in their own right.

UPTON SINCLAIR, *THE JUNGLE*, AND THE 1906 PURE FOOD AND DRUG ACT

Upton Sinclair's novel, *The Jungle* (1906), is quite possibly the saddest book ever written. The novel follows the plight of a Lithuanian immigrant family trying to make it in America in the early twentieth century. The Rudkus family endures unimaginable tragedy and suffering on every page due to the manipulation of con men, brutal industry foremen, and the generally horrible conditions of life for immigrants in America during the early 1900s. Sinclair, a socialist writer, knew exactly what he was doing with this book. He stated, in essence, that he was there to write the *Uncle Tom's Cabin* of the labor movement. Indeed, his novel did effect social change in that it exposed the gross and inhumane practices of such industries as the meat packing plants. Early on, managers at these plants would think nothing of mixing in a man's severed arm with a vat of diseased cow. What evolved from *The Jungle* and other texts was the Food and Drug Act of 1906, six months after the book was published, which called for regular inspections and regulations of all meat products. Literary exposés that led to legislation were nothing new, as Sinclair pointed out. Abraham Lincoln referred to Harriet Beecher Stowe, the author of *Uncle Tom's Cabin,* as "the little lady who started the big war." Of course, he was referring to the Civil War, which was in part fought for the abolition of slavery, a subject addressed in Stowe's novel.

VOICES NOT OFTEN HEARD: WOMEN AND BLACKS

While the years following 1900 were filled with optimism and hope for many individuals and groups, these years offered little optimism for blacks in the United States. Racial divisions that plagued the nation since its founding continued unabated.

Blacks and other non-Anglo citizens were denied their basic freedoms through violent intimidation, legal wrangling, and segregation. This volatile environment led to 214 blacks being lynched in 1900 and 1901, and an average of 100 a year through World War I.[9] The *Plessy v. Ferguson* (1896) case before the Supreme Court made segregation constitutionally legal and solidified the second-class status of African Americans. The court case upheld the idea of "separate but equal," which made discrimination legal if facilities and accommodations for whites and blacks were equal. Factories and shop floors were more open to immigrants than they were to blacks.

In this environment of fear, intimidation, and legal manipulation to keep blacks disenfranchised, African-American writers fought to have their voices heard. Even in the South, where local authors explored the distinct flavor of the region, black authors had little impact in comparison with their white counterparts. The reading public looked to white writers, such as Joel Chandler Harris (1848–1908), to interpret the rural South and the black culture. Harris published the best-selling Uncle Remus stories, written in African-American dialect and based on folk characters.

For the most part, women authors found it difficult to publish, especially writers of serious literature. Publishers and critics, who were mostly male, marginalized many top female writers or ignored them altogether. Immigrant and black female writers found it even tougher. Publishing houses also played a role in marginalizing women and blacks by not printing books that wouldn't garner a large audience. Often, as in the case of critically acclaimed African American author Charles Waddell Chesnutt, the few blacks and women who did get published only had a couple of chances to prove they could sell, or they would get dropped.

Some women writers, however, were able to find an outlet by producing popular fiction, mainly romance or historical romance works. Their success may be linked to the political attention women gained from the suffragette Susan B. Anthony before her death in 1906, and from social worker Jane Addams. In addition, the seemingly more open-minded stance of the Progressives might have also helped women writers gain some measure of acceptance.

Despite the rampant racism and sexism of the publishing industry in the 1900s, several outstanding female and African American writers were able to emerge, most notably Edith Wharton, Booker T. Washington, and W.E.B. Du Bois. Unfortunately, the works of countless other female and black writers were suppressed in the first decade of the twentieth century and have faded into oblivion.

Edith Wharton

Edith Wharton (1862–1937) emerged from an affluent family that tried to squelch her literary aspirations. At the time, many believed education to be a burden for upper-class women, ultimately weakening their constitution. After her marriage to Teddy Wharton, a wealthy Bostonian 13 years her senior, Wharton suffered from severe neurasthenia and did not recover until 1900. She later told a friend that for 12 years she experienced intense nausea and constant fatigue.

Wharton's first book, *The Decoration of Houses* (1897), written with architect Ogden Codman, examined household design. The empowerment she felt after the first book propelled Wharton toward her first book of fiction, published two years later, a collection of short stories called *The Greater Inclination*. Although well into her 30s, when most women of her class were tending to children and running the day-to-day affairs of their estates, Wharton embarked on a career as a novelist and writer. After her mother's death in 1901, the Whartons moved to Lenox, Massachusetts, where she built a mansion called "the Mount." Wharton designed the house to allow her the privacy to write without interruption.

Wharton produced nearly a book a year throughout the 1900s. In addition, she wrote short stories, travel accounts, and poems. Wharton set her first novel, a historical romance called *The Valley of Decision* (1902) in eighteenth-century Italy.

Though the book showed talent and earned praise from noted novelist Henry James, he urged her to write about the world around her, especially the high society of old New York. She followed his advice and wrote *The House of Mirth* (1905), which established her as a bestselling author and a respected member of the literary class.

The House of Mirth tells the story of Lily Bart, a woman of New York high society at the turn of the century. Trapped by her class, and expected to marry a man of status, she longs for escape. The satirical elements of the novel are scathing, fully illuminating what Wharton regarded as a vacuous world occupied by the rich. Longing to be free, Lily is pulled back by the trappings of her social class. Ultimately, she overdoses on sleeping medication—the only freedom she had power to grasp.

The House of Mirth established Wharton as a literary celebrity and the book broke sales records at the time, staying at the top of the best seller list for several months. It was released in October 1905, and by Christmas, 140,000 copies were in print.[10] In 1906, Wharton earned $27,000 from the royalties of *The House of Mirth* (more than $250,000 in today's dollars). Fellow authors applauded Wharton, including Henry James, Hamlin Garland, and William Dean Howells. Reviewers and critics also universally praised the work. Toward the end of her life, Wharton's critics charged her with being out of touch with contemporary America and not understanding the working class.

In her own life, Wharton defied the picture she painted of New York society. After years of a loveless marriage, she moved to Paris in 1911, divorced in 1913, and lived out a rich intellectual life. Wharton continued to publish and two of her later books are considered classics: *Ethan Frome* (1911) and *The Age of Innocence* (1920).

The Age of Innocence won the Pulitzer Prize in 1921. Two years later, Yale awarded Wharton an honorary doctorate, making her the first woman to receive such an honor from any American university.

Booker T. Washington

One of the first widely accepted black writers in the new century was Booker T. Washington (1856–1915). His autobiography, *Up from Slavery*

(1901), describes a life of overcoming enormous odds to achieve a semblance of the American Dream. As a child, Washington lived in a one-room shack with a dirt floor, and his stepfather forbade him to learn to read or write. Instead of retreating to a life of abject poverty, his early experiences pushed Washington to emphasize education and learning. Washington rose to become president of Tuskegee Institute and advised presidents and other leaders regarding race relations.

After Washington joined President Roosevelt for lunch at the White House in October 1901, a firestorm of protest erupted against both men. Ironically, neither Roosevelt nor Washington planned the meeting to make a point about racism. The intellectual Roosevelt simply wanted to meet with the black leader to discuss a wide-ranging set of issues. However, the public outcry over a simple lunch date showed how far the nation had to go to make any progress in regard to race issues.

W.E.B. Du Bois

Washington's approach to improving the lives of blacks through vocational training drew criticism from other black leaders, most prominently W.E.B. Du Bois (1868–1963). In Du Bois's mind, Washington supported a system that fundamentally denied African Americans their basic rights. Instead Du Bois favored blacks organizing their own businesses to achieve economic independence. He criticized Washington in an essay in his book *The Souls of Black Folk* (1903).

In contrast to Washington, Du Bois grew up in a middle-class family in Massachusetts and became the first black to earn a Ph.D. from Harvard University. Du Bois did not believe in civil rights as defined by other leaders. He urged Southern blacks to move north. After a bloody race riot in Springfield, Illinois, Du Bois and his followers held conferences at Harpers Ferry and Niagara Falls, which eventually led to the creation of the National Association for the Advancement of Colored People (NAACP). Du Bois served as the first editor of the NAACP journal, the *Crisis*.

Other Black Writers

Black writers asserted themselves as far as possible in a white-dominated publishing system. Poet Paul Laurence Dunbar (1872–1906) and novelist Charles W. Chesnutt (1858–1932) both gained fame during the 1900s. Booker T. Washington dubbed Dunbar, a native of Dayton, Ohio, as the "Poet Laureate of the Negro Race." Although talented writers, neither Dunbar nor Chesnutt enjoyed the fame or attention accorded their white contemporaries. Dunbar faced financial difficulties his entire life and eventually worked in the Reading Room of the Library of Congress. Chesnutt settled down in Cleveland, Ohio, and found success as a lawyer and legal stenographer.

While financial success eluded Dunbar most of his life, he became one of America's most popular poets during the 1900s and achieved international fame. Dunbar used black dialect and standard English in his poetry. He began publishing his verse in 1895, with *Majors and Minors*. With his first book, Dunbar grabbed the attention of William Dean Howells. The glowing review Howells gave Dunbar's dialectic poems, however, hindered the young man as he tried to break away from the genre. American literary critics accepted black poets only when they employed the dialectic of ex-slaves. To gain acceptance, Dunbar portrayed them as contented and free of the ills associated with racism, at least in part to ease white America's guilty conscience. A victim of tuberculosis, Dunbar died in 1906, cutting short a promising career. In addition to his volumes of poetry, he published four novels and four collections of short stories.

Born in Cleveland, Ohio, Chesnutt spent most of his life until age 25 in Fayetteville, North Carolina. Self-taught through rigorous studies, he served as a teacher and administrator in schools in North and South Carolina until moving north in the 1880s. Eventually, he moved to Cleveland. Chesnutt began writing short stories, many of which were published in newspapers. In 1887, one was published in the *Atlantic Monthly,* the first time a black writer's work was published in the magazine. His first two short story collections, both published in 1899, *The Conjure Woman* and *The Wife of His Youth,* explore the grim world of slavery. Chesnutt confronted issues of racial prejudice, including the actions of middle-class blacks in Cleveland, which he renamed "Groveland." As an African American writer in the 1900s, Chesnutt used irony to make points about racial stereotypes, and the short story served as his primary weapon.

Chesnutt published three novels during the 1900s: *The House Behind the Cedars* (1900), *The Marrow of Tradition* (1901), and *The Colonel's Dream* (1905). Collectively, these works examined interracial love, cooperation, and harmony. In Chesnutt's last novel, a Southern aristocrat tries to overcome the slave culture, but despite his efforts, he is driven out of the region.

Books

Racist Writers

Despite the efforts of Washington and Du Bois, blacks continued to fight against stereotypes and racism daily. The new century brought hope and optimism, but it did not deliver tolerance or harmony. White supremacists attacked blacks and used pseudoscientific methodologies, such as skull measurement, terminology, and supposed expert opinion, to support their position that blacks were physically and mentally inferior. William P. Calhoun's *The Caucasian and the Negro* (1902) and William Pickett's *Negro Problem* (1909), both racist works, attempted to justify the position of white supremacy. Whites, when they included black characters in fiction, most often portrayed blacks as savages or simpletons. These kinds of books flourished in the North and South.

Thomas Dixon Jr., a former Baptist minister wrote three racist books that were commercially successful: *The Leopard's Spots* (1902), *The Clansman* (1905), and *The Traitor* (1907). Dixon celebrated the racial violence of the Ku Klux Klan, lamented that the South had lost the Civil War, and criticized Reconstruction. Despite the nation's progressive political attitude, Dixon's works sold well, even prompting filmmaker D. W. Griffith to use *The Clansman* as the outline for his legendary film *The Birth of a Nation* in 1915.

MAGAZINES

At the end of the nineteenth century, technological improvements had lowered the prices of magazines and newspapers, making them affordable to a wider audience. The introduction of paper made from wood pulp, rather than rags, dropped costs dramatically, as did the use of photoengraving. The general expansion of the nation's school system fed new readers into the circulation cycle. School enrollment more than doubled from 7 million in 1860 to 15.5 million in 1900. Illiteracy dropped from 20 percent in 1870 to about 11 percent at the beginning of the new century.[11]

At the same time that reading became more commonplace, American businesses produced an array of consumer goods that needed publicity. A new style of magazine emerged that served as a vehicle for gaudy advertisements; half the space was devoted to ads. The combination of technological advances and money acquired through ad sales dropped the price of the general circulation magazines, in turn increasing circulation.

Women's magazines served an important role in the 1900s. They introduced American households to the growing consumer culture, while delivering domestic advice. The *Ladies' Home Journal,* under editor Edward Bok, advised women on everything from marriage and hygiene to architecture and interior decorating. The magazine also introduced readers to fiction written by Twain, Howells, and Jewett. *Good Housekeeping* set up a research institute in 1900 to test every product mentioned in its pages. The magazine introduced the Good Housekeeping Seal of Approval in 1909. Other magazines, imitating the pioneering work of *Good Housekeeping,* spread awareness of food quality nationwide.

As circulation figures rose at the *Journal,* so did Bok's influence. He banned suggestive advertising copy and all references to alcohol and tobacco. Although a conservative, Bok took a progressive stand on sex education. In a public battle, Bok joined with the Woman's Christian Temperance Union to oppose patent medicines, which contained high doses of alcohol and narcotic drugs. In 1904, Bok began printing the contents of the most popular patent medicines. He urged the estimated 80 million users to boycott the dangerous drugs. The $59 million industry fought back when Bok printed incorrect information about Doctor Pierce's Favorite Prescription and forced him to print a retraction and pay damages. Bok's advocacy helped popularize the legislation that eventually passed through Congress as the Pure Food and Drug Act of 1906.[12] (See Food of the 1900s.)

Publishers found an eager audience among children. Two publications stood out: the monthly

St. Nicholas (founded in 1873) and the weekly *Youth's Companion* (founded in 1827). *St. Nicholas* featured the work of Twain and L. Frank Baum, author of *The Wizard of Oz. Youth's Companion* had a circulation above 500,000 until 1907, when numerous changes were made and the magazine went into decline. Youth readers, especially boys, gravitated toward another type of magazine, called the dime novel, which were actually long short stories bound into five or ten-cent magazines.

The titles of these magazines were written to attract young male readers. They ranged from *Pluck and Luck: Stories of Adventure* to *Might and Main: Stories of Boys Who Succeed*. The greatest hero of the age was Frank Merriwell, created

This poster was published in 1903 to promote Fred R. Hamlin's musical extravaganza "The Wizard of Oz," to capture the great interest in the book. The Library of Congress notes that the costume designs featured in the poster are different from the popular illustrations in the book, published in 1900. Prints & Photographs Division, Library of Congress.

WORDS AND PHRASES

activism

bawl out

the berries (best, wonderful)

birds (women)

divvy (divine)

gratters/congratters (congratulations)

gummy (disgusting, terrible)

hard-boiled (heartless, strict)

muckraker

strenuous life (Roosevelt-promoted lifestyle consisting of outdoor activity, sports, and hard work)

Tin Pan Alley

by George Patten (alias Burt L. Standish) for *Tip Top Weekly*. A star athlete and student at Fardale Academy and Yale University, Merriwell embodied the ideal traits in a young man. For 20 years, he outwitted urban bullies, Texas bandits, and even Chinese hooligans. Even though Patten had an estimated 125 million readers a week, he received only $150 per issue and died in poverty.

Comics

As innovations in the color press improved during the 1890s, newspaper publishers added color supplements to their Sunday editions. Often, they reprinted color illustrations and art from various humor magazines. Comic strip artists realized the potential of the medium and were supported by publishers seeking a competitive advantage. The early comic artists mixed humor with social satire. Richard Felton Outcault, at one time a technical

NEW MAGAZINES

The Smart Set (1900)

Popular Mechanics (1902)

Redbook (1903)

Variety (1905)

Books

artist for Thomas Edison, began publishing a one-frame comic called "Hogan's Alley" in 1895. The comic featured a poor urban neighborhood and centered on a jug-eared toddler, dubbed the Yellow Kid, who captured the public's heart. Outcault's Yellow Kid fed a merchandising bonanza for Joseph Pulitzer's *New York World* and featured everything from Yellow Kid cigarettes to a Broadway musical.

Outcault eventually tired of the strip and grew frustrated at critics who declared that comic strips were crude. In 1902, Outcault created Buster Brown, an upper-class boy who terrorized everyone around him and created a constant wave of chaos. Each "Buster Brown" strip ended with a homily inspired by Ralph Waldo Emerson or Henry David Thoreau, explaining what Buster had learned in the course of his adventures. The success of his strips made Outcault wealthy, and he became caught in the battle between Pulitzer and his archenemy William Randolph Hearst, the owner of the *New York Journal.*

Entertainment

of the 1900s

In the 1900s, many families had excess leisure time and spending money for the first time. The billions of pages of Tin Pan Alley sheet music sold, and the plays, musicals, and concerts performed nationwide reflected an increasing demand for amusement. Later in the decade, a new form of entertainment, motion pictures or "flickering flicks," gained a large following.

The cult of celebrity propelled the public's desire to see theater—musicals, dramas, and comedies—in the early years of the new century. In New York City alone in 1900, there were 40 theaters, six vaudeville houses, and several stages specializing in entertainment for specific ethnic groups, such as the Yiddish theater. The emerging middle class put on their Sunday best and paid for the opportunity to cheer world-famous actor William Gillette as the methodical Sherlock Holmes, the legendary Sarah Bernhardt in Edmond Rostand's *L'Aiglon,* and perhaps the greatest actor of his day, Richard Mansfield, whose ego and tantrums matched his ability on stage in *Dr. Jekyll and Mr. Hyde.*

Working-class individuals often preferred a less sophisticated form of entertainment—vaudeville and burlesque. Nearly every town in America had a vaudeville theater in the 1900s. But like saloons, racetracks, and betting houses, vaudeville performances were a place where rich and poor mixed.

People across social classes also flocked (whether openly or secretly) to seedier forms of entertainment, such as "leg shows" and striptease acts.

Vaudeville houses in the biggest markets performed two shows a day to packed houses in glitzy theaters. In smaller cities and less glamorous locales, there might be as many as six shows a day. Theaters such as the Majestic in Chicago and the 27-house chain Orpheum Theatre, headquartered in Chicago with branches in Brooklyn and San Francisco, were first-run palaces in which families held reservations year after year for weekly performances. The popularity of vaudeville shows drew crowds away from more serious theater, but not as dramatically as movies soon would.

Theodore Roosevelt never realized the potential of film, although he was filmed on different occasions while he was president. When Henry Cabot Lodge suggested that Roosevelt use film in his upcoming campaign, the president sarcastically asked if he should do a dance for Thomas Edison's motion picture camera.

Movies came under fire in the 1900s from churches, reform groups, and social workers for loosening standards of morality. The fervor reached a peak in 1907 when New York City mayor George B. McClellan revoked the licenses of the city's 600 theaters after the clergy banded together to dispute films they deemed immoral and the practice of showing movies on Sundays. In response, production companies banded together to form a self-regulated overseeing body, known as the National Board of Review of Motion Pictures (NBR), which placed restrictions on movies in hopes that it would end censorship at the local level.[1]

The NBR, in cooperation with local municipalities, ushered in an unprecedented period of growth for the movie industry. As a result, former vaudeville theaters were renovated and turned into grand palaces where families could see movies. Business interests quickly realized the money-making potential of the movie industry and set out to legitimize the business.

BROADWAY

In 1900, Broadway was awash in electric light and the "Great White Way" was the mecca of the theater world. Critics cited an interesting contrast—weak plots, uninspiring performances, and manipulated emotion against lavish production elements designed for mass appeal. Basically, Broadway suffered from an abundance of style, but little substance, despite the number of playgoers who turned out for the performances. For middle-class citizens, going to the theater was a formal affair. Spectators donned their best attire to take in the glitter and pomp of plays, musicals, comedies, and dramas. The conservative middle-class audiences wanted damsels in distress and cookie-cutter heroes and villains. The theater scene degenerated to the point that in 1902 the *New York Times* questioned whether the musical theater would soon be "dead."

George Cohan came to Broadway's rescue and revived the musical comedy almost single-handedly. Born into a vaudeville family, Cohan had been on the road since the age of eight. The Four Cohans became one of the nation's most popular vaudeville acts. By the time he reached his late teens, Cohan was writing and choreographing most of the act. He wrote his first two musicals in 1901, but both were box-office failures. Cohan refused to give up, but he needed a financial backer to move up to bigger theaters in New York.[2]

Cohan found his backer in fellow theater enthusiast Sam H. Harris. Together, the two produced *Little Johnny Jones* (1904), the story of American jockey Tod Sloan, who rode in the previous year's English Derby. Cohan played the part of Sloan (fictionalized as Johnny Jones) emphasizing his patriotism, which appealed greatly to audiences. Cohan sang, "I'm a Yankee Doodle Dandy/ A Yankee Doodle do or die/ A real live nephew of my Uncle Sam/ Born on the Fourth of July." Although the show ran nearly five hours, Cohan introduced speed and fluidity into the musical, so the performance contained action throughout. Cohan also pioneered the use of slang in theater. In his show, women were called "birds," and lines included a waiter asking a customer, "Shall I call you a hansom [taxicab], sir?" to which the customer replied, "Call me anything you like." Despite its groundbreaking aspects, critics panned the show, and it lasted only 52 performances. Cohan, however, took the musical on the road, always honing and editing. When he returned to Broadway a year later, the show enjoyed two long runs.[3]

Cohan's next musical, *Forty-five Minutes from Broadway,* opened on New Year's Day, 1906. The successful show included one of the decade's most enduring hits, "Mary's a Grand Old Name."

Like so many other business endeavors in the 1900s, a trust, known as the Theatrical Syndicate, controlled financial backing on Broadway. The three men controlled the trust: Charles Frohman, Marc Klaw, and Abraham Erlanger. The Syndicate worked because theater owners received star-studded shows and, in return, merely had to book the performances through trust contracts. Any theater owner who chose to work outside the Syndicate was forced to book second-and third-rate shows. Anyone who balked at the system got blacklisted, which could cost performers their careers.

The Theatrical Syndicate forced playwrights to author plays showcasing a certain actor or actress, effectively stifling creativity. On the financial side, the trust collected 5 to 10 percent of each theater's gross income and set terms for all its members. While some actors, playwrights, and theater owners got rich from the monopoly, many more were exploited by the system. Some actors, actresses, and producers actively fought the trust, including Eugene O'Neill's father, James O'Neill, and producer-playwright David Belasco, one of the most popular producers in the United States in the period. Because actresses Minnie Fiske and Sarah Bernhardt took active stands against the Syndicate, they were forced to play in skating rinks and tent theaters during the height of the trust's power. A rival group, led by the Shubert brothers, began a monopoly of their own, and by 1910 the brothers had 1,200 theaters in their control nationwide.[4]

One of the most popular shows on Broadway during the decade was *The Merry Widow*

Sarah Bernhardt in the title role of the play "Theodora." Prints & Photographs Division, Library of Congress.

(1907). While walking down the streets of New York before the musical even opened, one could hear people whistling the music of a Viennese operetta, since the lack of copyright law made it possible to sell the sheet music before the show ever opened. The success of the sheet music "The Merry Widow Waltz," at five cents a copy, propelled huge advance ticket sales to the show. Soon, 100 companies were performing the show around the world.

The musical won widespread acclaim, and its popularity led to a fashion craze of *Merry Widow* products—the *Merry Widow* hat (a huge monstrosity topped by a bird of paradise), corsets, shoes, candies, cigars, and gloves. The success of the musical also led to six years of Broadway shows dominated by Viennese operettas, including Oscar Straus's *A Waltz Dream* and *The Chocolate Soldier* and Ivan Caryll's *The Pink Lady*.[5]

Some playwrights produced plays on serious topics based on real-world experiences. These playwrights followed in the path of the muckrakers and such realist writers as Theodore Dreiser and Frank Norris, who were concerned with the seedier aspects of daily life in the United States. (See Books, Newspapers, Magazines, and Comics of the 1900s.) After reading Ida Tarbell's *History of the Standard Oil Company* (1904), Charles Klein wrote the play *The Lion and the Mouse* (1906). The play, which examines the monopolistic tendencies of big business, centers around a main character who closely resembles oil magnate John D. Rockefeller. It enjoyed a two-year run on Broadway. Rachel Crothers wrote, from a feminist point of view, *The Three of Us* (1906) and *A Man's World* (1909). Other playwrights examined the social issues of labor struggles, poverty, and women's abuse.[6]

No matter what the subject of the play or musical was, audiences went to see their favorite stars. Actresses Lillian Russell and Anna Held, for example, were as famous in their day as the era's sports stars and athletes. Others became famous for one role, such as Maude Adams, whose performance as Peter Pan captivated audiences. Anna Held, backed by her common-law husband, Florenz Ziegfeld, captured the public's imagination as a Parisian beauty and seductress. Ziegfeld, a master of publicity, used his influence to make Held a huge star. He leaked stories to the press about Held's daily 40-gallon milk bath that supposedly preserved her creamy complexion, leading to an increase in milk sales across the country. The actress also persuaded Ziegfeld to put together a revue, which later evolved into *Ziegfeld's Follies*. In 1907, the *Follies* had a successful run on Broadway and then toured in Baltimore and Washington. For the year, the show made $120,000, which would translate into millions of dollars today.[7]

Florenz Ziegfeld's success made him a legendary figure in theater history. The basic inspiration for *Ziegfeld's Follies* came from a long-running Parisian revue that presented political and social commentary through skits, as well as other numbers that featured scantily clad women. When Ziegfeld Americanized the show, he added lavish production numbers, featured songs written by the nation's top composers, and organized a chorus of attractive women. Ziegfeld's show took the idea of minstrel theater, vaudeville, and cabaret and expanded them, while also adding an air of sophistication, ensuring that women would not be offended by the show.

The early success of the Follies in a small theater in New York led to the review being booked in the New Amsterdam, Broadway's largest and most attractive theater. Ziegfeld hired the best talent he could find, from set designers and technicians to musicians, writers, and actors. Ziegfeld's chorus

girls had glamorous costumes, designed by the era's best fashion mavens. He also made sure that the lighting and stage productions showed the women in the best light possible.

Later editions of the Ziegfeld Follies in the 1910s and 1920s featured talent as diverse as W. C. Fields, Will Rogers, and Eddie Cantor, and had songs composed by Irving Berlin. Ziegfeld himself gained such notoriety and fame that his story was made into a movie, *The Great Ziegfeld* (1936), which won an Academy Award for Best Picture.

VAUDEVILLE AND BURLESQUE

Vaudeville in the United States was a mixed bag of ventriloquists, jugglers, animal acts, singers, short one-act plays, and other more bizarre acts. The level of skill displayed by these early artists varied greatly. Most vaudeville players spent their lives on the road and made little money. Vaudeville performers expected a great degree of crowd interaction—some of which included throwing rotten fruits and vegetables at hapless stage acts. The Cherry Sisters, dubbed "America's Worst Act," sang with a net between them and the audience to protect the sisters from projectiles. On the other end of the spectrum stood the Three Keatons, a comedy act in which six-year-old Buster Keaton thrilled the audience as "The Human Mop" and teased his real-life parents, who contributed acrobatics and constant banter.

Those who once went to dramas or comedies now turned to vaudeville for its variety of features. At the famous Orpheum Theatre in San Francisco, a ticket had to be ordered days in advance for vaudeville performances.[8]

Some observers hoped that vaudeville would rise above its pedestrian roots. In a 1905 article appearing in *Cosmopolitan*, writer and playwright Israel Zangwill argued that vaudeville should stage the comeback of the one-act play and lamented that audiences were too comfortable with the lighthearted fare.

Many of vaudeville's top acts were multitalented performers who could sing, act, juggle, tell jokes, and do just about anything else to get a reaction from an audience. One of the early stars was Leo Carrillo, from one of California's richest families, who told Chinese dialect stories. Another big star,

---

NOTABLE THEATER OF THE 1900s

Florodora, 1900 (505 perfs.)

The Lion and the Mouse, 1905 (586 perfs.)

A Society Circus, 1905 (596 perfs.)

The Man of the Hour, 1906 (479 perfs.)

The Red Mill, 1906 (274 perfs.)

The Rose of the Rancho, 1906 (480 perfs.)

The Merry Widow, 1907 (416 perfs.)

The Man from Home, 1908 (496 perfs.)

The Fortune Hunter, 1909 (345 perfs.)

A Trip to Japan, 1909 (447 perfs.)

The Music Master, 1904 (627 perfs.)

Julian Eltinge, spoofed the famous Gibson Girl in 1907 with a female impersonation he called the Simpson Girl. Some major theatrical stars, including Sarah Bernhardt and Ethel Barrymore, joined vaudeville troupes between seasons.[9]

Public relations whiz Willie Hammerstein, cousin of composer Oscar Hammerstein, often used freak or stunt acts in his theater on West 42nd Street in New York City. Freak acts did not mean that the people in the acts were freaks; they were individuals the audience wanted to see because of their fame or notoriety. Often infamous criminals, who lamented their illicit ways, were part of vaudeville shows. Author and public speaker Helen Keller was a "freak" act, as was Dr. Frederick Cook, who discussed his adventures in the North Pole controversy.[10]

Burlesque began as musical productions making fun of current events or famous plays, which was said to be "burlesquing." The women who appeared in burlesque wore revealing tights to titillate the male audience. Beautiful scenery, music, and comedy were also used to attract men to the shows. While most people associate burlesque with striptease, that aspect only dominated the shows during its later years. The early years certainly featured sexually aggressive women spoofing the Victorian image of the dainty, submissive female. These acts were balanced with comedy and musicals, often spoofing Shakespeare or other cultural icons.

The greatest burlesque star of the 1900s was Millie de Leon, who mimicked Eva Tanguay's trancelike movements but also made physical contact with the audience. Like all great vaudeville and burlesque actors, de Leon used negative publicity to further her career. When she was arrested in Brooklyn in 1903, the charges against her

A poster for the "Hurly-Burly Extravaganza and Refined Vaudeville," ca. 1900. Prints & Photographs Division, Library of Congress.

NOTABLE ACTORS OF THE 1900s

Maude Adams, 1872–1953, stage actress

Ethel Barrymore, 1879–1959, stage actress

Sarah Bernhardt, 1824–1923, stage actress

Minnie Fiske, 1865–1932, realistic drama stage actress

William Gillette, 1853–1937, playwright and actor

Anna Held, 1872–1918, vaudeville performer

Richard Mansfield, 1854–1907, romantic actor

James O'Neill, 1845–1920, dramatic actor, father of Eugene O'Neill

Lillian Russell, 1861–1922, actress and singer

only spread her fame. She also spread rumors of alleged liaisons and affairs to keep the attention of audiences. She often took the stage without wearing tights, long before bare legs were acceptable for women in public.

By the mid-1900s, some promoters moved to make burlesque more respectable. In 1908, the Star and Garter opened in Chicago, offering "Clean Entertainment for Self-Respecting People," but burlesque remained scandalous and tawdry.[11]

Burlesque became a kind of minor league for vaudeville and musical comedy. Entertainers such as Sophie Tucker, Red Skelton, and W. C. Fields began their careers in burlesque, only to move up to vaudeville, radio, and movies in later years. In the 1920s, burlesque dropped many of its skits and comedy routines and focused on striptease, leading to burlesque's becoming more popular than vaudeville. Burlesque houses dominated Times Square in those days, until law enforcement cracked down on the striptease shows in the 1930s.

MOVIES

As early as 1894 and 1895, crude animated films were shown on screens in the United States. The first picture show in New York City took place at Koster and Bial's Music Hall on April 27, 1896. The early animations were difficult to see, but they fueled a great deal of curiosity.

The development of moving pictures was an outgrowth of advances in photography. By the turn of the century, millions of households had a stereoscope, a handheld device that made pictures look three dimensional. In 1901, the Underwood Company produced 25,000 stereo views a day and sold 300,000 stereoscopes. Stereo views were sold via catalogs, such as Sears, Roebuck and Company or door-to-door. The machines brought the events of the world to ordinary Americans. People collected stereo views of events ranging from the World's Fair to the flights of the Wright Brothers to the building of the Panama Canal.[12]

Meanwhile, George Eastman's handheld Kodak camera made it possible for anyone to take snapshots. In 1900, Eastman's chief designer, Frank Brownell, developed a cheap, easy-to-use camera made specifically for children—the "Brownie," which cost just one dollar. Kodak advertised the camera with illustrations of mythical creatures made popular by Canadian writer Palmer Cox in the children's magazine *St. Nicholas*. Kodak also set up camera clubs and sponsored photography contests to keep consumers interested in buying Kodak products.

Throughout the nineteenth century, inventors and artists searched for a way to represent motion, but it was not until Thomas Edison began working on film devices that the Kinetograph and Kinetoscope were born. After displaying these motion picture devices at the Chicago World's Fair, parlors were set up around the country featuring early motion pictures. Penny arcades allowed viewers to see short scenes of everyday life—a girl dancing or a man sneezing. The commercial prospects of Kinetoscopes developed as promoters realized they could make money if many people could watch a projected movie simultaneously.

The motion picture industry grew quickly, especially after Edison established the first studio in 1905, "Black Maria," a tarpaper-lined box that swung around to catch the sun for filming. Other groups raced to produce films, including the Vitagraph Company of Brooklyn, the Lubin Company of Philadelphia, and several firms in Chicago.

Early pictures varied from scenes of important cultural or political events, such as William McKinley's inauguration, or a simple prizefight or a moving automobile. In 1903, Edison may have filmed the first commercial, an advertising piece for the Lackawanna Railroad, showing company mascot Phoebe Snow riding the "Road of Anthracite" in a long, white dress to show how clean railroad travel had become. One of the first films to use narrative was Edwin S. Porter's *The Great Train Robbery* (1903), an 11-minute tale of a train robbery and the capture of the thieves. Porter, an early innovator in camera work, filmed one scene in which a robber fires his gun directly at the camera. The audiences, tricked by the technique, screamed, and some spectators passed out in terror.[13]

Porter created more visually stunning films over the next several years. *The Dream of a Rarebit Fiend* (1906) uses the camera to let the audience see the world through the eyes of a drunken man. Another Porter motion picture, *The Kleptomaniac* (1905) examines the way in which a wealthy woman shoplifter is handled by the authorities versus the brutal way they treated a poor woman who had stolen a loaf of bread.

Porter was an early innovator, but D. W. Griffith was the master filmmaker of the 1900s, despite his racist three-hour epic *The Birth of a Nation* (1915). (See Entertainment of the 1910s.) Griffith's first film, *The Adventures of Dollie* (1908), told the story of a child kidnapped by gypsies who is saved after floating down the river in a barrel. During his stint with the production company Biograph, which lasted until 1913, Griffith directed approximately 450 films. He was the first director to use many of the techniques we take for granted today, including the close-up and distant shots, the pan shot, the fade-out, and sustained suspense.

Most films lasted 15 to 20 minutes, short enough for people to fit them into their daily lives, especially children after school. Some families spent Saturday afternoons going from theater to theater to take in all the different films. Most early nickelodeons were located close to working-class and immigrant neighborhoods, often close to trolley lines and busy shopping streets. To keep up with the demand, theater owners imported nearly half of their films from overseas. France is generally credited with having the leading film studios in the 1900s.[14]

A 1908 report in *Independent* estimated that within the previous two years, a motion picture theater had opened in every town and village in the country.[15] By 1910, there were approximately 10,000 movie theaters servicing an audience of more than 10 million a week.[16]

DANCE

Dancing in the United States prior to the 1900s was regimented and had a sense of restraint—a holdover from the nation's early Puritan settlers. Formal dance, which had come from Europe, was considered high culture. On the other end of the social scale, public dances, held since the 1880s, were considered vulgar and a sign of lower-class standing. Working-class families were not as rigid, and young children often danced in the streets during playtime.

Despite these attitudes, and preconceived notions about the evils of dancing, a dance craze broke out at the turn of the century, fueled by young adults in the working class. After a full day in the factories, these young people flocked to neighborhood halls and saloons or ballrooms and danced the night away in their finest dress clothes. Children in working-class families were more likely to dance at an early age, so by the time they hit their teenage years, dancing was common. A survey conducted in 1910 revealed that nine out of ten girls between the ages of 11 and 14 claimed they knew how to dance, compared with only about one-third of the boys. Dancing offered young adults a chance to mix with the opposite sex without parental interference. Dancing also gave people an avenue for expressing themselves in public.[17]

For blue-collar workers, especially women under 20 years of age, participation in the dance craze was part of the courting ritual. Attendance at the dances increased as a young girl matured, then dropped off significantly after finding a boyfriend, and for most women ceased altogether after marriage. In New York City, every ethnic group had their own dance halls, and in one district, there was a dance hall every two and a half blocks.

Dancing encompassed many aspects of life in the working classes. People attending dances engaged in cultural and social dynamics that defined who they were. What dance steps groups favored, where they attended the events, how they interacted with one another, and what clothing styles they wore were important facets of their day-to-day lives.

As ragtime and Tin Pan Alley became more pervasive, the wild beat of the music ended much of the formal heritage of dance in America. Tin Pan Alley dictated which dance steps would become most popular, and new dances were invented for particular songs, leading to increased sales. Also, business interests took control of the public dance halls and the liquor being served. For example, 80 percent of the dance halls in the Lower East Side of New York City were adjacent to saloons. Hall owners made their profits from the liquor served, which led to a dance lasting anywhere from three to ten minutes, then an intermission lasting from 15 to 20 minutes, in which drinking was encouraged.

Hall owners also promoted social interaction to drive customers to their clubs. Some would give unescorted females discounted admission, while others let single women in free. As more and more large commercial dance halls opened, owners enticed patrons with bright lights, blaring music, and a carnival atmosphere. Middle-class reformers were outraged over the conduct of young people in the dance halls and warned against bawdy behavior, but most dancers were simply playing out the intricate social rituals to the best of their ability, given the staid nature of the day.

DANCE AS ART

Dance as an artistic outlet had been taught in the United States since the 1820s. Artistic dance was called Delsartianism after its creator, François Delsarte (1811–1871). Delsartianism focused on flexibility and natural movement, a graceful expression of the human form. Delsarte's ideas set off a dance craze in which young men recited poetry while prancing around gracefully. Females donned white robes and white face paint and held classical poses. Upper and middle-class Americans supported Delsartianism as a form of exercise.[18]

In the 1900s, Isadora Duncan (1878–1927) popularized Delsartianism and branched out to create her own unique form of dance, which audiences regarded as both scandalous and titillating. She shocked the staid audiences of the era, but at the same time she gave them a sense of liberation.

The San Francisco native enjoyed a classical education and was raised by an independent mother, both unusual during the waning years of the nineteenth century. Duncan's mother also encouraged her to express herself through dance. By her teenage years, Duncan had already focused her dance style on natural movements and graceful expressions of the human body. By the time she was 21 years old, Duncan had scandalized audiences by dancing with bare arms and legs. Some viewed her with disdain, but others recognized her artistry and embraced her as an avant-garde genius.[19]

Duncan spent most of her life in Europe and Russia. After touring Russia in the aftermath of the 1905 Russian Revolution, Duncan's views took a radical turn. She applied these thoughts to her dance, essentially liberating her body from the strict movements of traditional ballet. In 1921, while living in the Soviet Union, V. I. Lenin asked Duncan to create a school of dance in Moscow. Duncan used the school to promote art for the masses with political overtones. In 1922, on a trip to the United States, immigration officials detained Duncan because of her close ties to the Soviet Union. Newspapers quickly picked up the story, and headlines declared Duncan a Soviet provocateur. She was stripped of her citizenship and lived the rest of her life in France.[20]

Fashion

of the 1900s

In the 1900s, fashion and design melded together into one seemingly cohesive movement that swept through clothing styles, art, furniture, and architecture. In fashion, upper and middle-class men and women were still tied closely to European and Victorian styles from the 1890s. However, as industrialism sparked urban growth, fashion took on a utilitarian look that did not hinder work-related tasks. Young women working in factories or workshops could hardly wear frilly lace or don hats trimmed with flowers or fruit. Conversely, a proper "lady" would never leave the house without a tight corset or the right makeup, and an aristocratic man always wore a top hat and carried a walking stick.

Industrialism had another profound effect on fashion in the decade. As corporations mass-produced goods, they either fueled or created markets to purchase them, and advertisers pushed the message that the accumulation of goods equaled status. Searching for ways to get merchandise into the hands of consumers, companies like Sears, Roebuck and Company flooded the country-side with mail-order catalogs, while department stores and chain stores fed the machine in urban centers. Fashion took on a whole new meaning when women in small towns and villages could buy the same clothes that were available in cities. Industrialism brought democracy to fashion, al-

though, like its political counterpart, those with the money held the power and ultimately influenced future styles. The rich looked overseas or to the finest boutiques for their inspiration; the middle class purchased imitations through department stores and catalogs.

Clothing served as a measure in the widening gap between the rich and poor. While urban immigrants and rural farmers struggled to keep clothing on the backs of their families, wealthy families regarded clothing as a status symbol, merely another commodity.

A great clothing industry rose up to provide men and women with the mass-produced and handmade clothes they desired. In the 1900s, women spent more than $1 billion a year on clothes and accessories, including more than $14 million on corsets alone. The 1905 Sears catalogue offered 150 styles of the new shirtwaist blouse, ranging from 39 cents for a plain shirt to $6.95 for a fancy taffeta version.

When the 1900s began, fashion hinged on smallness—tiny waists "clasped with two hands," shoes a size or two too small, and small hats.[1] As the decade advanced, fashion rules became less rigid, but most people still adhered to earlier styles. In fact, upper and middle-class men and women both changed clothes several times a day. They treated the evening dinner as a formal

Thanks to mass production and mail order catalogs, more Americans, particularly those who lived outside of urban areas, were able to take advantage of ready-made fashions. As in previous eras, strict rules determined what was appropriate based on activity and time of day. Clothes remained a status symbol for the wealthy, while factory workers wore functional clothing. Among the highlights:

Women: Gibson girl look—long skirts, layers of ruffles and petticoats over corsets, big hats, long hair, shirtwaists (blouse worn with long skirts)

Men: large, boxy three-piece suits buttoned high up were everyday dress; hats; clean shaven

occasion and each changed for dinner, even if they were dining at home alone.

Styles in the 1900s centered largely on padding—the woman in layers of ruffles and the man in large, boxy suits. Even casual events were governed by strict guidelines, such as linen or flannel trousers in the summer for men and the ever-present corset for women. Both sexes wore hats just about everywhere, whether at work, on vacation, or at formal functions. As many of the stringent fashion rules of the decade fell to the wayside, people experimented with looser styles and more functional clothing, which came to symbolize the American spirit.

THE GIBSON GIRL

The ideal woman in the United States from 1890 to World War I was not Theodore Roosevelt's teenage daughter, Alice (although her every move was followed by the press), a star of the fledgling movie industry, or even a real person. Instead, the image every female idolized was illustrator Charles Dana Gibson's "Gibson girl"— an elegant, graceful, romanticized female of the age. Women imitated the style and fashions of the Gibson girl; men tried to be like her dashing suitors. The power of Gibson's illustrations rested in the air of dignity he conveyed and the detachment he captured in the Gibson girl's eyes.

For society at large, the Gibson girl was the ideal "new woman." The new woman broke through the barriers that had plagued women in earlier times. Generally, she had a college education, supported herself, and did not marry young like her mother's generation. Gibson encapsulated all the intrigue of the new woman in his illustrations and even the fear many people experienced regarding women's empowerment. Conservative traditionalists lashed out against the new woman movement. They attributed many social ills, such as soaring divorce rates, to the new woman.

Gibson's popularity, however, never wavered. The Gibson girl played golf and tennis, rode bicycles, made men swoon, and dressed in a simpler style. Typically, she wore a long skirt and a blouse, or "shirtwaist" as they were known in the era. She helped widen the appeal of the blouse over the frilly layers of heavy petticoats normally worn by women.[2] Gibson licensed the image of his drawings, so one could find her adorning china, silverware, pillows, or even whisk broom holders. Her image could be found everywhere, from pinups on college campuses to the Alaskan Klondike. Gibson's male characters papered the walls of many female boarding schools. Many young men decorated their apartments with Gibson girl wallpaper, the height of chic for bachelor pads.[3]

Gibson's serialized pen-and-ink sketches of the new woman in *Life* magazine appealed to women across class lines. Women from working-class families aspired to be like the Gibson girl and achieve a certain level of independence, perhaps as a telephone operator or social worker. Women from wealthy families found inspiration to do something meaningful, which the Gibson girl aspired to do.

The men in Gibson's drawings are almost as telling as the Gibson girl herself. Men hover over her, and older women scorn her for grabbing the men's attention. Almost embarrassed to be the focal point, she presents an air of supreme indifference. One young man—a dark-haired, square-jawed fellow—is usually depicted. His sadness is palpable. He knows he will never win the girl's hand, but he cannot keep himself from being near her.

Alice Roosevelt was a close incarnation of a real-life Gibson girl. Spirited and boisterous

A Charles Dana Gibson picture used as a cover for sheet music. The young woman is an example of the typical Gibson girl look. Courtesy of the Oakland Public Library, Oakland, California.

like her father, Alice flaunted many of the notions about "proper" behavior. She smoked in public, danced until dawn at social gatherings, and even danced the hula in Hawaii, a nearly immoral act at the time. There were songs written for her ("Alice, Where Art Thou?"), newborns named after her, and she even had her own color (Alice blue).[4]

Alice's popularity stretched around the world. European magazines followed her every move and published her picture on the cover of magazines. When she married Ohio Congressman Nicholas Longworth, it was the event of the year and followed by millions. She truly held the title of "America's Princess" in the 1900s.

WORKING WOMAN FASHION

Most women who worked in the 1900s found employment in department stores, factories, and offices. As a group, they were young, primarily urban, and single. For example, in New York City, 80 percent of the 343,000 working women in 1900 were single, and one-third were between the ages of 16 and 20. These women had quite a different set of jobs from those who had worked just a decade earlier, who usually labored as domestic servants or worked in small sweatshops. For young working women, clothing allowed them to express themselves and push beyond the limitations of urban, working-class life.[5]

Dressing up gave working women the ability to present themselves in a guise that took them out of the realm of the factories or department store floors, whether they were parading in the streets or enjoying a night on the town with a group of friends. Clothing allowed one to assert one's identity, even if that meant bending the supposed "rules" of fashion by dressing like upper-class women and putting on airs of wealth. Some observers believed women dressed like their wealthier counterparts in order to marry into a higher social class. Although there is some truth to this notion, the way working-class women dressed and the implications it entailed went beyond looking for a rich husband.[6]

Working women separated their clothes into work clothes and Sunday clothes, their nicer articles. What women wore to work depended on the job. A waitress might wear a white apron and matching cap, but a seamstress would wear older clothes that would not be ruined by sweat or grime from the shop floor. Sunday clothes, however, played an important social role. Women engaged in social activities in the community on Sundays. Without an acceptable set of Sunday clothes, women did not feel they could participate in these identity-building events. When new immigrants arrived in the United States, they acquired a set of nice clothes to help assimilate them to American culture.[7]

Although lumped together into one large group by the outside world, working-class females differentiated themselves through fashion, speech patterns, levels of schooling, and other yardsticks. Ideas about social status played an important role in clothing decisions, touching upon a family's thoughts about fitting into American culture and individual niches within one's own neighborhood or city.

Fashion

Some women gained an air of aristocracy from the Sunday clothes they wore at social gatherings. Women in New York bought cheap versions of the latest fashions from the clothing stores located on Grand Street. They also avidly read the fashion pages in the newspapers and saw upper-class women in department stores, and modeled their own dress on the basis of these encounters. The working class adopted other aspects of elite culture, such as calling other women "lady friends." They even used romance novels as a kind of guide to look inside the lives of women from the upper classes. The most important fashion development for women at the turn of the century was the shirtwaist, a simple blouse worn with a skirt. The shirtwaist, which allowed a full range of motion, did not restrict a worker's movement like cumbersome formal wear did, and it could be worn all day, a requirement for long hours at work. Both shirtwaist blouses and suits (usually called tailor-mades) gained momentum as a result of mass production. Companies produced both articles at prices workers could afford. The shirtwaist cost around $1.50; suits ranged from $10 to $20.[8]

WORKING-CLASS MEN

Working-class men wore sturdy, durable clothes that stood up against long hours and sweat-filled days. Mass production required men to work longer hours and toil at monotonous tasks, but it also made clothing less expensive. Other workers wore uniforms or clothing suited to their jobs. Railroad workers, construction crews, and those who worked primarily outdoors needed outerwear that kept them warm, but fit into their limited budgets.

Cheap materials, such as canvas, duck, corduroy, and leather were the primary materials used for most work clothes. Clothes made from these materials had two prerequisites: to keep workers warm and be roomy enough to permit the range of motion necessary to perform tasks. Often included in a workingman's uniform was a sheepskin vest, which provided another layer of protection against the elements.[9]

Workers in factories wore clothing that mirrored their counterparts in high society, except that the workers' clothes were obviously less expensive imitations. Photographs from the 1900s reveal workers on the shop floor wearing white, high-collared shirts and bow ties, vests, and hats, indicating the formal nature of the workplace. Even if the task at hand was not physical labor, men still had to have clothing that allowed them to labor at least 10 hours a day, six days a week.

Men who owned general stores or worked in the budding retail industry wore work aprons, which had developed over the years to feature various straps and pockets depending on one's occupation. Heavy-duty aprons had extra stitching and leather patches to increase durability. With the formality of clothing in a variety of professions, men donned aprons to protect their clothes against dirt and grime. They also used sleeve garters to keep extra fabric out of the way or cuff protectors to keep their white garments clean.[10]

WOMEN'S FASHION

Women who could afford to follow fashion looked to Paris and London for the latest styles. Women in the era donned corsets that produced S-shaped figures by pulling in the waist as tightly as possible and accentuating the bosom upward and the back end outward. Women looked as though their waists were pitched forward, while the rest of the body tilted backward.

Regardless of the pain of wearing them, corsets defined the look of affluent women in the 1900s. Meant to draw attention to the curve of the back, corsets used whalebone stays to force the body into this S-position. They were made from cotton or linen and worn over a vest of silky material, probably to absorb some of the chafing from the contraption. The corset laced in the back, which tied the body into the S-shape. Women added another layer with a corset cover, also made of fine material.

Women's dresses and petticoats were accentuated with lace, ribbon, or cord. The petticoats were stiff and worn over high-necked shirts that covered the entire neck area. Skirts were usually bell-shaped and had a slight train effect. Well-dressed women wore leather boots or suede shoes that fastened with buttons.

As the decade progressed, women's hats got larger and larger. By the end of the decade, hats

Fashion

A young woman standing outside a savings bank, wearing a big feathered hat, who is raising her skirt to insert a $5 bill inside her gartered stocking, ca. 1908. (This would have been a risqué picture for this era.) Prints & Photographs Division, Library of Congress.

had gigantic brims featuring ornate trains of feathers that hung down to the middle of the back and sometimes included lace to cover the woman's face. In 1905, Sears offered 75 different types of ostrich feathers to adorn women's hats. Milliners used a wide variety of bird feathers to decorate hats, including egrets, orioles, pigeons, doves, and wrens. Precariously balanced on the head or tilted to one side, the hats required countless hatpins to keep them in place.

COSMETICS

The use of cosmetics grew over the course of the 1900s, but makeup did not play a large role in women's lives. As late as 1916, one magazine estimated that only one in five people used toiletries, and the average spending per capita reached

just 50 cents per year. Magazines and mail-order catalog companies did not feel women should "buy their way to beauty," so they did not feature cosmetics as they did clothing, hairpins, and other beautifying products. Gradually, however, women's interest in makeup grew, bolstered by the department stores and chain stores that carried cosmetics.[11]

Despite the supposedly low number of women using makeup in the early 1900s, a growing number of women defied public opinion and began applying rouge and powder. The issue was contentious because up until that time, the only women who openly wore makeup were prostitutes and "sporting" women who frequented the dance halls, clubs, and cafes. The rise of urbanization, however, put more women out in public at night, and they began decorating their faces. Wealthy women followed the lead of French women who were using makeup regularly. Working women in urban centers wore makeup as an inexpensive means to distinguish themselves. However, until World War I, women simply did not have the freedom to wear makeup as they pleased. Societal norms excluded cosmetics, and women who wore makeup were treated as spectacles.

Although cosmetics took some time to catch on, the industry provided women with an opportunity to build their own businesses in the 1900s—one of the few entrepreneurial outlets available to them. Two famous African American entrepreneurs, Annie Turnbo and Sarah Breedlove, more commonly known as Madam C. J. Walker, built a thriving cosmetics businesses in the 1900s. Turnbo started her business in Illinois, but later relocated to St. Louis, which had a vibrant black community, before going national. The orphaned daughter of former slaves, Walker built a hair-care empire, eventually running national advertising campaigns and starting a mail-order business.

MEN'S FASHION

Men's fashion in the 1900s relied heavily on styles carried over from the Victorian era of the 1890s. Designers introduced innovative styles in the new century, but for the most part, men's clothes were dark and conservative. Men from the upper classes adhered to fairly rigid standards and rules about how they should dress and act in public.

Everyday wear centered on the suit, almost always three piece and buttoned high up the chest. Suits were basically long and loose, resulting in a bulky appearance. An average sized man required five yards of cloth per suit. Narrow, high lapels accentuated the boxy look, which made men look as though their shoulders were being held back. Men carried heavy gold pocket watches in their vests. A watch fob, a gold chain draped in front of and across the vest, connected the pocket watch to the other vest pocket.

Men's trousers were also cut large around the hips and waist, most likely to account for the portly stature of most wealthy men in the previ-

ous decades. Girth was a symbol of wealth in the Victorian era. Many politicians, lawyers, and civic leaders were immense by today's standards. Pants, called "peg-top" slacks, were pleated and cut to taper in sharply at the bottom. By 1905, cuffs were standard on most trousers in America.[12]

If a man could afford only one suit, he bought a sack suit in dark blue serge, a smooth twill fabric. Named for the formless shape of the jacket, it came in three or four-button styles, single-breasted, with high, short lapels. By 1907, fashionable men wore sack suits of varying colors and adopted a more youthful look by having the suit shaped at the hips and waist. The paunch of the 1890s was being pushed aside by the vigorous, energetic twentieth-century man exemplified by Theodore Roosevelt.

Fashion

Men posed wearing fall and winter business and theater fashions with overcoats and hats, against a backdrop of an interior view of the recently opened Library of Congress. Prints & Photographs Division, Library of Congress.

The growing number of businessmen in the United States forced designers to make a suit more formal than the sack variety. For this look, the coat extended down to just above the knees, an adaptation of the English walking coat suit. The proper accessories, such as a high silk hat, leather gloves, and walking stick, emphasized the formality of the suit. Also known as the business frock suit, the style quickly gained acceptance in the banking world. The suit signaled a move toward suits that were less bulky and more in line with current trends emanating from Europe.[13]

Formal evening attire for men included the tailcoat, which unlike the everyday suit, fit snugly against the body. The main feature of the coat, the tails, stretched below the knee. When attending the theater or dinner on the town, men wore stiff attached or unattached collars. One version of the collar, called the poke, had a slight curve in the front. The other style, the winged collar, came into fashion during the decade and is still the customary collar on men's tuxedo shirts today. Shirt studs were usually made of pearl, but they were spaced out on the shirtfront more than current styles. In addition to a heavy overcoat, formal wear called for high silk hats and a fashionable walking stick.

HAIRSTYLES

Women wore their hair long in the 1900s. As a matter of fact, to balance their gargantuan hats, women added artificial hair as padding. Critics of female hairpieces called them "rats" or "puffs."

A man and two women in typical bathing costumes at Daytona Beach, Florida, 1909. Courtesy of the Florida State Archives.

At formal occasions, women teased their hair into a pompadour, with the hair primped up on the side and a bun at the crown. As hats got bigger, women moved the bun from the top of the head to the back as an extra pin holder. Sometimes, women allowed tiny ringlets to hang down from the sides in front of their ears. Women used curling irons, waving irons, and other tools to style their hair in the 1900s. To keep it all in place, various hairpins, combs, and hairpieces were used.[14]

Men's hairstyles, whether on the face or on top of the head, went through many changes in the 1900s. Full beards were in style from the 1850s until 1901, but then they went out quickly. Mustaches were popular for most of the decade, spurred by Roosevelt's own walrus-like look, but many women disliked them. Many heroes of romantic novels wore long, blonde mustaches, which they stroked. The clean-shaven look served as an egalitarian symbol for men of all classes.

Hairstyles varied for men in the 1900s. Some wore their hair with a part on the side and a curled effect on top. Crew cuts were also popular, with short sides and varying lengths on the top. Sideburns were an option, especially on college campuses. Most men put some kind of tonic in their hair to accentuate their natural waves or to slick it back in order to add an air of sophistication.

Facial hair and hairstyles categorized the men in Charles Gibson's illustrations. The older men were portly, usually combing what little remaining hair they had over a bald spot, and they sported waxed mustaches with the ends curled up. Most of the younger dandies in Gibson's drawings, modeled after novelist, journalist, and adven-

A "Chanticleer" hat of bird feathers, ca. 1910. Prints & Photographs Division, Library of Congress.

turer Richard Harding Davis, were clean-shaven, with hair parted down the middle or on one side, slicked back to emphasize high cheekbones and square jaws.

Food

of the 1900s

In the first decade of the twentieth century, new technology gave farmers the ability to grow more food with less manpower. Thus, the sons and daughters of the farm were freed to move to the cities and provide the brute force needed to staff the growing factories.

Although historically farm families had been nearly self-sufficient, advertisers and manufacturers included them in the equation as they established a national consumer culture, which was based on purchasing mass-produced goods that decades earlier would have been either made by hand or done without. The Sears, Roebuck and Company mail-order catalog was a staple in the homes of America's farmers, reaching out to those unable to shop in the cities.

In addition to fueling consumer culture, the food industry played an important role in the development of the modern corporation. The first successful large-scale food producers processed perishable items. Meatpacking corporations, including Armour, Swift, Wilson, Morris, and Cudahy, were early examples of that national corporation and were followed closely by breweries, such as Anheuser Busch and Schlitz. Other leading food producers made cheap packaged goods using continuous-process machinery (Quaker Oats, Heinz, Borden's, Libby, and Coca-Cola).[1] Not only did these corporations establish

business processes, but they also stimulated the budding advertising and public relations industries.

The health and safety standards used in the manufacturing process came to light in author Upton Sinclair's *The Jungle* (1906), which examined the horrendous conditions in Chicago's meatpacking industry. He described the unsanitary methods used to make sausage and even insinuated that workers had fallen into the vats and become part of the product. Most food producers used some form of additives to enhance the flavor, smell, or coloring of products. Many additives turned out to be harmful, such as acids used to mask spoiled beef or hallucinogenic drugs added to headache remedies.

When congressional members first introduced pure food legislation, the food trusts used their collective lobbying skills and money to thwart any such attempts. It took a polemic tract like *The Jungle* and the subsequent full support of President Theodore Roosevelt to best the combined efforts of the food producers. In the end, the public outcry against unhealthy production methods and chemical additions led to legislation being passed.

Although legislators passed pure food and drug laws in 1906, food producers did not comply with the new regulations overnight.

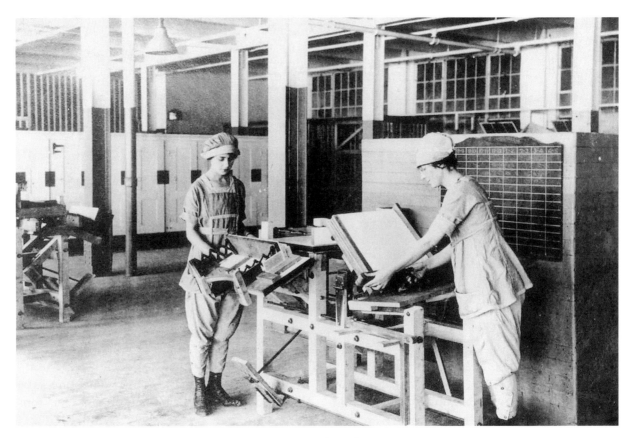

Two women sugar factory workers in Crockett, California (1905). Courtesy of the Contra Costa County Historical Society.

DIET AND INCOME

Studies of nutritional habits of working-class families in the 1900s have shown that variations in diet hinged on income. For most families, meals consisted of a handful of staples, such as large loaves of bread, stewed meats, potatoes, onions, cabbage, and condiments, like pickles. In the summer months, an abundance of fresh fruits and vegetables added diversity. Sociologists, nutritionists, and social workers in the 1900s studied dietary challenges from the perspective of immigrant status, usually delineating between native-born and non-native immigrants. They often overlooked the basic consideration of income and how that primary factor played into a family's ideas regarding food preparation and nutrition. Most nutritional experts felt that a remedy was to teach immigrants to "Americanize" their diets, when, in fact, giving them access to steady jobs that paid well would have eliminated their food-related problems.[2]

Changing the eating habits of immigrant families developed into something of a crusade in the 1900s. Immigrants were discouraged from eating spicy, mixed foods by home economists and social workers. Nutritionists believed that any diet that mixed foods together was inferior, since they thought that more nutrients were expelled in the preparation.[3]

Corporations undertook programs to force their foreign workers to adopt the habits of this nation. International Harvester, for instance, set up a program in its Midwestern plants that featured a "model workingman's home" to teach wives how to cook American style.[4]

These corporate initiatives continued up to World War II. Many companies, including the most famous attempt, Ford's Sociological Department, established divisions directly responsible for encouraging non-native workers to adopt an American way of life. Eventually, in striving for a middle-class lifestyle, many immigrants did become Americanized, but if there was one tie they kept to their homelands, it usually involved food.

The status of the United States as the world's leading agricultural producer helped families survive tough economic times. In the 1900s, industrialism pushed well beyond the country's steel mills and heavy manufacturing plants. Food production played an important role in establishing the United States as the world's exporter. Factories continued to manufacture foodstuffs in recessions, and the growth of the industry forced companies to find outlets, whether that meant cutting back prices or finding other alternatives.

THE FARM BECOMES A CORPORATION

In the decades leading up to the twentieth century, farming in the United States changed dramatically as a result of technological innovations. As railroads spidered across the West, settlers poured into the fertile lands and began cultivating wheat on the plains. Advances in harvesting and planting allowed farmers to increase their levels of production vastly.

The mechanization occurring on the farms and in the distribution process hurt many farmers. They had to buy new machinery and land continually to keep up with their competitors while the prices for their crops dropped. Large-scale production, freight costs, and machinery prices forced many farmers into tenant farming, especially in the South and Midwest. Laborers who did not own the land they tilled did 35 percent of all farming in the United States in 1900. Urban dwellers, however, benefited—they had a greater variety of fresher vegetables, fruits, and meats to choose from at affordable prices.

To feed the industrial machine, agrarians had to embrace the ideas of conglomeration and incorporation.[5] Commercial farmers entered into a period of unmatched prosperity in the 1900s. Industrialism and the subsequent transformation of farming into big business ushered in a new era for farmers, but countless small farmers were barely surviving.

As a result of the mechanization and organization of farmers, many became specialists. They produced one crop, often specific to the particular region they farmed. This ultimately increased

the divide between wealthy farmers (who had adopted the ideas of big business) and those who were left to their own devices. After 1900, big business, upset by the antibusiness rhetoric coming from the nation's farmers, actively courted farmers into an alliance that ultimately benefited both parties. Business interests, such as bankers, merchants, and the railroads, among others, had a large stake in the success of farmers, so it was only natural to invite an alliance among businessmen and farmers.

THE PURE FOOD AND DRUG ACT

Most people associate the drive for healthy, unadulterated food in the early twentieth century with the muckraking work of socialist author Upton Sinclair and his best-selling novel *The Jungle* (1906), but discerning citizens and watch groups lamented the state of American food production long before Sinclair's novel. The main critic of tainted food was Dr. Harvey W. Wiley, the chief chemist of the Department of Agriculture (1883–1912), who waged public skirmishes against large corporations and business enterprises.

In April 1900, Senator William E. Mason from Illinois wrote a long article in the *North American Review* lamenting the amount of food adulteration in the United States. Senator Mason placed the blame on the growing corporations. He pointed to a Congressional investigation into the flour industry, which revealed "very dangerous and absolutely insoluble substances were being used to adulterate flour."[6] In fact, the flour producers who were not using additives pushed for the inquiry because the offending companies tarnished the reputation of the entire industry, especially in the growing overseas market. American flour manufacturers could ill afford to have Europeans doubting the quality of their products.

Senator Mason called for national legislation that would prevent unhealthy materials from finding their way into the nation's food supply. He openly distinguished between additives, such as water, that diminished the health value of the product, versus adulterations that harmed consumers. Mason felt that consumers should be aware of every ingredient in the foods they buy,

Food

and manufacturers should be required to provide this information.[7]

Calling for the continuation of the pure food activism sweeping the nation, which led to a series of pure food congresses and investigations into additives, Mason touted the benefits of good-faith labeling. By encouraging the "honest manufacturer" and protecting them from dishonest competition, Congress would in turn offer protection to consumers, who would know what ingredients they were ingesting. Furthermore, Mason declared, the nation would establish a reputation for high standards regarding food products, which would increase the demand for American goods all over the world.

Practically every food manufactured in the 1900s contained some kind of chemical additive that was potentially harmful to consumers. Butcher shops used "Freezem" or "Preservaline" to deal with spoiled meat; ketchups, canned vegetables, chocolates, and skim milk all contained some kind of additive—sulphite, benzoate, and boric acid, among others. Food producers used science to mask unhealthy additives and preservatives, which contributed to noxious diets for many people.

While activists rallied against unhealthy products, politicians were less willing to fight the food companies. One of the first rallying points occurred when Edward Bok, editor of the *Ladies' Home Journal,* took up the fight against patent medicines. Bok waged the battle in the magazine, which had more than one million readers in the 1900s, but came up against an industry that had more than $59 million in sales in 1900. Although Bok proved many patent medicines contained opium, cocaine, alcohol, morphine, and other hallucinogenic drugs, his efforts did not produce the national legislation he hoped to see.

As early as 1898, farmers and chemists came together to fight unhealthy standards. They formed the National Association of State Drug and Food Departments. The group lobbied for stiffer regulations regarding food production and uniform food and drug laws across all states, so that farmers could meet one standard. Farmers who produced wholesome foods quickly realized that they were being hurt in the marketplace by doing so.

Wiley, the pure food movement's greatest activist, pursued the large corporations relentlessly during the 1900s. Taking the skirmish to the streets in 1903, Wiley fed volunteers foods to see if they were damaging. Dubbed the "poison squad," Wiley's experimentation drew others into the pure food movement, including many middle-class women. His fight eventually included working closely with certain food companies. Wiley got the publicity and funds he needed to drive the effort, while the companies, most notably Pittsburgh's Heinz, had their names associated with untainted food.

The many constituencies fighting for unadulterated food (doctors, chemists, women's groups, farmers, and so on) organized into a cohesive whole at the 1904 World's Fair in St. Louis. The activists took popular foods that were dyed to hide impurities and extracted the dye from the food. Then they used the coloring to dye pieces of silk and wool. This visual display got the fair's hundreds of thousands of attendees talking about the duplicity taking place among food corporations. The pure food exhibit at the World's Fair caused a national scandal, but big business still thwarted national legislation by outspending and outsmarting the activists. It took an even more pervasive event to get people incensed enough to act: the publication of *The Jungle* in 1906.[8]

Sinclair wanted *The Jungle* to open America's eyes to the evils of capitalism and big business. His grotesque depiction of the meatpacking industry—rancid by-products, acids, additives, and dead workers going into sausage-making vats—turned people's stomachs and created an outrage that could no longer be suppressed.

Outraged by the descriptions of the meatpacking industry, Roosevelt assigned Agriculture Secretary James Wilson, as well as Attorney General William Moody, to investigate the problem. Roosevelt realized that the dastardly conditions described in Sinclair's book made government look bad, especially his own administration.

The task force Roosevelt assembled learned that meatpackers were illegally using government inspection labels because the only real inspection occurred on the killing floors, not at any other stage of preparation. The commissioners reported back to Roosevelt, publishing a report explaining,

"We saw meat shoveled from filthy wooden floors, piled on tables rarely washed, pushed from room to room in rotten box carts, in all of which processes it was in the way of gathering dirt, splinters, floor filth, and the expectoration of tuberculous and other diseased workers."[9]

Roosevelt used this report to convince legislators and the public that the time had come for national legislation. After the president released the full report, no one questioned the need for regulation. With Roosevelt's full backing, various leaders in Congress introduced a series of bills that dealt with pure food and drugs, meat inspection, and labeling. Senator Albert J. Beveridge passed the first legislation in May 1906, which required government inspectors at every point in meat production, not just on the killing floors. Public uproar over the government report reached a crescendo. The Pure Food and Drug Act passed a month later by a vote of 240–17. The dissenters were Democrats who did not oppose the bill but protested under the belief that food regulation should be handled by state governments.[10]

Roosevelt's willingness to throw his weight behind pure food legislation served as a turning point. The president could clearly identify the villains and victims in the fight, and he used his public power to circumvent the collective money and influence of the beef trusts. One powerful foe, Congressman James W. Wadsworth of New York, supported by the food corporations, introduced weakened legislation, and then fought the president as he pushed amendments to it. His battle against Roosevelt ultimately cost him his seat in Congress, which he had held since 1881.

FOOD HIGHLIGHTS FROM THE 1900s

1902 Campbell's Soups expands its product line to 21 varieties—and stays at this number for the next 30 years.

1902 National Biscuit Company (later Nabisco) introduces Barnum's Animals—animal-shaped cookies in a box designed to look like a cage. The string attached to the box is intended to make it easy to hang on a Christmas tree. Showman extraordinaire P. T. Barnum has no connection to the product and receives no remuneration for the use of his name.

1902 In Philadelphia (followed soon in New York), Horn & Hardart opens the first automat, a machine-vended, self-service eatery promising a dining experience that is "Quick as a Click." For a couple of coins, customers can open various compartments and extract freshly prepared hot food and coffee.

1904 Campbell's Soups introduces Pork and Beans—specifically created to make use of worker downtime while soups are simmering.

1905 Neapolitan immigrant Gennaro Lombardi is credited with introducing the pizza in America when he opens a pizzeria on Spring Street in New York City, although pizza doesn't gain wide acceptance until the 1950s.

1905 Royal Crown Cola Company founded

1906 Kellogg's Corn Flakes invented

1908 James L. Kraft establishes a wholesale cheese business in Chicago.

1908 The Sunshine Biscuit Company launches its Hydrox chocolate wafer sandwich cookie, believing that a name that combines "hydrogen" and "oxygen" will have mass public appeal because it sounds "pure."

1909 Continuing a trend for cookbooks published by magazines, newspaper, and other media, *Good Housekeeping* magazine releases *The Good Housekeeping Woman's Home Cook Book*. Recipes include Compote of Marshmallows, Wigwam Pudding, and Picked-up Cod Fish.

Food

CHANGING DIETS

With a national dialogue regarding the consumption of healthy foods taking place in the 1900s, Americans adopted a simpler diet, based less on the heavy fare consumed in earlier decades. In fact, advertisers played on the consumers' desire for "pure" foods by stressing a brand's healthiness in national advertising campaigns in magazines and newspapers. The most notable example of this phenomenon occurred among breakfast foods. Breakfast food companies, such as Kellogg with Corn Flakes and Post with Grape-Nuts and Toasties, convinced consumers that they should substitute traditional meat-oriented breakfasts with highly processed grains.

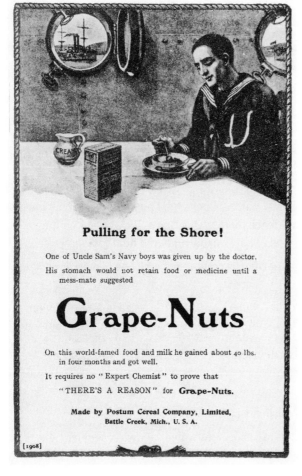

Reproduction of 1908 ad sponsored by Postum Cereal Company, Limited, showing sailor on ship seated at table eating Grape-Nuts cereal. Prints & Photographs Division, Library of Congress.

After many years of testing and failure, William K. Kellogg and his brother—Battle Creek, Michigan, sanatorium director Dr. John Harvey Kellogg—invented Corn Flakes as a vegetarian health food. Each later claimed to be the brains behind the creation. In turn, Battle Creek became the world capital of the Adventists, under the fiery leadership of Ellen Gould Harmon White. John Harvey Kellogg transformed the Battle Creek sanatorium into a thriving health resort catering to the nation's elite. Linking Corn Flakes with the hospital gave the cereal the kind of health food tie it needed to gain acceptance among a wider audience. Though the Kelloggs later broke with the mercurial White, the result of their experimentation turned the Michigan city into the world's breakfast cereal capital.[11]

The Kellogg sanatorium transformed into a hodge-podge of eccentrics, each pushing some wildly fantastic cure for a variety of ailments. Despite the circus-like atmosphere at the Kellogg retreat and the rich patrons flocking through its gates, Corn Flakes found success among middle-class consumers who linked the product with good health. Dr. Kellogg managed to stay above the fray despite the presence of the lesser healers and spiritualists, gaining an international reputation as a surgeon and medical guru.

One of Kellogg's ex-patients, St. Louis real estate magnate and food inventor Charles W. Post, began his own company and sold Grape-Nuts, clearly modeled after Kellogg's Corn Flakes. By establishing the Post Company near Kellogg's, Post gained from the connection to the sanatorium. The success of the two companies led to more firms establishing operations in Battle Creek. At one point there were 44 breakfast food companies and six companies making health drinks.[12]

The packaged breakfast foods gained wide acceptance because of middle America's concern about bacteria. Since the food came in a sealed container, the public assumed it was safe. Post marketed Postum cereal as "brain food" and claimed it cured malaria and loose teeth, among other things. Other cereals claimed to make red blood, cure blindness, and alleviate an inflamed appendix.[13] Even though breakfast food manufacturers came under fire for spouting such nonsense, as a whole they completely altered Americans' breakfast food.

William K. Kellogg, who took over the business aspects of the Kellogg company, realized that by using repetitive advertising and targeting children, he would be able to revolutionize the breakfast table. He pictured children on packaging, especially the instantly recognizable "Sweetheart of the Corn," a young girl who beamed up at the consumer with a bright smile while clutching a corn stock. Kellogg promoted the product by offering children prizes for collecting box tops, giving away free samples, and sponsoring corn shows in counties around the nation.

FOOD INNOVATIONS

With the rise of advertising and marketing to promote products and the public's increasing level of disposable income, food companies responded by introducing innovative products that soon became staples in the national diet. In the years just prior to 1900, Campbell's began producing canned soup after figuring out how to condense the contents, thus making storage and shipping practical. The next year, Campbell's first magazine ad appeared in *Good Housekeeping,* and it introduced Campbell's Pork and Beans.[14]

The decade was successful for Jell-O. By 1906, sales neared the $1 million mark. The company introduced its first trademark in 1903, the Jell-O Girl, who starred in all advertising promotions. She was shown playing in her nursery with Jell-O packages rather than toys. Over the next four years, the original Jell-O Girl graced magazine ads, store displays, and many items used as sales premiums, including spoons, molds, and china dessert dishes. In 1908, artist Rose O'Neill, the creator of Kewpie dolls, modernized the Jell-O Girl and gave her a more grownup look. Jell-O jumped on the pure food bandwagon in 1904 by producing its first recipe book and stating its approval by food commissioners. Chocolate, cherry, and peach flavors were added by 1907.[15]

Although Heinz introduced ketchup in 1876, the product did not find its true calling until 1900, when New Haven, Connecticut diner owner Louis Lassen placed a beef patty between two pieces of toast, and the hamburger was born. In 1901, the first hot dogs were sold at the Polo Grounds in New York, although they were not called "hot dogs" until 1906, when an artist drew a dachshund inside a bun for the *New York Journal.* The Pepsi-Cola Company was founded in North Carolina in 1902, and the first soda fountain was set up at Philadelphia's Broad Street Pharmacy in 1905. In 1904, David Strickler of Strickler's Drug Store in Latrobe, Pennsylvania created the banana split. Two years later, the hot fudge sundae was invented at C. C. Brown's ice cream parlor in Hollywood, California.

The 1900s also witnessed the rise of the chocolate empire of Milton S. Hershey. A native Pennsylvanian, Hershey began his career as an apprentice to a candy maker in Lancaster. After moving out on his own, he tried opening shops in Philadelphia, Denver, Chicago, and New York, but they all failed. Hershey finally found success when an importer wanted to introduce his caramels to England. By 1894, Hershey had built a thriving candy business.[16]

Hershey's big breakthrough occurred at the World's Columbian Exposition when he saw a German chocolate-making machine and decided he would make his own. In 1900, he sold all his other interests, including the caramel factory and his general candy division, and put all his effort into making chocolate. In 1903, Hershey bought a large tract of land in Derry Township, and then built a town around the central factory, later renamed Hershey, Pennsylvania. The candy maker experimented with a variety of ingredients until he devised his own secret concoction. He then turned his attention to the planned community around the factory, which would house his workers and their families. He built different styles of affordable housing for the workers, and also established churches, schools, and other institutions.[17]

Music

of the 1900s

In the early years of the twentieth century, music ranked just slightly behind literature as the most popular art form in the United States. By 1900, most major cities had orchestras or would establish them in the next decade. American classical musicians were steeped in the musical traditions of Europe and most classical composers trained there, although some innovative renegades hungered for a truly "American" sound. In the attempt to define a national music, these composers searched for the country's roots and unique folklore, or looked to the alternative forms blossoming in Russia and France. In deciding what American folklore actually meant, these artists turned to the types of music deemed most primitive: the music of American Indians and blacks.

During the decade, cities and towns built concert halls, opera houses, and theaters. Middle and working-class tastes ran toward the music found in outdoor concerts, saloons, dance halls, and vaudeville houses. Churches also served as an important source of music. Church-related social gatherings, such as choir practice, provided congregation members with a way to express themselves musically and spread song into the community.

Music filled many American homes as members of the played the piano, banjo, guitar, and harmonica and sang together. The availability of sheet music (containing both classical and popular compositions) spurred on these performances. Throughout the 1900s, publishing companies specializing in sheet music, concentrated in New York City on Tin Pan Alley, catered to the constant demand for new popular pieces people could play in their homes.

ORCHESTRAL MUSIC

Serious music in the 1900s was dominated by foreign influences, particularly those of Germany. Many of the most popular and renowned native-born composers trained in either Germany or Austria, then returned to the United States. The roots of the Germanic influence stretched back to the mid-1850s, when prominent European musicians performed with the New York Philharmonic, Chicago Symphony, and Boston Symphony.

A small group of influential American composers formed a tight-knit group. Many of them studied together at various times in their careers. The group included John Knowles Paine, Frederick S. Converse, Horatio W. Parker, Henry K. Hadley, and Arthur Farwell. The most famous and popular composer of the period, however, was Edward MacDowell. As the decade passed, most of the important composers linked themselves to large universities and budding music departments.

Paine (1839–1906) held the first chair of music at an American university when he won an appointment to Harvard in 1873. He also served as the college organist. An opera Paine composed, *The Pipe of Desire,* became the first American opera performed at the Metropolitan Opera House (1910). Parker became a professor of music at Yale in 1894, while working as the director of music at Boston's Trinity Church. Converse (1871–1940) joined Paine at Harvard and also taught at the New England Conservatory.

Edward MacDowell (1861–1908) was born in New York City and studied piano and composition in Paris and Frankfurt. In 1895, he became Columbia University's first professor of music. He taught at Columbia for the next nine years, until 1904, when he became embroiled in a public dispute with university officials and retired. MacDowell's composing also came to an end that year as a result of declining health, aggravated by a horse-cab accident, a growing problem confronting urban residents in the 1900s.

MacDowell composed works that expressed his vision of an idealistic life that could be inspirational. He believed that music should bring out the spiritual aspect of life and make people want to aspire to achieve great things. When composing, MacDowell worked tirelessly, both day and night, revising what he had previously written.

MacDowell's reputation, in part, rested on his prolific publishing output. He wrote symphonies, piano concertos, sonatas, and many other pieces, primarily for the piano. An avowed romanticist, MacDowell explored landscapes, seascapes, and medieval romance in his compositions. Among his works were a symphonic poem (*Lancelot and Elaine*), a suite for orchestra (*Les Orientales*), and childhood memories ("From Uncle Remus," *Woodland Sketches*).[1]

Arthur Farwell (1872–1952), a student of MacDowell, served as an early pioneer in establishing an American sound. He looked to Native American music, primarily Omaha tribal dances and songs. In 1901 Farwell established the Wa-Wan Press to encourage others to explore nontradi-

tional forms of expression and give them a forum for publication.

Farwell demanded that music education break free from German domination and that common people be given educational opportunities. Headquartered in Newton Centre, Massachusetts, the Wa-Wan Press scraped by on minimal funding and few profits, but gave younger artists a place to publish, mostly short piano pieces. In 1903, Farwell went on a combined concert/lecture tour to keep Wa-Wan afloat. Two years later, he established the American Music Society in Boston and opened centers in other cities across the nation. At the end of the decade, Farwell moved to New York City. He worked as a music critic, supervisor of the city's park concerts, and director of a music school settlement.[2]

Farwell concentrated on Native American music because he thought that they were connected to a universal creative spirit. The simplicity and spontaneity of Native American song, in Farwell's eyes, was a soothing contrast to the chaotic, money-driven music he thought was taking over the nation. Farwell also produced songs that contained African American spirituals and songs that combined the two, such as *Folk Songs of the West and South* (1905).[3] In 1914, Farwell sold the business to G. Schirmer. At that time, Wa-Wan published works by 37 composers, many specializing in Native American and black music.

Henry F. B. Gilbert (1868–1928) also championed the use of black music. He composed the operas *Comedy Overtures on Negro Themes* (1905) and *The Dance in Place Congo* (1906). Gilbert never undertook the formal musical training of his contemporaries, although he was a skilled violinist, but did study composition. His single goal was to make music that was strictly American and non-European.

Poor health forced Gilbert to work part-time on his musical career, but he helped Farwell run the Wa-Wan Press, which published six of his piano pieces and more than a dozen of his songs. Gilbert drew inspiration from popular authors, such as Mark Twain, Walt Whitman, Henry Thoreau, and Edgar Allen Poe. He also favored the use of humor in music.[4] Gilbert advocated a different point of view as a pioneer of American music. His

Music

music did not pander to the high society, but reveled in the minutia of everyday life.

ORCHESTRAS

The first important orchestra founded in the new century was the Philadelphia Orchestra. It was formed from two competing musical groups in the city—the Philadelphia Symphony Society and a smaller ensemble of professional musicians, the Thunder Orchestra. Fritz Scheel, a German active in New York, Chicago, and San Francisco since his arrival in the United States in 1893, served as the conductor. The group's first concert took place on November 16, 1900.

Backers found Scheel and the musicians so impressive that they set up a fund of $15,000 to fund the group. After a successful first season, the Philadelphia Orchestra Association formed, and the orchestra began touring nearby Pennsylvania towns. By the third season, the company had gained a great reputation, which led to performing concerts in Baltimore, Washington, D.C., and New York City.

The Boston Symphony opened a new concert hall in October 1900. From 1898 to 1906, Wilhelm Gericke conducted. Karl Muck, an outstanding musician and conducting genius, followed. Muck's first tour of duty with the symphony lasted only two years. In 1908, the German Kaiser Wilhelm demanded Muck return to Berlin's Royal Opera. In 1912, Muck returned to Boston where he continued his fine work with the symphony.

Boston operated as the ideological center of the musical world in the 1900s. Paine led a group of composers and musicians collectively known as the Second New England School; most were colleagues or students of Paine.

Collectively, the Second New England School, or the Boston Six, as they were also known, wished to produce indigenous American music, distinct from European composers. Members of the group, including John Knowles Paine, Horatio Parker, George Chadwick, Edward MacDowell, Amy Beach, and Arthur Foote, wrote the first substantial body of classical music in the United States. For example, Foote, who studied under Paine at Harvard, became widely known for chamber music, art songs, and music for choirs.

His early prowess led many critics to consider him the "Dean of American Composers" in the 1900s and 1910s.

SINGERS HIT THE HIGH NOTE

Concerts most often featured famous singers rather than instrumentalists. Even the early phonograph companies, including Columbia Phonograph Company (1887) and Victor Talking Machine Company (1901), specialized in recording opera stars.

The proving ground for many singers was Maurice Grau's Academy of Music in New York City. Grau let his operatic stars pick their own music, their own roles, and even allowed them to tinker with the score. He paid Polish tenor Jean de Reszke the princely sum of $2,500 a performance during the 1900–1901 season, even though the accompanying musicians barely made a living wage.

The most famous opera singers in the 1900s were Italian tenor Enrico Caruso and American soprano Geraldine Farrar. Caruso made his first appearance at the Metropolitan Opera on November 23, 1903. It was the first of his more than 600 performances with the Met. During the 1905–1906 season, Caruso sang *Faust,* his first French opera in New York.

The New York opera season of 1905–1906 ended more than $100,000 in the black. In an ironic twist of fate, the 1906 San Francisco earthquake erased the profit. The Metropolitan Opera was playing there and the resulting fire razed the company's scenery and costumes. Replacing them ate up the budget, and all the advance ticket sales had to be refunded.

On November 26, the opening night of the New York 1906–1907 season, the Metropolitan welcomed a 24-year-old singer named Geraldine Farrar, making her American debut after five successful years in Europe, wowing crowds from Berlin to Monte Carlo. In short notice, the Melrose, Massachusetts, singer became the only opera star who could equal Caruso as a box office draw.

TIN PAN ALLEY

The focal point of popular music in the 1900s surfaced on a single block in New York City at

28th Street between Fifth Avenue and Broadway. In 1903, Monroe Rosenfeld, a songwriter and journalist, researching an article on popular music for the *New York Herald,* dubbed the area "Tin Pan Alley." According to legend, Rosenfeld visited the famous songwriter Harry von Tilzer in his office and heard the distinctive von Tilzer sound, a tinny piano with paper wrapped around the strings to produce the effect. Soon, the term represented not only that area, but the entire music industry in the United States.

The nation's most powerful music publishers set up shop to be close to the stars and stages of Broadway. The first firm on Tin Pan Alley was M. Witmark and Sons, which opened offices at 49 West 28th Street in 1893. Shortly thereafter, the street was lined with music publishing firms trying to cash in on the demand for sheet music nationwide. Next, Tin Pan Alley swelled with an influx of pianists, arrangers, composers, conductors, and lyricists.

As the demand for new songs increased, the publishing companies blatantly copied words or themes. Tin Pan Alley has been described as a musical assembly line, so it is appropriate that many songs were written specifically to exploit the latest American technological achievements, such as airplanes, automobiles, and telephones. If a particular word or name gained popularity, dozens of writers grabbed the idea and many competing versions were created.

Tin Pan Alley cut a wide swath through American life. Songs celebrated the innovations of the United States, such as automobiles in "In My Merry Oldsmobile." "Meet Me in St. Louis, Louis" directed the nation's attention to the 1904 St. Louis World's Fair. Music played an important role throughout the period, bonding people together (often immigrants from vastly different cultures) and playing upon their patriotic heartstrings.[5]

Fortunes were made on Tin Pan Alley as million dollar sales grew increasingly more frequent. Von Tilzer (1872–1946), perhaps the most famous musician, composer, and publisher on Tin Pan Alley, had great success with "A Bird in a Gilded Cage" (1900), which sold over 2 million copies. Von Tilzer later claimed to have published more than 2,000 songs in his career. By the end of the decade, "In the Shade of the Old Apple Tree"

(1905) by Beth Whitson and Leo Friedman sold an astronomical 8 million copies. In all, nearly 100 songs sold more than a million copies of sheet music in the 1900s.[6]

The publishing companies used many strategies to get people to hear their songs. One avenue was to sell sheet music at department stores and five-and-dime shops. The publishing houses employed "pluggers" to give mini-performances, playing to the crowds who yearned to hear the latest music. The role of the plugger soon expanded to encompass duties similar to today's publicists and public relations specialists.

In addition to singing, pluggers exerted pressure on major stage stars to sing their songs. The ingenuity of a plugger pushed some songs to bestseller status. Mose Gumble prowled Coney Island, New York City amusement park and boardwalk, dance halls, ice cream parlors, and restaurants singing to the crowds. Some nights he even slept

Sheet music for "I Won't Be Home Until Late, Dear! (I've Some Real Pressing Business on Hand)," a racy song of the decade. Courtesy of the Oakland Public Library, Oakland, California.

on the beach to be there in the morning in an effort to persuade Coney Island singers to use his songs during that day's performances. In 1905, Gumble's efforts lifted Egbert Van Alstyne's "In the Shade of the Old Apple Tree" to one of the year's most popular songs.

When nickelodeons, a new kind of storefront theater showing films all day long, came into vogue, pluggers cajoled house pianists to play their songs, which served as the background for silent movies. Nickelodeons were a perfect venue for debuting songs since they featured fictional films, so the Tin Pan Alley hits became almost like soundtrack pieces. It was common to find pluggers singing songs prior to the beginning of the movie or during intermission. It was not unusual to find a plugger working up to eight theaters an evening and countless more on the weekend.[7]

THE KING OF RAGTIME

No craze swept the public's imagination in the 1900s more than ragtime, which first appeared on sheet music in 1893 in Fred S. Stone's "My Ragtime Baby." The term is most closely associated with Scott Joplin, who was known as the "King of Ragtime." In 1899, his piano piece "Maple Leaf Rag" became the first ragtime composition to hit best seller status. Joplin's success started a rage that swept the nation. Before long, ragtime tunes were played by piano bands and dance bands around the country and on player pianos, and enjoyed substantial sheet music sales.

Ragtime developed in the Mississippi Valley, the creation of mostly black pianists who lived and traveled through the region. Some scholars trace its origins to minstrel shows, while others believe that it developed from dance music and the Cakewalk, a burlesque dance performed primarily in Southern minstrel shows.

In its simplest form, ragtime is syncopated music that is often either high-spirited and danceable or slow and romantic. Ragtime's popularity in the seedy dance houses and saloons at the turn of the century fueled a national dance craze. While ragtime began as racy dance music, it slowly gained a measure of dignity. African American artists and composers used ragtime as a means of pushing into the music business.

Scott Joplin contributed more to the popularization of ragtime than any other single performer. Ironically, Joplin's contributions had almost been forgotten. When ragtime was "rediscovered" in 1974, following the success of the Paul Newman–Robert Redford film *The Sting,* Joplin's compositions again topped the charts. Modern filmmakers and contemporary historians can credit Scott Joplin with his accomplishments because he was able to leave a written record for musicians to reproduce. His ability to capture the African American vernacular tradition so ably, while relying on European notation and melodic methods, stands as one of the greatest achievements in the history of American popular music.

Joplin (1868–1917) was born in Texarkana, Texas. As did most blacks in the Reconstruction era, Joplin had a difficult childhood. His father, Jiles, was an ex-slave who worked on the railroad and later deserted the family.

Music played an important role in Joplin's early life. Reportedly, his father played the fiddle and his mother played the banjo, and he and his brothers were taught to sing along. The northeastern section of Texas called home by the Joplins was filled with people from the South who had brought their regional songs with them. Growing up in a biracial community also exposed Joplin to music from the white community, such as waltzes and polkas.[8]

Florence Joplin worked for a wealthy white attorney in Texarkana who allowed Scott to play the piano while his mother cleaned. The boy displayed an innate natural ability. Word spread quickly, and by the age of 11, he was receiving free lessons from a German teacher in sight reading and classical composition. His father managed to save enough money to buy a piano for the boy. Although Joplin's total immersion in music grew into a sore spot for Jiles, the youngster played at church gatherings and community events. He also played professionally, by himself and later with a local band.[9]

Joplin left Texas and toured the country as a professional musician. At the age of 24, he found himself in Chicago at the World's Columbian Exposition in 1893. The world of the exposition was a far cry from the small towns Joplin had lived in since leaving Texarkana. Jackson Park exploded with light from the glittery electric lights, and the midway pulsed with thousands of visitors from all over the world. The Columbian Exposition was the first time the young performer heard ragtime, with its roots in slave songs and complicated African cadences.

Joplin later moved to Sedalia, Missouri, where he took classes at the George R. Smith College for Negroes. While there, he taught piano and composition at the school. At night, Joplin played piano at the Maple Leaf Club, which he later immortalized in his most famous rag composition. In Sedalia, Joplin met John Stark, a music store owner, who served as his publisher. In 1900, the musician moved to St. Louis in an attempt to capitalize on his growing fame. The city was a mecca for black musicians, especially ragtime pianists.

Joplin's success in 1899 with "Maple Leaf Rag," which sold well for the next decade also helped, to some extent, to bridge the color barrier between the races.

Although Joplin wrote hit after hit in the 1900s, he still faced the limitations placed on black musicians. He wrote ballets, operas, and musicals during this period, but his publishers only wanted to see short, popular piano pieces. Though Joplin and Stark described his work as "classical ragtime" to separate it from other versions, in the end, Joplin could not move beyond ragtime.[10]

As a black man, Joplin achieved great wealth and fame. However, his color kept him from enjoying the success he deserved as a serious composer. Although ragtime is acknowledged as one of the first truly American forms of music and was all the rage in the 1900s, it also evoked images of slavery. The cover for Joplin's song "Original Rags" depicts an old hunched-over black man, smoking a corncob pipe in front of a ramshackle house with a mangy dog in the front yard. The cover of his song "The Easy Winner," however, cover shows sailboats, horse racing, and young whites playing football.

JAZZ

The nation's preoccupation with ragtime, based on African American music, gave rise to another uniquely American music—jazz. Born in a section of New Orleans where blacks gathered on Sundays, jazz sprang to life from the horn of Charles "Buddy" Bolden (1871–1931), who played dance

Ragtime music may have derived from minstrel shows, still popular at the beginning of the century. Here, a poster advertises William H. West's "Big Minstrel Jubilee," ca. 1900. Prints & Photographs Division, Library of Congress.

Music

music for the crowds. Bolden and other Louisiana musicians heard the syncopated melodies of ragtime and gave them an up-tempo beat. The earliest jazz blended dance music, the blues, and ragtime into one musical whole.

Bolden grew up in a social setting that set the stage for jazz to come alive. As a boy, he

The cover of the music for "The Jelly Roll Blues" by Ferd (Jelly Roll) Morton. Courtesy of the Oakland Public Library, Oakland, California.

Music

undoubtedly heard the brass bands that played in clubs around the black neighborhoods and heard the same groups at social gatherings, including the elaborate funeral marches played in the South. He would have also heard the field songs sung by plantation workers and the classical works played by educated Creoles. Bolden got his start playing in small string bands, which allowed him to experiment with bolder styles.[11]

By 1905, Bolden was famous around New Orleans for his swinging beat. Pianist Ferdinand "Jelly Roll" Morton, a young Creole who became an important figure on the jazz scene, remembered hearing the wail of Bolden's horn from all over the city, calling out the start of a dance in Lincoln Park. Bolden also had an impact on Louis Armstrong, who, as a young boy, listened to Bolden perform around New Orleans.

Bolden's success was short-lived. Even as his popularity peaked, he began experiencing severe mood swings and depression, which he tried to cure by drinking. In 1907, after experiencing fits of violence, Bolden was sent to a state mental institution, where he remained for the next 24 years.

Luckily, jazz survived Bolden's decline and did not go out of style. Other black horn players, notably Buddy Petit and Bunk Johnson, took up where Bolden left off. Bands around New Orleans set up shop on the back of horse-drawn wagons and played as they were pulled through the streets. Freddie Keppard, who formed the Olympia Orchestra in 1905, rose to prominence, playing both classical shows for high society gatherings and jazz at area dance clubs. Keppard later joined the Original Creole Orchestra, the first jazz band to play outside New Orleans, which traveled to San Francisco in 1913 and to Chicago a year later.[12]

HIT SONGS OF THE 1900s

"Strike Up the Band" (performed by Dan W. Quinn; written by Charles B. Ward and Andrew B. Sterling)—1900

"I Love You Truly" (written by Carrie Jacobs-Bond)—1901

"Arkansaw Traveler" (performed by Len Spencer)—1902

"The Entertainer" (written by Scott Joplin)—1902

"In the Good Old Summertime" (written by Ren Shields and George Evans)—1903

"Give My Regards to Broadway" (written by George M. Cohan)—1904

"Wait 'Til the Sun Shines, Nellie" (written by Andrew B. Sterling and Harry Von Tilzer)—1905

"You're a Grand Old Flag" (written by George M. Cohan)—1906

"Take Me Out to the Ball Game" (written by Jack Norworth and Albert Von Tilzer)—1908

"I Love My Wife, But Oh, You Kid" (written by Harry Armstrong and Billy Clark)—1909

Sports

and Leisure of the 1900s

In the 1900s, one man symbolized the athletic spirit of the nation—President Theodore Roosevelt. Roosevelt embodied what was then known as the "strenuous life," a phrase closely associated with him and also the title of a book of essays he published in 1900. For Roosevelt and, in turn, the nation, the strenuous life meant a dedication to outdoor activities and athletic endeavors on the one hand, but also to hard work and strife.

The president's outdoor exploits and active lifestyle were chronicled on the front pages of newspapers across the country. Roosevelt's feats did not seem contrived, but were manifestations of his true personality and the way in which he reared his own children. In his autobiography, Roosevelt discussed climbing steep cliffs with army officers and swimming in both Rock Creek and the Potomac River in early spring, with ice floating alongside.[1]

The nation eagerly bought into Roosevelt's call for a strenuous life. People had nostalgic feelings about rural life. The emphasis on outdoor living put them in touch with these seemingly gentler days. As a result, efforts were made in many cities to build parks and permanent green spaces for people to escape the density of their neighborhoods. As the automobile became more popular, people took day trips into the country, although this involved riding over rough country roads, leading to flat tires and other mechanical calamities.

The growth of the middle class in the 1900s led to greater wealth and an increase in leisure time for many. People had the time to attend football and baseball games, amusement parks, and horse races. In 1904, more than 22,000 spectators watched the annual Stanford–University of California at Berkeley football game on Thanksgiving Day. In 1910, attendance at major league baseball games reached 7.2 million, double the attendance in 1901. Newspapers also played an important role in turning fans into paying spectators. As the decade wore on, newspaper owners realized that they could significantly increase readership if they covered amateur and professional sporting events. The birth of the modern sportswriter can be seen in the 1900s, although a dedicated sports page would not become standard nationwide until the 1920s.

The rise of spectator sports had interesting consequences on the social order in the United States. Sporting events were a venue where rich and poor met and mingled, drawn by the common desire to see a favorite team or player. Saloons provided a space for upper and lower classes to interact, serving as both a male-dominated refuge and a place to wager on different contests. In the first two decades of the new century, saloons reached the height of popularity. For example, in Chicago, more than half the city's population frequented one of the city's 7,600 saloons every day on the average. Another rift in the social scene occurred when various professional athletes attained great wealth and were propelled into the upper classes.[2]

Most sporting activities at the turn of the century were geared toward men, although the two sexes looked to find entertainment venues in which they could interact without strict societal formalities. Dance halls, amusement parks, vaudeville houses, and movie houses gave young people a place to relax and spend time together, away from the watchful eyes of parents and elders. Soon, most cities had one or two amusement parks, which included dance halls, exhibits, band pavilions, mechanical thrill rides, swimming and bathing areas, and even circuses. Folks in small towns and rural areas enjoyed traveling carnivals and circuses.[3]

Cities set aside park areas for families to gather for picnics and community socials. Traditional places of formal social interaction, including churches, the YMCA, and municipal buildings also remained popular. Church members gathered in the evening for "ten cent socials," a time for frolicking and fun, but also for a good cause. The proceeds were donated to charity or used to aid the poor.

Lodges and union-sponsored social gatherings served as the primary form of entertainment for

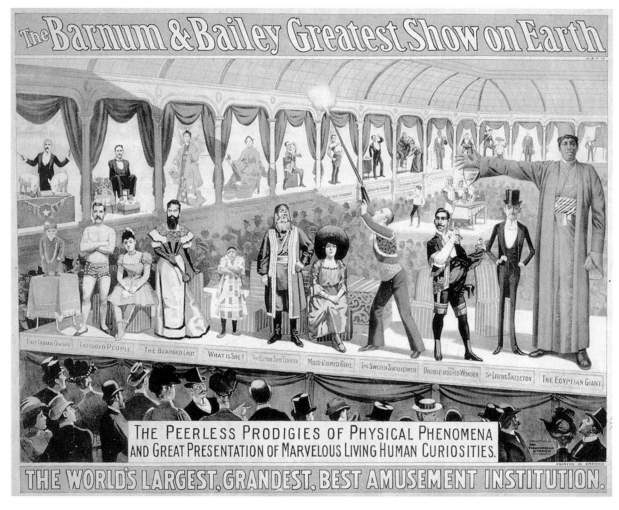

A poster for The Barnum & Bailey Circus, advertising "The greatest show on earth—the peerless prodigies of physical phenomena and great presentation of marvelous living human curiosities." Prints & Photographs Division, Library of Congress.

many families in the laboring classes. Men constituted the overwhelming majority of these groups, but women actively participated in some and benefited from the social aspects granted by their husbands' membership.

BASEBALL: THE NATIONAL PASTIME

Baseball was far and away the most popular sport in the 1900s. After both the American and National leagues began counting foul balls as strikes, pitchers dominated the game, leading the period to be called the "dead ball" era. The ball itself favored pitchers, since it had a rubber center and did not carry as far as today's cork-centered balls. Despite these balls and the prowess of great pitchers such as Cy Young, Christy Mathewson, Walter Johnson, and Grover Cleveland Alexander, many gifted hitters emerged. Perhaps the greatest hitter of all time, Tyrus Raymond "Ty" Cobb, set the record for highest career batting average (.367) from 1905 to 1928. Other feared hitters included Napoleon Lajoie and Honus Wagner, but it was not until Boston Red Sox George Herman "Babe" Ruth gave up pitching in 1919, was sold to the New York Yankees, and became the "Sultan of Swat" that people cheered long ball hitters.

Baseball clubs had formed in New York City as early as the 1840s and 1850s, including the New York Knickerbockers, under Alexander Cartwright, who established many of the rules of the game. The Cincinnati Red Stockings became the nation's first professional team in 1869, and seven years later the National League (NL) formed with eight teams. Baseball players were treated more like factory workers than superstars, with rigid restrictions on the players and limited movement between teams.

The National League dominated baseball before 1900, but faced financial challenges and had trouble finding enough qualified players and umpires. In an attempt to cut costs and deliver a better brand of baseball, the NL dropped six franchises and settled into an eight-team division in 1900. Cincinnati native and former sportswriter Byron Bancroft "Ban" Johnson, the president of the Western League, a secondary circuit operating primarily in midsized Midwestern cities, decided to challenge the NL. He adopted the name American League (AL) and moved quickly to scoop up the franchises dropped by the NL.[4]

Johnson and several big-name stars, including legendary managers John McGraw and Connie Mack, barnstormed the country to raise awareness of the new league and recruiting players. The AL signed more than 100 former NL players and two of the sport's biggest heroes and future Hall of Famers. First, pitcher Cy Young signed with the Boston club, then Napoleon Lajoie, a gifted hitter and infielder, joined Connie Mack's Philadelphia Athletics. The NL had a tight cap on salaries, which played into the hands of the AL owners. Both Young and Lajoie signed for $3,500, a princely sum in 1900.

The AL's first season in 1900 drew nearly 1.7 million fans, just 236,000 less than the senior circuit. Chicago won the championship behind player-manager Clark Griffith, an outstanding pitcher who won 24 games. In the NL, the Pittsburgh Pirates won the championship behind the hitting prowess of John "Honus" Wagner, one of the greatest players in baseball history.[5]

NL owners questioned the audacity of the new league in challenging their supremacy and resented the AL's poaching of their best players. Several court battles raged over players signing for more money to play in the AL, including a high-profile lawsuit involving Lajoie. A judge barred the star from the roster of the Philadelphia Athletics, but Johnson masterminded a trade to the Cleveland club, where Lajoie played for the rest of the decade. Both leagues quickly realized that if they continued stealing away each other's star players, it would hurt baseball as a whole.

The National Agreement of 1903 forced each side to accept the contracts of the other and formed a three-man National Commission to govern baseball as a whole. The agreement also set up the territorial boundaries of the minor league teams. In effect, the 1903 agreement took away the little bit of power players had over their own career moves. Players who were upset with their contracts had few options, since other teams could not sign them away. From 1903 to World War I, players attempted to exert some power by forming unions, but the efforts failed.

Arguably the best player of the 1900s was Georgia born Ty Cobb. In 1905, Cobb was a

Sports

minor league outfielder, but by 1907, he led the AL in batting average (.350), runs batted in, total bases, and stolen bases. From 1907 to 1919, Cobb averaged .378, and eclipsed the magical .400 mark in 1911 and 1912. By the end of his career, Cobb held 43 offensive records and set a career average record that probably will never be broken.

Cobb's fierceness on the field earned him few friends. He was sensitive about his Southern roots and the mysterious death of his father, who was killed by his mother when she thought he was an intruder in their home and shot him twice with a shotgun. Cobb also endured a great deal of hazing in his rookie season with the Detroit Tigers, a common practice in the big leagues, but difficult for the future star. Perhaps the greatest difference between Cobb and his fellow players was his intensity and will to power. Just over six feet tall and weighing approximately 175 pounds, he played far beyond his natural abilities on the basis of his competitiveness and internal fire.

Cobb captured Roosevelt's ideal of the strenuous life, playing the game with vigor and excelling beyond his natural abilities, but Cobb was also a racist and bully. He would climb into the stands and challenge fans physically. He carried a revolver off the field and used the gun to intimidate anyone who questioned his authority. His treatment of blacks unfortunately typified the racism of the day. On at least two separate occasions he hit black women, once kicking a hotel maid in the stomach. Although Ban Johnson fined him and attempted to discipline him, no one could control Cobb. One of the most famous men in America, he ate alone, traveled alone, and was despised by teammates and foes alike.

Ty Cobb and his fellow baseball players were among the nation's first celebrities, an entertainment class. Stadiums were built with dugouts to separate players from the fans. The press focused on the players and their exploits in an attempt to satiate the public's longing for the latest score or feature story about their favorite player.

The spectacle of baseball as the national pastime came together most strikingly in the World Series championships held between the AL and NL pennant winners. The first World Series in 1903, between the Pittsburgh Pirates and Boston Beaneaters (changed to the Red Sox the next year), was not officially sanctioned by either league. The animosity between the two leagues ran too deep at the time, resulting in no World Series the next year.

Led by Cy Young, the Boston team won the best of nine series in eight games. Young won two games for Boston, and Bill Dineen won three. Honus Wagner played poorly for Pittsburgh, batting only .222 and committing six errors. The first World Series vaulted the young American League and validated its place with the National League. Being the first championship of its kind in baseball, the game was followed primarily by the fans of the two cities, but it did draw over 100,000 spectators.[6]

Recognizing the moneymaking potential of the season-ending championship, the league presidents sanctioned the 1905 World Series, which pitted John McGraw's New York Giants against Connie Mack's Philadelphia Athletics. A pitching duel from the start, the series lasted five games with each team winning by shutout. Mathewson and Joe McGinnity blanked the Athletics to post four wins and clinch the series for New York. More important than the winning scores or the individual exploits of the players, the 1905 championship caught the imagination of the public.

WORLD SERIES

1903 Boston "Pilgrims" Red Sox (AL), 5 games; Pittsburgh Pirates (NL), 3 games

1904 No series

1905 New York Giants (NL), 4 games; Philadelphia Athletics (AL), 1 game

1906 Chicago White Sox (AL), 4 games; Chicago Cubs (NL), 2 games

1907 Chicago Cubs (NL), 4 games; Detroit Tigers (AL), 0 games

1908 Chicago Cubs (NL), 4 games; Detroit Tigers (AL), 1 game

1909 Pittsburgh Pirates (NL), 4 games; Detroit Tigers (AL), 3 games

BEISBOL: CUBA'S PASTIME

Baseball, the quintessential American sport, has almost as long a history in Cuba. American sailors are said to have played the game while docked in Havana in 1866, but for Cuban *beisbol* to take off, it needed encouragement from homegrown athletes and fans. In the mid-1800s, well-off Cuban families sent their sons to the United States for schooling. There, many of them learned the game.

By the early 1900s, baseball was flourishing in Cuba, and American players and soon entire teams came to the island for moneymaking exhibition games as soon as the U.S. baseball season ended. Starting in 1908, enthusiastic local fans flocked to the ballparks to see their own teams play—and more often than not beat—American major league clubs such as the Cincinnati Reds and the Detroit Tigers.

The foreign visitors noted that *beisbol* was everywhere one went in the island nation. Shop windows were filled with carefully displayed bats, balls, and gloves. In Havana, empty lots bustled with impromptu games, and in suburbs and rural areas, every hamlet had its own home team.

There was one stark contrast between Cuban and American baseball. The professional leagues in the U.S. were segregated—a strange concept to the racially mixed Cuban population. Cuban fans were equally welcoming to black American stars like Rube Walker and white players like Ty Cobb—although only light-skinned Cubans, like Mike Gonzalez of the Washington Senators, had any hope of playing for an American major-league team.

Over time, more and more white American ballplayers experienced racially mixed "winter ball" in Cuba, paving the way for integration. In 1947, when Jackie Robinson finally broke the color line for good, his debut with the Brooklyn Dodgers was preceded by the team's spring-training preseason in Cuba, where baseball never had a color.

FOOTBALL

In the 1900s, football was brutal—in 1905 alone, the *Chicago Tribune* reported the deaths of 18 football players and serious injuries to 159.

Many colleges took measures to deal with the brutality. Columbia abolished football in 1905; Stanford and California suspended play. Charles Eliot, president of Harvard, wanted to eliminate football altogether. In October 1905, President Roosevelt, a football supporter and proponent of the game, put together a committee to find a way to abolish the violence.[7]

Roosevelt's football commission formed the American Football Rules Committee, which designed plays to open up the game and move away from the power plays and wedges that brought together unprotected players in bone crushing collisions. Two important rules were developed: moving the first-down markers from 5 to 10 yards, and the forward pass.[8]

Despite the injuries, college football dominated the sport in the 1900s and increasingly became a focal point of collegiate life. In the early part of the decade, the teams of the University of Michigan outclassed the rest of the nation. In 1901, Michigan dismantled the University of Buffalo 128–0. Over the season, the Michigan team totaled 501 points without giving up a single point. In an attempt to determine the best team in the nation, a group of sports organizers put together the first Rose Bowl in 1902, pitting Stanford against Michigan. Michigan won 49–0, discouraging the Westerners to the point that they did not hold another Rose Bowl contest until 1916.[9]

BOXING

The *Baltimore Sun* reported on April 2, 1901, that Elizabeth Moore, a 24-year-old woman, had been arrested the prior night for attending the lightweight boxing match between the great Joe Gans (the first African American to hold a championship title) and Martin Flaherty. The official charge against Moore was "masquerading in male attire," but her real crime was invading the male-dominated bastion represented by professional boxing matches. Boxing, barely legal itself at the turn of the century, was no place for women according to societal norms.[10]

Despite its viciousness, seedy elements, and illegality in many states, boxing gained immense popularity in the 1900s. Many prize fights were basically bare knuckle brawls held secretly in saloons, gyms, or backwoods areas. Fans followed the sport closely and took great interest in the professional heavyweight division. Opponents of boxing, including Roosevelt, railed against the sport's gambling influences and outright brutality. At least four men died in 1901, although one can speculate that countless more died in illegal fights that were never reported. Even sanctioned boxing matches were vicious and often lasted 25 rounds or more.[11]

James J. Jeffries held the world heavyweight title at the start of the decade. He beat New Zealander Bob Fitzsimmons at the Coney Island Athletic Club in 1899 with an eleventh round knockout. Jeffries, six feet one inch in height and weighing 210 pounds, ruled the heavyweight division for the next four years. Jeffries, who defended his belt at every turn, voluntarily retired in 1905, at 30 years of age.

White boxers in the 1900s seemed to take a two pronged approach to competing with black contenders. On one hand, fight promoters and officials worked with the white champions and tried to deny blacks the chance to go for the title. At the same time, whites seemed to believe blacks were cowards and held the general belief that blacks were socially, physically, and mentally inferior. Interracial boxing matches took place in the 1900s and drew huge crowds because of the novelty. African American fighters, however, were discriminated against at nearly every turn.

Jack Johnson, a native of Galveston, Texas, would change white America's perception of black athletes in the 1900s. Johnson, who left school after the fifth grade, bounced from one menial job to another and traveled around the country. Settling in Dallas at the age of 16, Johnson worked at a carriage shop building horse-drawn buggies. His boss, Walter Lewis, was an ex-boxer and offered to teach the hulking Johnson to box. Johnson's first important fight was against noted heavyweight Joe Choynsky in 1901. Johnson was knocked out in the third round, and after the fight, both men were carted off to jail, as boxing was illegal in Texas at the time. For the next three weeks, the more experienced Choynsky gave Johnson boxing lessons.[12]

In 1903, Johnson beat "Denver" Ed Martin to win the Negro heavyweight championship. In 1903 and 1904, all Johnson's opponents were black, since the sport remained segregated. After beating Martin, Johnson gained the attention of the boxing world. In 1903, heavyweight champ Jeffries declared, "I will not fight a Negro! If Johnson wants to fight for the championship he will have to fight somebody besides me. If I am defeated, the championship will go to a white man, for I will not fight a colored man."[13] Since Jeffries would not fight him, Johnson began to question the champion's character publicly. Jeffries did not change his stance and chose to retire in 1905, claiming a lack of competition.

Johnson continued boxing and did not lose a fight in 1906 or 1907. He set his sights on the heavyweight championship, but the white titleholders continued holding to the color barrier. Johnson's most impressive victory during this time was a win over former champion Bob Fitzsimmons, the first time a black man beat a former titleholder. Johnson started chasing the new champion, Canadian Tommy Burns, all over the globe demanding a title shot. Newspapers jumped into the fray as well. Burns finally consented to a fight with Johnson. The fight date was set for December 26, 1908, with a total purse of $40,000; Burns would receive $35,000 and Johnson, only $5,000.[14]

Approximately 26,000 fans (including two women) watched Johnson—nearly six feet, two inches and 195 pounds—batter the heavyweight champion, who was six inches shorter and 15 pounds lighter. But it was not size that led to the pounding Burns took—it was Johnson's superior training and his desire to disprove the coward label that some had been pinning on blacks. Johnson knocked Burns down in the first round with a right uppercut, and by the eighth round Burns's eyes were swollen shut and he was bleeding from the mouth. Burns took more punishment through 14 rounds before the police called an end to the battle. Jack Johnson assumed the heavyweight championship of the world. Serving as ringside reporters were former champion John L. Sullivan and author Jack London. Immediately after the fight, London called out for Jim Jeffries to come out of retirement and defend the honor of whites. Soon, the cry for Jeffries as the "Great White Hope" took hold. Although retired for four

Sports

and a half years, the pressure and money were too much—Jeffries agreed to fight Johnson.[15]

On July 4, 1910, in Reno, Nevada, the two men came to the center of the ring to fight the battle of the ages. They did not like one another and agreed that there would be no traditional prefight handshake. By the thirteenth round, Johnson openly taunted Jeffries and laughed as he lunged after him. Two rounds later, Johnson repeatedly set Jeffries down to the canvas and then through the ropes. Jeffries's camp threw in the towel.

Johnson's victory set off a terrifying reaction against blacks across the nation. There were riots and fights in cities as diverse as Omaha, Philadelphia, Houston, New Orleans, and Macon, Georgia. In total, the carnage left 13 blacks dead and hundreds more injured. The public outcry against Johnson included banning films of the match and making it illegal to transport them across state lines.

Over the next several decades, Johnson faced prosecution by authorities in America, Europe, and Mexico. After trial for trumped-up charges for violating the Mann Act (transporting a person across state lines for immoral purposes) in 1912, Johnson was convicted on 11 counts, ranging from crimes against nature to prostitution and debauchery. He was sentenced to a year and a day in jail and fined $1,000. The case and trial caused another uproar, and white America even called on eminent black statesman Booker T. Washington to comment. Washington urged caution and suggested that Johnson act in nonthreatening ways. Black leaders feared violence and threats against the black middle class. Washington and W.E.B. Du Bois both felt that Johnson hindered race progress, but African Americans used every Johnson victory in the ring as a reason to rejoice. He gave them a sense of pride few blacks had experienced before.

GOLF AND TENNIS

Golf and lawn tennis gained in popularity in the 1900s. In 1894, the Amateur Golf Association was formed to standardize the game, and changed its name to the United States Golf Association (USGA) a year later. The first U.S. Open golf tournament was held in 1895, and by 1900, more than 1,000 golf clubs dotted the countryside. The game received a shot in the arm when three time British Open champion Harry Vardon toured America in 1900.

As the decade wore on, middle-class enthusiasts began to play golf. Amateur champion Walter J. Travis helped popularize the game by winning the national championship in 1900, 1901, and 1903. The following year, Travis became the first foreign player to capture the British amateur title. A wiry, small man, born in Australia, but making his home in Texas, Travis did not even begin playing golf until he was 35 years old. By 1905, he had his own magazine, *American Golfer,* and published *Practical Golf,* a guide to the sport. Jerome D. Travers, one of the first great American players, won amateur titles in 1907 and 1908, then again in 1912 and 1913. He also wrote numerous articles and several books on the sport.[16]

In 1874, New York socialite Mary Ewing Outerbridge, who saw British officers play lawn tennis while she was on winter vacation in Bermuda, introduced the game to the United States. She purchased a tennis set abroad but had to surrender the equipment to customs officials who did not know what it was. She used her family's ties in the shipping industry to get the items into the country. She had a tennis court set up at the Staten Island Cricket and Baseball Club, which her brother ran.

Unlike in golf, tennis players from both sexes competed with and against one another. Tennis was a rich person's game. The United States Lawn Tennis Association (USLTA) organized in 1881, and by 1900, the sport had its first great superstar, William A. Larned, who won seven national singles titles (1901, 1902, 1907–1911). More important for popularizing tennis, however, was the International Lawn Tennis Challenge Cup tournament, better known as the Davis Cup, after Dwight F. Davis, who donated the silver cup given to the winning team. Tennis's top players, including Davis, the national college singles champion, decided that an international competition would bolster the game's acceptance. The competition was first held between the United States and Britain, and later Australia was added. The U.S. squad won in 1900 and 1902, but the British held the cup until 1906, when the Australians took over through 1912.

Sports

Women competed on the national and international tennis stage. Strong American players included Myrtle McAteer, Elisabeth H. Moore, and Marion Jones, who earned a bronze medal at the 1900 Olympic Games. May Sutton became the first American woman to win Wimbledon, in 1905, and reclaimed the title in 1907. Decked out in all white, long sleeves, and a knotted tie, Sutton may have caused the biggest stir by wearing a dress that rose two inches above her ankles at the 1905 Wimbledon matches.

REBIRTH OF THE OLYMPIC GAMES

The father of the modern Olympics, Pierre de Coubertin, a French aristocrat served as the first secretary general and later president (1896–1925) of the International Olympic Committee (IOC). Coubertin designed the Olympic symbol of the five interlocking rings to represent the five continents and the colors of their national flags. He viewed the Olympics as games that exalted both the athlete's individualism and the patriotism felt for one's homeland. On a visit to the United States in 1889, he met U.S. Civil Service Commissioner Theodore Roosevelt. Recognizing in each other a focus on the strenuous life, the men quickly became friends and remained so for the rest of their lives.[17]

Coubertin organized numerous sports associations and then set his sights on reviving the Olympic Games. Several attempts had been made to revive the games, the most recent in Sweden in 1834, but people regarded the idea of the Olympics as sacred. When Coubertin lobbied in the United States to gain the support of the nation's sports leaders, including the secretary of the Amateur Athletic Union (AAU), he was told the idea was impossible. With the backing of England, Coubertin organized an international conference in France, which eventually led to the formation of the IOC. Its organizer decided that Athens should host the first modern Olympic Games in 1896.

The first modern games were fairly low-key. Some ceremony and ritual (King George I of Greece opened the event, cannons were fired, and doves were released over the spectators) were included, but there was little frenzy. Approximately 300 athletes and 40,000 spectators attended the games. The games were marked by indifference across most of the world and caused little stir outside Greece. Many of the American fans there were sailors on shore leave from the cruiser *San Francisco.*

Olympic winners received an olive branch, a certificate, and a silver medal; second-place finishers got a laurel sprig and a copper medal. American James Connolly was the first athlete to win an Olympic event, in the triple jump, leaping just under 45 feet.

The second Olympic Games were held in Paris, coinciding with the World's Fair in 1900, despite the protests of the Greek government, which wanted to host the games every four years. Rather than sparking the interest of fair attendees, the Olympic Games were hardly noticed. Organizers staged the events over the five-month duration of the fair, which diluted any interest in the outcomes. [18]

At the 1900 games, all 24 first-place gold medals were won by athletes from American and English teams. Alvin Kraenzlein, a German American, won four gold medals at the 1900 games, and John Tewksbury won two gold and two silver medals. The Paris Olympics were the first to allow women to participate. Margaret Abbott of Chicago had been studying art and music in Paris, but she entered and won the women's golf event and became the first American female gold medalist. Her prize was an antique Saxon porcelain bowl mounted in chiseled gold.

Although the cry throughout the land in 1904 was "Meet Me in St. Louis" for the World's Fair, relatively few European athletes were willing to travel to the American hinterland for the third Olympic Games. For the most part, they had never even heard of St. Louis and thought they might suffer from Indian attacks if they were to attend. Of the 554 athletes, 432 were Americans—not a single French or English athlete competed. Small teams from Austria, Canada, Cuba, Germany, Greece, and several other nations made the transatlantic trip and trek to St. Louis.

Opening day brought 5,000 spectators to the new Olympic stadium. The U.S. team completely dominated the events from start to finish. At St. Louis, American organizers originated the custom of awarding gold, silver, and bronze medals. In the end, the United States won 70 gold, 75 silver, and 64 bronze medals. The next closest competitor was Cuba with 5 gold, 2 silver, and

3 bronze. The 1904 St. Louis Olympics, like the World's Fair itself, was an exercise in nationalism in which the United States publicly thumped its chest and proclaimed itself the world's strongest nation.

HOW OTHERS SEE US

The 1904 Olympics: A Comedy of Errors

In its breathless American press coverage, the Olympic Games of 1904 were "a meet probably unequaled in the sporting annals of this or any other country." But the Games, held in St. Louis, Missouri, were the least international of all time. Only 12 nations sent athletes to the competition; of the 641 who participated, fully 80 percent of them represented the United States. Overshadowed by the World's Fair that was also being held in St. Louis that summer, the games became a glorified U.S. national track meet. Few European athletes were willing to travel so deep into the American continent. And though the local organizers had promised to send a ship across the Atlantic to pick up any teams that wished to attend, it never materialized.

The first Olympics to be held in the New World, the games were a comedy of errors. Pierre de Coubertin, founder of the Olympic movement, boycotted St. Louis on hearing rumors of a long-range tobacco juice spitting competition. That event never materialized, but the roque contest (an American croquet variant) sounded almost as strange to European ears. During the swimming races, the raft being used as a starting line sank repeatedly. In the marathon, competitors included a Cuban who had hitchhiked to St. Louis and ran in street shoes, a long-sleeved shirt, and trousers cut with scissors at the knee, as well as two Zulus who were in town as part of the Fair's Boer War exhibit and happened to have a free afternoon.

It would be nearly three decades before Coubertin would allow the Olympic Games to get so far beyond his control—or to be held anywhere outside Europe. And it would take even longer for Americans to shed the image of parochial bumpkinism that was only solidified that summer.

The IOC designated Rome as the host of the 1908 Olympic Games, but the eruption of Mount Vesuvius in 1906, which claimed 2,000 lives, forced the event to be moved to London. London built a new 70,000-seat stadium for the Olympics and adopted strict guidelines regarding what constituted amateur status for the athletes. The 1908 games were marked by protest, particularly regarding the way in which English officials treated Irish athletes, who wanted to compete under their own flag as a separate nation. Much of the protest came from American participants of Irish descent. Shot put champion Ralph Rose refused to dip the flag to the English king as flag bearer for the United States, sending a shock through the Olympic community.

The United States again dominated the track-and-field events, winning 15 of 27 contests. The marathon caused great consternation. An Italian runner, Dorando Pietri, staggered into the Olympic stadium and fell to the ground four times on the final lap. As American Johnny Hayes closed in on him, British officials dragged Pietri across the finish line first. American officials protested, which launched accusations of poor sportsmanship. The IOC overturned the decision and awarded the victory to Hayes.[19]

FAIRS, EXPOSITIONS, AND CARNIVALS

Since the 1890s, many people had more free time to spend in leisure, despite long work weeks. The most popular forms of entertainment were often the simplest—family picnics and community socials. Families also turned to commercial recreation, often sponsored by one's employer or a large corporation. This move toward commercial amusement gave people freedoms they had rarely experienced in earlier times. At places like Coney Island or Sandusky, Ohio's Cedar Point, young people were able to mingle without heavy parental supervision.

County or state fairs, usually held annually, began as celebrations of the year's agricultural harvest and livestock production, but later became showcases for American technological might, highlighting consumer products and innovations. In 1910, the Great Granger's Annual Picnic Exhibition at Williams Grove,

An open-air circus at Coney Island, New York. Prints & Photographs Division, Library of Congress.

A bird's-eye view of Coney Island, New York, showing that it was quite an amusement park as long ago as 1908. Prints & Photographs Division, Library of Congress.

Pennsylvania showcased 37 different types of washing machines. Proving to be moneymaking ventures and extremely popular, state and county fairs took on the characteristics of cities. Organizers replaced the flimsy, hastily constructed wooden buildings and tents with permanent structures made from brick and steel. They built machinery halls, auditoriums, concession stands, and retail stores.[20]

Popular entertainment became a fixture at fairs. Horse racing, music bands, circuses, vaudeville shows, and amusement rides gained in popularity as rural folks strolled down the fair's midway. With the success of fixed location amusement parks, most notably Coney Island, mechanical thrill rides were set up at rural fairs, including Ferris wheels, hot-air balloon rides, and, later, airplane rides. After dark, fairs took on a different role, enabling rural men and women to experience nightlife, as electricity lit up the night sky.[21]

The most popular diversion in America in the 1900s, in terms of attendance and grandeur, was the World's Fair. The United States caught World's Fair fever during the spectacle of the World's Columbian Exposition held in Chicago in 1893. Aided by state and federal governments, Buffalo organized a Pan-American Exposition in 1901. The theme of the Buffalo fair was to demonstrate the progress of civilization on both American continents. Unfortunately, the exhibits and innovations at Buffalo were overshadowed by the assassination of President McKinley at the event.

Other states and cities held their own expositions, including the Lewis and Clark Exposition in Portland in 1905, Jamestown in 1907, the Alaska-Yukon-Pacific Expo in Seattle in 1909, and two shows held in San Francisco and San Diego in 1915. Other cities holding expositions between the Chicago and St. Louis expositions were Atlanta, Nashville, Omaha, New Orleans, and Charleston.

The granddaddy of all expositions in the 1900s was the 1904 Louisiana Purchase Exposition held in St. Louis. The St. Louis Fair featured miles of electric light and countless acres of art and culture, as well as anthropological exhibits portraying real-life Indians (American and Eastern), Africans, Filipinos, Syrians, and other tribes. On the surface, planners designed the exhibits to show fairgoers how other people lived in their native habitats, but there was also a great deal of jingoism in the display.

Sports

Travel

of the 1900s

Mass transportation and personal means of travel advanced greatly in the 1900s. What had once been far-fetched ideas like the automobile or airplane became realities, opening a world of travel to people.

Whether emboldened by the westward movement, driven by a higher level of disposable income generated during the era, or in search of work, an unprecedented amount of travel occurred in the 1900s. Although there were fewer than 200 miles of paved roads in the United States in 1900, railways linked the coasts, and thousands of towns sprang to life to service the railroads. Cities across America were lined by growing suburbs, most within walking distance of railroad or trolley lines. Commuters made the daily journey aboard these trains into the city and back again in the evening. Many cities began electrifying their trolley lines to apply the latest technological innovation to city travel. Ferries also transported commuters and goods.

VACATION

Like their counterparts in Europe, affluent Americans traveled in the summer. Most often summer vacations meant residing in a second home—exclusive cottages in Newport and Narragansett, Rhode Island, Palm Beach, Florida, and Santa Barbara, California. The favored form of transportation was aboard private railroad cars, which offered luxury and shielded the wealthy from the general population. Countless resorts and spas sprang up in popular travel destinations, including Florida, California, Georgia, the Carolinas, and Virginia. Middle and lower-class travelers were enticed by reduced rate tours to Niagara Falls, Atlantic City, and other points along the seaside or lakeshore and in the mountains.

Vacations became common for middle-class Americans in the 1900s. The New York Department of Labor conducted a study of 1,500 factories and found that 91 percent gave their office staffs paid vacations, although hourly workers did not receive the same benefits. With their newfound leisure time, many Americans traveled widely. Studies show that in the two decades before the outbreak of World War I, more than 200,000 vacationers went to Europe annually. Travel agencies serviced a growing clientele and arranged for passage to Europe aboard passenger ships and tours of the Continent (costs ranged from $400 to $600 per person).[1]

The dizzying pace of life in the 1900s led many people to search out spas and resorts for their vacations. Diagnosed with neurasthenia—a psychological plight that caused nervousness, paranoia, fatigue, rashes, and other physical ailments—some of America's most influential artists, politicians, and business leaders sought vacations where they could relax and recover their health. People suffering from "American nervousness" ranged from writers Edith Wharton, Theodore Dreiser, and William and Henry James—and even President Theodore Roosevelt.[2] Under the watchful eye of doctors and therapists, these people were treated with hydropathy, a water therapy that made places like Hot Springs, Arkansas and French Lick, Indiana destinations for the mentally and physically exhausted.

Certain resort areas, especially ones on the ocean, became destinations for the rich and middle class alike. Atlantic City, New Jersey, offered gigantic piers bustling with music, vaudeville performances, theaters, and movie houses. The resort's seedier side featured lion tamers, snake charmers, and cheap trinket shops, as well as the flophouses and saloons.

Florida became a booming vacation site championed by Henry Morrison Flagler, a former partner of John D. Rockefeller. Flagler established a string of resort hotels on the eastern coast of Florida and linked them via a railroad. Flagler's tireless promotion of Florida as a vacation destination led to much of the state's future economic development.[3]

As a result of Theodore Roosevelt's call for leading an active life, many people vacationed in the mountains and open spaces. Roosevelt, perhaps the most conservation-minded president in American history, started a national park movement, which included Yellowstone, Yosemite, Grand Canyon, and Mount Rainier, among others. In 1903, Roosevelt traveled to Yosemite to publicize his vision of a national park and to meet Sierra Club founder and naturalist John Muir. Roosevelt was so eager to meet Muir that he called it "the bulliest day of my life."[4] Muir and Roosevelt believed that the national park system could offer city dwellers a way to fight the neurasthenic battle brought on by constant stress and wear from life in bustling cities.

In 1908, a group of millionaires ranked the most exclusive resorts in the United States. At the top of the list was Newport, Rhode Island, so exclusive that the report warned those just past the million dollar mark to beware—an entire fortune could be spent keeping up with the likes of Cornelius

Vanderbilt, coal baron E. J. Berwind, and John Jacob Astor. The rich in Newport built "cottages," although the most unassuming cottages could have 30 rooms and cost $1 million to build. Vanderbilt's magnificent 70-room Renaissance fortress, named "The Breakers," cost $5 million to build. William K. Vanderbilt's "Marble House" was built for $2 million, but he spent more than four times that much decorating it, including marble imported from Africa and a ballroom paneled in gold.[5]

High society in Newport centered on entertaining in a lavish, flamboyant style. The women of Newport prided themselves on entertaining 100 or more guests in an evening at their palatial cottages. Some families built brightly illuminated midways in courtyards surrounding the mansions, containing shooting galleries, dancers and singers, and other forms of entertainment similar to those offered at amusement parks. In 1902, Mrs. Cornelius Vanderbilt hosted a lavish dinner party with the featured entertainment provided by the cast of the Broadway musical comedy *The Wild Rose*. She simply had the cast and scenery shipped to Newport for the performance.

The opulent Hotel Alcazar in St. Augustine, Florida, ca. 1905. This hotel was popular when people who could afford them took vacations to warm areas of the country and to hot springs to recover from "American nervousness." Prints & Photographs Division, Library of Congress.

An interior view of plush railroad dining car filled with patrons, 1905. Prints & Photographs Division, Library of Congress.

Travel

TRAVEL IN CONGESTED CITIES

The turn of the century witnessed a huge building spree in many congested cities. City planners and officials elected to build trolleys and street railway systems. Electric engines were more economical and faster than steam engines and better adapted to the crowded terminals. From 1902 to 1907, more than 2,000 miles of track a year were laid out in congested cities. Both New York and Chicago built elevated steam-driven lines before 1900; Boston followed with its own in 1901. However, steam engines were not as practical as electric lines. New York adopted electricity for its elevated lines in 1901.[6]

With the crushing influx of people, primarily immigrants, cities like Boston, New York, Chicago, and San Francisco had to introduce inno-vative means of public transportation. Electric trolley cars, like the ones still used in San Francisco, first spread from downtown areas into the suburbs, then began linking communities. In 1906, the New York Central railway began electric operations from Grand Central Station, and two years later, lines ran all the way to Stamford, Connecticut.[7]

From 1900 to 1914, railroads added more than 4,000 miles of track annually. The advent of electric trolley lines and the growing influence of the automobile harmed the railroad industry, and after 1907 railroad profits slipped markedly.[8]

The Jacksonville Metropolis automobile was used in a 1909 endurance race from Tampa to Jacksonville and back. The Tampa *Daily Times* sponsored the event to show Florida citizens the need for a statewide highway system.

THE AUTOMOBILE

In 1900, automobiles (or "horseless carriages") were delicate machines, given to sputtering oil, fire, and smoke on a regular basis. Cars were also expensive—toys of the rich who could afford the exhaustive upkeep and repairs. Repairs were common because automobiles were forced to inch along dirt roads, trails, and paths. Many who favored horse-drawn carriages got a good laugh at the expense of automobile owners, often seen stuck in a muddy ditch or nearly overturned by a rut in a dirt road. There were no roadside gas stations or tow trucks to help drivers, who had to rely on their own ingenuity or the help of others to push their cars to safety.

In 1900, at the first car show held in the United States in New York City, nearly all the contraptions were electric or steam, despite the limitations of both types. Electric cars had a limited range of motion, since they needed to be renewed at electric charging stations; steam cars required an owner to get a steam engineer's license, since they were perceived as being very dangerous.[9]

Early automobiles often lacked much of a body. Henry Ford's first car, preserved in Dearborn, Michigan, looked like a bicycle, with four reed-thin wheels and a carriage seat. Later in the decade, passengers sat high above the engine and the wheels. The driver's side was on the right, and the front two seats looked like leather recliners. An ornate carriage seat took up the whole back of the car.

Despite the early design and fragility of automobiles, the machines grabbed people's imaginations. Soon, autos crowded the already jam-packed streets in American cities, and safety became an issue. An alarming number of pedestrians were injured or killed by auto enthusiasts. The outrage over vehicular deaths caused New York City officials to ban horseless vehicles from Central Park. In 1904, New York State passed a law setting the maximum speed limit at 10 miles per hour in built-up districts, 15 miles per hour in villages or outside congested areas, and 20 miles per hour elsewhere. Newspapers capitalized on anti-automobile public sentiment, but businesses that were affected by this outrage mobilized to resist the legislation.

The automobile profoundly affected the way in which people lived and interacted. Once automobile pioneers understood the impact the car could have, they moved quickly to make its influence a reality. In 1900, 4,192 automobiles were sold in the United States for a total of $4.89 million. Ten years later, the number jumped to 181,000 cars for $215.34 million.

Various inventors and engineers had tinkered with producing an automobile as far back as 1769, when French artillery officer Nicholas Cugnot made a primitive car that had three wheels and was equipped with a boiler and an engine. Charles E. and J. Frank Duryea built the first gas-powered car in Springfield, Massachusetts in 1893, while Ransom Eli Olds was credited with first attempting to build cars under a system of mass production in the late 1890s. The first Oldsmobile was manufactured in Lansing, Michigan in 1901, and 425 cars were sold that year; by 1904, Olds had sold 5,000 automobiles. Between 1904 and 1908, 241 auto companies were formed.[10]

Throughout the decade, automobiles were mainly for the wealthy. Early manufacturers advertised their cars with posters illustrating upper-class lifestyles, highlighting grandeur, speed, and power. Price was rarely mentioned in the classic automobile ads—if a person had to ask the price, he could not afford it.[11]

Cleveland-based Peerless Motor Car Company played on its slogan "All That the Name Implies" and showed rich women in big, feathered hats being carted around a department store by two chauffeur drivers. Another Cleveland auto company, the Baker Motor Vehicle Company, was an early pioneer in getting women interested in buying automobiles. Baker brought out the "Queen Victoria," an electric car that it touted as the "safest to drive" and "easiest to control."

Countless small businesses and parts suppliers helped fueled the growth of the industry. Entire cities began to cater to the growing auto manufacturers. Akron, Ohio, soon became known as "Rubber City" after a number of successful tire manufacturers, including Goodyear and Firestone, settled on the banks of the Cuyahoga River in northeastern Ohio.[12]

Just after the Civil War, Dr. Benjamin Franklin Goodrich, a surgeon by training and a burgeoning real estate developer, visited many cities in his search for a place to relocate his twice-failed New York rubber company. His financial backers stipulated that the new location had to be west of the Allegheny Mountains, where the company would not face competition from its Eastern rivals. While on a trip to Cleveland, Goodrich read an Akron Board of Trade brochure and scouted the city.

Goodrich was attracted to Akron's supply of coal and water, transportation system, and abundance of labor. In 1871, the machinery was shipped from New York to Akron. By 1888, the year B. F. Goodrich died, company sales reached nearly $700,000.

Other entrepreneurs rushed to imitate Goodrich's success and profit from the early devel-

opment of the automobile industry. By 1909, there were 14 rubber companies in Akron, including future giants Goodyear and Firestone. Five years later, rubber accounted for nearly 20,000 jobs and over 33 percent of the industry's yearly output.

HENRY FORD: THE FATHER OF THE AUTOMOBILE

Before the real car culture could grip America, someone had to make an auto the masses could afford to buy and maintain. The man who bridged the gap was Henry Ford, a farmer's son who was responsible for making the automobile affordable for the average man by perfecting the use of mass production. Although he did not invent the technology that made him famous,

Travel

The Jacksonville Metropolis automobile used in a 1909 endurance race from Tampa to Jacksonville and back. The promotional stunt sponsored by the *Tampa Daily Times* was to show Florida citizens the need for a statewide highway system. From the Louise Frisbie collection, courtesy of the Florida State Archives.

Ford perfected the assembly line, transforming the automobile from a luxury to a necessity.

Born in Dearborn, Michigan in 1863, Henry Ford had an early aptitude for machinery, but it was the sight of a coal-fired steam engine in 1876 that set in motion his later triumphs. By age 16, after leaving the family farm against his father's wishes, Ford apprenticed in a machine shop in Detroit. Next he joined the Westinghouse Engine Company, repairing old steam engines and setting up new ones.

Ford soon realized that steam engines were not the wave of the future. German engineer Karl Benz had developed a reliable internal combustion engine which ran on gasoline. Ford traveled around Detroit questioning its best engineers and later produced his own two-cylinder, four-cycle engine, which generated four horsepower. Ford mounted the engine on a borrowed chassis, and his "quadricycle" made its maiden run on June 4, 1896. It was a huge success. He sold his first for $200, then built a second bigger and more powerful one. Backed by investors, Ford opened the Detroit Automobile Company (soon reorganized as the Henry Ford Company). He was the first car manufacturer in "Motor City."

Ford entered his cars in races and won a reputation for speed and daring. Soon, he built racers that set speed records, and additional investors pumped money into the company, thus beginning the close union between the auto industry and auto racing. Over the years, the alliance led to overall improvements in car design and technology, benefiting the industry as a whole.

What makes Ford such a revolutionary business thinker is that he realized that everyone should benefit from his innovation. Ford proclaimed, "I will build a motor car for the great multitude," and he decided that the way to make them affordable was "to make them all alike, to make them come through the factory just alike." By 1908, he had bought out many and owned 58 percent of the company. In the fall of 1908, the first Model T rolled out. The car had several new features that made it more negotiable on country roads, and the engine was encased for protection. Ford set the price at $825, which to many was expensive, but he believed the price would fall through improvements in assembly-line technology. With Ford in control,

efficiency was the keystone of his operations. For 20 years, Ford produced only black Model T's (often called the "Tin Lizzie" or "flivver").

Ford sold 11,000 cars in 1908 and 1909, and sold 19,000 in 1910. Sales skyrocketed, reaching 248,000 in 1914, or nearly half the U.S. market.

TAKING TO THE SKIES

On December 17, 1903, Orville and Wilbur Wright, both wearing starched collars, ties, and dark suits, emerged from their small cabin at Kill Devil Hills, North Carolina, just four miles from the town of Kitty Hawk, ready to test their machine. For years, the brothers, who were bicycle mechanics from Dayton, Ohio, had dreamed of building an aircraft that would fly. The Wrights tinkered with various designs to test their theories, then headed to Kitty Hawk, which offered steady wind, open spaces, and, most important for the two patent-minded brothers, privacy.

In 1903, the Wrights started piecing together their "whopper flying machine" based on an engine they had designed and built, with a box frame that required the pilot to lie in the middle of the ship, using his hips to work the wings. As the world debated man's ability to fly, the Wrights put the finishing touches on their airplane. On December 17, they set up the plane's launching device, a 60-foot-long monorail that would send the plane skyward. Because it was a windy day, they set the monorail up on the beach, instead of on the hillside they had used in earlier efforts.[13]

With Orville lying down at the controls and Wilbur running alongside, balancing the machine as it gained speed, the chain-driven engine roared to life, shaking the entire plane. As it rolled down the monorail, the plane jerked into the wind. Forty feet down the track, the plane slowly climbed up to ten feet off the ground. In the 12 seconds it was airborne, the Wright's ship traveled 120 feet.[14] This moment was caught on film, but the small crowd who had gathered (mostly rescue swimmers from the nearby life-saving station) did not even cheer. The Wright brothers simply pushed the plane back to the starting blocks for another run. By the fourth flight, at noon that day, the plane stayed up for 59 seconds and traveled 852 feet.[15]

Travel

Amazingly, the national press reacted with complete indifference to the Wrights's feat. No newspaper reporters were present that day, and most did not run stories about the event. Only Norfolk *Virginian-Pilot* editor Keville Glennan understood the importance of the flight and printed the story on the front page. Ironically, the United States Armed Services did not consider the Wrights's achievement useful. In 1904, a representative of the British government approached the brothers, but U.S. services ignored their achievement until 1907.[16]

The Wrights finally received the coverage they deserved after they held a public demonstration of the airplane in 1908 at Fort Myer military base in Virginia. A crowd of 5,000 watched the plane turn in the air, fly over their heads, then land on the grassy field nearby. The demonstration flights received much press coverage, but it would be years before people really believed in man's ability to fly. In 1909, Wilbur put on an exhibition over New York Harbor that drew more than one million spectators. He delighted the crowd by flying along Manhattan and around the Statue of Liberty.

THE PANAMA CANAL

A passageway through Central America had long been a dream of American industrialists, and it was regarded as an important strategic move by the nation's governmental and military leaders. Connecting the oceans through the seemingly thin slice of land across Panama would cut weeks off the trip between New York City and San Francisco. Roosevelt bought the rights to the Isthmus of Panama from the French for $40 million, over the objections of the Colombian government, who disputed the French claim to the land.[17] The president saw building a canal as an assertion of American will—he would not be denied by lengthy negotiations with Colombia. Roosevelt

encouraged a revolution led by two French members of the Panama Company.[18]

Roosevelt sent American warships to a station off the coast of Colombia in a display of force. The maneuver sent a message, not only to the leaders of Colombia, but also to European nations: America would decide what happened in the Western hemisphere. The United States quickly recognized the rebel leaders and the new nation of Panama. The new canal treaty with Panama gave the United States rights to five miles of land on each side of the site, along with the right to build, operate, maintain, and defend a canal. After the U.S. Senate ratified the treaty on February 23, 1904, Congress set up a seven-member commission to organize the cutting of the canal.[19]

Almost immediately, construction began on the "Big Ditch." The decade-long project cost the nation $367 million, and more than 22,000 workers lost their lives to yellow fever and malaria in the disease-ridden swamps. Despite the lives lost, the site became a thriving vacation spot. In 1913, 20,000 vacationers went to Panama to gaze at the engineering wonders taking place. The Panama Canal, which stood as a symbol of American technological superiority, ranked as one of the nation's most impressive engineering feats.[20]

Medical knowledge played as important a role in the completion of the canal as engineering and technical skill. Colonel William Crawford Gorgas, the man who exterminated yellow fever in Havana, Cuba, was given the task of eradicating disease from the tropical swamps of Panama. Using methods similar to those he used in Havana, Gorgas had eliminated yellow fever by September 1905. Next he turned to malaria. He encouraged workers to eliminate stagnant water sources and ordered vegetation cut within a 200-yard perimeter around the construction crews. As a result, contraction rates fell from 40 percent to 10 percent between 1906 and 1913.[21]

Travel

Visual Arts

of the 1900s

The Progressive Era in America carried over into the nation's arts and culture. Although American artists still turned primarily to Europe for guidance on artistic styles and customs, their work began to encompass all aspects of society in the United States, from poor tenements to the manicured lawns of the leisure class and the sprawling mountains of the Western regions. Art critic Robert Hughes labeled the era stretching from the 1870s through the early 1900s the "American Renaissance" in visual arts.

In large cities, such as New York and San Francisco, support for the arts came from the wealthy, who filled their homes with works of art. They spared no expense in finding the next hot artist and buying artwork as fast as it could be commissioned.

The expanding middle class decorated their homes and parlors with lithographs, which were less expensive reproductions of famous works. Lithographs were extremely popular at the end of the nineteenth and the early part of the twentieth century. One firm, owned by Nathaniel Currier (later Currier and Ives) produced reproductions of 4,300 paintings between 1835 and 1907. Lithographs sold for between 20 cents and $3 apiece. Although some critics belittled lithographs as art by machinery, they exposed the middle class to the culture of the wealthy, but within their own social strata. Many members of the middle class also found that they had the leisure time to frequent museums subsidized by the rich.

In the 1880s and 1890s, photography inventor George Eastman began the process of photoengraving, which enabled large-scale reproduction of paintings from all around the world. For the first time, average citizens could see the works of European artists. In fact, the artists themselves used the new sources to inspire their own works.[1]

PAINTING

The first wave of painters in the American Renaissance traveled to Europe to take traditional training in Paris and elsewhere. As a result, much of the early work of American painters mimics the work of the Old World. Gradually, artists in the United States realized that they needed their own independent art scene.

In the years following the Civil War, painting gained importance in the United States. Fueled by the likes of J. P. Morgan and other incredibly wealthy collectors, American museums and private collectors acquired many of Europe's masterpieces. During the era, some American artists gained an international following, including Thomas Eakins (1844–1916), John Singer Sargent

(1856–1925), Winslow Homer (1836–1910), and James McNeill Whistler (1834–1903). For the most part, these artists achieved their fame at the end of the nineteenth century.

Impressionism dominated the art scene, influenced by the great impressionist painters of Europe—Claude Monet, Camille Pissarro, and others. Homer, Sargent, and Whistler all practiced the art of turning real images into a series of brushstrokes that came together to form an image softer than reality. The most important American female artist in the 1900s was Mary Cassatt (1845–1926). Her work, especially her paintings of domestic life, popularized Impressionism in the United States, although she lived in Europe, as did Whistler and Sargent.

Born in Lowell, Massachusetts as the son of a railway engineer, Whistler scorned the art world's distinction between European and American painting and the idea that Americans required Europe's guidance. For most of his life, Whistler lived overseas, studying in Paris, then moving to London, but he remained fiercely American in his attitudes. Whistler's reputation helped later American artists become accepted by European critics and audiences.[2]

Whistler believed in art for art's sake, not as a vehicle for moralizing or imparting romantic ideas. Thus, he called his most famous painting *Arrangement in Grey and Black, No. 1* (though it has been called "Whistler's Mother" because she was the sitter).

Many collectors snatched up Whistler's paintings and brought them home for display. Detroit railroad millionaire Charles Freer amassed hundreds of works by Whistler or collected by him, and he later donated the collection, and today it is housed in the Freer Gallery in Washington, D.C.[3]

The only American painter to rival Whistler's fame in the waning days of the 1800s and early 1900s was another expatriate, John Singer Sargent. Sargent was born in Florence and grew up in Italy, since his American parents had retired there. Sargent specialized in portraits, particularly of the cultivated set, and he soon became the most expensive and sought-after portraitist of his era.

Sargent escaped painting portraits by producing amazing watercolors and taking on commissions to paint murals in the United States and throughout Europe. His murals for the Boston Public Library and the Boston Museum of Fine Arts have been called the finest murals painted in the nation during the American Renaissance period.

Sargent traveled the world, recording his experiences in sketches and producing remarkable watercolors, although he remained American in spirit. He even refused a knighthood in Great Britain to retain his American citizenship.

While Sargent and other older painters plied their trade in Europe, a younger group of American artists returned from schools in France to bring Impressionism back to the United States. The primary group called themselves Ten American Painters or, more commonly, "The Ten." They sought to apply the skills they had learned overseas to American scenes and atmosphere.

Founded in Boston by Frank Weston Benson, The Ten also included Joseph De Camp, Childe Hassam, Thomas Dewing, Robert Reid, Willard Metcalf, Edmond Tarbell, J. Alden Weir, Edward Simmons, and John Twachtman. William Merritt Chase joined the group after Twachtman's death in 1902. As a group, The Ten were tired of the conservative attitude among the established art organizations in America, the large exhibits forced upon painters, and the multitude of styles presented at the exhibits. Worst of all, American collectors bought French Impressionist works and practically ignored American pieces. In 1897, The Ten signed an agreement to exhibit together in small galleries around New York City. Benson's works sold the best among the group and his reported annual income exceeded six figures, although the reputations of Chase and Hassam have carried more weight into modern times. In fact, Hassam is widely regarded as America's premier turn-of-the-century Impressionist.

Chase's work as a teacher (among his many students were Georgia O'Keeffe and Edward Hopper) and his fanciful lifestyle made him immensely popular. Chase also created a public image of himself. He could be seen parading down the streets of Fifth Avenue dressed in a cutaway coat, topper, and a jeweled neck scarf, with Russian wolfhounds on a leash. Chase also dressed a black servant as an African prince. These gimmicks

Arts

worked wonders for Chase, who became one of New York's most sought after portraitists.[4]

Hassam's first works in the genre captured his friend, the writer Celia Thaxter, on Appledore Island, off the New Hampshire coast. Hassam's works gained popularity, in part, because of a wave of nostalgia America felt for its colonial past. His Impressionistic paintings recalled a softer, quainter lifestyle.[5]

As the 1900s progressed, other painters, driven by the excitement and technological innovations of the new century, created new forms of artistic expression.

The Ashcan School

A group of artists came together in New York City to form a group called The Eight, or the Ashcan school (because they could find art in the "ashcans" of dirty cities). Led by Robert Henri, The Eight included George Luks, William Glackens, John Sloan, Everett Shinn, Arthur B. Davies, Maurice Prendergast, and Ernest Lawson. The Ashcan artists disdained academic pretensions in the established art world and they never formed a society or a school. Many had worked as illustrators at magazines or newspapers, which contributed to their approach of looking at everyday life through the lens of a journalist. Critics, who did not want to see such vulgarity displayed in art, called the group the "Revolutionary Black Gang."[6]

The Eight held their first exhibition of their own works in 1908. In 1910, they held another show that was so popular and sensational that riot police had to be called in to subdue the crowd of 1,500 spectators. However, the true impact of the Ashcan school on the international art scene did not occur until three years later when they put on the Armory Show, by some accounts the most important art exhibit ever held in the United States (see Art of the 1910s).[7]

The two most important members of the Ashcan school in the 1900s were Robert Henri (1865–1929) and his student George Bellows (1882–1925). Henri was the son of a Mississippi riverboat card shark. After working as an illustrator for a newspaper, he entered the Pennsylvania Academy of Art in Philadelphia. In the late 1880s,

Henri studied in Paris for three years and started down the Impressionist path.[8]

Henri began teaching at the New York School of Art, headed by Chase. After several years, Chase resigned and Henri became head. In 1904, Bellows enrolled at the school and worked directly with Henri.

Henri and the other members of the Ashcan movement looked to Winslow Homer as their spiritual guide. Henri also looked to the great poet Walt Whitman for inspiration. Henri insisted on his pupils finding their own vision—developing the instincts that would drive them toward truth. Although Henri had gifts as an artist, his real importance was as an agitator and rebel. He fought the established art leaders of the 1900s and brought the Ashcan school into a loosely knit association that stood up to its critics.[9]

Henri's own paintings resembled Impressionism, but darker. His *Snow in New York* (1902) is a murky view of a snowy street barely lit by a single lamppost among the skyscrapers lining each side of the street. The shadowy figures in the painting seem to be in a losing battle with the wintry New York night.

Between arriving in New York City in 1904 to his death in 1925, Bellows became the most famous and highly regarded American artist of his day. It is estimated that he produced more than 700 works in his career, an average of more than 33 a year from 1904 to 1925. Bellows turned down a chance to play professional baseball to pursue a career as an artist. In his first summer in New York, while his friends returned home or searched for ways to make cash, Bellows played semi-professional baseball with a team in Central Park.[10]

Henri invited Bellows to his house every Tuesday evening for informal gatherings with the other members of the Ashcan group. Bellows spent the other summer evenings traveling in the slums of New York, seeing firsthand how the poor struggled to survive. This prepared him for the intellectual discussions that took place at Henri's meetings.

Bellows's art seemed to embody the spirit of the age—Roosevelt's plea for a strenuous life, combined with a raw, big view of the world around him.[11] Bellows shocked the Pennsylvania

Arts

Academy in 1908 with his painting *Forty-Two Kids,* depicting 42 young street urchins swimming naked in the polluted East River. The judges found the subject matter offensive (not the nudity, rather that the subjects were street children). Bellows used dark hues to create a somber scene of boyish frivolity, though the river ominously engulfs them. In other paintings, Bellows continued his portrayal of the underbelly of urban life. Both *River Rats* (1906) and *Cliff Dwellers* (1913) show urban America as chaotic and fast-paced. A common pastime among upper-class Americans in the 1900s was to go "slumming," touring the working-class neighborhoods to glimpse the downtrodden. The way people viewed the poor, with a kind of detached sentimentality, contributed to Bellows's popularity, although he did not hold these convictions. By this time, he had become a Marxist.[12]

Bellows began painting the excavations underway to build Pennsylvania Station. His first in a series recording the digging was finished in January 1907. Designed by the architectural firm McKim, Mead, and White, Penn Station was one of the city's largest urban projects. The tunnel leading to the terminal required digging under both the Hudson and East Rivers and demolishing four city blocks. The only hole ever dug that size was the recently completed Panama Canal (see Travel of the 1900s).

Although Bellows's New York street scenes were critically acclaimed, he gained his fame and lasting reputation on the basis of his boxing paintings, which is remarkable, since he produced only five boxing works. Although boxing was illegal in New York in 1907, Tom Sharkey's saloon, just across the street from Bellows's studio, evaded the law by converting the bar into a club for the evening. The cheap dues allowed "members" into the back room to observe the fight. Bellows's friend, Ed Keefe, invited him to see a match at Sharkey's. From this first visit, Bellows painted *Club Night,* revealing his ability to portray brutal energy and strength.[13] From the thick calf muscles and biceps of the combatants to the puffy face and misshapen nose of the fighter on the left, Bellows seems to have caught a punch being thrown in midair. An observer can almost feel the pain of the boxers in *Club Night.* The painting also highlights the dichotomy between the beaten and battered fighters and the ringside spectators, arrayed in formal attire. The faces of the fans are hideous and devilish. *Club Night* led to other boxing paintings including *Stag at Sharkey's* (1909) and *Both Members of This Club* (1909).

PHOTOGRAPHY

In the 1900s, art patron Alfred Stieglitz, who is credited for introducing modern painting to America by debuting shows featuring the works of Henri Matisse, Pablo Picasso, and Paul Gauguin, broke ground in another blossoming art form—photography. It became his mission to have photography accepted as the equal of painting or literature. In this role, Stieglitz mentored young photographers and founded the photography journal *Camera Work* (1903).

Born in New Jersey to wealthy Jewish parents, Stieglitz (1864–1946) learned photography in Germany in the 1880s. Stieglitz ruled the American art scene with an iron fist, arrogance, and a sharp tongue. He encouraged the development of a uniquely American art that characterized the conditions of life.

In the 1890s, Stieglitz began his campaign for photography as a "pictorialist," a person who attempts to make photos look like paintings. He preferred the "hard" school of pictorialism, a realistic look, as opposed to the soft branch that tried to make photos seem like watercolors or oil paintings. The hard pictorialists derisively called the soft photographers "fuzzyographers." Similar to Impressionist painting in that it emphasized suggestion over detail, Stieglitz's photography helped usher in a wave of modernism to the United States.

In 1902, Stieglitz formed the Photo-Secession group, along with friends and colleagues Edward Steichen, Clarence White, and Gertrude Kasebier. The group rebelled against the stringent academic thinking that dominated the arts in the 1900s and the bad photography they felt soft pictorialism represented. Stieglitz founded *Camera Work* in 1903 to showcase the group's photographs. The group's first exhibit at the National Arts Club Show in New York City was a great success and placed them in the forefront of the art photography movement.

The powerful painting *Stag Night at Sharkey's,* 1909, by George Bellows. © The Cleveland Museum of Art, 2001. Hinman B. Hurlbut Collection.

From 1902 to 1905, Stieglitz and his cohorts exhibited at galleries around the United States, Canada, and Europe. Next, under Stieglitz's leadership, they set up a permanent gallery at 291 Fifth Avenue in New York, which became known throughout the art world simply as "291." Until 1907, 291 showed nothing but photography, following Stieglitz's lead.[14]

The 291 served as a hub for avant-garde artists and became known as a place for experimentalists who were shunned by the art community. From 1908–1911, the list of artists who displayed works at the 291 reads like a who's who of the world's greats, including Picasso, Matisse, Renoir, Cézanne, Rodin, and Toulouse-Lautrec. In his own time, though, Stieglitz pushed too far ahead of the pack to effect great change on the nation as a whole.

While Stieglitz carried on his modernist crusade, other photographers used their lenses to capture realistic pictures of everyday life, revealing the real spirit of the age. Frances Benjamin Johnston, from her studio in Washington, D.C., traveled to Hampton, Virginia, to capture stills that represented the progress African Americans had made since the Civil War. As one of the most successful photographers of the 1900s, Johnston could have easily turned down such a commission. A member of the well-to-do society in the nation's capital, she photographed diplomats and government officials, including Admiral George Dewey and Secretary of State John Hay.[15]

Johnston, a free spirit, led a group of artists and writers in Washington called The Push, who captured their parties on film. In a revealing self-portrait, Johnston posed as a "new woman," a beer stein in one hand and a cigarette in the other. Her skirt is hiked up above her knees, and a rogue's gallery of jilted suitors stares down from her mantle. Her playful demeanor and ability to catch magical, informal moments made her reputation. This ability led to the commission she received from Thomas J. Calloway, the agent in charge of finding work for the "Negro Exhibit" at the 1900 Paris Exposition.

By the spring of 1900, Johnston had shot more than 150 images for the exhibit. She contrasted the photos of enterprising young Hampton Institute graduates with ones of elderly African Americans struggling to survive. When Calloway saw the photos, he immediately wrote Johnston to tell her that he felt they were the best at the Paris exhibit. By contrasting the young college-educated blacks with their poorer brethren, Johnston constructed a portrait of African American life at the turn of the century that proved how little blacks had advanced as a whole, but still contained some hope for the future.[16]

SCULPTURE

Augustus Saint-Gaudens

American sculpture in the 1900s revolved around Augustus Saint-Gaudens, not only the greatest sculptor of his time, but possibly in all American history. The Irish-born Saint-Gaudens (1848–1907) came to the United States with his parents during the potato famine while he was still a baby. He grew up in New York City, and took night classes at Cooper Institute and the National Academy of Design. In 1867, he traveled to Paris, then Rome to study sculpting.[17]

The sculptor's first important commission upon returning to the United States in 1881 was a statue of Admiral David Farragut to be placed in Central Park. This early work spawned a series of

American sculpture in the early 1900s revolved around Augustus Saint-Gaudens, not only the greatest sculptor of his time, but possibly in all American history, 1908. Prints & Photographs Division, Library of Congress.

Arts

commissions for the young artist. In 1897, Saint-Gaudens unveiled a Civil War memorial on the edge of Boston Commons that immortalizes Colonel Robert Shaw and his men, the Union's Fifty-Fourth Massachusetts Regiment, who were all black volunteers, some of whom had been slaves. The powerful work shows the men marching to their final battle at Fort Wagner in South Carolina. In 1863, the regiment attempted to take the fort, despite the overwhelming odds against them, an almost suicidal mission. They all died in the battle and were buried in a mass grave. The commission marked the first time an American sculptor had been asked to represent blacks as heroes. The memorial was also the first American sculpture to commemorate a group, rather than an individual.

In 1903, Saint-Gaudens unveiled his gold-leaf statue of General William Tecumseh Sherman and Nike, the goddess of victory. On the southeast edge of Central Park, near Fifth Avenue and Fifty-ninth Street, Sherman rides a great war horse, with Nike by his side, her right arm outstretched and leading the general forward. In 1907, Saint-Gaudens designed a twenty-dollar gold eagle, which has been called the most beautiful coin ever minted. He made 70 different versions before deciding on the best one.[18]

Frederic Remington

Another form of sculpture in the 1900s was less formal and perhaps more popular with the general public: Native American and frontier works. Frederic Remington (1861–1909), also a painter and illustrator, created powerful works of cowboys and horses that rival Bellows's boxing paintings for their raw energy and vitality.

From an early age, Remington loved the outdoors. He studied art at Yale, but left for the West, where he visited Indian camps, cavalry posts, and cowboy ranches. Remington repackaged the West with heavy doses of nostalgia. He even fabricated a story about fighting in the Indian wars with the American cavalry. He settled down in New York but made frequent trips west in search of material. In his lifetime he produced more than 2,700 paintings.

By the early 1900s, his paintings and sculptures came to symbolize the West for many observers. His status as an artist grew steadily throughout

Frederic Remington's *A Bucking Bronco,* 1908. Prints & Photographs Division, Library of Congress.

the decade. His friendship with Theodore Roosevelt bolstered his sales and his image as a hard strewn Westerner. Over the course of the 1900s, Remington produced his sculptures *The Cheyenne* (1901), *Comin' Through the Rye* (1902–1904), and *The Cowboy* (1908).

ENDNOTES FOR THE 1900s

OVERVIEW OF THE 1900s

1. E. Benjamin Andrews, *History of the United States: From the Earliest Discovery of America to the End of 1902,* vol. 5 (New York: Charles Scribner's Sons, 1903), 359–364; Sean Dennis Cashman, *America in the Age of the Titans: The Progressive Era and World War I* (New York: New York University Press, 1988), 8.
2. Mark Sullivan, *Our Times: The United States, 1900–1925,* vol. 1 (New York: Charles Scribner's Sons, 1927), 561.
3. Robert H. Wiebe, *The Search for Order, 1877–1920* (New York: Hill and Wang, 1967), 168–170.

4. Howard Zinn, *A People's History of the United States, 1492–Present* (New York: Harper Perennial, 1995), 346.

5. Quoted in Chambers, *The Tyranny of Change,* 184; Zinn, *A People's History of the United States,* 341–346.

6. Roosevelt, "Fourth Annual Message," 175–176.

7. Mansel G. Blackford and K. Austin Kerr, *Business Enterprise in American History,* 2nd ed. (Boston: Houghton Mifflin, 1990), 174–179.

8. Quoted in Daniel Gross, *Forbes' Greatest Business Stories of All Time* (New York: John Wiley, 1996), 59–63.

9. Quoted in Gross, *Forbes' Greatest Business Stories,* 67.

10. David Montgomery, *The Fall of the House of Labor: The Workplace, the State, and American Labor Activism, 1865–1925* (New York: Cambridge University Press, 1987), 310–315.

11. Quoted in Zinn, *A People's History of the United States,* 324.

12. Daniel A. Okun, "Drinking Water and Public Health Protection." In *Drinking Water Regulation and Health,* ed. Frderick W. Pontius (New York: John Wiley & Sons, 2003), 12.

13. Cashman, *America in the Age of the Titans,* 170–172.

14. Thomas J. Schlereth, *Victorian America: Transformations in Everyday Life, 1876–1915* (New York: HarperCollins, 1991), 288–289.

15. Sullivan, *Our Times,* 380.

16. Ray Ginger, *Age of Excess: The United States from 1877 to 1914, 2nd ed.* (Prospect Heights, IL: Waveland Press, 1989), 314–315.

17. Judy Crichton, *America 1900: The Sweeping Story of a Pivotal Year in the Life of the Nation* (New York: Henry Holt, 1998), 211–215.

18. Crichton, *America 1900,* 215.

19. George Lane Jr., "The Day Arcadia Burned," History, Desoto Co FLGenWeb Project, http://www.roots web.ancestry.com/~fldesoto/arcadia.htm (August 11, 2008).

20. Wagenknecht, *American Profile,* 123–124.

21. Wagenknecht, *American Profile,* 128.

ADVERTISING OF THE 1900s

1. Juliann Sivulka, *Soap, Sex, and Cigarettes: A Cultural History of American Advertising* (Belmont, CA: Wadsworth, 1998), 94.

2. Susan Strasser, *Satisfaction Guaranteed: The Making of the American Mass Market* (New York: Pantheon, 1989), 93–97.

3. Strasser, *Satisfaction Guaranteed,* 97–102.

4. Sivulka, *Soap, Sex, and Cigarettes,* 96–97.

5. Strasser, *Satisfaction Guaranteed,* 210.

6. Strasser, *Satisfaction Guaranteed,* 210–211.

7. Sivulka, *Soap, Sex, and Cigarettes,* 95.

8. Strasser, *Satisfaction Guaranteed,* 212–213.

9. Strasser, *Satisfaction Guaranteed,* 212–213

10. Strasser, *Satisfaction Guaranteed,* 213–214.

11. Strasser, *Satisfaction Guaranteed,* 128–129; Wagenknecht, *American Profile,* 141–142.

12. Wagenknecht, *American Profile,* 144.

13. Fox, *The Mirror Makers,* 46.

14. Sivulka, *Soap, Sex, and Cigarettes,* 99–100.

15. Wagenknecht, *American Profile,* 150–152.

16. William Wrigley Jr., "The Story of the Wrigley Company," http://www.wrigley.com/wrigley/about/about_story.asp (August 11, 2008).

17. Quoted in Fox, *The Mirror Makers,* 61.

18. Quoted in Fox, *The Mirror Makers,* 61.

19. Sivulka, *Soap, Sex, and Cigarettes,* 117–119; Jackson Lears, *Fables of Abundance: A Cultural History of Advertising in America* (New York: Basic Books, 1994), 156.

20. Wagenknecht, *American Profile,* 137–138.

21. Wagenknecht, *American Profile,* 140.

22. Sivulka, *Soap, Sex, and Cigarettes,* 119–120.

ARCHITECTURE OF THE 1900s

1. Stern, *Pride of Place,* 255.

2. Robin Langley Sommer, *American Architecture: An Illustrated History* (New York: Crescent Books, 1996), 70.

3. Wagenknecht, *American Profile,* 99–100.

4. Sommer, *American Architecture,* 71.

5. Sommer, *American Architecture,* 75.

6. Spiro Kostof, *America by Design* (New York: Oxford University Press, 1987), 38–39.

7. Daniel M. Mendelowitz, *A History of American Art* (New York: Holt, Rinehart and Winston, 1960), 405–407.

8. Shi, *Facing Facts,* 174–178.

9. Kathy Peiss, *Cheap Amusements: Working Women and Leisure in Turn-of-the-Century New York* (Philadelphia: Temple University Press, 1986), 34–35.

10. Ezra Bowne, ed., *This Fabulous Century, 1900–1910* (Alexandria, VA: Time-Life Books, 1969), 169.

11. Meryle Secrest, *Frank Lloyd Wright* (New York: Knopf, 1992), 169.

BOOKS, NEWSPAPERS, MAGAZINES, AND COMICS OF THE 1900s

1. Peter Conn, *Literature in America: An Illustrated History* (New York: Cambridge University Press, 1989), 297–301.

2. Wagenknecht, *American Profile,* 209.

3. Shi, *Facing Facts,* 104–107.

4. J. Leonard Bates, *The United States, 1898–1928: Progressivism and A Society in Transition* (New York: McGraw-Hill, 1976), 9–10.

5. Henry James, *The American Scene* (London: Chapman and Hall, 1907), 131, 231.

6. For an extended discussion of neurasthenia, see Tom Lutz, *American Nervousness, 1903: An Anecdotal History* (Ithaca, NY: Cornell University Press, 1991), 38–62.

7. Faulkner, *The Quest for Social Justice,* 260.
8. Wagenknecht, *American Profile,* 219–221.
9. Faulkner, *The Quest for Social Justice,* 11.
10. Margaret B. McDowell, *Edith Wharton,* rev. ed. (Boston: Twayne, 1991), 8.
11. Institute of Education Sciences. National Center for Education Statistics. U.S. Department of Education. "National Assessment of Adult Literacy" (1993), http://nces.ed.gov/naal/lit_history.asp.
12. Cashman, *America in the Age of the Titans,* 81–82.

ENTERTAINMENT OF THE 1900S

1. Schlereth, *Victorian America,* 204–205.
2. Hollis Alpert, *Broadway!: 125 Years of Musical Theater* (New York: Arcade, 1991), 41.
3. Alpert, *Broadway,* 43.
4. Faulkner, *The Quest for Social Justice,* 300.
5. Alpert, *Broadway,* 45–48.
6. Faulkner, *The Quest for Social Justice,* 302–303.
7. Alpert, *Broadway,* 48–54.
8. Richard Schwartz, *Berkeley 1900: Daily Life at the Turn of the Century* (Berkeley, CA: RSB Books, 2000), 275.
9. Wagenknecht, *American Profile,* 265.
10. Wagenknecht, *American Profile,* 266.
11. Wagenknecht, *American Profile,* 268.
12. Schlereth, *Victorian America,* 196.
13. Schlereth, *Victorian America,* 202–203.
14. Schlereth, *Victorian America,* 204.
15. Schlereth, *Victorian America,* 200.
16. Faulkner, *The Quest for Social Justice,* 296.
17. Peiss, *Cheap Amusements,* 88.
18. Fredrika Blair, *Isadora: Portrait of the Artist as a Woman* (New York: McGraw-Hill, 1986), 16–18.
19. Blair, *Isadora: Portrait of the Artist as a Woman,* 30.
20. Blair, *Isadora: Portrait of the Artist as a Woman,* 400–401.

FASHION OF THE 1900S

1. Quoted in Sullivan, *Our Times,* 388.
2. Chambers, *Tyranny of Change,* 33.
3. Bowne, *This Fabulous Century,* 182–183.
4. Bowne, *This Fabulous Century,* 180.
5. Kathy Peiss, *Cheap Amusements: Working Women and Leisure in Turn-of-the-Century New York* (Philadelphia: Temple University Press, 1986), 34, 62.
6. Peiss, *Working Women,* 63.
7. Peiss, *Working Women,* 63.
8. Caroline Rennolds Milbank, *New York Fashion: The Evolution of American Style* (New York: Harry N. Abrams, 1989), 48.
9. O. E. Schoeffier and William Gale, *Esquire's Encyclopedia of 20th Century Men's Fashions* (New York: McGraw-Hill, 1973), 124.
10. Estelle Ansley Worrell, *American Costume, 1840 to 1920* (Harrisburg, PA: Stackpole Books, 1979), 145.
11. Kathy Peiss, *Hope in a Jar: The Making of America's Beauty Culture* (New York: Henry Holt, 1998), 50–51.
12. Schoeffier and Gale, *20th Century Men's Fashions,* 2–3.
13. Schoeffier and Gale, *20th Century Men's Fashions,* 4–5.
14. Worrell, *American Costume,* 146–149.

FOOD OF THE 1900S

1. Cashman, *America in the Age of the Titans,* 40–42.
2. Harvey A. Levenstein, *Revolution at the Table: The Transformation of the American Diet* (New York: Oxford University Press, 1988), 98–103.
3. Levenstein, *Revolution at the Table,* 104.
4. Levenstein, *Revolution at the Table,* 105–108.
5. Chambers, *Tyranny of Change,* 38.
6. William E. Mason, "Food Adulterations," *The North American Review* 170 (1900): 548–549.
7. Mason, "Food Adulterations," 549–553.
8. Cashman, *American in the Age of the Titans,* 83.
9. Quoted in Cashman, *American in the Age of the Titans,* 87.
10. Brands, T. R., *The Last Romantic,* 550–551; Cashman, *American in the Age of the Titans,* 88–89.
11. Levenstein, *Revolution at the Table,* 33; Wagenknecht, *American Profile,* 144–145.
12. Wagenknecht, *American Profile,* 144–146.
13. Wagenknecht, *American Profile,* 146–147.
14. Wagenknecht, *American Profile,* 148–149.
15. Kraft Foods, "The History of the Wiggle." http://kraftfoods.com/jello/explore/history/.
16. Wagenknecht, *American Profile,* 152–153.
17. Wagenknecht, *American Profile,* 153–154.

MUSIC OF THE 1900S

1. H. Wiley Hitchcock, *Music in the United States: A Historical Introduction* (Uper Saddle River, NJ: Prentice-Hall, 1974), 141.
2. Nicholas E. Tawa, *Mainstream Music of Early Twentieth Century America: The Composers, Their Times, and Their Works* (Westport, CT: Greenwood Publishing, 1992), 120.
3. Tawa, *Mainstream Music of Early Twentieth Century America,* 123.
4. Tawa, *Mainstream Music of Early Twentieth Century America,* 106–108.
5. Wagenknecht, *American Profile,* 121.
6. Ewen, *All the Years,* 154.
7. Ewen, *All the Years,* 155.
8. Susan Curtis, *Dancing to a Black Man's Tune: A Life of Scott Joplin* (Columbia: University of Missouri Press, 1994), 35.
9. Curtis, *Dancing to a Black Man's Tune,* 38.

10. Curtis, *Dancing to a Black Man's Tune,* 129–145.

11. Grace Lichtenstein and Laura Dankner, *Musical Gumbo: The Music of New Orleans* (New York: W. W. Norton, 1993), 26–27.

12. Lichtenstein and Dankner, *Musical Gumbo: The Music of New Orleans,* 28–29.

SPORTS AND LEISURE OF THE 1900s

1. Theodore Roosevelt, *An Autobiography* (New York: Macmillan, 1913), 52.

2. Benjamin G. Rader, *American Sports: From the Age of Folk Games to the Age of Televised Sports,* 2nd ed. (Upper Saddle River, NJ: Prentice-Hall, 1990), 119.

3. Rader, *American Sports,* 120.

4. G. Edward White, *Creating the National Pastime: Baseball Transforms Itself, 1903–1953* (Princeton: Princeton University Press, 1996), 48.

5. Quoted in Charles C. Alexander, *Our Game: An American Baseball History* (New York: Henry Holt, 1991), 78–79.

6. Alexander, *Our Game,* 85–86.

7. Allison Danzig, *Oh, How They Played the Game: The Early Days of Football and the Heroes Who Made It Great* (New York: Macmillan, 1971), 149.

8. John Durant and Otto Bettmann, *Pictorial History of American Sports: From Colonial Times to the Present* (New York: A. S. Barnes, 1952), 110–111; H. W. Brands, *T.R.: The Last Romantic* (New York: Basic Books, 1997), 553–554.

9. George Gipe, *The Great American Sports Book* (Garden City, NY: Doubleday, 1978), 177.

10. Gipe, *The Great American Sports Book,* 171.

11. Gipe, *The Great American Sports Book,* 168.

12. Arthur R. Ashe Jr., *A Hard Road to Glory: A History of the African-American Athlete, 1619–1918* (New York: Amistad, 1988), 30–32.

13. Ashe, *A Hard Road to Glory,* 32.

14. Ashe, *A Hard Road to Glory,* 33.

15. Ashe, *A Hard Road to Glory,* 34.

16. Faulkner, *The Quest for Social Justice,* 289–290.

17. Allen Guttmann, *The Olympics: A History of the Modern Games* (Urbana: University of Illinois Press, 1992), 1–10.

18. Guttmann, *The Olympics,* 22–23.

19. Guttmann, *The Olympics,* 28–31.

20. Thomas J. Schlereth, *Victorian America,* 233–234.

21. Thomas J. Schlereth, *Victorian America,* 234.

TRAVEL OF THE 1900s

1. Schlereth, *Victorian America,* 214.

2. Lutz, *American Nervousness,* 1–30.

3. Quoted in Schlereth, *Victorian America,* 216–217.

4. Quoted in Lutz, *American Nervousness,* 90.

5. Brown, *This Fabulous Century,* 216–219.

6. Faulkner, *The Quest for Social Justice,* 141.

7. Faulkner, *The Quest for Social Justice,* 142.

8. Faulkner, *The Quest for Social Justice,* 143–144.

9. Sullivan, *Our Times,* 488–490.

10. Cashman, *America in the Age of the Titans,* 268–269.

11. For several examples of classic automobile posters targeting affluent consumers, please see Brown, *This Fabulous Century,* 237–240.

12. Bob Batchelor, "The Rubber City," *Inside Business,* October 1998, 22.

13. Walter Lord, *The Good Years: From 1900 to the First World War* (New York: Harper and Brothers, 1960), 91–94.

14. Walter Lord, *The Good Years: From 1900 to the First World War* (New York: Harper and Brothers, 1960), 94–98.

15. Chambers, *The Tyranny of Change,* 124–125.

16. Lord, *The Good Years,* 99–100.

17. Schlereth, *Victorian America,* 26.

18. Wiebe, *The Search for Order,* 244.

19. Cashman, *America in the Age of the Titans,* 442–444.

20. Schlereth, *Victorian America,* 26–27.

21. Cashman, *America in the Age of the Titans,* 444–446.

VISUAL ARTS OF THE 1900s

1. Davidson, *History of the Artists' America,* 251.

2. Davidson, *History of the Artists' America,* 251.

3. Hughes, *American Visions,* 242.

4. Hughes, *American Visions,* 261–264.

5. Hughes, *American Visions,* 265–266.

6. Davidson, *History of the Artists' America,* 252–253.

7. Hughes, *American Visions,* 353–357.

8. Hughes, *American Visions,* 323.

9. Shi, *Facing Facts,* 252–259.

10. Donald Braider, *George Bellows and the Ashcan School of Painting* (Garden City, NY: Doubleday, 1971), 24.

11. Hughes, *American Visions,* 330.

12. Joyce Carol Oates, *George Bellows: American Artist* (Hopewell, NJ: Ecco Press, 1995), 18–20.

13. Braider, *George Bellows,* 39–43.

14. Hughes, *American Visions,* 352.

15. Crichton, *America 1900,* 92–93.

16. Crichton, *America 1900,* 94.

17. Wagenknecht, *American Profile,* 293–294.

18. Hughes, *American Visions,* 210.

1910s

Timeline

of Popular Culture Events, 1910s

1910

February 8: The Boy Scouts of America is chartered by William D. Boyce.

March 17: The Camp Fire Girls is chartered by Dr. & Mrs. L. H. Gulick.

Florence Lawrence declared the first genuine movie star as the "Vitagraph Girl."

Architect Frank Lloyd Wright completes work on the Robie House, Chicago, Illinois.

May 18: Return of Halley's Comet passes sun without disastrous consequences that were predicted.

June 4: Jack Johnson becomes the first black heavyweight champion of the modern era with a 15th-round knockout of Jim Jeffries.

June 25: The Mann Act passed, outlawing the transportation of women across state lines for any "immoral purpose" (i.e., prostitution). Also known as the "White Slavery" Act.

November 8: Washington State adopts women's suffrage.

The National City Planning Association is founded to help designers better coordinate architectural and landscape designs into American cities.

Morris and Rose Michtom found the Ideal Novelty & Toy Company.

1911

March 25: Triangle Shirtwaist Fire kills 146 workers in Lower Manhattan.

May 15: Supreme Court orders dissolution of Standard Oil Company.

December 14: Roald Amundsen of Norway beats Robert Scott to the South Pole.

Edith Wharton publishes *Ethan Frome.*

The magazine *Masses* is rechristened with Max Eastman as editor.

Walter Dill Scott publishes *Influencing Men in Business,* which defines the methods of modern advertising.

Crisco shortening is introduced by Procter & Gamble.

The U.S. Children's Bureau is established by President William Howard Taft to investigate and report on infant mortality, orphanages, juvenile courts, and other concerns.

Gordon Craig publishes *The Art of the Theatre,* describing the latest trends in staging and performing live theater.

Irving Berlin publishes hit song "Alexander's Ragtime Band."

The Kewpie doll, created by Rose O'Neill, appears.

The state of Illinois becomes the first to pass laws providing aid to mothers with dependent children.

Frank Lloyd Wright completes Taliesin, his home, studio, and retreat, near Spring Green, Wisconsin.

The Mona Lisa is stolen from the Louvre in Paris, France.

Pennsylvania Station completed in New York City by architects McKim, Mead, and White.

Galbraith Rodgers takes 82 hours—over seven weeks—to fly across the United States in an airplane.

The Gideon Organization of Christian Commercial Travelers begins placing more than 60,000 Bibles in hotel rooms.

President Taft goes on a diet, his weight dropping from 340 to 267 pounds, in an effort to appear "healthy" for the upcoming presidential election.

1912

April 14–15: The ocean liner *Titanic* strikes an iceberg and sinks, killing 1,523 passengers and crew.

May 12: The Girl Scouts of America are founded by Daisy Gordon.

June 19: Eight-hour labor law extended to all federal employees.

Poetry, a Magazine of Verse is first published in Chicago, Illinois.

Maria Montessori publishes *The Montessori Childhood Education Method,* describing new techniques in preschool education.

Mack Sennett founds the Keystone Company to produce comedy motion pictures.

Carl Laemmle forms Universal Pictures.

Richard Hellman begins marketing his "Blue Ribbon" mayonnaise.

Will Marion Cook composes and publishes *A Collection of Negro Songs.*

Novella *Tarzan of the Apes* is published by Edgar Rice Burroughs.

Woodrow Wilson is elected the twenty-eighth president of the United States.

1913

February 17: The Armory Show of Modern Art is staged in New York City.

February 25: The Sixteenth Amendment to the Constitution is passed allowing for a federal income tax on those making more

than $3,000 per year (fewer than 600,000 of 92 million Americans are affected).

May 14: John D. Rockefeller donates $100 million to create the Rockefeller Foundation.

Congress designates the second Sunday in May as Mother's Day.

Sigmund Freud and Carl Jung engage in speaking tour of the United States.

Dancers Vernon and Irene Castle debut in America.

A third professional baseball league, the Federal League, is founded to compete with the National and American Leagues. The Federal League folds in 1915.

The Oreo cookie is introduced.

James Reese Europe becomes one of the first African Americans to secure a record deal, with Victor Records.

Clarence Crane introduces a hard candy called the Life Saver. His first flavor is Pep-O-Mint.

A. C. Gilbert begins marketing the Erector set.

Amateur Francis Ouimet, the 20-year-old son of a recent immigrant, defeats two British professionals to win the U.S. Golf Association Open, propelling the game of golf into a national sensation.

George Herriman's cartoon strip "Krazy Kat" premieres in the *New York Journal.*

The Mona Lisa is recovered in Florence, Italy, and returned to Paris unharmed.

Willa Cather publishes *O, Pioneers!*

The Height of Buildings Commission of New York City regulates the city's skyscrapers, mandating the famous "setback" design of the decade.

The Woolworth Building is completed in New York City.

1914

February 13: Tin Pan Alley songwriters organize the American Society of Composers, Authors, and Publishers (ASCAP) to protect their financial interests through royalty payments.

July 28–August 26: World War I begins in Europe.

July 29: First transcontinental telephone service between New York City and San Francisco is successful.

Robert Frost publishes *North of Boston.*

The magazine the *New Republic* is first published.

Charlie Chaplin becomes a national star after the release of *Kid Auto Races at Venice;* "Charliemania" sweeps the country.

Tinkertoys are introduced.

W. C. Handy introduces America to the blues with the publication of the St. Louis Blues.

Women in eleven Western states and the territory of Alaska are allowed to vote in state and local elections.

Construction begins on the Lincoln Memorial, Washington, D.C.

Mary Pickford becomes a national sensation after starring in D. W. Griffith's *Tess of Storm County.*

By the end of the year, it took the Ford Motor Company only one hour, 33 minutes to construct a new Model T; the firm produced more than 300,000 vehicles this year.

Margaret Sanger publishes *Family Limitation,* introducing many to the values of birth control.

The Harrison Drug Act is passed to restrict access to narcotics in the United States. The federal government estimates that 4.5 percent of the American public is addicted to drugs.

Gold is discovered in Alaska, leading to the last gold rush in American history.

1915

February 6–20: Panama-Pacific exposition held in San Francisco.

May 7: The *Lusitania* is hit by torpedoes fired from a German U-boat, killing 1,193 passengers, including 128 Americans.

July 1: Cost of telephone calls in New York City is reduced to a nickel.

July 24: The *Eastland* steamer capsizes in Chicago, killing 841 people.

September 29: The first transcontinental telephone call is placed. Direct wireless service is established between the United States and Japan.

December 18: Widower President Woodrow Wilson marries widow Edith Bolling Galt at her home in Washington, D.C.

D. W. Griffith releases his landmark film *The Birth of a Nation.*

Vice President Thomas R. Marshall suggests, "What this country really needs is a good five-cent cigar."

Edgar Lee Masters publishes *Spoon River Anthology.*

Carl Sandburg publishes *Chicago Poems.*

"Jelly Roll" Morton publishes the "Jelly Roll Blues."

R. J. Reynolds creates one of the most successful brand-name advertising campaigns in modern history by introducing Camel cigarettes.

The Victor Talking Machine Company begins selling phonographs to the public.

Ford Motor Company produces its one-millionth Model T.

The state of Nevada passes the first no-fault divorce law, which requires six months of residency in the state.

1916

January 1: First permanent annual Rose Bowl football game.

June 3: Louis Brandeis becomes the first Jewish person selected to serve on the U.S. Supreme Court.

August 25: The National Park Service is created.

September 1: The Keating-Owen Child Labor Act regulates working conditions for many child laborers and, through penalties to industry, severely limits the employment of children under fourteen years of age.

October 16: Margaret Sanger opens the first birth control clinic in Brooklyn, New York, and is arrested for distributing "obscene" materials.

Architect Irving Gill completes the important early modern Dodge House in Los Angeles.

Piggly-Wiggly, the first self-service grocery store, is founded by Clarence Saunders in Memphis, Tennessee.

D. W. Griffith films and releases the motion picture *Intolerance.*

Georgia O'Keeffe premieres at Alfred Stieglitz's New York Gallery, known as 291.

The Provincetown Players move from Cape Cod, Massachusetts, to Greenwich Village, New York, and become the most influential Little Theatre of the decade.

Jeannette Rankin, of Montana, becomes the first women elected to the U.S. Congress.

Norman Rockwell illustrates his first cover for the *Saturday Evening Post.*

Fortune cookies are introduced to the world by David Jung, a Los Angeles noodle maker.

A polio epidemic strikes the United States; more than 29,000 are affected and more than 6,000 die.

Woodrow Wilson is re-elected president.

1917

February 23: The Smith-Hughes Vocational Education Act provides federal money to found many of the nation's first professional vocational schools.

April 1: Ragtime pioneer Scott Joplin dies.

April 6: The United States enters World War I.

April 14: The Committee on Public Information is created to censor news and issue propaganda for the war effort.

December 18: The Constitutional amendment prohibiting the manufacture, sale, and use of alcohol passes Congress and is sent to the states for ratification.

The National Birth Control League, later Planned Parenthood, is created by Margaret Sanger.

The New Orleans group known as the Original Dixieland Jazz Band is "discovered" while playing at Reisenweber's Restaurant, New York City, introducing the town to the jazz sound.

The *Saturday Evening Post* earns more than $17 million in advertising revenues alone.

1918

August 12: The first airmail flight occurs between Washington, D.C. and New York City.

November 7: World War I ends in an armistice.

A national outbreak of influenza begins in September and kills 588,000 Americans.

The first installment of Irish writer James Joyce's *Ulysses* is banned by the U.S. Post Office.

The Raggedy Ann doll, created by Johnny Gruelle, is introduced.

1919

January 29: The Eighteenth Amendment, prohibiting the manufacture, sale, and consumption of alcohol, is ratified.

April 17: United Artists is founded by Charlie Chaplin, D. W. Griffith, Douglas Fairbanks, and Mary Pickford.

Severe civil and economic unrest shake the United States. More than three million are unemployed while more than four million workers participate in 2,665 strikes.

Race riots affect 26 cities, and 70 lynchings are confirmed.

Eight members of the Chicago White Sox take bribes to throw the 1919 World Series, resulting in the "Black Sox scandal."

The first transoceanic flight is successfully completed.

George "Babe" Ruth hits 29 home runs, shattering the old record. The next year Ruth will hit 54 homers, more than any other single *team* previously.

The Actors' Equity Association goes on strike.

Peter Paul Halajian of the Peter Paul Candy Company introduces the Konabar.

Lincoln Logs, a toy building set, are introduced.

Overview

of the 1910s

For the average American, everyday life seemed to be in a constant state of change during the 1910s—from eating and dressing to entertainment and travel. But while the commercialization of everyday life during the 1910s was greater than that in previous decades, it was the challenge to America's traditional sense of itself that was the most significant. In a country that was consciously aware of its rural, democratic, and largely Western European heritage, the growth of an urban, commercial, and multiethnic popular culture generated deep anxieties and tensions in many citizens.

New and old technologies were made more common to the average American. For example, motion pictures changed from being a new pastime to a $735 million industry by 1920, which altered trends in fashion, public opinion, and even conversation. In 1910, 458,000 automobiles were registered in the country; by the end of the decade, this number exceeded eight million. While the population grew at a moderate rate (from 92 to 106 million in ten years), the economic output nearly tripled (from $35 billion to $92 billion) and the average salary increased from $750 to $1,226 per year, which furthered the pace of commercialization.[1]

PROGRESSIVISM

That most Americans were actively engaged in deciphering the meaning of these changes is a key characteristic of the decade. While Progressivism meant different things to different people, it was driven by the forces of everyday life and was experienced by all sectors of the American public, especially at the local level. Progressivism was an optimistic faith in the ability of science and rational thought to address the worst abuses of modern life. It also attacked traditional racial, ethnic, class, and gender prejudices. New York City workers and labor organizations had vocally identified the dangerous working conditions, low pay, and health problems associated with the garment industry, but it was not until the 1911 Triangle Shirtwaist Company fire, which claimed the lives of 146 people (mostly young women) that reform of the trade became a national issue. Once stirred, however, reformers such as Florence Kelley, Frances Perkins, and Al Smith radically redesigned both the inspection and operation of other work sites in the city, state, and throughout the country.

Broadly defined, the Progressive movement sought to accomplish three goals. The first was to limit the worst abuses of power associated with the concentration of capital. By using trust-busting and workplace inspections, and by organizing workers, reformers attempted to identify monopolies and to empower interest groups. Second, Progressives hoped to amplify the tendency of Americans to see ourselves collectively, as a nation and a people, rather than as competitive individuals struggling against each other. Jane Addams and Florence Kelley pioneered settlement houses in an effort to lend the talents of educated, active American women to impoverished immigrants (mostly women). Kelley and Lillian Wald brought the same ideals to the U.S. Children's Bureau in 1912. Finally, Progressives intended to benefit from the abilities of technical specialists to reorganize and improve society. Reformers created a number of institutions, associations, commissions, and other bodies to lend authority to America's professionals. In business, efficiency experts improved management techniques, wages, and working conditions to get the most out of industry, thereby maximizing profits, improving quality, and creating a better work environment. While all three goals of Progressivism addressed specific areas of concern, often reforms were a mixture of these and other factors.

LIFE IN RURAL AND URBAN AMERICA

While the decade saw an increase in the population of urban, industrial laborers (from 16 to 29 million) and a slight decrease in rural workers (from 11 to 10.4 million), the period was an affluent time in rural America, with the doubling of gross farm income and the tripling of farm values. Productivity enhancements (such as fertilizers, improved breeds, and machinery), easier access to world markets (which had become a near monopoly with the start of war in Europe), and an improvement in farm living conditions (due to the use of automobiles, electricity, and water pumps) contributed to the boom.

Local civic improvements, most notably in roads and schools, increased, and greater investments were made in local churches and other private functions. These efforts augmented the Progressive Country Life Movement, which began as an investigation into why, in spite of such good times, Americans were continuing to move from the countryside to the city. Of course, those who did not directly benefit from by commercial farming, such as black tenant farmers and day laborers, were not greatly affected by the reforms. Stagnant rural incomes for African Americans in the South was one of the reasons for the Great Migration north during World War I.

The Country Life Movement went to the heart of Progressive anxieties during the decade. The fear of lower agricultural productivity was the gravest concern. Rising farm prices would make it more difficult for America to trade abroad, and cheap food prices were essential to maintaining prosperity at home. Moreover, a consensus emerged that rural people were not properly educating their young and were instead using children as unskilled family laborers. An urban curriculum, which included a greater emphasis on the arts and humanities and physical education, was intended to offset the worst problems of provincialism. Formal vocational training, rather than the practical experience gained on the farm, was initiated with the passage of the Smith-Hughes Act of 1917.

Millions of working-class people lived in the nation's cities. By the end of the decade, 60 percent of urban dwellers were immigrants and their children, arriving most recently from Italy, Poland, Greece, and Eastern Europe. Few of these people wanted to settle in the countryside—many were fleeing rural poverty or persecution—and many hoped to earn enough cash to improve their lot in Europe, where they hoped to return. During the 1900s and 1910s, Progressives became aware of the difficult conditions that these Americans faced in their daily lives. From unsanitary conditions and less than subsistence wages to crime and substance abuse, the urban working poor were forced to live within an inhospitable environment.

Muckraking journalists and reformers addressed the issue of housing reform and sanitation less to benefit the working poor and more as a way to highlight the corruption of big city machines. When, in the 1910s, Progressives argued that the government had a stake in "saving" urban children or in providing "decent" recreational facilities, increasing numbers of citizens found themselves in agreement.

At the same time, the suburbs were growing and becoming more significant. For the most part, suburbs were split between regions that were serviced by regular streetcar facilities, populated largely by the native-born working class, and areas that required personal means of transportation, dominated by professionals, owners, and the upper-middle class. Suburbs favored single-family detached homes. With the growth of the automobile industry, higher industrial wages, and cheaper, more functional housing, the suburbs had become an increasingly popular and affordable option for many by the close of the decade.

PROGRESSIVE POLITICS

Progressive politics remained a fundamentally local phenomenon throughout the era. Local city or county governments became the focus of reformers. Such reform ranged from environmental improvements of housing and sanitation to such far-reaching projects as the City Beautiful campaign, which sought to redesign urban America by building parks and playgrounds for the social betterment of its citizens.

The turn toward directly elected city commissioners, managers, or other administrative officials attempted to "rationalize" the operation of city government. By 1917, more than 500 American cities and towns had opted for such a structure. The resulting efficiency and social welfare programs had a direct and immediate effect on everyday life. St. Louis prosecutor Joseph Folk, who later was elected Missouri's governor, was typical in cleaning up the city council, passing pure food legislation, curbing organized crime, setting standards for industry and labor, and promoting the transfer of ownership of many utilities (such as the streetcars) to municipal governments.

At the state level, leaders such as Wisconsin's Robert La Follette Sr. expanded these initiatives onto the national stage. La Follette, whose career included stints as a U.S. congressman and a governor, cobbled together effective coalitions of voters which included farmers, small businessmen, and industrial workers. From this base, he promoted issues such as tax reform, the direct election of U.S. senators, primary elections, and railroad regulation. He trusted and relied on experts in higher education, beginning a tradition of tapping into these academic resources for public service.

When Progressivism entered the national political stage, it became the central platform for change. In 1912, four presidential candidates each claimed a mandate to lead based on their Progressive agenda. While the incumbent president,

William Howard Taft, had considerable Progressive credentials—appointing activists such as Philander Knox, Henry L. Stimson, and Charles Evans Hughes to his administration—he was not progressive enough to withstand challenges from Theodore Roosevelt, Woodrow Wilson, and Socialist Eugene V. Debs. Roosevelt even left the Republican Party and formed the Progressive Bull Moose Party in 1912 based on his vision of New Nationalism, which called for a chief executive dedicated to the distribution of social justice.

Woodrow Wilson, the victor in 1912 and 1916, was the dominant Progressive force at the national level for most of the decade. Wilson wanted government at all levels to be more open and representative and for business to be free from the evils of large, influential corporations. His administration reformed tariffs, advocated a national income tax, extended loans directly to farmers, established the Federal Reserve system and the Federal Trade Commission, passed banking and investment reform, banned child labor and mandated an eight-hour day in many industries, and helped pass the Clayton Antitrust Act, which legalized the formation of unions.

INTEREST GROUPS AND THE "NEW WOMAN"

The formation of associations by professionals and other like-minded individuals was part of the Progressive impulse to rationalize and bureaucratize social organization. While groups like the American Medical Association and the National Association of Manufacturers were created to protect specific economic or specialist niches, other interest groups formed to provide a more powerful voice for traditionally underrepresented populations. Two sectors in particular, African Americans and women, were especially active in the 1910s.

Since emancipation, blacks had struggled to find equality in America. Following the advice of Booker T. Washington, many African Americans quietly suffered the outrage of segregation in order to achieve economic self-sufficiency. By 1910, however, many black intellectuals, including W.E.B. Du Bois and William Monroe Trotter, were finding it hard to accept the arguments of racists. In 1909, Du Bois and a number of white supporters founded the National Association for the Advancement of Colored People (NAACP) and a monthly journal titled *Crisis*. Spurred by contemporary events, such as the success of the openly racist film *The Birth of a Nation* (1915), segregation and unfair practices during World War I, the Great Migration north, and the race riots of 1919, the NAACP provided a rallying point for citizens unwilling to accept second-class status. The group focused on constitutional protections, most notably the Fourteenth Amendment, setting in motion the modern civil rights movement.

The "New Woman" in America, who was increasingly engaged in public life, was both a political force and something of a stereotype. She was portrayed in popular culture as a cigarette-smoking, dancing, sexually liberated free spirit, but members of the movement were more typically average working women and women's club members. Margaret Sanger's crusade to provide birth control to working women was an attempt to free all women, particularly the working poor, from the primary biological factor (i.e., reproduction) that limited female independence. Settlement houses added to the number of committed activists, which included Jane Addams, Florence Kelley, and Alice Paul, and expanded reforms into child care, urban pollution, global peace, and consumer protection.

Women's suffrage both reflected and limited the effect of the New Woman on society. Led by organizations such as the National American Women's Suffrage Association and, later, the National Women's Party, the suffrage movement created a heightened awareness among American women. In November 1910, the state of Washington passed a referendum legalizing women's suffrage. Over the next two years, California, Arizona, Kansas, and Oregon enacted similar legislation. When Illinois became the first state east of the Mississippi River to pass women's suffrage, it was clear that the movement was more than simply a Western remedy to a low voter base, and that a majority of men wanted to enfranchise women.

Still, the push for universal female suffrage, which was finally accomplished in 1920 with the ratification of the Nineteenth Amendment, was not without considerable compromise. "Radicals" like Alice Paul picketed, paraded, and underwent hunger strikes to demand equality based on the promises made in the Constitution. Moderates, like Carrie Chapman Catt and Anna Howard Shaw, used less dramatic means and linked women's suffrage to a host of previously unconnected issues, such as the war in Europe, immigration, and nativism to secure their goals.

CRIME, VICE, AND PERSECUTION

In the 1910s, "victimless crimes," such as prostitution, became intolerable—but mob violence proceeded without much opposition. The murder rate grew by nearly 50 percent from 4.6 to 6.8 deaths per 100,000 people.[2] No doubt, this was aided by the rapid pace of urbanization during the decade.

Prostitution, while illegal, had been a regular feature of everyday life in the United States since its inception. By 1910, reformers increasingly took note of the red-light districts (places where sex was commercialized), seeing them as a sign of the dangers and moral depravity of the inner cities. Vice fighters tried to save women they believed had been trapped into a life of prostitution by using police crackdowns and by publicizing the names of men who frequented the brothels. There were other reasons for these campaigns, ranging from the growing real estate values of the inner city and better wages for female industrial laborers to changes in the family and an increase in premarital sex by America's youth.

The Mann Act, also called the White Slave Traffic Act, passed in 1910 and was typical of a Progressive solution to a crime like prostitution. Assuming that all women who engaged in the trade were coerced either by violence or drugs, the act used federal resources to locate and break up the rings which allegedly abducted women, raped them, and then transported them across state lines to serve as prostitutes. Between 1910 and 1918, more than 2,000 ring members were found guilty of violating the Mann Act.[3]

The combined effect of federal and local enforcement of these vice laws generally was not beneficial for the women who practiced prostitution.

While few brothels were still owned by women in the 1910s, the vice districts did allow for some form of protection for the average professional. Following the crackdowns, many of the best run and highest paying brothels were closed. The women were forced out into the streets and were increasingly exposed to greater physical dangers from small-time pimps, corrupt policemen, and the general public.

Alcohol use also underwent a profound change in the 1910s. Aided in part by the vast grain surpluses of the country, as well as traditional alcohol use by native-born and immigrant alike, alcohol was readily available to adults and minors. The rise of the Women's Christian Temperance Union and the Anti-Saloon League, as well as the efforts at women's suffrage, provided the necessary catalysts for the passage of a number of state-based alcohol reforms. Tinged with fears of immigrant (largely Catholic and Jewish) cultures that periodically used alcohol, reformers portrayed the waste of spending one's wages on alcohol and the social costs of family violence, absenteeism, and chronic poverty. By 1916, 23 states and numerous municipalities had prohibited the manufacture of alcohol. World War I probably provided the final incentive for national action because some items needed for the production of alcohol were rationed and many prominent German families were at the forefront of the brewing industries. Congress passed the Eighteenth Amendment to the U.S. Constitution in December 1917. Ratified two years later and enforced through the 1920 Volstead Act, prohibition made the manufacture, sale, and transportation of intoxicating liquors (more than 0.5 percent alcohol) a federal crime.

The unintended result of such criminalization was that average citizens began to accept greater lawlessness in order to secure a casual glass of beer (the preferred drink of most lawbreakers). Because of the complexity and capital-intensive nature of manufacturing, selling, and transporting alcohol, organized crime was the beneficiary. Most notable were the various syndicates which emerged in the larger cities and the men who rose to prominence, including Frankie Yale in New York City and "Big Jim" Colosimo, John Torrio, Dion O'Banion, and Al Capone in Chicago. Chicago's municipal government fell under the influence of such men as "Bathhouse" John Coughlin and "Hinky Dink" Michael Kenna. Many rationalized police corruption, gangland murder, expanded racketeering, and rigged elections for the sake of providing a thirsty public with the "hospitality" they craved.

A willingness to turn a blind eye to outright criminal behavior had a lasting effect on other crimes. Violence targeting racial and ethnic groups was widespread throughout the decade. Lynchings in the South and a revival of the Ku Klux Klan created tension between blacks and whites, which frequently escalated to violence. Race riots in East St. Louis (1917) and Chicago (1919) resulted in the deaths of hundreds, the destruction of entire black communities, and racial scars that would last generations. Few were ever brought to justice, but there were unintended benefits. Following the war, the NAACP was increasingly vocal about the prevalence of summary justice (the punishment of suspected offenders without a proper trial) and racial violence.

Fear of ethnic radicals, especially socialists, was another excuse to resort to violence. Inspired by new publications, such as the *Masses,* and intellectual trends, American socialists were mobilized by the Progressive movement, victories at the ballot box, and a rebirth of labor activism. Radical strikes in Paterson, New Jersey (1913), and in Ludlow, Colorado (1914), and the success of the Industrial Workers of the World (IWW) led to a conservative backlash. Under cover of the war, civil liberties were suspended as hundreds of people were arrested, beaten, or killed in violence for being "un-American." The Bolshevik Revolution in 1917 unnerved many legislators, who authored numerous laws aimed as such seditiousness. By 1920, hundreds of people, including presidential candidate Eugene V. Debs, were rounded up, arrested, or deported as a result of the Red Scare. During that same year, Nicola Sacco and Bartolomeo Vanzetti were tried and convicted of first degree murder on evidence that established little more than their immigrant status and radical social views. Their execution, in 1927, was such a travesty of justice that there was a worldwide condemnation of America's seemingly warped sense of justice.

THE GREAT WAR

World War I loomed large in the 1910s. While the United States did not formally enter the conflict until April 6, 1917, most Americans closely followed events in Europe after Gavrilo Princip, a Serbian nationalist, assassinated Archduke Franz Ferdinand, the heir to the Austrian empire, on June 28, 1914, precipitating the "Great War" several weeks later. Questions of American neutrality greatly affected the average citizen. America emerged from nearly 100 years of isolation and committed itself to forming a new world.

When President Wilson called on Americans to be neutral "in thought as well as in action," he knew that the request was an ambitious one.

The country was closely linked to English traditions and home to a large number of immigrants from Germany and Ireland (a nation seeking independence from England, with a long history of hatred and violence between the two). Still, the public saw through many of the efforts to exploit ethnic hatred and often became more supportive of American isolation as a result. Humanitarian efforts to ease the suffering in Belgium, a neutral country which was mercilessly invaded by the Germans, suggest a general pro-Allied stance by the public, but nothing more. Most believed that the fighting should remain "over there."

By contrast, American businesses were deeply involved in the conflict. U.S. banks were increasing loans to England and France who, in turn,

U.S. Army infantry troops, African American unit, marching northwest of Verdun, France, in World War I, 1918. Despite serving bravely in one of the most difficult wars on record, African American veterans of the war came back to racism and lack of opportunity. Prints & Photographs Division, Library of Congress.

used the money to buy American food and manufactured goods. Soon the United States had an economic incentive to see that the Allies were capable of repaying their loans. An effective blockade of trade with Germany, as well as a near monopoly in trade to Latin America, expanded the gap. By 1917, U.S. loans to the Allies neared $2.6 billion; less than $35 *million* was extended in credit to Germany and its compatriots.

The effect of the U.S. supplies was not lost on the German military leadership. When it became clear that an embargo of war munitions from the United States was ineffective at stopping the flow of munitions to England, the Central powers announced a policy of unrestricted submarine warfare near and around the British Isles. On May 7, 1915, a German submarine sunk the passenger liner *Lusitania,* killing 1,153 people, including 128 Americans.[4] That the ship was warned about a potential attack and that it was probably carrying munitions was ignored by an American public, who suddenly felt the loss of war. Repeated confrontations with the Germans in 1916 heightened tensions.

During that presidential election year, the question of America's involvement in the war became paramount. Strong isolationist and peace movements, led by Progressives and women's suffrage advocates, helped to propel Wilson to reelection under the banner that "He Kept Us Out of War." Unfortunately, the situation in Europe had deteriorated to the point that the nations at war were willing to risk any gamble in an effort to gain the upper hand. Germany reasoned that a final, massive assault in the spring of 1917 could turn the tide. In order to prevent supplies from reaching the Allies, total submarine warfare would be unleashed on all vessels in the Atlantic. Hoping to win the conflict before an inevitable declaration of war was made by the United States, German official Arthur Zimmermann secretly approached the state of Mexico with an offer of post-war assistance in return for their attack on the United States. Coupled with the sinking of seven U.S. merchant vessels in March alone, the publication of the Zimmermann Telegram turned the tide against isolation. On April 6, 1917, the United States formally declared war on Germany and its allies.[5]

THE WAR OVER HERE AND OVER THERE

Although more than 24 million Americans registered to serve in the armed forces, and more than two million did serve, America's involvement in the conflict was relatively minor. Fresh troops, abundant supplies, and a renewed sense of victory buoyed the spirits of the Allied powers and had the reverse effect on the Central powers. Russia, an ally, was the first to crack politically (France and Italy were barely maintaining their political stability) while German territory remained unoccupied when the armistice was finally signed between the Germans and the Allies in 1918. The effects to the United States pale to near insignificance when compared to Europe: the total war dead was about 116,000 for the United States and more than 24 million for Europe; the governments in Russia, Austria, and Germany were totally destroyed.[6] Nevertheless, the effect of the war at home was considerable. Federal oversight of the economy began almost immediately, with the War Industries Board dictating prices, profits, wages, and supply of materials. Congress began massive war bond and rationing programs. The government borrowed nearly $22 billion from the American public through the sale of Liberty Bonds. Income tax reform (expanding the number of those who were required to pay), a federal police force (the FBI [Federal Bureau of Investigation] was founded in 1917), and an active propaganda division (Committee on Public Information, which distributed more than 75 million pamphlets throughout the war) were examples of how the government expanded its role in and helped to standardize modern American life.

Wartime industrialization expanded employment opportunities for blacks, Mexican Americans, and women. During the Great Migration, more than 500,000 African Americans left the rural South. Women earned the right to vote largely as a result of their support of the administration during the war. Even moderate labor unions, like the American Federal of Labor (AFL), benefited by the sense of common cause that was generated in the United States. On the other hand, those who opposed the war, including the IWW, were treated harshly. Issues such as an eight-hour workday, a minimum wage, and collective bargaining were resolved by those willing to support the war effort.

Given the enormity of World War I, the peace process accomplished very little. When the nations agreed to an armistice on November 11, 1918, they had little notion of how to deal with the war's devastation and no idea of how to deal with the Bolsheviks in the newly christened Soviet Union. Wilson's proposal was to reshape international politics to "make the world safe for democracy." Such ideals contrasted sharply with V. I. Lenin's call for a worldwide social and economic revolution, and did little to quell Allied bitterness over the war. The Wilsonian doctrine—calling for self-determination, free speech, an international body of arbitration, and new ethnic nations in Europe—remained U.S. policy for much of the twentieth century, but it could not prevent a punitive peace treaty from alienating and pauperizing Germany. The result was the rise to power of Adolf Hitler fourteen years later.

At home, peace forced Americans radically to retool their economy. Layoffs and shrinking profits led to a series of bitter strikes, which affected almost a fifth of the nation's workers in 1919. In Seattle, New York, and Boston, strikes shut down key segments of the economy, even entire cities, for long periods of time. The rising fear of bolshevism led to a Red Scare, which weakened many of the gains in civil liberties that had been secured by the Progressives. Racial and ethnic violence erupted across the country. When Warren G. Harding called for a "return to normalcy" in the 1920 presidential election, he reflected the fear that something had been lost in America as a result of America's experiences in the war.

THE *TITANIC* AND OTHER SHIP TRAGEDIES

Relying on multiple steam-turbine engines driving three or four screw propellers, shipping companies like the English owned White Star and Cunard lines launched dozens of ships in the first two decades of the twentieth century to meet the growing demand for transatlantic travel. The largest of these were White Star's new line which included the *Olympic*, *Britannic*, and *Titanic*.

Ironically, *Titanic* was designed for safety and comfort, rather than speed. The ship could travel a respectable 22 knots, but was protected by 16 watertight compartments (spanning the length of the ship) and 15 transverse bulkheads (spanning the width). Electrical generators powered emergency, watertight doors that would make the vessel nearly unsinkable in the event of a hull breach. The number of lifeboats, which figured prominently in two of the three great shipping disasters of the decade, was mandated by the tonnage of the vessel, not by the capacity. All ships of over 10,000 tons were required to carry 16 lifeboats (each capable of carrying from 60 to 80 people). These regulations were followed, but *Titanic*'s weight of more than 46,000 tons suggests how outdated such regulations were. The fact that the ill-fated ship carried four additional collapsible lifeboats was seen as further deference to the safety of its passengers. It was assumed that even the direst of emergencies would not sink the vessel, and that the lifeboats could handle a large number of passengers who could then wait for a speedy rescue.

First and second-class patrons enjoyed luxurious suites, mahogany-lined restaurants, ballrooms, golf links, gymnasiums, and baths as part of the basic amenities of travel. Servants catered

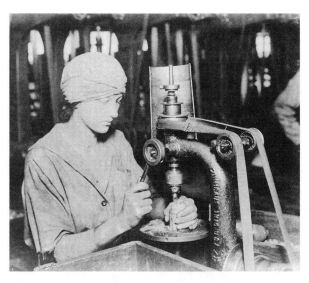

Woman countersinking a detonator tube hole and filling the hole in a hand grenade at Westinghouse Electric & Mfg. Co., East Pittsburgh, Pennsylvania. Women worked in factories in World War I for the war effort, as they would again later in World War II. Prints & Photographs Division, Library of Congress.

to their every need, from personal physicians and activities directors to valets and tailors. While prohibited from using the elite accommodations, "steerage" passengers did enjoy modern and sanitary eating, dining, and bathroom facilities and generally were free from the overcrowding common earlier. More important, the size of the superliners made the journey smooth and tolerable even for the most claustrophobic. Still, class differences were stark. Patrons did not mix socially and were treated differently when an emergency did arise.

On its maiden voyage, *Titanic* left Southampton, England at noon on April 10, 1912, piloted by the White Star line's most well-respected and best-liked captain, Edward J. Smith. Officially, 2,227 passengers and crew were on board when, around 11:40 p.m. ship's time on April 13, the ship struck a massive iceberg. The iceberg ripped an opening in the hull 250 feet long that transversed six separate compartments, opening *Titanic* to the North Atlantic. Smith ordered a visual inspection of the damage. Twenty minutes later he was apprised that the liner was terminally wounded. He gave

orders to swing out the lifeboats and abandon ship only 30 minutes after contact occurred.

The tragedy, which, in a matter of hours would result in the death of 1,523 passengers and crew, was due to a series of mistakes. Certainly, the lack of rescue boats and emergency preparedness lead the list. The *Titanic* was carrying over 2,200 people, but the ship's lifeboats could safely support less than 1,200. When the last lifeboat was freed from the ship, at 2:05 in the morning, more than 1,500 people remained on board with no chance of survival. Moreover, despite Smith's reputation as an accomplished captain, *Titanic*'s navigation department was poorly run. Warnings and sighting reports of numerous large icebergs were routinely broadcast over the wireless telegraph. Still, in spite of *Titanic*'s treacherous route, the wireless operator failed to take note of repeated warnings (a technical malfunction that afternoon led to a backlog of notes), which included another ship's report, only 50 minutes before the collision, that they had taken the extreme action of ordering a full stop due to the number and size of the

The *Titanic* at sea, from a photo taken in 1912. Prints & Photographs Division, Library of Congress.

icebergs in the region. Smith and nearly 500 other crew members paid for this error with their lives.

More troublesome was the role that class played in the determining who was rescued. Of the first-class passengers, 96 percent of the women and children were saved, 89 percent of second-class women and children, and 47 percent of steerage-class women and children. When Americans learned that "women and children first" meant the rich first, a vocal debate emerged.[7]

Defending the skewed survival rates were traditional nativists and other bigots who valued the lives of the propertied classes over those of the poorer immigrants. When the list of wealthy victims was released, including millionaires John Jacob Astor, Benjamin Guggenheim, and Charles M. Hays, many praised their unselfish devotion to duty. Ignoring the aloof luxury these men choose for themselves on their journey, many suggested that the rich were actually better at making sacrifice and exhibiting valor than those without means. A report that the ship's band played "Nearer My God to Thee" as *Titanic* underwent its final destruction was fabricated (none survived to report what the band played at the last moments). Still, the story resonated with upper-class Americans who saw their kind not as pampered idlers but as the righteous enablers of God's plan for the American economy.[8]

Many were appalled at the distorted death tolls as well as the cavalier way in which many poorer victims went unnoticed or were listed simply by their occupation, such as "a maid." Working-class newspapers mocked stories of how industrialists "saved" poorer *Titanic* passengers while they were seemingly unconcerned with the thousands of workers who had toiled for them for years. More heroic to their minds than the rich who refused to get into lifeboats (many because they did not believe that the ship would sink and therefore did not want to endure a cold trip in a lifeboat) were the boilermen and stokers who worked to keep power to the ship (which maintained electricity and prevented panic) despite their certain death.

In comparison to *Titanic,* the reaction of the American public to the *Eastland* and *Lusitania* disasters was tame. The *Eastland,* another mammoth steamship, was designed for travel and tourism along the Great Lakes. The *Eastland* was built for speed with a narrow, streamlined hull that could cut through the relatively calm waters of the inland lakes. To make room for its nearly 2,500 passengers, the substructure of the *Eastland* was redesigned to add seating capacity above the waterline. In 1904, a fully loaded and underway *Eastland* began to list to the starboard (right) by nearly 25 degrees. While the ship remained in service, this structural instability led to rumors that the boat was unsafe. Repeated inspections, certifications, and claims by *Eastland* engineers assured the public that it was seaworthy. The final modification, one that quite possibly led to its fatal instability, was, ironically, the installation of additional lifeboats at the top of its maindecks.

On July 24, 1915, these faults led to the death of 841 passengers. In the aftermath, it was clear that the victims could have been anyone, not only the elite or the poor immigrant. The *Eastland* was one of six boats chartered by the Western Electric Company for their annual employee picnic in Chicago. Entire families, from infants to grandparents, arrived early to board the *Eastland* hoping to secure coveted window seats below deck on the recently remodeled "Speed Queen of the Lakes." Passengers first entered at 6:40 a.m., and the vessel began listing almost immediately. The crew attempted to compensate by flooding ballast tanks, but by 7:20, with 2,572 people on board, the *Eastland* began swaying from one side to the other, all while docked in a sheltered river with little or no wind. The port (left) list became so bad, nearly 30 degrees, that water began to enter in the lower level windows. Below decks, the crew worked to rebalance the human cargo while engineers worked above to do the same with the ballast. Neither knew what the other was doing. Within eight minutes, the list was nearly 45 degrees. By this time, the passengers began to realize the seriousness of the problem and a slight panic ensued. Unable to maintain their position on the tilted decks, even more people slid to the left. Those on the right jumped from the ship, which only added to the imbalance. At 7:30, the *Eastland* rolled the final 45 degrees and settled on its left side, trapping everyone who was inside below the water line. Entire families, all intending to enjoy a simple day trip on Lake Michigan, were wiped out.[9]

The public outcry began immediately and centered its blame on state regulators and the *Eastland* crew. Only inept or corrupt regulators and ballast-tank operators, specialists whose job it was to keep the public safe from technical malfunction, could possibly explain why such a horror was visited on the public. The fact that such travel—especially with capacities running in the thousands—was inherently dangerous was never admitted or discussed. The final legal outcome was resolved in 1935; no criminal or civil liability was cited.

By contrast, the sinking of the *Lusitania* earlier that same year (1915) was a premeditated act of war. Built in 1906 to win the coveted Blue Riband prize for the fastest transatlantic crossing, Cunard's *Lusitania* and its sibling the *Mauretania* were the largest ships of their day and could easily achieve 25 knots in calm seas. While christened as a luxury liner, each ship was outfitted with moorings to house 6-inch guns to serve as armored troop transports or merchant cruisers should the need arise.

The neutrality of the United States in the Great War led to the destruction of the British *Lusitania*. Fearing a German torpedo boat, Captain William Turner hoisted and sailed under the American flag in January 1915, prompting an international incident. Unwilling to fire upon an American liner, the Germans declared in April that ships known to be chartered by belligerent countries would no longer receive the protection of American neutrality should they be found in contested waters. *Lusitania* left New York on May 1, 1915, after a published warning by the German government, and entered the "danger zone" off the English coast carrying nearly 2,000 passengers and crew six days later. As with *Titanic*, these patrons included a large number of wealthy and influential people who regarded the liner as the finest and fastest in service. At 2:15 p.m., as the ship approached Liverpool, *Lusitania* was believed to be struck by a single torpedo, which was soon followed by a powerful internal explosion. The blasts caused the stricken vessel to list badly to the right, rendering the portside lifeboats

From the *Sphere,* a London newspaper, 1915: "The doomed *Lusitania:* how the Irish rescuers hurried to the scene of the tragedy. The boats pulling away…and the rescuers approaching from Kinsale and Queenstown." Prints & Photographs Division, Library of Congress.

inoperable (they could not be lowered) and many of the starboard boats unreachable as they swung out over the open ocean. The electrical power failed immediately, creating near total darkness within the ship, and the craft sank in 18 minutes. The severe conditions accounted for 1,193 passenger deaths, including 128 Americans.[10]

Again, unlike the *Titanic,* interpretation of the disaster was without class recriminations for the passengers or their luxurious mode of travel. The German navy became a symbol of treachery and heartlessness, despite the fact that the *Lusitania* was known to be carrying war provisions and was sailing within a known corridor of U-boat activity. The fact that the 31,000-ton liner sank in less than half an hour after being struck by a single torpedo (compared to *Titanic*'s three hour ordeal, which was caused by hitting a mountainous iceberg) strongly supports the theory that *Lusitania* carried munitions as well as passengers and other cargo. The United States threatened to enter the war as a result of the sinking, but it was two more years before a formal declaration was issued. Still, the tragedy galvanized moderate public opinion in the United States firmly against Germany and significantly influenced the activities of both the Allied and Central Powers during the conflict.

Advertising

of the 1910s

At the start of the decade, ad campaigns were primitive, hit-or-miss affairs relying on little more than the instincts of the copywriters or manufacturers. Following the war, many national promotions involved intensive market analysis and the services of dozens of professionals. The explosive growth of ads in the 1910s anchored the many new forms of popular culture, reinforcing the desire to go to the ballpark, buy a new car, or see the latest movie.

ADVERTISING MODERNITY

Advertising during the 1910s needed to address the fact that American society had modernized. For example, the rapid expansion of railroads and a banking infrastructure made a mass consumer market a possibility. Population growth sustained this marketplace, while the great improvements in literacy allowed their appeals to be read. Finally, the majority of Americans now worked and lived in cities, thereby thrusting themselves into a rapidly changing social and economic environment.

As a result, advertising in the decade revolved around three key themes. The first was an effort to help the individual find meaning in an increasingly complex and bureaucratized world. Modern comforts and lifestyles were in sharp contrast to the production of basic needs—food, clothing, and utensils—which had previously occupied the lives of most Americans. Even the new industrial workers, less profoundly influenced than the growing white-collar population, found that they were less involved in creating a tangible product than in performing a mechanized routine. In such a setting, citizens needed new meaning for themselves, their work, and their lives. Advertising addressed this need by providing significance, however fleeting, to consumer goods.

Second, advertising offered "solutions" to many of modern life's newest problems. Frustrations with modernity and the faster pace of living were common, and advertisers sought to ease these psychological pressures by assuring their clients that their goods were the latest and most progressive products available. As a result, the advertising styles changed markedly throughout the decade. Ads that provided simple information about a product gave way to those that demonstrated, often visually, how the item could solve basic problems of modern living.

Finally, ads helped to create a new standard of conduct. Urban living, industrialization, and the move toward bureaucratic hierarchy made social interactions more complex. What were the new standards of conduct? Was how one dressed as important as one's character? In many ways, these were the sort of guides that many wanted

ADVERTISING SLOGANS OF THE 1910s

"I Want You," U.S. Army, 1917

"The skin you love to touch," Woodbury Soap, 1911*

"When it rains it pours," Morton Salt, 1911*

"Say it with flowers," American Florist Association, 1910s

"The penalty of leadership," Cadillac, 1915*

The instrument of the immortals," Steinway & Sons, 1919*

---

* Among *Advertising Age's* 100 Best Ads of 20th Century. http://adage.com/century/.

Two women pasting billboard posters, Cincinnati, May 1912. Prints & Photographs Division, Library of Congress.

when confronted with the mysteries of fast-paced urban living. Most Americans first confronted novel technologies, fashions, and fads through national advertising.

The manner and scope in which advertising expanded during the 1910s illustrates these changes. Total advertising volumes in the United States increased from approximately $256 million in 1900 to about $682 million in 1914, and then reached $1,409 million by 1919.[1] While little is known about revenues for local newspapers, direct mail campaigns, or local publicity efforts (such as sandwich board walkers), the numbers provide a clear indication of the rapid expansion of national advertising.

NEWSPAPERS AND BILLBOARDS

Newspapers played an active role in the growth of the industry. Daily and weekly presses had, for decades, relied on the revenues from their sales copy to augment their subscription earnings. But typesetting technology limited innovation and, as a result, most ads were restricted to certain preformatted sections of paper (usually the front page), changed copy infrequently, and used few pictures or other imagery.

Bill posters (advertising posters) were potential sources for advertising growth. Standardizing on three formats in 1900, and seeking to regulate itself through the Associated Bill Posters' Association, the industry did not suffer from lack

of imagination or limited artistic formats. Almost any artist could publicly display his or her pitches regardless of taste or quality. The public outrage over the more vulgar attempts, aided by monthly editorials in competing advertising forums such as magazines and newspapers, forced the industry to seek greater controls. By creating a national licensing system, a classification for bill quality, and an oversight board to suggest policies for improved public relations, the bill posters industry eliminated much of the antagonism directed against their efforts. Although active in the 1910s, particularly during the war years, billboard advertising hit its stride only in subsequent decades when Americans took to the roads in their automobiles.

MAGAZINE ADVERTISING

The premiere advertising forum of the 1910s was the periodical. By and large, the earliest magazines were financed through subscriptions by individual consumers. Advertisers were convinced that active consumers were, in fact, avid readers of specific publications. The advertising style began to mirror the editorial content of each publication, reasoning that what attracted a reader to an article might also persuade them to purchase a new product. The most prolific advertisers were those who sold relatively common products (such as soap, shirt collars, or cigarettes) to a broad yet selective audience. Gossipy, casual publications such as *Cosmopolitan, Ladies' Home Journal,* and the *Saturday Evening Post* seemed the most logical choice for such advertisements. Now that they had access to an urban middle class eager to understand trends quickly and cope with the complexities of modern life, advertisers soon poured millions of dollars into the glossy monthlies. In 1917 alone, the *Saturday Evening Post* earned more than $17 million in advertising revenues.[2] More than half of the pages of the typical magazine, which usually extended to 100 pages per issue, were devoted to advertisements.

The vast influx of advertising revenues allowed publishers to sell their journals at nearly the same cost that it took to print them—and occasionally below cost, thereby expanding circulation. This then compelled other advertisers to spend their money likewise. Occasionally, demand outstripped supply, and many publications lost money by undercharging advertisers. As a result,

AFRICAN AMERICAN MAGAZINES

Many periodicals intended for non-middle-class and white audiences struggled to find the necessary sponsorship that would propel circulation. For example, magazines intended for the African American community repeatedly struggled, usually in vain, for survival. Up to 1910, the two biggest of these were *The Colored American* and *Voices of the Negro*. Neither journal claimed more than 20,000 paid subscribers. While divisive debates surrounding Booker T. Washington's accommodation of Jim Crow legislation did not help, it was the lack of advertising subsidies that kept most magazines struggling. When W.E.B. Du Bois, a professor at Atlanta University, took the post of director of the newly founded National Association for the Advancement of Colored People (NAACP) in 1910, he founded what was probably the strongest African American publication of the era: *Crisis: A Record of the Darker Races*. Circulation grew from 9,000 in 1911 to more than 35,000 by 1915, but Du Bois could rely on little outside support beyond the subscription funds funneled to him by the NAACP.

John Tebbel and Mary Ellen Zuckerman, *The Magazine in America: 1741–1990* (New York: Oxford University Press, 1991), 131–39.

magazines and advertising agencies became closely linked in their goals.

REFORMING MADISON AVENUE

While newspapers, billboards, and magazines were essential in the spread of advertising, it was the evolution of professional advertising agencies and their new advertising styles that revolutionized the industry in the 1910s. The large agencies, centered in New York, Chicago, and Philadelphia, were the driving force behind the modernization of advertising pitches.

The chief obstacle threatening the success of these agencies was the pervasive fear that advertising was little more than trickery. Tensions mounted in the 1900s as muckrakers and other Progressive reformers exposed the impurities and toxic additives routinely contained within the nation's food

An ad for Manoli's Gibson Girl cigarettes. Color poster by Lucian Bernhard, 1883–1972. Prints & Photographs Division, Library of Congress.

and drug supply. Advertising agencies, which had been extolling the virtues of many of the worst offenders, were connected with these villains.

The Progressive crusades in the 1900s did two things to help advertisers in the 1910s. First, the largest advertising firms came to follow the editorial lead of the most prominent periodicals. Editors such as the *Ladies' Home Journal's* Edward Bok dictated many of the products that they were willing to market on their pages. With the forced exclusion of many of the most egregious offenders, such as alcohol products and patent medicines, the largest agencies were able to free themselves from the negative connotations associated with these products. Second, self-regulation such as the Associated Advertising Clubs of America (1911) was created with the goal of freeing the medium from falsehoods and deceptions. The strong connections between editors and publishers created an unwritten but powerful layer of censorship, which served as reform for the decade. Just as the *Ladies' Home Journal* could set the boundaries, so too could advertisers now claim to be acting in the best interests of the consumer. This new public legitimacy freed agencies to experiment with new and aggressive advertising styles in the 1910s. When, during World War I, the U.S. government added its blessing to advertising, it solidified the trust and confidence of willing consumers.

COMMUNICATING THROUGH ADVERTISEMENTS

The 1910s saw the widespread use of images, pictures, and icons to facilitate this new form of communication. Unlike traditional ads, which promoted specific products, sales events, or prices (in other words, promotions that were tied to a concrete reality), new, largely national advertising avoided any mention of specifics and focused their appeal on abstractions. Abstract words printed in newspapers and magazines allowed consumers to pour their own hopes, fears, and illusions into the products. The people characterized in ads represented how people wanted to be seen rather than how they appeared in reality.

Two dominant styles of advertising were used during the decade. The more common was the reason-why or hard-sell approach. Based on "plain speaking," these pitches hoped to cloak their products in honesty and virtue, dispelling the fear that one might be taken in by fancy sales talk. They suggested that suppliers were simply in the business of meeting consumer demand, as opposed to creating demand, as many had begun to fear.

Reason-why advertising was often referred to as "salesmanship on paper" because it supposedly conveyed the same information a hired representative might convey if given the opportunity to meet with every consumer. Typical reason-why ads prominently displayed the product at the center of the pitch. Little space was wasted in elaborate or unclear imagery that did not directly reflect upon the product. An example of such an approach was the Ivory Soap campaign from 1907 to 1909, which showed the bar of soap as the

A straightforward approach to explaining the benefits of Ivory Soap are seen in this ad. © Corbis/Bettman.

foundation for such well-known structures as the Washington Monument, the Great Pyramid, and the Arch de Triumphe. The ad copy is presented as straightforward and "honest." Consumers could feel confident that Procter & Gamble had a high level of trust in Ivory Soap and, by extension, so should they.

The soft-sell, or impressionistic, approach was laden with atmosphere and meaning. Extensive artwork, detailed layouts, and clear associations between the product and human feeling characterized the ads. Generally these promotions placed human actors at the center of the ads, showing how the products might be used to benefit consumers. Soft-sell advertisements were a new and profoundly revolutionary form of commercial expression during the 1910s.[3]

More than any other format, the atmosphere advertising style was best able to take advantage of the complexity and insecurity generated by modern living. For example, Arrow collars and shirts were sold with little more than pictures of men smugly secure within this new society. Others, such as the advertisers of Pebesco Tooth Paste and Odorono, took a more threatening stance. Promising to prevent "Acid-Mouth," which inevitably led to the loss of teeth, a Pebesco ad showed a young woman smiling in disbelief as an old toothless man warned, "I once had good teeth like yours, my dear." Odorono, an antiperspirant for women, humorlessly provided "a frank discussion of a subject too often avoided." Showing an attractive woman in close contact with a dashing suitor, the copy warned that "fastidious women who want to be absolutely sure of their daintiness have found that they could not trust to their own consciousness," however, Odorono would ensure a woman's "perfect daintiness." In each case, the product offered a solution to a modern problem that most became aware of only by reading these ads.

EFFECTIVENESS OF ADVERTISING

Most advertising agencies and manufacturers in the 1910s used a mixture of both styles of advertising. Promoters themselves had little sense of what was most effective, and many were wary of spending the ever-increasing sums needed to stay

in the public eye. Henry Ford, for example, alternated between a grudging acceptance of mass advertising and outright hostility.

Another problem for manufacturers during the decade was the relative novelty of their wares. For example, a range of electrically powered products were introduced for home use, including refrigerators, toasters, irons, fans, sewing machines, washing machines, and even dishwashers. Electricity, however, was available in only a small number of homes. It was not until 1910 that a standard electrical current was agreed upon by power providers. These limitations did not stop manufacturers, such as the Hoover Suction Sweeper Company, who advertised their new electric vacuums in the most important national magazines. Stressing modernity, cleanliness, and ease of use, the Hoover ads were, in a sense, preparing a marketplace for their products as electrification came to more homes.

Coca-Cola

Soft drinks originated as inexpensive consumer indulgences that were made to order at drugstores and specialty soda fountains. Initially, most of these syrups were the result of failed experiments at creating useful medicines. Pharmacist John Pemberton created just such a potion, sometime between 1880 and 1886, to cure headaches. In 1886, Willis E. Venable began serving Pemberton's creation at his soda fountain in Atlanta, which he named Coca-Cola Syrup and Extract. Two years later, wholesale druggist Asa Candler, also from Atlanta, took control over production and began exporting and advertising the popular syrup around the country. When Candler retired from the firm in 1916, his net worth exceeded $50 million.

As a product that originated as a patent medicine, Coca-Cola was susceptible to the consumer pressures that resulted from the 1906 Pure Food and Drug Act. While the firm claimed in 1916 that the soft drink contained only "pure water sterilized by boiling,"[4] sugar, flavoring extracts, caramel, caffeine, and citric and phosphoric acids, regulators were concerned that the drink included other substances, ranging from cocaine (which was present in small quantities until the turn of the century) to alcohol (which had never been used). The name Coca-Cola referred to coca and cola leaves, which were the source of the extracts. By the 1910s, however, most of these constituents were far removed from the production of the syrup. Other products also relied on these seemingly simple naming conventions: Pepsi-Cola was thought to contain pepsin to aid digestion; Palmolive soaps were taken from the oils of palm and olive plants. Still, in 1909, Dr. Harvey Wiley, head of the Bureau of Chemistry of the Department of Agriculture, accused Coca-Cola, whom he termed "dope peddlers," of violating the Pure Food and Drug Act because their product contained *no* coca and very little cola.[5] The suit was eventually settled in the soft drink company's favor in 1918.

Early Coca-Cola ad using the baseball personality Napoleon "Nap" Lajoie for product endorsement. The ad shows Lajoie on the baseball grounds as members of the audience drink Coca-Cola, January 1, 1910. Photo by Transcendental Graphics/Getty Images.

The evolution of Coca-Cola's advertising illustrates the transformation of the industry as the firm moved from strong, reason-why promotions to more subtle and effervescent ones. The firm clearly believed that its product, which contained caffeine, provided a functional relief from headaches and drowsiness. Reflecting their roots as a soothing and inexpensive indulgence, ads in the 1900s provided brief and well-reasoned justifications for its consumption. In 1904, one spot proclaimed "Coca-Cola is a delightful, palatable, healthful beverage." The following year, the product was hailed because it "revives and sustains." By the 1910s, however, the promotions began to appeal to more emotional, less factual benefits. For example, advertisements asked consumers to "Enjoy a glass of liquid laughter" (1911), drink "The Best beverage under the sun" or "The Best drink anyone can buy" (1913), because the beverage was "Pure and wholesome" (1914).

Model T

Automobile advertisements also used both the hard and soft-sell approaches. The growth of the industry drove the need for greater product differentiation. When little more than 4,100 cars were manufactured in 1900, there was not a great need to distinguish a Packard from a Chalmer from a Pierce. As these production figures began to balloon—from 181,000 cars in 1910, to 895,500 five years later, to almost two million units by 1920—manufacturers turned to advertising to spur their sales.[6] Appealing to the consumers of such expensive and durable goods was more difficult than convincing Americans to spend a nickel for a cold soda. Were the purchasing decisions of consumers influenced more by technology—in which case a reason-why approach might be more useful—or did people buy for prestige?

Impressionistic copy seemed to predominate. The Jordan Automobile Company, for example, claimed their car allowed modern drivers freedom to yield "to the whims of the moment."[7] In 1917, the Overland Car Company pictured the "Four Greatest Events" in the life of the average American as getting married, buying a home, having a baby, "and buying your Overland."

Ford Motor Company went the furthest from this industry trend in its advertising between 1910 and 1919. The source of this difference can generally be attributed to Henry Ford's goal to provide a truly low-cost yet quality product. Ford's development of the interchangeable assembly-line production process was critical to this approach. In 1910, it took his firm an average of 12 hours and 28 minutes to complete work on one auto. With the completion of his new Highland Park assembly plant in 1913, however, this number fell dramatically. By 1914, it took Ford only one hour and 33 minutes to construct a Model T. As a result, more than 300,000 cars were manufactured that year, half a million the following year, and more than two million in 1923. With mass production came lowered costs, and the price of a Model T fell from $440 in 1915 to $290 in 1925.[8]

Henry Ford believed that it was his "better car," not some esoteric and psychological need on the part of consumers, that sold his cars.

Ford also looked to benefit from free publicity which, in essence, did much of the emotional promotion for him. For example, his well-noted and liberal minimum wage and maximum daily hour policies, commencing in 1914, earned the firm much public praise. Moreover, Ford successfully battled the Association of Licensed Automobile Manufacturers, a trust consisting of such heavyweights as Cadillac, Oldsmobile, and Packard, to obtain the rights for a gasoline-powered engine. This image of Ford as trustbuster and populist, combined with the car's low cost and reliability, freed the firm to pursue more hard-hitting, reason-why promotions when the competition was headed in the opposite direction. According

Henry Ford, standing between the first and ten-millionth Ford cars made. Prints & Photographs Division, Library of Congress.

CIGARETTE ADVERTISING

Tobacco consumption in the United States increased significantly during the latter 1910s. Prior to this time, most tobacco consumers either chewed plug tobacco or smoked the shredded leaves in a pipe. In 1881, James B. Duke introduced a mechanized roller that could produce more than 100,000 cigarettes per day. "Buck" Duke parlayed his production advantage into market dominance when he formed the American Tobacco Company (ATC) in 1890. As a trust, ATC was busted in 1911 into the new American Tobacco Company, Liggett & Meyers, R. J. Reynolds Tobacco, and P. Lorillard and Company, and these four maintained market dominance throughout the decade.

As with soft drinks and automobiles, cigarettes were advertised both for the rational and emotional reasons to smoke them. Consumers were advised to try American cigarettes because they were milder on the throat than the Turkish varieties, and since they were pre-rolled, they were convenient to smoke. However, critics were already charging that cigarette usage was unhealthy and unappealing. Noteworthy individuals and groups—including Henry Ford, Thomas Edison, the Women's Christian Temperance Union, and Marshall Field—were undermining much of the reason-why cigarette ads.

Rather than continue a losing campaign over the health benefits derived from smoking, many suppliers turned to impressionistic appeals. The makers of Pall Mall cigarettes pitched their brand as the smoke of the rich globe-trotter. R. J. Reynolds came up with one of the most successful campaigns for their brand Camel. Beginning in newspapers, Reynolds started a cryptic campaign of announcing, in 1915, "The CAMELS are coming." Modeled after a smiling dromedary named "Old Joe" from the Barnum and Bailey circus, the camel became an emblem of an inexpensive, mild cigarette made from Turkish and domestic tobaccos and intended for a mass audience. Reynolds completed the picture of brand loyalty with the slogan, "I'd walk a mile for a Camel," and showed people willing to go to great lengths to ensure that they obtained their one true choice. These appeals had their intended effect. By 1919 Camel was the most popular ready-rolled cigarette in the world. Liggett & Meyers, ATC, and R. J. Reynolds controlled more than 82 percent of the market by 1925.

James D. Norris, *Advertising and the Transformation of American Society,* Contributions in Economics and Economic History, no. 110 (Westport, CT: Greenwood Press, 1990), 138–39, 141; Charles Goodrum and Helen Dalrymple, *Advertising in America: The First 200 Years* (New York: Harry N. Abrams, 1990), 195.

to historian James D. Norris, by 1915 "when Ford's advertisement for the Model T simply showed a picture of the 'Tin Lizzie' touring car model with the caption 'BUY IT BECAUSE IT IS A BETTER CAR,' most Americans believed him." Many auto makers were forced to rely on ads that highlighted the social status and prestige of their cars because of Ford's dominance at the low-end of the market spectrum.[9]

ADVERTISING THE WAR

American advertising was certainly modern by the time the United States entered World War I. As a result, the war did not transform advertising as much as it promoted its efficacy in the larger business community. As manufacturers shifted to wartime production and lost opportunities to sell to the public, they had an even greater need for subtle advertising that allowed them to remain visible without appearing to be callous.

Ironically, while manufacturers increasingly soft sold their products during the war, the U.S. government used hard-sell advertising to sell the conflict to the American public. In the first days after war had been declared, President Woodrow Wilson selected George Creel to head the Committee on Public Information to accomplish this task. Creel, a muckraker from Kansas City and Denver, was so effective that his name became synonymous with the committee. Most notable were Creel's "four-minute men," a veritable army of propagandists who gave more than 75,000 short, patriotic public lectures. The Creel Committee generated nearly 75 million pamphlets and more than 6,000 press releases.[10] The Red Scare and ethnic and racial intolerance evidenced after the war suggest that there were a few unintended consequences of the Committee's powerful messages.

The modern advertising styles were most obvious in the Division of Pictorial Publicity headed by artist Charles Dana Gibson, but also including such notables as Howard Chandler Christy and James Montgomery Flagg. Playing off the hardest sell of all—human life—the poster artists tugged repeatedly at Americans' sense of duty, patriotism, and humanitarianism. Flagg's legendary portrayal of "Uncle Sam" unflinchingly demanding "I Want You" leaves little to the imagination and almost defies the viewer to not buy into the war effort. While most war art played off of these positive values, others played off of the not-very-subtle racial and ethnic biases of most American citizens.

In 1918, the trade journal *Printers Ink* concluded, "The war has been won by advertising, as well as by soldiers and munitions. It has been a four-year strife between the powers of repression and concealment and the powers of expression and enlightenment."[11]

Architecture

of the 1910s

Of all architectural forms, the skyscraper is undeniably the most American. Introduced in the late nineteenth century, high-rise buildings represented a unique American blend of progress, commerce, culture, and democracy. The stunning heights of these massive structures, rising more than 800 feet from the ground by the 1910s, became a symbol of American optimism and ingenuity.

At the same time, the rise of affordable housing communities, such as Allwood in Passaic, New Jersey, or Goodyear Heights and Firestone Park in Akron, Ohio, and the growing availability of the private automobile in the 1910s had long-term implications for domestic architecture. Less obvious reforms, such as the 1913 Constitutional amendment that created a graduated income tax, sapped the unlimited spending of many of the very wealthy. Finally, the war cut many of the ties between the American and European branches of the profession, and many fewer aspiring designers traveled to Paris's École des Beaux-Arts after 1914.

FORM AND MEANING

American architects in the 1910s found themselves torn between providing a building that was serviceable for the people who would use it and the desire to make a lasting artistic impression. The type of structure under consideration figured greatly in the amount of latitude a designer had. For example, vernacular or folk architecture, which relied on tried and true methods of construction that were passed on informally from generation to generation using readily available materials, produced little artistic variation in form. Most early nineteenth-century houses, for example, are quite uniform throughout the country. By contrast, academic or high-art architecture looked for particular ideas and emotions to be delivered by buildings specifically commissioned for construction. Relying on historical motifs, these designers used the symbols of the Gothic cathedral or the Greek and Roman temple, for example, to signify a particular theme. By the 1910s, American architects mixed and matched these well-known motifs to create a style all their own. The rise of mass production and, especially, the use of modern building materials in both vernacular and academic design blended the relationship between form and function even further.

The best term to describe the architectural style of the 1910s is eclectic, that is, a selection of components from various other sources. To critics, this characteristic suggests that there was no particular style of the 1910s. In actuality, the eclectic style was a distinct method of design in that it avoided *one specific* historical model. The decade saw a greater tolerance of informal design elements that many connoisseurs found distasteful. Spanish influences from California and Florida, Pueblo motifs from the Southwest, and Creole styles from New Orleans, for example, were added to the palettes of architects throughout the decade. Traditional vernacular and academic designs remained strong, but it was now much more likely for a suburb or city to contain a hodgepodge of styles rather than merely variations on a central theme.

The four mainstays of the era were Classical, Gothic, Renaissance, and Romanesque design. Each had its own specialized treatments, such as the neoclassical and beaux arts classical. The Classical style refers to a Roman temple design that raises the base of the foundation off the level of the ground, uses a four-column portico or entryway, and has simple, unadorned moldings. The Gothic style is noted for its steeply pitched roofs, multiple dormers, relatively simple lines, and use of stone exteriors. Renaissance and Romanesque architecture are decidedly more formal and academic in composition. The Renaissance style is characterized by a strictly repeated regularity in rectangular window and door designs and strong horizontal belts for each floor. Each floor is also distinguished by a slight but noticeable change in the treatment of the brick exterior. The roof line is either flat or augmented by a balustrade or railing. Romanesque design is set off by the repeated use of archways, brick or stone exteriors, towers at the corners, and, in the case of the Richardsonian Romanesque, an intentional sense of great mass and volume. During the 1910s, architects often mixed these elements within single buildings.

These standard forms provided not only guidance for designers, but also a "standard vocabulary" for the public. When comparing the Classical, Gothic, Renaissance, and Romanesque forms above, one might just as easily have called these the bank, church, townhouse, and university styles, respectively. Increasingly in the 1910s, architects

Municipal Building, Des Moines City Hall. Designed in the Beaux Arts classical style of civic architecture, it was built in 1911. Prints & Photographs Division, Library of Congress.

created new combinations using standard materials, shapes, ornamentation, and proportions.

When used without restraint, eclecticism tended to degenerate into mad collections of styles and ornamentation. Mass-produced woodwork and other accessories undermined the academic architects' claim that historical design uplifted and educated the citizenry. When, from 1900 to 1920, elite draftsmen began to downplay and soften the historical elements of their buildings, the road was paved for modernists to discard them.

MODERN MATERIALS

Several powerful forces that were changing the architectural and social landscape of America. The first of these was the development of new and better building materials. By 1900, most suppliers of wood had standardized their millwork, allowing architects to order a wider variety of wood types with the assurance that a "two-by-four" or standard joist was the same regardless of the lumberyard. Mechanized millwork also improved, so moldings, doors, shutters, blinds, gables, and trim arrived at job sites in a much more polished and uniform state. Brick presses fashioned masonry in a variety of designs and colors. Finally, the spread of affordable pane glass reduced the traditional reliance upon the small and expensive rows of glass seen in many preindustrial structures. Providers often sold completely framed windows and doors, trimmed in the specific style requested by the designer.

The increased availability of affordable steel led to larger, taller buildings. A steel frame distributed the load throughout the structure and practically eliminated height constraints. The use of steel support beams also meant that internal spaces could now be opened, allowing for larger rooms without walls. The resulting structure was lighter and therefore could be built higher, and it was also more open to air and light.

Safety elevators, telephones, electricity, and incandescent lighting made these vast interior spaces functional. By 1910, architects relied heavily on these basic technical and engineering innovations in their construction.

A change in the training of architects also led to changes in the field. Most nineteenth-century American architects were trained informally, apprenticed at an established firm, in studios, or with construction companies. Here they absorbed the basic historical vocabulary of design. It was not until the latter part of the 1800s that standard skills were developed by the American Institute of Architects and formal training was provided by such universities as Massachusetts Institute of Technology, Yale, the University of Illinois, and Cornell University.

Good architecture fit into and augmented a larger, citywide plan. Seeking to place a structure within a "proper" environmental setting, natural designers, such as Frederick Law Olmsted, Calvert Vaux, and Charles Adams Platt formed the American Society of Landscape Architects in 1899 to help designers to see the building within its "natural setting" (which was often manufactured, as in the case of Central Park in New York City). The connection between the structure and its immediate environment had been recognized by most academic architects by 1910.

City planning was formalized around 1900, and noteworthy commissions were formed in cities such as Cleveland, Chicago, Washington, D.C., and San Francisco. In 1910, the National City Planning Association was founded to help designers incorporate their plans better into the larger needs of the metropolis. Led by Charles Mumford Robinson, advocates believed in a "science" of city design, which provided tangible benefits to the city's residents. By 1916, New York City became the first municipality to zone its space for specific purposes (e.g., residential, commercial), a trend that spread rapidly to other towns and, later, the suburbs.

ÉCOLE DES BEAUX-ARTS

While architecture, landscape design, and city planning were well understood by most architects, no American institution had the cultural or intellectual authority to unify designers into a single school of thought. As had been the case throughout the nineteenth century, the best and brightest American architects turned to Europe, in particular to France, for guidance and leadership. The École des Beaux-Arts in Paris became the most influential institution in American architectural design. Many of the most prominent American designers either attended the Beaux-Arts or worked in partnership with architects who had. While it too changed over time, the central mission of the French school was to unify the theory of the design (called the *parti*) with both the rational needs of the structure and city and the emotional or artistic desires of the architects and patrons.

American students seemed intent on fashioning their own unique solutions while using the traditional methods countenanced by their European masters. It was here that the eclectic style was born. For example, after influential architect Ernest Flagg studied at the Beaux-Arts for nearly three years, he felt he had absorbed as much academic classicism and structural rationalism as possible. Flagg, however, had no interest in remaining in Europe or in earning any of the prestigious prizes awarded to the most accomplished students. What Flagg and the other Americans seemed most impressed with was the *parti*.

The work of these French-influenced draftsmen was soon seen across the United States through a variety of popular and trade presses. By 1910, only the most isolated vernacular architects were unaware of the *parti* and the freedom of eclectic design. Periodicals included the *American Architect and Building News, American Architect,* the *Architectural Record,* the *Brickbuilder, American Builder's Companion,* and the *Modern Builder's Guide.* The last two of these addressed the needs of builders and contractors rather than those of the design artists. Mass magazines, such as the *Ladies' Home Journal* and *Better Homes and Gardens,* began to highlight "ideal homes" and designs, further popularizing and supporting eclecticism and the architects who favored it. Many popular writers and critics gained fame by popularizing and critiquing the latest designs. Finally, the vernacular pattern books, which provided pictorial indexes of most of the major styles of exterior and interior treatments, were wildly popular with the public.

PUBLIC BUILDINGS

The most forceful American architectural expression of the decade was clearly the skyscraper.

As historian Carter Wideman noted, "They are, after all, the way Americans explain how high Superman can leap in a single bound."[1] While height is, in itself, an impressive characteristic of building design, very often early designers lost sight of proportion.

New York's Singer Tower was an unfortunate example of this type of problem. Designed by Ernest Flagg and completed in 1908, the 47-floor, 612-foot structure was for a short time the tallest building in the world (and later the tallest building ever torn down, in 1968). Flagg appended a needlelike tower to his conventional, mansard-roofed, Beaux-Arts design. The exaggerated French Baroque design was highlighted by a garish green and red terra cotta exterior.

The Singer Tower is notable for its role in bringing about new urban zoning laws. While construction for Singer Tower was under way, City Investing Company began work on an equally tall structure on the same block. It soon became apparent that the buildings would crowd each other out for attention, and also for the much-needed natural light and breezes. Flagg approached city planners with a proposal to restrict the amount of vertical space a building could claim based on the area of the structure at the ground level and the width of the streets servicing the region. Opposed by prominent designer D. Knickerbocker Boyd, who wanted shorter but more spacious towers, discussion continued at the Heights of Buildings Commission of New York City from 1913 until 1916. When a resolution was passed by the planners, the city's set-back or wedding-cake building design became law. It decreed that after a developer had reached 25 percent of the lot area, it could build a skyscraper of any height. On 25 percent of the lot, a developer could build a slender tower, which is what happened in New York and throughout other cities.[2]

For the remaining quarter, there were no height restrictions. The New York zoning law was soon copied by many other cities, giving the American urban landscape a unique, ziggurat-like appearance that would last until the 1960s.

The Woolworth Building demonstrated how the eclectic style could result in a true work of art. Financed entirely in cash by retailing mogul Frank Woolworth (and retained by the company until 1998), the structure was designed by Cass Gilbert and engineered by Gunvald Aus from 1910 to 1913. Unlike the Singer Building, which relied on embellishments for dramatic effect, the Woolworth Building used a seemingly traditional Gothic motif to soar 57 stories, or 792 feet, above the streets of New York. Gilbert softened the heavier elements of the Gothic style, removing most of the horizontal breaks that would prevent an observer's eye from rising with it. At the top, the Gothic finials, gargoyles, and flying buttresses were oversized so as to be seen and experienced from the streets below. The Gothic theme is carried into the interiors, lending a sense of wholeness to the structure and leading Reverend S. Parkes Cadman, who attended the opening ceremonies with dignitaries including President Woodrow Wilson, to dub the Woolworth Building the "Cathedral of Commerce."[3] In many ways, the Woolworth Building was the fulfillment of the eclectic style. Employing the most modern technology (including a bank of 30 elevators that could reach the top floors in less than a minute) and built with contemporary materials, the building could be stripped of its Gothic exterior and be indistinguishable from the emerging International Style.

Numerous other public buildings of note were either constructed or completed in the 1910s. Pennsylvania Station, designed by the New York firm of McKim, Mead, and White, suggested that neoclassicism could still provide utility while conferring beauty and tranquility to an important civic space. Covering two entire city blocks, the central rail station of New York relied on the same steel girder construction as did its loftier neighbors. The external colonnade design, completed in 1911, complemented the internal vaults which took passengers and visitors more than 45 feet below street level. For the nation's largest rail station to remain functional, McKim varied the internal spaces so that areas that were to provide swift passage were small and low-ceilinged, while the ticketing and debarkation points, places where people might linger, were large and high. Razed in 1963, the site is now occupied by Madison Square Garden. Pennsylvania Station's less impressive relation, Grand Central Terminal (in essence, an inner-city depot of the station),

constructed in 1913, was designated a National Historic Landmark in 1976.

The New York Public Library was completed during the decade. Founded in 1886 by the largess of Samuel J. Tilden, who bequeathed about $2.4 million to create and maintain a public reading resource, the city library merged with two semiprivate collections in 1895 to form the base of the current institution. The library immediately sought a permanent home to accommodate its immense collection (now second only to the Library of Congress). Although the foundation was laid in 1902, the final construction of the library, including the placement of the now famous lions, was not completed until 1911. Commissioned to the relatively obscure firm of Carre're and Hastings, the exterior was patterned along the relatively traditional Beaux-Arts style. It was the public nature of the space, providing access to books to tens of thousands of readers and visitors on its very first day, which makes the New York Public Library such an extraordinary building.

Finally, the architecture of many semipublic institutions was also greatly shaped by American eclecticism. Many colleges were either opening or augmenting their campus facilities. The eclectic genre melded nicely with the needs of the university as developers were asked to design unified campuses that showed both deference to the past and confidence in the future. Rice University in Houston, Texas, and the Massachusetts Institute of Technology in Boston, provide excellent examples of this widespread architectural trend in the 1910s; however, perhaps American eclecticism was best applied at the U.S. Military Academy at West Point, New York. Ralph Adams Cram won the commission for the academy in 1903, and construction continued until it was completed in 1910. Cram's selection of a neo-Gothic motif for the main hall and chapel gave West Point a clean, Spartan, and decidedly masculine atmosphere.

Public monuments were also key architectural legacies of the decade. Most prominent among these was the Lincoln Memorial, commissioned in 1911 by Congress and constructed between 1914 and 1922. Henry Bacon's design, like that of Charles McKim for Pennsylvania Station, used traditional Classical motifs, in this case a Greek, Doric-columned temple. As was typical with the eclectic style, Bacon modified the form to keep the best elements—giving the structure an openness and serenity that was suitable to Abraham Lincoln's memory—while maintaining functional access for the public. Such simple modifications as rotating the axis of the building by 90 degrees to allow for a more dramatic facade to face the reflecting pool, also under construction, created symmetry with the existing Washington Monument and anchored the Washington Mall area. The massive sculpture of a seated and peaceful Lincoln, completed by Daniel Chester French, was assembled at the site near the end of 1919. Combined with the president's two most cited speeches (the Gettysburg Address and his Second Inaugural) and symbolic references to the Union that Lincoln helped to preserve, Bacon's memorial became one of the most popular and solemn public places in the nation's capital.

PRIVATE BUILDINGS

By the turn of the century, home ownership had become an important civic characteristic of the middle class. Tenement-style living was still rare, and the single-family detached home accounted for from between half and three-quarters of all housing starts from 1890 to 1930. The styles employed in designing these homes were the visible markers of an owner's relative "respectability."

The earliest suburbs of the nation's largest cities drew families disproportionately from the upper economic categories. Towns such as Oak Park or Evanston, near Chicago, and Brookline, near Boston, declined offers by the major cities to annex them. This growing population of wealthy clients offered architects new places for them to design their ideal structures. Moreover, the advent of new technologies—such as electricity and indoor plumbing—removed many of the restraints to design that led developers to accept the limits of vernacular design without challenge.

By the 1910s the many heavily ornamented suburban Queen Anne and Eastlake homes were beginning to look dated. The affectations of domesticity seemed silly in an era when modernity was quickly outdating old traditions. The consumer revolution brought new, disposable products and ready-made foods, which eliminated the need for large work spaces in the home. Parlors and large hallways seemed foolish in an era when formal private visitations were disappearing in favor of more public entertainments. In the new decade, simplicity had replaced formality, and the Victorians were most certainly not simple.

The search for simplicity consumed residential architects for most of the 1910s. The focus on honesty in form and presentation was termed by practitioners an "organic" style, which attempted to build structures appropriate for the owners, the site, and the community. Organic architectural styles favored lightly treated natural surfaces, such as wood and stone, and intrinsic colors rather than the ornate and painted millwork that festooned most Victorian homes. Minimalism was also a quality of organic home design, as architects tried to reduce the need for expensive upkeep and cleaning while making each room multifunctional. Floor plans also changed significantly. Most first floor layouts were now circular, allowing easy access to every room. Kitchens were dramatically reduced in size, and back staircases and servants' quarters were eliminated. Upstairs, it was rare to find homes with more than three simple bedrooms, instead of the four or five bedrooms typical of the Victorian. Even for the least expensive new homes, built-ins were used wherever possible, including closets, which replaced free-standing armoires, laundry chutes, and bathroom fixtures. Such a house was less of a social statement and more a place for a family to care for its needs efficiently so that they might make their statements elsewhere in the increasingly public American life. These trends in organic and minimalist styles led directly to a standardization of home production and, as a result, a lowering of the cost for home ownership.

FRANK LLOYD WRIGHT

Frank Lloyd Wright continued as a leader in architecture, and in particular, in organic design. A Midwesterner by birth, Wright was ambitious, self-assured, and an architectural genius. Trained informally as a commercial architect with some of the era's greatest designers, Wright won international fame largely on the basis of his residential structures, which came to define the "Prairie school" of design. (See "Architecture of the 1900s.") While the esthetic of the Prairie school is profound, Wright was equally capable in using the newest technologies and building theories. The Tokyo Imperial Hotel, built from 1916 to 1923, is a case in point. Wright's use of steel and concrete opened the doors for innovations in a multitude of buildings.

Wright designed and erected Taliesin, his home, studio, and retreat, in 1911 at his family's estate near Spring Green, Wisconsin. At 37,000 square feet, Taliesin had ample space and a strong emotional connection to the land, which allowed Wright's architectural imagination to run free. Significantly, he placed his home not on the crest of the hill (which would have lifted the structure away from its natural environment) but on the "brow" of the hill. (*Taliesin* is a name meaning "shining brow" in Welsh.) Unfortunately, fires have left little of the original structure intact. As Wright rebuilt, he remained true to his vision of an organic structure that was both part of nature and also the product of a man's hand.

In the 1910s, the Prairie school design principles were well demonstrated by a host of Wright's apprentices. George Elmslie, Dwight H. Perkins, George Maher, and Walter Burley Griffin, and others, continued and expanded the new style in places well outside of Wright's Midwest. The basic characteristics of these homes remained relatively consistent, and included a minimal number of rooms, a close integration between site and structure, few interior walls, exterior walls replaced with windows whenever possible, built-in utilities and many built-in furnishings, minimal extraneous ornamentation, and no "fashionable" (i.e., non-Prairie) decor within the structure.

THE ARTS AND CRAFTS MOVEMENT

Wright and the Prairie school of design were not the only ones discovering the simple, organic forms of natural materials. The Arts and Crafts movement, begun in England but championed by Gustav Stickley in the United States, mirrored many of the same trends of the Prairie school but traced a different lineage. (See "Architecture of the 1900s.") While his simply hewn furniture remained popular during the 1910s, it was easily copied by those less committed to hand craftsmanship. While not immediately recognizable as a Stickley or Wright-inspired design, the California style of

A model of proposed Imperial Hotel, Tokyo, designed by Frank Lloyd Wright, with Japanese and English text. Prints & Photographs Division, Library of Congress.

Architecture

HOW OTHERS SEE US

Frank Lloyd Wright's Tokyo Imperial Hotel

Iconic American architect Frank Lloyd Wright was in some ways a surprising choice to design the Tokyo Imperial Hotel in 1916. Wright and his work were strongly associated with the American Midwest. Yet Wright was also a great adapter who often borrowed the architectural vocabulary of other cultures, and he was fascinated by Japanese art. He lobbied hard to get the hotel project.

Completed in 1923, Wright's ornate and mannered design fused elements of Japanese, Mayan, and Egyptian decoration and architecture, as well as his own Prairie Style, to form a massive complex that was a center of the city's social scene. Its "uncommon unity" was a point of special praise: viewers were said to "stand in mute admiration" at its "mass of details" that managed to coalesce into "a graceful oneness." Its legend was enhanced by the fact that it stayed standing during the devastating 1923 Great Kanto Earthquake, a magnitude 7.9 temblor that destroyed many of Tokyo's modern-style buildings and killed at least 100,000 people.

Wright lived in Japan for much of the hotel's six years of construction, and during that time he exhorted local architects and builders to fight the European-style modernism that was creeping into Japan's urban landscape. "There is no reason whatever why the Japanese style of architecture, as seen both in the temples and private dwellings, should not be adapted to the needs of modern Japan," he lectured. He incorporated such Japanese elements as rigorous symmetry, reflecting pools, serene plantings, and cantilever-supported roofs into his Imperial Hotel design. But Japanese architects continued to look to Western modernist styles for their main inspiration, particularly in the massive rebuilding efforts after World War II, leaving Wright's vision of a uniquely Japanese modern architecture unrealized.

the 1900s and 1910s soon gave birth to one of the most novel, most popular home designs of the twentieth century: the American bungalow.

Architects and brothers Henry and Charles Greene were certainly influenced by the work of Wright, Stickley, and the other leading Eastern designers. Trained at M.I.T. and suffused with Beaux-Arts classicism, the Greenes designed mostly Colonial and Queen Anne homes for the wealthy until the turn of the century. Near the end of the 1900s, they began experimenting with cantilevered eaves and historical craftsmanship. By the time the partners had created the D. L. James house in Carmel Highlands, California, in 1918, the design had matured from being a derivation of others' ideas into a more natural, native creation.

The fusion of styles visible in the Greenes's work was typical of early vernacular design in California. Entire communities, such as Pasadena, imbued the Arts and Crafts style in uniquely Western ways. The inclusion of Arroyo Seco cultural objects such as blankets, pottery, and jewelry, or the use of natural forms from the desert were just two of the ways in which the California style differentiated itself. One of the state's most

important residential architects, Irving Gill, drew deeply upon the multicultural history of Southern California. By mixing reinforced steel with traditional adobe, Gill constructed a number of homes for both the elite and the masses.

These native historical traditions, academic eclecticism, and vernacular design elements all merged in the 1910s to produce a boom in California bungalow construction. Simple, versatile, casual, inexpensive, and closely linked to a love of the outdoors, the bungalow became a hit across the country. In its ideal form, the bungalow featured a low-pitched roof, an ample porch, and an open, single-floor interior. Popularized by Henry L. Wilson's *Bungalow Book* (1908) and Henry H. Saylor's *Bungalows* (1911), the bungalow was appreciated for its low cost and basic usefulness. The few rooms were spacious but easy to clean and maintain by working couples. The basic design was readily modified through the use of dormers, chimneys, roof lines, and windows to encourage a sense of individuality in a society that was rapidly homogenizing. By the end of the decade, developers could design and build a simple bungalow for as little as $900, making home ownership and middle-class respectability a reality for millions of working families.

With such democratic advantages, the bungalow quickly became the favorite style of real estate developers and even mail-order houses. The Southern California Standard Building Company, for example, sold and financed hundreds of standard bungalow designs on small lots. California speculators also originated bungalow courts, consisting of a ring of homes surrounding a central grassy area. Prefabricated bungalows were hot sellers for the Sears, Roebuck and the Montgomery Ward mail-order firms after 1910. In 1918, Sears offered a 146-page catalog of various bungalow styles from which to choose. These mail-order bungalows were prefabricated and quickly assembled, often in less than a day. Other large national suppliers included Pacific Ready-Cut, the Aladdin Company of Bay City, Michigan, Harris Brothers of Chicago, and the Gordon-Van Tine Company of Davenport, Iowa.

While seemingly never a vital concern for most architects, California designers did show an extraordinary interest in providing inexpensive and functional housing for low-income Americans. For example, in 1910, Irving Gill developed Lewis Courts, in Sierra Madre, California, to house 11 moderate-income families. The prefabricated homes were placed within a common, terraced courtyard with a communal play area for children and a large public porch. These small neighborhoods soon became so successful that developers were able to raise rents, which drove away tenants of modest means.

Books

Newspapers, Magazines, and Comics of the 1910s

Literary artists, unlike other artists in the 1910s, were largely free of the direct control of European stylists. Certainly, European writers were considered more refined and intellectually challenging simply because of their home, but Americans had developed their own written traditions using a language that was particularly their own.

The new writers built upon this growing anxiety about the world Americans saw around them, while tapping into two well-established traditions of previous transcendentalist authors. First, these earlier artists understood that change was an important component of American popular culture. Second, writers in the 1910s borrowed the strong sense of individuality that ran through the works of nineteenth-century writers such as Herman Melville, Nathaniel Hawthorne, Henry David Thoreau, Walt Whitman, and Ralph Waldo Emerson. This inner strength was highly democratic and rewarded those most willing to take risks. As a result, many realist writers concentrated on the very wealthy, not because they were technically "better" than the rest of the public, but because the wealthy were better able to demonstrate their individual mettle, since their wealth freed them from the distress of poverty.

The list of writers and literary publications that came of age under these conditions is remarkable. In fiction, they include Willa Cather, Sherwood Anderson, Gertrude Stein, and Theodore Dreiser. In criticism, publications like the *Masses* (1911), *Poetry* (1912), the *Smart Set* (1914), and the *New Republic* (1914) were founded, and writers such as John (Jack) Reed, Max Eastman, and H. L. Mencken gained wide circulation. In poetry, Ezra Pound, T. S. Eliot, Robert Frost, Carl Sandburg, and Edgar Lee Masters were first published.

The shift in American literature was slow due to a number of factors. First, the contrast between the soaring optimism in the world in 1910 and the bleak reality of world war knocked the breath out of the movement in its earliest years. Stein would later call the group of writers most directly affected by the war a "lost generation," hinting at their alienation and disillusionment. Second, many of these creative authors chose to live in Europe, which had an unintended effect of slowing the pace of literary change in the United States. Dwarfing these factors was the realist tradition which kept many writers grounded in everyday life. Realism absorbed, modified, and pacified many of the most revolutionary artistic innovations of the decade, but it also changed significantly throughout the decade.

REALISM AND MODERNISM IN NONFICTION

Literary realism was both a revolutionary reappraisal of life in America and a simple acceptance of the forces of industrial capitalism. Writers focused on the complexities of mass society and created fictional worlds where impersonal forces overwhelmed the hopes and dreams of their subjects. Typically, the drama of a realist work flowed from everyday events such as losing or taking a job, moving to a city, or making money, rather than contrived, overly emotional plot devices. Significantly, the setting of these works was almost always modern and, as a result, readers found the narratives familiar and very powerful.

The appearance of a number of influential nonfiction works focused on the concrete reality of life supported this overall trend in the 1910s. The leading books of the decade include *Twenty-Years at Hull-House* by Jane Addams (1910), *My First Summer in the Sierra* by John Muir (1911), *The Montessori Method* by Maria Montessori (1912), *An Economic Interpretation of the Constitution* by Charles and Mary Beard (1913), *The Negro* by W.E.B. Du Bois (1915), and *America's Coming of Age* by Van Wyck Brooks (1915).

Fictional works followed an equally realistic pattern. Typically, a narrative introduced a young and idealistic hero who was thrown into a setting that overwhelmed his or her ability to respond. Try as he or she might to strike out against conformity, by the end of the piece, the character was usually broken in spirit and incapable of further resistance. As noted above, the focus on the very wealthy was common in the works of early realists like William Dean Howells, Theodore Dreiser, and Frank Norris. Here were men who had the inner drive to succeed in the new economy yet who ultimately had to face the reality that they could not control the markets that had made them rich.

"Modernism" is a recognized literary style separate from realism. Where realists usually depict characters struggling to employ traditional moral values to their problems, modernists suggested that these values were no longer valid. As a result, the dramatic tension realists portrayed *between* different members of society and their values was transformed to the dramatic tension *within* a single person torn between his or her own values. Realists suggested the need to adapt traditional morality to modernity, while modernists hinted that the old views of morality no longer even applied. During the 1910s, modernists tended to rely more upon everyday language, portrayed less balanced characters (both emotionally and economically), and blurred the traditional linear narrative progression of their works.

NEW MAGAZINES
Boys' Life (1911)
Masses (1911)
The New Republic (1914)
Detective Story Magazine (1915)
Forbes (1917)
True Story Magazine (1919)

Magazines

Muckraking exposés and general interest magazines remained popular in the decade, but the magazine business transformed into big business, fueled by advertising dollars and an eager public. As a result, confessionals and gossip-heavy books—forerunners to modern tabloids—grew in popularity. Consumer demand for a certain genre led to a vicious circle of more of the same type being pushed onto the public, because the publishers were motivated by profits. Titillating and shocking content became a mainstay of magazine content.

At the other end of the spectrum, lifestyle magazines featured the latest fashions and goods that catered to the wealthy. Heavy on slick photographs and splashy illustrations, magazines such as *The Smart Set* and *Vanity Fair* appealed to wealthy readers. Condé Nast, a pioneering ad man and publisher, bought *Vogue* in 1909 and turned it into the nation's most profitable magazine by emphasizing fashion and advertisements aimed at wealthy readers. In 1913, Nast purchased *Vanity Fair* and *House and Garden,* followed by a

Books

British edition of *Vogue* in 1915 and a French version in 1920.

THE "NEW CRITICISM" AND NEW MAGAZINES

Before the 1910s, critics usually overlooked the values contained within a work provided that the artist conformed to traditional literary rules. If a verse was constructed in the proper meter or if prose developed an emotionally moving drama, the author was rarely held accountable for his or her views on society. By contrast, New Criticism and the publications that published these reviews, focused intently on the cultural assumptions of the writer and directly challenged works that were based on values that they felt were unsupported in the modern era.

The birth of the *Masses*, a magazine of social and artistic criticism in 1911, reflected this trend. The magazine began tentatively by humorously needling the genteel values that were already struggling to survive in the twentieth century. The magazine was soon reconstructed to address explicitly the role of art in the modern industrial world.

Critical to the success of the *Masses* was its dedicated stable of talented contributors. Many of these, including Charlotte Perkins Gilman, Colonel Edward House, and Mary Heaton Vorse, were Progressive reformers and muckrakers interested in popularizing the plight of the working poor in the United States. Others, like Upton Sinclair and Jack Reed, were more committed to the militant and inspired actions of the Industrial Workers of the World (IWW) and a true socialist government. Reed, the son of a wealthy Oregon family and educated at the best schools, reveled in the violent labor strikes in Paterson, New Jersey, and Ludlow, Colorado. His passionate writing provided a human face to the threatening revolutions in Mexico and Russia (*Ten Days That Shook the World* was published in 1919). Reed's activism led him to the Soviet Union, where he died in 1920.

While the *Masses* staked a claim as representative of the enlightened worker, other publications sought less rigid ideological ground. Most notable was the *New Republic*, a "journal of opinion" started in 1914 by Herbert Croly with funding by heiress Dorothy Straight. More centrist in tone, the *New Republic* advocated neutrality in the war and backed the modest reforms put forth by Theodore Roosevelt's Progressive Party, although the periodical maintained its focus on cultural expression, particularly literature. The *New Republic* hoped to enlighten its readers with writing and criticism that expressly connected literary trends—which advanced a new understanding of one's place and role in society—and the intense political activity of the decade.

Finally, the decade saw the growth of more sophisticated and discerning literary magazines. For decades, such popular publications as the *Ladies' Home Journal*, the *Saturday Evening Post, Cosmopolitan, Munsey's*, and *McClure's* had offered middle-class readers a taste of the newest trends in literature. These magazines greatly aided in the development of the short story in America.

Still, in general, commercial publishers shied away from the more experimental. As a result, many specialty magazines, such as *Little Review* (1914), *Others* (1915), the *Seven Arts* (1916), and the *Dial* (1916), were founded to cater to these needs. Harriet Monroe started *Poetry: A Magazine of Verse* in 1912 in Chicago to provide a forum for modernist poets, such as Joyce Kilmer, Vachel Lindsay, and Carl Sandburg. More important, these magazines opened the public to a more pressing criticism of modern literature.

H. L. Mencken

As a journalist, critic, and editor, Henry Louis Mencken (1880–1956) used his corrosive but humorous wit to dissolve pretentiousness, inequality, and ignorance, although he was not without his own prejudices. While frequently contemptuous of democracy and impatient with those of lesser intellectual capacity, Mencken was always honest and straightforward in his writing.

Mencken had little use for female reformers or the Women's Suffrage movement. He had even less tolerance for African Americans, partly due to his Southern upbringing, but also because he believed blacks were undereducated as a result of their own lack of resolve, a common error of the day. Mencken also was an unabashed supporter of science and a critic of organized religions.

Mencken wrote prolifically for newspapers in Baltimore and elsewhere; for journals (such as the *Smart Set,* where he began working as a literary editor in 1908, and which he began editing with George Nathan in 1914); and he wrote a number of books. As a critic, he wrote 182 book reviews spanning a wide range of offerings. He loved the works of such realist novelists as Theodore Dreiser, Sherwood Anderson, and Willa Cather, and he advanced the poetry of Edgar Lee Masters and Ezra Pound.

REALIST AND MODERNIST NOVELS

The 1910s saw the creation of some of the best realistic, popular, and modern novels of any decade in American history, including works by Upton Sinclair, Jack London, Edith Wharton, Willa Cather, and Ellen Glasgow. Theodore Dreiser's works are perhaps the best examples of the American realist style.

Drieser's breakthrough came with the publication of *Sister Carrie* (1900), a gritty account of how people followed the sensual pleasures on obvious display in the large cities. (See Books, Newspapers, Magazines, and Comics of the 1900s.) He continued to explore materialism and the darker aspects of contemporary life in *Jennie Gerhardt* (1911), a bestseller, and his trilogy based on the life of railroad magnate Charles T. Yerkes—*The Financier* (1912), *The Titan* (1914), and *The Stoics* (written in 1916 but not published until 1947). Objects were magical possessions and people like Yerkes, who had so much and wanted so much more, became superhuman—unburdened by pointless middle-class morals and fears of sin, lacking human warmth, and wholly manipulative of others.

The experimental modernism of Gertrude Stein was certainly as influential as Dreiser's realism. Born in 1874, educated at Radcliffe College and then medical school at Johns Hopkins University, Stein left the United States in 1902 to live in Europe. She returned only for visits until her death in 1946, but she always considered herself a Yankee. Stein was an adventuresome writer who willingly sacrificed book sales for greater freedom in her prose. In *Three Lives* (1909) and then *Tender Buttons* (1913), she experimented with repetitive sentences and new speech patterns. She largely abandoned traditional narratives for an immediacy of presentation—shifting tenses within her writing so that all action (past, present, or future) was directly connected to the psyche of her characters. Stein saw the stream-of-consciousness style as typically modern and more typically American. As a critic, Stein strongly supported the work of Hemingway, William Faulkner, Eliot, and others.

LITERARY TRENDS AND THE POPULAR NOVEL

While Dreiser's realism and Stein's modernism were important indicators of the direction of American literature, popular novels were more loosely associated with these schema. Writers of popular fiction, Edgar Rice Burroughs and Zane Grey, for example, understood that these more respected authors were widening the possibilities of their own craft. In addition, regional writers, such as Midwestern authors Willa Cather and Sherwood Anderson, achieved popular acclaim while driving the realist and modernist literary movement in unforeseen directions. All told, the public taste in novels both supported and limited the more artistic trends in American literature during the 1910s.

Zane Grey, born Pearl Zane Gray in 1872, began publishing in 1903 and became successful with his book *The Heritage of the Desert* (1910). Throughout his life, Grey published 85 books that sold more than 40 million copies. He used predictable melodramatic plots and simple characters speaking in flat dialog, all contained within a loose, realist style.[1]

Grey's writing was based on a love of the mythic West, themes he had absorbed from his numerous fishing and sightseeing excursions to Arizona's Painted Desert. *The Heritage of the Desert* was typical of his early experiences. It is the story of an Easterner who is transplanted in the West who, through a rapid series of improbable yet hair-raising events, proves his mettle to the satisfaction of the heroine and validates his claim to be a real man. In *Riders of the Purple Sage* (1912), Grey pilloried Mormonism to show how institutional religion and traditional notions of community undermined the natural dignity of the cowboy. Grey established the stock Western character of the "reluctant gunman," an honorable individual who was forced to become a killer because of encroaching civilization.

Grey's pseudo-historical novels were also popular during the decade. *The U. P. Trail* (1918) and *The Desert of Wheat* (1919) dealt with the contests between man and nature in building the transcontinental railroad and supplying the world with wheat. Both novels drew upon the same cast of stock characters as in his earlier works, but he used the natural drama of history to lend gravity to his stories. The reliance upon current events and heavies like the IWW and Imperial Germany gave his work the appearance of realist literature without the complexities that gave the realists their lasting reputation.

In a different vein, Edgar Rice Burroughs rose to fame in the 1910s as the creator of *Tarzan of the Apes,* a novella published in the October 1912 issue of the *All-Story* magazine. By the end of Burroughs's career, he had penned 23 additional Tarzan stories (and more than 50 others).[2] Like Grey, Burroughs took advantage of the realist style to pit man against nature. Influenced by Rudyard Kipling's *Jungle Book,* Teddy Roosevelt's call for a more "strenuous life," and popular novels emerging from the colonization of Africa, Burroughs devised a scenario whereby an English aristocrat was tested by the wildest of jungles. Lord Greystoke (i.e., Tarzan) might have been raised in the jungle, but in Burroughs's hands he soon proved his evolutionary worth by teaching himself to read and laying claim to being the king of the beasts. Burroughs knew that what he was writing was not "literature"; he spent most of his creative energies marketing his Tarzan stories to moviemakers and the comic books. As with Grey, his series were short on credible dialog and plots and long on action.

His rise to fame shows the fate of a typical writer more clearly than that of an author with the artistic talents of Dreiser or Stein. Short stories such as Tarzan were in great demand by the pulp fiction magazines (so called because of the coarse and inexpensive paper that was used) which became popular in the 1890s and sold for a nickel or dime. By 1910, all-fiction magazines such as *Popular Stories, Short Stories, Top Notch,* and *All-Story* were commercially successful. They demanded a steady stream of authors for hackneyed but surefire plots and would burn through a writer's creative imagination in a matter of months. By 1912, Burroughs had already submitted several short stories, including "A Princess from Mars" (1911), a thriller which combined the Old West and outer space while staying true to the formula of the pulp magazines. In his sequel to Tarzan's popular premiere, Greystoke battled Russian spies in the Sahara. Originally titled "Monsieur Tarzan," the chronicle was published as "The Return of Tarzan" in *New Story* magazine in 1912. Two years later, Burroughs published *Tarzan of the Apes* as a novel, and in 1918 it was transformed to the silent screen (where the character was significantly altered from Burroughs's original conception).[3]

THE MIDWESTERN RENAISSANCE

Grey and Burroughs sacrificed artistic realism for commercial success. Their treatment of their fictional worlds limited their ability to incorporate a more serious analysis of the relationship of their characters to their environment, the very basis of realistic writing. Much of the work of The Midwestern Renaissance of the 1910s was commercially successful, however, showing that it was possible to merge artistry with business in popular American literature.

The success of writers emerging in the Midwest in the 1910s was phenomenal. Coupled with the arrival of the Chicago School of architecture and the importance of Midwestern musicians, the term renaissance may not be an overstatement. The list of stellar writers included Hamlin Garland, Willa Cather, Sherwood Anderson, Sinclair Lewis, Ring Lardner, F. Scott Fitzgerald, and T. S. Eliot. The region was reaching its apogee of economic importance for the United States and, lacking any real indigenous cultural tradition, these writers tended to create one. Focusing on the power of the land, shared rural roots, and the unbridled economic optimism of the region, Midwestern writers provided works that were robust, confident, and wholly original.

Willa Cather

Willa Cather never needed to travel to pick up local color; she was emotionally and spiritually a part of it. In fact, while she wrote poetry, prose, and criticism in a variety of styles, her body of work is hard to classify as a single school or theory. While she clearly represented the realist and modernist trends of novels in the era, she also incorporated the symbolism of poetry and the political optimism that gave life to the Progressive movement. If there is a single source of power in her words, it comes from the faith that she took from the land.[4]

Willa Cather was born in Virginia in 1873. When she was 10 years old, her family moved to Red Cloud, Nebraska, an immigrant town where native-born Americans were a minority. Cather attended the University of Nebraska, where she began her professional career as a writer and teacher. She moved first to Pittsburgh and then to New York where she became an editor for *McClure's* magazine in 1906. While in New York, she became close friends with a group of writers and activists who challenged her thinking and tightened her skills as a creative writer. Her writing reflected a strong, female-centered appreciation for the Midwest, a rarity for accomplished writers of the era.

Cather was an intensely private person, and she directed that most of her private correspondence and all of her unfinished manuscripts be destroyed after her death. This relative lack of biographical material has forced scholars to come to terms with Cather through her fiction alone, and it is here where she earned her distinguished reputation.

Cather felt that her first major published work, *Alexander's Bridge* (1912), was too shallow and artificial to merit much attention. Still, she began to demonstrate her infatuation with the subject of youth which coursed through her entire body of work. In the novel, a young architect, Bartley Alexander, must choose between his youthful dreams and his adult responsibilities. Torn between the two, Alexander is killed when his bridge collapses from its structural instability.

These efforts paid handsome dividends in the 1910s with the publication of *O Pioneers!* (1913), *The Song of the Lark* (1915), and *My Àntonia* (1918)—the first and the last of which are considered to be part of the canon of American literature. Cather considered *O Pioneers!* to be her first true novel. The story is of an immigrant woman transplanted to Nebraska who suffers through the precarious fate of most prairie settlers. Cather's sparse style spends little effort describing the plains, focusing instead on the nearly tangible spirit of the land. Surrounding this immigrant girl were dozens who committed themselves to chasing the illusion of success through materialism and transient pleasures. By contrast, while the heroine was tormented in life, she was sustained by the timeless peace, cycles, and surety of the physical earth. In style and subject matter, *O Pioneers!* was unique, and it established Willa Cather as an author of note.

In *My Àntonia,* the most autobiographical of all her novels, Cather transformed her presence in the novel into a young, male, romantic, native-born railroad lawyer named James Burden. Burden narrates the novel and recounts how he came to understand a Bohemian immigrant girl from Nebraska by the name of Àntonia Shirmerda and how his Àntonia restored his faith in himself and in the world around him. Again, Cather's style is Spartan, and the dramatic elements of this novel are completely ordinary. Àntonia is seen to go through four stages of life: a spirited youth, a troubled young woman, an abandoned mother, and, finally, a fulfilled matriarch of a stable and fertile extended family. While suffering the suicide of her romantic father, the hypocritical gossip of "respectable" society, and the lies of a native-born lover, the immigrant sees the joy of life connected to the natural and living rhythms of the land. Burden, the typical American, sees through Àntonia that he had lost this faith. By the end, however, he knows where to look to recapture his youthful optimism; he knows again that all things are possible.

Sherwood Anderson

Sherwood Anderson achieved his literary fame with the publication of *Winesburg, Ohio* in 1919 when he was 43 years old. Anderson had worked as a laborer, served in the Spanish-American War, and worked in advertising, all the while dreaming of writing fiction. After suffering a nervous breakdown in 1912, Anderson came to Chicago and became friends with a small group of struggling

Books

writers including Edgar Lee Masters, Carl Sandburg, and Harriet Monroe. This was an auspicious time for creative writing in the city as both *Poetry* and the *Little Review* gave a forum for new and experimental poetry and prose.

Anderson experimented with novels and, in 1916, he published his first book titled *Windy McPherson's Son*. One year later, *Marching Men* was released. Both books examined small-town America, the effects of modernization, and the alienation of thinking men in such a society. The books sold poorly, so Anderson turned to shorter, more focused studies about particular individuals. Several of his short character studies were published in the *Masses* and the *Seven Arts*. These pieces formed the core of his anthology of stories which he published under the name *Winesburg, Ohio*.

Winesburg, Ohio contains 22 separate stories, usually related by or observed through the eyes of a local reporter who represented an idealized version of the author. A town just emerging from the Civil War and going into the tempest of modernization, Winesburg has no sense of the future and no trust in the past. Most of the characters are emotionally and psychologically scarred. Their lack of self-awareness and their reliance on moral clichés only deepens these wounds in others. Anderson used modern vocabulary, a frank discussion of sex and sexual drives, and a merciless focus on the tottering genteel values of small-town America to lend power and substance to his work.

Anderson did not set out to attack village life. His characters in *Winesburg* are a mixed bag of transients, locals, the urbane, and provincials. Moreover, some of his characters display strong moral values which are developed and often reinforced through their contact with fellow citizens. What Anderson disliked was not the physical reality of small-town U.S.A., but rather the self-righteousness and lack of self-criticism that come from a population that never stops to evaluate its own morals. In *Winesburg*, characters are trapped and tortured by the very institutions and belief systems held most dear by the citizens: family, rectitude, and Christian morality. While most of his characters struggle against conforming to the wishes of others, the battle leaves them broken

and their individuality "grotesque." Winesburg is a claustrophobic town, where its peoples' hopes and dreams are turned into fears and nightmares from the realities of modern living.

Winesburg, Ohio was a critical and financial success for Anderson. He used his fame to promote the work of other talented modern writers such as Ernest Hemingway and William Faulkner. Moreover, Anderson proved that the modernist style of using colloquial speech, short, simple sentences, and poetic imagery could be fashioned into a powerful yet popular novel.

BEST-SELLERS, AND THE GREAT WAR

Lying between the extremes of experimental modernism and the adventure stories of Burroughs and Grey, novelists Edith Wharton, Booth Tarkington, and Arthur Guy Empey filled a unique niche of American literature in the 1910s. Wharton was perhaps the most influential of these novelists. Born to wealth in 1862, she struggled with a failed marriage and the conservative elite culture of New York City, often making this culture the subject of the 47 volumes she wrote. Wharton popularized the struggles of the upper classes to retain their footing upon the shifting sands of modern society.

Wharton continued upon her literary success of the previous decade. *Ethan Frome* (1911) was her most popular book of the 1910s. In it, two selfish and materialistic women destroy the ideals and the very life of the title character. In the critically acclaimed *The Custom of the Country* (1913), Wharton's subject was a social climber who was trapped by the shallowness of the moneyed class. In addition, Wharton published *Tales of Men and Ghosts* (1910), *The Reef* (1913), *Xingu and Other Stories* (1917), and *Summer* (1919), and most of these were best sellers. While *The Age of Innocence* (1920) earned Wharton the Pulitzer Prize, many of her critics contend that her work had become nostalgic and uncritical by this date.

Other bestselling authors wrote impressive works throughout the decade. The best of these followed traditions already in place before the decade began, such as Joel Chandler Harris's *Uncle Remus and the Little Boy* (1910) and Finley Peter

Edith Wharton. Prints & Photographs Division, Library of Congress.

NOTABLE BOOKS

Howards End, E. M. Forster (1910)

Ethan Frome, Edith Wharton (1911)

Mother, Kathleen Norris (1911)

The Harvester, Gene Stratton Porter (1912)

Riders of the Purple Sage, Zane Grey (1912)

O Pioneers!, Willa Cather (1913)

Pollyanna, Eleanor Hodgman Porter (1913)

The Spoon River Anthology, Edgar Lee Masters (1915)

A Portrait of the Artist as a Young Man, James Joyce (1916)

Rhymes of a Red Cross Man, Robert W. Service (1917)

Diet and Health, Lulu Hunt Peters (1918)

The Magnificent Ambersons, Booth Tarkington (1918)

Winesburg, Ohio, Sherwood Anderson (1919)

The Four Horsemen of the Apocalypse, V. Blasco Ibañez (1919)

Dunne's *Mr. Dooley Says* (1911) and *New Dooley Book* (1912). Booth Tarkington, too, solidified his reputation as a talented narrator with *The Turmoil* (1915)—a story of economic exploitation—and *Seventeen* (1916)—a story of teens coming of age. Bestsellers also included Jeffrey Farnol's *The Broad Highway* (1911), Gene Stratton Porter's *The Harvester* (1912), Harold Bell Wright's *The Eyes of the World* (1914), and H. G. Wells's *Mr. Britling Sees It Through* (1917).

Wells's novel, which seeks meaning from death in World War I, was typical of many popular novels during the war years. The meaning of the war became a contested terrain for writers. During the 1910s, the majority of these books tended to the see the conflict as a way for young men to test their bravery, honor, patriotism, and masculinity. Author Alan Seeger was an unfortunate example of this trend. Graduating from Harvard in 1910, Seeger went to Paris in 1912 and joined the French Foreign Legion when the fighting began in 1914. Seeger was stationed on the front. While he fought, he wrote popular dispatches for the *New York Sun* and the *New Republic.* Killed in action in 1916, his posthumous memoirs became a best seller in 1917, as Americans marveled and wept over his selfless sacrifice for "the cause."[5]

The field was open for a large number of guts-and-glory memoirs or fictionalized accounts. Arthur Guy Empey's *Over the Top* (1917) was typical. Telling the story of his experiences as a machine gunner, Empey used realistic descriptions and jargon to suggest that frontal assaults on fortified gun nests were the height of glory for young men. The book sold 350,000 copies its first year and was soon turned into a movie. Empey became a featured speaker at patriotic rallies throughout the country. Other best sellers included Robert W. Service's *Rhymes of a Red Cross Man* (1917), Alan Seeger's *Poems of Alan Seeger* (1917), Ian Hay's *First Hundred Thousand* (1917),

Francis W. Huard's *My Home in the Field of Honor* (1917), Edward Guest's *Over Here* (1918), James W. Gerard's *My Four Years in Germany* (1918), and Lt. Pat O'Brien's *Outwitting the Hun* (1918).

AMERICAN POETRY

The trends in poetic verse in the 1910s underscored the shifts seen in popular fiction and criticism. When Ezra Pound called for a conscious *risorgimento,* or reorganization of poetic styles, in 1909, he was asking poets to reformulate their approach in ways that rejected the formal complexities of traditional verse. Pound, who was born in Idaho and lived most of his early life in Pennsylvania before emigrating to England in 1908, was a great promoter of American poets who he believed were attempting to make this crossover, including T. S. Eliot, William Carlos Williams, e. e. cummings, Hilda Doolittle (who published her works by her initials, H. D.), and Robert Frost.

Pound's greatest ally was Thomas Stearns (T. S.) Eliot. Born in St. Louis and educated at Harvard, the Sorbonne, and Oxford, Eliot permanently relocated to England in 1910. Neither he nor the other expatriates abandoned their American roots; rather, they regarded Europe as a cultural oasis in which they could pursue their craft more freely than in the more materialistic States. Eliot championed a symbolist style that had been gaining influence since the turn of the century. His greatest work of the decade was *The Love Song of J. Alfred Prufrock,* published as a compilation titled simply *Prufrock,* in 1917. He used common language to establish new patterns of rhythm within his text. The subject matter was expanded to include all forms of human behavior, particularly those considered too crude for Victorian poets. The mood of the piece was usually established by images and tones rather than glaring emotions or contrived dramatic flourishes. Finally, Eliot's writing was meticulously crafted, often to the point that the work became near parodies. After the release of *The Waste Land* (1922), a poem of incredible influence, Eliot added footnotes in an effort to guide readers to the sources of his imagery.

Concurrent with the rise of a regional voice in American novels, poets found that their experiences in the United States granted them a unique artistic perspective. The Midwest Renaissance sparked just such a movement. Edgar Lee Masters, who was born in Kansas and raised in Illinois, came to Chicago in the 1890s to practice law but made his name as an accomplished poet with the publication of *Spoon River Anthology* in 1915, his third book of verse. In this classic, Masters introduced his readers to the ghosts of former residents of the region. Being dead afforded the narrators the freedom to be honest. In their confessions, Masters related how they believed they had wasted much of their lives on petty grievances, fleeting sexual pleasures, and a fruitless search for understanding. As with Anderson and, later, Sinclair Lewis, the work is often misconstrued as a focused attack on small-town America. In actuality, these writers used their experiences in small towns to show how these frustrations were magnified by close contact within the provincial village, but that the experiences were no less present in the city. In many ways, the small town inhabitants were at least able to identify their frustrations.

Carl Sandburg, who like Masters was first published in the Chicago-based *Poetry* magazine, was the son of a Swedish blacksmith from Galesburg, Illinois. After moving to Chicago in 1913 and taking a series of odd jobs which brought him into contact with Chicago's polyglot society, Sandburg was able to capture the distinct regional and American values of citizens toward work, society, and the country. While often overly sentimental toward the wisdom of the public, Sandburg translated the raw power of America's industrial and economic might into lyrical and moving verse. His frequently quoted description of Chicago, from *Chicago Poems* (1916), as "Hog Butcher for the World, Tool Maker, Stacker of Wheat, Player with Railroads…Stormy, husky, brawling, City of the Big Shoulders" revels in the sweaty accomplishments of workaday living. These are again hailed in his later works, *Cornhuskers* (1918) and *Smoke and Steel* (1920).

While some critics of the Midwest Renaissance take exception to the accomplishments of these poets, it is clear that regionalism had become a distinguishing characteristic of American poetry in the 1910s. The success of Robert Frost's works is telling proof of this assertion. Frost, who was born in San Francisco in 1874, moved to New Hampshire with his family when he was 11 years old. There he absorbed the local diction and environment and began writing poetry. After attending Dartmouth and then Harvard, Frost emigrated to England in 1912 where his work was noticed and supported by literary activists Pound and Stein. In England, Frost began to publish his regional American verse, first with *A Boy's Will* (1913) and then the critically acclaimed *North of Boston* (1914).[6]

Frost's work is often regarded as homage to rustic simplicity and folksy wisdom. In reality, he used the picturesque New England countryside and vernacular to examine and attack the same genteel traditions that were bombarded by other modernist poets. For example, while his popular poem "The Road Not Taken," published in *Mountain Interval* (1916), seems to cherish the man who took the road "less traveled by, and that has made all the difference," he also suggests that an American will justify *any* action in hindsight as the most adventuresome and least conforming. In "Mending Wall" (*North of Boston*), Frost seems to lament the need for boundaries between citizens but concluded, with one of his characters, that "Good fences make good neighbors."

NEWSPAPERS AND COMICS

The influence of advertisers crept into newsrooms in the 1910s. Will Irwin exposed the relationship between the two in a 14-part series published in *Collier's* magazine in 1911. One of the major influences Irwin uncovered was the agenda-driven work of powerful editors who had almost complete control over how news was gathered. However, at the same time, the emphasis on journalism as a profession (fueled by the investigative work of the muckrakers and the lurid reporting of the yellow papers) led to a code of ethics emerging among reporters. These reporters emphasized their responsibility to the public.

Comics

Newspaper comic strips were popular through the 1910s, with humorous drawings being by far the most popular form of illustrations throughout the decade. Moreover, the visual and written humor contained within the illustrations reinforced or questioned many traditional assumptions about American society.

Regular cartoons began in the 1880s primarily in the sports and editorial sections of the newspapers. Most of these were single-panel drawings relying on verbal jokes for their humor. The characters were mostly underdeveloped and did not repeat from day to day.

In the 1890s, the comics became more consistent when newspapers owned by E. W. Scripps, William Randolph Hearst, and Joseph Pulitzer began forming national chains, or syndicates. These affiliated dailies standardized their editorial and reporting content and employed a regular stable of comic illustrators. By the 1910s, their comics were running in hundreds of papers, making the art form a common point of reference

Mutt and Jeff by Bud Fisher. In this 1917, war-era strip, Mutt and Jeff, as sailors, on deck of ship, are receiving knitted muffler and socks from ladies. Prints & Photographs Division, Library of Congress.

for many readers. Popular comics included Hogan's Alley (originally drawn by Richard Felton Outcault, now drawn by George Luks) James Swinnerton's "Little Bears," and Rudolph Dirks's "Katzenjammer Kids."

The first true comic strip was introduced in 1907 in the *San Francisco Chronicle.* Titled "A. Mutt" (meaning a rather unimportant person) and penned by Bud Fisher, the strip was a series of cartoons that told narrative and increasingly visual jokes spread out across the newspaper page. The strip was an innovation in several ways. First, by using frames, Fisher was free to develop multiple gags within a strip, which allowed character development. The use of speech balloons allowed characters to interact within each frame, rather than deliver extended speeches at the bottom of a single illustration.

The humor of the strip was aimed at the sporting man who read the sports pages of the *Chronicle.* It was not until 1910, with the regular appearance of a second, more sympathetic character, "Jeff," that the strip matured into an accessible and popular feature for the paper. Jeff, who appeared when Mutt was thrown into an asylum as a result of his gambling addiction, thought he was heavyweight boxing champion Jeff Jeffries. Jeff proved to be the perfect foil for Mutt; one an irrational idealist, softhearted and innocent, the other a crafty materialist. In 1916, the strip was retitled "Mutt and Jeff" to reflect the popularity of the diminutive newcomer. Fisher had the foresight to copyright his creations. When he left the *Chronicle* for better pay at Hearst's *Examiner,* the former publication attempted to continue the strip under the same name using the same characters. Fisher sued and won, in 1915, establishing the right of comic artists to maintain control over their intellectual property.

Strips also loosened the bounds of typical graphic humor. The need for a gag or slapstick in comics was lessened as artists sought more emotionally interesting ground. George Herriman was well ahead of his contemporaries in creating abstract humorous content in "Krazy Kat" (1913). Herriman, born to a mixed-race couple in New Orleans, created a strip for Hearst's *New York Journal* that was never immensely popular.

It was featured in only 48 papers while more popular cartoons were usually syndicated in hundreds.

"Krazy Kat" remained in print solely because William Randolph Hearst liked it. When Herriman died, in 1944, the panel was discontinued. Still, the strip is regarded today as one of the best examples of how the visual arts both reflected and influenced popular culture.

The content of "Krazy Kat" is absurdly simple yet compellingly complex. Three central characters are involved in an unrequited love triangle, a topic that clearly indicates that, like his contemporaries, the audience was the adult reading public and not children. Krazy Kat is love with Ignatz the mouse. Ignatz hates Krazy and expresses his frustrations by hurling bricks at the confused cat, who assumes these to be expressions of love. Offissa Pup, torn between *his* love for Krazy and his duty to uphold the law in stopping Ignatz's behavior, stumbles between the two, incapable of achieving either objective. The plot, if indeed there was one, was simply how Ignatz would find ways to lob his missiles. The humor was in how all three characters accepted the absurdity of their lives while remaining true to their hopes of love and independence. Herriman interjected

---

WORDS AND PHRASES

ace (cool)

air conditioning

beans! (nonsense!)

big shot

buzz-off

chow (food)

civvies (casual clothes)

copycat (noun)

crabby

cushy

duck soup (easy)

floozy (loose woman)

heebie jeebies

Tin Lizzie/flivver (Model T)

popular slang, Yiddish, Bronx accents, and even Shakespearean dialect into a surreal yet familiar speech.

Even the most conventional strips tended to reinforce the popular culture of the day. For example, *Chicago Tribune* publisher Robert McCormick wanted his readers to become more comfortable with the automobile. As a result, illustrator Frank King was asked to create a strip in 1918, which he called "Gasoline Alley," that eventually became one of the longest running, most successful series in cartooning.

Strips also began to portray kids as relatively simple and honest pranksters intent on having fun. In line with the reform of children's play, strips like Merril Blosser's "Freckles and His Friends" (1915) and Carl Ed's "Harold Teen" (1919) all showed youth and youth culture as non-

threatening and potentially redeemable. Blooser's work ran for 50 years in more than 700 newspapers. "Harold Teen" was the first to begin identifying older children as intrinsically different from their more innocent younger siblings. Until 1959, when the strip ended, Harold also provided readers a daily dose of teen slang, humor, and trends that no doubt proved to be useful for parents confused by the growing generation gap.

These popular cartoonists commanded phenomenal sums. George MacManus was a multimillionaire as a result of "Bringing Up Father." Former shoe salesman Gene Byrnes, who penned "Reg'lar Fellas," was making $25,000 per year by 1920. "Mutt and Jeff" creator Bud Fisher earned over $1,000 a week, owned a stable of horses, and was frequently seen in the company of movie starlets and showgirls.

Books

Entertainment

of the 1910s

During the 1910s, the performing arts seemed to both support and undermine many of the prevailing values and behaviors of American society. Many still believed in the moral simplicity of Victorianism—that good and evil were easily identified, and that poverty and social inequality were indicators of individual character. Yet the complexities and social realities of modern life were quickly dissolving the foundation of this bias. Technology freed performers from the bounds of the traditional productions, allowing artists to probe more psychologically complex issues on the stage.

THE EUROPEAN ROOTS OF MODERN AMERICAN DRAMA

The greatest influence on the changes that overtook the American stage in the 1910s was the new intellectual trend in European drama. Most of the tension that existed for European playwrights was due to the rising intellectual dissatisfaction with bourgeois or middle-class rationalism.

George Bernard Shaw, an Irish-born literary critic and writer, who was prominent from the 1890s until his death in 1950, took a satirical and humorous approach in his early playwriting. Shaw demonstrated through his characters that a life of critical self-awareness and humanitarianism could address many of society's ills. World War I obliterated his sense of progressive optimism, and Shaw's work took on darker, more fatalistic tones with the publication of *Heartbreak House* (1919).

Russia's Anton Chekov tapped into the social frustrations of the aristocratic, landholding elite. Incapable of accepting a place among the common people, many of Chekov's characters harbored deep-seated frustrations at the limits of modern society and the emptiness of their class system.

Shaw, Chekov, and others opened the format of the staged play to new possibilities. Still, there remained one large and serious problem: how to produce a show which effectively related the seriousness and complexity of the written word. Theaters were designed primarily to cope with traditional repertory productions. These houses had actors who trained for and performed a set number of classical or Shakespearean dramas. Konstantin Stanislavsky found that he needed to retrain nearly all of the Moscow Art Theatre's performers. His "actor's studio" worked to prevent artists from using clichéd, overly dramatic outbursts that previously had clued an audience into the emotional state of a character. Instead, he wanted to allow the themes and dialog to set the mood.

It was not until details of the new production methods had been translated into English that these plays received serious consideration in the United States. Stage director Adolphe Appia and theater connoisseur Gordon Craig made this possible in the 1910s. Appia wrote several influential books detailing the use of three-dimensional scenery, special effects, and variations in lighting (both color and brightness) and sound to help set the emotional tone of a production. Craig popularized these techniques in *The Art of the Theatre* (1911), *Towards a New Theatre* (1913), *The Theatre Advancing* (1919), and in a theater periodical titled *The Mask,* which was published from 1908 to 1929. Craig's criticism of the powerful producers who restricted the development of experimental theater gave courage to a number of less influential theater companies to produce more daring plays.

A final, and unexpected, source of change was in the world of psychology. From 1900 to 1905, Sigmund Freud and his leading disciple, Carl Jung, set the scientific and medical communities on their ears by demonstrating the link between dreams, the subconscious, and human sexual behavior.

"ART" COMES TO THE AMERICAN DRAMA

By 1910, American critics of the theater had begun to create alternatives to the commercial stage, although it was not until the late 1920s and early 1930s that these trends converged to transform drama in America.

The result of this haphazard transformation was a period of intense experimentation in dramatic realism. Sparked by the new European attitudes, the artificiality of the traditional theater became the target of reform. This experimentation, at times, distracted the audience more than it enhanced the performance. American theater lacked directors; no one was capable of coordinating the wide range of new artistic expressions. Previously, the closest equivalent to the director was the stage manager, an administrator whose job responsibilities included ticket sales, music, stage design, and the temperature of the theater. While some experienced Europeans, like Max Reinhart, did lend their talents to the American cause, it was not until the 1920s that the current form of the stage director emerged.[1]

Equally problematic was the generally poor state of dramatic writing in America in the 1910s. In general, writers tended to modify existing narratives or relied on fanciful tales of transformation. For example, Alice Gerstenberg adapted Lewis Carroll's story of Alice in Wonderland into a play titled *Alice* in 1915. While some writers exposed American audiences to the exciting possibilities of the new style, they provided little motivation for the public or producers to move American theater in this direction.

THE LITTLE THEATRE MOVEMENT

The growth of small, experimental theaters in the United States provided the necessary space and audiences for America's modern playwrights to develop their skills. Under the new rules, the barren stage designs of these small, underfunded theaters became a virtue. The lack of extravagant sets, complex musical numbers, and top-named actors meant that production costs could be kept low, making it easier for the company to take risks. In addition, the tiny audiences were usually drawn from the local arts and academic communities, who tolerated a greater freedom of expression than those who paid top dollar for Broadway productions. Critic and writer Maurice Brown termed these noncommercial venues "Little Theatres," a name that was proudly displayed by their founders.

The Little Theatre movement was the most influential trend in American drama during the 1910s. Beginning in 1912, local writers, actors, and enthusiasts opened Little Theatres throughout the country. By 1917, more than 50 Little Theatres were in operation throughout the United States.

The style of the Little Theatres was a complete departure from the more mainstream stage. The Little Theatres rejected melodrama, star appeal, and extravaganza, and created their own "off Broadway" qualities. Novelty and experimentation were paramount. The traditional repertoire was reinterpreted to highlight mental complexities. The focus on simple, quiet, and realistic stage designs stood in stark contrast to the glitter and blaring orchestras at most commercial venues.

The Provincetown Players was an important Little Theatre during the decade. Moving from

Entertainment

Cape Cod, Massachusetts to Greenwich Village in 1916, the Players drew upon the talents of such notables as John Reed, Robert Edmund Jones, Eugene O'Neill, and George Cram Cook and his wife, Susan Glaspell. They drew upon a variety of sources for their inspiration, including labor radicalism and the Armory Art Show. When disbanded in the 1920s, the company had produced 97 original plays written by 47 American authors.[2]

Certainly the most accomplished writer to come from the Little Theatre movement was Eugene O'Neill, the son of acclaimed Broadway actor James O'Neill. By the time he joined the Provincetown Players, in 1916 at the age of 28, O'Neill had already composed 16 one-act plays that had been rejected by the commercial theater. He also had several years of formal training at Harvard. His true gift was in crafting natural dialog and rhythm within plays of great emotional depth. His work was unsparing in its attacks on those who rationalized their feelings or attempted to develop artificial states of happiness. In one of his most acclaimed plays of the era, *Beyond the Horizon* (1918), which won the Pulitzer Prize in 1920, O'Neill portrayed the lives of two brothers in love with the same girl, each of whom took on the values of the other to disastrous consequences. The play stunned critics with its emotional power, contemporary language, lack of dramatic gimmickry, and, most of all, American authorship. While with the Players, O'Neill either staged or wrote some of his most accomplished plays, including *Long Day's Journey into Night*, *Bound East for Cardiff*, *Anna Christie* (which also won the Pulitzer Prize), and *The Emperor Jones*.

COMMERCIAL THEATER

Critics of commercial theater were frustrated by the continued success of so many seemingly identical Broadway productions. The success of the daring Theatre Guild and the rising popularity and recognition of writers such as O'Neill was evident to all who made their living through drama. Experimental works and "serious" plays were produced for the commercial stage in the latter half of the decade. The best of these were written by Clyde Fitch, Booth Tarkington, William Vaughan

Moody, Sinclair Lewis, Martha Morton, and Josephine Preston Peabody. The problem, however, was that few of these productions (and almost no works of lesser quality) succeeded in making money for their commercial producers.

Theatergoers demonstrated little interest in complex Freudian dramas, favoring instead light comedy and trendy musicals. They usually attended plays based on the stars appearing in the production, rather than on innovative writing or staging methods. The arrival of the little and community theaters provided enthusiasts of the modern style the perfect forum for experimental productions. It is highly probable that the inability of the commercial theaters to profitably stage experimental dramas only added to the off-Broadway movements of the decade.

The main stages were most successful when they provided extravagant, lighthearted, and lavishly expensive productions. America's taste for melodrama, while widely rejected by the artistic community, remained overwhelmingly popular. Preachy morality plays and tear-jerking dramas written and performed by American artists found ready support.

The very popular operetta *Robin Hood,* with Katherine Gault and Alexandro Cautacuzene. Prints & Photographs Division, Library of Congress.

It is possible to grant the commercial theater some credit for innovations. Most notably, the Broadway musical comedy became an authentic national art form in the first decades of the twentieth century. Operettas and light opera, such as those written by W. S. Gilbert and Sir Arthur Sullivan in the 1880s and 1890s, had been providing Europeans with memorable songs and soul-stirring arias. Composers and librettists, such as Reginald De Koven (whose operetta *Robin Hood* ran for 3,000 consecutive performances), Victor Herbert (who wrote the successful *Naughty Marietta* in 1910), and Jerome Kern, were instrumental in this transition from high art to popular entertainment in the United States.

Kern's career shows this evolution. Beginning in 1912, he, like most other American composers, stayed close to the European method. Yet Kern soon found that, in order for his work to connect with American audiences, it needed to be more accessible and believable. Kern wrote songs for shows at the Princess Theatre and, later, for Florenz Ziegfeld's *Follies*. Supported by talented librettists, such as Guy Bolton and P. G. Wodehouse, Kern soon perfected an American style that established a close and direct relationship with the crowd through songs that used common language, natural humor, and believable experiences. His more artistic operettas, *Very Good Eddie* (1915) and *Sally* (1920), were commercially successful and laid the groundwork for his collaboration with Oscar Hammerstein II, which produced *Showboat* in 1927.

ORGANIZATIONAL INNOVATIONS OF BROADWAY

As with other economic endeavors of the Progressive Era, mass entertainment saw a dramatic increase in the amount of money needed to produce their product. The construction of large and expensive theaters, as well as the skyrocketing costs of stage technologies, required internal organization and accounting that was uncharacteristic of the medium's entrepreneurial roots. Major productions cost hundreds of thousands of dollars before a single ticket was sold. Managing this uncertainty, while spreading the general availability of popular shows nationwide, was an important legacy of Broadway during the 1910s.

The obvious example of this management style was the operation of a group of production companies collectively called "the Syndicate." Formed in 1896 by the owners of the biggest theaters in the country, the Syndicate offered regional theaters a full season of high-quality, popular shows if they would stage only these productions. Nonconformists were blacklisted, making it unlikely that named actors and writers would be willing to work for non-Syndicate members. The Syndicate effectively blocked experimental dramas, but did ensure that high-quality works made it to the interior of the nation. By stabilizing and augmenting the cash flow into the dramatic arts, the Syndicate also encouraged the construction of new theaters and the implementation of new technologies—such as high-wattage electric lighting and multiuse stages.

The success of the Syndicate led to the growth of rebel organizations. David Belasco, who opened the Stuyvesant Theatre in 1907 (renamed the Belasco Theatre in 1910), effectively challenged the Syndicate when his production of *The Governor's Lady* began to tour the country in 1912. Belasco appealed to the public's desire for spectacle when he pioneered the use of modern electric spotlights and reconstructed a working restaurant on stage. The Syndicate backed down, allowing regional affiliates to show *The Governor's Lady*. The rise of national chains of theaters, such as those owned by brothers Lee and Jacob J. Shubert, gave writers and actors viable alternatives to the Syndicate by 1913. When Frohman died in the 1915 sinking of the *Lusitania*, the trust lost its most effective advocate, and the Syndicate was soon broken.

The downfall of the Syndicate had unforeseen consequences on the labor relations among actors, directors, and managers on the New York stage. Directors, still minor players, tended to wield power indirectly. Actors had influence and could compete for what were at that time astronomical salaries if they could prove their "star power" in drawing patrons to their shows. Most actors, however, had virtually no leverage and were paid only for performing before an audience, not for rehearsals. Another nightmare (partially addressed by the Syndicate) was the speculative touring company that failed to meet expenses. Managers could and did stop productions in mid-tour, stranding dozens of people without work or pay. In 1896, the Actor's Society was formed to pressure managers to establish a fairer, more reliable payment method. The union failed, but it was replaced in 1913 by the Actors' Equity Association, which expanded demands to include Sundays off and paid layoffs during Holy Week, a traditionally slow week for theaters.

In 1919, Equity members went on strike. Several factors were responsible for the final outcome. First, by the end of the decade, theaters were increasingly facing competition from movies. Second, the Red Scare, which followed the Bolshevik Revolution of 1918, harassed and often silenced many of Equity's more radical members. While these variables seemed to favor management, the third change was a growing support of the union by Broadway stars. Either swayed by sympathy for their fellow actors or the threat to their profession from the silver screen, the star actors' support provided Equity with the courage to demand fair treatment for all. When managers refused even to meet with the actors, a general strike began just before the curtain was called on August 6, 1919. Entire casts walked out, closing every major theater in New York (the cooperatively run Theatre Guild was a lone exception). Managers, led by George M. Cohan, claimed that Equity's demands would ruin the industry. Star actors, including Ethel Barrymore, Ed Wynn, Lillian Russell, and W. C. Fields, walked the picket lines and appealed to the emotions of the public. In the end, it was the stagehands and musicians (who respected the actors' picket line) who convinced the managers that they had no alternative but to settle. The Producing Managers' Association, losing fortunes every week that the theaters remained closed, on September 6, recognized the Actors' Equity Association and signed a contract, which yielded to almost every demand.

THE PEOPLE'S THEATER

The more widely attended popular or "people's theater" was also important to the direction of the performing arts. From minstrel shows and vaudeville to revue artists and the "girly shows" of Florenz Ziegfeld, popular theater was both independent of and closely linked to the more prestigious stage productions of the decade. The minstrel or coon shows probably were the most representative—and reprehensible—popular theater of the 1910s. Usually starring whites wearing blackface makeup, the shows parodied and exaggerated African American culture, speech patterns, and physique. Since the 1830s, minstrel shows had sold bigotry to white audiences. By 1910, the growing popularity of these performances in Northern cities suggested that the shows acted to dissipate—in a mean-spirited, but nonviolent way—much of the growing fear associated with the internal migration of blacks.

While the minstrel performances did much to advance satire, slapstick, and ad lib comedy in the United States, they did so at great cost to the few black performers able to find employment. Bob Cole and Will Marion Cook, both classically trained musicians, found work by composing coon songs for white casts. Bert Williams and George Walker, educated black actors, were typecast into self-denigrating roles that mocked the efforts of many African Americans to assimilate into the closed, racist white culture.

African Americans attempted to combat racism on the stage. The National Association for the Advancement of Colored People (NAACP) actively promoted the work of black playwrights, helped stage their work, and openly condemned the obvious hatred that supported such plays as Edward Sheldon's *The Nigger* (1910) and, later,

---

> ### NOTABLE THEATER OF THE 1910s
>
> *Peg O' My Heart,* 1912 (603 perfs.)
>
> *Within the Law,* 1912 (541 perfs.)
>
> *Potash and Perlmutter,* 1913 (441 perfs.)
>
> *The Boomerang,* 1915 (522 perfs.)
>
> *The Man Who Came Back,* 1916 (457 perfs.)
>
> *Maytime,* 1917 (492 perfs.)
>
> *Oh, Boy,* 1917 (463 perfs.)
>
> *East Is West,* 1918 (680 perfs.)
>
> *Everything,* 1918 (461 perfs.)
>
> *Lightnin',* 1918 (1,291 perfs.)
>
> *Irene,* 1919 (675 perfs.)

movies such as *The Birth of a Nation*. W.E.B. Du Bois, a driving force in the NAACP, authored *The Star of Ethiopia* in 1913, and Ridgely Torrence wrote *Three Plays for a Negro Theatre* (1917) to highlight racial tensions and inequality. African American writers and actors found a more welcome reception in the experimental Little Theatres, such as Anita Bush's Lafayette Players, who staged a number of works written by and starring blacks. Eugene O'Neill's critically acclaimed *The*

Emperor Jones (1920) starred African American Charles Gilpin in the title role. Still, these were limited and largely symbolic protests against the widespread bigotry of the era. It was not until the Harlem Renaissance and Jazz Age of the 1920s that significant change in the attitudes of white audiences and artists occurred on the American stage.

Vaudeville had deep connections to American society in the 1910s. Permanent vaudeville

A cast of scantily clad but artistically arranged Ziegfeld girls in "Midnight Frolic." Edna French and others. Prints & Photographs Division, Library of Congress.

theaters replaced the touring revue shows around the turn of the century. Most typical productions included eight or nine separate acts, which included comedians, singers, dancers, acrobats, jugglers, and ventriloquists. Headliners included starts such as W. C. Fields, Will Rogers, Eddie Cantor, the Marx Brothers, or Fanny Brice.

By 1910, Chicago had 22 vaudeville theaters, Philadelphia, 30, and New York City, nearly 40. While chains similar to the Syndicate attempted to lock in the best acts, the need for fresh material and a surplus of unusual acts generally kept the forum open. Audiences could be ruthless in their rejection of performers, and managers used hooks to pull failing performers from the stage. Conversely, positive audience responses could sustain a talented but repetitious act for years. Many of those who succeeded became known for their consummate skill and masterful delivery. As a result, the vaudeville stage often was the best location for experimental European and American artists to demonstrate their crafts. Well-known performers such as Sarah Bernhardt and Anna Pavlova also toured with vaudeville companies during the decade. Popular vaudeville actors such as Charles (soon to be Charlie) Chaplin were hesitant to turn to film because it was not considered as "respectable" as the people's theater.

Two of America's most popular vaudeville performers were Al Jolson and George M. Cohan. Jolson, known today largely as the star of the first synchronized sound film, *The Jazz Singer* (1927), was perhaps the most energetic and well-loved stage figure of the 1910s. Performing in a one-man show, punctuated by others during his breaks, at the Shubert's Winter Garden Theatre in New York, Jolson sang, danced, performed minstrelry, and told jokes.

The so-called girly shows also reflected the changing tastes of American theatergoers. Certainly, the appeal of young and attractive females on stage was not unique to the 1910s. Rather, it was during this decade that producers first capitalized on this temptation while remaining within the accepted norms of polite society. At the fore was Florenz Ziegfeld, born in Chicago, trained in vaudeville, and dedicated to his motto, Glorifying the American Girl. Ziegfeld's revue, called the *Ziegfeld Follies,* created a glamorous, exciting, and refined show for young women that would remain a standard for decades. He demanded that "his girls" have ample hips, perfect teeth, and an effervescent stage personality. The well-choreographed production numbers featured exotic costumes of feathers, chiffon, and color, which often cost thousands of dollars. Despite the arduous training required, Ziegfeld received more than 15,000 applications a year from women interested in an audition—in part a reflection of the grandeur the country saw in the New York stage. While Ziegfeld had little interest in the comedy presented between dance numbers, his shows featured some of the country's most talented performers. By 1917, one could see Fanny Brice, Bert Williams, Leon Errol, Ed Wynn, W. C. Fields, Eddie Cantor, and Will Rogers in a single show performing routines they had perfected on the vaudeville stage.

AMERICAN DANCE

Formal American dance saw few changes in the 1910s. While dance numbers remained part of the vaudeville, theater, and film repertoire, few of these productions qualified as anything more than glorified marches parading pretty women across the stage. One noteworthy exception was the extraordinary dance team of Vernon and Irene Castle, who appeared in 1914 in the Broadway musical comedy *Watch Your Step.* The Castles's elegance and energy on stage was augmented by their willingness to coordinate their movements closely to the rhythm of the music. In addition, the Castles developed an engaging presence in the emerging nightclub and cabaret scene of New York City. The Castle walk was one of the first styles to be transported from the stage to the popular dance studios. The fox trot, popularized by vaudeville comedian Harry Fox while at the *Ziegfeld Follies,* also achieved notoriety by 1913.

Up until 1910, theater, vaudeville, and nightclubs avoided being labeled as vulgar pastimes in large part because they successfully segregated their audience based on class, race, and gender. At that time, it would have been considered scandalous to be seen dancing in public because of the threat to these strong social norms. The cabaret settings smashed these taboos. New York clubs such as the Sans Souci, launched by the Castles in 1913, provided venues for women to practice public dancing during afternoon "teas," and then for the tony late night set to dance until dawn.

The more academic forms of public dance, such as ballet, were nearly nonexistent in the United States. As with drama, ballet was experiencing a renaissance in Europe. On May 29, 1913, Russian dancer Vaslav Nijinsky's brilliant yet abrasive interpretation of Igor Stravinsky's *Le Sacre du Printemps* (The Rite of Spring) led to a near riot at the Paris ballet. In Saint Petersburg, Moscow, and Berlin, there were equally daring changes. Only rare appearances, such as the tours by the Ballet Russe, were made in the United States, and these often were seen only on the popular vaudeville circuit—hardly an ideal location for serious appreciation. Some dancers did find the American markets profitable during the 1910s, such as Anna Pavlova, Mikhail Fokine, and Mikhail Mordin.

Paralleling the changes in music and an influx of immigrants, popular dance began the process of borrowing and synthesizing that would lead to an explosion of creativity in the coming decade. In addition to the customary waltzes and polkas of the old country, American barn dances, two-steps, and marches were widely known and practiced at music halls and family gatherings throughout the country.

Finally, the decade saw the emergence of a small number of black tap dancers on the vaudeville stage. Tap dancing, pioneered on the stage by men like Willie Covan, was well suited to the rapid pace of vaudeville and the sound of modern America. By 1917, after a lifetime of touring, Covan was accepted into many of the more popular vaudeville theaters on a regular basis. The majority of adult black performers, however, rarely broke through to success at commercial theaters.

THE BUSINESS OF MOTION PICTURES

No single decade was as consequential to American cinema as the 1910s. By 1910, it was estimated that more than 25 million Americans (out of a total of 92 million) attended a movie *every day* of the year. By the middle of the decade, gross annual revenues for the industry were more than $735 million, exceeding that of automobiles and trailing only the railroad, textile, steel, and oil industries. When Mary Pickford, an experienced but typical stage actress, signed with Biograph Pictures in 1909, she earned $175 per week. By 1917, First National Films had agreed to pay her $1 million to work in three of their pictures. Two years later, the entrepreneur joined her husband, Douglas Fairbanks, Charlie Chaplin, and D. W. Griffith to form United Artists.

Seeking to unify the largest manufacturers into a trust, Thomas Edison created the Motion Picture Patents Company (MPPC) in January 1909, which included Biograph, Vitagraph, Essanay, Selig, Lubin, Kalem, two French companies, and Edison's Western Electric Company. The MPPC sought to monopolize the American market by licensing all projection equipment and by establishing an exclusive arrangement for film stock through Eastman Kodak.[3]

The film industry experienced phenomenal growth and complexity by 1910. The first projection motion picture theater opened in 1902, and by 1910 there were approximately 8,000 to 10,000. Operated in small storefront operations, usually with nothing more than a series of benches and a crude screen, the theaters soon took the collective name "nickelodeons" as a reflection of the typical cost for admission. Largely as a result of the entertainment "rules" established by vaudeville, patrons demanded a variety of styles of performances in their shows. Theater owners wanted a reliable availability of films to rent. Distributors emerged to purchase films and circulate them for rent to the theater owners.[4]

The MPPC hoped to standardize and control the production, distribution, and exhibition of film through their trust. The control over the production of movies seemed the easiest to secure. Preventing filmmakers from buying raw stock or cameras not controlled by the trust was fairly straightforward in most Eastern cities like Chicago and New York (where most movies were made). Some filmmakers moved to Oklahoma, Texas, and the burgeoning city of Los Angeles, which had nearly perfect natural conditions for filming as well as easy access to contraband cameras and film from Mexico. The MPPC threatened to remove exhibitors' projectors or cut off the supply of films unless exhibitors paid the weekly licensing fees and showed only MPCC movies. For distribution, the trust created a film exchange clearinghouse, called the General Film Company (1910), which circulated and underwrote the production of many films. By 1912, the Motion Pictures Patent Company controlled all but one of the 58 existing distribution companies in the United States.[5]

The MPPC's restricting of free trade had some positive effects. The trust increased the quality and general availability of films nationwide. They also lowered the price for most films and stabilized the acting, directing, and producing talent pools. Their willingness to remove damaged films and projectors from circulation and their ability to rent rather than sell their motion pictures supported the young industry.

Two firms finally broke the grip of the MPPC during the 1910s: Carl Laemmle of Independent Motion Picture (IMP) Company and the Greater New York Film Rental Company, the lone remaining independent distribution company, owned by William Fox. Both men were immigrants who made their fortunes in operating strings of small nickelodeons. In 1912, Laemmle formed Universal Pictures, which combined IMP with a host of smaller independent producers, and moved to Los Angeles. He began to sign and promote popular movie stars and feature-length films which Americans could see only at independent theaters. Fox experimented with novel production and presentation methods that appealed to moviegoers' desires for a more exciting theater experience. Both men used Americans' distrust of monopolies to their advantage. They filed antitrust suits and used newspapers to discredit the MPPC. By lowering costs and making better films, the two effectively undermined the power of the trust.

THE STYLE OF EARLY MOVIES

With few exceptions, movies made before 1910 were quickly forgotten. Limited to single reels, which provided less than ten minutes of screen time, and filmed in a day or two, early movies spent little time in developing good stories or sympathetic characters. Much of the material

produced was vulgar, and respectable actors generally shunned the medium until the last years of the 1900s. Most films, sold by the foot, were little more than a series of stunts, travelogs, or hackneyed melodramas. David Wark (D. W.) Griffith, for example, directed more than 400 single-reel films between 1908 and 1913.[6] While this groundbreaking director would go on to completely redefine the style and structure of film, only rare glimpses of his genius are evident in these early offerings.

While the urban working class made up a sizable percentage of filmgoers, by 1910 rural and urban middle-class citizens also frequented movies in great numbers. As with vaudeville, these diverse audiences demanded high quality and excitement. One incorrect assumption that people hold today is that the films of the 1910s suffered from poor production values—scratchy images, action that was too fast, and, of course, no sound. In reality, reproductions today do not recreate how the films were originally shown. The film quality was very good, and the finished prints were often tinted with colors and used extensive in-theater sound accompaniment. The versions that exist today are black-and-white reproductions of second or third copies of originals, which were usually saved only after long runs in theaters. The reproducing equipment, by the 1930s, ran at a faster pace than the original, hand-cranked cameras captured the action.

Finally, movie acting and narratives took on decidedly different forms from those used in live theater. When the accomplished actress Sarah

---

NOTABLE MOVIES

Gertie the Dinosaur, 1914

Kid Auto Races at Venice, 1914

The Perils of Pauline, 1914

The Birth of a Nation, 1915

Intolerance, 1916

The Poor Little Rich Girl, 1917

Rebecca of Sunnybrook Farm, 1917

Tom Sawyer, 1917

Broken Blossoms, 1919

Bernhardt starred in the movie *Queen Elizabeth* (1912), her actions seemed exaggerated and foolish. Many other early actors in film used the same overly expressive stage style with similar results. The new reality was that the closeness of camera canceled the need for dramatic embellishment. Viewers could see the actors clearly and the words were printed for all to read. Storytelling also changed because writers and directors could cut scenes that did not further the plot.

THE STAR SYSTEM AND FEATURE FILMS

The combined growth of Hollywood, the spread of the star system, the use of feature-length (multireel) films, and the rise of the new movie theaters signaled the true emergence of modern film in the United States. By 1911, when the major independents and even some of the licensed production companies moved to California, the effective control of the MPPC had been broken. George Spoor and his business partner, Gilbert Anderson, founders of Essenay (named after their initials), were the first to relocate in 1910, and they began to produce hundreds of traditional film shorts. By 1914, 52 companies were purchasing vast tracks of land from the nearby lemon and orange growers. While competition between the firms was fierce, Hollywood provided movie producers enough space, actors, and set locations for most to concentrate on reaping the profits of the era.

The spread of the star system also helped to undermine the MPPC. Before this, most actors were paid by the day for their service and rarely received screen credit for their work. When actors did catch the eye of the public, either for their looks or acting abilities, they received fan mail addressed to "the Vitagraph Girl," "Biograph Girl," or, nicknames such as American Sweetheart, Mary Pickford. The appearance of fan magazines such as *Motion Picture Story Magazine* and *Photoplay* helped propagate the glamour of film stars. In June 1910, Florence Lawrence was labeled the first motion picture star by fan magazine *New York Dramatic Mirror*. Lawrence was also the first actor "stolen" by another producer, Carl Laemmle, for the then unheard of sum of $175 a week. When

Pickford followed Lawrence to IMP, it signaled the start of intense bidding wars for the biggest tars.

Feature-length films also placed pressure on established producers accustomed to mass-produced shorts. While the idea of using multiple reels to show a film was not new, what producers showed on these films was. Longer films meant more complex narratives, which required artistic directors to tell the story visually in ways that conveyed the appropriate emotions at the designated time. Features also created stronger bonds between the audience and stars, quickening the cycle between the public's demand for their favorite actors and the studio's production of films.

The expansion of film content allowed studios to standardize their fare while giving artists a creative new medium. Genre or type films first appeared in the 1910s as a result of the feature. Probably the best example of this was the success of the movie serial. Each week in these serials, the stars were placed in harm's way, only to be rescued in the next installment in ways that were ever more daring. With little plot development, idiotic characters, and corny morality, the serials were easy to produce and proved to be popular with the public. The most famous of these, *The Perils of Pauline* (1914), starred Pearl White in a role that she would reprise, under different character names but always blindly trusting the villain, until 1923. While cliffhangers certainly brought people back to the theater, they did little to advance the craft.

Finally, the appearance of luxurious movie palaces throughout the decade signaled a qualitative shift in how Americans experienced the movies. While the MPPC retained control over many of the smaller nickelodeons, by 1910 moviegoers were becoming increasingly dissatisfied with these small outfits. Few exhibitors had plans to invest money in more comfortable seats, better screens, or ambience. By contrast, movie houses were designed to seat hundreds of patrons comfortably in an environment of luxury.

Certainly, the sudden appearance of Hollywood, the star system, feature films, and the new cinemas had a destabilizing effect on the MPPC organization. The trust was undermined in its efforts to control the industry by entrepreneurs who relied on the public's willingness to pay for a better form of entertainment. Yet until the end of the decade, no rival structure existed to compete with the MPPC for supremacy. As a result, the stars and film content of the 1910s played a pivotal role in the nature and direction of motion pictures. Pioneers in both acting and directing emerged during the decade, with profound consequences for American popular culture.

THE STARS

During the 1910s, female stars both expanded the perceived boundaries of Victorian righteousness while they also strengthened them. Dorothy and Lillian Gish, both of whom became celebrities under the direction of Griffith, personify this creative tension. Dorothy, the older sister, was less popular than her sibling, but since fewer of her earliest films survive, it is unclear who was the better actor. Usually Dorothy was assigned supporting roles that built upon her ability to project warmth, mischief, and female sensuality.

Lillian Gish was one of the eminent performers of the era. She played the leading female role in D. W. Griffith's most critically important films, such as *The Birth of a Nation* (1915), *Intolerance* (1916), *Hearts of the World* (1918), and *Broken Blossoms* (1920). Lillian, who had been performing on the stage since childhood, played fragile, youthful beauties with a deep but tragic strength. She served as Griffith's unofficial and uncredited assistant director throughout most of these productions.

If Dorothy and Lillian Gish represented the warm and demure Victorian woman-child ideal, then Theda Bara characterized the threatening and sexually charged, liberated woman. Bara, who was born Theodosia Goodman to middle-class parents in Cincinnati, Ohio, was rumored in the fan magazines to have immigrated from northern Africa with a mixture of Egyptian and Arab blood and an ancestry that traced back to the Ptolemies. She appeared in *A Fool There Was* (1915) as a "sexual vampire" who seduced and ruined unsuspecting men. She played a vamp in almost all of the 40 movies she made at Fox. William Fox orchestrated a publicity campaign that took full advantage of the sensational movie. It was leaked to the press that her stage name was an anagram

for "Arab Death," and her hobbies were listed as astrology and alchemy. Bara made one attempt to break out of her typecast when she played a sweet and likable lead in *Kathleen Mavoureen* (1919). It was both a critical and commercial disaster.

While Dorothy and Lillian Gish and Theda Bara all three portrayed women who were publicly confident and intellectually capable, their screen personas contained strong support for the prevailing biases toward the "proper place" of women in American society.

Mary Pickford

While these examples suggest that Hollywood's star system constrained, rather than freed, dramatic artists on the screen, the careers of Mary Pickford and Charlie Chaplin provide strong counter-evidence: the "New Personality" film stars were able to puncture many of society's strongest prejudices and intolerance. Pickford was born Gladys Mary Smith in Toronto in 1893. Following her father's death, she and her siblings performed on the stage, where they changed their names. Pickford's small frame and noble bearing gave her a strong stage presence, and she rose to prominence in the New York theater by 1909. Facing a rare stretch of unemployment, Pickford decided to augment her stage income with performances in film. While her movie roles were similar to many other young women's, her pixie-like appearance gave her a special sympathetic quality. Lacking any credits, she became known as "Little Mary" or the "Biograph Girl" in most of her fan mail.

Pickford took full advantage of the economic potential of the star system. Stolen away from Biograph by Carl Laemmle, Pickford jumped from IMP to Majestic, then back to Biograph, next to Famous Players, then American Film, and finally First National. With each new contract, her salary and creative freedom increased, from $175 per week while first at Biograph to the million dollar contract from First National in 1918.

Pickford's screen characters remained fairly constant throughout the decade. While usually the unfair victim of poverty, society, or an abusive male, Mary showed strength and resilience in her ability to overcome obstacles. Because of her

Actors Mary Pickford and Charlie Chaplin seated on shoulders of Douglas Fairbanks, ca. 1915. Prints & Photographs Division, Library of Congress.

small size, large eyes, and curly hair, Pickford was repeatedly cast as an adolescent. Even her much publicized divorce of Owen Moore and marriage to Douglas Fairbanks in 1919 did little to damage the luster of America's Sweetheart.

Her association with D. W. Griffith solidified her star status. Early movies and her successful stage run in *The Good Little Devil* (1913) established her charm and gentility. But it was with Griffith in *Tess of Storm County* (1914) that the Little Mary persona was firmly established. Griffith's strong direction and exceptional eye for editing captured the rebelliousness, independence, and energy of youthful freedom that was so appealing to moviegoers. While her later productions, such as *Rebecca of Sunnybrook Farm* (1917) and *M'liss* (1918), demonstrated an actor of wide range and immense depth, she never strayed far from her central character.

In both her business dealings and screen roles, Pickford tapped into a growing awareness by American women of their potential for

independence from men. Her contract battles, public appearances, weekly newspaper column, and national advocacy for women's suffrage demonstrated to America a new and self-aware modern woman. While she acted in films that were written and directed within the milieu of strong Victorianism (especially under Griffith), her star power and screen presence usually overshadowed the stagy morality of the stories.

Charlie Chaplin

Between 1914 and 1918, Chaplin not only dominated American cinema but also appeared in popular music, children's games, cartoons, and other forms of popular entertainment. In July 1915, New York City hosted 30 Chaplin amateur nights where dozens of Derby-wearing tramps waddled across local stages. By the end of the decade, Chaplin counted among his friends and professed admirers Albert Einstein, Winston Churchill, Mahatma Gandhi, James Joyce, and Pablo Picasso.[7]

Charles Chaplin was born in the slums of Lambeth, London in 1889. Charles and his half-brother, Sydney, earned jobs with the celebrated Karno pantomime company, which toured the American vaudeville circuit in 1911 and 1913. In May 1913, Mark Sennett offered him a lucrative one-year, $150-per-week contract with the Keystone Company, which lured a hesitant Chaplin to the slightly disrespectful movie industry.

While with Keystone, Chaplin made 35 films in which his character tended to mock the stereotypic English gentleman (a role Chaplin had perfected over the years). In his second film for Sennett, *Kid Auto Races at Venice* (1914), Chaplin displayed his tramp character for the first time. He assembled the outward appearance of the character—false mustache, loose and ill-matched clothes, the Derby hat—from castaway props found on the Keystone lot. The character evolved from an abrasive and slightly contemptible man to a lovable and honorable free spirit that captured the attention of moviegoers.

The combination of Sennett's productivity and the actor's skill established "Charlie" Chaplin as a star. While a January 1915 poll of readers of *Motion Picture Magazine* failed to cite him in their

Entertainment

Charlie Chaplin as the Little Tramp. Prints & Photographs Division, Library of Congress.

top one hundred actors, competing production companies noted the packed theaters and rising anticipation for Chaplin's work. That month, he left Sennett for Essanay for $1,250 per week and a $10,000 signing bonus. One year later, Mutual signed him for $10,000 per week and a $150,000 bonus. In 1918, Chaplin signed with First National for $1 million and complete creative control as producer, director, writer, and star.[8]

Almost all of Chaplin's films of the era made large profits, and many are regarded as classics today. His best work during the decade stems from the Mutual years and includes *One A.M.*, *The Pawnshop*, *The Rink*, *Easy Street*, *The Immigrant*, and *The Adventurer*, all released between 1916 and 1917. In each, Chaplin deepened and strengthened his character's empathy for the world around him. For example, in *Easy Street*, he examines social reform movements, and in *The Immigrant*, he examines the problems of capitalism. In these films, Chaplin was able to make his audience aware of class tensions and poverty without preaching or losing his ability to entertain.[9]

In many ways, the recognition of Chaplin's "genius" and the seemingly easy way in which he moved through society provided theorists with an example of how to connect the arts with the masses in ways that were meaningful for both. The lack of sound probably helped Chaplin, who was adept at using his expressions, body, and props to convey emotions. When sound did arrive in the movies, Chaplin was unwilling to put words in the tramp's mouth and continued to rely on his visual communication skills.

Chaplin interjected a subtle criticism of American society that resonated with the experiences of millions. In many of his films, Chaplin portrayed law enforcement officials as cruel and menacing rather than as agents of justice. Institutions such as businesses, the church, and government show little concern for the real suffering of the people. While Charlie applies a bandage to the problems—often with only a smile, some food, or a well-placed kick in the pants—frequently his movies ended with him departing honorably beaten, or with his character awakening from a dream. In either case, the problems were on public display and left to be solved by an audience which probably had only stopped in for a good laugh.

While Chaplin's personal life and opinions would distract from his international fame in the coming decades, in the 1910s the only dark cloud that hovered over him was World War I. As a British citizen (he never pursued U.S. citizenship) in a country that was decidedly anti-German, Chaplin was regarded as slighting his country in its hour of need. As a result, Chaplin became very active in wartime propaganda both in selling Liberty Bonds and in filmmaking. In May 1918, he released *Shoulder Arms* which had Charlie going through boot camp, in the trenches, and assaulting a German position. Significantly, Chaplin did not portray the Germans as subhuman beasts, but rather suggested that it was the war itself that was the root of human suffering.

THE POWER OF THE FEATURE FILM

Feature, or multireel, films also had a decisive effect on the collapse of the MPPC. By expanding the format of film, independents opened the door to creative talents. The shift from strict rental fees to a smaller lease with a percentage of the box-office receipts ensured exhibitors that the new, longer films would always have the interests of the ticket buyers in mind. As a result, cinematic story-telling became more complex and the characters more real. In the case of the career of D. W. Griffith, this innovation allowed for radical changes in the ways in which films could be structured as well as how the public would receive them.

Not all feature films led to significant change. In the case of the portrayal of African Americans, for example, the feature-length movie simply amplified many of the prevailing biases. In *Confederate Spy* (1910), *For Massa's Sake* (1911), and the first version of *Uncle Tom's Cabin* (1914), African Americans were categorized as acceptable only when they served whites faithfully and unquestioningly, and were quick to turn to God and not against racist America in order to deal with their suffering. In *How Rastus Got His Turkey* (1910), which spawned a host of serials, blacks were portrayed as simpletons without a care other than the next meal or the next song and dance.

When combined with the artistry of a director like D. W. Griffith, such imagery could be harnessed as a powerful incentive for whites to lash out at the powerless.

D. W. GRIFFITH

D. W. Griffith was a movie director who first gave meaning and artistry to the feature film. His editorial prowess, sharp eye for talent, and, above all, willingness to take risks in his films resulted in some of the most important movies of all time. Today Griffith is seen as the key to understanding the development of American *and* European narrative film; his movies are required viewing as sources of inspiration and enlightenment. Yet his social agenda included racism, a rejection of the modern independent woman, and an utter disregard for historical fact. When Griffith died in 1948 he was not only destitute, but also largely ignored by the cinematic community for his outdated prejudices and sappy Victorian morality.

Griffith, born in Kentucky in 1875, began his career in films by accident. Intending to write

melodramatic plays for the stage, he turned to acting and screen writing out of financial necessity in 1907. Within a year, Biograph offered him the chance to direct. From his tentative beginning until 1913, Griffith produced more than 450 shorts for Biograph. While the scripts he followed were no better than others, his filming, editorial, and technical abilities were being honed. In addition, he became an astute judge of talent, surrounding himself with natural actors such as Pickford and the Gish sisters, and gifted cameramen like Billy Bitzer, who could translate his cinematic vision into actual film scenes.

Griffith made it easier for directors to tell complex and emotional stories which did not rely on dense written or verbal communication. Griffin frequently changed camera positions to give single-room scenes greater depth, panned across the room, or mounted the camera on tracks to achieve a rolling effect. He pioneered the use of close-ups and faraway shots, fades in and out, and variable lighting, and he used scenes consisting of three-dimensional props, the outdoors, buildings, and other objects to create mood. The dynamic emotional power unleashed by crosscuts, which allowed the viewer to see action taking place at several locations at the same time, were simply impossible to duplicate in live theater.

His novel approach to filming did not happen by accident. Griffith's experienced crews of actors and technicians remained with him for long stretches of his career. Billy Bitzer served as Griffith's chief cameraman from 1908 to 1924. Lillian Gish acted in most of his films of the 1910s and performed many of the duties of an assistant director. Griffith pressured his film companies to retain the services of these craftsmen as their market value increased over the years. He also held expensive and time-consuming dress rehearsals for his films, something undreamed of in an era when most movies were shot in about a week. Moreover, beginning in 1912, Griffith began to seek out longer, more difficult scripts and subjects to film. By late 1913, while he was acknowledged as a uniquely talented director, Biograph balked at the added expense of his films. Unlike movie stars, directors did not yet draw patrons to the cinemas. Griffith left for the independent Mutual Company, taking with him his entire cast and crew, with an agreement giving him complete creative control over some films provided that he mass-produce others.

The Birth of a Nation

Griffin intended for *The Birth of a Nation* (1915) to consummate the merger of his technical virtuosity with the power of a modern epic. Knowing that European directors had experimented with monumental feature films, such as the eight-reel *Quo Vadis* (1913) released in Italy with a cast of thousands, Griffith began work on a similar project intended to dramatize the historic sweep of the Civil War and Reconstruction in the United States. Griffith chose for his landmark film a book written by Thomas Dixon Jr., titled *The Clansman: A Historical Romance of the Ku Klux Klan* (1905). The novel portrayed members of the KKK as heroes bent on returning the South to white rule. Racist to the core, the text was immensely popular with Southerners such as Griffith, whose father served in the Confederacy. Griffith shot the work in nine weeks, after six weeks of rehearsal. Costing $110,000 and running 13 reels, the movie premiered in New York under the title *The Clansman* on March 3, 1915. After viewing the magnificent epic, Dixon suggested that the title be changed to reflect the importance of the film's thesis.

The critically acclaimed movie was a great financial success for Griffith. Reviews nationwide suggest it was not Griffith's directorial organizational and editing, but rather the offensive racial stereotyping that affected white audiences powerfully. The "brutal black buck" typecast was everywhere, from sex-crazed crowds of freed blacks to an armed renegade named Gus who pursued a fair woman to her death, while black bumpkins used their time in the state legislatures to get drunk. Central to the drama was the assumption that there were "proper places" for blacks in America, and that the mixture of races inevitably led to chaos. Only the bravery of the Klan was able to restore white supremacy temporarily.

The response by fair-minded Americans was swift and loud. Progressives such as Jane Addams labeled the film an abomination. The NAACP or-

ganized massive demonstrations in Chicago and Boston, and the movie was eventually banned in five states and fifteen cities.

Griffith was stung by the criticism. To him, it was the unnatural conditions of Reconstruction, not innate depravity in blacks, that led to the fictional and devilish behavior on the part of his characters (all played by white minstrels). That this message was equally racist, historically incorrect, and never once made explicit in the two hour plus movie escaped Griffith's notice.

Intolerance and Beyond

Seeking to distance himself from the roiling domestic politics in the United States, Griffith made *Intolerance* (1916). Using four separate narratives—the trial and death of Jesus, the Saint Bartholomew's Day Massacre of Protestants in medieval France, the fall of Babylon, and the persecution of a reformed criminal in contemporary America—and an enigmatic mother rocking a cradle, Griffith hoped to draw historical

---

NOTABLE ACTORS OF THE 1910s

Roscoe "Fatty" Arbuckle, 1887–1933

Theda Bara, 1885–1955

Ethel Barrymore, 1879–1959

Lionel Barrymore, 1878–1954

Fanny Brice, 1891–1951

Charlie Chaplin, 1889–1977

George M. Cohan, 1878–1942

Douglas Fairbanks Sr., 1883–1939

W. C. Fields, 1880–1946

Dorothy Gish, 1898–1968

Lillian Gish, 1893–1993

Al Jolson, 1886–1950

Tom Mix, 1880–1940

Mary Pickford, 1893–1979

Lillian Russell, 1861–1922

Florence E. Turner, 1885?–1946

Ed Wynn, 1886–1966

Entertainment

connections between the common ways societies have overridden the rights of their citizens because of ignorance, hypocrisy, and, of course, intolerance. Running more than three hours, the film was amazingly complex with all four narratives combined together. Griffin's continuing mastery of editing, filming, understated acting, and lighting techniques nearly carried the film, but mixture proved too confusing for audiences to follow and the pacifist message ran counter to a period when the drums of war were beating loudly in the United States. The fortune that Griffith earned for *Birth* was lost.

Griffith's directed several more commercially successful films, including *Broken Blossoms* (1919) and *Isn't Life Wonderful?* (1924). Still, after 1916, his career went into a decline and in 1924, he lost creative control over his projects.

Griffith's eventual failure was largely due to the narratives he chose to film. *Birth* and *Intolerance* were stiff morality plays that favored Victorian sensibilities. In addition, his movies suggested that easy answers were possible if people would simply return to these values. Most of Griffith's popular films were remembered because of the actors who appeared in them, although *The Birth of a Nation* proved that Americans would accept complex (and long) movies that appealed to their intellect as well as their emotions. The power of his imagery and editing skills, so evident in *Intolerance,* was soon grafted to even the most formulaic Hollywood offerings.

Fashion

of the 1910s

In the 1910s, the newly rich sought ways to flaunt their wealth conspicuously through their clothing and accessories. Styles included the use of expensive ornamentation and accessories. While department stores and mail-order catalogs provided knockoff styles for the masses, those without disposable income strove for function, not fashion in their clothing.

By the close of the decade, fashion trends had abandoned much of clothing's layered garishness for a newfound freedom of movement and expression. The rise of international fashion trends and the expansion of popular entertainment made much of the old bundled look seem obsolete. In addition, World War I and the changes to notions of women in America contributed to the shift in fashion.

FASHION TRENDS

With the changing seasons, fashion trends fell into a regular pattern. Each year, new styles were introduced in the spring and fall and were adopted, rejected, or modified by the coming season. Clearly, not every American changed his or her wardrobe with every new design. Many used embroidery, appliqués, and accessories to modify existing clothing. Still, by 1910, it was considered unwise for most women to have a large inventory of clothing going into late summer, as the fashions were no doubt about to change.

In 1910, the Gibson girl S-shaped silhouette still held sway in American women's fashion. (See Fashion of the 1900s.) Designers highlighted small waists, large bosoms, and curved rears through the use of corsets and multiple layers of heavy fabrics. By the following year, the style was on the decline as the work of Paul Poiret, a Parisian fashion designer, focused on a lighter, more natural look. The hobble skirt, with its tight gatherings at the knees and ankles, enjoyed a brief popularity owing to its controversial design and a censure from the pope. In 1911, necklines were lowered, the "Greek" style was introduced, and full-length fur coats became popular in the wealthier crowds. Influenced by the movies, turbans and "tray hats" adorned with plumage were considered fashionable. Throughout these early years of the decade, men's fashion remained predictable: striped pants, vests, starched shirts, and high collars. Tweed jackets and other blazers were more common, but gloves, hats, a gold watch with chain, a cane or walking stick, studs, and tie pins were still required for all occasions.

In 1913, slits appeared on the sides of day skirts and on the backs of evening dresses, exposing more of the leg and leading to more interesting and comfortable stockings and hosiery. The dance craze (led by the tango) had pioneered new "sensible" shoes, a flounced skirt, and pantaloon suits (with looser arms and legs to ease movement).

With the start of hostilities in Europe, Americans turned to more conservative fashion statements, including lower hemlines, natural waists, broader skirts and jackets, and simpler colors and prints. Military themes and khaki colors were also introduced. American female suffragists popularized dresses, suits, and coats with multiple pockets. The jumper-blouse (called simply a jumper by 1919) could be worn with a skirt or suit. In addition, men's fashion also became more relaxed. Jackets were rarely padded, trousers were slimmer, slash pockets replaced patch pockets, and, overall, there were fewer pleats.

During the war, men and women wore what was available and were less likely to buy new, seasonal clothing. The styles were dominated by function and comfort, and the colors were almost entirely muted (forced upon them by a lack of German-made dyes). After the war, the return of brighter colors and patterns, the use of formerly scare materials such as wool, leather, and silk, and the availability once again of ribbons, fringes, and feathers set the stage for a rebound in fashion.

Women's Clothing

Women's attire during the 1910s was more formal, but also more daring. Unlike men, nonworking women from families of more than modest means changed their clothes three or four times a day in 1910. The phases were divided among specific duties that these women might perform. In the morning, women wore coordinated outfits of shirts and short jackets that provided functional yet stylish cover while they shopped, managed their homes, and made frequent yet informal social visits. In the early afternoon, tea dresses were donned. These were made of lighter fabrics and had long, free-flowing skirts that did not require corsets or other bulky undergarments. Women formally received guests in their tea gowns, but it was also a time for them to be more relaxed without the need to act in a certain way or to be seen in public (in most romance novels of the era, it was during tea time and in tea dresses that married

Double ripple suit of tricotrine or serge (by Russek), March 22, 1918. Prints & Photographs Division, Library of Congress.

women entertained their lovers). The afternoon break divided the day and led to the third and possibly fourth change of clothes. Women and men dressed for dinner. If there were guests or after-dinner activities were planned, wives often changed after eating. Many dresses were satin, silk, or taffeta and featured low necklines, pleats, extensive costume and real jewelry, elaborate beadwork, feathers, and furs.

Hemlines rose throughout the decade, revealing ankles that had traditionally been concealed. Tight sleeves and bodices showed a greater willingness by women to reveal their figures. The wardrobe of a truly wealthy woman might contain scores of outfits complete with matching accessories. Even for those of moderate means, a young woman would expect to begin her adult life with at least "[t]welve evening gowns, two to three evening wraps, two to four street costumes, two coats, twelve hats and four to ten house dresses."[1] The evening gown was the most public form of fashion for women and, as a result, it varied greatly throughout the years.

Women's Undergarments

In the 1910s, women's undergarments were restrictive and often painful to wear (by contrast,

Women's fashions. A race gown, to be worn to a horse race, designed by Paquin, 1914. Prints & Photographs Division, Library of Congress.

Fashion was still strongly dictated based on the time of day and the activity. The wealthy changed clothes numerous times a day; poorer people sought functionality.

Women: Gibson Girl's corseted look, but hemlines rose slightly; hobble skirts; dresses featured tight sleeves and bodices; large hats; girls wore long hair down until they turned 18; makeup started becoming acceptable for "nice" females to wear.

Men: suits and hats were worn for everyday wear, but were less formal; young men wore dusters, goggles, gloves and caps; moustaches popular among youth.

men's undergarments consisted of a sleeveless T-shirt, boxer shorts, and hose supporters or garters to hold up their socks, which did not yet contain elastic bands). Women's undergarments took quite a bit of time and, for the most, required the assistance of another woman (family member, friend, or servant) to fasten and align them properly. The first layer consisted of white cotton drawers and a short silk slip (chemise), which were fastened behind with dainty ribbons and adorned with lace and embroidery.

Next came a corset made of heavyweight cotton twill, reinforced with steel or whalebone, and held together with hefty stud and loop fasteners. These artificially contoured women's bodies to create the desired "S-shape," which accentuated the bust, minimized the stomach, and highlighted the rear. Achieving this "natural look" through the use of corsets led not only to discomfort but also disfigurement. Bones could break and internal organs could be malformed as a result of these bindings. The best corset makers tailored their product to avoid these problems, but for those who could only afford over-the-counter varieties, an ill-fitting corset could mean hours of pain. (See Fashion of the 1900s.)

Rounding out these hidden outfits were supporters or suspenders, which kept the stockings from falling. These were needed since once corseted, a woman could not bend to reach her stockings. The stockings, made of cotton, wool, or silk, were often elaborately decorated with inlays and embroideries. Given that most of the leg remained hidden from view, the designs were usually concentrated on the foot and ankle, and they were coordinated with the cut, style, and color of the shoe.

Mary Phelps Jacob, a New York socialite, found that her corset prevented her from wearing the latest sheer fabrics being used in evening wear. In 1913, Jacob, with the help of her maid, devised a rudimentary brassiere using handkerchiefs, ribbon, and some cord. The following year, after requests from her friends for a similar article, Jacob patented the Backless Brassiere, but due to her lack of business acumen she could not profit from its manufacture and sale. She sold the patent to the Connecticut-based Warner Brothers Corset Company, who began to market the product successfully throughout the country. By 1920, there were dozens of suppliers using slightly modified designs. Women, especially young women, preferred the lighter, cooler, and less constraining brassiere.

Women's Accessories

Accessories that coordinated an outfit were also important for the fashionably dressed female. Affordable jewelry included hair combs made of tortoiseshell and adorned with feathers. Paste diamond (rhinestone) or glass earrings, tiaras, and choker necklaces were also common. Silver and bronze adornments such as buttons, lockets, and brooches were worn, but bracelets and rings were rarely worn. Purses, shoes, gloves, and bags in the 1910s coordinated or accentuated evening wear. Always matching the dress in color, purses were small and often made of delicate, impractical fabrics. Shoes rose just above the ankle and were secured with straps or buckles and had heels of middling height. Leather and suede gloves, also colored to match the dress, were either short or barely reached the elbow and often included modest glass, paste, or buttoned detail. For the true elite, these accessories were required for each of a woman's many outfits, extending to include furs, umbrellas, parasols, walking sticks, and fans. Most women, regardless of economic status, wore hats. Usually large (measuring nearly a yard across for the most radical), women's hats

THE GIBSON GIRL BECOMES THE NEW WOMAN

At the start of the decade, the "Gibson Girl" look was still the rage for most young women. Established by magazine illustrator Charles Dana Gibson in the 1890s, the look focused on the elegant and refined beauty of the well-dressed female. Corsets and other undergarments were required to generate the typical S-shaped curves. Hats, high collars, gloves, and other accessories framed a woman's face and body in ways that highlighted the "appropriate" features.

In the 1910s, this constructed image began to change in significant and long-lasting ways. Young women increasingly turned to more liberating undergarments. The "New Woman" was active, mobile, and more comfortable with her place in society. Other shifts in women's behavior added to this trend. For example, the spread of automobile travel gave rise to dusters, caps, and goggles. Sporting attire, which became popular for golf, tennis, croquet, and skating, allowed movement and flattered a woman's natural body shape, which the steel-and-whalebone construction of the Gibson look did not.

Ironically, one of the more prominent fashion crazes among young urban women was the "hobble skirt." With very tight gatherings at the knees and ankles, the dress was named for the way in which women were forced to walk when they wore them. When, by 1915, public dancing became the rage for this population, the hobble skirt faded from view. Dance also doomed the large hats, corsets, and voluminous dresses that had dominated women's fashions.

were adorned with a wide variety of plumage, beads, fringe, and pom-poms. The rage for feathers went so far as to prompt bird lovers, such as those of the Audubon Society, to attempt to limit the number and types of animals harvested to feed the fickle fashion industry.

Hairstyles and Cosmetics

Hairstyles and cosmetics contributed greatly to fashion in the 1910s. While men's styles were mainly conservative, grooming was very important. Hair was kept short and well trimmed. Moustaches were typical for young men and beards only for older gentlemen. Barbers applied dyes to color grey hair, and a variety of techniques were used to hide baldness or thinning hair. By contrast, women's coiffures were more creative. Girls wore their hair long until reaching their eighteenth birthdays. After "coming out" in society, young ladies curled, braided, and otherwise sculpted their long locks. For women who had thin hair, a postiche (hairpiece) was considered acceptable. These small wigs, often called "rats" by critics, were attached with ornate pins and combs. With the demise of large hats, hairstyles became of even greater importance.

Cosmetics and perfumes were also intended to be used as fashion accessories by the modern woman. The rise of cosmetics use in the United States followed a lengthy cultural battle over whether it was proper for a woman to "paint" herself or "put on a face" for public display; something, it was thought, that only prostitutes or lower-class women did. The heightened public presence of women in everyday life, including the stage, screen, and the many advertisements in pages of magazines and newspapers, made makeup acceptable. The cosmetics industry used medical terms to promote "beauty aids" that would highlight "natural" tone. Women such as Elizabeth Arden, Helena Rubenstein, Annie Turnbo, and the famous Sarah Breedlove (known to most by her marketing name of Madame C. J. Walker) were pioneers in the promotion, sales, and expansion of cosmetics in the modern era. Breedlove, an African American entrepreneur, created an economic empire through her employment of females who traveled door to door to meet the needs of the underserviced black population. Her pyramid marketing relied on trained saleswomen, often neighbors and family members, to lend legitimacy to the use of cosmetics in a large number of skeptical consumers. By the 1920s, cosmetics were enshrined in female culture.

MENSWEAR

While men claimed no less extensive of a wardrobe than women, the cut of their clothing was less varied. As a result, stylishness and fashion became even more important to distinguish a man from his peers, all of whom wore similar clothing to similar events. Unlike women, most men were not viewed as old-fashioned if they were seen in public wearing last year's styles (with the exception of the very wealthy, who closely followed the latest styles).

The average American male's typical dress consisted of trousers, shirt, collar, tie, and jacket. For formal occasions, gentlemen wore black morning coats (including tails which fell to the back of the knees), a heavily starched white shirt with studs and a high collar (some approaching three inches), a double-breasted waistcoat (vest), and striped grey or blue trousers, with a top hat, white gloves, and a grey or black frock coat for outdoor activities. The double-breasted frocks fell to or slightly below the knee and were made of a warm, durable material such as wool. Highly polished black patent leather shoes were worn by nearly all to formal occasions. An ornate cane, white boutonniere, or tightly wound umbrella often completed the ensemble. Some men still wore monocles, held by long and finely worked gold chains, but the practice was rare and certainly passed by 1919.

The style of lapels, the shape of collars, the number of buttons (on the coat and shirt), the cut of the cuffs (on shirts and pants), and the cut of the leg (baggy or straight) changed only slightly throughout the decade. Generally, men's attire became less formal and less physically restrictive. For example, the tighter lines of the double-breasted suit gave way—on informal occasions only—to the lounging suit (today called a business suit), which was tailored using a single-breasted style, without a vest, often with pants made of matching fabric. Tweed jackets and blazers were increasingly worn in public. These loose-fitting, pocketed lounge jackets remained popular in the United States despite being shunned by most men in Europe. Pants were generally cut narrow with small, half-inch cuffs. Even formal attire was toned down by Americans, who came to prefer the short and looser dinner jacket to the vest and morning coat combination.

Most men wore fur-collared Chesterfield overcoats or capes in cold weather. The Mackintosh, a raincoat imported from England, was popular because the waterproof garment did not exude the oily, rubber smell associated with other waterproof coats. The automobile duster, which consisted of a light cotton overcoat and usually extended to the ankles, was worn with matching caps, goggles, and gloves. Younger men began to wear the duster even when they were not driving. Sporting events, too, required a specific outfit depending upon the activity. Combinations of flannel trousers, blazers, knitted wool sweaters, and cotton shirts were used for outdoor casual entertainment. While men did not have a formal "tea" outfit, as did women, they wore velvet smoking jackets embellished with gold braided cord on the shoulders to lend the coats a masculine, military look. Silk ascot ties and cravats were common before 1914, but by the end of the decade were replaced by small, patterned bow ties and neckties made of silk or wool. Most men also carried a pocket watch (maintaining the need for vests), but by 1920 the trend was clearly moving toward the wristwatch.

FASHION IN STORES AND IN PRINT

The styles that were regularly worn by members of one's immediate social set generally set fashion trends. Ensembles and accessories would be standardized for at least the season (cold and warm weather months). Many popular magazines and newspapers of the era, such as *Life*, *McClure's*, *Good Housekeeping*, and *Ladies' Home Journal* helped Americans become comfortable with the quicker pace of change in the modern era. Many of their images highlighted the increased freedom in women's attire and suggested that the properly clad lady could achieve considerable social mobility. Fashionable women were viewed both as objects of desire and as individuals who had gained considerable control over men through their sexual power.

More traditional outlets for fashions were local dress shops, mail-order catalogs, and department stores, which had become common by 1910. Dressmakers adapted the fashion styles portrayed in the publications. Tailors to the very elite could command great prices, and access to their studios became limited by social status and time. In less

elite settings, the dressmakers did the best they could to copy the latest styles, convince their patrons of the need for change, and adapt these patterns to different body shapes. Paper patterns and complex written instructions were followed to allow women to dress in the latest style. Mail-order catalogs provided ready-made dresses and accessories for the masses that could be amended at home to fit the needs of the consumer. "Trimming" stores were common, offering a variety of bows, ribbons, buttons, feathers, and other accessories with which to personalize their wardrobes. Rarely did the lower classes fully copy the styles of the elite. Not only were these fashions impractical and expensive, but many people regarded dressing beyond "one's station in life" as presumptuous and in "bad taste."

The most important source of fashion for the typical shopper was the department store. By 1910, stores such as Marshall Field and Company, the Boston Store, and Wanamaker's had dedicated several floors of their massive emporiums to clothing and accessories. B. Altman and Company's Fifth Avenue showcase was typical. Their first floor—the most public space of the building—housed silk and velvet goods, laces, embroideries, women's neckware, gloves, hose, millinery, notions, umbrellas, handkerchiefs, and jewelry, as well as men's hats, coats, and shoes. On the upper floors, Altman's sold ready-made clothing, attire for children and infants, outfits for maids and nurses, coats, furs, shoes, undergarments, and specialty sports or active wear. The busy hive of activity on each floor, complete with floorwalkers, salespeople, and patrons, only added to the excitement felt by shoppers.

FASHION'S INFLUENCES

Some shifts in fashion were sparked by events traditionally not seen as part of the fashion world. For example, the rise of automobile travel for the average American led to entirely new outfits comprising dusters, gloves, caps, and goggles for both men and women. The success of the Ballet Russe, which toured the country throughout the decade, and the Post-impressionist art movement led to a variety of fads, including a simplified "Greek look" featuring straight lines, a lack of adornment,

Fashion

and vibrant colors. The movies popularized new styles that mirrored the childlike innocence of Mary Pickford or the sensual exoticism of Theda Bara. Even cigarette makers set fashion trends when they included picture postcards in their packs. While these tended to reinforce traditional styles such as the Gibson girl look, some introduced a more active, aggressive, and adventuresome female attire that cigarette makers thought more fitting for the woman who smoked.

The phenomenal popularity of dance partners Irene and Vernon Castle, after 1913, led to several changes to American fashion. In particular, the freedom and grace of Irene Castle's dancing provided women with new standards of beauty. The overdressed, staid looks of society matrons, who donned expensive clothing and accessories, were replaced by less constricting, certainly less layered styles. Castle's lithe body shape and youth also added to the new look. Younger consumers followed her wardrobe changes through the style magazines, and when Irene Castle cut her hair short before she underwent surgery, thousands of girls followed suit.

Such fashion trends had important social consequences in the United States. Women became more comfortable displaying their sexuality in public. While most sought to emulate the "wholesome and fresh" looks of the new woman portrayed in the popular periodicals, the looser clothing freed many women from the constricting confines of the corset. Even though most female performers, such as Irene Castle, maintained a studied pose of elegance while on stage (largely to separate themselves from the more "degenerate" forms of popular culture performed by women of color), their style allowed for a new sensuality. Even Vernon Castle, who rarely deviated from black formal wear, influenced men's wear by showing how the male dancer could be debonair without losing his masculinity. The trend toward wearing wristwatches (often considered bracelets by men) was accelerated when it became clear that Vernon wore his at all times.

Formal fashion designers also gave direction and legitimacy to these new trends. Most notable were Paul Poiret, a Parisian and the most influential fashion designer of the decade, and London's Lady Duff Gordon, also known as Lucille. Poiret,

who began in 1903, popularized the leaner look of the 1910s, simplifying dress design, and added to the move toward more natural beauty. His design house is credited with helping to end the reign of corsets in women's fashion and initiating the use of new colors and patterns. Poiret broke the reliance on the traditional colors of cream or white, pastel mauve, pink, or sky blue, and black, grey, and purple for all serious occasions. His palette included a wide range of hues, including the natural tones that are more common today. Lucille, too, while less dramatic than Poiret (she wore corsets), erased many of the more artificial curves in women's designs in favor of more flowing, drape-like dresses. Poiret also introduced formal fashion photography as both a promotional and artistic tool for designers.

In the United States, fashion-conscious women such as Edna Woolman Chase, editor in chief of

Fashion photograph for *Vogue* magazine, 1920. Prints & Photographs Division, Library of Congress.

Vogue, helped promote these designers through their publications and social contacts. After the outbreak of war in 1914, Chase held a series of fashion fêtes to raise money for the stricken fashion houses of Europe. Held at Henri Bendel's New York department store, the gatherings did more to advance the work of young American-based designers, including Maison Jacqueline, Tappé, Gunther, Kurzman, and Mollie O'Hara, than they helped the French industry. While the war lowered the output of European fashion designers, Poiret, Lucille, Gabrielle "Coco" Chanel, and others remained active and largely unchallenged in their world leadership.

Fashion

Food

of the 1910s

The foods and eating habits of Americans during the 1910s did not change in any dramatic way. The appearance of new foods, new production methods, and new dining options were in keeping with trends that extended both before and beyond the decade. Prepackaged goods, popular sweets, and simplified cooking directions suggest that modernity was having a lasting effect on the way in which Americans fed themselves. Americans experienced public eating as a form of popular entertainment, and being seen eating was often as important as actually doing the eating. Taken together with other shifts in popular culture, food patterns of the 1910s support the notion that Americans were increasingly more comfortable with using the material culture around them to define who they were to themselves and to others.

DIETARY CHANGES

Americans during the 1910s came to appreciate food in new and highly modern ways. The nutritional value of foods—including calories, compositions, and benefits—was of increasing interest to researchers looking for the best diet. The most noteworthy new discovery was that of vitamins. A wide variety of diseases, including scurvy, rickets, beriberi, and pellagra, were caused not by infection but, it was learned, by the lack of certain nutrients in the diet. Work in Europe led the research into vitamin nutrition, but American biochemists such as Casimir Funk also contributed to the identification of both the water and fat-soluble varieties of these compounds. Funk isolated the chemicals known as B1, B2, C, and D between 1912 and 1915. Later, he connected vitamins with hormones in identifying several other common diseases and maladies. When World War I broke out in 1914, the knowledge of vitamins was incorporated into the food rationing that was soon required by many European nations. Hoping to prevent widespread malnutrition in their populations—it was found that 41 percent of English recruits were considered in poor health as a result of nutritional deficiencies—governments attempted to balance the types of foods needed to provide an adequate amount of calories, proteins, minerals, and vitamins. It was not until the 1950s, however, that nutritional research was underwritten by the U.S. government and that food analysis was professionalized in this country.[1]

More typical for the decade and the country were nostrums and pseudo-scientific studies of proper nutritional and eating habits. Diet and nutritional books were not yet common, but many suggestions were adopted by the public. In 1910, Victor Hirtzler published *The St. Francis Cookbook*. Hirtzler was the head chef at the St. Francis Hotel in San Francisco where he became enamored of the lighter cuisine that was popular locally owing to the easy access to fresh fruits and vegetables. This California cuisine substituted salads, natural herbs, and vegetable and fish oils for the heavy meats, breads, and animal fats found in most existing fare. While not a best seller, Hirtzler's contribution began the development of a uniquely American style in cooking which would become an international sensation by the end of the century.

In general, the trend toward lighter dining was in keeping with more active pastimes, like dancing, which became popular during the decade. As social role models became younger and more energetic—such as ballroom dancers Irene and Vernon Castle or actors Mary Pickford and Douglas Fairbanks—the gluttony common at the turn of the century became passé. Perhaps no single man epitomized these old ways better than railroad tycoon "Diamond Jim" Brady. Eating as many as five or six meals a day, Brady's eating (as well as his clothing, female accompaniment, and jewelry, from which came his nickname) bordered on obscene. A typical breakfast for Brady included several quarts of orange juice, eggs, half a loaf of bread, a large steak, fried potatoes, onions, grits, bacon, muffins, coffee, and a full stack of pancakes. For Brady and his corpulent colleagues, eating was a public act intended to display their wealth. When Brady died in 1917, an autopsy showed that his stomach had enlarged to over six times that of an average man his height. By contrast, the lighter breakfast of toast and a single soft-boiled egg became the traditional morning meal of most chic diners in the 1910s.

Certainly, the contingencies caused by World War I contributed toward this trend in lighter eating. Shortages and rationing in the supply of certain foods—particularly meat, eggs, and wheat—led many to plant gardens at home. The introduction of fresh vegetables, herbs, and meatless dishes into the diet caused many cooks to rethink the traditional meals that they served before the war.

FOOD HIGHLIGHTS OF THE 1910s

1911 Procter & Gamble applies the relatively new process of hydrogenating liquid oils using hydrogen gas to produce Crisco, the first vegetable-based shortening that stays solid regardless of temperature. The Crisco can is sold in a white paper overwrap to emphasize its purity.

1912 The National Biscuit Company introduces Oreo Cookies, which are destined to become the best-selling American cookie of all time.

1912 Cracker Jack, already enshrined in the 1908 song "Take Me out to the Ball Game," begins inserting a toy in each package and using the slogan "A Prize in Every Box." Brand icons Sailor Jack and his dog, Bingo, appear on packaging four years later.

1916 James L. Kraft patents a processed cheese formula, based on milk solids, and calls it "American Cheese." He succeeds in selling 6 million pounds of the product to the U.S. Army.

1916 A schoolboy submits the winning drawing in a contest sponsored by Planters, and thus Mr. Peanut is born.

1916 In an effort to discourage copycat beverages, the Coca-Cola Company sponsors a contest to design a bottle so distinctive it could be recognized by feel in the dark. The Root Glass Company of Terre Haute, Indiana, comes up with the winning design for a "contour" shape still used by Coke in the twenty-first century.

Food

FOOD CULTURE: HOW FOOD WAS USED

For the most part, changes to food culture in the home during the 1910s were incremental, but they did shift how food was produced and consumed. Improved devices for food storage and cooking, new prepared foods, and the growth of suppliers able to furnish these goods accelerated trends toward greater convenience, flexibility, and reliability in American foods.

Probably the most important change to how food was prepared in the 1910s was the spread of electric devices for the kitchen. Following the Electric Exhibition at New York City in 1911, several new and innovative machines, including electric skillets, toasters, mixers, and waffle irons, became commonly available for affluent and upper middle-class consumers. The KitchenAid brand of noncommercial mixers, which combined rotating beaters with a bowl that moved in the opposite direction, was the most popular but far from an everyday convenience. Priced at nearly $200 when it debuted in 1919, it was not until the 1920s that the mixer was reduced in size and cost and mass marketed to the typical homemaker. Similarly, Frigidaire and General Electric introduced lines of electric refrigerators for domestic use by 1915.

New cooking devices also expanded the range of food options for the typical home cook. Thermostatic ovens (either gas or electric), introduced in 1915, enabled bakers to maintain a constant oven temperature. The introduction of new baking materials was also important. Most notable was borosilicate, or Pyrex, bakeware for the home. Pyrex, a trademark for a specific type of glass, is resistant to heat and electricity. Because its chemical properties allow Pyrex to expand about a third less than conventional glass, it is less likely to break when taken from the oven or refrigerator. These conveniences gave the typical cook the confidence to try new menus.

The rise of department stores and self-serve markets allowed shoppers to buy fresher foods and a wider variety of products. Department stores, as well as other providers, supplied consumers with these new kitchen products through installment credit plans. Installment credit expanded rapidly during the 1910s, causing many to question its effects on the average consumer. While

Women being trained in canning methods doing World War I. Prints & Photographs Division, Library of Congress.

fears of excessive debt and class pretentiousness remained, by the end of the decade most Americans felt comfortable with and had acquired many of these kitchen "necessities" through installment credit.

More important was the spread of the self-service grocery store. These emporiums expanded the food options, while making shopping a more private and efficient process. The first of these, Piggly-Wiggly, was founded by Clarence Saunders in Memphis, Tennessee, in 1916. Saunders allowed his customers to roam the aisles of his store selecting products of their own choice rather than submitting a grocery list to be filled by a store clerk. Piggly-Wiggly developed a reputation for stocking a wide variety of named items—thousands of goods increasingly desired by America's more brand-conscious consumers. Saunders's success was quickly copied throughout the country.

Of course, these new products and outlets were only as good as the food that was available to cook, store, and sell. In the 1910s, Americans became accustomed to a wide variety of new convenience foods, ranging from food preparation products to new cooking oils.

Many of the food items first introduced in the 1910s became popular simply because they were packaged in new and convenient ways. The tea bag (1910) allowed consumers to brew a single cup of the beverage rather than an entire pot as

Shelves in a Piggly Wiggly self-service grocery store in or near Memphis, Tennessee, approximately 1917. Piggly Wiggly was the first grocery store to offer self-service so that customers did not have to ask for products from a clerk at a service counter. Prints & Photographs Division, Library of Congress.

was customary. Other goods, such as Ocean Spray cranberry sauce (1912), fruit cocktail (1914), and Campbell's soups (Cream of Celery, 1913; Beef Vegetable, 1918), placed a previously perishable, time-consuming product within easy reach of the average shopper. While traveling with his family on a hunting expedition to the Labrador coast, Clarence Birdseye discovered that rapidly frozen foods (such as venison, which froze in a matter of minutes in the Arctic air) retained much of their original flavor. Birdseye perfected an artificial process which replicated these conditions, placing packaged foods in devices that could be quickly cooled down to −50 degrees Fahrenheit. While several ventures failed in the 1910s—owing to the lack of freezers in most grocery stores—Birdseye's method became wildly successful in the coming decades.

Other foods changed American eating and cooking habits more drastically. For example, the marketing of a granulated, "pourable" table salt by the Morton Salt Company in 1912 allowed cooks and restaurants to reduce the amount of salt used in their meals, allowing diners to salt their own food to taste. Similarly, Richard Hellmann began mass marketing his wife's Blue Ribbon mayonnaise in 1912. Hellmann, a German immigrant and deli operator on Columbus Street in New York City, had first tested his sandwich spread on customers, who then rated his varieties. To meet a largely local demand for his product, Hellmann opened his first factory in Queens in 1915 and a second one in Long Island in 1920 to supply the growing regional demand. His ready-made mayonnaise allowed many to turn ordinary bread and cold cuts into an appetizing specialty sandwich. It was not until 1927, however, when Hellmann sold his concern to General Foods, that the product became truly national in scope.

The introduction of Crisco in 1911 dramatically changed America's food preparation habits. Crisco, manufactured by Cincinnati-based Procter & Gamble, was a solidified shortening product made entirely of vegetable oils. A special manufacturing process allowed Crisco to remain solid yet soft throughout all seasonal conditions. By contrast, before Crisco, most cooks relied on butter or animal fats (lard) which quickly spoiled or frequently became too runny for many baking

needs. The product was an instant hit for both domestic and commercial bakers. Crisco was so new that Procter & Gamble published their own cookbooks, recipes, and tips that made it easy to bake "from scratch" by standardizing and making predictable the key blending products in most baked goods.

Certainly no meal was changed more drastically during the 1910s than breakfast. Typically, before the 1900s, the morning meal consisted of leftovers from the previous night or, if one were dining out, fried clams, mushrooms, grilled plover, steak, or the occasional egg. The arrival of the active, healthy lifestyle of the era expunged the desire for such heavy fare. Suppliers of nutritious, quick, and lighter breakfast alternatives quickly became popular. Cereals offered under brand names, such as Kellogg's Corn Flakes (1915), 40 percent Bran Flakes (1915), and All-Bran (1916); Quaker Puffed Rice (1913); John Campbell's Malt-O-Meal (1919); or C. W. Post's Grape Nuts (1897) and Post Toasties (1904), soon created new morning rituals throughout the United States. (See Food of the 1900s.)

AMERICA'S SWEET TOOTH

Of course, not all of America's new eating habits fostered better nutrition. During the 1910s, the nation first gave evidence of a penchant for sweet snacks. Before then, most lovers of candies and cookies were content with a periodic visit to the confectioners or with a special batch of homemade treats. By contrast, the rise of "penny and nickel candies" sold at the counters of many shops and store-bought packaged cookies made this consumption more regular. Often advertised as "instant energy," the diverse confections of chocolate, caramel, nuts, dried fruits, and a variety of other products reflected the novelty of new processed foods.

Chocolate bars were not new in 1910. As early as 1875, Henry Nestlé and Daniel Peter had perfected the manufacture of milk chocolate, which could be processed, transported, stored, and sold without losing too much of its flavor. German chocolate making was displayed at the 1893 World Columbian Exposition in Chicago, where Milton S. Hershey observed chocolate-making techniques and then began integrating them into his caramel factory in Lancaster, Pennsylvania in 1894.

Hershey's success in selling his milk chocolate bars in the late 1890s and early 1900s led many to experiment with ingredients and packaging. Frank Mars introduced the Milky Way bar in 1923. Peter Paul Halajian had more immediate success with his Konabar in 1919, a candy made of dried fruit, nuts, coconut, and chocolate. In 1922, Peter Paul introduced his most successful candy, the Mounds bar. Similarly, in 1919, Christian Nelson and chocolate magnate Russell Stover experimented with other ways to apply chocolate directly to ice cream. Using cocoa butter in the preparation, Nelson premiered the Eskimo Pie in 1921.

David Little Clark, who was selling gum to retailers in the early part of the 1910s, developed his own product, called the Clark Bar, which contained a core of roasted peanuts covered in milk chocolate. He mass marketed the candy to U.S. soldiers as a nutritious, quick energy food in 1917. The connection between candy sales and World War I was not accidental. The U.S. Army Quartermaster Corps shipped an average of 40 pounds of chocolate each week to the American bases in Europe. Broken into smaller lots on the battlefield, many servicemen grew accustomed to the easy availability of sweets. When they returned home, they not only provided a ready market for the goods but also sanctioned the practice of snacking as something that was acceptable for men.

Non-chocolate-based sweets were also introduced during the decade. For example, Clarence Crane, a Cleveland-based chocolate manufacturer, was looking for a product which was not as messy as chocolate but could still satisfy America's developing sweet tooth. In 1912, he developed a hard peppermint candy which he fashioned into a circle. Crane turned his product, called Pep-O-Mint, into a commercial sensation by packaging fourteen mints in easy to dispense rolls and naming them Life Savers, after their characteristic shape.

Perhaps the greatest novelty confection of the 1910s was the marshmallow. The appearance of the Moon Pie and Mallomars during the decade were the most successful of these. Found primarily along the East Coast, Mallomars were first sold in 1913 as a combination of cookie, marshmallow, and dark chocolate. The Moon Pie, which was a larger version of the same medley of goods, was introduced in 1917 by the Chattanooga Bakery Company in Tennessee; it has remained the favorite of Southerners. In 1917, Archibald Query began selling his Marshmallow Fluff door to door around Sommerville, Massachusetts. Hard sales work by Allen Durkee and Fred Mower, who bought the recipe from Query in 1919, landed their Toot Sweet Marshmallow Fluff on the shelves of local groceries. By 1927, the product was being mass produced.

Packaged cookies rounded out the list of new sweets that were available to American consumers. For example, Lorne Doone cookies, a simple shortbread, premiered in 1912. Novelty cookies sold more quickly. The greatest of these during the 1910s was the Oreo chocolate sandwich cookie, which was heavily promoted by the National Biscuit Company, later Nabisco. Probably the most novel of the new cookies was the fortune cookie, invented in the United States by David Jung, a Los Angeles noodle maker, in 1918. When production was mechanized in the 1920s, fortune cookies became standard fare at most Chinese restaurants and were soon exported from America to China and Hong Kong.

Food

CIGARETTES

At the turn of the century, Americans were already consuming more than four billion cigarettes per year. Opposition to tobacco use was widespread, with many concerned that the product was adulterated, containing opium or arsenic. By 1912, Dr. I. Adler had demonstrated a strong connection between cigarette smoking and lung cancer. The American Society for the Control of Cancer, later the American Cancer Society, was founded in 1913 to promote antismoking campaigns. Business leaders frowned on the use of the product by their employees, and leaders such as Thomas Edison and Henry Ford openly prohibited smoking at their factories (Edison refused to hire smokers). Others feared for the safety of children and women, who were legally barred from smoking in many states. In 1909, baseball star Honus Wagner withdrew his name and image from use by cigarette companies, including the baseball cards that came with their products. As a result, the Honus Wagner card remains today one of the rarest of collectibles.

Still, the tobacco industry, led by James B. Duke's American Tobacco Company, was a powerful force in American business and government. The tobacco lobby successfully kept nicotine off the list of controlled substances passed with the 1906 Food and Drug Act. Many began adding potency to their product by spraying the young plants with nicotine as an insecticide. Even after the American Tobacco Company was broken up as a trust into the American Tobacco Company, R. J. Reynolds, Liggett & Meyers, and Lorillard in 1911, the industry thrived. Driving these trends were two things. The first was the successful advertising campaigns of the 1910s. Liggett & Meyers's Chesterfield brand led the field when, in 1912, they pioneered the use of such simple slogans such as, "They satisfy." In 1915, R. J. Reynolds debuted Camels and, two years later, the American Tobacco Company brought out Lucky Strikes. By 1917, cigarettes were being targeted to women as a means for suppressing the appetite. World War I provided the second key component to the success of cigarettes. Along with candy, servicemen were provided cigarettes as part of their daily rations. The boost in U.S. production of tobacco—aided by a blockade of Turkish tobaccos—provided a market advantage which allowed most producers to lower their retail charge to either a dime or fifteen cents for a pack of twenty cigarettes.

DINING OUT

Growing public amusements—including vaudeville, dance halls, and the movie theater—provided Americans with additional reasons to consume food outside their homes. Restaurant menus and style of service changed markedly during the 1910s. These trends continued to alter the traditional form of public eating in ways that laid the groundwork for the rise of many fast food establishments in the decades to come. Nathan Handwerker opened "Nathan's" hotdog stand at Coney Island in 1916.

Most Americans did not frequent upscale restaurants; commonplace establishments continued to feed the majority of the nation's public. Known as chophouses, these locations typically specialized in steaks, chops, and other cuts of meat with a serving of potatoes, bread, and, nearly invariably, oysters and a schooner of beer. Many taverns offered patrons a free lunch included with the purchase of at least two drinks. Women found repast in tearooms and other women's restaurants which typically served omelets, light chicken dishes, and salads.

At more upscale, but still middle-class, establishments, a typical dinner in 1910 included at least two courses. The first included either turkey, duck, or chicken, a variety of sweets, smaller dishes of fruits (usually apricots or apples), and a starchy vegetable like corn or peas. The second, or main, course included a choice of soups, fish, a larger portion of meat, vegetables, and breads or pastries. While tame in comparison to the meals of the upper class, these dinners indicate that lighter dining was still just a trend.

Elite dining underwent more interesting changes. As early as 1860, wealthy Americans could find restaurants like Delmonico's where

The elegant Waldorf-Astoria Hotel offered exclusive dining for well-to-do New Yorkers in the 1910s. Prints & Photographs Division, Library of Congress.

they could be treated and fed like royalty. As with the more pedestrian, middle-class restaurants, the elite diner could expect culinary excess. A typical meal might include an appetizer of clams or oysters, a clear soup, and a tray of rich hors d'oeuvres, including olives, canapés, caviar, and anchovies. A first course might contain fish, potatoes, and a cucumber salad, and often included terrapin, (more) oysters, crab legs, lobster, shrimp, and frogs. Concluding the meal were large servings of roasted meat, vegetables, bread, a fruit punch, and lighter side dishes. The post-meal dessert, served with coffee, topped off the dining experience. Many wealthy socialites would then set off to the evening's activity only to end—after the show—with a midnight banquet of champagne and lobster at the so-called lobster palaces that ringed the city's many theater and entertainment districts.[2]

Why the wealthy and affluent consumed food in this way is related to a number of factors. Most important, food consumption was a visible indication of one's status in society. The more one ate, and the more luxurious the dishes, the higher one could position himself in the social hierarchy. In addition, restaurants offered the younger elites new public places where they might interact, freed from the cloistered confines of the many balls and parties held by their economic peers. Finally, public restaurants provided new spaces for women to be freed from the confines of polite society.

While not an era for grand cuisine, the 1910s did see the expansion of more ethnic cooking across the spectrum of restaurants. Hungarian goulash and a wide variety of Italian pastas were sampled for the first time. With the growth in immigration, until the war prevented safe passage, came Italian, German, Chinese, and Jewish cooking. Many of these styles were loosely appropriated into American cuisine. As a result, the decade saw the introduction of a number of new types of foods and preparations, including chop suey, crab Louis, fettuccine Alfredo, and vichyssoise. In spite of their exotic names, all of these dishes originated in the United States. Vichyssoise, a chilled soup made from potatoes, leeks, and cream, was created by Louis Diat of the Ritz-Carlton Hotel in 1917.

Food

Music

of the 1910s

Popular music was one of the first entertainment media to cross over successfully from distinct, usually class, cultural, and racially influenced styles, to a more generic and inclusive American format. In the pre-radio years, crossover artists relied solely on the interest generated from fusing the old with the new. From the concert hall to the nightclub, popular musicians integrated African American musical styles while, at the same time, they built upon the rich European heritage of notation, composition, and melody.

The acceptance of African American styles and performers created opportunities for new talent. African Americans found a means to excel in U.S. society—means that were acceptable to dominant white tastes. The arrival of radio in 1920 provided the technological breakthrough that was needed to catapult this fusion into a truly mass phenomenon.

THE EUROPEAN INFLUENCE ON AMERICAN MUSIC

The cultural importance of European academic training and the classical works of masters, such as Ludwig van Beethoven, W. A. Mozart, and J. S. Bach, influenced white musicians. This approach valued formal arrangements of traditional instruments to produce an appealing melody. By 1910, these influential European trends began to move away from the strong Romanticism of German composers such as Richard Wagner—who first introduced vernacular folk music into the academic realm—toward more subtle, impressionistic effects. French composer Claude Debussy was one of the most adventuresome of these innovators. From his first public performance in 1902 until his death in 1918, Debussy challenged European critics and audiences to listen to new styles and moods of music, which allowed performers to experiment with unconventional methods.

By accepting the vernacular tradition, academic composers in Europe made it possible for audiences to consider these "lesser" works as true art forms. Moreover, European arrangements forced composers to find ways to incorporate the nonconventional styles of folk music, which in the United States was driven largely by rhythm, into the highly structured and melody-based methods of academic notation. Throughout the decade, leading composers, such as Béla Bartók (*Allegro Barbaro*, 1911), Arnold Schoenberg (*Pierrot Lunaire*, 1912), and Igor Stravinsky (*Le Sacre du Printemps*, 1913), borrowed themes taken directly from the American vernacular tradition. By contrast, American composers such as Frederick Converse and Horatio Park continued within traditional patterns and, as a result, their work is largely forgotten today. While Stravinsky was clearly distant from popular musicians in the United States—he had never even heard an authentic ragtime band before he wrote *Ragtime for Eleven Instruments* in 1918—the fact that European classicists were openly interested in American folk music gave credence to the work of public performers in the 1910s.

THE AFRICAN INFLUENCE ON AMERICAN MUSIC

African musical styles are unique in that the rhythm, and not the variation of pitch, dominates. Unlike a piano, which has a number of differing tones, the sound of percussion instruments, such as the drum, vary mostly by the beat. African performers were adept at using both hands to construct contrasting yet supportive rhythms on their instruments. In addition, artists relied upon an audience's ability to maintain a base rhythm, termed a "metronomic sense" (e.g., toe tapping, which keeps a beat even if the musicians do not play one), to add further complexity to their music.

The communal use of music in African culture was vital to the development of these intricate rhythms and the emerging American sound. Africans used musical performances in rituals and ceremonies, and while at work to build cohesion in the group as well as to communicate and establish a mood. As a result, the music is both participatory and extremely powerful in evoking emotional responses.

African styles are more elaborate than European styles. Where European artists relied on *either* a double or triple meter pattern within a single work, African stylists routinely mixed the two. Where European artists allowed the formal and noted melody to set the emotional tone for a composition, African performers shifted and improvised their works to respond to the audience in immediate and powerful ways.

Based on a seven-note, half-step European scale, musicians were unfamiliar and ill-equipped to write African sounds that were rooted in a scale of five notes with no halves. While European stylists were not ignorant of rhythm, they were unaccustomed to giving over so much control to the response of an audience.

Of course it was not African, but *African American* music that directly influenced popular music in the United States. The peculiar position of blacks in late nineteenth-century America—as a vital labor force living in large communities but as disenfranchised citizens who were ostracized from the mainstream culture by widespread racism—nurtured their distinct musical heritage. Segregation allowed African American music to thrive, and this style transformed the nation's music in the modern era.

African Americans conserved their African and Afro-Caribbean musical heritage as well as possible under slavery and through emancipation. In the latter half of the nineteenth century, blacks learned to sing or play a homemade instrument in order to earn additional income or simply to earn the respect of neighbors. Such training developed skills of improvisation and a heightened ability to respond to the changing mood of an audience rather than an ability to read music or perfectly recreate a tune time after time. Spirituals and work songs, the forerunners of the blues, relied heavily on call-and-response improvisation.

While African Americans fought against their second-class status in the United States, most white composers were willing to profit off of the rampant racism of the era. White minstrels singing "coon songs" exaggerated the "exotic" nature of African American lives. Coon songs portrayed black males as ignorant, cowardly, lazy, petty thieves, and women as shallow and sexually indiscriminate. While reprehensible and slightly pathetic, these white performers did introduce an element of African American music into the mainstream culture. As the popularity of lively rhythmic songs grew in the 1880s and 1890s, some black artists were allowed to perform more authentic versions of the craft. Musical pioneers like W. C. Handy, Bessie Smith, and Bert Williams all got their first taste of the white entertainment business through the minstrel shows.[1]

It was not the white misappropriation of African American music but rather the cumulative efforts of generations of black artists that eventually led to its acceptance and success. The New Negro movement of the 1910s supported the work of these artists by rejecting notions of cultural inferiority and an inherent submission to white

Music

authority. Activists, inducing A. Phillip Randolph, Chandler Owen, and Hubert Henry Harrison, gave voice to a growing desire to reject assimilation and to support authentic black culture. Such an approach created great conflicts within the black community and placed many middle-class African Americans in the difficult position of either supporting the advancement of their race or the economic well-being of their families. Moreover, the heightened cultural consciousness of blacks no doubt added to the paranoia of many white Americans following World War I.

African and African American styles proved to be extremely significant to the development of popular music in the United States through the widespread use of syncopation—the musical practice of unequally dividing beats into long and short notes to create multiple cross rhythms within a musical piece.

ACADEMIC MUSIC

By 1910, European composers had provided academic artists with some leeway in the type of materials considered acceptable for performance. Moreover, from 1890 to 1910, urban Americans invested heavily in supporting local symphonies, conservatories to train musicians, and opera houses. European conductors and musicians, such as Anton Phillip Heinrich, Louis Moreau Gottschalk, and the renowned Antonín Dvořák, came to America in search of students capable and willing to explore the rich musical folk traditions of this country. The stage was set for American composers to expand their repertoire beyond the European masters and to include newer, domestic works.

Unfortunately, few composers proved willing or able to move beyond the classic symphonies. One of these was Harry Burleigh. An African American who studied under Dvořák, Burleigh became an accomplished soloist and composer who relied upon his knowledge of spirituals. Burleigh published a number of significant compositions, including *From the Southland* (1914) and *Southland Sketches* (1916) for violin and piano, before he became the music editor for Ricordi and Company. Burleigh also published a number of songs based on these works, including "The Young Warrior" (1916), which was eventually translated into Italian and became something of an anthem for Italian troops during World War I. Burleigh's greatest work was an anthology of spirituals, published under the title *Jubilee Songs of the United States of America* (1916), which he later performed before such luminaries as President Theodore Roosevelt and King Edward VII of England. Will Marion Cook, also a black man, studied first in Berlin and then at the National Conservatory of Music in New York City. Cook composed a series of musicals, many songs, and published *A Collection of Negro Songs* in 1912.

Lacking such a purposeful musical foundation, white academics struggled in their efforts to create a style that was not derived from their European masters. Arthur Farwell was one example of a white composer who understood the limits of his European education. Born in St. Paul, Minnesota, Farwell developed his skills as a violinist, pianist, and composer first at the Massachusetts Institute of Technology, then in Germany and France. Farwell was deeply motivated by African American, Native American, and folk Western music, but he was unable to turn his fascination into a respected academic anthology of composition. (See Music of the 1900s.)

Edward McDowell and Charles Tomlinson Griffes also attempted to fashion a genuine indigenous classical style. MacDowell, born in New York and trained overseas, unsuccessfully sought to meld Native American songs with the romantic classics. Griffes published a variety of tone poems throughout the decade, including *Three-Tone Pictures* (1915), *Roman Sketches* (1917), and *Five Poems of Ancient China and Japan* (1917). His efforts at symphonic composition, which resulted in *The Pleasure-Dome of Kubla Khan* (1917), were first performed by the Boston Symphony in 1919 and occasionally ever since. Still, as compositions, the works of Farwell, MacDowell, and Griffes pale by comparison with those of such modern European composers as Debussy, Stravinsky, and Modest Mussorgsky.

Charles Ives is the era's one true lasting classical voice, partly because he did not fear the rejection of contemporary audiences. Growing up in an affluent home in Danbury, Connecticut, attending Yale University, and becoming successful as an insurance executive, Ives was free from the financial pressures that could compromise an artist's creativity. Rarely did Ives perform his works (only one was ever played in public before 1919, and he stopped composing in 1923). His isolation allowed him to develop his own unique sound and produce a vast quantity of hymns, songs, tone poems, and symphonies, but he never had to face the criticism and rebukes of a hostile and provincial season ticket holder.

Building on his appreciation for sounds rather than harmonious tones or melodies, Ives created works of intense contrasts and jarring musical discord. Ives sampled from others' works, scored intentionally off-key sections, and interjected passages within his works using a variety of motifs. Much as the successful European modernists, Ives intended his works to be appreciated as organic wholes, but from a multitude of perspectives.

ARRANGEMENTS FOR POPULAR ORCHESTRAS AND BANDS

Perhaps because public orchestras and bands were less self-consciously patterned after the European ones, popular musicians displayed a greater freedom in performing a more American variety of sound in the 1910s. No artist more closely represented this difference than John Philip Sousa. Born in 1854 to immigrant parents, Sousa reveled in his role as a representative of the American Dream. Formally trained by the U.S. Marine Band, he took leadership of the ensemble in 1880 and for twelve years led the group in a number of world tours. As a composer, Sousa excelled at marches and other two-step numbers, including "Semper Fidelis," and his signature work, "The Stars and Stripes Forever" (1896).

Sousa's contribution to American music in the 1910s demonstrated that the white public had a taste for well-performed vernacular arrangements. His concerts introduced much of the country to ragtime and African American songs. He gave "black music" a national platform and included African Americans, such as Arthur Pryor, in his band. By using unconventional orchestral instruments, such as the banjo, Sousa lent legitimacy to the smaller ethnic groups.

Of these new performers, none was as talented and potentially revolutionary as James Reese

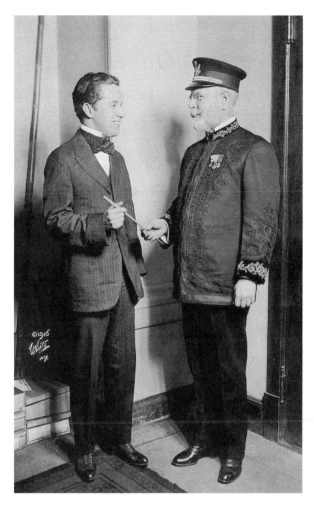

John Philip Sousa, right, in uniform, talking to Charlie Chaplin. Prints & Photographs Division, Library of Congress.

Music

Europe. Born in Alabama in 1881 to a musically accomplished family, Europe moved to Washington, D.C. and then to New York City as a young man, where he gained both formal training and real-world experience. In 1910, he formed the Clef Club Symphony Orchestra, which was partly a band but also functioned as a union representing and finding work for black musicians and entertainers. As an African American, Europe was instrumental in staging authentic vernacular music played on the original instruments. When he played Carnegie Hall in 1912, Europe premiered ragtime marches and songs from black composer Will Marion Cook.

At the height of its popularity, the Clef Club earned more than $100,000 a year. By 1914, Europe was tapped as the bandleader for the influential dance team of Irene and Vernon Castle. The Castles credited Europe with introducing many of the songs that led to their international fame. He was one of the first African Americans to secure a record deal, with Victor Records in 1913. When he and his famed vocalist, Noble Sissle, performed overseas during the war (Europe had enlisted in the 369th U.S. Infantry), the Old World was introduced to modern *American* music for the first time. Sissle later recounted how 60-year-old French women, German prisoners, and even other orchestra members spontaneously broke into dance when they heard them play.

Following his return to the United States, Europe continued to promote this new style. He either composed or cowrote such big hits as "Good Night Angeline," "On Patrol in No Man's Land," and "I Wish I Had Someone to Rock Me in the Cradle of Love." In performance, Europe was restrained and professional, rejecting the over-the-top behavior that characterized most black performers in the minds of many whites. It seemed that, by 1919, James Reese Europe was about to revise completely the role of African American artists in the United States. Unfortunately, in 1919 one of Europe's own musicians stabbed the bandleader with a knife after being scolded by Europe for crossing the stage during the performance. Europe either refused or was denied medical treatment, and he bled to death that evening.

TIN PAN ALLEY

While Europe and Sousa were able to borrow from vernacular traditions to give life to an anemic musical field, the same process elevated show music, termed Tin Pan Alley, from cultural obscurity to the pinnacle of popular music. (See Music of the 1900s.) Tin Pan Alley composers could not rely on the ready-made legitimacy afforded to writers of classical pieces. Intended to support popular theater and vaudeville acts, Tin Pan Alley artists needed first to entertain before they could be concerned with the formal arrangement or the artistic aesthetics of their music. As a result, these composers borrowed heavily from both white and African American vernacular sounds. Known for the "tinny" sound generated by the upright piano,

the region became home to songwriters who wanted to tap into the new, lighter, and more urbane style. Melding catchy lyrics, melodies, and toe-tapping, syncopated rhythms, the sale of Tin Pan Alley sheet music brought stardom to a number of innovative writers, including Jerome Kern, Harry Von Tilzer, and Irving Berlin.

Hit songs were usually sold as sheet music in the lobbies of the theaters, clubs, and vaudeville acts that performed them. In an age when most children were taught to read music in school and when many American families owned pianos or other instruments, printed musical scores sold widely. Tens of millions of sheets were sold annually by 1910. The typical hit could expect to sell nearly 100,000 sheets. Priced from thirty to forty cents each, the royalties from the sale of a single hit sustained many performers for a lifetime. When 170 Tin Pan Alley writers organized the American Society of Composers, Authors, and Publishers (ASCAP) in 1914, the recovery of royalties for the public performance of copyrighted materials increased the monetary value of their work.

Phonographs, which reproduced music through either recorded cylinders or discs, were a growing influence. By 1909, more than 27 million records and cylinders had been sold with royalties protected by the U.S. Copyright Act of 1909. Ten years later, two million players had been sold and nearly 100 million recordings. While not as influential as the spread of radio after 1920, the sales of sheet music and recordings brought the popular musical style of Tin Pan Alley out of the theaters, nightclubs, and brothels and into American homes.

The topicality of the songs was their key appeal. Unlike more structured works, popular tunes could be constructed in time to meet or anticipate the public's curiosity with current events. For example, inventions such as the airplane, telephone, and automobile became the subject of hit songs, including Fred Fisher's "Come, Josephine, in My Flying Machine" (1910) and Maurice Abraham's "He'd Have to Get Under, Get Out and Get Under, to Fix Up His Automobile" (1913). World War I provided composers with a way to combine their craft with patriotism and a sort of public relations boost. War songs such as "Over There," "It's

You know all these people

They are but a few of the great stars of opera, drama, concert and vaudeville who are at your command—not merely once in a while, but *whenever you wish*, when you own the

Edison Phonograph

The talent behind the Edison Phonograph comprises the *very best* in every branch of entertainment. The perfect reproduction of the Edison *itself* brings these stars to your home absolutely true to life. The Edison repertoire provides

Advertisement showing composite of phonograph and portraits of Sophie Tucker, Stella Mayhew, Nat M. Wills, Victor Herbert, Lauder, Sousa, Sylva, Slezak, Carmen Melis, Anna Chandler, Ada Jones, and Billy Murray, 1912. Prints & Photographs Division, Library of Congress.

a Long Way to Tipperary," and "Keep the Home Fires Burning" were performed numerous times on stage, at home, and in the foxholes.

Several artists from this genre stand out for their influence and success. Harry Von Tilzer, known as the "man who launched a thousand hits" wrote formulaic songs loved by the public. Introducing Latin American sounds into his tunes, such as "The Cubanola Glide" (1909), or African American styles into songs, such as "Under the Yum Yum Tree" (1910), Jerome Kern turned out catchy tunes with syrupy lyrics. His fame spread after a string of hit songs from 1912 to 1914. By then, Kern had moved to musical comedy. None of these have the polish or depth of emotions that Kern later would be remembered for, following the 1928 premiere of *Showboat*. While not the most talented composer of Tin Pan Alley, George

M. Cohan was the most successful at turning his songs into national hits. His most popular songs, "The Little Millionaire" (1911), "Hello Broadway!" (1914), "The Voice of McConnell" (1918), and "The Royal Vagabond" (1919), were typical light entertainment of the era.

By far the greatest Tin Pan Alley composer was Irving Berlin. He was born in 1888 in Russia, as Izzy Baline, and immigrated to the United States with his family. By 1902, he was making a living in New York City as a singing waiter and piano player. Berlin had no formal training as a musician (he could neither read nor write music and played the piano using only a single key, F#), but by 1910, Berlin was emerging as a leading force in American popular music. Berlin tapped into the sentimental optimism that was so closely held by many Americans. His hits of the decade included "Alexander's Ragtime Band" (1911), "Everybody's Doin' It Now"(1911), "A Pretty Girl Is Like a Melody" (1919), and the wartime hit "Oh How I Hate to Get Up in the Morning" (1918).

The most likely reason for the success of Tin Pan Alley was that it drew upon the well-developed and mature vernacular styles that existed in the United States. The reliance upon ragtime piano pieces is a good case in point. Berlin's "Alexander's

HIT SONGS OF THE 1910s

Song and performer unless otherwise noted.

"Let Me Call You Sweetheart" (Peerless Quartet)—1910

"Some of These Days" (Sophie Tucker)—1911

"When Irish Eyes Are Smiling" (Chauncey Olcott)—1912

"Ballin' the Jack" (Prince's Orchestra)—1913

"St. Louis Blues" (written by W. C. Handy)—1914

"Carry Me Back to Old Virginny" (Alma Gluck)—1915

"O Sole Mio" (Enrico Caruso)—1916

"Poor Butterfly" (Victor Military Band)—1917

"Rock-A-Bye Your Baby With a Dixie Melody" (Al Jolson)—1918

"A Pretty Girl Is Like a Melody" (John Steel)—1919

Music

Ragtime Band" and later "The International Rag" (1913) were ragtime *songs,* but not ragtime music. Ragtime music was formally structured and syncopated, and used conventional European harmonies. By contrast, ragtime songs were much looser, intending to give *feeling* to the music without being tied to its arrangement.

Tin Pan Alley musicians borrowed an emotive sense of African American music without attempting to create a lasting work of art. For example, when Berlin composed "Alexander's Ragtime Band," he revitalized the original style for a number of years. Tin Pan Alley songs aided black artists by shunning the derogatory coon-song style of previous white composers.

RAGTIME

"Ragtime" means the timing of a traditional piece of music is "ragged" through the inclusion of syncopated rhythms and an informal playing. The style was common for unschooled African American musicians who played by ear, taking well-known melodies and performing them in their own way. The key to a rag was how well the music merged with vernacular dance—the so-called cakewalks and reels that were common to African American gatherings. Ragtime is a combination of African American styles and European methods of notion and melodies. When innovators such as Scott Joplin, Joseph Lamb, Tom Turpin, Eubie Blake, and James Scott began the process of writing ragtime composition, they also initiated the first true musical fusion of international styles into a uniquely American sound. (See Music of the 1900s.)

Combined ragtime styles became immensely popular in the United States from 1900 to 1920. Coinciding with the growing sales of home pianos (which peaked in 1909) and the maturing sheet music industry, ragtime emerged as the sound for urban performers in a nation that was increasingly looking to cities for its evening entertainment. The development of the player piano helped ragtime, for the machines could effortlessly reproduce the difficult sound of the works. That ragtime was seen as fresh "youth music" only added to its attraction.

Hit ragtime songs of the 1910s include Jay Roberts's "The Entertainer's Rag" (1910), George Botsford's "Grizzly Bear Rag" (1911), Edward B. Claypoole's "Ragging the Scale" (1915), and George L. Cobb's "Russian Rag" (1918). The fact that all of these men were white and that the subject matter had shifted away from African American culture or derogatory coon songs suggests how far the medium went toward providing black artists with national respectability.

Of course this acceptance did not occur without dissent. Legitimate opponents included educators, critics, and performers who simply did not like the new musical style when compared to the old European masters. The ironic reality—that modern European musicians were also deeply impressed by ragtime—was missed. Moreover, the line between an honest dislike of the new style and hidden racial prejudice was hard to distinguish.

More common were foes who openly admitted their prejudice that the rise of African American culture posed a threat to white domination and control. Such cultural critics believed that the acceptance of black music displayed a loss of critical judgment in the public that would eventually lead to a population that could not distinguish between good and evil.

Still, in spite of these concerns, ragtime fundamentally shifted the nature of popular music in America away from European sources and toward our own domestic vernacular roots. Ragtime was the first true America genre, a fusion of Old World styles into a modern, New World sound. Moreover, it opened the doors for African Americans to perform before people who were less likely to see them as caricatures and more as cultural educators about everything from clothing styles to dance steps. Ragtime also ushered in many other modern musical styles, especially jazz and the blues, as artists such as "Jelly Roll" Morton and others took the stage as rag artists but finished their careers as jazz pioneers.

Scott Joplin, known as the "King of Ragtime," wrote chart-topping music throughout the 1900s. In doing so, he influenced many others in the 1910s, most notably James Scott and Joseph Lamb. Scott, aided by Joplin, published numerous bestsellers, including "Ragtime Oriole" (1911), "Efficiency Rag" (1917), "New Era Rag" (1919), and the most acclaimed "Pegasus: A Classic Rag"

Ragtime

While it drew on some of the conventions of European music, ragtime is seen by most historians as the first truly American popular music form to find widespread commercial acceptance, and the first to be exported. The rousing syncopation of ragtime, owing much to the marches of John Philip Sousa but written mainly for piano, lent itself to dancing, and early American hits like Scott Joplin's 1899 "Maple Leaf Rag" helped establish the modern music industry with huge sales of its sheet music—75,000 copies in the first six months.

Within a few years, British music hall performers were singing American ragtime hits in their acts, and in 1912 a band called the American Ragtime Octette toured England in response to a full-blown craze that soon spread to the Continent. By 1913, American visitors to Europe were reporting that, going by all the ragtime songs that could be heard in London, Paris, Vienna, or Berlin, they could have sworn they'd never left home.

Some critics, such as J. B. Priestley, expressed alarm that Europe's importation of such a patently American musical form could only mean one thing: eventual American cultural dominance. But there was no stopping the flood tide of popular culture, especially not when there was money to be made (London established its own "Tin Pan Alley" style music publishing industry toward the end of the 1910s). Composers like Claude Debussy incorporated ragtime conventions into new piano suites; poets like T. S. Eliot quoted popular ragtime lyrics in such works as "The Waste Land." Such widespread acceptance of ragtime laid the groundwork for the future introduction of jazz, blues, and other American musical innovations.

(1919). Lamb, who was white, learned ragtime from Joplin's sheet music. Lamb's style, published by John Stark (based on a recommendation by Joplin), led to a ragtime craze along the Eastern seaboard. From 1908 to 1919, Lamb published twelve rags for Stark, most notably the "Ragtime Nightingale" (1915) and "Top Liner Rag" (1916).

THE BLUES AND JAZZ

While the links between ragtime, the blues, and jazz are still debated, it is certain that the formation of the blues and jazz was influenced by the growing commercial and artistic acceptance of ragtime. Fortunately, neither the blues nor jazz suffered the fate of ragtime—that of being absorbed and weakened by commercial composers on Tin Pan Alley. This was probably true for the blues because the medium was so closely linked to African American performances. Using distinct "blue notes," a flat third and seventh, few chord changes, odd modes, and only three-line verses, the blues remained a strongly vernacular sound that was nearly impossible for composers to capture on paper. The trembling blue notes were particularly discernible in black performances, a characteristic tracing its lineage back to African and Caribbean roots. Always deep in meaning, the style was intended to be used to combat depression, not wallow in it.

The ability to manipulate the same song into many unique forms was typical of the improvisational character of the blues. When the blues were finally published in 1912, the genre created a line of popular music which was both separate from and connected to that of ragtime.

William Christopher (W. C.) Handy is credited as being the "father of the blues," in large part because he was able to compose music that retained the ephemeral qualities of the style. Because recordings of blues performances did not begin until the 1920s, Handy's compositions provide the earliest evidence of the format free and clear of commercial influence. Handy was a formally trained musician who learned as much from his everyday performances as he did from his instructors. While he began his career playing marches, rags, and popular orchestral pieces, he soon earned local fame from his renditions of "authentic" African American music. In 1909,

Music

while performing in Memphis, he was asked to turn one of these into a campaign song for a local politician. The result, first termed "Mr. Crump," was later polished and rechristened "The Memphis Blues." Although not published until 1912, this date serves as a useful starting point for the birth of the blues. Throughout the decade, Handy continued to produce compositions that sold millions of copies, including "St. Louis Blues" (1914), "Joe Turner Blues" (1916), and "Beale Street Blues" (1917). While these received great attention from white entertainers, Tin Pan Alley proved incapable of bottling the lightning of black performers.

The blues were also unique in that they provided an opportunity for African American female singers to flourish. Women such as Ma Rainey, Bessie Smith, Chippie Hill, and Ida Cox dominated the early blues market. With a wider vocal range and a greater ability to shift between blues notes and traditional major notes, women were able to navigate the difficult performances while still articulating the all-important lyrics. Bessie Smith was probably the best of this strong group. Smith's fame and fortune had to wait until the 1920s, when the recording industry began to take the genre seriously and the listening public developed an ear for the new sound.[2]

Jazz, too, gained popularity in the 1910s. Whether generated from ragtime or, as many claim, more directly from the blues, jazz soon developed a style all its own. The connection to ragtime is less secure, as the formal structure and strict composition of rags were contrary to the improvisational style of jazz performances. In addition, ragtime performances were limited to those who could read music and, usually were performed before mixed or all-white audiences. By contrast, jazz musicians typically played by ear, with no two renditions exactly alike, and before crowds more likely to be dominated by African Americans. As a result, the tunes were played "hotter," with a faster pace that was, like the blues, difficult for white composers to copy and exploit on Tin Pan Alley. Still, the careers of ragtime, blues, and jazz composers hint at the intricate ways in which these three threads of African American music were woven together.[3]

Jazz certainly originated in the urban black subculture of New Orleans. Based on the "hot," performances of African American musicians hired to entertain customers at the local bars and brothels of Storyville, "jazzed" tunes were highly improvised. The city aided in the development of this sound in several ways. The tolerance of red-light districts such as Storyville provided steady work for a large number of musicians. The Creole culture of New Orleans also gave blacks greater freedom to intermingle with whites, which translated into greater access to their entertainment dollars. Finally, the port city provided a source of cheap brass instruments, many left over from the Spanish-American war, for impoverished but talented black musicians.

Musicians not native to the region had a hard time imitating the effect. The style favored combos containing a trombone, cornet, clarinet, drums, and piano—each capable of syncopating and improvising. Jazz was also a performing art rather than a written or composed one. Virtuoso performances, not sheet music sales, were the mark of a great performer. Finally, early jazz bands developed almost accidentally as talented musicians moved from gig to gig, looking for steady pay and reliable partners. As a result, most jazz bands of the 1910s rarely lasted long. It was not until 1915 that "Jelly Roll" Morton cut the first jazz records, and not until the 1920s that these recordings began to provide enough money to support professional jazz bands.[4]

Around 1909, New Orleans jazz bands began to migrate north, first to Kansas City and Memphis and later to Chicago, Oklahoma City, and Detroit. When in 1917, during World War I, the U.S. Army ordered the closure of most brothels in Storyville, the slow but steady trickle of musicians became a torrent. From 1918 until the mid-1920s, distinct jazz styles (such as Chicago jazz) evolved in many of these secondary cities. It was largely from these regional expressions that white performers such as Jimmie McPartland, Lionel Hampton, Bix Beiderbecke, Gene Krupa, and Benny Goodman learned their jazz sounds.

The first recorded jazz band, the Original Dixieland Jazz Band, was composed of white musicians. Leaving New Orleans in 1915, the band became a sensation in Chicago and was "discovered" in 1917 while playing at Reisenweber's Restaurant, in New York City. Recorded on

February 26, 1917, and led by cornetist Dominic James LaRocca, the Original Dixieland Jazz Band sold over a million copies of their songs "Livery Stable Blues" and "Dixieland Jass [sic] Band One-Step." While later recordings by the group showed little originality or improvisation, their early work certainly was the product of, and accurately reflected, the New Orleans sound. Although it may be unfair that the quintessential contribution of America to world music was originally credited to white musicians, the music that they produced was the product of African American artists.

Regardless of who was recorded first, black performers soon dominated the field. Sidney Bechet, a Creole from New Orleans, toured the country, and went on to Europe and worldwide fame. Joseph "King" Oliver, also a product of New Orleans, played cornet with Storyville legends such as Bunk Johnson before achieving stardom in Chicago. Oliver's departure opened the door to a young prodigy by the name of Louis Armstrong, who redefined and further elevated the genre in the coming decades. "Jelly Roll" Morton probably best defines the African American jazz performer of the 1910s. A product of rag, blues, and jazz traditions, "Jelly" experimented with a variety of sounds, techniques, and arrangements before settling on a recognizable (and marketable) jazz style. A product of the New Orleans urban subculture, Morton was a Creole who worked as a pimp and a gambler before settling on music. His first composition, "Jelly Roll Blues" (1915), was a hit that contributed to an irregular but generally productive career which lasted for the next twenty years. Still, Morton's broad-based musical background included ragtime, blues, classical, jazz, spirituals, and opera; he performed from New Orleans to California in clubs ranging from two-bit brothels to some of America's greatest halls.

Music

Sports

and Leisure of the 1910s

During the 1910s, Americans displayed, through their participation in or consumption of these sports, games, and fads, a greater commitment to individual expression than in previous generations. These activities validated the broader Progressive ideals of fair play, democracy, and civic advancement, thus redefining what it meant to participate in American life.

SPORTS AND RECREATION

In the 1910s, Americans continued to debate and redefine what sports and recreation meant. Earlier generations had found exercise in their daily lives (if from no other activity than walking), and they considered play and recreation to be a waste of time. By 1910, play was regarded not only as a useful pursuit, but as an essential one in the training of young minds. The focus on children was especially sharp, as the drive to expand recreation and sport merged with efforts made by reformers to save immigrant children from the harsh environmental conditions of the inner cities. Proper civic values, such as a respect for fair play, self-help, and an avoidance of class biases, were thought to be foreign to the millions of immigrants and their children.

Armed with a greater awareness of inner-city social problems—the direct result of the reports by muckrakers and Progressives like Lewis Hine and Jane Addams—advocates believed that opportunities for "organized play" would have a significantly positive effect not only on America's youth, but also on the ability for others to accept these new citizens as equal members of society. In 1911, when Milwaukee residents were asked to describe the typical day of the urban child, more than half assumed that they were "doing nothing" with their time. Two years later, a similar poll in Cleveland showed that 40 percent of respondents believed that youth were wasting the day, possibly leading to juvenile delinquency. In the 1900s, many towns and cities had passed ordinances prohibiting any type of child's play on city streets.[1]

The rising fears of gang activity also supported the need to take a second look at recreation and sports. Social reformers had found that teenagers generally joined gangs as a way to achieve an independent identity that was separate from parental (or state guardian) authority. While in these gangs, youths were educated to believe that their particular race, ethnicity, religion, or social status was the single most important social characteristic in their lives. As they aged into young adults, many gang members proved unwilling to accept their place within a society of equal individuals because of the values instilled by the gang.

A maypole dance, a common event for children, in celebration of May Day, May 1. Prints & Photographs Division, Library of Congress.

By contrast, reformers claimed that organized play and team sports undermined the tendency to form factions and supported the idea that fair play and respect for others were rewarded in modern society. Individual transgressions of the rules penalized the entire group.

Finally, international events reinforced these efforts to extol the virtues of play. The revival of the Olympic games in 1896—along with the 1904 St. Louis Olympics—merged nationalism with physical skills in ways that suggested the positive good of sports. The activities of American servicemen in World War I also promoted the organized play movement. To develop physical fitness, inductees and volunteers spent countless hours at military bases playing volleyball, baseball, hockey, and basketball. Boxing, wrestling, and swimming were also championed by the U.S. Army. As a result, Americans became more accepting of claims that sports and physical fitness would lead to decency and honor.

Ultimately, proponents of organized play tapped into these fears and opportunities in an effort to reform a child's "wasted time" into useful, civically beneficial activities. The play movement was essentially a progressive reform intended to save children from the vices of the inner city and to develop the civic values many believed the immigrant culture lacked. This was not an insignificant shift in the minds of many native-born Americans. Cooperation and group development ran counter to many of the intellectual trends of the past fifty years. In addition, many opposed the Progressive notion that environmental conditions of poverty were the leading causes of vice.

PARKS, PLAYGROUNDS, AND THE PLAY MOVEMENT

The challenge of dealing with overcrowded tenements, crime, and inner-city pollution gave rise to recreation and sports facilities. Certainly, some

Sports

efforts had been made before the 1910s to develop parks and recreational facilities. Landscape architect Frederick Law Olmsted constructed New York City's Central Park in 1867 to provide contemplative, natural settings for urban citizens. Unfortunately, these facilities were rarely accessible to the working class, nor were they friendly to those who wanted to use them for exercise. As late as the 1900s, many municipal parks expressly forbade walking on the grass, much less organizing a baseball game on the grounds. In 1910, Boston had only 14 places for the public to swim and seven public gymnasiums. Similarly, small, local playgrounds were appearing in the inner city, but usually in regions that were populated by wealthier Americans—and only when the land was not claimed by developers interested in erecting more housing.

Still, urban reformers convinced of the social benefits to be derived from organized play were planning facilities that could be used by those of more moderate economic means. Chicago's South Park System, begun in 1903, comprised 10 separate parks, all located in the poorest parts of the city. Funds were made available for the maintenance of these grounds and for the construction of a number of playgrounds, tracks, pools, and gyms. It was estimated that in its first few years of operation, the South Park System serviced nearly five million people annually.[2]

Such concentrated efforts remained rare, however; less than 40 parks had been constructed nationwide. Moreover, the movement lacked a coordinated, national voice. This changed in 1906, with the rise of the Playground Association of America (PAA). Led by Henry Curtis, Joseph Lee, Jane Addams, Jacob Riis, and Luther Gulick, and funded from money provided by the Russell Sage Foundation, the PAA combined the moral suasion of the settlement house movement, the medical profession, and the presidency (Theodore Roosevelt acted as the honorary leader of the PAA until 1908). With its organization centered in New York City, the PAA focused their efforts on the larger, industrial cities with amazing success. By the 1910s, the group coordinated the work of 744 full-time and more than 5,000 part-time play directors. They oversaw the construction of thousands of playgrounds, costing

localities a combined $100 million, which arranged age-specific activities for children from 4 to 18 years old. By 1917, the PAA claimed it had initiated 3,940 playgrounds and recreational programs with 8,748 directors in 481 cities and towns throughout the country.[3]

CLASS AND THE RISE OF MODERN SPECTATOR SPORTS

The aspiring middle class exerted great influence on the development of modern sports. Increasingly, by 1900, white-collar workers and professionals could find the time and money to spend on leisure pursuits. The meritocracy of sports, which valued the best player on the field, not the wealthiest one, worked well with the mindset of the increasingly confident middle class. The rationality of sports—as well as its strict organization, set rules, equality of competition, and fascination with statistics—was in keeping with the search for order craved by many new professionals. Finally, sports seemed to provide the middle class access to new and largely open opportunities for social advancement. One could hobnob with industry leaders, discussing noncontroversial sports-related topics that were the focus of such popular new magazines as *Field and Stream, Sports Afield,* and *Outing,* or demonstrate their skills on the golf course or tennis court without having to discuss one's parents, occupation, or country of origin.

Such activities had interesting and unintended consequences in the field of spectator sports. For example, golf was long held as an elite pursuit as it required time, equipment, and access to rural or suburban courses. But with the rise of the upper middle-class professional, golf began to emerge as a more popular pastime in 1910. Soon, every good-sized town could boast of a local golf course, especially in the suburban areas lining the great cities on the Eastern seaboard.

In 1913, at the U.S. Golf Association Open, golf became a national sensation. The unlikely star of the tournament was Francis Ouimet, the 20-year-old son of a recent immigrant who had learned to play golf as a caddie and by sneaking onto the exclusive Brookline Country Club in a Boston suburb. He had won six amateur events

Champion golfer Marion Hollins, swinging a golf club in 1916, was typical of wealthy Americans who enjoyed golf. Prints & Photographs Division, Library of Congress.

and legitimately qualified for the selective Open. Ouimet stunned the sports world when he tied British stars Harry Vardon and Ted Ray after three rounds. The following day, Ouimet fell behind, but rallied to force a fifth round the following day. He then bested Vardon by five strokes, and Ray by six.

Working-class Americans did have popular pastimes, but rarely were they accorded the respect given a "sport." The need for time and some disposable income were significant determinants of who participated or watched sporting events. While real wages were rising by 1910, the typical industrial laborer still worked 10 hours per day, 6 days a week. As a result, the sports that originated in neighborhood saloons, like boxing, pool, and illegal blood sports, expanded quickly in the working-class regions of the city. The growth of pool halls throughout the decade was phenomenal. More than 42,000 halls were legally registered by 1920. Although less numerous, bowling alleys were popular with the upper working classes because they allowed for family entertainment that included both men and women.

PROFESSIONAL BASEBALL

Baseball emerged as the first true mass spectator sport intended for the average American. Professional baseball survived a difficult decade: numerous splits in the professional leagues, a world war, and a scandal that included one of its greatest players in the World Series.

Baseball owners were quick to catch onto the ideals of organized play that were capturing the attention of reformers. It was argued that following baseball could make one a better citizen. Its rules, sense of fair play, meritocracy, and honesty made buying a ticket to the ballpark nearly a civic duty. Rooting for the home team helped recent immigrants develop a greater sense of civic pride.[4]

One important component ball clubs needed to make this argument more persuasive was a sense of permanence. A club that moved from town to town was unable to attract and retain a base of fans. The construction of modern parks went far to provide this stability. As a result, the decade saw new fields constructed in Pittsburgh (Forbes Field), Philadelphia (Shibe Park), Boston (Fenway Park), Detroit (Tiger Stadium), New York City (the Polo Grounds), Brooklyn (Ebbets Field), and Chicago (Comiskey and Wrigley Fields). These ballparks were not just monuments to the team's stability and commitment to the locale. They also assuaged the fears of many fans. Fires in Chicago, Cleveland, and New York stadiums were well chronicled in the newspapers, and old wooden stands occasionally collapsed under the weight of the crowd. Given the heightened competition from movies, vaudeville, and dance halls, improvements were required for baseball to continue growing in the 1910s.

The mammoth size of these modern arenas created a new type of public space. The Polo Fields, when opened in 1911, seated more than 32,000 people before it was expanded to hold 54,000.[5] One result of these large structures was that the baseball crowd tended to be more diverse and representative of America than almost any other popular sport. Women regularly attended the games, as did people of color. The arrival of the American League in 1901 opened play on Sundays, giving access to workers who were otherwise occupied on Saturdays (leading to a middle class–working class split between the fans of National and American League teams). While the game was still played only by white men, outsiders felt more comfortable within the anonymity of the large parks. As a result, baseball crowds tended to be much more orderly than those of almost any other sport.

By 1912, there were 46 minor leagues and two major leagues with teams throughout the United States. Nearly 6.8 million people attended a baseball game each year by 1910 (double that of the previous decade). This grew to 9.3 million per year by the close of the decade.[6]

The greatest direct threat to the professional leagues came in 1913, when the Federal League was born. This professional association was created by entrepreneurs who felt they had been excluded from the game by the current owners of National and American Leagues. By and large, the new teams were created in markets where clubs already existed. Many tried to attract the biggest talents of the established leagues through higher salaries or other incentives. This gamble proved to be too risky, and by 1915 the Federal League agreed to disband. The established professional club owners offered each Federal League club that agreed to fold $600,000, the possibility of buying into an established club at a discount at some future date, and admission to their league for the two most successful Federal clubs: in Chicago and St. Louis. In 1919, the Federal League franchise in Baltimore sued, claiming that the American and National Leagues constituted a national monopoly, or trust, over professional baseball and therefore should be regulated by the federal government as any other interstate business. In a landmark decision for professional baseball, the U.S. Supreme Court ruled in 1922 that while teams certainly traveled between states, the "product" of baseball (i.e., games) did not cross state lines. Baseball was not subject to federal oversight.

A second potential problem during the decade was the owners themselves. Their commitment to winning and sharing their success with the players varied greatly. For example, Frank Farrell and Jacob Ruppert were both owners of the New York Highlanders, soon to be renamed Yankees, during the 1910s. Farrell bought into the new American League using the proceeds from his network of more than 200 gambling outlets and pool halls. While he proved to be one of the most financially resourceful of all owners, many suspected that his connections to illegal wagering held potentially

Floyd "Rube" Kroh, Chicago Cubs, National League, 1910. Prints & Photographs Division, Library of Congress.

explosive problems for the game. When Ruppert, a millionaire socialite and brewing magnate, purchased the team from Farrell for $460,000 in 1915, he wanted to rename it after a line of his beer. In the end, both men proved to be beneficial to the organization. Indeed, Ruppert's lavish spending on his players and facilities—for example, on January 5, 1920, he "purchased" George Herman "Babe" Ruth from the Boston Red Sox for $125,000, and in 1923 he built Yankee Stadium—created the baseball dynasty. Less wealthy owners soon found themselves at a disadvantage. Moreover, owners ruled without opposition and, as was the case with the Chicago White Sox, their personal biases and intransigence could have disastrous consequences.[7]

Ultimately, it was the rise of the star system in baseball that secured its success. With the arrival in 1901 of the American League, and then in 1913 of the Federal League, the best ball players could market their services to a larger pool of bidders. By 1910, the average major leaguer was making a respectable $3,000 per year; that rose to around $5,000 by the end of the decade. The best players' salaries topped $10,000 per year, on par with doctors and lawyers. Each year, individual contracts kept driving the prices higher. Honus Wagner signed with Pittsburgh for $18,000 in 1910,

Ty Cobb was paid $20,000 annually by Detroit, and in 1922 Babe Ruth made $56,000 for his service to the Yankees.[8]

It appears that these salaries were well spent. The 1910s saw some of the best players in the game, including Cobb, Wagner, Ruth, Christy Mathewson (New York Giants), and Walter Johnson (Washington Senators). In 1919, Ruth hit 29 homers, shattering the old record (the next year he hit 54, more than any single *team* had previously) and become a national sensation. Many consider Johnson to have been the greatest pitcher in the game. While Cy Young won more games throughout his career (he retired in 1911 with 511 wins), Johnson earned his victories with a team that was a perennial loser. Johnson had ten consecutive 20-win seasons and twice topped 30. In 1913, his record was an astonishing 36–7; he pitched 56 consecutive scoreless innings, delivered 243 strikeouts, gave up 38 walks and an average of 1.09 runs per nine innings. Mathewson was an outstanding pitcher, but it was his behavior on and off the field made him a role model for baseball. At the peak of his career, Mathewson volunteered for duty in World War I, was gassed in combat, and died in 1925, largely as a result of related injuries. When the Baseball Hall of Fame was established in 1936, the five "Immortals" selected on the first ballot were Cobb, Wagner, Ruth, Mathewson, and Johnson—and all but Ruth made their most lasting mark playing during the 1910s.[9]

Stars, high pay, and modern stadiums led to escalating interest and attendance. Good players were lauded for how well they exemplified American values. Rising salaries and, in 1912, the formation of a new player's union (the Fraternity of Professional Baseball Players of America) gave strong encouragement for others to avoid brawls and obvious alcohol abuse. Managers began to require that their players dress and act as professionals while in the public eye. Clubs looked to hire college-educated athletes, many of whom—like Jim Thorpe—had already made a name for themselves nationwide. By 1920, nearly 20 percent of all rookies came from the college ranks.[10] Umpires were paid better and abused less. This professionalism boosted the faith that middle-class Americans put into baseball.

When viewed in this light, the 1919 "Black Sox" scandal could have been potentially lethal to professional baseball. The Chicago White Sox were owned by Charles Comiskey, a former player and manager who toiled all his life under cheap owners. When Comiskey himself became an owner, first in Sioux City, Iowa, and then, in 1900, in Chicago, he proved to be even more petty. Joining the fledgling American League in 1901, Comiskey's team (which took the name White Sox after it had been discarded by the National League's Chicago team, which shifted from White Sox, to Nationals, to Colts, and finally the Cubs) won pennants in 1901, 1906, 1917, and 1919. While the team was well supported by the city, Comiskey paid his players less than half of the national average and much less to his star players. The greatest player of the White Sox was "Shoeless" Joe Jackson. A lifetime .356 hitter, Jackson came to Chicago in 1916 after a stellar career in Cleveland. His batting stance was thought to be nearly perfect, and numerous major league players (including Babe

Ty Cobb and Joe Jackson, two of the best baseball players of the era. Prints & Photographs Division, Library of Congress.

Ruth) patterned themselves after the consummate hitter. His skills were so well regarded that Comiskey was forced, in 1919, to extend a three-year guaranteed contract to Jackson. That year, supported by a strong team, Jackson propelled the White Sox to the World Series, where they were heavy favorites to beat the Cincinnati Reds.

The links among organized crime, professional gamblers, and baseball had always been close. Baseball offered gamblers many ways to wager, and collusion by only a few players could have great consequences. After winning the pennant, White Sox first baseman Chick Gandil was approached by a professional gambler named Arnold Rothstein and offered $100,000 to throw the series. Gandil agreed and was helped by seven of his teammates, including Jackson, who later admitted to taking $5,000. While Jackson played well, batting .375 and driving in six runs, the White Sox lost the World Series three games to five (in a best of nine contest).

Many, including Comiskey, suspected that the "fix was in" by the second game. Comiskey had evidence of a bribe only weeks after the series ended. He said nothing. It was not until 1920, after a Chicago Cubs regular-season game was thrown, that Illinois Attorney General MacClay Hoyne impaneled a grand jury to investigate gambling and baseball in the state. Hoyne subpoenaed eight suspected White Sox players. In their testimony before the grand jury, Gandil, Jackson, and the others admitted they had taken money. This was enough to convince the jurists that a felony had been committed, and Hoyne was advised to press charges. The trial had the potential to ruin the White Sox, smear the reputation of baseball, incarcerate Rothstein and the players, and drive Comiskey from the game. Yet when the trial began, the incriminating testimony mysteriously disappeared. When the eight refused to testify in open court, the prosecution was left without evidence and the "Black Sox" were acquitted.

The damage to the reputation of baseball went to the core of its self-professed values. Only the heavy hand of the baseball commissioner—a former federal district judge—Kenesaw Mountain Landis prevented the situation from deteriorating further. In spite of the acquittal, Landis permanently banned the players from professional baseball. Jackson was also permanently barred from admission to the Hall of Fame as a result (to date, he has the third highest lifetime batting average in all of baseball and the highest of any player not currently enshrined at Cooperstown). Landis's swift and decisive action, coupled with the hitting prowess of Babe Ruth, allowed baseball to emerge relatively unscathed by the incident.

Many believe that Comiskey was the man in the center of the controversy. Had he paid his players even an average salary or treated them with the respect that entertainment professionals earned in the United States by 1919, the team members in all likelihood would not have been tempted by the numerous gamblers who loitered around America's ballparks. Comiskey's character deficiencies were revealed more fully in 1924 when, after being sued for his failure to honor Jackson's guaranteed contract, he produced the "lost" grand jury confession. By proving that Jackson had admitted taking a bribe, Comiskey showed that Jackson had breached his contract

WORLD SERIES

1910 Philadelphia Athletics (AL), 4 games; Chicago Cubs (NL), 1 game

1911 Philadelphia Athletics (AL), 4 games; New York Giants (NL), 2 games

1912 Boston Red Sox (AL), 4 games; New York Giants (NL), 3 games

1913 Philadelphia Athletics (AL), 4 games; New York Giants (NL), 1 game

1914 Boston Braves (NL), 4 games; Philadelphia Athletics (AL), 0 games

1915 Boston Red Sox (AL), 4 games; Philadelphia Phillies (NL), 1 game

1916 Boston Red Sox (AL), 4 games; Brooklyn Dodgers (NL) 1 game

1917 Chicago White Sox (AL), 4 games; New York Giants (NL), 2 games

1918 Boston Red Sox (AL), 4 games; Chicago Cubs (NL), 2 games

1919 Cincinnati Reds (NL), 5 games; Chicago White Sox (AL), 3 games

and therefore was not entitled to the remainder of his salary. Many have concluded that Comiskey and Rothstein planned and carried out the pilfering of these confessions in 1920. Comiskey never admitted his role in the crisis nor did he change his tightfisted ways.

BOXING

Prize fighting represented one of the rare instances in which a once disreputable working-class pastime was transformed into an accepted national spectator sport. The emergence of respectable fighters, including Jack Dempsey, the "Manassa Mauler," and Gene Tunney, who perfected his boxing skills while with the American Expeditionary Force in World War I helped lead to this acceptance.[11]

Jack Johnson continued to be one of the most prominent boxers of the decade, following his earlier successes beginning in the later 1890s. One of the first African American heavyweight champions of the modern era, Johnson earned his title in 1910 with a fifteenth-round knockout of James Jeffries. (See Sports and Leisure of the 1900s.) After Johnson earned $60,000 for winning the fight, Johnson's mother proudly claimed that her son "said he'd *bring home the bacon,* and the honey boy has gone and done it,"[12] thereby adding a new slang phrase to the American language. In an era of overt racism, Johnson stood as a proud

Jack Johnson (right) and James Jeffries (left) at the World Championship Battle, Reno, Nevada, July 4, 1910. Prints & Photographs Division, Library of Congress.

symbol for African Americans: able to excel as a champion based on merit, second to no one regardless of his skin color. Johnson's drinking and womanizing, typical for prizefighters of that era, and his marriage to an 18-year-old white actress and model, Lucille Cameron, however, stoked racial hatred. Nearly every competitor of Johnson's was labeled a "great white hope," and race riots broke out across the country when Johnson sent his opponents reeling. Johnson, exiled from the United States for supposedly violating the Mann Act through his marriage to Cameron, lost his crown in 1915 to Jess Willard while fighting in Havana, Cuba.

BASKETBALL

Essentially a new sport, created by Dr. James Naismith in 1891, basketball showed signs of growth in the 1910s, but remained small compared to baseball and football. Much of the enthusiasm for the game grew out of collegiate contests. Several college conferences began play in the 1900s, and more established games in the following decade, including the Southwest (1915) and Pacific Coast (1916). Wisconsin, under the tutelage of innovative coach Walter "Doc" Meanwell, stood as national collegiate champions in 1912, 1916, and 1917.

Professional basketball did not have a central organizing body in the decade. The Original Celtics, founded in 1918 by promoters Jim and Tom Furey, helped consolidate the hodgepodge by luring the best players to one team. The Furey brothers signed star players, such as Henry "Dutch" Dehnert and Joe Lapchick, to individual contracts based on play for an entire season, thus limiting a player's ability to switch to another league or team midway.

FOOTBALL

Football was originally a sport of the upper class; the game was the chosen recreation of most college-bound sons of America's elite. Despite these aristocratic roots, by 1900 football was found throughout the country and was vying for recognition as *the* national game.

Football's popularity on college campuses was primarily due to the fact that the typical college

Sports

student at the time was male, young, affluent, and in a relatively uncontrolled environment for the first time. These sons of the rich, well trained to sacrifice for the good of the group, were eager to show the world that they could lead the "strenuous life" needed to take control of an emerging industrial giant like the United States. The rituals of the weekend games, either as a player or as a spectator, also served to release pressure after a week's worth of classes in which one's place in the future social order was being determined. Accordingly, America's most prestigious universities had some of the fiercest and most selective football programs in the country, followed closely by the large Midwestern universities that now make up the Big 10 football conference.

A large part of the appeal of the game was the violent release of energy that occurred on the field. Unfortunately and probably inevitably, young men driven to such levels of excitement were often unable to contain this violence. At times, the game turned deadly. Fortunately for the hundreds of student athletes, Walter Camp, the head of the American Collegiate Football Rules Committee (the precursor to the National Collegiate Athletic Association, NCAA), set to work modify the basic rules of the game. Among other changes, Camp wanted to create more opportunities to score and, in 1912, he changed the number of points for a touchdown to six and reduced the scoring of field goals to three points. (Before that the average score for most games had been in the single digits.) He legalized the forward pass and separated the teams by a line of scrimmage to give the players more time to develop complex scoring strategies. Camp also outlawed the unstoppable, bone-snapping, flying wedge as being simply too dangerous.

Almost immediately, these changes had their intended effects. Deaths became less and less common, and the fans were treated to a more wide-open, enjoyable game. In some ways, scoring became too easy for the better schools. Georgia Tech's impressive 1916 and 1917 teams rolled up massive margins against their opponents, including a 41–0 win over Pennsylvania, and a 222–0 victory over Cumberland (Tennessee), a game in which Tech's kicker booted 18 extra points in the first half alone. The changes also allowed

innovative and daring football tacticians to take on the giants of the game. Most noteworthy was the small, wholly outmatched team from Notre Dame, a little and largely unknown Catholic college, who utilized the forward pass to stun Army 35–13. Their quarterback, Gus Dorais, relied on the quickness and intelligence of his key receivers, including Knute Rockne, to befuddle the impenetrable wall that was Army's defensive line. That same year, University of Chicago's Amos Alonzo Stagg began numbering his players' jerseys as an aid to the public, who were beginning to take an intense interest in the revived sport.

During the 1910s, the immense popularity of football began attracting fans across the nation. Colleges began constructing large stadiums: The newly constructed Yale Bowl, in New Haven, Connecticut, held 60,000 fans when it opened in 1914. That same year, colleges invested over $2 million nationwide for new arenas. The decade also saw the growth of football stardom for such players as Rockne, George Gipp, Jim Thorpe, and coaches including Stagg and Glen Scobie "Pop" Warner. In 1915, the second Tournament of Roses football game was played in Pasadena, California. The first, held thirteen years earlier, was a failure. After 1915 the Rose Bowl became an important and much discussed contest between the best teams of the East and West, and it signaled the arrival of college football as a national preoccupation.

While no doubt aided by the innovative tactics of his coach, "Pop" Warner, and the skills of his fellow teammates at Carlisle Indian School, Jim Thorpe's exceptional athletic skills set him apart from all others. During his freshman year, Thorpe's smaller teams defeated such goliaths as Pennsylvania, Chicago, Army, and, in one of the greatest upsets of all time, Harvard in 1911. Thorpe solidified his reputation as "the world's greatest athlete" at the 1912 Olympic Games held in Stockholm, Sweden, where he won nearly every event in both the decathlon and pentathlon and won gold medals in both. When it was later reported that Thorpe had earned $15 a week for playing semi-professional baseball in the summer of 1909, a common practice for most college athletes, the Olympic Commission stripped him of his medals, an offense that was not corrected until 1980, 27 years after his death. Regardless of this slight, Thorpe popularized football as Babe Ruth did in baseball. His professional football career motivated many Americans to attend their first spectator sport.

OLYMPICS

Stockholm, Sweden hosted the 1912 Summer Olympic Games. Nearly 2,500 athletes partici-

JIM THORPE

Jim Thorpe, born with a twin brother, Charles, in the Oklahoma Territory in May of 1888, was primarily descended from the Sac and Fox tribes. After the sickly Charles died at age eight, Thorpe went on to excel in sports at a young age, earning All American honors at Carlisle Indian Industrial School in Pennsylvania. A member of the Olympic team in 1912, Thorpe won gold medals in the pentathlon and decathlon and set a 200-meter hurdling record that stood for 36 years. During the awards ceremony the king of Sweden, Gustave V, exclaimed, "Sir, you are the greatest athlete in the world." Later, Thorpe was stripped of his medals in 1913 due to his playing professional baseball in 1909 and 1910 in the East Carolina league. Thorpe went on to play baseball for the great New York Giants under the irascible John McGraw. When his manager hurled a racial slur at him one day, Thorpe chased him across the infield, and only his teammates prevented him from giving his manager a severe beating. At the beginning of the 1919 season, Thorpe decided to quit baseball, deliberately striking out with a smile on his face. McGraw fired him on the spot. During his baseball career he played professional football as well, ultimately becoming the American Professional Football Association's first president in 1920. Thorpe played pro football for 14 teams including one composed of mostly Native Americans. Thorpe was the first of the two-sport athletes who came later, such as Bo Jackson and Deion Sanders. His achievements in sports as a Native American during the pre-civil rights era became legendary.

From Mike Coppock, "The 20th Century's Greatest Athlete," *American History* 42, no. 5 (2007).

pated from 28 countries. The host nation won the most total medals (65), followed by the U.S. (63), and Great Britain (41).

The 1912 Games caused an international uproar when officials decided to include women's swimming and diving events. James E. Sullivan, the powerful head of the AAU, forbade American women from competing in the Stockholm festival. Despite the puritanical reaction of the U.S., many nations allowed women to compete.

The 1916 Summer Games scheduled for Berlin were cancelled when war broke out in Europe. Despite calls to change the venue, founder of the modern Olympic movement Pierre de Coubertin would not change the location.

GAMES AND TOYS

In the fall of 1917, the Council of National Defense held hearings in Washington, D.C., to debate a topic that was a child's worst nightmare: whether to cancel Christmas. The council, made up of powerful industrialists and policymakers, was not debating the merit of observing the Christian celebration. Rather, given America's entry into World War I in April of that year, the council was questioning the rampant consumerism that had grown in conjunction with the holiday. The council hoped to conserve critical war materials, such as steel and copper, as well as to instill the need for personal sacrifice.

The production and sale of toys were not significant components of the U.S. economy in the 1910s. Most stores did not even carry toys regularly on their shelves; nearly two-thirds of toy purchases were made around the Christmas holiday. It was the toy industry's lobbyists, not children or their parents, who were most vocal about the potential ban.[13]

For the most part, up to 1910, typical toys and games were constructed at home or were limited to small, relatively inexpensive purchases. Homemade dolls, blocks, jigsaw puzzles, and dice were the basis for most children's toys. For girls, cutout dresses for paper dolls taken from newspaper advertisements or last year's catalogs were common. For boys, a rare figurine or wheeled miniature was standard—and these typically were handed down through the generations.

Sports

The vast majority of purchased toys were made in Germany, England, or France. There, suppliers had perfected the process of working tin into a variety of shapes and styles. Tin plate provided a smooth, flat surface that was easy to bend and could easily be assembled using either solder or metal tabs. More important, tin allowed for metal lithographing, which applied a variety of colors and patterns to a toy's surface.

American manufacturers did excel, however, in the production of cast-iron toys. Perhaps because of their weight, which prohibited easy overseas transport from Europe, the market for cast-iron goods remained under the control of U.S. suppliers. Initially these goods were cruder than the European imports, but they were easier to mass produce and hence cheaper for the consumer. The quality of these goods varied greatly. Expensive toys were finely finished and packaged in handsome wooden boxes. Cheaper goods, much cruder, were packed in cardboard or not at all.

During the 1910s, as prices fell and casting techniques improved (allowing for greater detail), consumers became mesmerized by sturdy mechanized banks and the spring-driven vehicles. Cast-iron replicas of boats, fully functioning steam engines, miniature sewing machines, and other mementos of the machine age became increasingly easy for manufacturers to mass produce. The craze for all things on wheels, from automobiles to fire engines, helped spur the growth of sales. When the war broke out, miniature cast-iron airplanes, dirigibles, and artillery pieces became popular among children. By the end of the decade, the Arcade Manufacturing Company (Freeport, Illinois) was issuing an annual catalog, listing over fifty pages of cast-iron toys.

Stuffed toys also became increasingly popular in the 1910s. While rag dolls and stuffed animals

Sports

Teddy bears, made in New York, 1915. Prints & Photographs Division, Library of Congress.

had always been made for children, the popularity of the teddy bear drove the markets to new heights throughout the decade. The toy, named for Teddy Roosevelt, who in 1903 refused to shoot a tethered grizzly bear cub, became the rage after the *Washington Post* promoted the incident. Typical of the period, it was a German toymaker, Margarete Steiff, who produced the first teddy bears in 1904. It was estimated that more than a million of the toys were sold by 1910. In the United States, Morris and Rose Michtom, Russian immigrants and toy retailers, began manufacturing the stuffed bears domestically in 1907. By 1910, the Michtoms had closed their store to focus on production and founded the Ideal Novelty & Toy Company. Ideal was one of the first suppliers to begin using cotton for their stuffing, rather than the traditional straw, kapok (a silky fiber imported from Malaysia), or granulated cork. As a result, they developed a reputation for quality that previously had been reserved for European imports.

Stuffed dolls kept pace with the teddy bear. Cute figurines such as Baby Bumps, Negro Baby Bumps, and dolls representing the Campbell Kids—a cherub-faced boy and girl who were depicted on the popular soup labels—were promoted in newspapers and the periodicals. The advertising tie-in between one product and a seemingly unrelated toy, as was the case with Campbell's campaign in 1911, was an early indication of the profound changes that were driving choices of many consumers. When Rose O'Neill began marketing her Kewpie dolls, chubby dolls with a topknot of hair, in 1911, it was not to toy stores or other retailers but directly to the readers of the *Ladies' Home Journal.*

The single most influential new doll of the decade was Raggedy Ann, introduced in 1918. The creation of Johnny Gruelle, a political cartoonist, Raggedy Ann (and her friend Raggedy Andy, unveiled in 1920) was patented in 1915 through a series of children's stories written and illustrated by Gruelle. The doll was based on a rag doll created by Gruelle's mother, to which the son added the characteristic button eyes and triangle nose. Gruelle found a publisher willing to package a doll with each book sold. The firm, Volland Publishing Company of Chicago, found that the product tie-in greatly enhanced their sales. By the end of the decade it was the doll, and not the story, that drove Raggedy Ann's popularity.

Board games were also played by children and young adults, but with an important difference. In the 1910s, board games were regarded as ways in which to instill proper values which would prepare youngsters for the responsibilities of adulthood. These goals included fair play, rational thought, and honest competition—meaning that the winner was determined based solely on his or her merits.

The Singer Sewing Machine Company did much the same thing in marketing a toy sewer that was fully functional. They advertised the child's diversion as both "Practical and Instructive." Such functional thinking was typical of the era's approach not only to games and toys, but also to children's recreation and sport.[14]

One popular board game of the decade—Ouija—was diametrically opposed to this trend. The game was not really intended for children, but rather for adults. The title combines the French and German words for "yes" (*oui* and *ja*). Ouija was first created in the 1880s following an occult craze. The game was played by two people who, eyes closed, placed their fingers lightly on a three-cornered "planchette," which held a pencil. After asking the board a question, the planchette allegedly moved across letters or to a "yes" or "no" corner to indicate a response. William Fuld, a Baltimore toy maker who marketed Ouija in the United States, sold more than a million copies of the game in 1918 alone.

The most innovative and inventive children's games of the era, however, stayed true to educational goals. The Erector Set, developed by A. C. Gilbert, was the most significant. This construction toy was intended to allow a child to develop his imagination. Introduced in 1913, the Erector Set was sold under the slogan, "Hello, Boys! Make Lots of Toys!" Born in Salem, Oregon, Gilbert excelled at sports, including track, gymnastics, wrestling, and football, earning both an Olympic gold medal in 1908 and a scholarship to Yale. While at Yale, Gilbert focused on physical education, studied medicine, and eventually earned an M.D. Although well steeped in the Progressive values of a strenuous, healthy lifestyle, Gilbert also enjoyed practicing magic. He used this skill to earn

Sports

additional money as a performer and to start a small mail-order business that catered to amateur magicians. Gilbert's prospering magic supply business led him to open retail establishments selling these and other toys. In 1911, while traveling from New Haven to New York City, Gilbert was intrigued by the steel girders used to support the electrical lines that propelled the streetcars. He envisioned manufacturing a set of small construction pieces, including electric motors, cogs, and other moving parts, which would allow children to build their own toys. After experimenting with a number of designs throughout 1912, he finally arrived at a working solution which he patented and began to market the following year.

Gilbert's partners in magic were unwilling to participate in this gambit. Meccano, a rival construction set manufactured in England, had already sold poorly in the United States. Nevertheless, Gilbert believed that proper promotion and the inclusion of moving parts would ensure success. Venturing out on his own, Gilbert spent more than $12,000 to advertise the toy in such national magazines as *American Boy, Good Housekeeping,* and *Saturday Evening Post.* Gilbert highlighted the educational features of his product, and his Erector Set became an overnight sensation. Over the next twenty years, Gilbert expanded the options available through the sets and forayed into other "educational toy" markets such as microscopes, telescopes, and chemistry sets.

Other creative toys followed throughout the decade. Most notable was the arrival of Tinkertoys in 1914 and Lincoln Logs in 1916, which were originated by John L. Wright, son of architect Frank Lloyd Wright.

FADS AND HOBBIES

Most fads were initiated by the need to be the first on one's block to own new products, such as washing machines, floor sweepers, hair dryers, and pop-up toasters. Probably the most innovative was the handheld camera perfected and marketed by George Eastman. His first Kodak camera, which retailed for $25, was available for only $2 in 1913 and provided higher quality and better reliability than almost any other camera on the market.

Being the first to recognize cultural trends was also prized by many. Following the expansion of popular musical forms, ranging from Ragtime to Tin Pan Alley, dance crazes swept the country in the 1910s. By 1912, there were dozens of particular dance steps—including the fox trot, horse trot, crab step, kangaroo dip, camel walk, fish walk, chicken stretch, turkey trot, grizzly bear, and bunny hug—which rose and fell from popularity.

Fads during the 1910s were usually closely connected to new products or services rather than to new ideas or behaviors, and most were popular across racial, class, and gender lines. In addition, for the first time, American fads were exported around the globe. Americans developed a cultural pride, a sense of themselves as being separate from Europe through their unique manias. The fact that others could belatedly share in these passions lent strength to their movement through U.S. society.

Given the immense popularity of the automobile, it is not surprising that the car developed its own culture throughout the 1910s. More important, the popularity of Ford's Model T turned this once elite luxury into an everyday desire. When unveiled in 1908, the Model T retailed for $850, a modest price for a typical automobile. But when mass production lowered the cost of Ford's cars to $600 by 1912, middle-class Americans and the higher-paid working class were able to join in the fun. By 1914, every other new car purchased was a Ford.[15]

While still a major acquisition, Ford's consumers quickly personalized the Model T to suit their own style. Particularly for the young, riding clothes, goggles, running boards, rumble seats, cloth tops, and other accessories became mandatory to differentiate their (or their father's) Model T from the thousands of others. Model T joke books, which focused on the frequent breakdowns or slow speeds of the vehicle, soon proliferated across the country.

The speed of automobiles also took hold of America's imagination, although poor roads and congested urban traffic limited most speeds to ten to twenty miles an hour. Still, the potential for rapid transportation captured the minds of many. As early as 1906, Fred Marriot navigated a steam-powered automobile (called the Stanley Steamer)

Sports

over Daytona Beach at more than 127 miles an hour. More expensive internal combustion cars, such as Pierce Arrow or Panhards, could travel over fifty miles an hour on good roads. As a result, the 1910s saw the development of ways to limit the eagerness of drivers to drive fast. Most cities established speed limits (usually twenty miles per hour); in 1914, Cleveland became the first city to employ traffic lights to force drivers to yield to others at major intersections. Probably most indicative of America's love of speed was the Indianapolis 500, inaugurated in 1911 and won by Ray Harroun, who averaged 74 miles per hour.

Pilots also competed in popular time trials which were often sponsored by newspapers. Flight records were repeatedly set and broken throughout the decade. In 1912, Captain Albert Berry became the first American to jump successfully from an airplane aloft using a parachute. In 1919, an English pilot and an American navigator became the first to perform a nonstop transatlantic flight. After the war, former military aviators toured the country recreating perilous dogfights and performing death-defying tricks with their biplanes. The fad reached its height in the decade when, in 1919, couples began taking their wedding vows while riding on planes.

Sports

Travel

of the 1910s

A number of significant innovations and long-lasting changes were made to the ways in which Americans traveled during the 1910s. From the novelties of the airplane to the everyday travel of streetcars, getting from one place to another was easier and quicker. The variety of transportation ranged from the automobile and ocean liner to traditional horse carts and railroads. Soon, driving a car or taking an elevated train came to represent one's relative status in society. Even when disaster struck, such as during the infamous maiden voyage of RMS *Titanic* in 1912, Americans read into the tragedy criticisms about modern society and culture rather than the seaworthiness of the White Star Line's massive flagship.

DESTINATIONS

People still planned weekend visits to relatives, day trips to local amusements, and annual vacations to regional resorts. By the end of the decade, however, these visits were increasingly farther away from one's home and required more cash outlays. For example, in 1910 a typical vacation ocean cruise could be purchased for less than $60 per person (a price well within the range of the typical worker), which included a berth and meals for a 12-day round-trip voyage from New York City to Halifax, Nova Scotia. Similar

trips were available for runs along the Atlantic seaboard to Florida and the Caribbean. For more money, one could travel to Europe or Latin America via regular, and increasingly quicker, boats. Railroads provided access to a number of popular attractions, including Niagara Falls and the Grand Canyon, which previously had been visited by those within a relatively small radius. In conjunction with the growth of these junkets was the spread of hotel accommodations. For around one dollar a day, travelers could find comfortable lodging in most American cities.

Cars also gave Americans access to a growing movement known as the Chautauqua. The Circuit Chautauqua, which first appeared in the 1870s in southwestern New York State, was a traveling troupe of actors, motivational speakers, and religious revivalists. Largely independent of formal associations, the Chautauquas varied greatly by region and local economy, but in general appealed to families seeking educational and cultural entertainment. A typical Chautauqua might last three days and include a selection from a Shakespeare play or a dramatization of Dickens, a noted speaker (such as William Jennings Bryan), music, movies, poetry readings, and social commentary by both humorists and reformers. The popularity of the events (estimates range as high as 30 to 45 million people attending by the

Camping became more popular in the 1910s because there were more options for transportation. The National Park Service was created in 1916. Prints & Photographs Division, Library of Congress.

mid-1920s) led to great competition between the tours. The movement ebbed by the 1930s, largely due to radio, which provided similar entertainment in the home, the Great Depression, and the automobile, which provided a wider array of entertainment options.

Camping, too, became more widespread as a result of growing transportation options. The desire to experience the great outdoors became almost a national passion in the 1910s. The combined effects of Progressive reformers, who spoke against the poor quality of life within the cities, the growing access to unspoiled natural environments throughout the country, increased promotion by railroad companies hoping to spur a tourism boom, and the interest generated by the formation of a National Park system led many to strike out for the wilds. While Congress had set aside parts of the Yosemite Valley in California, as well as parks in Yellowstone in Montana and Wyoming, in the nineteenth century, protected regions expanded greatly in the 1910s. The creation

of a National Park Service, in 1916, gave control of more than 14 preserves, mostly in the West, to the Department of the Interior. The service built roads, hotels, museums, and camping facilities within these domains to control the environmental impact of the thousands of new park visitors.

THE AIRPLANE

Air travel had come far since Orville and Wilbur Wright made their first flight in 1903. By the close of the 1910s, air travel was no longer a novelty and had become a key strategic technology for modern military forces.

In 1910, most airplanes were flimsy crafts allowing short journeys and carrying only a limited amount of weight. By 1913, the biplane (which used two sets of staggered wings) had become the standard model. The increase in lift and decrease in drag, due to the streamlined, enclosed fuselage, was accompanied by an engine that steadily increased in power. In England, in 1913, A. V. Roe

Travel

and Tom Sopwith constructed the first military training aircraft, a move that furthered the drive toward greater speed and agility. By the start of the war, Sopwith's "Camel" could climb more that 15,000 feet in less than 10 minutes, carry an effective military payload, and travel at over 200 miles per hour.

Pilots quickly gained experience throughout the decade. Novelty displays, which were popular with the public, led to a greater knowledge of what the plane could do. Parachute drops, water landings, loop-de-loops, inverted flight, and endurance flights (of speed, distance, and height) all were pioneered in the 1910s to the gaping awe of the audience.

When, in January 1914, P. E. Fansler used a Benoist flying boat to ferry passengers and freight from Tampa and Saint Petersburg, Florida, he launched the first commercial airline. While Fansler's firm lasted less than three months, more than a thousand people took the 22-mile excursion. On the ground, legal battles between the Wright brothers and Glenn H. Curtiss were being closely followed. Curtiss, a public aviator and builder, made his fame by setting speed records and winning a distinguished flying contest from Albany to New York City, in 1910, sponsored by Joseph Pulitzer's *New York World*. He converted his motorcycle factory to airplane production, but was blocked by patents held by the Wrights. In 1913 and then again in 1914, the federal courts upheld the Wright patents (in the process, recognizing them as the "first in flight"). In response, Curtiss began working closely with English and French designers, incorporating their modifications into his American planes, including the first gyroscopic automatic pilot, retractable landing gear, and a number of useful instruments.

The outbreak of war in 1914 profoundly affected the evolution of air travel. While the American military was initially hesitant to invest heavily in combat-ready aircraft (partly because the United States was not at war until 1917), European fighters like Frenchman Roland Garros and Germany's Lt. Manfred Von Richthofen (the "Red Baron") established the lethal and strategic advantages gained by an air force. Aircraft provided direct visual reconnaissance of an enemy's movements and their reinforcements. They could deliver minor, but strategic, attacks against an enemy's most vital positions (such as supply depots or command centers). They could sustain numerous hits while remaining aloft and capable of landing in many locations (on August 2, 1917, E. H. Dunning became the first pilot to land a plane on a *moving* ship, on the deck of HMS *Furious*). The only real threat to these aircraft was other pilots. Richthofen was credited with more than 80 kills before he was killed himself, in 1918, in a dogfight with Canadian pilot Roy Brown. American Eddie Rickenbacker shot down 26 enemies in the short time he saw action.

During the war, the American military chose a standard military training plane: the Curtiss Model JN (or Curtiss "Jenny") in 1914. The Jenny, a sturdy biplane, remained a standard for American aviation for nearly a generation. With America's entry into the war, Congress appropriated more than $640 million to "darken the skies" of Europe with more than 20,000 aircraft. While only a fraction of these were ever commissioned, the American war effort lent the aircraft industry the technical and financial justification to begin the construction and operation of a safe and affordable civilian air fleet in the 1920s.[1]

TRAGEDY AND CLASS IN OCEAN TRAVEL

In the decade that saw the sinking of the *Titanic,* the *Lusitania,* and the *Eastland* (which, technically, was a boat designed for lake travel and capsized rather than sank), ocean travel had become regarded by many as the ultimate example of the arrogance of Progressive society. The "unsinkable" designs of these mammoth ships relied on science and technology to provide patrons with the latest in consumer conveniences, including speed, at supposedly no cost. Of course, such thinking was not confined to the great ships, as World War I proved. But still, the opulence and strong class lines reflected in these liners suggested to many that the wealthy were willing to take great risks in order to maintain their place in society.

The luxury cruise ship the *Titanic* sank overnight on April 14–15, 1912, with more than 2,200 people on board. More than 1,500 died. The *Eastland*

Lusitania out in harbor, 1908–1914. Prints & Photographs Division, Library of Congress.

was a lake excursion ship that carried more than 2,500 passengers on a Chicago company picnic in Lake Michigan. It capsized in 1915, killing 841 of its passengers. The *Lusitania,* a luxury ocean liner owned by the Cunard Steamship company, was torpedoed by a German ship on May 7, 1915, off the coast of Ireland as it approached Liverpool. It sank, killing 1,193 people, including 128 Americans, and turned public opinion in the U.S. against Germany, although the U.S. did not enter World War I until 1917. (See Overview of the 1910s.)

EVERYDAY TRAVEL

Streetcars

Although less glamorous, rail travel in the 1910s was certainly more important to the average American than the opulence of the ocean liners. For the very wealthy, cross-country rail travel did not require a sacrifice of comfort. Personal cars ordered from the Pullman Company offered magnates like James B. Duke all the luxuries of

home without the need to rub shoulders with the common folk. For average Americans, rail transportation improved in quality and regularity while generally decreasing in cost. The introduction of safety features, such as the air brake and stronger alloys for key parts, decreased the likelihood of fatal accidents.

Within cities, horse cars and cable cars transported the masses on a daily basis. Horse cars seated about 20, and during peak hours, people hung from the sides and stood in the aisles. Pulled by teams of two to six horses, the service was slow and dirty. It was estimated that the horses in service in a typical city the size of Milwaukee produced over 133 tons of manure a day. When the overworked beasts collapsed and died, their bodies were left alongside the road for days. In 1912, the city of Chicago reported the destruction of nearly 10,000 draft horses per year.

Cable cars, introduced in 1883, used an underground system of steel cables to pull the attached vehicles at a fixed rate of speed. Suffering from mechanical failure, high expense, inefficiency, and an inability to speed up service during times of high usage, cable cars were only briefly the popular choice for municipal mass transit. Still, more than 373 million passengers per year used cable cars throughout the country by the turn of the century.

The arrival of the electric streetcar, or trolley, in the late 1880s added to the growth of the modern city. Trolleys were clean, safe, dependable, and cheap. At a speed of over twenty miles per hour, the streetcar was faster than other forms of urban travel, and capable of accelerating and slowing to accommodate open or congested areas. Terminating at ballparks, race tracks, beer gardens, or beaches, the trolley lines saw more than a doubling of service during the weekends, suggesting that Americans used the utility in ways that allowed them to access new usable spaces within the city.[2]

During the 1910s, America's light rail system was more developed and serviced more people than any other transportation system in the world. In 1911, New York City had ten times the mileage of Tokyo, a city that was over twice its size in population. In 1919, New York's peak year of trolley service, more than 1,344 miles of track were in use. Nationwide, more than 70,000 miles serviced

Travel

The beautiful interior of the Chicago and Alton Railroad cars. Prints & Photographs Division, Library of Congress.

billions of passengers annually.[3] In the largest cities, Americans rode the trolley an average of once every other day of the year. Unfortunately, the pressure to retain the nickel fare overrode the need of most lines to keep up with inflation, which ran rampant during the war years. Moreover, automobiles and auto manufacturers (who purchased trolley lines only to replace service with motorized buses) soon undermined the monopoly held by electric rail in the cities.

Automobiles

Automobile travel grew relatively slowly in the United States before 1910. Most cars were primarily intended for use by the wealthy. As late as 1905, there was only one car for every 1,078 Americans.[4]

There were many reasons for the slow growth of the U.S. auto industry before 1910. The size of

the country and the rapid growth of public transportation were certainly factors. In addition, restrictive legislation, the generally poor state of roads, the lack of directional signs and maps, and the need for filling stations made automobile use inconvenient for any travel beyond one's immediate neighborhood.

In the 1910s, the relationship between Americans and their cars fundamentally changed. By 1913, there was one car per eight people.[5] There were more cars registered in Michigan than in all of England and Ireland. Henry Ford is credited with leading to this transformation. Ford's desire to "build a motor car for the great multitude," and his ability to do so made him a legend. (See Travel of the 1900s.)

Ford faced an auto industry that had not standardized a single source of power. Electric and steam-powered automobiles were widely available

Woman boarding a New York City streetcar by jumping onto the running board, 1913. Prints & Photographs Division, Library of Congress.

and offered competitive advantages that were not easily addressed by the internal combustion device. Steam cars, led by Francis and Freelan Stanley, who in 1906 built a Stanley Steamer that traveled at 127.66 mph, were simple and relatively cheap to own.[6] While inconvenient to operate, once underway the steam car far outperformed its gasoline-powered rivals. Electric cars were quiet, clean, and favored by wealthy women, both for their ease of operation and for the status (the best electric cars ranged in price from $2,600 to $5,500). However, electric cars were limited in range and power and required a new charge every evening. The massive batteries and boilers for both styles made the cars heavy and hard to maneuver in the heavily rutted roads. In the end, neither platform met the needs of the average consumer: low cost *and* ease of operation.

Patent laws were a third obstacle to Ford's vision of a "universal car." The patent for the internal combustion engine (actually, for a two-cylinder device that was never used to power a car) was held by the Association of Licensed Automobile Manufacturers (ALAM), which charged a nominal royalty for all gasoline-powered engines. Ford was bothered by the infringement and sued the ALAM in 1903. When, in 1911, he won his case (ALAM retained the rights for the nearly useless two-cylinder product), Ford Motor Company was able to develop future lines of cars without the need for prior legal approval.

By 1911, Ford had already developed his universal car in the Model T. Experimenting with a number of combinations of cylinders, chassis sizes, and production methods, the Model T was introduced in 1908 and was, in many ways, the culmination of Ford's engineering talents. The success of the "Tin Lizzie" or "flivver" lay in the fact that the car was relatively affordable (it premiered at $825), easily repaired by the average operator, could traverse poor roads well, and could be modified by farmers to perform a variety of tasks. Three foot pedals, two hand levers,

and a throttle switch were needed to operate the vehicle. In order to start the car, one needed to set the hand brake, set the spark and gas throttle to their "proper" positions (which varied by climate and even by car), hand crank the engine until it caught, then race back to the cabin to reset the spark and fuel mixtures. One of the endearing qualities of the "Lizzie" was its powerful reverse gear. Given that the gasoline flowed from the rear tank to the engine by gravity alone, it was common to see Ford drivers backing up hilly roads at a lively pace.

While reliable, affordability made the Model T the vehicle of choice for many first-time buyers. Ford was able to lower the price of his car by developing a system of production previously unseen in American manufacturing. Called "Fordism," or the just-in-time moving assembly line, which delivered parts to workers just as they needed them in the assembly process, the technique was pioneered at his new plants in Highland Park (1910) and River Rouge (1919), Michigan. Unlike Ford's earlier efforts, which produced between 2,000 and 3,000 cars per year, the miles of conveyor belts at his new factories allowed production at a scale previously unimaginable. In 1910, before Highland Park was in production, Ford could build only hundreds cars per day and had to raise the price of his cheapest car to $900. In 1914, he

Busy traffic in Detroit. Prints & Photographs Division, Library of Congress.

Travel

was producing 300,000 cars per year and the price fell to $590. By 1916, it was $345. While the war caused a brief jump in prices, by 1924 Ford Motor Company was manufacturing more than 9,000 cars per day and had lowered the price of a new car to $290.[7]

Pivotal to Fordism was the level of control Henry Ford exerted in his plants. He had bought out all other investors by 1919. One minority investor, who had purchased $1,000 of stock in the original firm, sold his ownership to Ford for $30 million. Ford Motor Company remained a privately held concern until 1956, making it uniquely manageable.

Ford also recognized the need to reduce employee turnover. He wanted a labor force that could turn out quality work in record numbers.

Traditionally, younger industrial laborers would change jobs several times per year. In January 1914, Ford announced an eight-hour work-day and a pay raise for employees with at least six months of experience on the job to $5 per day (more than double that of the best paid industrial worker).[8] The offer instantly galvanized many workers to Ford. While he demanded loyalty, and even used a variety of underhanded means by which to test this loyalty, Ford created a stable workforce that could produce his product the way that he wanted. The fact that the average Ford worker earned $1,500 per year, when his neighbors averaged only a third of this, and when even white-collar professionals earned only slightly more, made his employees remarkably agreeable.

Travel

Visual Arts

of the 1910s

Visual arts in the 1910s displayed a tremendous variety. Visual artists used images to communicate messages that both reinforced and challenged American society. While disparate, these visual arts reinforced the processes of modernization that were underway throughout American culture and served to blend many of these cultural trends in new and provocative ways.

As with the other expressive humanities in the decade, realism was the dominant theme in the visual arts. The sensibilities of realism were quite provocative, given the general genteel traditions that dominated American culture in the 1910s. Showing life "as it is" meant portraying the harsher qualities of modernity, including vice, poverty, and a growing sense of alienation.

Realist painters and illustrators believed their work was a direct refutation of the fawning stance taken toward European standards by most leading American institutions. The exclusive National Academy of Design (NAD), which could make or break the career of a young artist, jealously guarded its cultural authority and passed its approval only onto those willing to follow its lead.

Realist portrayals gave viewers easy access to art through the use of familiar images and emotions, which helped educate and reassure the country. Trends, social problems, and other elements of mass culture could be seen, talked about, and better understood through the realists' work. Although by 1920, the realist style was considered obsolete, throughout the decade it remained the most influential and popular form of expression.

MAGAZINE ILLUSTRATIONS

The 1910s are seen by many as a golden era in magazine illustration. Wider magazine circulation and a commitment to print advertising had reached their peak, while radio and television were still in the future. Most important, the technical process of mass producing high-quality and often colored illustrations had been perfected by the start of the decade. While the shift from wood engravings to photographic engraving had occurred by the early 1900s, it was not until the first decade that "line" or "halftone photoengravings" were made affordable.

In addition to technological improvements, soaring magazine circulation provided greater exposure and more work for graphic artists. Established fiction and opinion magazines, such as *Harper's* and *Atlantic Monthly*, were joined by a host of fashionable women's and popular literary magazines. By 1910, the most notable illustrated magazines included *Century, Harper's, McClure's,* and *Scribner's. Good Housekeeping, Ladies' Home Journal, Pictorial Review, Collier's, Saturday Evening Post, Youth's*

Companion, and the humorous weeklies *Life, Puck,* and *Judge* included dozens of illustrations in each week's issue. Adding to the demand was the growth in print advertising. More than half of these 100-page monthly publications were purchased by the advertisers who used illustrations to draw attention to their products.[1]

Finally, the literature that provided inspiration for these illustrations was becoming more engaging and lively. Realist writing gave artists an opportunity to delve into images and subjects thought to be beyond the staid traditions of previous illustrators like Charles Dana Gibson, whose Gibson Girls were immensely popular in the 1900s. The strong emotions of realistic literature were captured by the illustrators as they looked to find the essence of life's highly dramatic moments.

Illustrators received fan mail and were often considered celebrities in high society. Top illustrators could earn tens or even hundreds of thousands of dollars per year. By 1919, at the age of 25, Norman Rockwell was a millionaire as a result of his magazine and advertisement illustrations in the *Saturday Evening Post* and other popular publications.

The most prominent magazine illustrators of the 1910s included Arthur William Brown and Frederic Gruger (*Saturday Evening Post*), Coles Phillips and Jessie Smith (*Good Housekeeping*), George Plank (*Vogue*), Harrison Fisher (*Ladies' Home Journal*), Maxfield Parrish (*Collier's*), Wallace Morgan (*Collier's* and *Saturday Evening Post*), and James Montgomery Flagg. Gruger developed the medium to its full potential, injecting life, emotion, and meaning into his work in ways that escaped the camera. The fact that Flagg, Gruger, and many others were exhibited by the NAD as

Drawing for magazine cover shows men, some possibly holding racing forms, in a grandstand cheering, 1912. Prints & Photographs Division, Library of Congress.

"Fact and Fiction" (old man reading newspaper beside young woman reading book) by Norman Rockwell, 1917. Prints & Photographs Division, Library of Congress.

NORMAN ROCKWELL

Norman Rockwell was the best-known magazine illustrator to get his start during the 1910s. Born in New York City to affluent parents in 1894, Rockwell demonstrated an aptitude for drawing early in life. In 1912, he was commissioned for his first professional illustrations in the newspapers. Soon, he was contributing to the popular children's *Tell Me Why Stories* and *Boys' Life* magazine. By 1913, he was a regular contributor to *Youth's Companion, Everyland, American Boy,* and *St. Nicholas* magazines, and produced more than 100 drawings for the *Boy Scouts' Hike Book.* From 1914 to 1916, Rockwell became a major illustrator, garnering work in *Collier's, Life, Leslie's, Judge, Country Gentleman, Literary Digest,* and, at age 22, the cover of *Saturday Evening Post* in 1916. By 1919, Rockwell was a featured artist for the publication and began illustrating a series of Christmas covers that would continue until 1943. The illustrations were remunerative, but Rockwell made his greatest wealth as a named illustrator for such products as Maxwell House coffee, Encyclopedia Britannica, and Massachusetts Mutual Life Insurance.

Rockwell's images told stories that were easily understood by his audience and created an immediate sense of empathy for his subjects. These visual narratives were almost invariably optimistic, inoffensive, and nostalgic for an age of innocent youth. His style spotlighted the minor, awkward moments when people are faced with their own fallibility. Tempering these episodes with youthful subjects (90 percent of his *Post* covers included children before 1919), Rockwell was able to balance the painful feelings of loss with an emotional hope for learning and growth.

Rockwell's commitment to technical realism remains at the heart of his artistic legacy. For example, his first *Post* cover depicted a boy wearing his Sunday best, pushing a baby in a carriage. The youth's pained expression, as he passes his friends on their way to playing baseball, those of his tormenters, and even the bottle of milk stuck hastily in his breast pocket all convey the strong yet simple emotions such a child might feel. Rockwell's sentimental assemblage of stock emotions and nostalgia for family, country, and youth's innocence proved to be the most successful combination of artistic realism and commercialism of the decade.

serious artists underscores the respect they provided the medium.

World War I provided unique opportunities for these illustrators. Many, like Harvey Dunn, Wallace Morgan, Harry Townsend, and Walter Jack Duncan, were commissioned in the American Expeditionary Force, lived on the Front, and conveyed to the country the striking realities and horrors of the war. Others, like James Montgomery Flagg, remained at home to lend their talents to the Committee on Public Information, a federal propaganda program intended to promote patriotism at home. Flagg's famous portrait of Uncle Sam declaring, "I Want You" (actually a self-portrait) remains the most famous of these efforts. He also created less publicized work on Liberty Bonds, local advertising campaigns, and billboards and posters. The power of these images, especially those depicting the brutality of

the German-led enemies, was based largely on the talents of illustrators, well-honed by years of magazine work.

THE FINE ART REVOLUTION

The fine arts witnessed what can only be described as a revolution in the 1910s. Given that the decade experienced a collision among the conservative yet powerful NAD, members of the modern American realists (the so-called Ashcan school), works by the most influential modernist painters of Europe (such as Picasso and Cézanne), the public, and a host of critics, it is not surprising that art historians regard the 1910s as *the* decade in which modern American art was born. When the Armory Show of Modern Art was staged in February 1913 at the 69th Infantry Regiment Armory in New York City, these contradictory forces were compelled to resolve the growing gulf between their divergent aesthetic sensibilities. The effects of the Armory Show, probably the single most important exhibition of fine art in American history, were profound.

This clash was contingent on the efforts of a number of individuals, groups, and trends of the 1910s. Efforts by leading American artists, such as Robert Henri, Arthur B. Davies, and Alfred Stieglitz, figured greatly in determining when and how this conflict would be resolved. Moreover, World War I served as a critical backdrop to the rise of modern art in the United States—first in shaping the work of the European artists, then by validating their vision and providing U.S. artists with time to absorb these values into their own distinctive style.

Origins

While American visual artists took their cue from the European art world, rarely were they comfortable with pioneering new forms. The NAD was no exception. First established in 1825, the NAD split into several rival groups in the 1870s, and then re-emerged united in 1906. Members of the academy were American artists whose works were deemed to best represent classical European styles: rigid compositions, strict representations of form and color, and traditional models of the past (particularly Greek mythology or biblical allegory). NAD membership was required for artists to secure commissions, to be included in exhibitions, and to attract the attention of wealthy patrons.

Not all American artists were comfortable with the NAD. Robert Henri was the most important opponent of the NAD and the reason for the growing acceptance of realism in the fine arts by 1910. An accomplished artist, Henri studied at the Pennsylvania Academy of Art, was familiar with the Impressionist style, and had exhibited and sold his work in the Old World. In 1901, Henri joined the New York School of Art and began recruiting other promising realists to his classes. Henri tapped into talents that were being developed not by the NAD but by the popular newspapers and magazines of the day. By 1906, these included George Luks, John Sloan, William

Glackens, Everett Shinn, George Bellows, Arthur B. Davies, Rockwell Kent, Glenn Coleman, Edward Hopper, and Walter Pach.

Henri implored his students to simply "observe and record," to build upon the skills they had learned as newspapermen and illustrators, and to work quickly to capture the feeling of a scene rather than to worry about formal composition.

By 1907, Henri was the most influential teacher in New York City In 1908, Henri organized a showing at the Macbeth Gallery in New York City of "unknown and experimental" art by American painters. The show highlighted the work of Henri, Sloan, Glackens, Luks, Shinn, Davies, Ernest Lawson, and Maurice Prendergast. Known as "the Eight," the painters formed the core of what was later to be termed the Ashcan school. While critics were merciless in their censure of their work, the popularity of the show ensured that other exhibitions would be staged. By 1910, Henri's students seemed to be everywhere, and the spirit of change was in the air.

Henri might have been the first to call for the NAD to open its eyes to the new art, but he was not alone. Americans abroad, who were exposed to and could appreciate the trends in European Post-Impressionism were aware of the "storm on the horizon" for the visual arts in the United States. More than anyone, Alfred Stieglitz created the conditions whereby this modern art could be critically regarded by Americans. Under Stieglitz, American modern artists such as Marsden Hartley, Max Weber, John Marin, Arthur Dove, Charles Demuth, and Georgia O'Keeffe (who later married Stieglitz) were not only introduced, but also "Americanized."

Stieglitz established a magazine of photography and modern art, titled *Camera Work,* in 1903, and then in 1905 opened a gallery in New York City named The Little Galleries of the Photo-Secession but referred to as "291," the street address on Fifth Avenue, by almost everyone. As a result, 291 introduced the American art community to some of the most revolutionary and influential artists of the era: the first exhibition or one-man shows of Auguste Rodin (1908), Henri Matisse (1909), Francis Picabia (1913), and Constantin Brancusi (1914). For American artists, 291 debuted John Marin and Alfred Maurer (1909),

Oscar Bluemmer (1915), and Elie Nadelman (1915); staged comprehensive shows of Marsden Hartley, Arthur Dove, and Max Weber (1910), Gino Severini (1917), and Stanton Macdonald-Wright (1917); and introduced the work of Georgia O'Keeffe (1916). Following the Armory show, which led to the collapse of the NAD and the triumph of modernism, Stieglitz half-joked that he would be willing to show the work of older, conservative artists if they found no exhibition space available elsewhere.

The Armory Show

The Armory Show in New York City not only completely overturned the conservative NAD but also swept aside the modern American realists. The staid academic artists in America were easy targets for a style that had already overturned the European conservatives, who had enjoyed even greater social prestige than their Western counterparts. Yet Henri, the other members of the Eight, and their converts were completely unprepared for the lasting transformation that was unleashed upon them. Milton W. Brown, a distinguished historian of the era, noted that, by the close of the Armory Show, the one-time mavericks were "blind to the fact that [their work] had already become irrelevant."[2]

The bitter irony was not lost on these contemporary artists. The Armory Show was organized by the Association of American Painters and Sculptors (AAPS), supporters of the Ashcan movement, to highlight the many changes wrought by American realists. It was assumed that patrons would be found for and canvases sold by these American visionaries. Their success would force the NAD to recognize the significance of their contribution. But the intense comparison brought about by the show between the Americans and the Post-Impressionist Europeans marginalized their work, seemingly aging the compositions overnight.

The AAPS was founded in November 1911, by Jerome Myers, Elmer McRae, Walt Kuhn, and Henry Fitch Taylor. Joined by Henri, Glackens, Lawson, Bellows, Davies, Alden Weir, Gutzun Borglum, and Jonas Young, the association represented some of the finest and most respected artists in the country (seven of the 25 founders were also members of the NAD). They resolved to field an exhibition of the best modern works, regardless of nationality and NAD membership. Fearing an open war with the powerful NAD, Weir declined the presidency in January 1912, and the office fell to Arthur B. Davies.

Davies was an exhibited painter with strong connections to American and European art patrons and dealers. In the late summer of 1912, Davies, aided by Walter Pach, traveled throughout Europe securing the loan of modern works and the cooperation of a number of galleries in The Hague, Munich, Paris, and Berlin. Returning in November, Davies and the AAPS set about funding the project, arranging the various halls, printing more than 50,000 catalogs and pamphlets, and scheduling delivery for and hanging more than 1,300 works of art (a third of which were produced by foreign artists).

More than 4,000 people attended the show's opening on February 17, 1913. When it closed in New York, conservative estimates suggested that at least 75,000 had seen the exhibit. The show's motto—The New Spirit—was evident in the breadth of the display. The first galleries displayed the "Old" modern masters van Gogh, Paul Gauguin, Seurat, and Cézanne; the mood then shifted toward the more daring works of Picasso, Matisse, Georges Braque, Marcel Duchamp, and Wassily Kandinsky. The American modernists were numerically superior and included the works of the Eight as well as such later notables as Edward Hopper, Joseph Stella, and Charles Sheeler. Still, the American pieces seemed more provincial and derivative than they had realized when compared to more mature, daring, and brazenly confident European offerings. Given the lack of knowledge of the European movement, it was amazing that the AAPS was capable of presenting such a high-quality breadth of works.[3]

On March 15, the New York show closed and about 500 pieces moved on to the Art Institute of Chicago. The exhibit was seen by another 200,000 people in less than 25 days. By the end of April, approximately 250 works continued on to Boston's Copley Hall where they were shown to dwindling audiences. When the Boston exhibition closed, on May 19, the organizers agreed to end the tour.

Internal dissent over the (generally negative) effect of the show on American artists had split the AAPS by 1916. The association never staged a second exhibition after the Armory Show. Its one production had fundamentally transformed the fine arts in America.

The Critics

Most individuals who attended the Armory Show were impressed by the magnitude of the display. A few were openly supportive of the new and modern aesthetics. The majority of critics, however, were unsure of exactly *what* to think; it was all amazingly new. The new visual culture challenged America's tastes and personal assumptions about art. When evaluating the evaluators, then, we look not only for their artistic interpretation, but also their cultural biases and reactions.

Grudging acceptance or hidden bemusement might best describe the typical response of the Armory Show visitor. Characteristic was Theodore Roosevelt, who attended the New York showing on March 4, not coincidentally the very same day that his rival for the presidency in 1912, Woodrow Wilson, was being inaugurated. Roosevelt published his response in *Outlook,* titled "A Layman's View of an Art Exhibition." In the essay, Roosevelt showed considerable flexibility and a liberal spirit for most of what he saw. Yet Roosevelt was also uncomfortable with what he regarded as a lack of common reference points for the viewing audience. For the former president, and many others, the work of these avant-garde artists was too far afield to even be considered art.[4]

Many other critics simply tried to laugh at what they did not understand. Marcel Duchamp's *Nude Descending a Staircase, No. 2* (1912) was described by many as an explosion in a shingle factory, and it inspired popular jingles and cartoons. Many came to the show simply to see the canvas and laugh.[5]

Many critics took special comfort in the odd personal histories of the leading artists. For example, Cézanne was an incompetent businessman before turning to painting, van Gogh had mutilated himself by cutting off an ear, and Gauguin had deserted his family and friends for a life in Tahiti. Clearly these individuals were as "mad" as their paintings suggested them to be "failures" both as artists and men. Many noted that the relative sanity of the American works spoke well for this country's reputation around the globe.

By far, the responses of the instructors and students at the Art Institute of Chicago were the most acrimonious. Because of the intense criticism emanating from the New York debut, Chicago's artists were primed to hail the newcomers as "fakers," "madmen," and "degenerates." Near the show's close, students were further incited by their teachers to burn images of Matisse, Brancusi, and Walter Pach in effigy. It was not the professionals but the laymen who believed that the immediate condemnation of the show and burning of artist images was simply un-American.

Ironically, while most Americans defined themselves as an individualistic society, modern painters earned the wrath of the American art community for taking this same spirit into the visual arts.

Elitism and the Fine Arts

The question of elitism has shown great longevity in the ways in which the American public embraced or rejected the fine arts since 1913. The new styles seemed to be all subjectivity and perspective. Moreover, for fans of the American modernist movement, these temperaments were decidedly European and undemocratic.

Most modern artists had (and have) a different interpretation than these critics. Many would claim that the new art more clearly relates the individualistic world around them than those works that use "common images" heavily laden with symbolic meaning, often created by those in power for their benefit. The modernists' conclusion, that science and modernity had killed realistic representation, is best seen in the ready-made art of Marcel Duchamp. Duchamp displayed everyday items in galleries and at exhibitions, simply calling them works of art. His most (in)famous was *Fontaine,* displayed at 291 and the Independents' Exhibition (1917). The item was once a working urinal, but by placing it on display Duchamp hoped to show how life and art were one. The public, according to Duchamp, does not need critics, art academies, or their biased aesthetic filters to recognize that "art" surrounds them.[6] In this way, the new art could claim to be radically democratic and emancipated from the control of others.

By contrast, charges of elitism emerged. Nowhere was this sentiment more pronounced than on the pages of the *Masses*. The magazine, home to many influential American realists, believed in a clear connection between art and social uplift. Much like Stieglitz, who held that the new art could change the world, contributors to the *Masses* were concerned when they saw the Armory Show diverge so forcefully from accessible visual culture. If artists were simply taking stock of their own irrational and functionally useless opinions of the modern world, what reason would the real masses have to seek their council? To them, the Postimpressionists spoke in a foreign language wholly indecipherable by anyone else. Such elitism ran counter to their basic values and was soundly condemned by established American modernists.[7]

The Post-Armory Years

The success of the Armory Show spawned numerous exhibitions and new modern art galleries. Large museums, such as the Carnegie Institute in Pittsburgh, the Taylor Galleries in Cleveland, and the Carroll Gallery and National Arts Club in New York City, and many smaller ones now spent their energies and resources in developing American artists with Postimpressionist styles. In 1916, the Forum Exhibition at Anderson Galleries on Park Avenue held its second major show of American modernism, followed, in 1917, by the Independents' Exhibition of more than 2,500 works by 1,300 artists. Most of the major collectors (including John Quinn, Arthur Jerome Eddy, Lillie P. Bliss, Walter Arensberg, Albert C. Barnes, and Stephen C. Cook) purchased aggressively during the show. Of the 250 works sold, however, more than 200 were by foreign artists. By 1918, most "official" American academies (such as the NAD) and art schools had lost their prestige and, with it, their power to control the content of exhibitions. The central fatality of this change was the modern realist style of the Ashcan school. Ostensibly the reason for the Armory Show, these artists were

quickly marginalized and often forgotten in the immediate aftermath of the show.

Judging from the output, cubism, abstraction, and expressionism became the dominant form of most fine artists in America. Max Weber, Marsden Hartley, Man Ray, John Covert, and Arthur Dove were the most notable of a large group. Stuart Davis became the most original and inventive. A former Ashcan artist and contributor to the *Masses,* Davis merged expressionism with ready-mades into a form that heralded the pop art movement of the 1950s and 1960s. Thomas Hart Benton, Joseph Stella, Morgan Russell, and Stanton MacDonald-Wright all experimented with synchromatic art, and were exhibited at the Carroll Gallery in 1914. Stella's *Battle of Lights, Coney Island* (1913) and *The Bridge* (1918) remain testaments to the group's talents and ambitions. Georgia O'Keeffe, the youngest of the new artists, melded synchromism, abstraction, and Southwestern themes. She was one of the few artists who developed a particularly American style in the 1910s. Unfortunately, the Armory Show led many artists simply to copy the newer European styles. Still, the show and the subsequent war jumpstarted American modern art, enabling domestic painters to equal and then surpass their colleagues overseas.

ENDNOTES FOR THE 1910s

OVERVIEW OF THE 1910s

1. The statistical data presented in this chapter is compiled and taken from a number of sources, including Donald B. Dodd, comp., *Historical Statistics of the United States: Two Centuries of the Census, 1790–1990* (Westport, CT: Greenwood Publishing Group, 1993); John Milton Cooper Jr., *The Pivotal Decades: The United States, 1900–1920* (New York: W. W. Norton, 1990); Forrest E. Linder and Robert D. Grove, *Vital Statistics Rates in the United States, 1900–1940* (New York: Arno Press, 1976); Lois Gordon and Alan Gordon, *The Columbia Chronicles of American Life, 1910–1992* (New York: Columbia University Press, 1995); and Nell Irvin Painter, *Standing at Armageddon: The United States, 1877–1919* (New York: W. W. Norton, 1987).
2. Gordon and Gordon, *The Columbia Chronicles of American Life,* 2, 754.
3. Timothy J. Gilfoyle, *City of Eros: New York City, Prostitution, and the Commercialization of Sex, 1790–1920* (New York: W. W. Norton, 1992), 308–309.

4. Thomas H. Johnson, *The Oxford Companion to American History* (New York: Oxford University Press, 1966), 490.
5. David M. Kennedy, *Over Here: The First World War and American Society* (New York: Oxford University Press, 1966), 10.
6. John Mack Farragher et al., *Out of Many: A History of the American People*, 3d ed. (Upper Saddle River, NJ: Prentice-Hall, 2000), 657.
7. Gilfoyle, *City of Eros*, 308–309.
8. Farragher et al., *Out of Many*, 657.
9. George Hilton, *Eastland: The Legacy of the* Titanic (Stanford, CA: Stanford University Press, 1995).
10. Johnson, *The Oxford Companion to American History*, 103.

ADVERTISING OF THE 1910S

1. Jackson Lears, *Fables of Abundance: A Cultural History of Advertising in America* (New York: Basic Books, 1995), 159–162.
2. John Tebbel and Mary Ellen Zuckerman, *The Magazine in America: 1741–1990* (New York: Oxford University Press, 1991), 140–146.
3. Marchand, *Advertising the American Dream*, 11.
4. Cecil Munsey, *The Illustrated Guide to the Collectibles of Coca-Cola* (New York: Hawthorne Books, 1972), 8–10, 39–40.
5. Lears, *Fables of Abundance*, 159.
6. U.S. Department of Commerce, *Bureau of the Census, Historical Statistics of the United States: Colonial Times to 1970*, vol. 2 (Washington, D.C., 1975), 716.
7. Lears, *Fables of Abundance*, 212–213.
8. James D. Norris, *Advertising and the Transformation of American Society, 1865–1920*, Contributions in Economics and Economic History, no. 110 (Westport, CT: Greenwood Press, 1990), 151.
9. Norris, *Advertising and the Transformation of American Society*, 161–165.
10. Lears, *Fables of Abundance*, 219.
11. Lears, *Fables of Abundance*, 220.

ARCHITECTURE OF THE 1910S

1. Carter Wiseman, *Shaping a Nation: Twentieth-Century American Architecture and Its Makers* (New York: W. W. Norton, 1998), 48.
2. Columbia University. "The Architecture and Development of New York City with Andrew S. Dolkart." "The Birth of the Skyscraper." http://ci.columbia.edu/0240s/0242_2/0242_2_s7_text.html (accessed August 12, 2008).
3. Mardges Bacon, *Ernest Flagg: Beaux-Arts Architect and Urban Reformer* (Cambridge, MA: MIT Press, 1986), 43.

BOOKS, NEWSPAPERS, MAGAZINES, AND COMICS OF THE 1910S

1. Carlton Jackson, *Zane Grey* (Boston: Twayne Publishers, 1973), 8.
2. John Taliaferro, *Tarzan Forever: The Life of Edgar Rice Burroughs, Creator of Tarzan* (New York: Scribner, 1999).
3. Taliaferro, *Tarzan Forever*, 75.
4. Jamie Ambrose, *Willa Cather: Writing at the Frontier* (New York: Berg Publishers, 1988), xiii.
5. David M. Kennedy, *Over Here*, 180–181.
6. Geoffrey Moore, "American Poetry and the English Language, 1900–1945," in *American Literature Since 1900: The New History of Literature*, ed. Marcus Cunliffe (New York: Peter Bedrick Books, 1987), 91.

ENTERTAINMENT OF THE 1910S

1. Ethan Mordden, *The American Theater* (New York: Oxford University Press, 1981), 56.
2. Adele Heller, "The New Theater," in *1915: The Cultural Moment: The New Politics, the New Woman, the New Psychology, the New Art, and the New Theatre in America*, ed. Adele Heller and Lois Rudnick (New Brunswick, NJ: Rutgers University Press, 1991), 220, 231.
3. Gerald Mast, *A Short History of the Movies*, 5th ed. (New York: Macmillan, 1992), 5–28.
4. Mast, *A Short History of the Movies*, 57.
5. Geoffrey Nowell-Smith, ed., *The Oxford History of World Cinema* (New York: Oxford University Press, 1996), 25–27.
6. Nowell-Smith, *The Oxford History of World Cinema*, 30–31.
7. Nowell-Smith, *The Oxford History of World Cinema*, 84–85.
8. Mast, *A Short History of the Movies*, 93.
9. Charles J. Maland, *Chaplin and American Culture: The Evolution of a Star Image* (Princeton, NJ: Princeton University Press, 1989), 25.

FASHION OF THE 1910S

1. Valerie Mendes and Amy de la Haye, *20th Century Fashion* (London: Thames & Hudson, 1999), 28–29.

FOOD OF THE 1910S

1. Reay Tannahill, *Food in History: The New, Fully Revised, and Updated Edition of the Classic Gastronomic Epic* (New York: Crown Publishers, 1988), 334.
2. Lewis Erenberg, *Steppin' Out: New York Nightlife and the Transformation of American Culture, 1890–1930* (Chicago: University of Chicago Press, 1981).

MUSIC OF THE 1910s

1. James Lincoln Collier, *The Making of Jazz: A Comprehensive History* (Boston: Houghton Mifflin, 1978), 23.
2. Collier, *The Making of Jazz,* 114.
3. Lynes, *The Lively Audience,* 105–107.
4. Lynes, *The Lively Audience,* 105.

SPORTS AND LEISURE OF THE 1910s

1. Bernard Mergen, "Games and Toys," in *Handbook of American Popular Culture,* ed. M. Thomas Inge, vol. 2 (Westport, CT: Greenwood Press, 1980), 169.
2. Dominick Cavallo, *Muscles and Morals: Organized Playgrounds and Urban Reform* (Philadelphia: University of Pennsylvania Press, 1981), 29–30.
3. Cavallo, *Muscles and Morals,* 16–45.
4. Steven A. Riess, *Touching Base: Professional Baseball and American Culture in the Progressive Era, Contributions in American Studies, no. 48* (Westport, CT: Greenwood Press, 1980), 46–53.
5. Riess, *Touching Base,* 220–221.
6. Riess, *Touching Base,* 14–20.
7. Riess, *Touching Base,* 53–66.
8. Riess, *Touching Base,* 86–91.
9. Riess, *Touching Base,* 24.
10. Riess, *Touching Base,* 88–90.
11. Elliot J. Gorn, *The Manly Art: Bare-Knuckle Prize Fighting in America* (Ithaca, NY: Cornell University Press, 1986), 205.
12. Randy Roberts, *Papa Jack: Jack Johnson and the Era of White Hopes* (New York: The Free Press, 1983).
13. Inez McClintock and Marshall McClintock, *Toys in America* (Washington, D.C.: Public Affairs Press, 1961), 421.
14. Blair Whitton, *The Knopf Collector's Guide to American Antiques: Toys* (New York: Alfred A. Knopf, 1984), 113.
15. Foster Rhea Dulles, *America Learns to Play: A History of Popular Recreation, 1607–1940* (New York: Appleton-Century, 1940), 310.

TRAVEL OF THE 1910s

1. James M. Morris, *America's Armed Forces: A History,* 2d ed. (Upper Saddle River, NJ: Prentice-Hall, 1996), 189–191.

2. Kenneth T. Jackson, *Crabgrass Frontier: The Suburbanization of the United States* (New York: Oxford University Press, 1985), 103.
3. Jackson, *Crabgrass Frontier,* 112.
4. Allan Nevins, *Ford: The Times, the Man, and the Company* (New York: Charles Scribner's Sons, 1954), 135–142, 252–255.
5. Jackson, *Crabgrass Frontier,* 157–158.
6. David J. Wilkie, *Esquire's American Autos and Their Makers* (New York: Esquire, Inc., 1963), 70.
7. Nevins, *Ford,* 447–480.
8. Jackson, *Crabgrass Frontier,* 160–161.

VISUAL ARTS OF THE 1910S

1. John Tebbel and Mary Ellen Zuckerman, *The Magazine in America: 1741–1990* (New York: Oxford University Press, 1991), 140–146.
2. Milton W. Brown, "The Armory Show and Its Aftermath," in *1915: The Cultural Moment: The New Politics, the New Woman, the New Psychology, the New Art, and the New Theatre in America,* ed. Adele Heller and Lois Rudnick (New Brunswick, NJ: Rutgers University Press, 1991), 164.
3. Milton W. Brown, *The Story of the Armory Show,* rev. ed (New York: Abbeville Press, 1988), 86.
4. Brown, *The Story of the Armory Show,* 119.
5. Brown, *The Story of the Armory Show,* 138–139.
6. Edward Abrahams, "Alfred Stieglitz's Faith and Vision," in *1915: The Cultural Moment: The New Politics, the New Woman, the New Psychology, the New Art, and the New Theatre in America,* ed. Adele Heller and Lois Rudnick (New Brunswick, NJ: Rutgers University Press, 1991), 190.
7. H. Wayne Morgan, *The New Muses: Art in American Culture, 1865–1920* (Norman: University of Oklahoma Press, 1978), 164; Rebecca Zurier, "The *Masses* and Modernism," in *1915: The Cultural Moment: The New Politics, the New Woman, the New Psychology, the New Art, and the New Theatre in America,* ed. Adele Heller and Lois Rudnick (New Brunswick, NJ: Rutgers University Press, 1991), 209.

1920s

Timeline

of Popular Culture Events, 1920s

1920

January 2: Department of Justice agents arrest some 4,000 suspected communists and radicals in 33 American cities as part of what becomes known as the "Red Scare."

January 16: The Eighteenth Amendment, prohibiting the manufacture, transportation, and sale of alcohol, goes into effect.

February 12: The Negro National Baseball League is founded.

April 20: Grand Canyon National Park is dedicated.

August 26: The Nineteenth Amendment, granting women the right to vote, is ratified.

September 17: The American Professional Football Association is founded (renamed the National Football League in 1922).

September 28: Eight members of the Chicago White Sox are indicted for conspiring to throw the 1919 World Series, resulting in the so-called "Black Sox Scandal."

November 2: Warren G. Harding is elected the twenty-ninth president of the United States.

November 2: Station KDKA, East Pittsburgh, Pennsylvania, inaugurates regular radio broadcasting.

F. Scott Fitzgerald publishes his first novel, *This Side of Paradise.*

The Baby Ruth candy bar is introduced.

Transcontinental airmail service begins between New York and San Francisco.

1921

February 6: Charlie Chaplin's first feature-length film, *The Kid,* premieres.

March 10: The first White Castle hamburger restaurant opens in Wichita, Kansas.

May 23: *Shuffle Along,* the first all-black Broadway musical of the decade, opens.

May 31–June 1: A riot erupts in Tulsa, Oklahoma, during which white mobs kill at least 85 African Americans and burn to the ground much of the black business district.

September 8: Margaret Gorman wins the first Miss America Pageant in Atlantic City, New Jersey.

September 15: Silent film comedian Roscoe "Fatty" Arbuckle is indicted for manslaughter after aspiring actress Virginia Rappe dies under suspicious circumstances in a San Francisco hotel.

October 31: *The Sheik,* starring Rudolph Valentino, premieres.

November 2: The American Birth Control League is founded.

November 9: President Harding signs into law the Federal Highway Act, providing states with matching federal funds to construct a national network of two-lane highways.

November 11: The Tomb of the Unknown Soldier is unveiled in the Rotunda of the U.S. Capitol.

The polygraph, or lie detector, is invented.

The Washburn-Crosby Company of Minneapolis creates Betty Crocker, a fictional model homemaker, to promote its Gold Medal brand flour.

Wonder Bread is introduced.

The Eskimo Pie ice cream bar sells more than one million units during its first year on the market.

1922

February 5: *Reader's Digest* publishes its first issue.

April 15: The U.S. Senate launches an investigation into the alleged illegal activities of Secretary of the Interior Albert B. Fall, in what becomes known as the "Teapot Dome Scandal".

May 5: French fashion designer Coco Chanel introduces her signature perfume, Chanel No. 5.

May 23: *Abie's Irish Rose,* the longest running Broadway play of the 1920s, opens.

May 30: The Lincoln Memorial is dedicated in Washington, D.C.

October 3: Rebecca Latimer Felton, age 87, of Georgia, becomes the first woman to serve as a U.S. senator, when she is appointed by the governor of Georgia to fill the remaining term of Senator Thomas Watson, who died in office; her term lasts only one day.

November 4: Archaeologist Howard Carter and his excavation team discover King Tutankhamen's tomb in the Valley of the Kings, near Luxor, Egypt.

Fruit, Garden and Home begins publication (renamed *Better Homes and Gardens* in 1924).

George Squier invents Muzak, first developed in order to calm anxious elevator riders.

Emily Post publishes *Etiquette in Society, in Business, in Politics and at Home,* which becomes a national best seller.

Sinclair Lewis publishes his most famous novel, *Babbitt.*

The first A&W Root Beer stand opens in Sacramento, California.

The Klondike (ice cream) Bar is introduced.

1923

February 16: Bessie Smith makes her first recordings, "Down Hearted Blues" and "Gulf Coast Blues," for Columbia.

March 3: *Time,* the nation's first weekly news magazine, publishes its first issue.

April 1: Alma Cummings wins the first American dance marathon, held at the Audubon Ballroom in New York City.

April 5: Louis Armstrong makes his first recording, "Just Gone," as a member of King Oliver's Creole Jazz Band, for the Gennett label.

April 18: Yankee Stadium opens.

August 2: President Warren G. Harding dies in office.

August 3: Vice President Calvin Coolidge succeeds Harding as president of the United States.

October 29: *Runnin' Wild,* an all-black musical revue, introduces the song "Charleston" and the dance of the same name.

December 4: Cecil B. DeMille's epic biblical film *The Ten Commandments* premieres.

John D. Hertz founds the Hertz Drive-Ur-Self Company.

Neon advertising signs are introduced.

Mars Candies markets its first candy bar, the Milky Way.

Jacob Schick receives a patent for the first electric razor.

Reese's Peanut Butter Cups are introduced.

The nonsensical "Yes! We Have No Bananas" becomes a major hit song, to the annoyance of countless Americans.

The Bell and Howell Company introduces a 16-mm camera, marking the advent of home movies.

1924

February 14: The Computing-Tabulating-Recording Company, founded in 1911, formally changes its name to International Business Machines (IBM).

February 24: George Gershwin's jazz concerto *Rhapsody in Blue* premieres at Aeolian Hall in New York City.

March 10: J. Edgar Hoover is appointed acting director of the Bureau of Investigation (later renamed Federal Bureau of Investigation).

May 26: The National Origins Act passes, restricting the annual number of European immigrants to 165,000 and prohibiting all Asian immigration to the United States.

August 5: *Little Orphan Annie* comic strip debuts in the *New York Daily News*.

September 19: Nathan Leopold Jr. and Richard Loeb are sentenced to life imprisonment for the kidnapping and murder of 14-year-old Bobby Franks.

November 4: Calvin Coolidge is elected the thirtieth president of the United States.

Macy's department store sponsors its first Thanksgiving Day parade.

The Kimberly-Clark Company introduces Kleenex, the first disposable facial tissue.

Flagpole sitting becomes a national fad.

Richard Simon and Max Schuster publish *The Cross Word Puzzle Book*, launching a major fad.

Wheaties breakfast cereal is introduced.

The Popsicle is invented.

1925

January 5: Nellie Taylor Ross is elected governor of Wyoming, thus becoming the first woman governor in U.S. history.

February 16: The corpse of Floyd Collins is recovered amidst a national media frenzy. Collins died after being trapped underground for 18 days in Sand Cave in Barren County, Kentucky.

February 21: *The New Yorker* begins publication.

June 26: *The Gold Rush*, starring Charlie Chaplin, premieres.

June 26: Walter Chrysler incorporates the Maxwell Motor Car Company as the Chrysler Corporation.

July 21: High school science teacher John T. Scopes is convicted in Dayton, Tennessee, of violating a state statute prohibiting the teaching of evolution in public schools.

August 8: Forty thousand Ku Klux Klan members hold a mass rally in Washington, D.C.

September 3: The navy dirigible *Shenandoah* crashes in a storm near Ava, Ohio, killing 14 crew members.

November 28: The *WSM Barn Dance* (renamed *The Grand Ole Opry* in 1927) begins its Saturday night broadcasts in Nashville, Tennessee.

Alain Locke publishes the Harlem Renaissance collection *The New Negro*.

Bruce Barton publishes *The Man Nobody Knows*, a pseudo-biography of Jesus that becomes a national best seller.

The Goodyear Tire and Rubber Company launches its first advertising blimp, *The Pilgrim*.

F. Scott Fitzgerald publishes his most acclaimed novel, *The Great Gatsby*.

1926

May 9: Rear Admiral Richard E. Byrd and Floyd Bennett become the first aviators to fly over the North Pole.

May 23: Western Air Express, later renamed Trans-World Airlines (TWA), begins passenger service.

August 6: Gertrude Ederle becomes the first woman to swim the English Channel.

November 15: The National Broadcasting Company (NBC), the nation's first radio network, premieres.

The Book-of-the-Month Club is founded.

The Butterfinger candy bar is introduced.

Ernest Hemingway publishes his novel *The Sun Also Rises*.

1927

April 7: The first demonstration of long-range television transmission, from a signal in Washington, D.C., to a receiver in New York City, occurs.

May 21: Aviator Charles Lindbergh completes the first solo, non-stop flight across the Atlantic Ocean.

August 12: Paramount's *Wings*, which later wins the first Academy Award for Best Picture, premieres.

August 23: Italian anarchist immigrants Nicola Sacco and Bartolomeo Vanzetti, convicted of murder in 1921, are executed in Massachusetts.

September 18: The Columbia Broadcasting System (CBS) begins broadcasting.

September 22: Gene Tunney defeats Jack Dempsey to retain his heavyweight boxing title in a match made famous by its "Long Count."

September 30: New York Yankees slugger Babe Ruth hits his 60th home run of the regular season, a major league record that will stand until 1961.

October 6: Warner Brothers' *The Jazz Singer,* the first feature-length motion picture with synchronized speech and music, premieres.

December 2: The Ford Motor Company introduces its new Model A automobile.

December 27: The Broadway musical *Showboat* premieres.

Kool-Aid (originally spelled Kool-Ade) is introduced.

1928

November 6: Herbert Hoover defeats Alfred E. Smith to become the thirty-first president of the United States.

November 18: *Steamboat Willie,* Walt Disney's black-and-white animated cartoon featuring Mickey Mouse and synchronized sound, premieres.

Peter Pan peanut butter is introduced.

Gerber baby food is introduced.

Dubble Bubble, the nation's first bubble gum, is introduced.

Kraft introduces Velveeta, a processed cheese food.

1929

January 7: The first science-fiction comic strip, *Buck Rogers in the 25th Century A.D.,* debuts.

January 17: Cartoonist Elzie C. Segar introduces a sailor character named Popeye in his *Thimble Theatre* comic strip.

February 14: Six members of "Bugs" Moran's gang, along with a mechanic, are gunned down in a Chicago garage in what becomes known as the "St. Valentine's Day Massacre."

May 16: The first Academy of Motion Pictures Arts and Sciences Awards ceremony is held in Hollywood, honoring films for the years 1927 and 1928.

August 19: The comedy radio series *Amos 'n Andy* premieres on the NBC network.

October: The New York Stock Exchange crashes on "Black Thursday" (October 24), with 13 million shares sold, and again on "Black Tuesday" (October 29), with 16 million shares sold.

The Museum of Modern Art opens in New York.

Overview

of the 1920s

While everyday life in the 1920s became more comfortable for most Americans, it also became increasingly complicated and harried. A consumer goods revolution fueled the nation's flourishing economy, and increasing reliance on new technologies and mass media transformed the daily lives of millions of ordinary Americans.

Middle-class consumers enthusiastically embraced the newfangled accoutrements of modern life, from automobiles, refrigerators, and electric razors to motion pictures and radios. However, others yearned for a simpler world where their lives moved at a slower pace and there was less pressure to keep up with others.

THE AGE OF REPUBLICAN DOMINANCE

Three Republican presidents led the United States during the 1920s, and each had to confront the repercussions of a modern mass society that was expanding and changing faster than ever before. Each administration strongly encouraged cooperation between government and big business, thus contributing to an era of extraordinary production and consumption.

Warren G. Harding, elected in 1920, had appealed to a nation weary of war, foreign policy squabbles, and progressive reforms by campaigning with the slogan, "Back to Normalcy." Unlike his idealistic, intellectual predecessor, Woodrow Wilson, Harding was a friendly, good-natured man who liked to play poker and, it was widely reported, to drink bootleg liquor. Unfortunately, Harding's administration was riddled with scandal and corruption. Several political cronies he appointed to high-level cabinet positions accepted bribes and committed fraud.

Harding's successor, Calvin Coolidge, was more solemn and introverted, which earned him the nickname "Silent Cal." Coolidge presided over a nation that was rapidly expanding its industrial production and consumer wealth. Coolidge approved legislation that assisted corporations and lowered income tax rates, especially for the wealthy. When he declined to run for reelection in 1928, Herbert Hoover, his secretary of commerce, accepted the Republican nomination and assumed the presidency after handily beating New York Democrat Alfred E. Smith, the first Roman Catholic to run on a major party ticket. Hoover's administration, begun with optimism and promise, soon saw the stock market crash of 1929 and the onset of the Great Depression. Hoover's mishandling of the crisis, coupled with his seeming lack of sympathy for the homeless and unemployed,

A couple listening to the radio, ca. 1925. Prints & Photographs Division, Library of Congress.

ruined his reelection bid in 1932 against New York Governor Franklin D. Roosevelt.

THE RISE OF BIG BUSINESS

Although often remembered for its unprecedented prosperity, the 1920s began with the nation gripped in a serious economic recession. After the end of World War I, industrial productivity declined, unemployment rose, and consumer spending dwindled. The sluggish economy rebounded in 1922, due in part to the manufacturing industries that produced automobiles, radios, and other consumer goods. Throughout the rest of the decade, industrial production nearly doubled. Purchasing merchandise on credit lost its stigma as millions of Americans bought big ticket items such as cars, furniture, pianos, and

radios on credit. Modern advertising, a nearly $3 billion-a-year business by 1929, encouraged shoppers to purchase newly invented products or ones that previously seemed unnecessary, including vacuum cleaners, electric razors, canned soup, mouthwash, and deodorant. Rising rates of mass production and consumer sales propelled the American economy into a spectacular period of prosperity.

The Coolidge and Hoover administrations' pro-business policies, combined with the support of federal and state governments, also fueled the nation's economy. In 1921, Congress reduced taxes on corporations and then, the following year, raised tariffs on imported goods. Federal regulatory agencies, which had been established during the Progressive Era to oversee and control big business, instead cooperated with these corporations. The Supreme Court and the Justice Department protected businesses from unions by striking blow after blow against organized labor. Lobbyists hired by professional organizations, manufacturers, retailers, and other special interest groups intensified their efforts to gain support from legislators at every level. Not all Americans reaped the benefits of the booming economy. The nation's farmers, textile workers, and coal miners did not generally share in the prosperity of the 1920s. Neither did railroad and streetcar employees, since revenues generated by these forms of transportation declined with the widespread ownership of automobiles. Many small merchants lost business or were driven into bankruptcy by the rise of chain grocery stores, drugstores, and department stores. Nevertheless, the overall standard of living rose for most Americans, as salaries and wages increased in many occupations, and the length of the average workweek shortened.

SOCIAL CLIMATE

During the 1920s, the lives of most middle-class Americans improved as a result of mass production and technological advancements, but other powerful forces also influenced the attitudes and behaviors of ordinary Americans. Millions of native-born, white Americans harbored intense fears that communism would spread to America, immigrant hordes would seize their jobs, and African Americans would integrate their racially homogeneous communities. These anxieties heightened pre-existing racial and ethnic tensions and led to the outbreak of repressive and often violent clashes between Americans of different races, religions, and political beliefs.

The Red Scare

Between 1919 and 1920, escalating ethnic and political tensions in the United States erupted in a wave of mass paranoia and repression known as the "Red Scare." The Bolshevik Revolution of November 1917 in Russia sparked fears that a communist coup was imminent in the United States. The American economy was in recession, unemployment was high, and living costs were even higher. More than 3,300 labor strikes broke

out across the nation in 1919, including a nationwide strike by steelworkers, many of whom were Southern and Eastern European immigrants. The Boston police force also went on strike, forcing Governor Calvin Coolidge to enlist the state militia to protect the city and prevent looting. Several highly publicized bombings and attempted bombings of politicians and business leaders, including an explosion on Wall Street in September 1920 that killed 38 people, fueled the public's general sense of pandemonium. Most Americans blamed these incidents on communist and socialist aliens.

In January 1920, the General Intelligence Division of the Bureau of Investigation (renamed the Federal Bureau of Investigation in 1935), operating under orders from Attorney General A. Mitchell Palmer, launched what became known as "Palmer Raids." Federal agents, in cooperation with local police officers, raided homes, newspaper offices, and meeting halls in 33 cities across the nation without search warrants, and arrested more than 4,000 alleged radicals on the suspicion that they threatened national security. Many of those arrested were held in custody without access to counsel for weeks and even months, and while most were eventually released without ever being charged with a crime, almost 600 aliens were deported. Although the Palmer Raids drew criticism from those Americans who recognized that these tactics violated basic civil liberties and even the Constitution itself, many groups and organizations, including the American Legion (founded in 1919), supported any government action, however drastic, that combated the perceived threat of communism in the United States.

Immigration Patterns

Between 1890 and 1914, more than 17 million immigrants came to the United States, many of them from Russia, Italy, Austria-Hungary, Poland, and Germany.[1] The outbreak of World War I severely reduced the number of immigrants arriving from Europe. After the war ended, immigration levels returned to prewar levels, but new concerns about continued strike waves and radical aliens, coupled with anti-foreign resentment and demands for "One Hundred Percent

Americanism," prompted the federal government to clamp down drastically on immigration. In 1921, Congress passed the Quota Act, which capped the total number of immigrants allowed to enter the United States at 385,000 per year. Three years later, the passage of the National Origins Act imposed an annual immigration ceiling of 165,000, and gave preference to applicants from Northern European, chiefly Protestant countries. Asian immigration was entirely prohibited. In

1929, Congress restricted annual immigration to only 150,000 people.[2]

RACE RELATIONS

During the 1920s, at least 700,000 African Americans left the South for northern urban industrial centers like Harlem, Chicago, St. Louis, and Detroit.[3] Most of these migrants moved north to find higher paying jobs and to escape segregation, sharecropping, and racial violence common in the South. The flood of African American newcomers heightened competition with white workers for jobs, housing, and public facilities, and set off a surge of race riots.

Unfortunately, well-paying jobs were scarce for black workers in northern and Midwestern cities, and racist practices led to segregated schools, theaters, housing, and other facilities. Although the 1920s saw a tremendous flowering of African American arts, particularly in Harlem, the decade overall was one of tense, turbulent, and sometimes violent relations between black and white Americans. In 1921, for example, two days of rioting engulfed Tulsa, Oklahoma, where white mobs killed at least 85 African Americans and torched much of the city's flourishing black business district. In 1923, a mob of white racists wiped out the small, predominantly black community of Rosewood, Florida. Between 1918 and 1922, according to records kept by Tuskegee Institute, mobs lynched almost 300 African Americans, more than 90 percent of them in the South, for a wide range of real and alleged crimes, including murder and sexual assault. After this surge, the number of lynchings dropped off throughout the rest of the 1920s to an average of around 17 per year,[4] but racist mobs employed increasingly brutal methods to execute African Americans, including setting their victims on fire, torturing and dismembering them, and sexually mutilating their corpses.

The Revival of the Ku Klux Klan

The resurgence of the Ku Klux Klan during the 1920s aggravated already strained race relations in the United States. The original Klan, which emerged shortly after the end of the Civil War, was a racist organization dedicated to terrorizing

---

HOW OTHERS SEE US

Storm of Protest: The Sacco and Vanzetti Case

The trial, conviction, and execution of Nicola Sacco and Bartolomeo Vanzetti was a cause célèbre in the Boston area and throughout the United States. Sympathizers in Canada, Europe, Asia, and South America also rallied to the defense of the two Italian immigrants accused of armed robbery and murder on flimsy evidence. Neither defendant had a prior criminal record, but both were members of anarchist organizations.

In the years between the men's 1921 trial and their 1927 deaths, their case united political activists around the world—particularly those connected with the anarchist, socialist, or communist movements—in a common cause fed by intense newspaper coverage. Protesters denounced the American judicial system, as well as a judge and jury that were said to be biased against both immigrants and those on the political left (the accused were followers of the Italian anarchist Luigi Galleani).

Tokyo's activists, for example, posted leaflets throughout the city calling for boycotts of American goods and the expulsion of American missionaries; they urged the Japanese people to join against American imperialism and capitalism. Threatening letters, one written in blood, arrived at Tokyo's American embassy and warned of bombings and other violence. This pattern was repeated in city after city: Brussels, Prague, Sofia, Lisbon, London, and Paris. American consulates in Buenos Aires and Montevideo were bombed.

recently emancipated African Americans and their white Republican allies. This organization disbanded after 1870, but in 1915, an Atlanta evangelist and businessman named William J. Simmons revived the Klan in a cross-burning ceremony on Stone Mountain, Georgia. This resurrected Klan preached that white supremacy was under assault and that the increasing diversification of American culture was serving to "mongrelize" and therefore undermine native-born, white Protestant dominance. The Klan targeted not just African Americans but also immigrants, communists, union leaders, Catholics, and Jews. They pledged their devotion to protecting the American family, and meted out vigilante justice to bootleggers, wife-beaters, adulterers, and other perceived threats. By 1924, at the height of its power, the Klan boasted two million members nationwide, many of whom were small urban businessmen and recent rural migrants. The Klan dominated the political scene in Oklahoma, Texas, Colorado, and particularly Indiana, where an estimated 10 percent of the entire population belonged to the organization. Every one of Indiana's 92 counties contained a Klan chapter, and Governor Ed Jackson was himself a Klansman. But in 1925, David C. Stephenson, the Grand Dragon of Indiana, was arrested and convicted of the rape and murder of a 28-year-old state welfare worker. The conviction of such a high-ranking Klan officer decimated popular support for the organization, and Klan membership in Indiana plummeted from 350,000 to 15,000 within a year.[5] By 1926, the Ku Klux Klan was in serious decline nationwide. Many Klansmen elected to office in 1924 had not proven particularly effective, and the general prosperity of the nation made it difficult to continue to scapegoat African Americans, Jews, Catholics, and immigrants. Furthermore, strict immigration quotas had been passed—a major victory for white supremacists. Nevertheless, actual or threatened violence by Klansmen continued to influence American race relations throughout the rest of the 1920s.

Marcus Garvey and Black Nationalism

During the 1920s, hundreds of thousands of African Americans joined black nationalist organizations that celebrated race pride and racial self-determination. The most powerful of these groups was the Universal Negro Improvement Association (UNIA), founded in 1914 by Marcus Garvey, a charismatic Jamaican immigrant. Garvey promoted the UNIA by publishing a black-oriented newspaper, *Negro World,* and founding the Black Star shipping line to assist African Americans in emigrating to Africa. By the early 1920s, the UNIA claimed more than one million members worldwide. In 1922, when the Black Star line floundered, thousands of investors lost their money, and charges of corruption and the mishandling of funds tarnished the organization's reputation. Garvey was arrested for mail fraud in 1923, convicted and imprisoned two years later, and finally deported to Jamaica in 1927. The UNIA collapsed, but Garvey's message of black pride and separatism inspired hundreds of thousands of working-class African Americans to strive for fiscal and social independence from white society.

The New Negro

Although the phrase "New Negro" dates to the late nineteenth century, it was not until the 1920s that this label gained currency as a description for middle-class African Americans who advocated a new sense of militancy and racial pride. Alain Locke, an African American philosopher, critic, and editor, titled his Harlem Renaissance literary anthology *The New Negro* (1925) to signal these powerful currents of black artistic consciousness, renewed civil rights advocacy, and racial solidarity. The National Association for the Advancement of Colored People (NAACP) and other organizations waged court battles in an attempt to secure African Americans' civil and political rights. Black writers, musicians, and artists, especially those who resided in Harlem, used their work to celebrate African American culture and challenge racist stereotypes. Above all, "New Negroes" attempted to participate fully in American culture, while resisting white America's attempts to cast them as a "problem" that somehow needed to be solved.

NATIONAL PROHIBITION

On January 16, 1920, the Eighteenth Amendment to the U.S. Constitution went into effect.

Group of policemen posed with cases of moonshine, Washington, D.C., 1922. Prints & Photographs Division, Library of Congress.

The amendment, passed in 1919 and also known as National Prohibition, prohibited, "the manufacture, sale, or transportation of intoxicating liquors within, the importation thereof into, or the exportation thereof from the United States." In 1919, Congress had also enacted what became known as the Volstead Act, which defined "intoxicating liquor" as any beverage containing a minimum of one-half of one percent alcohol. So-called "padlock laws" allowed enforcement agents to close down any illegal drinking establishment for one year, and the government could seize and sell any vehicle used to transport liquor illegally. However, the Prohibition Bureau, a division of the Treasury Department created by the federal government to enforce its anti-alcohol laws, remained underfunded and understaffed throughout the 1920s, and most cities and states refused to appropriate enough money to hire additional officers to enforce these laws. In fact, 30 states appropriated no money at all to support the Volstead Act, choosing instead to leave the entire responsibility of law enforcement to the federal government.

Drinking During Prohibition

Although beer, wine, and spirits became more difficult to obtain during National Prohibition, and many people did drink less, Americans could still usually obtain liquor. Illicit bars called speakeasies sprang up in cities and towns across America, and moonshiners (producers of homemade distilled spirits), rumrunners (alcohol smugglers), and bootleggers (alcohol distributors) quickly found a lucrative market. The cost of liquor skyrocketed—drinks that once cost a nickel before Prohibition could cost 50 cents or more.

Although the price of alcoholic beverages rose, the quality declined. Bootleggers frequently adulterated genuine scotch, rye, and gin by diluting them with water and adding coloring, flavoring, and more alcohol. As a result, cocktails became popular during the 1920s, as drinkers used ginger ale, tonic water, or fruit juices to mask the unpleasant taste of low-grade liquor. Cocktail parties also became fashionable during Prohibition, since hosts could serve alcohol in their homes without much fear of being raided by Prohibition agents. People who could not afford bootlegged liquor often drank homemade beer, wine, or moonshine, and some desperate people resorted to concoctions of Sterno, aftershave lotion, hair tonics, over-the-counter medicines, and other alcohol-based household products. Adulterated alcohol poisoned or blinded tens of thousands and even killed people—mostly poor and working-class drinkers who could not afford to buy their liquor from reliable bootleggers.

Americans could purchase illegal liquor at underground commercial establishments. The urban saloon evolved into the popular "speakeasy" that hid in plain sight among legitimate businesses in most cities and towns. According to one study, New York City contained more than 30,000 speakeasies by 1927.[6] Some were located in elegant upscale surroundings and catered to the fashionable society set. For example, the 21 Club operated in a posh Manhattan townhouse and sold authentic—and expensive—smuggled Canadian liquor. Most speakeasies, however, were modest establishments that operated behind locked doors in apartments, out-of-the-way commercial properties, or the back rooms and basements of legal businesses. Prior to 1920, most women who entered working-class saloons were prostitutes, but after the enactment of Prohibition, it became acceptable and even fashionable for respectable middle-class women to drink in speakeasies, as long as a male companion accompanied them.

Prohibition and Crime

Prohibition laws led to a dramatic rise in the scope and scale of organized crime, motivating powerful gangsters, including George Remus in Cincinnati, Al "Scarface" Capone in Chicago, and Salvatore "Lucky" Luciano in New York, to exploit bootlegging as a new and lucrative business. George Remus—allegedly the inspiration for F. Scott Fitzgerald's character Jay Gatsby in the novel *The Great Gatsby* (1925)—made so much money from bootlegging that he would leave $100 bills under his guests' plates at dinner parties and once even gave brand-new Pontiac automobiles to all 50 of the female guests who attended one of his social gatherings. In 1928 alone, Al Capone made an estimated $105 million—reportedly the highest income in the United States—from his bootlegging, gambling, and prostitution rackets. Gangland bootleggers occasionally paid for their crimes through jail time and fines, but to a great extent they lived beyond the reach of the law. Mob bosses would pay corrupt police, federal agents, and even judges in exchange for protection from interference and prosecution. Gang-related violence repeatedly made headlines during the decade, and Americans were especially shocked by the 1929 "St. Valentine's Day Massacre," in which

---

PROHIBITION AND POPULAR CULTURE

National Prohibition influenced virtually every aspect of American culture during the 1920s. Hundreds of new words entered the American language to describe drinking, drinkers, and various forms of alcohol. Terms such as *happy sally, yack yack bourbon,* and *cherry dynamite* referred to various kinds of moonshine, and terms such as *shellacked, fried, potted,* and *crocked* described being drunk. Prohibition inspired dozens of popular songs, many of which parodied already familiar tunes. Among the most memorable titles were "If I Meet the Guy Who Made This Country Dry" (1920) and "It's the Smart Little Feller Who Stocked Up His Cellar (That's Getting the Beautiful Girls)" (1920). Until the late 1920s, when the motion picture industry began to self-censor movies with questionable moral content, Hollywood films frequently showed glamorous young men and women patronizing a speakeasy or attending a cocktail party.

Capone's henchmen, disguised as police officers, mowed down six members of rival George "Bugs" Moran's gang and an innocent bystander at a Chicago garage.

The Repeal of Prohibition

By the early 1930s, widespread disregard for the law, combined with the added social and economic pressures of the Great Depression, made the futility of the Prohibition laws evident to all but the most ardent temperance supporters. On December 5, 1933, President Franklin D. Roosevelt signed into law the Twenty-First Amendment to the Constitution, repealing the Eighteenth

Amendment (the only constitutional amendment ever repealed).

WOMEN'S ROLES

While many women, especially young women, broke from tradition when it came to hairstyles, clothing, and social behaviors, most still adhered to traditional gender roles. Young, unmarried women might flirt and "play the field" more than their mothers and grandmothers had, but the majority still dreamed of marrying, settling down, and raising children. While women entered colleges and universities in unprecedented numbers throughout the decade, relatively few planned to pursue careers outside the home after they were married.

The birthrate of middle-class families continued to decline as birth control became more widely available and more frequently practiced. The passage of more liberal laws made it easier to get a divorce, which prompted a rise in the divorce rate. In 1900, about eight percent of marriages ended in divorce, but by 1928, that number had increased to 16.6 percent.[7] Increasing numbers of married women worked outside the home, usually out of economic necessity, and by 1930, more than three million married women were in the workforce. Still, the great majority of families followed traditional sex roles; the husbands were the principal breadwinners, and the wives had primary responsibility for cooking, cleaning, and caring for the children.

In previous decades, middle-class Americans often employed at least a part-time maid or cook, but advances in such technologies as electric washing machines, vacuum cleaners, hot and cold running water, and refrigerators, coupled with the dwindling supply of domestic servants, made it customary for middle-class women to do their own housework. So-called labor-saving devices may have created more work for women, as washing machines and vacuum cleaners, for example, helped to raise common standards of cleanliness. And technological changes came far more slowly to homes in rural America. By 1930, only 10 percent of the nation's farms were wired for electricity, and only 33 percent had running water.[8]

A happy young flapper putting a flask in her boot, Washington, D.C., 1922. Prints & Photographs Division, Library of Congress.

Women at Work

During World War I, with more than 3.6 million men engaged in military service, American business and industry actively recruited women to work in factories, office buildings, and munitions plants. Wartime propaganda celebrated these female employees as patriots who were doing their part for the common good, but after the war ended, critics charged that working women neglected their husbands and children and took jobs that belonged to them. As a result, even many single women lost their jobs to returning veterans. Unions did little to protect women workers, largely because they, too, believed it inappropriate for women to compete with men for jobs. In fact, the great majority of wage-earning women worked as domestic servants, secretaries, telephone operators, typists, hairdressers, or department store clerks, or in other female-dominated occupations. College-educated women also tended to enter the "nurturing" professions of teaching, nursing, or social work. Overall, few women worked for their own gratification; rather, their income was needed to help support their families. Nevertheless, many employers believed that working women worked only to acquire pocket money, which justified their lower wages. During the 1920s, white women, on average, earned about half of what men earned for similar work, and black women earned about half of what white women did. Barriers for advancement remained high, and many women labored in mills and factories for years with little hope of a raise or a promotion. A small number of women became doctors, professors, lawyers, scientists, and business leaders in their communities, but lucrative jobs in management and administration eluded most women during the 1920s, regardless of their talent, education, or intelligence.

Women and Politics

In 1920, the Nineteenth Amendment was ratified, guaranteeing women the right to vote. Many political observers predicted that women would vote in a cohesive bloc and thus initiate dramatic reforms in American government and society; however, this quickly proved not to be the case.

After the passage of the suffrage amendment, the women's movement, whose diverse factions had united behind this common cause, once again splintered into dozens of political camps. One major divisive issue was the proposed Equal Rights Amendment (ERA), introduced in Congress in 1923, which read, "Men and woman shall have equal rights throughout the United States and every place subject to its jurisdiction."[9] Members of the National Women's Party (NWP) and other feminist groups believed that the ERA logically extended the political rights granted to women by the Nineteenth Amendment. Opponents feared that the amendment would endanger or prohibit legislation specially designed to protect and assist women, such as the Sheppard-Towner Act (1921), which distributed federal matching grants to the states for prenatal and child health clinics, midwife training, and visiting nurses for pregnant women and new mothers. Although the ERA was reintroduced in Congress three times in the 1920s, it never made it out of committee.

RELIGION AND FUNDAMENTALISM

By the 1920s, modern influences had infiltrated virtually every aspect of American society, Reverend Harry Emerson Fosdick and other liberal Protestant clergy rejected literal interpretations of the Bible and embraced the notion that Christianity could co-exist with science. They emphasized the moral and ethical teachings of the "historical Jesus" and encouraged church members to seek the counsel of their ministers on both spiritual and personal matters. They de-emphasized the supernatural and miracle-working aspects of Christianity and concentrated instead on dispensing practical advice about living as a Christian in an increasingly secular, materialistic world.

The rise of modern religion triggered a strong backlash among more traditional Protestant Christians. Conservative clergy preached about the dangers of modernity and warned their followers not to stray from biblical teachings. Their reaction became known as Fundamentalism, named after a series of pamphlets called *The Fundamentals* (1909–1914), which insisted on the literal truth of the Bible and Jesus Christ's critical role in saving humanity. Fundamentalism spawned a related movement called Pentecostalism, which appealed primarily to poor and working-class Americans, especially those in the Midwest and South. Pentecostals believed in faith healers and speaking in tongues, which, to them, signified the presence of the Holy Spirit. Both groups believed that the modern world had become morally corrupt and that its emphasis on money making, consumerism, leisure, and science had seduced weak-willed Christians. Thus, leaders in these churches tended to preach "old-time religion" that stressed conservative morality and the truth of biblical stories.

The Fundamentalist movement produced several famous ministers who, ironically, used modern show business techniques. During the 1910s and 1920s, Billy Sunday, a former professional baseball player turned evangelist, toured the country with his vaudeville-like revivals, converting sinners and denouncing the evils of the modern world. Aimee Semple McPherson, a dynamic Pentecostal preacher and bona fide celebrity, proved that Fundamentalist religion could seamlessly incorporate many elements of modern life. In 1923, McPherson established the 5,300-seat Angelus Temple in Los Angeles, dedicated to a religion she called the Foursquare Gospel, which promoted the ideas of divine healing, regeneration, baptism in the Holy Spirit, and the second coming of Jesus Christ. Her services incorporated elaborate stage sets, jazz music, animals, and actors playing various parts. Beginning in 1924, she broadcast her sermons and religious programs over her church-owned radio station, KFSG. In 1926, she claimed that she was kidnapped from a California beach, drugged, and held against her will in Mexico for several weeks until she could escape. Journalists attempted to prove that she had actually slipped away for a tryst with a married man, but her devoted followers still believed that McPherson was a selfless servant of the Lord.

Evolutionary Science and the Scopes Trial

Fundamentalists stressed the literal truth of the Bible as God's divinely ordained word, so evolutionary teachings, which clearly contradicted the story of Genesis, became a particular target of wrath and condemnation. Between 1921 and 1922, legislatures in 20 states introduced bills banning the teaching of evolution in public schools. When Tennessee passed such a law in 1925, the American Civil Liberties Union (ACLU) offered to provide legal representation for any teacher willing to challenge this law in court. John T. Scopes, a high school biology teacher in Dayton, Tennessee, accepted the offer. After he explained Darwin's theory of evolution to his students, he was arrested, sparking one of the most famous and sensational trials of the decade. William Jennings Bryan, former secretary of state, three-time presidential candidate, and a leader of the Fundamentalist movement, argued for the prosecution. Clarence Darrow, a famous liberal trial lawyer and professed agnostic, assisted with Scopes's defense. The trial, held in July 1925, attracted thousands of spectators and reporters to the small town of Dayton.

Throughout the 12 day trial, Americans were riveted to the case, which had essentially devolved into the question of whether Darwin or Genesis was "right." Camera crews sent daily newsreel footage of the trial to movie theaters across the country. Hundreds of thousands of people listened to the proceedings carried by WGN, Chicago—the first trial ever broadcast live on radio. Darrow, who was forbidden by the judge from introducing any expert scientific testimony, called Bryan, a self-proclaimed expert on the Bible, as his only witness. Darrow proceeded to humiliate Bryan, who testified to the literal accuracy of biblical stories (including the tale of Jonah's being swallowed by a big fish and Joshua's making the sun stand still) and exhibited his vast ignorance of science. Sophisticated Americans thought Bryan ridiculous, and reporters such as H. L. Mencken, writing for the *Baltimore Sun*, lampooned Bryan and what they saw as the idiocy and backwardness of Fundamentalists in particular and southerners in general. In the end, a jury found Scopes guilty of breaking the law and fined him $100, but the Tennessee Supreme Court later overturned the case on a technicality. Nevertheless, anti-evolution laws prohibiting the teaching of Darwinism remained on the books, and evolution-free biology textbooks continued to dominate classrooms in high schools across much of the South. .

Defense Attorney Clarence Darrow (center, wearing suspenders) during the Scopes Trial, Dayton, Tennessee, 1925. Prints & Photographs Division, Library of Congress.

TECHNOLOGICAL ADVANCES

The 1920s saw the rapid development of new technologies. By 1928, approximately 17 million homes—out of about 27 million homes—were wired for electricity. These homes contained approximately 15.3 million electric irons, 6.8 million vacuum cleaners, 5 million washing machines, 4.5 million toasters, and 755,000 electric refrigerators.[10]

Telephone ownership increased from 14.3 million in 1922 to 20.3 million in 1930, and in 1926, phones were first manufactured not as two separate pieces connected by a cord, but with the transmitter and receiver in a single handset.[11] Even experimental television made headlines. The first demonstration of long-range television transmission, from a signal in Washington, D.C., to a receiver in New York City, took place in April 1927. The image projected was the face of then Secretary of Commerce Herbert Hoover. Two years later, the NBC radio network began broadcasting a regular television schedule, but a low-resolution signal, and few receivers made this effort commercially unsuccessful.

During the 1920s, a series of medical breakthroughs improved the state of medicine. Doctors first used insulin to treat diabetes in 1922, British scientist Alexander Fleming discovered penicillin in 1928, and advances in the treatment of scarlet fever and measles helped bring these dangerous diseases under control. In 1928, Dr. George Papanicolaou, a Greek immigrant, published news of his medical breakthrough, the "Pap smear," which could detect cervical cancer in women. Newly invented medical equipment included the electrocardiograph in 1924, the "iron lung" respirator in 1928, and the electroencephalograph in

1929. Despite these advances, medical care in the United States during the 1920s was spotty at best. Relatively few doctors lived in the rural South and Midwest, and residents of those regions were most likely to suffer from hookworm, pellagra, rickets, and other diseases caused by nutritional deficiencies. Americans living in urban centers or near medical schools enjoyed better access to advanced health care, but doctors still relied more on bedside comforting and commonsense remedies than they did on pharmacological cures. Still, by the end of the 1920s, increased understanding of nutrition and preventive health care had considerably lessened infant mortality rates and increased life expectancy.

NATIONAL NEWS STORIES

The phenomenal growth of mass-circulation magazines and newspapers during the 1920s prompted Americans to follow national news stories with great interest. For example, when spelunker Floyd Collins became trapped in Sand Cave (near Cave City, Kentucky) in 1925, more than 150 reporters descended upon the area. For two weeks, radio broadcasts and front-page newspaper articles chronicled the heroic but futile attempts made by Louisville firefighters and local volunteers to rescue him. Some 15 days after he had become trapped, Collins died, but that did not mark the end of national attention. Later that year, hillbilly singing star Vernon Dalhart recorded "The Death of Floyd Collins," and picture postcards were printed of the tragic scene, including at least one that pictured Collins's corpse being removed from the cave. Mass media had tapped into the nation's fascination with such sensational news.

The 1920s saw many dramatic and highly publicized trials, including the Scopes trial. Another sensational trial was that of Nathan Leopold and Richard Loeb, which later inspired Alfred Hitchcock's 1948 film *Rope*. Eighteen-year-old Loeb and 19-year-old Leopold, the privileged sons of two wealthy and prominent Chicago families, conspired to commit what they believed to be the "perfect murder." Their plan resulted in the kidnapping and brutal bludgeoning death of 14-year-old Bobby Franks in May 1924. A pair of Leopold's

eyeglasses, inadvertently left near Franks's body, eventually led police to the two young men. Leopold and Loeb pleaded guilty to murder, and Clarence Darrow, the famous defense lawyer, argued passionately and successfully to keep his clients from receiving the death penalty. Throughout the course of the month-long hearing, Americans closely followed newspaper and radio coverage of the case, simultaneously repelled and mesmerized by this motiveless "thrill killing."

TIME MAN OF THE YEAR

1927 Charles Lindbergh (aviator)

1928 Walter Chrysler (founder of Chrysler Corp.)

1929 Owen D. Young (foreman of Second Reparations Conference)

Tabloid newspapers, which enjoyed higher circulations than most serious papers, cashed in on Americans' appetite for crime and scandal by reporting, in lurid and titillating detail, shocking sex scandals and murder trials. Readers followed the breaking developments of trials in the pages of the tabloids as if they were following the convoluted plot twists of a Hollywood film. For example, when silent film comedian Roscoe "Fatty" Arbuckle was arrested and charged with the rape and murder of actress Virginia Rappe in 1921, he was effectively tried and convicted in William Randolph Hearst's chains of newspapers. In April 1922, after two trials that resulted in hung juries, Arbuckle was acquitted of all charges in a third trial, but the negative publicity irreparably damaged his film career. Other scandalous murder trials also fascinated the public. In 1927, a Queens, New York, homemaker named Ruth Snyder and her lover, a salesman named Judd Gray, murdered her husband, Albert Snyder. A frenzy of newspaper reportage kept readers glued to the trial. Both Snyder and Gray were convicted and executed in 1928, with Snyder being the first woman ever electrocuted in the state of New York.

THE STOCK MARKET CRASH

When Herbert Hoover was elected president of the United States in 1928, the country appeared to have a bright future. Part of this optimism came from the astounding rise in the stock market. Stocks had been trading well above their market value, and investors had been purchasing these inflated stocks "on margin," providing a minimal down payment—sometimes as little as 10 percent—and then borrowing the rest of the money at high interest rates. The loan, in theory, would be paid back out of the profits from the stock, whose value, people believed, would never stop rising. Indeed, the market value of all stocks, which stood at about $27 billion in 1925, had climbed to $87 billion by 1929. The stock market seemed like the perfect place to make easy money, and even middle-class Americans began to speculate on Wall Street. But on October 24, 1929—"Black Thursday"—the stock market collapsed. Orders to sell poured into the New York Stock Exchange, and stock prices plummeted. Panicked brokers began calling in their customers' debts, which led to more sell orders. Some stocks, which found no buyers at any price, became worthless. The worst was yet to come. Five days later, on October 29, so-called "Black Tuesday," a record 16 million shares of stock traded hands. By November, $30 billion in stock values had vanished. Companies were wiped out, banks were drained, and investors saw their life savings disappear.

Many factors caused this devastating stock market crash. The economy appeared healthy, but in fact industrial production far outpaced consumer demand, and tremendous amounts of inventory were accumulating in warehouses. Overseas markets for American-made products had dwindled as a result of a severe depression in postwar Europe, and many American businesses were buried in debt. Middle-class and especially working-class Americans saw their paychecks grow at a much slower rate. And while large segments of the

"History of 1929" cartoon by Daniel Fitzpatrick, *St. Louis Post-Dispatch,* December 31, 1929. Courtesy of the State Historical Society of Missouri, Columbia.

population, primarily farmers, textile workers, and coal miners, lacked sufficient income to meet their basic needs, 60 percent of the nation's wealth lay in the hands of just two percent of the American people. The stock market crash did not directly cause the Great Depression, but it did accelerate the collapse of an already unstable economy and the onset of the worst economic crisis in American history. "Black Tuesday" marked the end of the prosperous and flamboyant Jazz Age and the beginning of a new era in American history, the Great Depression.

Advertising

of the 1920s

During the 1920s, sophisticated professional salespeople, graphic designers, and copywriters bombarded Americans with attractive, persuasive advertising campaigns. Modern advertising sought to convince consumers that the key to increased status, health, happiness, wealth, and beauty existed in the mass-produced goods available in department stores, chain stores, and mail-order catalogs. In prior decades, Americans had tended to define themselves at least in part based on factors such as race, ethnicity, region, religion, and politics. During the 1920s, however, Americans increasingly defined themselves through the houses, cars, clothes, and other goods and services they purchased.

MASS CONSUMERISM

During World War I, the government encouraged Americans to conserve food and fuel and to sacrifice for the good of the war effort by consuming only basic necessities. But during the 1920s, the increasing prosperity of the American middle class led to soaring levels of consumerism. Between 1922 and 1927, the average per capita income rose by 30 percent, and although a serious depression continued to plague agriculture, most aspects of the American economy seemed to be healthy and growing prior to the October 1929 stock market crash. As Americans earned more disposable income, companies offered a wider variety of goods at comparatively low prices.

American consumerism also exploded in part due to the increasing popularity of affordable installment plans. Buying a home, of course, often required a mortgage, and other large purchases such as automobiles sometimes involved financing, but it wasn't until the 1920s that ordinary middle-class consumers began buying large numbers of more expensive items on installment. In fact, between 1920 and 1929, installment purchases quintupled, and in 1929 accounted for 90 percent of all vacuum cleaner, radio, and refrigerator sales, 70 percent of furniture sales, and 60 percent of auto sales.[1] Advertisers contributed to the erosion of the old ethos of avoiding debt by emphasizing the ease with which consumers could pay merely $5 a week for a fur coat or $20 a month for living room furniture, all the while enjoying the merchandise.

THE MODERN ADVERTISING INDUSTRY

Most Americans not only had more money during the 1920s than they had in previous decades, but they also increasingly equated personal success with material goods. Modern advertising

ADVERTISING SLOGANS OF THE 1920s

"Always a bridesmaid and never a bride," Listerine, 1923

"Reach for a Lucky instead of a sweet," Lucky Strikes cigarettes, 1928

"The Pause That Refreshes," Coca-Cola, 1929

Burma-Shave signs, 1925

"I'd walk a mile for a Camel," Camel Cigarettes, 1921

"Somewhere west of Laramie," Jordan Motor Company, 1923

Source: *Advertising Age's* 100 Best Advertising Campaigns of 20th Century. http://adage.com/century

fueled this new attitude. Billboards, newspapers, magazines, and radio commercials touted the virtues of their various advertisers' products, and companies poured enormous sums of money into advertising. Collectively, American companies spent around $700 million on advertising in 1914, but by 1929 that figure ballooned to nearly $3 billion.[2] Advertisers attempted to convince consumers that choosing their product instead of one sold by a competitor would enhance their health, safety, beauty, even the quality of their lives. Companies quickly found that advertising paid. For example, after an extensive advertising campaign, the American Tobacco Company, the manufacturers of Lucky Strike cigarettes, saw its earnings swell from $12 million in 1926 to $40 million in 1930.[3]

Modern advertising flourished during the 1920s. The modern advertising agency consisted of teams of professional salesmen, graphic designers, and copywriters who created sophisticated advertising campaigns and then placed them in appropriate venues. Many modern ads created associations between a product and such desirable traits as youthfulness, attractiveness, intelligence, and popularity. These ads encouraged Americans to buy newly developed or "improved" items that they had never before considered necessary. Companies developed persuasive advertising campaigns that taught consumers regularly

to purchase brand-name, often nonessential products.

As late as the early 1920s, some print advertisements still functioned largely as informative declarations of a particular product's merits. These advertisements sought to create a subtle but positive impression on consumers. As the 1920s progressed, however, copywriters developed advertisements that appealed more overtly to consumers' psychological needs and fears. Increasingly, ads featured people enjoying a product, rather than merely showing the product itself. The language of advertisements became more personal and intimate, essentially encouraging American consumers to judge themselves and each other based not on strength of character but rather on the brand-name products they purchased.

During the 1920s, most advertising professionals were men, but about 10 percent were women, most of whom worked as assistants or copywriters. Many of the men who joined advertising firms were college graduates, and some had even earned degrees from the new business schools or advertising programs that flourished in the 1920s. Many of these university-trained advertisers gravitated toward the emerging field of market research and learned how to track consumer reactions to particular products and advertisements using statistics, surveys, and other analytical methods.

ADVERTISING STRATEGIES

By the 1920s, advertisers and retailers knew that while men were ordinarily the primary wage earners in their families, women did most of the actual purchasing. As a result, a considerable percentage of advertising in the 1920s targeted females. Print advertisements appeared in the mass-circulation women's magazines of the day, such as *Ladies' Home Journal* and *Good Housekeeping*, touting everything from food products, clothing, and electric kitchen appliances to cosmetics, anti-aging creams, and weight-loss regimens. Many advertisers suggested that buying a certain product would make them better wives and mothers. Some print ads blatantly correlated the intensity of a mother's love with the purchase of a particular brand of soup, toothpaste, or

Do wives think differently today?

Changing habits prove they do

Doesn't it seem only yesterday that wives were so busy with household cares that they found but little time for anything else?

How different is the new order that has been ushered in. Today, your wife finds opportunity to vary her interests . . . to be a companion to your children . . . to study closer your welfare. She has won a new freedom and happiness in her daily life.

What has brought about this change? Your wife will tell you . . . thinking differently . . . thinking of housekeeping in much the same terms as you think of your business problems . . . discarding time-worn ideas and old-fashioned methods in favor of a new-day efficiency in home management.

Whenever wives meet, these modern methods of homekeeping are discussed. Particularly, do they speak of how one important problem—that of food buying—has been simplified.

No longer do you find these women visiting store after store in search of goodness and value in foodstuffs. They confine their purchases to the one store which experience has taught them provides both the good foods and the good values they seek.

Daily they go to the A & P, knowing that a few minutes spent selecting foods solves what was formerly a vexing problem. For A & P's shelves are filled with the finest foods that a great world-wide buying organization can secure . . . nationally advertised brands . . . the choicest imported luxuries . . . foods locally famous. And women have learned that substantial savings go hand in hand with this quality.

This changing habit in food buying—the result of wives thinking differently today—is nation-wide in scope. Like guideposts along the highways, A & P stores everywhere point the way to good foods and good values.

At the A & P she is sure to find the popular, nationally advertised brands of groceries.

THE GREAT
ATLANTIC & PACIFIC
TEA COMPANY

"Do wives think differently today?," asks this A & P grocery store ad. *The Saturday Evening Post,* July 14, 1928.

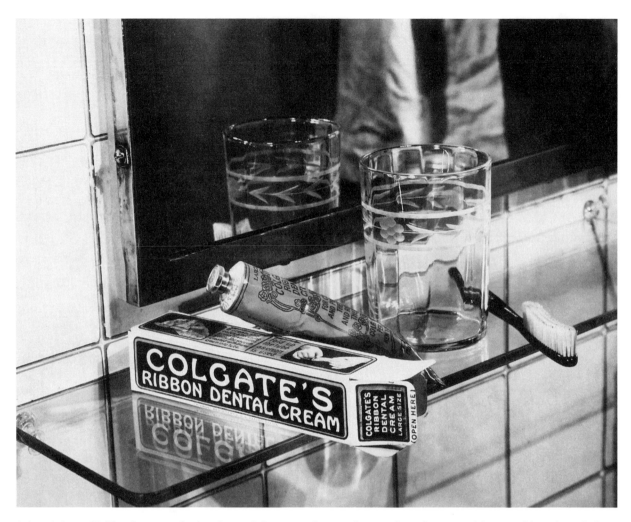

Advertising still-life photograph showing a Colgate toothpaste box and toothpaste with a toothbrush and glass on a shelf in a bathroom, 1922. Prints & Photographs Division, Library of Congress.

detergent, suggesting that choosing a rival product would jeopardize the health or safety of one's children. Other companies tempted homemakers with promises that buying their products would streamline meal preparation and lighten their domestic workload.

One of the most successful and ubiquitous advertising techniques during the 1920s was the relentless appeal to modernity. Modernity equaled progress, and whatever was new was often seen as automatically desirable. The Campbell Soup Company, for example, exhorted homemakers to try its condensed soups because opening a can was not only fast and easy but also the "modern way of 'making' soup." Other advertisements warned consumers that appearing old-fashioned or outdated could actually result in some personal tragedy—anything from losing a suitor to losing a job to losing one's self-respect.

Advertisers also exploited a different aspect of modernity—the intense anxiety that some Americans experienced in response to a faster-paced lifestyle, mass consumerism, intrusive technologies, and the erosion of long-standing traditional values. Although progress was largely heralded as positive and healthy, certain aspects of modern life did seem overwhelming to ordinary Americans. "Anti-modern" advertisements for products that were intended to reduce stress and tension abounded. For example, one Post Bran Flakes advertisement featured a picture of a harried businessman rushing to work. This cereal, the ad suggested, promoted good health and regularity despite living a modern life.

SEEKING BEAUTY WITH AN UNUSUAL PRODUCT

Advertisers helped to fuel the 1920s trend of worshiping youthfulness. Fashions, particularly women's fashions, emphasized a slim, youthful figure, and the cosmetics industry boomed as millions of American women tried all sorts of products that promised to restore the eyes, hair, and skin of their younger years. For example, one 1928 advertisement for Lysol disinfectant pictured two fashionable young women, clad in smart cloche hats and fur-trimmed coats, glancing back at a couple who has just walked past them. One woman comments to the other, "She looks old enough to be his mother." The advertisement's copy explains how this unfortunate woman, who is actually five years younger than her husband, has succumbed to the ravages of age by not relying on Lysol for her feminine hygiene needs (which is not only amusing in its sexism, but shocking to women of the twenty-first century who know Lysol only as a rather strong disinfectant for cleaning floors, sinks, and toilets). Lysol was also used by some women in the 1920s and later years as a contraceptive, though in the 1930s, some public medical criticism of its use had begun. The ad also sadly notes that, "in this enlightened age, so often a woman has only herself to blame if she fails to stay young with her husband and with her woman friends." Likewise, an ad campaign for Palmolive soap exploited the notion that women of all ages ought to "keep that schoolgirl complexion" and that Palmolive soap provided the foundation of "modern beauty culture."

From: Rachel Lynn Palmer and Sarah K. Greenberg, *Facts and Frauds in Woman's Hygiene; A Medical Guide Against Misleading Claims and Dangerous Products* (Garden City, NY: Garden City Publishing, 1938), 142–157; Roland Marchand, *Advertising the American Dream: Making Way for Modernity, 1920–1940* (Berkeley: University of California Press, 1985), 15, 181.

Not all Americans needed to be told that they were unique individuals. Some successful advertising campaigns took the opposite approach and appealed to consumers based on their perceived need to hop on the proverbial bandwagon. The Campbell Soup Company, for example, launched a series of ads during the 1920s for canned pork-and-beans that explains that "Years ago tastes for beans varied in different parts of the country. Certain sections were justly proud of the way they cooked and served them. But today there's no doubt whatever about the pork-and-beans the whole country prefers."[4] Rather than see homogenization as a disadvantage, advertisers urged consumers to take comfort in the fact that millions of Americans could not be wrong, and so choosing what the masses chose was a wise decision.

Some ads of the 1920s traded on "snob appeal," intimating that only consumers of wealth, culture, and class would be interested in, or even deserved to own, such a tasteful product. Other advertisements offered scientific information and medical advice or even warned about the hazards of unsanitary conditions.

SPOKESPERSONS

Although celebrity endorsements of consumer products were not new in the 1920s, they carried considerable weight in a nation highly attuned to the behaviors of its favorite movie stars and sports idols. When Hollywood sex symbol Clara Bow lent her name to a line of hats, for example, or football hero Red Grange's image appeared on a candy bar, American consumers paid attention—and bought. Lucky Strikes cigarettes launched a highly effective celebrity endorsement campaign in the late 1920s that combined Americans' fears of being overweight with their desires to emulate their beloved stars. The American Tobacco Company, the cigarette's manufacturer, hired famous actors, singers, athletes, and even military heroes to recommend that consumers watch their figures and "Reach for a Lucky instead of a sweet." Lucky Strikes also touted its cigarettes as "[t]he modern way to diet! Light a Lucky when fattening sweets tempt you.... The delicately toasted flavor of Luckies is more than a substitute for fattening sweets—it satisfies the appetite without harming the digestion."[5] As smoking became increasingly popular among women, advertisements carried testimonials from famous women such as aviator Amelia Earhart and actress Constance Talmadge.

124   *THE SATURDAY EVENING POST*   *August 18, 1928*

DON'T FOOL YOURSELF

Since halitosis never announces itself to the victim, you simply cannot know when you have it.

Halitosis makes *you unpopular*

It is inexcusable . . . . . . can be instantly remedied.

NO matter how charming you may be or how fond of you your friends are, you cannot expect them to put up with halitosis (unpleasant breath) forever. They may be nice to you—but it is an effort.

Don't fool yourself that you never have halitosis as do so many self-assured people who constantly offend this way.

Read the facts in the lower right-hand corner and you will see that your chance of escape is slight. Nor should you count on being able to detect this ailment in yourself. Halitosis doesn't announce itself. You are seldom aware you have it.

Recognizing these truths, nice people end any chance of offending by systematically rinsing the mouth with Listerine. Every morning. Every night. And between times when necessary, especially before meeting others.

Keep a bottle handy in home and office for this purpose.

Listerine ends halitosis instantly. Being antiseptic, it strikes at its commonest cause—fermentation in the oral cavity. Then, being a powerful deodorant, it destroys the odors themselves.

If you have any doubt of Listerine's powerful deodorant properties, make this test: Rub a slice of onion on your hand. Then apply Listerine clear. Immediately, every trace of onion odor is gone. Even the strong odor of fish yields to it. Lambert Pharmacal Company, St. Louis, Mo., U. S. A.

> The new baby—
> LISTERINE SHAVING CREAM
> —you've got a treat ahead of you.
> TRY IT

READ THE FACTS
⅓ *had halitosis*

68 hairdressers state that about every third woman, many of them from the wealthy classes, is halitoxic. Who should know better than they?

LISTERINE
The safe antiseptic

A 1928 ad for Listerine plays on readers' fears of being unpopular. *The Saturday Evening Post,* August 18, 1928.

Advertisers soon realized that spokespersons need not be famous—or even real. A popular advertising gimmick of the 1920s was to invent an imaginary figure, usually a woman, to function as a spokesperson for a particular product or company. In 1921, the advertising department of the Washburn-Crosby Company created a fictional model homemaker and nutrition expert named Betty Crocker for use in an advertising campaign promoting its Gold Medal flour. She was so named by combining a popular woman's name, "Betty," with the surname of the retired company director, William G. Crocker. Originally, the company used Betty Crocker's name to sign letters written in response requests it received from homemakers seeking baking advice. Her signature, company executives believed, offered a more personal and authoritative touch to these letters, and a secretary who had won a handwriting contest among the company's female employees supplied Betty Crocker's signature. The Washburn-Crosby Company soon began to publish cookbooks under her name and established the Betty Crocker Kitchens, in which a team of home economists tested and created recipes used the company's Gold Medal flour. By the late 1920s, many fictitious spokespersons were endorsing brand-name products. The Postum Company invented Carrie Blanchard, who received thousands of letters from fans. And Libby Foods created Mary Hale Martin, whose name was signed to advice columns in Libby's advertisements as well as to "personal replies" sent in response to consumers' letters.

ADVERTISING AND RACE

Not all company spokespeople were as culturally inoffensive as Betty Crocker. Since the late nineteenth century, advertisers had tapped into familiar Old South racial stereotypes to sell their products. Images of happy, docile African American servants eager to serve their masters (i.e., the consumers) proliferated on brand-name packaging of the 1890s and endured into the 1920s and beyond. Among the best known of these fictional spokespersons were Aunt Jemima, a "mammy" figure who advertised self-rising pancake flour for the Davis Milling Company (later acquired by the Quaker Oats Company), and Rastus, the

black chef featured on Nabisco's Cream of Wheat box. Both of these figures still appear on packaging today. Although Aunt Jemima has lost her headkerchief in the process of being "updated," the image of Rastus remains virtually unchanged. Other popular racial stereotypes employed in advertising during the 1920s were the Gold Dust Twins—two little black children who appeared on Gold Dust soap powder labels. These twins became synonymous with the product they represented, and they came to life between 1923 and 1926, when white actors impersonating the twins starred in *The Gold Dust Twins,* a musical-variety program broadcast on WEAF, New York.

During the 1920s, Aunt Jemima and Rastus were visible brand-name characters designed to appeal to white consumers who found comfort in old-time images of happy, nonthreatening black domestics who "knew their place" and served their white employers with a smile. A brief, fictionalized biography of Aunt Jemima, which appeared in a 1920 *Saturday Evening Post* advertisement, described a supposed 1864 encounter she had with a Confederate general, during which she prepared him a heaping plate of her delicious pancakes. Cream of Wheat ads featured Rastus dressed in white chef's apparel, grinning as he served white children steaming bowls of cereal.

PUBLICITY STUNTS

Some companies relied upon attention grabbing and often bizarre publicity stunts to attract attention. One popular publicity stunt was the look-alike contest, which attracted crowds of people who dressed up like Jackie Coogan, the child star, or Charlie Chaplin, the "Little Tramp," often in exchange for complimentary movie tickets. In 1927, Douglas Fairbanks and Mary Pickford participated in a famous publicity stunt when they became the first movie stars to plant their footprints in the wet cement on the sidewalk in front of Grauman's Chinese Theatre in Hollywood. Over the years, other celebrities have added their handprints or footprints to the Hollywood "Walk of Fame."

Even before Charles Lindbergh's historic transatlantic flight in 1927, aviation-related events attracted extensive media coverage. Advertisers hired pilots to fly airplanes towing promotional banners, and found new ways to capitalize on the advertising potential offered by the airplane. In 1923, for example, Otto Schnering, the owner of the Curtiss Candy Company, hired a pilot to drop thousands of his new Baby Ruth candy bars, each attached to a tiny parachute, over Pittsburgh, Pennsylvania. This promotional gimmick proved so successful that he later expanded his candy bar drops to metropolitan areas in 40 other states.

In 1924, Procter and Gamble launched the first Ivory soap carving competition, which became a tremendously successful and long-running advertising stunt. Thousands of people carved statues out of blocks of soap, and the winning sculptures toured the nation in a traveling exhibit, attracting even more attention for Ivory soap. Also in 1924, Macy's department store sponsored its first Thanksgiving Day parade. Originally called a Christmas parade, though held around Thanksgiving, the procession included floats and displays of all the latest toys, which, of course, were for sale in Macy's toy department. In 1927, the parade began to feature the familiar enormous helium balloons, with the first ones shaped like Felix the Cat and the Toy Soldier.

Another popular publicity stunt during the 1920s was flagpole sitting, and Alvin "Shipwreck" Kelly, a professional Hollywood stuntman, reigned as the undisputed king of flagpole sitters. In 1929, he perched atop a pole in Baltimore for 23 days and seven hours. The following year, he spent 49 days aloft above the Atlantic City, New Jersey boardwalk. More often, though, he would balance on a flagpole as a paid publicity stunt for movie theaters, car dealerships, and other businesses. The large crowds that such an event attracted were full of potential customers, and the media coverage also drew attention to the sponsoring store or theater. Adventuresome teens and college students also participated in the craze for the personal celebrity it briefly bestowed upon them.

ADVERTISING VENUES

The rapidly increasing circulations of the larger national magazines and newspapers provided retailers with the chance to advertise their brand-name products coast-to-coast. As the new

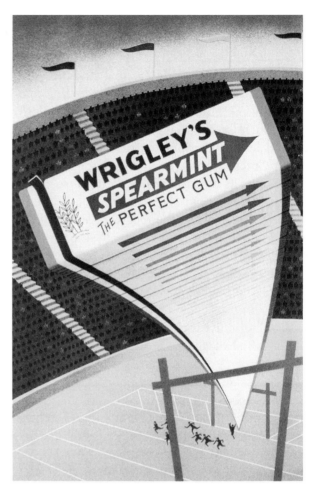

Poster showing pack of gum being kicked over goal posts in a football stadium, ca. 1925. Prints & Photographs Division, Library of Congress.

medium of radio became more popular, companies broadcast their commercial messages over the nation's airwaves. Eye-catching billboards along roads and highways promoted everything from the newest typewriter to breakfast cereal. In 1925, the Burma-Vita Company launched its famous billboard advertising campaign for Burma-Shave shaving cream. The company's first billboards were erected in Minnesota, but soon Burma-Shave signs were dotting the roadways across the nation. Streetcar ads catered to the industrial laborers who rode the cars back and forth to work. Neon signs, first introduced in 1923, provided a modern, high-tech look that made it easier to advertise products at night. Department stores began hiring professional window dressers to present merchandise in appealing and creative ways. Comic strip characters hawked dolls and toys in the pages of the "funny papers." Small-scale advertising also continued, as hired boys walked the streets of cities and towns wearing sandwich boards to promote a restaurant's lunch special or a department store's big sale. Giant corporations sponsored early "commercials" that ran in motion picture theaters before feature presentations. Even architecture itself became a form of advertising, as roadside restaurants developed unique architectural designs to catch the attention of passing motorists. A coffee shop in the shape of an enormous coffee pot or an ice cream stand built to resemble a giant milk bottle was sure to attract customers.

Print Advertisements

The most popular and powerful national print advertising venues during the 1920s were mass-circulation magazines, which, by the end of the decade, collectively sold more than 200 million copies a year. Magazine publishers quickly realized that profits lay not in subscriptions or newsstand revenues, but in the sale of valuable advertising space. *The Saturday Evening Post, Ladies' Home Journal, Collier's Weekly, Life, Vanity Fair,* and *Scribner's* all sold for about one-fourth to one-fifth the actual cost of printing them, yet their publishers raked in enormous profits from the many advertisers. In 1917, for example, *The Saturday Evening Post's* circulation was just under 1.9 million and generated advertising revenues of about $16 million. By 1928, circulation had risen by about 50 percent (to about 2.8 million), but advertising revenues had increased 300 percent (to more than $48 million).[6] Women's magazines, including publications such as *Ladies' Home Journal, Good Housekeeping,* and *McCall's,* earned more than $75 million in advertising revenues in 1928.

As advertisers strove to distinguish their brand-name products from those of their competitors, print advertisements in magazines became more eye-catching and colorful. As late as 1924, more than three-quarters of the advertisements in most popular magazines were still printed solely in black-and-white; however, during the mid-1920s, the production of color advertisements rose significantly. The Coca-Cola Company, for example,

ran four-color magazine ads and billboard posters, employing slogans such as "Enjoy Thirst" and "Refreshment Time." In 1929, Coca-Cola's advertising department created its legendary slogan, "The Pause That Refreshes," which first appeared in a series of advertisements in *The Saturday Evening Post.*

Daily newspapers represented another important advertising venue, but newspaper ads tended to be smaller and less elaborate than magazine ads. Nevertheless, newspapers did aid advertisers and retailers by promoting local businesses and sales. Grocery stores were one of the primary industries to capitalize on daily newspaper advertisements. In the early 1920s, the Kroger grocery store chain began printing its weekly food prices and special sales in newspapers; by the end of the decade, this practice became widespread in the grocery industry. In fact, by 1929, the manufacturers of drugs, toiletries, food, and beverages spent more

ADS BASED ON INSECURITIES

The roaring 1920s marked a brand of idealism in America not seen since the first settlers set eyes on the new land. The early postwar years transformed a society that was learning how to live in the city from production to consumption. For many whites, the American Dream was at hand. American idealism and the idea that nearly every American who was white, male, and not fresh off the boat had a shot at being successful was not lost on those looking to cash in on the greenbacks burning holes in the pockets of the flappers and philosophers. Advertisements catered to the anxiety existent in those worried about maintaining status. Personal hygiene was chief among the characteristics of the wealthy, and those that wanted to be wealthy had to appear wealthy. Further, advertisements targeted women indirectly in that the dawn of sex as marketing tool was born. Advertising based on insecurities continues today unabashed. From smart pills, to Spanish fly equivalents, to soda that makes one look like the latest star, there is a product out there that will fulfill any desire. One needs only to watch TV for 20 minutes to see all the things he or she doesn't have.

money on newspaper ads than did any other industry.

Radio Advertisements

At the beginning of the 1920s, the radio industry was still in its infancy. Radio hobbyists listened to crystal sets with earphones, and few had any inkling that this new medium would soon become such a powerful force. As broadcast signals reached farther and farther, and radio's popularity soared, the public first believed that the airwaves were a public trust that should be kept free from commercial sponsorship. This was not the case for long. In 1922, a real-estate corporation became the first paid radio sponsor on WEAF, New York, signaling the advent of commercial radio advertising.

Initially, the commercial radio industry remained wary of alienating listeners who might find on-air advertisements intrusive and annoying. The magazine industry, who considered radio advertising unwelcome competition, warned against cluttering the airwaves with unwanted commercial messages. Critics of radio advertising argued that listeners would directly support their favorite stations, and thus the stations themselves would need no advertising revenue, however, few radio listeners wanted to pay for a service currently provided free of charge.

Still, the radio broadcasting industry proceeded cautiously, and for several years prohibited blatant "commercials" that directly offered or described merchandise. Rather, radio program sponsorship attempted to boost the name recognition of participating companies and their products. One common advertising practice was for companies to hire a band, orchestra, or other musical act to perform on a program named after the sponsor and then hope that listeners who enjoyed the show would purchase the company's products. In 1923, for example, the New York chain of Happiness Candy Stores hired two popular recording and vaudeville stars, Billy Jones and Ernest Hare, to team up on radio as the Happiness Boys. Jones and Hare sang songs and told stories during their half-hour music-and-comedy program called *The Happiness Boys,* and in doing so promoted Happiness candy. Beginning in 1923, the A&P

chain of grocery stores sponsored *The A&P Gypsies,* which featured a band that played distinctive and recognizable exotic music, first for New York listeners and then, after 1927, for nationwide audiences on the NBC network. By the mid-1920s, the B. F. Goodrich Company was financing *The Goodrich Silvertown Orchestra,* and the Cliquot Club Ginger Ale Company was promoting *The Cliquot Club Eskimos.* The Eskimos evolved into a full-fledged dance orchestra and, as early as 1926, developed what is considered to be the first radio show theme song, "The Cliquot Foxtrot March."

As early as 1923, the National Carbon Company, the manufacturer of Eveready Batteries, began to sponsor the first major radio variety show, *The Eveready Hour.* This hour-long program, which aired on WEAF in New York and featured a mixture of music, news, drama, and comedy, proved an immediate hit with radio audiences. In 1926, the NBC network picked up the show for broadcast on more than 30 stations across the country. Top celebrities such as Will Rogers and D. W. Griffith made guest appearances, and regular cast members toured the nation to promote Eveready products. Between 1927 and 1928, Eveready spent $400,000 on the program, but its battery sales skyrocketed.

Radio advertisers quickly realized that women made up the largest segment of the listening audience. Thus, radio advertisers soon devised strategies to appeal specifically to female consumers. The first women's radio programs, sponsored by companies that produced items commonly purchased by homemakers, were largely instructional in nature. Daytime programs about cooking and sewing offered suggestions about incorporating a particular brand of food into one's menu planning or about using a particular company's clothing patterns to sew the latest fashions. These programs frequently touted the reliable advice of their "experts," who taught ordinary women how better to shop, keep house, entertain company, and generally care for their families.

By the late 1920s, women listeners regularly tuned in to hear their favorite experts give advice about homemaking. On the NBC network, a woman impersonating the fictional Betty Crocker had her own radio cooking show, during which she lauded the foodstuffs produced by her "inventor," the Washburn-Crosby Company (later General Mills). "Aunt Sammy," another fictional radio figure, offered opinions on everything from how to clean linoleum to how to cook a meatloaf. Her popular program, *The Housekeeper's Half-Hour* (later titled simply *Aunt Sammy*), was sponsored by the U.S. Department of Agriculture. Rather than promote particular brand-name products, Aunt Sammy passed along helpful hints and general information about nutrition, cooking, and housekeeping. Ida Bailey Allen, a real dietician and cooking instructor, attracted a wide audience of American housewives with *The National Radio Home-Makers' Club* program, during which she dispensed wisdom on nutrition, menus, and beauty. Unlike most other 1920s radio programs, which were supported by a single commercial sponsor, Allen's show was underwritten by several smaller companies, each of which funded only a portion of her entire program—one of radio's first examples of "spot advertisements."

ADVERTISING SWINDLES

The advertising industry attracted a great deal of controversy. Advertisers were often derided as mere hucksters and charlatans. This kind of low public opinion led, in 1911, to the founding of the Associated Advertising Clubs of America, which launched the "Truth-in-Advertising" movement. The movement marked the industry's first attempt to regulate itself, to minimize occurrences of consumer fraud, and to enhance its credibility with the American public. Advertisers felt compelled to assuage public fears that their industry would stop at nothing to sell products and that promotional claims were often purposefully misleading and not necessarily rooted in fact or science. The movement's immediate targets consisted of loan sharks, real estate speculators, and other confidence men who knowingly swindled their customers. Well-established corporations—regardless of how far their advertisements strayed from the truth—were seldom prosecuted.

Despite the good intentions of the Associated Advertising Clubs of America, advertising swindles bilked tens of thousands of Americans out of their life savings during the 1920s. One of the most notorious swindlers was the Italian immigrant Carlo "Charles" Ponzi, who launched his most famous fraudulent business scheme in Boston in December 1919. Ponzi claimed that he and his associates could make enormous sums of money for investors by taking advantage of favorable international monetary exchange rates. He promised his "clients" that he would return their capital investment, plus 50 percent, in fewer than 90 days, and this get-rich-quick scheme suckered approximately 40,000 people into handing over anywhere from $10.00 to $50,000. He did fulfill his promise to the first wave of investors, but, like all pyramid schemes, his investment business required increasing numbers of new investors to provide the money to pay off previous investors. Within a few months, Ponzi's whole scheme collapsed, and in August 1920, he was arrested for using the mails to defraud. Investigations revealed that more than $13 million of the $15 million he had collected had mysteriously disappeared and Ponzi's name became synonymous with any pyramid scheme.

Another costly investment debacle in the decade was the Florida land boom (and bust). During the early 1920s, real-estate speculators purchased large tracts of land in Florida and built grand hotels and vacation homes in the hopes of luring middle-class American families. Advertisers glamorized the image of life in Florida and enticed investors with stories of how easy it was to make money speculating in real estate. Land bought in 1920 or 1921 could be sold to another investor in 1924 or 1925 at enormous profit—sometimes 100 times more than its original purchase price. In 1925, the *Miami Daily News* published a 504-page issue that consisted almost entirely of real-estate advertisements. Readers from across the nation, most of whom never had and never would set foot in Florida, sought out realtors who were all too happy to accept their down payments by mail. Of course, this land boom could not last forever. By the mid-1920s, Florida land prices were so inflated that speculators could no longer sell their real estate at a profit, and buyers all but disappeared. To make matters worse, a devastating hurricane hit the Florida coast in 1926, destroying over 13,000 homes and killing nearly 400 people. The glamour of Florida faded in the minds of most Americans, and the land boom came to an inglorious and unprofitable end.

Architecture

of the 1920s

American architectural styles of the 1920s encompassed both traditionalism and modernism. Old-fashioned designs still appealed to those architects and consumers who appreciated, for example, the classic beauty of colonial homes and Gothic office buildings. On the other hand, new architectural trends shaped many of the homes and commercial buildings constructed during the 1920s.

ARCHITECTURAL STYLES

Art Deco

During the 1920s and early 1930s, an eclectic design style emerged that later became known as Art Deco, a name derived from the 1925 Exposition Internationale des Arts Décoratifs et Industriels Modernes, held in Paris. The purpose of the exposition was to forge a relationship between art and industry, and although American architects did not directly participate in the event, its influence reverberated in the United States for decades. The exposition featured exhibits that combined industrial technology with earlier design styles, and the result was a stylized look that juxtaposed angular, geometric forms with designs found in nature, such as sunbursts, flowers, and stars. France remained the center of Art Deco innovation until the late 1920s, but

American architects and designers soon began borrowing Art Deco themes to design everything from movie theaters and hotels to furniture and clothing. Bevis Hillier, a British art critic and historian, coined the term *Art Deco* in 1968. Prior to that, this style was often called Modernistic or Style Moderne.

Art Deco usually refers to a hodgepodge of elegant, sophisticated styles from the 1920s and 1930s, and it can describe any dramatic combination of modern technological styles and ancient artistic influences. Art Deco designs are often characterized by simplicity, dramatic geometry, and vibrant colors, and sometimes incorporate exotic patterns and iconography culled from Mayan and Aztec cultures, as well as from West Africa, India, and the Far East, and ancient Egypt, Greece, and Rome. The golden, jeweled treasures discovered when English archaeologist Howard Carter unearthed King Tutankhamen's tomb in 1922, for example, became an important source of inspiration for Art Deco design. Art Deco became fashionable for everything from earrings to skyscrapers.

Some of the most enduring examples of Art Deco style are found in the American architecture of the 1920s. Architecture historians often divide the Art Deco period into two major categories: decorated Art Deco, popular primarily between

Chrysler Building, New York City, 1930. Prints & Photographs Division, Library of Congress.

1926 and 1936, and streamline Art Deco, popular throughout the 1930s. While streamline Art Deco buildings look simple, with rounded corners, small windows, and wide, smooth expanses of metal or glass, decorated Art Deco buildings tend to be highly ornamented with abstract, geometrical, or floral designs inspired by the 1925 exposition. New York City's elaborate Chrysler Building, constructed between 1928 and 1930, remains perhaps the most famous American example of decorated Art Deco architecture from the 1920s.

The International Style

The International Style of architecture originated in Europe, but its influence pervaded the United States during the 1920s and 1930s. Its leaders included Walter Gropius, Ludwig Mies van der Rohe, and Charles-Edouard Jenneret (who went by the name Le Corbusier). Among the early American proponents of the International Style were architects Raymond M. Hood, Albert Kahn, Richard J. Neutra, and George Howe. The term derived from a 1932 book called *The International Style* by historian and critic Henry-Russell Hitchcock and architect Philip Johnson. The book, along with the 1932 International Exhibition of Modern Architecture at New York's Museum of Modern Art, generated widespread publicity for this style.

The International Style exerted considerable influence on American architecture, particularly office buildings and skyscrapers, during the 1920s. International Style buildings tended to be geometric and streamlined, with flat roofs and smooth facades, and were constructed primarily of inexpensive, mass-produced modern materials such as concrete, steel, and glass. Many resembled enormous boxes, which is essentially what they were. Even today, the skylines of American cities contain streamlined International Style banks and office buildings that lack any superfluous decoration. Although some critics considered International Style buildings boring and unimaginative, others saw beauty in the clean, crisp lines and sharp angles of these functional buildings.

SKYSCRAPERS

The technology of steel skeletons and elevators ushered in towering urban structures, and no buildings represent more fully the dramatic changes and sweeping optimism of Jazz Age America than these majestic skyscrapers in cities across the United States. By 1929, the nation had 377 skyscrapers taller than 20 stories; 188 were in New York City.[1] Skyscrapers symbolized both the nation and a particular company's innovation and power. Old buildings were razed and new landmarks were erected, including New York's Barclay-Vesey Building (1923–1927), the

Architecture

McGraw-Hill Building (1929–1930), the Chrysler Building (1928–1930), and the American Standard Building (1923–1924); Chicago's Tribune Tower (1922–1925); and San Francisco's Pacific Telephone and Telegraph Building (1924–1925). These magnificent structures declared to the entire world the spectacular success of American business.

As new skyscrapers vied for the title of tallest building in various cities, Americans became increasingly attracted to the ever-rising skylines of the urban landscape. Indeed, much of the attraction of skyscrapers lay in their awe-inspiring appearance, for seldom did they garner immediate profits for their owners. Designing and building a skyscraper was tremendously expensive, and once constructed, the rents paid by the tower's tenants often barely covered the elevator and maintenance costs. Nevertheless, the buildings' psychological appeal proved irresistible, and dozens were designed and planned during the boom years of the 1920s, although many were not completed until the 1930s.

A turning point for American skyscraper design came in 1922, when the Chicago Tribune Company sponsored a design competition for the construction of a new office tower. The *Tribune's* owner, Colonel Robert R. McCormick, offered a prize of $50,000 for the most beautiful and functional design, and the contest drew 281 entries from around the world. The winners were Americans John Mead Howells and Raymond M. Hood, who designed a huge Gothic tower topped by a tall, narrow spire. The architectural world, however, preferred the second-place entry, submitted by the Finnish architect Eliel Saarinen (the father of architect Eero Saarinen, who later designed St. Louis's Gateway Arch). Saarinen's design looked almost like a mountain and its crown looked more like a gently tapering pyramid. Although the Howells-Hood design was used, Saarinen's design exerted a more powerful influence on future American skyscraper design.

The Philadelphia Savings Fund Society Building (1929–1932), often considered the first truly modern American skyscraper, incorporated the sleek geometry of the European-influenced International Style. Designed by the American George Howe and the Swiss William Lescaze, the building combined modern style with urban practicality. It housed small shops on the ground floor, with the banking floors rising above it and offices above that. It was only the second skyscraper in the nation to offer air-conditioning as a standard feature in its rental property and was one of the first constructed with a dropped ceiling of acoustical tile.

Skyscrapers of the 1920s varied widely. Some featured crowns that resembled terraced pyramids, while others were flat-roofed, rectangular slabs. Architects who designed skyscrapers in New York City also had to contend with the city's 1916 zoning ordinance that, to prevent tall buildings from blocking too much sunlight from the streets below, required building walls progressively to set back from the building line as they rose from the base. When the setback building had been reduced to one-quarter of the size of the entire site, the building could continue to rise upward without getting any smaller. Architects responded by designing buildings that tapered toward the top, in a stair-step or ziggurat fashion, thus admitting plenty of sunlight to the surrounding city blocks. Although city laws imposed no actual limitations on a skyscraper's height, the required setbacks effectively constrained building heights because, after a certain point, it was not economical to build tall, thin buildings with limited commercial space on the upper floors.

The most famous skyscraper designed during the 1920s was New York City's Empire State Building. The building, begun in 1930 and completed in 1931, incorporated striking Gothic styles and elaborate outside detailing, including a mast intended for mooring dirigibles (the mast was never used for this purpose, although it later served as a television antenna). The plans for the 1,250-foot, 102-story Empire State Building—at the time the tallest building in the world—were approved only one month before the October 1929 stock market crash. As a result of the severely depressed economy, builders drastically compressed the construction schedule—the entire structure was completed in only 410 days and came in well below its estimated $50 million budget.

The 1,046-foot, 77-story Chrysler Building, designed by architect William Van Alen, is a notable example of Art Deco architecture as well

Typical skyscraper construction of the period. Shown here, a building going up in St. Louis, Missouri. Prints & Photographs Division, Library of Congress.

as an important New York City landmark. The building boasted an innovative heating system and 32 high-speed elevators, inlaid with exotic woods from around the world. The exterior ornamentation reflected the new technology of the automobile, with enormous decorative car wheels, radiator caps, and steel eagle gargoyles—replicas of the 1929 Chrysler hood ornament. The spire on top emerged from shiny crescent-shaped steps designed to resemble a silver sunburst—a popular Art Deco motif.

CHURCHES AND TEMPLES

The 1920s saw a new trend in American church architecture: the skyscraper church. The bottom few floors of these high-rise churches

were devoted to the church itself, while the upper floors were reserved for offices and apartments. The rent from the upper floors helped to finance the operation of the church below. One of the more impressive skyscraper churches was the Chicago Temple of the First Methodist Episcopal Church, completed in 1924. This 568-foot skyscraper was, at its completion, both the tallest church in the world and the tallest building in Chicago. The lower five floors comprised the 2,000-seat church, along with a gymnasium, classrooms, and meeting rooms. An illuminated revolving cross atop the church's spire could be seen for miles. The floors between the church and the spire were rented to various companies. Other skyscraper churches were erected in Detroit, San Francisco, and several other major cities. The Northwest Methodist Temple in Minneapolis, for example, generated revenue from a hotel that occupied one entire wing and most of the building's 300-foot tower. These skyscraper churches combined traditional religious devotion with the new cult of American business prosperity.

Church architects were generally slow to adapt to architectural innovations, and most churches constructed during the 1920s featured more traditional Gothic, Roman Classic, Baroque, or Georgian styles. For example, All Souls' Unitarian Church in Washington, D.C. (1923), was built in classic Georgian style. And some churches in the West and Southwest, such as St. Vincent de Paul Catholic Church in Los Angeles (1925), adopted architectural styles derived from Spanish traditions.

UNIVERSITY, GOVERNMENT, AND INDUSTRIAL ARCHITECTURE

The construction of college and university buildings soared in the United States as enrollment in higher education increased. Between 1920 and 1930, the number of students enrolled in the nation's colleges and universities increased from approximately 600,000 to almost 1.2 million students.[2] Clearly, more classroom buildings were needed to accommodate such a flood of undergraduates. Wealthy industrialists and businessmen gave educational institutions money to construct new buildings, dormitories, and libraries.

An old stereo print of the Lincoln Memorial, for 3-D viewing, which had just been finished in 1922. Prints & Photographs Division, Library of Congress.

Although several major institutions of higher learning were founded during the 1920s, many existing colleges and universities expanded their campuses. Much of this university construction incorporated older, more traditional styles rather than the new look of Art Deco or International Style architecture. For example, the Harkness Quadrangle at Yale University, designed by James Gamble Rogers in the Beaux-Arts Gothic style, added a dramatic focus to the campus when it was built in 1921. The Harvard Business School's design competition in 1925 led to a cluster of new red-brick Georgian buildings. In 1924, James B. Duke, the founder of the American Tobacco Company, established a $40 million endowment to create Duke University in Durham, North Carolina, on the site of what was formerly a small school called Trinity College. The Duke family spent $19 million rebuilding the old campus and adding 11 Georgian-style buildings, made of red brick and white marble, between 1925 and 1927. This campus housed the undergraduate college for women. Between 1927 and 1930, a new campus, built in the Tudor Gothic style out of native North Carolina stone, was constructed one mile to the west of the original campus to house the undergraduate college for men and the professional schools.

Federal, state, and local governments constructed impressive new monuments, courthouses, and office buildings. Architect Bertram Grosvenor Goodhue's innovative 1920 design for the Nebraska State Capitol included a 400-foot tower rising from a low, square base. Construction was completed in 1928 for just under $10 million. The 1920s also saw the federal government commission the construction of a new building for the Department of Commerce. In 1929, President Herbert Hoover, the secretary of commerce during the Coolidge administration, laid the cornerstone for the building, which, when completed in 1932, was the largest office building in the world.

During the 1920s, the innovative design of new manufacturing plants increased the productivity of these factories. Automobile tycoon Henry Ford was only one of the American industrialists who sought to incorporate the most modern design elements into his factories. Industrial architect Albert Kahn designed the Ford Motor Company's enormous River Rouge plant (constructed between 1918 and 1926) on the outskirts of Detroit, Michigan. Kahn developed well-proportioned, bright, and efficient plants, which took into account how assembly lines functioned, at the 2,200-acre River Rouge complex. The entire complex was self-sufficient and contained everything necessary for the production of automobiles, including blast furnaces, steel mills, foundries, an engine plant, a glass factory, a tire plant, and its own power generators.

LINCOLN MEMORIAL

Commissioned in 1867 by Congress, the Lincoln Memorial did not undergo construction until 1911, when President William Taft signed a bill to begin the project. Eleven years later, and 57 years after Lincoln's assassination, the memorial of our sixteenth President was completed in all its glory: 36 Doric columns (representing the 36 states that were members of the Union at the time of Lincoln's assassination) each measuring 37 feet in height, a 19-foot statue of Abe himself, and two 60-foot long murals representing the achievements of the Savior of the Union. The memorial was designed by architect Henry Bacon, the magnificent sculpture of a seated Lincoln was carved by Daniel Chester French, and the murals were painted by Jules Guerin.

A number of notable events have occurred at the memorial, from African American contralto singer Marian Anderson's Easter Sunday performance in 1939, to Dr. Martin Luther King Jr.'s famous "I Have a Dream" speech in 1963, to, the Rockettes, swinging their legs on the steps of the memorial for President G. W. Bush's 2001 inaugural celebration. The memorial has also been featured in dozens of popular films, including *Mr. Smith Goes to Washington* (1939), *JFK* (1991), *Forrest Gump* (1994), *National Treasure* (2004), and *Wedding Crashers* (2005). So popular has Honest Abe's marble tribute become that several urban legends have developed around it. One such legend proclaims that Lincoln is forming his initials in sign language with each hand. Another insists that Robert E. Lee's face is etched on the back of Lincoln's statue. Although dispelled as just myths, such widespread buzz surrounding a national monument only gives credence to the stature of Lincoln's legacy. As his gaze rests contemplatively over the reflecting pond in the National Mall, tourists regularly crowd the platform securing his chair for a photo op with the Great Emancipator.

Other automobile manufacturers, including General Motors, soon constructed similar plants.

RESTAURANTS

During the 1920s, restaurant architecture, especially the interiors of lunchrooms and cafeterias, reflected the modern styles. While lunchrooms and cafeterias were often located in larger downtown buildings of varying architectural styles, the interiors of these restaurants typically featured simple, sanitary, and functional designs. Often walls and ceilings were painted gleaming white to emphasize the cleanliness of the restaurant. Floors were covered with easy-to-clean tile or linoleum. Counters, tabletops, and stools were made of porcelain enamel, which was impervious to grease and dirt. Refrigerators, stoves, sinks, dishwashers, and coffee urns were clad in sparkling stainless steel. The most up-to-date restaurants even installed air-conditioning systems. This emphasis on new, shiny, man-made materials made these modest restaurants some of the most modern-looking public places in the 1920s.

The White Castle hamburger chain, which was founded in Wichita, Kansas, in 1921, launched the multi-billion-dollar fast-food industry. White Castle became the first American restaurant chain to develop its own recognizable architectural style. The first White Castle buildings, freestanding structures modeled after the architecture of Chicago's famous Water Tower, were constructed of rusticated concrete blocks—a cheap and popular building material. The tops of the walls were built like the ramparts of a medieval castle, and one end of the building sported a corner turret. Throughout the 1920s, White Castle experimented with other building materials, including stucco and white enameled brick, before finally settling on durable, prefabricated porcelain-enameled steel panels. The restaurant chain's combination of distinctive medieval architecture and inexpensive, fast-food service proved tremendously popular with American diners. Most importantly, although these restaurants started out small—only 10 by 15 feet—they were easily identified by passers-by. By the end of the 1920s, other restaurant chains had adopted their own distinctive architectural styles.

MOVIE PALACES

Unlike the standardization of restaurant chains, the grand movie palaces built during the 1920s each boasted a unique design. The large movie theaters found in the downtown business districts of major cities featured some of the most opulent and ornate architecture of the decade, and their luxurious interiors created the sensation that attending a film was a special experience. The Roxy Theatre (billed as America's "Cathedral of the Motion Picture"), built in 1927 near New York City's Times Square, seated nearly 6,000 patrons. Its immense lobby and foyers contained a dozen five-story green marble columns and an oval rug, woven to order, that weighed more than two tons. Movie palaces featured lavishly appointed smoking lounges, rest rooms, and powder rooms, and many were among the first public buildings to install air-conditioning systems. Babysitting facilities were included in the price of admission at

America's "Cathedral of the Motion Picture," the Roxy Theater, with a view of the orchestra pit and stage, New York City, 1927. Prints & Photographs Division, Library of Congress.

many movie palaces, and some featured kennels in which to board patrons' pets during the film. The largest theaters, such as the Roxy and San Francisco's Fox Theatre (built in 1929), even had adjoining hospitals to tend to patrons' medical emergencies. Even small theaters tried to furnish elegant surroundings and amenities.

Most palaces, particularly their exteriors and lobbies, were inspired by classical European architecture. In fact, many theater exteriors and interiors replicated Old World churches, monuments, and palaces. La Salle de Spectacle, the eighteenth-century opera house at Versailles, served as the model for the Ringling Theatre, constructed in Baraboo, Wisconsin, in 1915. The theater lobby featured a one-third-scale replica of the frieze decorating the choir gallery in the cathedral at Florence. The lobby of San Francisco's spectacular Fox Theatre boasted throne chairs, statuary, and a pair of vases once owned by Russian czars. Its picture gallery was an exact replica of a Versailles chapel, and the curtain was made out of gold kidskin, padded lamé, 2,500 glass reflectors, and silk rope fringe.

Foreign influences also included Egypt and the Far East. Grauman's Egyptian Theatre (1922), built by Sid Grauman in Hollywood, featured a forecourt lined with massive Egyptian columns, hieroglyphics, and huge dog-headed Egyptian god statues. Employees dressed as robed Bedouins carrying spears paced the building's parapet all day long. Grauman's Chinese Theatre, which opened a few blocks away in 1927, resembled a giant red pagoda and had images of huge silver dragons on the ceilings.

One of the most important and influential theater architects of the 1920s was the Scottish-born Thomas W. Lamb, who designed more than 300 movie houses (mostly for Loew's theater chain) during his career. Many of Lamb's elegant movie theaters contained elaborately decorated domed ceilings constructed to resemble nineteenth-century European opera houses. His Loew's State Theatre, constructed in St. Louis in 1924, incorporated Corinthian columns, marble balustrades and staircases, and ornate fountains. In 1927, he designed the incredibly lavish Loew's Midland Theatre in Kansas City, Missouri. This 4,000-seat baroque and rococo temple contained more than six million square inches of silver and gold leaf, mahogany walls topped by plasterwork cherubs, a dome hung with two elaborate crystal chandeliers, and valuable antiques purchased from tycoon William K. Vanderbilt's demolished New York City townhouse.

In 1923, Austrian-born John Eberson created another style of movie palace when he designed the Houston Majestic, the nation's first "atmospheric" theater, in Houston, Texas. Atmospheric theaters could be built for just a fraction of the cost to build a standard domed theater, because their ceilings consisted of a plain concrete surface that was painted midnight blue. By projecting images onto the ceiling with a device called the Brenograph magic lantern, these theaters gave audiences the sensation of watching a film under a night sky filled with clouds, moon, stars, and even an occasional airplane. Other visual images could also be projected onto the ceiling, including the Northern Lights, angels, butterflies, fire, lightning, rainbows, and volcanoes. The walls of the atmospherics were usually decorated to resemble open courtyards in various exotic locales. Chicago's Avalon Theatre (1927), one of Eberson's most elaborate projects, combined Middle Eastern decor with projected ceiling images to suggest the feeling of being in a Persian mosque. Loew's Paradise (1929), built in the Bronx for $4 million, contained an auditorium that was designed to give moviegoers the impression they were sitting in an extravagant Venetian palace.

GAS STATIONS

Prior to World War I, most filling stations were little more than a shed with a gas pump out front. But beginning around 1917, larger gas stations began to appear, with multiple pumps and indoor offices. Since filling stations competed to sell products—gas and oil—that were virtually indistinguishable from station to station, owners soon realized that they had to attract consumers based on the facility itself. During the early 1920s, most gas stations were built to resemble small, neat houses. These homey structures blended in with the houses in surrounding residential neighborhoods and projected an image of friendliness. Just as some of the nation's leading restaurant chains

attempted to create their own unique architectural style, some oil companies hired architects to design a particular style of gas station that motorists could readily identify with their brand of gasoline. For example, the Pure Oil Company built filling stations that looked like charming English cottages, and Socony-Vacuum built its stations to look colonial houses, Chinese pagodas. Other companies designed stations to look like Chinese pagodas, suburban bungalows, Spanish haciendas, or mini-Tudor mansions.

During the mid-1920s, many filling stations began to expand their services to include not only gasoline fill-ups and oil changes but also engine repairs, tire changes, battery and headlight replacements, and other services. Filling station added service bays and storage rooms onto their existing structures, which soon required an architectural style different from that of a little house. Architects created the "box-style" station, which contained an office, bathroom, utility room, service area, and one or more garage bays configured in a rectangular layout. The gasoline pumps were usually located on islands a short distance away from the service area. These box stations remained the standard in gas station architecture until the 1930s, when those constructed in the Streamline Moderne style eclipsed them in popularity.

MIMETIC ARCHITECTURE

During the 1920s, motorists would occasionally encounter freestanding buildings that resembled enormous windmills, Indian heads, root beer barrels, pigs, cows, castles, tepees, coffee pots, and other fanciful designs. This architectural style, known as mimetic or programmatic architecture, was intended to provide publicity for a business and to attract customers. Typically, the shape of the building in some way represented the business housed within. For example, a Dayton, Ohio, business that sold Liberty Bonds during World War I was built in the shape of an enormous cash register, and the Big Pump, a Maryville, Missouri, filling station, was constructed to look like a big gas pump. The famous Brown Derby restaurant in Hollywood, completed in 1926, resembled a gigantic hat. While mimetic architecture existed prior to the 1920s, this style became popular as modern advertising techniques increasingly pressured Americans to consume.

RESIDENTIAL ARCHITECTURE

The overwhelming majority of American homes built during the 1920s reflected traditional, conservative architectural styles. In particular, middle-class Americans preferred homes that reminded them of a English cottage, an Spanish villa, a French farmhouse, or a colonial mansion. Homeowners gravitated toward these classic styles, even as they filled their traditional-looking houses with the latest electric appliances and modern conveniences. Of course, a few American houses were built in the modern Art Deco or International Style.

Many subdivisions across the nation contained row upon row of bungalows, which featured an efficient floor plan arranged around a central living room, a low sloping roof, wide eaves, and a prominent front porch supported by two or more columns. Porches were perhaps the most consistent feature of bungalow houses, providing comfortable spaces for people to cool off in hot weather and to visit with their neighbors.

During the 1920s, many new houses were built in either the American Four-Square or Prairie Box styles, both of which featured a simple box-shaped floor plan. These houses were taller than regular bungalows—usually two or two-and-a-half stories high—with four rooms on each floor. American Four-Square homes often featured a large dormer window on the front of the house, and, like the popular bungalow, a large front porch. Inside, they resembled the bungalow with their open floor plans and built-in shelves and cabinets. Like bungalows, Four-Square houses were popularized by the sale of blueprints in pattern books, catalogs, and mail-order kits.

Colonial Revival houses were also common sights in the American suburbs of the 1920s. These houses were usually shaped like rectangular two-story boxes, and they often incorporated elements of Federal or Georgian architecture from the late eighteenth and early nineteenth centuries. Tudor-style houses, based on architectural

"Own Your Own Home." This ad from Sears Roebuck and Co. promotes their home building plans.

styles from sixteenth-century England, also became fashionable during the 1920s. These houses usually featured steeply pitched, front-facing gables, tall windows, and distinctive ornamental half-timbering. Tudor-style houses were traditionally clad with stucco or masonry, but in the 1920s, with the advent of new masonry veneering techniques, many of these homes were built to resemble the look of brick or stone without their considerable expense.

The Spanish Colonial Revival style (sometimes called Spanish Eclectic) took its inspiration from the Spanish churches, forts, and houses of the American Southwest. Many homes in Florida, California, and the Southwest that were built in this style featured red tile roofs, arched windows, decorative railings, and stucco siding. This style of residential architecture gained popularity after the 1915–1916 Panama-California Exposition held in San Diego. This style reached its zenith in the 1920s and early 1930s but fell rapidly out of favor during the 1940s.

INTERIOR DESIGN

Middle-class Americans during the 1920s consciously decorated their homes and offices to reflect their personal style and taste. While Art Deco and the International Style exerted considerable influence on those individuals most attuned to architectural and stylistic trends, most Americans favored more traditional design styles. General advice about interior decorating was easy to find. *House Beautiful, Arts & Decoration, Fruit, Garden and Home* (founded in 1922 and renamed *Better Homes & Gardens* in 1924), and other national magazines offered suggestions about how to arrange furniture, acquire antiques (or reproductions), and generally make one's home more attractive. Even fashion magazines such as *Vogue* and *Harper's Bazaar* published occasional articles about interior design. Eager to capitalize on the newfound interest in home decorating, publishers released dozens of interior design guidebooks, including Ethel Davis Seal's famous *Furnishing the Little House* (1924). Wealthy and fashionable homeowners often hired professional designers to provide them with interior decors that were elegant, tasteful, and harmonious.

Although few people completely furnished their homes with Art Deco objects, this style did creep into the living rooms, bedrooms, and kitchens of millions of ordinary Americans. Oriental-looking lacquered screens, stylized ceramic statues, geometrically patterned floor coverings, inlaid dressing tables, and goods constructed of man-made materials such as plastics, glass, and chrome all represented the new Art Deco look. Certain mass-produced items, such as sleek tubular furniture and objects made of colorful Bakelite plastic, also contributed to the elegant and sophisticated look of Art Deco interior design that became fashionable in middle-class American homes.

Albert Kahn

Albert Kahn (1869–1942) was the most influential and prolific industrial architect of the 1920s. He specialized in designing automobile factories and, despite his lack of a college education or professional training, designed more than 1,000 buildings throughout the course of his career, many of them for Ford, Chrysler, Packard, and other major automobile manufacturers. Born in Germany, Kahn and his family immigrated to Detroit in 1880, when he was 11 years old. He apprenticed with a Michigan architect, George D. Mason (a partner in the Detroit firm of Mason and Rice), and started his own architectural firm in 1895. In 1904, while designing his tenth Packard automobile factory, Kahn suggested using a new building technique—reinforced concrete. His innovative design solidified Kahn's career in industrial plant design.

In 1918, Kahn began constructing the Ford Motor Company's enormous Rouge River plant, which, when completed in 1926, became the largest single manufacturing complex in the United States. Kahn relied on simple geometric shapes and modern materials, such as steel roof trusses and glass walls, to create facilities that were as pragmatic and efficient as the assembly lines they housed. Although Kahn became particularly well known for his bright, well-proportioned factories, he also designed and built office buildings, banks, and even private homes, including Edsel Ford's estate in Grosse Pointe Shores, Michigan.

What made Kahn great was that he had no formal educational training. Where most of the other draftsman could boast of degrees from prestigious schools, Kahn could only boast of his grit and determination, which he did not. Kahn went on to build well over 1,000 buildings in his lifetime, including many enormous industrial buildings for manufacturers like Chrysler, in addition to Ford. He impressed later artists and thinkers like La Corbusier, who was interested in expressions of modern life.

Raymond M. Hood

Raymond M. Hood ranks as one of the most renowned architects of the Art Deco period. Born in Rhode Island, he attended Brown University, the Massachusetts Institute of Technology, and the premier architecture school in the world at the time, the École des Beaux-Arts in Paris. Hood's first major commission came when he (along with John Mead Howells) won the *Chicago Tribune* Company's architecture contest in

1922, and they subsequently designed the Gothic skyscraper. Hood's success led to other important commissions, including the auditorium and foyer of New York City's Radio City Music Hall, the RCA Building at Rockefeller Center, and the Daily News Building.

William Van Alen

William Van Alen is best remembered as the innovative designer of the Chrysler Building in New York City, arguably the greatest Art Deco skyscraper ever built. Van Alen studied in Brooklyn at the Pratt Institute and then, after spending several years working in various New York architectural firms, won the 1908 Lloyd Warren Fellowship, which allowed him to travel to Paris to study at the École des Beaux-Arts. Upon returning to New York in 1911, he earned a reputation for designing commercial structures that defied traditional conventions. Van Alen was one of the first architects to use stainless steel over a large exposed building surface, as exhibited on the Chrysler Building. Even today, the Chrysler Building's shiny tower remains one of the Manhattan skyline's most recognizable landmarks.

Paul Revere Williams

Paul Revere Williams, a Los Angeles native, was one of the foremost commercial and domestic architects of southern California and the first African American architect to be admitted as a fellow in the American Institute of Architects. His numerous commissions to design homes for Hollywood celebrities led to his nickname, "the Architect to the Stars." His clients included such motion picture and television stars as Lon Chaney, Bill "Bojangles" Robinson, Tyrone Power, and, in later decades, Frank Sinatra, Lucille Ball and Desi Arnaz, and Zsa Zsa Gabor. Over the course of his career, Williams designed close to 3,000 homes, commercial buildings, and government structures and became one of the most successful African American architects of the twentieth century.

Frank Lloyd Wright

In 1922, Frank Lloyd Wright finished supervising the construction of the impressive Imperial Hotel in Tokyo, Japan, which was built on an innovative "floating foundation" designed to withstand earthquakes. (See "Architecture of the 1910s.") Later that year, after returning to the United States, Wright began to experiment with architectural forms and structures based not on the traditional rectangles and squares but on circles, spirals, arcs, and angles. He also spent considerable time during the decade corresponding with leading European architectural thinkers, and his work and ideas were widely disseminated in architectural and design journals throughout the world. In 1928, Wright began writing his autobiography (first published in 1932 as *Frank Lloyd Wright: An Autobiography*), which explained his complex theories of architecture.

Books

Newspapers, Magazines, and Comics of the 1920s

The 1920s was a decade of innovative, experimental, modernist writing. Many important writers and poets found their first audiences during the 1920s, including F. Scott Fitzgerald, Ernest Hemingway, William Faulkner, T. S. Eliot, Ezra Pound, and e. e. cummings. African American writers such as Langston Hughes, Zora Neale Hurston, and Claude McKay also entered the literary scene, in a movement now known as the Harlem Renaissance. Readers' tastes varied from popular best-selling fiction to serious works of non-fiction to splashy pulp magazines.

BOOKS

Best-Selling Novels

Although dozens of literary masterpieces were published during the 1920s, few were reading T. S. Eliot's *The Waste Land* (1922) or William Faulkner's *The Sound and the Fury* (1929). Authors who combined romance, history, and intrigue in their novels often attracted a large fan following. Best-selling fiction writers of the 1920s included Sinclair Lewis, Zane Grey, Edna Ferber, Dorothy Canfield, Booth Tarkington, Temple Bailey, and Edith Wharton.

The advent of subscription book clubs in the 1920s boosted the careers of many writers and brought millions of books into American homes. In 1926, Harry Scherman started the Book-of-the-Month Club, which became an immediate hit among regular book buyers. Members received a novel each month that had been selected by literary "experts," and the success of this club spawned a number of rival organizations, including the Literary Guild, founded in 1927. Subscription book clubs attracted tens of thousands of members and helped influence the books that made the bestseller lists. The Book-of-the-Month Club's first selection, in April 1926, was the British writer Sylvia Townsend Warner's debut novel, *Lolly Willowes* (1926), a story about an unmarried woman in post–World War I Britain.

Novels by such female writers as Edna Ferber, Temple Bailey, Gene Stratton-Porter, Mary Roberts Rinehart, and Kathleen Norris regularly topped the book sales charts. Many of these novels feature sexually liberated heroines who had adopted the radical, freethinking philosophies commonly associated with the rebellious flapper. For example, Diana Mayo, the sensual heroine in E. M. Hull's *The Sheik* (1921), and Lorelei Lee, the sexy gold-digger in Anita Loos's *Gentlemen Prefer Blondes* (serialized in *Harper's Bazaar* in 1925), each embody certain aspects of the "New Woman," who could live an independent life and enjoy sex just as much as men. These heroines were more liberated than the typical fictional protagonists of the day. The majority of popular women's novels center on young women who had adopted the trappings of flapperdom, but by the story's conclusion, they become devoted wives and mothers.

BEST-SELLING WRITERS

Sinclair Lewis

Sinclair Lewis was an American writer who appealed to both general audiences and literary critics of the 1920s. A prolific novelist, playwright, satirist, and social critic, Lewis became, in 1930, the first American to receive the Nobel Prize in literature. He was nominated for the Pulitzer Prize for *Main Street* (1920) and *Babbitt* (1922) and won it for *Arrowsmith* (1925). He declined the award, however, claiming that the award was intended to honor a novel that celebrated American wholesomeness, and his novel did no such thing. Indeed, much of Lewis's fiction satirized what he saw as America's preoccupation with crass materialism, and he ridiculed how unbending conformity to small-town ideals could stunt one's potential. Audiences responded enthusiastically to Lewis's biting social commentary, and several of his popular novels were made into movies, including *Main Street* (1923), *Babbitt* (1924 and 1934), and *Arrowsmith* (1931).

Lewis' greatest literary success was *Main Street,* the top-selling novel in 1921. The novel traces the story of Carol Kennicott, a freethinking modern woman who finds herself in constant conflict with the expectations of the local townspeople of Gopher Prairie (a town based loosely on Lewis's hometown of Sauk Centre, Minnesota). After marrying the young town doctor and settling down in his hometown, she attempts to bring what she considers beauty, art, and other forms of cosmopolitan "culture" to the community. Carol's efforts are frustrated by the pettiness of the townspeople, and through her story Lewis satirizes the narrow-mindedness of small-town life and attacks the unyielding conformity and dulled intellect of its residents.

Lewis's next novel, *Babbitt,* considered by many critics to be his finest work, made the best seller

lists in both 1922 and 1923. The novel focuses on real estate agent George F. Babbitt, a modern-day slave to consumerism, advertising, and social status, who resides in the Midwestern town of Zenith. Babbitt takes such inordinate pride in his middle-class home, his automobile, and his zealous Zenith "boosterism" that the term *Babbittry* soon became synonymous with unthinking conformity and shallow, materialistic values. Lewis's next best seller, *Arrowsmith,* depicts the life of a medical doctor caught between idealism and commercialism. Lewis had two other best sellers in the 1920s: *Elmer Gantry* (1927) and *Dodsworth* (1929).

Zane Grey

Perhaps the single most popular author in America during the post-World War I years was Zane Grey, although he never garnered the critical acclaim that Sinclair Lewis did. Grey wrote more than 60 novels in which he presented the landscape of the American West as a moral battleground that had the power either to destroy or to redeem his characters. His stories usually dealt with settlers, cowboys, desperadoes, Indians, cattle drives, family feuds, and other familiar aspects of Western lore. Grey achieved widespread acclaim with the release of *Riders of the Purple Sage* (1912), which sold over two million copies and was adapted for motion pictures three times. During the 1920s, Grey hit the best seller lists with *The Man of the Forest* (1920), *The Mysterious Rider* (1921), *To the Last Man* (1922), *The Wanderer of the Wasteland* (1923), and *The Call of the Canyon* (1924), all of which were adapted for the silver screen. Grey sold over 17 million copies of his novels during his lifetime, and some estimates suggest that more than 100 films have been based on his stories.

Edna Ferber

Although Edna Ferber began publishing novels in 1911, her first best seller, *So Big* (1924), solidified her popular success. The inspirational story of Selina DeJong, a young woman struggling to raise her son on a small farm outside Chicago, *So Big* won the Pulitzer Prize in 1925 and was immediately made into a silent film (other movie adaptations followed in 1932 and 1953). A number of Ferber's novels were translated into popular movies during the 1920s. *Show Boat* (1926), the story of three generations of the Hawks family on board a Mississippi riverboat, was made into several films, a successful musical, and a radio program. *Cimarron* (1929), a Western dealing with the opening of the Oklahoma Territory, was filmed for the first time in 1931. While Ferber was a popular novelist, literary critics appreciated her writing style far more than that of most other popular writers of the 1920s.

Mary Roberts Rinehart

Mary Roberts Rinehart was a tremendously popular mystery and detective writer during the 1920s. One of her books produced the famous whodunit phrase, "The butler did it," and in her heyday she was more famous than her chief rival, British writer Agatha Christie. *The Circular Staircase* (1908), the first of Rinehart's many mystery novels, established her as a leading writer of the genre; in 1920, this novel was adapted into a film titled *The Bat*. In the 1920s, Rinehart wrote primarily romantic fiction including *A Poor Wise Man* (1920), *The Breaking Point* (1922), and the suspenseful *Lost Ecstasy* (1927).

Non-Fiction Best Sellers

Several historical studies, particularly military ones, hit the non-fiction best-seller lists during the decade, including Philip Gibbs's *Now It Can Be Told* (1920), H. G. Wells's *The Outline of History* (1920), and Hendrik Van Loon's *The Story of Mankind* (1921). Bruce Barton, a veteran salesman and advertiser, published his best-selling *The Man Nobody Knows* (1925), which portrayed Jesus Christ as a dynamic salesman who, with his staff of 12 managers, founded a highly successful global organization called Christianity. Diet and health guidebooks also sold well. Dr. Lulu Hunt Peters's *Diet and Health, With Key to the Calories* was originally published in 1918, and by 1922, it had already gone through 16 editions. *Diet and Health* ranked among the best-selling non-fiction books every year between 1922 and 1926, the first

American diet book to do so. Cookbooks were also big sellers during the 1920s. For example, Fannie Farmer's *The Boston Cooking-School Cook Book* made the best seller list between 1924 and 1926. Readers also sought help from Emily Post's *Etiquette in Society, in Business, in Politics and at Home* (1922), which today is in its seventeenth edition.

Self-help books were a relatively new phenomenon in the 1920s. Émile Coué, a French psychotherapist, published the first popular self-help book in America, *Self-Mastery Through Conscious Autosuggestion* (1922). He posited that self-suggestion could boost confidence and motivation and recommended that his followers chant the optimistic mantra: "Day by day, in every way, I am getting better and better."[1] Coué founded institutes to teach his principles.

Perhaps the most unusual non-fiction best seller of the 1920s was the first book published by Simon and Schuster: *The Cross Word Puzzle Book*

Books

NOTABLE BOOKS

Main Street, Sinclair Lewis (1920)

The Age of Innocence, Edith Wharton (1920)

Ulysses, James Joyce (1922)

The Waste Land, T. S. Elliot (1922)

The Velveteen Rabbit, Margery Williams (1922)

Etiquette, Emily Post (1922)

The House at Pooh Corner, A. A. Milne (1923)

The Voyages of Doctor Doolittle, Hugh Lofting (1923)

A Passage to India, E. M. Forster (1924)

The Cross Word Puzzle Book (1924)

The Great Gatsby, F. Scott Fitzgerald (1925)

The Sun Also Rises, Ernest Hemingway (1926)

Winnie-the-Pooh, A. A. Milne (1926)

Coming of Age in Samoa, Margaret Mead (1928)

The Sound and the Fury, William Faulkner (1929)

All Quiet on the Western Front, Erich Maria Remarque (1929)

A Room of One's Own, Virginia Woolf (1929)

A Farewell to Arms, Ernest Hemingway (1929)

(1924). This was the first book devoted to crossword puzzles, and although booksellers initially balked at stocking this unconventional volume, it sold hundreds of thousands of copies, sparked a national craze for crossword puzzles, and ensured Simon and Schuster's success. (See "Sports and Leisure of the 1920s.")

MODERNIST FICTION

Some of the best-known American literature from the 1920s falls under the category of "modernism," which is a term used to describe literature that addresses the perceived breakdown of traditional society and culture under the pressures of modernity. Modernism traces its roots to Europe and was inspired, in part, by the devastating effects of World War I. Modernist literature could take a number of forms, from the dense, allusive poetry of T. S. Eliot to the sparse, minimalist dialogue of Ernest Hemingway. Modernist stories and poems omit many details and explanations, often end without resolution, and challenge readers to interpret for themselves a work's ultimate meaning. A common effect of this fragmented style of writing is that the work often appears to lack continuity, a unified plot, or easily identifiable heroic figures. Not surprisingly, most readers passed over great modernist works of fiction and instead reached for their favorite Zane Grey western or Mary Roberts Rinehart mystery.

One of the foremost modernist writers, Mississippi-born novelist William Faulkner, wrote magazine stories and published his first two novels, *Soldier's Pay* (1926) and *Mosquitoes* (1927), to little popular acclaim. Faulkner experimented with language, psychology, and point of view in *The Sound and the Fury* (1929), but this now-celebrated novel was not particularly well received in its time. Novelist and short story writer Ernest Hemingway fared considerably better during the 1920s. His first novel, *The Sun Also Rises* (1926), catapulted him to international celebrity and resulted in a wave of American tourists traveling to Spain to see the Pamplona bullfights that he so glamorously immortalized in the book. Hemingway soon became known for his distinctive writing style, which was characterized in part by short, stripped-down sentences in which much

was left unsaid, yet still allowed careful readers to comprehend exactly what was meant.

F. Scott Fitzgerald

F. Scott Fitzgerald, the darling of the American literary scene during the 1920s, managed to bridge the gap between popular fiction and serious literature. His name was often associated with all-night partying and carousing during the Jazz Age, an era that he himself named. Fitzgerald commanded high prices for his short stories, which he frequently placed in *The Saturday Evening Post, The Smart Set,* and other magazines. His first novel, *This Side of Paradise* (1920), portrayed the flamboyant exploits of self-indulgent, pleasure-seeking, college age youth. He followed with three collections of short stories—*Flappers and Philosophers* (1921), *Tales of the Jazz Age* (1922), and *All the Sad Young Men* (1926)—and two more novels—*The Beautiful and Damned* (1922) and his best-known work, *The Great Gatsby* (1925). Scott and his wife Zelda (Sayre) Fitzgerald, also a

Ernest Hemingway. Prints & Photographs Division, Library of Congress.

F. Scott and Zelda Fitzgerald on their honeymoon, from a photograph taken in 1920. Prints & Photographs Division, Library of Congress.

THE GREAT GATSBY

The Great Gatsby, written by F. Scott Fitzgerald and published in 1925, is regarded by some critics and readers as one of the greatest novels of all time. A staple in high school and college curricula, the novel has become synonymous with the roaring twenties and the high time had by many after World War 1. Indeed, Fitzgerald referred to the 1920s as the great cocktail party, and the Depression of the 1930s, the hangover. The story is told from the first person peripheral point of view of Nick Carraway, a would-be banker with a literary bent, who moves east and rents a house next to the mysterious Jay Gatsby. Gatsby embodies the American Dream gone awry. Born to a poor family, Gatsby falls in love with a girl named Daisy, Nick's third cousin, before the war, only to be jilted because of his financial prospects. From that point forward, Gatsby devotes his life to becoming rich and winning Daisy. At the outset of the novel, Daisy is married to athletic, racist, and rich Tom Buchanan. The two live in a luxurious home next to Gatsby, who has purchased a mansion next door in hopes of impressing Daisy with his wealth. The novel unfurls in a brutal tragedy whereby Gatsby is shot and killed, his material aim in life seemingly all for nothing. *The Great Gatsby* may be both a cautionary tale, warning of the perils of greed and avarice, and a beautifully observed story of ambition, careless wealth and power, yearning, and love.

talented writer and artist, personified the mood of the 1920s—they were a fun-loving, irreverent, adventuresome pair who loved to party and to spend money recklessly.

POETRY

The American poetry scene was remarkably diverse in the 1920s. Modernist poets such as Ezra Pound, T. S. Eliot, Amy Lowell, Wallace Stevens, and William Carlos Williams developed innovative verse forms and techniques (such as free verse and imagism), while more traditional poets such as Robert Frost, Edna St. Vincent Millay, and Edward Arlington Robinson were more popular with critics and the public. The most acclaimed poet of the 1920s was Edward Arlington Robinson, who won the Pulitzer Prize three times during the decade: *Collected Poems* won in 1922, *The Man Who Died Twice* won in 1925, and *Tristram* won in 1928. Poet Conrad Aiken, winner of the Pulitzer Prize in 1930 for his *Selected Poems* (1929), edited and published the *Selected Poems of Emily Dickinson* in 1924 and effectively launched her posthumous literary reputation.

Robert Frost ranked as one of the most popular American poets during the 1920s, in part because he wrote what appeared to be folksy, traditional poems. Unlike the deliberately difficult poems of Pound and Eliot, Frost's poems evoked nostalgic scenes of the farms, forests, and country people of New England that readers found a refreshing change from their increasingly urban surroundings. In 1924, Frost won the Pulitzer Prize for his *New Hampshire: A Poem with Notes and Grace Notes.*

Edna St. Vincent Millay, the first female poet to win a Pulitzer Prize (for *The Ballad of the Harp Weaver* in 1923), became famous during the 1920s as much for her bohemian lifestyle in Greenwich Village, New York, as for her poems. Although she wrote about seemingly "old-fashioned" subjects, such as nature, romantic love, death, and even poetry itself, she also dealt candidly with issues of sexuality, rebellion, and the liberated woman. Her outspokenness, as well as her combining of traditional verse forms with quintessentially modern sensibilities, garnered her a larger audience than most other American poets of the decade enjoyed.

Books

THE HARLEM RENAISSANCE

The Harlem Renaissance, sometimes called the Negro Renaissance or the New Negro Movement, describes the period roughly between the end of World War I and the onset of the Great Depression, during which African Americans produced a vast number of literary, musical, and artistic works. The artists associated with the Harlem Renaissance attempted to create new images of African Americans and celebrate their traditions in order to destroy old racist stereotypes. The works they created were, for the most part, confident, positive, and optimistic about the future of black Americans.

During the 1920s, approximately 700,000 African Americans left the South for Harlem and other northern urban-industrial centers, where, they believed, they would find greater freedom and better job opportunities. [2] Thousands of black families crowded into Harlem, a large neighborhood in upper Manhattan loosely defined in the 1920s as the area between 110th and 155th streets. New York City's black population soared from more than 152,000 in 1920 to nearly 328,000 by 1929. [3] Harlem became an important cultural crossroads, as young African Americans flocked to Harlem to join the growing colony of black intellectuals fueling the Harlem Renaissance.

Writers including Langston Hughes, Countee Cullen, Claude McKay, Zora Neale Hurston, Jean Toomer, Walter White, Rudolph Fisher, Nella Larsen, and Wallace Thurman produced poems, novels, short stories, essays, and plays that encouraged readers to appreciate African American culture and its folk roots. African American journals such as *The Crisis, The Messenger,* and *Opportunity* published essays, articles, and stories by black writers. In 1925, Alain Locke, an African American philosopher, critic, and editor, published *The New Negro,* the first literary anthology of the Harlem Renaissance. Contributors included McKay, Hughes, Toomer, Cullen, W.E.B. Du Bois, James Weldon Johnson, and Gwendolyn Bennett. The works in this volume gave voice to the African American cultural revolution that was taking place in metropolitan black communities across the country.

Black culture fascinated many white people, who believed that it was inherently exotic,

Zora Neale Hurston in 1938. Photo by Carl Van Vechten. Prints & Photographs Division, Library of Congress.

primitive, and exciting. Wealthy white New Yorkers and tourists came to Harlem in droves during the 1920s, "slumming," as they called it, in jazz cabarets and speakeasies. White readers regularly purchased books written by Harlem Renaissance authors, and white writers frequently penned laudatory introductions to these volumes. A number of white writers even incorporated what they believed to be African American themes of exoticism and sensuality into their own writing, most notably playwright Eugene O'Neill, who wrote *The Emperor Jones* (1920) and *All God's Chillun Got Wings* (1924), and novelist Carl Van Vechten, whose 1926 *Nigger Heaven* sparked considerable controversy among both black and white readers. Some wealthy white patrons provided living expenses and small stipends to black writers, thus allowing them to pursue their art without having to hold down regular jobs at the same time.

ZORA NEALE HURSTON (1891–1960)

Author Zora Neale Hurston was a member of the New Negro Movement of the 1920s and 1930s, later called the "Harlem Renaissance," during which African American artists representing a variety of fields began creating work that was representative of the African American experience, rather than imitative of white artists. Hurston spent her childhood in Eatonville, an all-black community in Florida, where she observed African Americans in leadership roles in the town, and her unusual environment played a major role in shaping her personality and literary style. Her happy childhood came to an end when her mother died when Hurston was 13, and problems with her stepmother led her to go off and struggle on her own to survive. Eventually, she won a scholarship to Barnard College in New York. After receiving a degree in anthropology in 1928, Hurston began publishing essays, poems, plays, and books, first in school magazines and later for a national audience. Hurston's work often explored aspects of rural African American life and proved appealing to both African American and white readers. Among her most lasting works was the novel *Their Eyes Were Watching God,* published in 1937, which told the story of Janie Crawford, a young African American woman who, over the course of the novel, engages in three romances, each a unique blend of passion and tragedy. When her work began to lose favor in the late 1940s, she took a succession of jobs to support herself, but died in poverty in Fort Pierce, Florida. Author Alice Walker brought Hurston's work to academic prominence in 1975, after it had been largely forgotten, calling *Their Eyes Were Watching God* Hurston's most important book. While some criticized Hurston for pandering to white audiences with her tales of "quaint" African American life, others, like Walker, praised her for creating works that reached across color lines with passionate prose and a timeless view of human culture.

By most accounts, the heyday of the Harlem Renaissance ended with the stock market crash of October 1929.

MAGAZINES

American readers purchased popular magazines in record numbers during the 1920s, and hundreds of new magazines were founded.

General Audience Magazines

In February 1922, DeWitt and Lila Wallace began publishing *Reader's Digest,* a compilation of news, entertainment articles, and fiction that had been culled from other magazines and reprinted (often abridged). The magazine was marketed as a convenient way to manage the overwhelming amount of information available in the modern age. *Time,* the nation's first weekly news-magazine, debuted in March 1923. Its founders, Yale graduates Henry Luce and Briton Hadden, believed that Americans needed a magazine that covered a broad range of general news,

from international affairs and science to religion and business developments. *Time's* relatively short, easy-to-read articles enabled busy readers to stay abreast of their fast-changing world, and the magazine's early foray into radio advertising (in 1926) helped boost its weekly circulation to nearly 200,000 readers by the end of the decade. *The Saturday Evening Post* also emerged as one of the more popular magazines in the 1920s. Editor-in-chief George Horace Lorimer hired some of America's most talented writers and illustrators, including Sinclair Lewis, Ring Lardner, F. Scott Fitzgerald, and Norman Rockwell. *The Saturday Evening Post* is considered by many readers and historians to be an accurate reflection of the pro-business and consumerist values of white middle-class Americans. *Life,* although primarily a humor magazine, also included book and theater reviews, verse, sketches, light articles, and illustrations by some of the finest artists of the decade. It struggled during the Great Depression, and, in 1936, was sold to Time, Inc., which reinvented *Life* as a photojournalism magazine.

"Teaching old dogs new tricks." A *Life* magazine cover by John Held Jr., showing a young flapper and an elderly man dancing the Charleston, 1926. Prints & Photographs Division, Library of Congress.

Women's Magazines

A number of periodicals were specifically marketed to middle-class women during the 1920s, including *Good Housekeeping, McCall's,* and *Women's Home Companion.* These magazines featured short stories and serialized novels, recipes, dress patterns, and household tips. Other popular women's magazines, such as *Harper's Bazaar* and *Vogue,* focused primarily on clothing and fashion. The undisputed giant among women's magazines, however, was *Ladies' Home Journal,* which, in 1904, became the first American magazine to reach a circulation of one million readers. *Ladies' Home Journal* targeted a readership of married, white, middle-class women who took their roles as wife, mother, and homemaker seriously. The magazine offered short stories, household and decorating tips, and recipes. As a matter of principle, it refused to run advertisements for alcohol, tobacco, playing cards, patent medicine,

or other products considered of questionable moral value.

Magazines for the Smart Set

The so-called smart magazines, such as *The Smart Set: A Magazine of Cleverness* (1900), *Vanity Fair* (1913), *American Mercury* (1923), and *The New Yorker* (1925) found a receptive audience in the 1920s. These witty and entertaining periodicals catered primarily to educated, middle

WORDS AND PHRASES

bee's knees

bingo! (as an interjection)

boho (Bohemian, unconventional)

boogie-woogie

delish

dream team

fat cats

flapper

gaga

gut-buster

heebie-jeebies

intergalactic

It girl

jeepers (interjection)

jive

magic bullet

mojo

nifty

recycle

ritzy

robot

superstar

tearjerker/weepie (for a sad or tragic film)

whoops

wimp

wisecrack

wow

and upper-middle-class readers. Amid articles about restaurants, fashion, theater, art, and other topics, smart magazines published early works by F. Scott Fitzgerald, Dorothy Parker, Theodore Dreiser, Eugene O'Neill, and Edna St. Vincent Millay. Smart magazines managed to walk a fine line between highbrow magazines such as *The Atlantic Monthly* and *Harper's Monthly* and the more highly commercialized, broad-based magazines such as *The Saturday Evening Post* and *Life*. Smart magazines appealed largely to those who wanted to read more intellectual material than the mass-circulated periodicals provided.

Little Magazines

Small, non-profit literary magazines of the 1920s, such as *Poetry: A Magazine of Verse* (founded 1912), *The Little Review* (1914), *The Dial* (1917), *Broom* (1921), *The Fugitive* (1922), *Transition* (1927), and *Hound and Horn* (1927), were known as "little magazines." The magazines' limited circulations marked them as "little." These magazines experienced a renaissance in popularity in the 1920s. Editors of little magazines were usually willing to publish avant-garde and experimental literature. They were often the first to publish the work of modern writers and critics, such as T. S. Eliot, Gertrude Stein, William Carlos Williams, and James Joyce. Because commercial success was not a primary objective of these periodicals, little magazines tended to generate small circulations and often went out of business only a handful of issues.

Pulp Magazines

Pulp magazines, a periodical genre that flourished between the 1920s and the 1940s, were lurid, mass-produced fiction magazines. Pulp magazine covers were made of smooth, shiny paper stamped with colorful pictures of beautiful women, hard-nosed detectives, rugged cowboys, and even monsters from outer space. Inside pages were made of cheap, porous "pulp" paper, which kept publishing costs down and which gave the magazines their nickname. The pulp paper yellowed and began to disintegrate within months,

which makes many of these magazines tremendously valuable to collectors today. Only black ink was used inside the magazine, but many stories were lavishly illustrated with line drawings. Pulp magazines ranged in price from 5 to 25 cents—less than half the price of a typical periodical—and attracted huge numbers of readers from all walks of life, especially the working classes.

By the 1920s, hundreds of pulp magazines were being published. Some pulp magazines enjoyed large subscription circulations, but most of them survived on newsstand and drugstore sales. Most pulp magazines can be classified into a handful of general categories, but some magazines appealed to a narrow target audience, including *Secret Service Stories* (1927), *Firefighters* (1929), and *Railroad Man's Magazine* (1929).

Crime fiction and detective story magazines attracted large numbers of readers. *Detective Story Magazine* (1915) was the first fiction pulp to dedicate itself to this particular genre of story, and it

Cover of *Weird Tales: The Unique Magazine,* April 1924. Prints & Photographs Division, Library of Congress.

soon spawned dozens of imitators. In 1920, H. L. Mencken and George Jean Nathan, the editors of the sophisticated but unprofitable magazine *The Smart Set,* introduced the highly successful *Black Mask.* Several famous detective fiction writers, including Dashiell Hammett, Raymond Chandler, and Erle Stanley Gardner, received their literary start by publishing in *Black Mask* and other detective pulps. Hard-boiled private eyes such as Race Williams and Sam Spade were born in the pages of these magazines, and Hammett's *The Maltese Falcon* first ran as a 65,000-word, five-part serial novel in *Black Mask* (from September 1929 to January 1930). By the end of the 1920s, dozens of pulps, including *Real Detective Tales and Mystery Stories* (1925), *Clues* (1926), and *Detective Fiction Weekly* (1928), featured crime and detective stories.

Other genres of pulps abandoned all sense of reality. Audiences fascinated by stories of horror, fantasy, and the supernatural could read *Weird Tales* (1923), *Ghost Stories* (1926), or *Tales of Magic and Mystery* (1927). These magazines launched the literary careers of several well-known American authors, including H. P. Lovecraft, Robert E. Howard, Ray Bradbury, and Edmond Hamilton. In 1928, *Weird Tales* published the first story by 14-year-old Thomas Lanier "Tennessee" Williams, who went on to become a celebrated American playwright. Science fiction—then called "scientification"—found outlets in publications such as *Amazing Stories* (1926), *Science Wonder Stories* (1929), and *Air Wonder Stories* (1929). *Amazing Stories* also fostered the formation of some of the earliest science-fiction fan clubs. The magazine published a readers' column that included the mailing addresses of its correspondents. Soon, science fiction enthusiasts began contacting one another directly and started to form fan clubs across the nation.

Pulp magazines such as *The Argosy* (1882) and *Action Stories* (1921) offered stories about strapping he-men engaged in thrilling situations in the South Sea Islands, the Amazon, and other far-off locales. *The Argosy* actually began as a general fiction magazine, but in the 1920s its focus shifted to adventure stories. The top adventure magazines always strove for as much realism as possible and often hired real-life travelers and explorers to contribute their most exciting tales. Edgar Rice Burroughs, one of the most popular pulp writers, contributed his famous *Tarzan of the Apes,* in its entirety, to the October 1912 issue of the adventure pulp *All-Story Magazine* (1905). This inspired a national Tarzan craze that lasted throughout much of the 1920s, even though by that time Burroughs had gone on to write hundreds of other adventure tales. *Adventure* advertised a "membership" that supplied each reader with an identification card. If the reader were killed or injured while carrying the card, according to the magazine's publicity, someone coming upon the body could contact the magazine, which would then contact the person's next of kin. This became a tremendously successful marketing ploy, and some of these card-carriers eventually formed the Adventurers' Club of New York.

Several pulp magazines commemorated the drama, tragedy, and heroism of World War I. Publications such as *War Stories* (1926), *Battle Stories* (1927), *Air Stories* (1927), *Flying Aces* (1928), *Navy Stories* (1929), and *Submarine Stories* (1929) glorified the military engagements of the Great War and cashed in on a sense of nostalgia that certain Americans felt for the first war of the modern industrial age.

Western and cowboy pulps, including *Western Story Magazine* (1919), *The Frontier* (1924), *Cowboy Stories* (1925), and *Wild West Weekly* (1927),

NEW MAGAZINES

Architectural Digest, 1920

Black Mask, 1920

Better Homes and Gardens, 1922

Reader's Digest, 1922

Time, 1923

True Romance, 1923

True Detective, 1924

New Yorker, 1925

Amazing Stories, 1926

Parents, 1926

Weekly Reader, 1928

Business Week, 1929

provided adventure stories about cowboys, out-laws, and frontiersmen. Some western pulps, including the 15-cent *Western Story Magazine,* sold as many as 500,000 copies a week. Many of the writers for these pulps had never actually *seen* the American West, but readers didn't seem to notice. Stories ranged from nostalgic, pastoral recollections of pioneer life to tales about the violent, gunslinging world of horse thieves and Indian attacks.

Stories about love and romance also played an important role in the pulp magazine industry. For the most part, these pulps targeted a female readership, with titles such as *Love Story Magazine* (1921), *Lover's Lane* (1923), and *Heart Throbs* (1928). The female protagonists were inevitably positive and appealing characters who, after a series of trials and setbacks, usually ended up either engaged or married to their true love. A few love story magazines, such as *Ranch Romances* (1924) and *Western Romances* (1929), blended genres in order to tap in to the widespread popularity of cowboy stories.

Sex pulps—a sensational spin-off of the love story pulps—also flourished during the 1920s. These magazines typically sprinkled their stories with obvious sexual innuendos, lengthy descriptions of beautiful, semi-clad women, and racy "true confessions" stories. Although Americans of every background purchased these titillating publications, sex pulps were primarily targeted toward working-class male audiences and were usually sold under the counter at cigar stores, as opposed to the newsstands, where most other pulps were available. To dodge the authorities during a decade when various "blue laws" were intended to limit, if not eliminate, the trade in sexual literature, these magazines relied on such euphemistic titles as *Snappy Stories* (1912), *Pep Stories* (1916), and *Saucy Stories* (1916), the latter of which, like *Black Mask* and the sex magazine *Parisienne* (1915), was edited by H. L. Mencken and George Jean Nathan. These pulps also included sex-advice columns, book reviews, humorous pieces, letters from readers, and advertisements for lingerie and sex merchandise such as performance-enhancing tablets and breast-augmentation products.

One sub-genre of the sex pulps was true-confession magazines, which started with the

H. L. MENCKEN (1880–1956)

Henry Louis Mencken, an American newspaperman, author, and literary and social critic was born and lived in Baltimore, MD. During his heyday, the decade of the 1920s, he was one of the most influential figures on the American Scene. Mencken, a prolific writer who wrote over ten million words in his career, had many interests. He wrote on food and drink, books, music, philology, politics, religion, and a myriad of other topics. Mencken's prose is usually a delight to read, and much of it is extremely funny—a detriment, as it has led some critics to class him as a humorist and to ignore his serious thought. He scorned and ridiculed pretension and provincialism, but he was also, at times, racist and anti-Semitic in his writings.

An ardent and vocal opponent of Prohibition, Mencken wrote letters and essays railing against the Volstead Act and was quoted as saying, "I drink exactly as much as I want, and one drink more." A frank enthusiast of Friedrich Nietzsche, Mencken's influence can be seen in critics such as Harold Bloom and others who are not afraid to champion less-favored ideas, especially liberal trends.

For just some of the information available on Mencken and his writing, see The Mencken Society Home Page. http://www.mencken.org/.

founding of *True Story Magazine* in 1919. By the mid-1920s, monthly sales of *True Story Magazine* reached two million, making it one of the best-selling pulps. Ordinary people, not professional writers, supposedly wrote for true-confession magazines, which were characterized by first-person accounts of shocking rendezvous and scandalous encounters. Among the most famous titles were *True Confessions, True Experience, True Romance,* and *Secrets.*

NEWSPAPERS

During the 1920s, more than 2,000 dailies were published. In 1920, an estimated 27 million Americans regularly read newspapers; 10 years later, that number had climbed to almost 40 million.[4] But as circulation skyrocketed, the overall number of American newspapers declined. Giant newspaper chains, the largest of which were owned by William Randolph Hearst and the Scripps-Howard chain (led by E. W. Scripps and Roy W. Howard), began acquiring and then consolidating small-town papers across the nation. The central office of each syndicate provided its chain of newspapers with common stories, columns, editorials, and features written for a national audience. Thus, many newspapers during the 1920s shifted their focus from covering exclusively local news to following more national and international events. Some critics complained about this "standardization" of American newspapers and the decline of local news coverage, but the widespread availability of Hollywood gossip, box scores, comic strips, and financial news appealed to many readers.

While serious journalism thrived during the 1920s, tabloid journalism emerged as the newspaper industry's equivalent of the lucrative pulp magazines. Tabloid journalists concentrated on sensational stories about celebrities, murder trials, sex scandals, and public tragedies, such as when silent screen legend Fatty Arbuckle was charged with raping and murdering a young actress in 1921, and when millionaire bootlegger George Remus shot his wife in 1927. Tabloids, which were only half the size of regular newspapers and full of photographs, began when Joseph Medill Patterson launched the New York *Illustrated Daily News* in 1919 (later the *New York Daily News*). By 1924, his paper had garnered a circulation of 750,000 customers—the largest newspaper circulation in the nation. Rival tabloids soon emerged, including William Randolph Hearst's New York *Daily Mirror* (1924) and Bernarr Macfadden's *New York Evening Graphic* (1924), nicknamed the "Evening Pornographic" for its lurid illustrations and photographs. The *Evening Graphic* became particularly famous for its use of "composographs," or photographs superimposed on one another to create an entirely new (and often ludicrous) image. For example, after film sensation Rudolph Valentino died in 1926, the tabloid ran a "photograph" of Valentino in heaven, standing next to his deceased Italian countryman, opera star Enrico Caruso, who had died in 1921. Because of their immense profit-

ability, tabloid newspapers soon spread beyond New York City, but all could be characterized by their shocking headlines and lurid stories of sex, scandals, violent crimes, sports, and gossip.

ILLUSTRATION

The expansion of book publishing, modern ad campaigns, and mass circulation magazines led to an increase in the use of illustrations. Many artists and painters turned to commercial illustration, which could be an extremely lucrative profession, and some became household names during the 1920s.

Of all the artists and illustrators of the 1920s, nobody better captured the gaiety and freewheeling spirit of the Jazz Age than did illustrator John Held Jr. His images of the long-legged, long-necked, short-skirted flapper and her round-headed, spindle-necked boyfriend adorned the covers and pages of *Life, The New Yorker, Cosmopolitan,* and other national magazines. These characters were often depicted engaged in such activities as joy riding, smoking, dancing, or golfing. Held also drew dozens of satirical (and inaccurate) maps for *The New Yorker* that poked gentle fun at, for example, the plethora of antique shops in a particular location or the thousands of bootleggers and rumrunners that surrounded the nation's borders during National Prohibition. Additionally, he created memorable advertisement illustrations for Van Heusen shirts, Planter's Peanuts, and Packard automobiles, among others.

Artist and illustrator Ralph Barton's subjects often included movie stars and other celebrities, and his drawings appeared in books and magazines such as *Vanity Fair* and *The New Yorker.* Barton's illustrations for Anita Loos's best-selling book *Gentlemen Prefer Blondes* (1925) brought to life one of the decade's most famous fictional flappers, Lorelei Lee.

Norman Rockwell continued to be one of the most popular illustrators and painters. Rockwell had begun to work professionally in the 1910s and went on to create thousands of images for magazines, posters, advertisements, and calendars during his more than 40-year career, including more than 300 covers for *The Saturday Evening Post.* Rockwell also worked as the primary illustrator for a series of youth magazines, including *Boy's Life, Youth's Companion, St. Nicholas,* and *American Boy.* His wholesome, conservative images of white middle-class experiences represented, for generations of citizens, mainstream American life.

N. C. Wyeth illustrated dozens of adventure books, including a new edition of *Robinson Crusoe* (1920), and contributed hundreds of story illustrations to such magazines as *McCall's* and *The Saturday Evening Post.* Neysa McMein painted every cover for *McCall's* magazine between 1924 and 1936, as well as oil portraits of such notables as President Warren Harding, film comedian Charlie Chaplin, and poet Edna St. Vincent Millay.

CARICATURE

After World War I, the popularity of caricature grew dramatically. *Vanity Fair* routinely commissioned hundreds of these entertaining images of interesting personalities. The popularity of this irreverent, witty drawing during the 1920s was

Caricatures became popular in the 1920s. The Broadway actress Marie Cahill is shown in a caricature by Al Hirschfeld in 1927. Prints & Photographs Division, Library of Congress.

closely related to the rise in the culture of celebrity in general.

Artist Al Hirschfeld became famous for his distinctive line drawings and caricatures of actors and theater performances. He sold his first caricature to the *New York Herald Tribune* in 1926. Hirschfeld's drawings appeared in several newspapers until 1929, when he signed an exclusive contract as a caricaturist for the *New York Times.* His artwork ran in the *Times* for nearly seventy-five years, until his death at age 99 in 2003. Other caricaturists also specialized in theatrical personalities, including Alex Gard, who, in 1927, began sketching caricatures of famous actors. Eventually, these celebrated images decked the walls of Sardi's Manhattan restaurant.

COMICS

By 1924, approximately 84 percent of urban children and teenagers regularly read the Sunday funny papers.[5] Comic strips often dealt with absurd, fantastical situations, such as George Herriman's *Krazy Kat* (1916), which followed the obsessive and futile love triangle of a dog, a cat, and a mouse. (See "Books, Newspapers, Magazines, and Comics of the 1910s.")

Other strips helped Americans to make sense of their fast-changing modern world. For example, *Chicago Tribune* publisher Robert McCormick thought that a comic strip that regularly featured the automobile might make his readers more comfortable with these new contraptions. He asked illustrator Frank King to create such a comic, and the result, the long-running *Gasoline Alley* (1918), initially focused on men's interest in cars. Martin Branner's *Winnie Winkle the Breadwinner* (1920) featured a young, single secretary trying to provide for her family and find herself a good husband, marking the advent of strips featuring modern wage-earning women.

Buck Rogers in the 25th Century A.D.

In 1929, writer Philip Nowland and artist Dick Calkins introduced the first science-fiction comic strip, *Buck Rogers in the 25th Century A.D.,* effectively launching a craze for science fiction. Earlier in the 1920s, pulp fiction magazines had begun to explore the area of scientific fiction or "scientification," as it was called, but *Buck Rogers* exposed a much larger audience to outer-space exploits. The comic followed the adventures of pilot Anthony "Buck" Rogers, who initially was trapped in an abandoned Pennsylvania coal mine where radioactive gases put him into a state of suspended animation. When he awoke in 2419 A.D., he found that China controlled the world. Rogers joined the guerrilla movement and, with the help of Wilma Deering, a tireless freedom fighter and Buck's love interest, freed his nation from its conquerors. Rogers went on to face evil aliens and other adversaries with futuristic technologies such as laser beams, anti-gravity flying belts, robots, ray guns, and atomic weapons. *Buck Rogers* spawned a number of toys and books, as well as a radio program, a television program, and a series of films.

Tarzan

Coincidentally, the *Tarzan* comic strip debuted on the very day that the first *Buck Rogers* strip appeared: January 7, 1929. The character of Tarzan, however, was already 17 years old by then. Author Edgar Rice Burroughs published his short novel, *Tarzan of the Apes,* in its entirety in the October 1912 issue of the adventure pulp *All-Story Magazine.* (See "Books, Newspapers, Magazines, and Comics of the 1910s.") The story follows the adventures of John Clayton, whose parents, Lord and Lady Greystoke, are marooned on the coast of Africa. Lady Greystoke dies soon after the birth of her son, and Lord Greystoke is later killed by a band of apes. A female ape named Kala adopts the infant John and names him Tarzan, meaning (supposedly) "white skin." Tarzan, raised by apes yet constantly wrestling with his true identity, starred in more than 20 novels and more than 50 films. When *Tarzan* first premiered as a comic strip, it was essentially a graphic rendering of Burroughs's first novel, with none of the customary dialogue balloons. The text, adapted from the novel, ran below the illustrated panels, drawn by Hal Foster. During the 1930s, the *Tarzan* comic

strip was changed to incorporate dialogue and sound effects.

Little Orphan Annie

Little Orphan Annie debuted in 1924 in the *New York Daily News.* Written and illustrated by Harold Gray, *Little Orphan Annie* tracked the adventures of Annie, a spirited orphan from New York who is adopted (along with Sandy, her canine companion) by Oliver "Daddy" Warbucks, a fabulously wealthy, childless tycoon. Unlike many other comic strip characters, Annie did not possess super powers or live in the future, but she had grit, determination, and a cheerful sense of self-reliance. Annie, drawn with curly red hair and empty, pupil-less eyes, introduced her famous catchphrase "Leapin' Lizards!" into the American vernacular. The strip became increasingly political during the 1930s, as the staunchly conservative Gray infused his story lines with attacks on President Franklin D. Roosevelt's New Deal. Annie's popularity launched a popular radio serial in 1930 and a line of merchandise in the 1930s and 1940s.

Popeye

Popeye, the cartoon sailor man, made his debut in 1929 as a minor character in Elzie Crisler Segar's comic strip *Thimble Theatre.* The strip, which first appeared in 1919, followed the adventures of the Oyl family: Cole and Nana Oyl and their children Castor and Olive. In 1929, Segar introduced Popeye in a series of strips, and readers soon took to the uncouth, squint-eyed, pipe-smoking sailor. Segar made him a recurring character and then, finally, the star of the strip, which Segar renamed *Thimble Theatre Starring Popeye.* Other memorable characters included the hamburger-mooching J. Wellington Wimpy, Alice the Goon, baby Swee'Pea, and, of course, Bluto and Brutus, Popeye's archenemies and rivals for Olive's affection. Eating canned spinach gave Popeye superhuman strength, a fact that nutritionists credited in the 1930s for dramatically increasing the consumption of spinach in the United States.

Entertainment

of the 1920s

During the 1920s, commercial radio and Hollywood motion pictures attracted audiences in unprecedented numbers, but vaudeville theater declined dramatically in popularity. Socializing, especially among young Americans, frequently revolved around motion pictures, vaudeville shows, theater performances, nightclub acts, or at home "radio parties."

THEATER

Broadway Drama

While vaudeville dwindled in popularity, New York City's Broadway theater district experienced a surge of expansion. Between 1924 and 1929, 26 new theaters opened, bringing the total number of theaters to 66. Over the course of the decade, an average of 225 new shows were produced every year—a total that has never been equaled. Of course, not every New York City resident or tourist could afford to attend a Broadway show. Theater tickets sometimes cost as much as $3.50—more than 10 times the price of an average movie ticket. But hit Broadway songs were broadcast widely on commercial radio, and Hollywood studios adapted many popular theatrical productions for the silver screen, thereby boosting the influence and attraction of Broadway theater.

Critically acclaimed productions did not always attract the largest audiences. The longest running Broadway play of the decade was a critically panned comedy called *Abie's Irish Rose* (1922) which ran for 2,327 performances. The story, written by Anne Nichols, revolves around a "mixed" marriage between Abie Levy, a Jew, and Rosemary Murphy, an Irish Catholic. Despite antagonism between their families, Abie and Rosemary wed. The debate about whether the couple's first child should be raised Jewish or Catholic occupies much of the rest of the play, and the issue is conveniently resolved when Rosemary gives birth to twins.

Of course, not all Broadway theater relied on such flimsy material. Battles over censorship escalated dramatically. Religious leaders, conservative politicians, reform organizations, and even newspaper magnate William Randolph Hearst railed vociferously against theatrical depictions of content they deemed immoral, including prostitution, white slavery, and homosexuality. Eugene O'Neill's *Desire Under the Elms* (1924) and Sidney Howard's *They Knew What They Wanted* (1924), among others, prompted organizations such as the Actors' Association for Clean Plays and the Society for the Suppression of Vice to lodge formal complaints, alleging that these performances were indecent and should therefore be shut down.

NOTABLE THEATER

The Bat, 1920 (867 perfs.)

The First Year, 1920 (760 perfs.)

Peg O' My Heart, 1921 (692 perfs.)

Abie's Irish Rose, 1922 (2,327 perfs.)

Seventh Heaven, 1922 (704 perfs.)

Rain, 1924 (648 perfs.)

The Student Prince, 1924 (608 perfs.)

Is Zat So?, 1925 (618 perfs.)

Broadway, 1926 (603 perfs.)

The Ladder, 1926 (640 perfs.)

Show Boat, 1927 (572 perfs.)

Street Scene, 1929 (601 perfs.)

In 1927, the New York state legislature passed the Wales Padlock Law, which gave police broad powers to arrest the producers, playwrights, and actors involved in a production that appeared to be morally offensive. Under this law (which was repealed in 1967), if a court subsequently declared the play obscene, the theater could be closed for up to a year.

Eugene O'Neill was the most talented and influential American playwright of the decade. The son of a popular romantic actor, O'Neill accompanied his family on theatrical tours when he was a child. He began writing plays in 1913, and his first major production of the 1920s, *Beyond the Horizon* (1920), won the Pulitzer Prize. Other successes quickly followed: *The Emperor Jones* (1920), *Anna Christie* (1921, which also won the Pulitzer Prize), *The Hairy Ape* (1922), *All God's Chillun Got Wings* (1924), *Desire Under the Elms* (1924), *The Great God Brown* (1926), and *Strange Interlude* (1928). O'Neill experimented by dramatizing the emotions and memories of his characters and finding new ways to express these feelings onstage. He sacrificed realism to achieve a more emotional effect—sometimes his characters wore masks or addressed the audience directly. At other times, he had two actors play the same character, or he introduced ghosts or choruses into the story. Several of his plays feature main characters who undergo an experience so intense that they

psychologically deteriorate into their primitive, chaotic selves.

Serious dramatic theater experienced a renaissance during the 1920s. In the years surrounding World War I, more than 100 plays about the war appeared on Broadway, such as *What Price Glory* (1924), by Maxwell Anderson and Laurence Stallings. Other serious plays tackled racism, women's rights, big business, the Red Scare, and other central concerns of modern American life. Experimental dramas appeared on Broadway with regularity, and many playwrights dabbled in non-realistic portrayals of human experience. Despite the substantial success of "serious theater," many theatergoers preferred a world of song and dance.

Musical Theater

Americans audiences of the 1920s were drawn to the spectacle of musical theater. The popularity of musicals may have evolved from the well-loved vaudeville shows, or from the extravagant sets, glamorous costumes, elaborate dance numbers, and happy endings. Whatever the reason, musicals became steady favorites during the decade and paved the way for the lavish Hollywood movie musicals of the late 1920s and 1930s.

Most Broadway musicals emphasized great music and memorable dance routines rather than coherent, well-developed plotlines. For example, *No, No, Nanette* (1925) featured a forgettable story line, but some unforgettable hit songs by composer Vincent Youmans and lyricist Irving Caesar, including "Tea for Two" and "I Want to Be Happy." Occasionally, big budget musicals did take on more sophisticated, complicated plots. *Show Boat* (1927), based on Edna Ferber's 1926 novel of the same name, tackled racism and miscegenation. Its tremendous musical score, written by composer Jerome Kern and lyricist Oscar Hammerstein II, included such classic songs as "Ol' Man River" and "Make Believe." *Shuffle Along* (1921) was the first musical of the decade to be written, produced, directed, and performed entirely by African Americans. It offered the hit songs "Love Will Find a Way" and "I'm Just Wild About Harry," by composer Eubie Blake and lyricist Noble Sissle. *Shuffle Along* gave a number of talented black performers, including Florence Mills, Josephine Baker, and Paul Robeson, their first big break in show business. It also opened the door for other black musicals to appear on Broadway. Many hit musicals of the 1920s were quickly adapted to the silver screen, thus bringing their catchy songs and new dance steps to a national audience.

Musical Revues

Light musical revues—theatrical performances consisting of a series of unconnected musical acts—also remained audience favorites throughout the 1920s. Perhaps the most famous and best-loved theatrical revue of the day was *The Ziegfeld Follies,* produced by Chicago native Florenz Ziegfeld Jr. (See "Entertainment of the 1910s.") Essentially a sophisticated variety show, the show featured a rotating cast of singers, dancers, and comedians who spoofed the social and political "follies" of the day. *The Ziegfeld Follies* were inordinately expensive productions, and Ziegfeld constantly changed his roster of stars and songs to keep the show fresh and to encourage repeat customers. One aspect of the revue, however, remained constant: the chorus line of stunning young women known as the "Follies Girls"—long-legged women dressed in scanty costumes. Changes in popular taste, including Americans' insatiable love for the new talking motion pictures, caused the revue to falter in the late 1920s, and Ziegfeld produced his final *Follies* in 1931.

The George White Scandals (1919–1939), produced by George White, featured such major stars as singer Rudy Vallee and dancer Ann Pennington. Between 1912 and 1924, J. J. Shubert produced annual versions of *The Passing Show*—a revue that copied the format of *The Ziegfeld Follies* and featured headliners such as dancers Adele and Fred Astaire, singer Marilyn Miller, and comics Ed Wynn and Willie and Eugene Howard. John Murray Anderson staged a popular revue series called *The Greenwich Village Follies* (1919–1928), which became so successful that it eventually moved to Broadway.

Revues featuring African American casts also flourished, including *Runnin' Wild* (1923), the *Plantation Revue* (1922), and *Hot Choco-*

lates (1929). The most popular African American revue was the *Blackbirds* series, produced and directed by the white impresario Lew Leslie. *Blackbirds,* which premiered in 1926, introduced a series of hit songs by composer Jimmy McHugh and lyricist Dorothy Fields, including "I Can't Give You Anything But Love" (1928), "Diga Diga Do" (1928), and "Doin' the New Low Down" (1928). Black performers often traded on then-popular racist caricatures of the country bumpkin "Jim Crow," the knife-wielding urban "Zip Coon," and undomesticated children, referred to as "pickanninies" or "picks." Although these images are offensive, some African American performers of the 1920s understood that the success of a show depended on pleasing white audiences, who demanded familiar, hackneyed—and therefore "safe"—portrayals of African Americans.

DANCE

During the 1920s, professional, academic dance such as ballet did not exert much cultural influence, and in fact little high-quality ballet was performed in the United States, except by touring foreign dance troupes. The fledgling genre of modern dance was just beginning to attract audiences, largely due to the influential Denishawn School of Dance, founded in 1915 by Ruth St. Denis and her husband, Ted Shawn. Two of Denishawn's most famous and talented students, Doris Humphrey and Martha Graham, introduced dance lovers of the 1920s to the creative choreography of modern dance.

Popular Dance

Social dancing at nightclubs, dance halls, speakeasies, and in private homes became an all-consuming activity during the 1920s. The availability of hit records, the increasing affordability of radios, the popularity of vaudeville and Broadway musicals, and the ever-increasing influence of Hollywood movies combined to offer Americans unprecedented access to trendy, danceable music and models of great dancers and dances. For example, the brother-and-sister dance team of Fred and Adele Astaire helped popularize tap dancing in the Broadway musicals of the 1920s, and chorus line dancers, vaudevillians, Broadway entertainers, and movie stars all taught the American public how to fox-trot, shimmy, and tango. Being a good dancer became one avenue to popularity, particularly among high school and college age youth, so many people enrolled in dance lessons at local studios. Arthur Murray invented a correspondence course that taught customers the steps to the latest popular dances by using a lesson book with footprint diagrams and accompanying instructions. By 1925, an estimated five million people had learned to dance using the footprint diagrams they received in the mail. Later that year, Murray opened his first studio in New York City, and he began to franchise his dance studios in 1938.

Most social dancers diligently and enthusiastically imitated the dancers they saw on the movie screen or the vaudeville stage. One of the first new dance trends of the decade was the tango, sparked in part by film star Rudolph Valentino, who performed this classic Latin-American dance in the sexy opening scene of *The Four Horsemen of the Apocalypse* (1921). The early 1920s also witnessed

the rise of the shimmy, which Gilda Gray popularized in *The Ziegfeld Follies of 1922*, but nothing better symbolized the carefree spirit of the Jazz Age than the Charleston, a high-stepping version of the fox-trot that became a nationwide craze between 1923 and 1926. Although its origins remain uncertain, the Charleston was probably based upon a dance step popularized by African Americans in Charleston, South Carolina. Dancer Elizabeth Welch introduced it to the public in the 1923 all-black musical revue *Runnin' Wild*. The Charleston, which could be danced solo, with a partner, or as a group, soon took the dancing public by storm. Hotel ballrooms, cabarets, and dance halls across the nation staged Charleston contests, and Tin Pan Alley songwriters turned out dozens of new Charleston songs, such as "I'm Gonna Charleston Back to Charleston" (1925) and "Charleston Baby of Mine" (1925).

The Black Bottom, which eventually eclipsed the Charleston in popularity, was another wildly popular dance. First introduced in the all-black musical *Dinah* (1923), the Black Bottom did not become a national sensation until white dancer

A Charleston dance contest, St. Louis, Missouri, 1925. Courtesy of the Missouri Historical Society, St. Louis.

HOW OTHERS SEE US

The Charleston

The provocative Charleston—which, to the horror of an older generation, encouraged young women to dance alone and with disturbing abandon—became a full-blown craze in the United States in 1925. The dance's energetic syncopation meshed well with the hot jazz that was popular at the time, and within a year the fad crashed onto foreign shores.

As in America, reactions to the Charleston ranged from disgust to delight. The young and the fashionable latched on to the dance immediately. The Prince of Wales, a global style icon, made headlines multiple times as he danced the Charleston at balls in London and around Europe. In Paris, a world congress of dancing masters voted, albeit reluctantly, to sanction the dance as worthy of instruction, if only it could be "purified" of its "eccentric" kicks and improvisations (the very things that had made it so popular in the first place).

But in the Soviet Union, the Charleston was seen as an "immoral manifestation of bourgeois luxury" to such a degree that a Moscow choreographer was commissioned to invent a more proletarian craze. In South Africa, Christian clergymen denounced it for its similarities to Bantu and other traditional dances that missionaries were attempting to stamp out. And the District Council of Leyton, a London suburb, banned the Charleston from its local dance halls, claiming that its high kicks made it dangerous to other dancers and sparked dance-floor fights. As one impassioned speaker put it, the "fools" who attempted these perilous moves were clearly "balmy."

Ann Pennington performed it in *The George White Scandals of 1926*. Other dance crazes followed, including the varsity drag (introduced in the 1927 Broadway musical *Good News*) and the raccoon (popularized by the 1928 song "Doin' the Raccoon"). The Lindy hop, first made popular by George "Shorty" Snowden at a 1928 dance marathon, was named for aviator Charles Lindbergh. This swing dance rose to even greater popularity during the Big Band Era of the 1930s and 1940s. But the perennial favorite dance of the 1920s remained the fox trot, which had been introduced—and perhaps invented—by the nationally known dance team of Irene and Vernon Castle during the 1910s.

Many of these new dances disturbed clergymen, social workers, and older, conservative Americans, who considered them to be immoral. Some of these dances required couples to cling to each other with their cheeks and bodies touching, while other like the Black Bottom were explicitly sexual. Automobile mogul Henry Ford believed that modern dances such as the Charleston, along with jazz music, corrupted America's youth. Ford tried to revive old-time fiddling and square dancing, both of which he believed embodied the nation's wholesome, conservative values. In 1926, he staged a national fiddling contest through his Ford dealerships, offering cash prizes and automobiles to winners. He also engaged 200 dance instructors to teach square dances, polkas, and waltzes to his employees and their families. As a result, fiddling and square-dancing did witness a brief revival.

HOLLYWOOD MOTION PICTURES

After World War I, movies replaced vaudeville theater as the most popular form of commercial entertainment. By the mid-1920s, most small towns had a theater. Major cities such as New York and Chicago boasted hundreds. In 1928, the nation contained an estimated 28,000 movie theaters, which charged moviegoers 10–50 cents per ticket. The entertainment might include a newsreel, perhaps a comedy short or two, and then the feature attraction. Since films contained no synchronized sound until the advent of the "talkies" in 1927, actors and actresses conveyed emotions through pantomime acting, while a minimal number of printed intertitles between the scenes conveyed written dialogue and helped explain the plot. Most neighborhood theaters featured a pianist or organist who supplied musical accompaniment. Grand movie palaces offered large orchestras, which might contain as many as 100 members, to set the mood and heighten the drama onscreen.

HOW OTHERS SEE US

Talkies in Europe: Cinema "Degenerates"

In the early days of the film industry, critics on both sides of the Atlantic saw the cinema as a wholly new, almost magical art form. Films made in the United States and in Europe were equally prestigious and worthy of aesthetic study. And then came talkies.

With the massive popularity of 1927's *The Jazz Singer,* the first feature with significant amounts of spoken words and recorded sound, European critics in particular were taken aback. What had been a highbrow art form became quite suddenly lowbrow, in their estimation. The disappointment of the intellectual elite was palpable. British director Alfred Hitchcock thought that films with sound were merely "photographs of people talking," even as he created the first British talking picture. Critics blasted the talkies as "aesthetically reactionary," "escapist," "degenerate," and worst of all, "commercial."

The British and continental movie-going public, on the other hand, flocked to the theaters to see this new wonder—that is, when they could. Few cinemas were equipped with sound systems, and the changeover to the new technology was painfully slow. By 1930, fewer than 100 theaters in all of France could show talking pictures, and Germany had only 200 sound-ready cinemas. British theater owners were quicker to adopt the new technology, in part because the steady flow of American sound films gave them many English-language talkies to show (although occasional protests against the American accents in these films were reported).

Elsewhere, however, governments took action to prevent American cinematic dominance. For example, Italian dictator Benito Mussolini banned English dialogue in any imported movies. Soviet authorities had been accepting of American silent films, but Hollywood talkies were not allowed to be shown to Russian audiences.

During the 1920s, the Hollywood motion picture companies developed the so-called studio system. Under this system, a handful of studios—Metro-Goldwyn-Mayer (MGM), Paramount Pictures, Fox Film Corporation, Warner Brothers, and RKO Pictures—controlled every aspect of the production, distribution, and exhibition of their own films. These giant studios, nicknamed the "Big Five," owned and operated nationwide networks of movie theaters that screened only films produced by their parent company. The studios also created a subsidiary market for their movies by employing the "block booking system," which required independent theater owners to show all of a particular studio's films if they wanted to show any of them. This system guaranteed the giant studios reliable outlets for exhibiting even their low-budget films and generated annual profits that ran into the tens of millions of dollars.

Prior to World War I, studios produced films that were intended chiefly to entertain urban working-class audiences. As the industry expanded, however, Hollywood began to market its films primarily to middle-class Americans. To attract them, studios produced a greater number of big-budget epic movies with glamorous stars, sophisticated camera shots, complex plots, better-developed characters, and elaborate costuming and sets. MGM's epic *Ben-Hur: A Tale of Christ* (1925), for example, which was filmed in both Italy and southern California, cost a record $4.5 million to make. Feature films such as *Ben-Hur* usually ran between one and two-and-a-half hours, and while most were shot in black-and-white, a few of them, such as *The Black Pirate* (1926), used an early version of Technicolor. These blockbuster films increasingly celebrated the nation's newfound fascination with glamour, sex appeal, exoticism, and urbanity, and audiences loved them. By 1922, Americans purchased an average of 40 million movie tickets each week.

Hollywood motion pictures exerted a profound influence on popular culture. Americans copied the hairstyles, clothing, speech, and behavior of their favorite actors or actresses. Hollywood films not only dictated many fads and fashions, but also

NOTABLE ACTORS OF THE 1920s

John Barrymore, 1882–1942

Lionel Barrymore, 1878–1954

Clara Bow, 1905–1965

Lou Chaney, 1883–1930

Charlie Chaplin, 1889–1977

Jackie Coogan, 1914–1984

Douglas Fairbanks Sr., 1883–1939

Lillian Gish, 1893–1993

Al Jolson, 1886–1950

Buster Keaton, 1895–1966

Harold Lloyd, 1893–1971

Tom Mix, 1880–1940

Mary Pickford, 1893–1979

Norma Shearer, 1900–1983

Gloria Swanson, 1899–1983

Norma Talmadge, 1893–1957

Rudolph Valentino, 1895–1926

NOTABLE MOVIES

The Last of the Mohicans (1920)

The Four Horsemen of the Apocalypse (1921)*

The Sheik (1921)

The Ten Commandments (1923)*

The Thief of Bagdad (1924)

Ben-Hur (1925)*

The Big Parade (1925)*

The Gold Rush (1925)

The General (1927)

Flesh and the Devil (1927)

It (1927)

The Jazz Singer (1927)

Metropolis (1927)

The Crowd (1928)

The Wind (1928)

The Broadway Melody (1929)

Gold Diggers of Broadway (1929)

* Among the highest grossing films of the decade.
Source: www.filmsite.com.

ACADEMY AWARD WINNERS

1928 Picture: *Wings*

Director: Frank Borzage, *Seventh Heaven;* Lewis Milestone, *Two Arabian Nights*

Actor: Emil Jannings, *The Way of All Flesh; The Last Command*

Actress: Janet Gaynor, *Seventh Heaven, Sunrise, Street Angel*

1929 Picture: The Broadway Melody

Director: Frank Lloyd, *The Divine Lady*

Actor: Warner Baxter, *In Old Arizona*

Actress: Mary Pickford, *Coquette*

helped to fuel mass consumption and taught millions of young people about dating and sex.

Silent Film Genres and Stars

Hollywood studios released around a thousand movies each year throughout the 1920s. The most popular genres were biblical epics, melodramas, romances, historical adventures, Westerns, and comedies. Cecil B. DeMille, the single most influential director of the decade, directed and produced two great biblical epics, *The Ten Commandments* (1923) and *The King of Kings* (1927). He also made a series of lurid melodramas such as *Why Change Your Wife?* (1920), *The Forbidden Fruit* (1921), and *The Affairs of Anatol* (1921), which frankly addressed themes of sexual desire, infidelity, divorce, and other problems plaguing modern married couples. Moviegoers flocked to see romances, especially the box-office hit *Flesh and the Devil* (1927), which starred John Gilbert and Greta Garbo, one of the Jazz Age's greatest pairs of screen lovers. Garbo, a Swedish émigré

who came to the United States in 1925, established herself as a mysterious, sultry sex symbol in a series of Hollywood films, including *The Temptress* (1926), *The Mysterious Lady* (1928),

Composite of two photographs of Greta Garbo, full-length portraits; 1922 photo, wearing a swimsuit; 1931 photo, as Hollywood movie star. Prints & Photographs Division, Library of Congress.

and *A Woman of Affairs* (1929). Other romantic leading men and women included Rudolph Valentino, John Barrymore, Charles Farrell, Gloria Swanson, Clara Bow, and Janet Gaynor.

Some motion pictures of the 1920s tackled important social and cultural issues, such as World War I films like King Vidor's *The Big Parade* (1925) and Raoul Walsh's *What Price Glory?* (1926), but most box-office attractions consisted of escapist entertainment. Several classic Westerns were produced during the 1920s, such as John Ford's *The Iron Horse* (1924) and Victor Fleming's *The Virginian* (1929), starring Gary Cooper, one of Hollywood's rising leading men. In addition, studios churned out dozens of popular serial Westerns, which often featured "cliffhanger" endings. Many of the smaller independent studios produced dozens of low-budget horror films and science

fiction thrillers. By the late 1920s, gangster films increasingly captivated moviegoers, reflecting the nation's fascination with crime, corruption, and gangland warfare.

Another popular film genre was slapstick comedy, which traded on sight gags, acrobatic stunts, and physical comedy, often made even more ridiculous by wildly exaggerated acting styles. Harold Lloyd, one of the most successful silent film comedians typically portrayed an innocent "everyman" who was forever getting into improbable, but funny, situations. His comedic masterpiece, *Safety Last* (1923), features a spectacular scene in which he dangles from the hands of an enormous clock eight stories above the city street below (Lloyd did most of his own stunt work, including this scene). Another great film comedian was Buster Keaton, known as "the Great Stone

Face" for his deadpan, stoic expressions. During the 1920s, Keaton wrote, directed, and starred in a series of classic comedies, most notably *The Three Ages* (1923), *Sherlock, Jr.* (1924), *The Navigator* (1924), and the Civil War comedy *The General* (1926). The 1920s also saw the screen debut of two of the most influential comedy teams of all time. In 1927, Stan Laurel and Oliver Hardy starred in *Slipping Wives,* the first of the 105 comedies the duo would eventually make, and the Marx Brothers shot their first feature-length film, *The Cocoanuts,* in 1929. Ironically, of all the Hollywood film genres of the 1920s, slapstick comedies often contained the most biting criticisms of America's political conservatism and crass materialism.

By nearly every account, the greatest genius of silent film comedy was British-born Charlie Chaplin. (See "Entertainment of the 1910s.") One of the biggest international celebrities of the 1920s, Chaplin wrote, produced, directed, starred in—and sometimes even composed the musical scores for—some of the most critically acclaimed comedies in American cinema. A former London vaudevillian, he began working in 1914 as an actor and director in one-and two-reel comedy shorts for a series of Hollywood studios. In 1921, Chaplin directed and starred in his first feature-length film, *The Kid,* which also launched child star Jackie Coogan's career. *The Gold Rush* (1925), widely considered by cinema historians to be one of the greatest films of all time, contains two classic Chaplin routines. In one scene, snowbound and starving in an Alaskan blizzard, he dines on a Thanksgiving feast consisting of a boiled boot, and in the other, he entertains the girl he loves with a pair of dancing dinner rolls stuck on the ends of forks. Chaplin's many responsibilities on the movie set and his meticulousness as a filmmaker limited the number of films he could produce. As a result, Chaplin made only five feature films during the 1920s, the last of which, *The Circus* (1928), took him two years to complete.

All the comedies Chaplin made during the 1920s featured him in the role of his signature character, "the Little Tramp," whom he had introduced in *Kid Auto Races at Venice* (1914). His kindhearted tramp sported a toothbrush mustache, an ill-fitting suit and baggy trousers, oversized shoes, bowler hat, and a bamboo cane. Chaplin was a master of making audiences laugh, but through this innocent, trusting character, he also leveled some of the most strident social criticism seen in American film. In the guise of a tramp—a social outsider—Chaplin challenged those capitalist values of respectability, industriousness, and self-control that dominated modern American life during the 1920s and 1930s. For almost a decade after the advent of talkies, Chaplin continued to make silent films, including *City Lights* (1931) and *Modern Times* (1936), which contained only synchronized music, sound effects, and sparse dialogue (Chaplin himself has no spoken lines). He did not make his first wholly sound picture until *The Great Dictator* (1940), a savage satire of Adolf Hitler.

During the 1920s, African American directors, actors, and actresses found it exceedingly difficult to break into Hollywood's studio system. In the late 1920s, African American actors and actresses did begin to land occasional roles in mainstream films. Still, most of these roles consisted of stereotypical bit parts as butlers, maids, and "plantation darkies." Often, they played comical buffoons, shiftless ne'er-do-wells, or chicken thieves, which represented then-current racist caricatures of African Americans. For example, during the late 1920s and early 1930s, Stepin Fetchit emerged as the first bona fide black Hollywood star, but he did so largely by portraying dim-witted, shuffling "coon" characters. Late in the 1920s, several Hollywood studios exhibited a new but limited wave of interest in exploring the African American experience. In 1929, for example, Fox released the critically acclaimed *Hearts in Dixie*, an experimental talking film featuring an all-black cast, and MGM followed with *Hallelujah!* (1929), another all-black feature film.

Despite Hollywood's racist, exclusionary practices, African American cinema did succeed during the 1920s. Black actors found work in low-budget "race pictures" produced for African American audiences. Most of these movies addressed themes of African American life and racial issues seldom depicted in mainstream Hollywood movies. Small, independent black film companies, many of them founded in the late 1910s and early 1920s, produced the bulk of these movies, which featured all-black casts, including Edna Morton, billed as "the Colored Mary Pickford," and Lorenzo Tucker, "the Black Valentino." The most famous director and producer of race pictures was the pioneering African American filmmaker Oscar Micheaux. Micheaux, a pulp fiction writer, founded his own production company in 1918 in order to make a movie based on his novel, *The Homesteader* (1917). In 1920, he released *Within Our Gates,* which tackled the controversial subject of lynching. Throughout the 1920s, he made more than a dozen feature films, including *The House Behind The Cedars* (1923), an adaptation of Charles W. Chesnutt's novel, and *Body and Soul* (1924), the first film of actor Paul Robeson.

The Hollywood Star System

The fledgling Hollywood star system matured into a full-blown cultural phenomenon during the decade. Studios aggressively promoted their film stars to capitalize on the nation's fascination with celebrities. Consequently, millions of moviegoers came to idolize the glamorous movie stars. More than 25 mass-circulation magazines, such as *Motion Picture, Screenland,* and *Photoplay,* offered the latest Hollywood news, scandals, and gossip. Studio publicists kept their celebrities in the headlines by issuing press releases, staging publicity stunts, and scheduling interviews and personal appearances. Studio executives knew that the more publicity an actor or actress could generate, the more movie tickets Americans would purchase. In May 1929, in one of the industry's many efforts at self-promotion, the Academy of Motion Picture Arts and Sciences (founded in 1927) hosted the first Academy Awards ceremony at a banquet in Hollywood's Roosevelt Hotel. Those awards, which honored the films produced during 1927 and 1928, went to Emil Jannings for Best Actor, Janet Gaynor for Best Actress, and the blockbuster war epic *Wings* for Best Picture.

One of the nation's most popular actresses in the 1920s was the diminutive, golden-curled Mary Pickford, who was known as "America's Sweetheart." Pickford often starred in wholesome melodramas such as *Pollyanna* (1920) and

Sparrows (1926), in both of which she portrayed innocent young girls. Pickford's dashing, athletic husband, Douglas Fairbanks, whom she married in 1920, starred in a series of swashbuckling historical adventures, including *The Mark of Zorro* (1920), *The Three Musketeers* (1921), and *Robin Hood* (1922). Lon Chaney, known as "the Man of a Thousand Faces," thrilled moviegoers as the monstrous hunchback Quasimodo in *The Hunchback of Notre Dame* (1923) and the horribly disfigured composer Erik in *The Phantom of the Opera* (1925), one of the earliest American horror films. One of the biggest box-office draws was a German shepherd named Rin Tin Tin, whom an American officer had found as a puppy in Western Europe during World War I. From 1922 until his death in 1932, Rin Tin Tin appeared in a series of popular serials and feature films.

Playing against type, the usually demure Mary Pickford is more exotic in the movie *Rosita,* 1923. Prints & Photographs Division, Library of Congress.

The most celebrated romantic lead of the 1920s was Rudolph Valentino, an Italian immigrant—billed as "the Great Lover"—who emerged as one of Hollywood's first great male sex symbols. His darkly handsome good looks and his sexy Latin exoticism captivated millions of female moviegoers, who were said to swoon and faint at the sight of him. After his breakthrough lead performance in *The Four Horsemen of the Apocalypse* (1921), Valentino starred in more than a dozen movies, including his most famous, *The Sheik* (1921), before he died suddenly in 1926 at the age of 31. Clara Bow, the greatest female sex symbol of the decade, broke into the film industry in 1921 by winning a national contest sponsored by *Motion Picture* magazine. Over the next six years, she played a series of flappers in such movies as *Daughters of Pleasure* (1924) and *Mantrap* (1926), before becoming a silent screen sensation in *It* (1927). "It" was a euphemism for sexual attraction and self-confidence, and Clara Bow had plenty of both. With her curly, bobbed red hair, translucent white skin, and scarlet pouting "bee-stung" lips, she became the epitome of the sexy Jazz Age flapper and was known as the "It Girl" for the rest of her film career.

The Advent of the "Talkies"

The introduction of synchronized sound in 1926 revolutionized the movie industry. The most sensational early talking motion picture, though not the first, was Warner Brothers' feature film *The Jazz Singer,* released in October 1927. Although the film featured synchronized sound in only six musical numbers and in one snippet of dialogue—its star Al Jolson's famous line, "Wait a minute! Wait a minute! You ain't heard nothing yet"—*The Jazz Singer* demonstrated the

Clara Bow, the "It" girl. Prints & Photographs Division, Library of Congress.

Al Jolson, three-quarter length portrait, facing front, in blackface, kneeling on one knee, in *The Jazz Singer*. Prints & Photographs Division, Library of Congress.

enormous potential of this new technology and whetted movie audiences' appetite for talkies.[1] Studios continued to produce silent films into the 1930s, but talking films represented the film industry's future, and by mid-1928, some 300 theaters across the nation were wired to exhibit sound films. The advent of sound motion pictures boosted ticket sales. By 1930, American movie-goers were purchasing an estimated 100 million tickets each week—at a time when the nation's population was approximately 123 million.[2]

ANIMATED CARTOONS

Since the mid-1910s, short, animated cartoons lasting between one and seven minutes were often shown before feature films. Many animated cartoons, such as the *Krazy Kat* series, brought to life already-popular comic strip characters. Animated cartoons, like the films they preceded, did not incorporate synchronized sound until the late 1920s.

Felix the Cat

Felix the Cat, created by Otto Messmer and Pat Sullivan, was the first American star of animated cartoons. Felix made his debut in 1919 in *Feline Follies* and went on to appear in approximately 150 short films. Much of Felix's comedy came from his remarkable ability to transform various body parts into useful tools with which he could solve problems. Throughout the 1920s, Felix's image was licensed to toy manufacturers, cigarette companies, and other industries. He also appeared in a newspaper comic strip called *Felix the Cat* (1923), and was the subject of a popular novelty song, "Felix! Felix! Felix the Cat" (1928). When synchronized sound was introduced to cartoon animation in 1928, Felix's final silent film cartoon, aptly titled *The Last Life,* appeared in 1928. Despite a few unsuccessful attempts at a talking Felix, the cat had disappeared from the silver screen by 1930.

Walt Disney and Mickey Mouse

In 1922, Walt Disney founded an animation company in Kansas City, Missouri, called the Laugh-O-Gram Corporation, which specialized in making short, animated fairy tales. When the company went bankrupt in 1923, Disney headed to Los Angeles with his brother, Roy, where they founded the Disney Brothers Studio (later renamed the Walt Disney Company). The brothers created a series of short films based on *Alice in Wonderland,* which juxtaposed a live Alice with a cartoon background and supporting cast of animated characters. This popular series, called *Alice in Cartoonland* (1923–1927), included dozens of popular short films that were released in movie theaters nationwide.

In 1927, Disney created a new cartoon character, Oswald the Lucky Rabbit, who starred in more than 20 short animated films, but a New York distributor copyrighted the character and Disney lost control of the rabbit's image. In 1928, when he created Mickey Mouse, Disney copyrighted the mouse for himself, but his colleague, artist Ub Iwerks, was the illustrator. Mickey Mouse appeared in two 1928 silent cartoons, *Plane Crazy* and *Galloping Gaucho,* but he did not speak in his famous squeaky falsetto voice until *Steamboat Willie,* the first animated cartoon with synchronized sound, was released later that year. *Steamboat Willie* was an overnight sensation. Audiences were delighted to hear Mickey whistle, as well as play the xylophone on a cow's teeth and the bagpipes on a sow's udder. Disney began work on the *Silly Symphonies* animated series, with the first film released titled *Skeleton Dance* (1929).

RADIO

In the 1920s, radio emerged as a powerful and broadly appealing commercial mass medium. On November 4, 1920, KDKA, in East Pittsburgh, Pennsylvania, became one of the first stations in the nation to begin regularly scheduled radio broadcasts when it carried the results of the presidential election between Warren G. Harding and James M. Cox. Although only a few thousand listeners owned radio receivers at the time, this historic election-night broadcast is widely considered the birth of commercial broadcasting in the United States. Over the course of the next few years, commercial radio underwent phenomenal growth. The number of licensed radio stations operating in the United States jumped from four at the beginning of 1922 to 576 by the end of that year.[3] The sale of radios and radio equipment soared from $1 million in 1920 to $400 million in 1925.[4]

In 1926, the Radio Corporation of America (RCA) formed the nation's first radio network, the National Broadcasting Company (NBC), which actually operated two networks: NBC-Blue and NBC-Red. Originally, NBC linked 24 affiliate stations located between New York and Kansas City, but by the end of 1928, its almost 70 affiliated stations were broadcasting coast-to-coast. The Columbia Broadcasting System (CBS), established in 1927, soon created its own network of 49 affiliate stations. Before the creation of national networks, local programs showcased local talent and reflected local interests. Increasingly, though, as the influence of the networks grew, radio listeners across the nation heard many of the same programs and personalities. Network radio programs carried corporate-sponsored shows, such as *The Eveready Hour, The Majestic Theatre of the Air,* and *The Voice of Firestone,* many of which featured such national celebrities as Eddie Cantor and Will Rogers. These network shows crowded out many of the local personalities and performers who had once provided the bulk of radio entertainment, homogenizing American radio. By 1929, commercial radio had developed into a large-scale industry consisting of three national networks and some 618 stations.

Although listening to radio was essentially a private activity conducted in one's home, in many ways this new medium inspired a variety of social activities. Neighbors and friends often gathered around a family's receiver in the evening for "radio parties." Young people rolled up the rug, moved the furniture out of the way, and danced to the latest jazz sounds. Families tuned in on Sunday mornings to listen to nationally famous preachers and church services. Many listeners even scheduled their daily activities around their favorite radio shows. By 1929, according to one survey, more than 33 percent of American families owned a radio set, and of those, a reported 80 percent listened to their sets daily.[5] Thus, less than a decade after its advent, commercial radio had become an integral part of everyday life for millions.

Stations generally featured live music performed in the studios by singers and musicians. By 1924, many stations also aired so-called "remote" broadcasts (that is, those made from locations outside of the radio studio) of bands and orchestras performing in opera houses, concert halls, and hotel ballrooms. Throughout much of the decade, classical music programs, such as *The Atwater-Kent Hour* and *The Voice of Firestone,* dominated the airwaves, but eventually popular music, particularly jazz, filled daily broadcasting schedules. In 1925, music constituted approximately 70 percent of all airtime, according to one study.[6]

Radio stations required significant resources to finance operating costs. In 1922, WEAF, New York, in 1922, ran the first commercial ad, and soon advertising emerged as the primary form of revenue. Most advertising involved corporate sponsorship of programs, often musical shows. The companies included their product's name in the title of the show, such as *The Happiness Boys* (named for a candy manufacturer), *The Clicquot Club Eskimos* (named for a ginger ale maker), and *The Gold Dust Twins* (named for a scouring powder manufacturer). Network radio, on which

RADIO ACT OF 1927

The Radio Act of 1927, enacted during the presidency of Calvin Coolidge, decisively took the airwaves from the public and delivered them into the hands of the federal government. The Act outlawed anyone to broadcast any sort of radio communication without a license, and with the help of the previous Radio Act of 1912, stripped most existing licenses. Clearly, the U.S. government feared that during and since World War I, enemies home and abroad were using radio to communicate and conspire against the United States. In stripping the public its right to radio, the government set a precedent that resonates today. Nevertheless, today one can find the spirit of independent radio alive and well in college towns. Pirate radio stations all over the country are broadcasting the latest music with little or no punishment.

national corporations advertised their brand-name products, earned an estimated $40 million in revenues by 1929. In fact, between 1928 and 1934, as the number of newspaper and magazine ads declined, radio advertising leaped 316 percent.[7]

Radio also provided local and national news, market reports, weather forecasts, political speeches, public lectures, sports scores, household hints, and recipes. Broadcasts of sporting events boosted the popularity of college and professional sports and turned athletes such as Babe Ruth, Jack Dempsey, and Red Grange into heroes. Even broadcasters, particularly NBC sportscaster Graham McNamee and CBS news commentator H. V. Kaltenborn, became celebrities.

Other Programming

Special news events, such as the 1925 Scopes trial, which Chicago's WGN covered live via remote broadcasts from Dayton, Tennessee, formed an important part of broadcasting. An estimated audience of 30 million radio fans listened to NBC's extensive coverage of Charles Lindbergh's celebrated return to the United States after his historic 1927 transatlantic flight. Millions of housewives listened to homemaker shows, cooking programs, and home economics lectures as they performed their household chores.

By the late 1920s, radio networks offered more innovative and sophisticated programs, including Westerns, detective shows, soap operas, comedies, children's shows, romances, and variety shows. Particularly popular were serial comedies and dramas, which featured a cast of characters involved in an ongoing story line. In August 1929, NBC launched *Amos 'n Andy,* a 15-minute weekday show that is widely considered to be the first serial program on network radio. This program, sponsored by Pepsodent Toothpaste, starred Freeman Gosden and Charles Correll, two white vaudevillians. It recounted the adventures of the title characters, a scheming Amos Jones (played by Gosden), and a buffoonish, manipulative Andrew H. "Andy" Brown (played by Correll), black southern migrants living in Chicago who were obsessed with moneymaking schemes. Gosden and Correll wrote the scripts and performed all

RADIO DEBUTS OF THE 1920s

"The Happiness Boys" (1921): the vocal duo of Billy Jones and Ernie Hare present comic songs like "Barney Google" and "Does the Spearmint Lose Its Flavor on the Bedpost Overnight?"

"The A&P Gypsies" (1924): musical program starring Harry Horlick and his jazz band. Sponsored by the food-market chain A&P, this is the first of many sponsored radio shows to go into national syndication.

"National Barn Dance" (1924): country-music broadcast that helped establish the careers of Gene Autry, Andy Williams, George Gobel, and others.

"Grand Ole Opry" (1925): live Nashville concert program that became the premier showcase for country music, as well as the longest-running radio show in American history, continuing its broadcasts to the present day.

"Rambling with Gambling" (1925): news and talk program hosted by three generations of John Gamblings, from 1925 to 2000.

"Father Coughlin" (1926): controversial sermons on political and economic themes from a Roman Catholic priest with isolationist, anti-Semitic, and Fascistic opinions.

"Amos 'n Andy" (1928): popular situation comedy-drama about two Chicago men and their circle that drew on broad stereotypes of black life and culture.

"The Goldbergs" (1929): long-running serial about a poor family in the Bronx, New York.

"The Rudy Vallee Show" (1929): also known as "The Fleischmann's Yeast Hour," a musical and variety series hosted by singer-bandleader Rudy Vallee.

"The Guy Lombardo Show" (1929): musical broadcast featuring Guy Lombardo and his swing band.

of the characters (sometimes as many as 10 different people in a single scene), and the show's roster of minor characters eventually reached into the hundreds. Despite its racist, stereotypical characterizations, and the fact that white performers portrayed African Americans, *Amos 'n Andy* was an immediate sensation, and historians credit the show's popularity for a 23 percent surge in radio sales in 1929. Restaurants played the nightly episodes over loudspeakers in order to appease their customers, and movie theaters scheduled the showing of films around the program. After being petitioned by their employees, the managers of 40 textile mills in Charlotte, North Carolina, agreed to end their shifts 15 minutes early so that workers could listen to *Amos 'n Andy*. Expressions regularly used on the program—such as "holy mackerel," "check and double-check," and "ain't dat sumpin?"—became popular catchphrases. Within a few years, the show had spawned a syndicated comic strip, a series of phonograph recordings, a candy bar, two books, and a motion picture. In 1931, at the height of the show's popularity, an estimated 40 million fans tuned in each night, or roughly 60 percent of all radio listeners. *Amos 'n Andy* remained on the air until 1955, despite mounting protests from the National Association for the Advancement of Colored People (NAACP), and the show was also translated into a short-lived CBS television series during the early 1950s.

Fashion

of the 1920s

During the 1920s, the notion of keeping up with fashion trends and expressing oneself through material goods seized middle-class Americans as never before. Purchasing new clothes, new appliances, new automobiles, new *anything* indicated one's level of prosperity. Being considered old-fashioned, out-of-date, or—worse yet—unable to afford stylish new products was a fate many Americans went to great lengths to avoid.

FASHION AND POPULAR CULTURE

By the 1920s, the postwar explosion of magazines, newspapers, modern advertisements, radio commercials, and Hollywood films dramatically accelerated the pace of fashion developments. Americans looked to national celebrities and glamour magazines as guides to what clothing and hairstyles were in. Fashion shows and beauty contests—including the Miss America Pageant, founded by H. Conrad Eckholm in 1921 in Atlantic City, New Jersey—received widespread media coverage and showed the latest fashion trends. In 1927, Sears, Roebuck and Company advertised boots endorsed by Gloria Swanson and hats modeled by Clara Bow and Joan Crawford, knowing women would imitate their favorite Hollywood stars.

Many American consumers justified clothing expenditures as a necessary and prudent invest-

ment in one's future, reasoning, for example, that a well-dressed woman would more likely to attract a suitable husband. Older, more conservative Americans interpreted this dedication to fashion trends as another example of the recklessness and self-indulgence of the modern "flapper." Over the course of the decade the carefree flapper came to symbolize the flamboyant, reckless spirit of the Jazz Age. Perhaps more than any other icon, the flapper epitomizes those fast-changing cultural trends that many people commonly associate with the 1920s—a young woman with bobbed hair, wearing a straight, slim dress and a long, beaded necklace, drinking gin, and dancing the Charleston to the wild syncopations of a jazz band. Flappers, according to the stereotype, were daring and uninhibited trendsetters who wore their stockings rolled down and their hemlines just below the knee and let their unlaced galoshes flap around their ankles.

Despite the seeming extravagance of purchasing trendy clothing, the latest fashions were actually more affordable and accessible to ordinary Americans than they had ever been before. During the 1920s, women's clothing fashions were largely dictated by French haute couture. Of course, few people could afford haute couture, but American clothing manufacturers and buyers regularly traveled to Paris to attend fashion shows hosted by famous French designers. Back in the United States, they recreated the latest Parisian designs in inexpensive fabrics and sold them as ready-to-wear fashions. Clothing retailers sprinkled their advertisements with French phrases, since fashion-conscious shoppers devoured anything with a Parisian flair. For the first time, high fashion became accessible to even the working classes, as cheap factory-made clothing and inexpensive sewing patterns for up-to-date styles were widely available.

WOMEN'S FASHIONS

One of the primary changes in women's clothing during the 1920s stemmed from a dramatic shift in American standards of beauty and fashion. Prior to World War I, the so-called Gibson girl, with her hour-glass figure, long, upswept hair, floor-length skirt, and high-collared blouse, represented the model of American beauty and femininity. (See "Fashion of the 1900s.") In contrast,

Fashionable young woman posed beside a roadster, 1926. Prints & Photographs Division, Library of Congress.

the most desirable female figure during the 1920s was a flat-chested, slim-hipped look of the flapper. Because the slim, long-waisted dresses that were fashionable looked attractive on only the slenderest bodies, millions of women went on severe diets.

Yet wasn't enough to be thin—one had to be *young* to be fashionable. Shorter skirts and longer waists were reminiscent of little girl fashions, but bare legs, bold, short haircuts, and scarlet lipstick suggested an openly sexual youthfulness. With the addition of a stylish heel to the child's Mary Jane shoe, women juxtaposed juvenile fashions with the rolled-stocking, bared-knee sexuality of the modern woman. The short hair, brief outfits, and brazen use of cosmetics scandalized many older Americans, who argued the look was unladylike and immoral.

During the 1920s, women's clothing caused countless scandals, but it also freed women from the discomfort of corsets, pointed shoes, and impossibly large hats. The simpler fashions also meant women could drastically reduce the time they spent washing, ironing, and mending elaborate dresses, hats, and undergarments.

FASHION TRENDS OF THE 1920s

The 1920s saw a shift from the corseted, hourglass "Gibson girl" to the flapper style with its slim dresses with dropped waists and raised hems.

Women—straight, slim dresses; long, beaded necklaces; cloche hats; fur trim; trousers late in decade; functional, one-piece swimsuits; makeup acceptable; hair bobbed with marcel waves or permanent waves.

Men—suits consisting of jacket, trousers, vest, and tie; fedoras or peaked cap for casual; top hats and bowlers for formal occasions; "collegiate style" with raccoon coats or belted trench coat; baggy flannel trousers, sports jackets; wristwatches rather than pocket watches.

RETAIL CLOTHING

By the 1920s, most Americans wore ready-made clothing, although the wealthiest urban dwellers still bought couture fashions and the poorest rural dwellers still wore homemade clothing. Of course, many middle-class women continued sewing some of their own and their family's clothing, and widely available pattern books and magazines made it easy for them to create the latest fashions.

During the 1920s, department stores such as Gimbels, Marshall Field's, Wannamaker's, and Macy's offered shoppers a wide variety of merchandise arranged in attractive combinations. These department stores commonly used mannequins to display clothing that had already been assembled into eye-catching outfits to tempt shoppers into purchasing an entire ensemble. Similarly, departments were grouped together in order to encourage multiple purchases.

Mail-order catalogs sold ready-to-wear clothing, especially to rural families. America's most widely distributed mail-order catalog was published by Sears, which claimed to be "the World's Largest Store." Sears produced its first catalog in 1896 and, by the 1920s, its biannual publication represented an important aspect of consumer culture. The Sears Winter/Fall catalog of 1927 featured 11 pages of women's hats, and about 60 sewing patterns, costing around 20 cents apiece, for everything from infant clothes to women's party dresses.[1] The fashions did not necessarily reflect cutting-edge haute couture, but they kept families of moderate means stylishly clothed.

WOMEN'S DRESSES

During the 1920s, lavish evening gowns became an obvious symbol of the wearer's wealth and social standing. Made of luxurious fabrics such as velvet, satin, crepe de chine, or silver and gold lamé, evening dresses were decorated with metallic embroidery, beads, rhinestones, and fringe. Formal evening gowns were appropriate attire for balls, the opera, the theater, elegant dinner parties, and upscale restaurants. Gowns were designed in the basic shape of a sleeveless tube, with either deep U-or V-shaped necklines or high-cut, wide, boat-style necklines. After about 1926, plunging necklines were cut into the backs of gowns, and women sometimes draped long necklaces of beads or faux pearls down their exposed backs. Early in the decade, waistlines fell to about hip-level, and hemlines rose to just below

the calf. By around 1925, dress hemlines inched up to just below the knee—as short as they would get during the decade.

Stylish women wore afternoon dresses to luncheons, teas, matinees, and daytime dances. Sometimes called "tea-gowns," these dresses featured long flowing sleeves in the early 1920s. By 1925, the afternoon frock had become more streamlined and slender, with a knee-length skirt and short or fitted sleeves. They came in a variety of bright colors and patterns and were often adorned with narrow belts, sashes, bows, or artificial flowers at the dropped waist. In 1926, French designer Gabrielle "Coco" Chanel introduced what remains a fashion staple: the simple but elegant "little black dress." During the late 1920s, French designer Madeleine Vionnet pioneered dress design using the "bias cut" (the fabric was cut on the diagonal) to soften the severe angular shapes of fashionable dresses.

Women's suits contained many of the same features found in men's clothing styles. Women's suits were usually made of wool, with straight, hip-length suit jackets worn over straight matching skirts, and typically came in navy, brown, tan, or black, possibly with white pinstripes. Jackets might be single-or double-breasted, or "edge-to-edge," which meant that the two front panels just barely came together and were fastened with a single metal link button. Skirt silhouettes were very narrow, although they might include box or knife pleats. Coco Chanel introduced the classic Chanel suit: a boxy jacket trimmed with contrasting ribbon or braid, worn over a straight skirt. The jacket was lined in the same material as the matching blouse, and the jacket and skirt were made of soft jersey or tweed. Women's suits were considered appropriate attire for work or for travel, but not typically for entertaining.

Women wore informal morning dresses or housedresses, usually made of cotton in various striped, plaid, or checked patterns, while they did their domestic chores. By 1925, housedresses were shorter and slimmer than they had been before.

WOMEN'S SPORTSWEAR

During the 1920s, women, particularly those of the middle and upper classes, increasingly engaged in sports such as tennis, golf, boating, and swimming. Designers largely appropriated men's fashions to create women's outdoor clothing, including serge or tweed knickers to wear while hiking and flared jodhpurs to wear while horseback riding. Women golfers wore pleated, knee-length skirts topped with patterned sweaters. Tennis players wore white hose and short, slim white dresses. Coco Chanel introduced loose, bell-bottomed trousers made of silk, cotton, or crepe de chine for women to wear while boating. Women soon began wearing these wide-legged pants, known as "beach pajamas," over their bathing suits at the beach.

For ordinary casual wear, women wore long, soft blouses that were often banded or belted at the natural waist. Women also adopted the middy blouse, which resembled the top half of a sailor's uniform and was a traditional style for children's clothing. The vest-style blouse, patterned after a man's vest, had long or short sleeves and a notched collar. The lumberjack shirt, made of wool plaid and typically worn with knickers, was also popular. In cool weather, women (and men) donned colorful Fair Isle sweaters, popularized in 1922 by Edward, Prince of Wales, or coat sweaters, introduced by Coco Chanel, which were cardigan-style sweaters with a high shawl collar, pockets, and sometimes a belt.

WOMEN'S BATHING SUITS

Prior to World War I, "bathing costumes" were modest garments made of itchy woolen fabric. Men wore sleeveless knit tunics over (or sometimes attached to) knit shorts that reached several inches down the thigh. Women's costumes usually consisted of a loose overblouse, a knee-length skirt, and stockings. Although women's bathing costumes were not conducive to swimming, this was not a problem, since few swam.

In the 1920s, three major bathing suit manufacturers, eventually known as Jantzen, Cole, and Catalina, succeeded in popularizing beach fashion and breaking down older prohibitions on suitable bathing garments. Danish immigrant Carl Jantzen, along with his partners John and Roy Zehntbauer, invented a machine that could knit a stretchy fabric that was ribbed on both sides.

This fabric was much more elastic than ordinary jersey, the fabric most commonly used to make swimwear, and it clung to every curve of the body. In 1921, Jantzen began developing one-piece bathing suits that looked as if they were actually two pieces. These tubular maillot suits, sometimes called "California-style" suits, consisted of a scoop-necked, sleeveless top that was sewn at the waist to a pair of trunks. Often these unisex suits were embellished with bold, colorful stripes across the chest, hip, and thigh. Jantzen founded the Jantzen Swimming Association in 1926 and launched a national campaign called "Learn to Swim," which offered free swimming lessons across the country, certificates of completion, local competitions, and endorsements from champion swimmers. By 1930, Jantzen was the world's largest producer of bathing suits, selling more than 1.5 million suits a year.

While Jantzen's Oregon-based company specialized in athletic-looking suits that were actually suitable for swimming, Fred Cole's company in Los Angeles focused on creating dramatic suits that were designed primarily for glamorous sunbathing. In 1925, Cole began marketing the "Prohibition Suit," which had a low-cut neckline and tiny skirt that was shockingly revealing for the time. Catalina Swimwear offered a range of swimsuits that were sexier than Jantzen's but less daring than Cole's. Catalina introduced the nearly backless bathing suits that became immensely popular among women in the late 1920s. Catalina also served as the official swimsuit provider for the Miss America Pageant.

The evolution of form-fitting swimwear caused significant controversy during the 1920s, as directors of public beaches, resorts, and country clubs implemented strict dress codes. Violations were punishable by fines and, occasionally, imprisonment. Typically, dress codes specified the number of inches above the knee that that trunks (or bloomers) and skirts could rise. Sometimes female bathers were required to wear stockings, usually rolled above the knee. Some public beaches and resorts hired "beach censors" to maintain order and enforce dress codes. Chicago's Clarendon Beach employed a female "beach tailor" who stitched up loose armholes and sewed longer, more modest skirts onto too-short bathing suits. Men's

Fashion

Bill Norton, the bathing beach policeman, measuring distance between knee and bathing suit on woman, Washington, D.C., 1922. Prints & Photographs Division, Library of Congress.

swimwear was also regulated, but the dress codes for men were enforced less stringently than they were for women.

WOMEN'S UNDERGARMENTS

Women's underwear became lighter and less constricting during the 1920s. Old-fashioned corsets were still worn, particularly by older women, but were replaced over time by less burdensome corsets and lightweight rubber girdles. By the end of the decade, many women opted for the brief new "step-ins" or "cami-knickers," which were a silk or rayon camisole stitched to a pair of thigh-length panties.

Most brassieres manufactured during the 1920s were intended to flatten rather than accentuate women's breasts. These cupless brassieres were made of cotton, silk, or rayon, and fitted snugly against the woman's body in order to smooth her silhouette under the straight, narrow dresses of the day. Some bras during the mid-to late-1920s, however, were designed to separate and lift women's breasts. In 1922, Ida Cohen Rosenthal developed the support bra and founded the Maiden Form Brassiere Company (later renamed Maidenform). These "uplift" brassieres often featured elastic inserts and were widely advertised as preventing the bust from sagging.

WOMEN'S SHOES AND HOSIERY

The shorter skirts of the 1920s exposed more of women's legs, so shoes and hosiery became important accessories. At the beginning of the decade, many shoes featured pointed toes and two-inch, curved heels, broad one-and-three-quarter-inch "military" heels, or one-inch "walking" heels. Comfortable rubber soles and heels, introduced during World War I, gained in popularity throughout the 1920s. As the decade progressed, women's shoes with rounded toes and chunky, two-inch "Cuban" heels or slender "spike" or "Spanish" heels became common. Dressy women's shoes often featured a strap across the top of the foot, often made of brocade, satin, or another delicate material. The straps buttoned on one side of the shoe, and fashionable button covers made of enamel, rhinestones, silver, gold, or brass added flair. These strapped shoes also prevented women from accidentally kicking them off during an exuberant dance. A plain pump was also a popular footwear choice. In the early 1920s, most women's shoes were brown, tan, black, white, or gray. As the decade wore on, however, women began to sport shoes in silver, gold, red, green, and other dramatic colors.

Rising skirt hemlines led to black cotton and lisle stockings being replaced by beige or tan hose made of silk or, after 1923, rayon (then called "artificial silk"). While a pair of plain silk stockings could be purchased for about a dollar, fancier silk hose could cost six dollars or more per pair. Women wore garter belts to keep their thigh-high stockings from sagging or falling down. Sometimes women rolled the tops of their stockings over garters worn just above the knee, but flapper fashion dictated that stockings be rolled down to expose delicately powdered knees. More conservative Americans considered bare knees the epitome of immoral dress, but as the 1920s progressed, stockingless knees became increasingly common.

WOMEN'S HAIRSTYLES

Although popular conceptions of the Jazz Age suggest that every fashionable woman bobbed her hair, some women wore their hair long. Long-haired women usually pulled their hair back to the nape of the neck and wound it into a smooth chignon or knot. Another fashionable style at the beginning of the decade involved coiling long hair

into a bun behind each ear. This hairstyle, known as "earphones" or "cootie garages," fell out of favor by the mid-1920s. The bob, cut short and straight at about chin-length, was introduced in the United States by dancing sensation Irene Castle shortly before World War I. When other celebrities such as Coco Chanel and Hollywood film star Louise Brooks also adopted the haircut, women across the United States followed suit. Many women had their hair cut by men's barbers, since some hairdressers, fearing that short, simple hairstyles would put them out of business, refused to shear off women's long tresses. The bob could be worn with or without bangs, and was often accompanied by side curls plastered to the cheek or by a single curl dramatically set in the middle of the forehead. Around 1923, the standard bob haircut began to evolve into different, even shorter styles. The shingle haircut, or "boyish bob," tapered to a point at the nape of the wearer's neck and often featured waves or short curls on the sides. The more radical "Eton crop," which was trimmed above the wearer's ears and shaved in back, appeared in 1926. These streamlined haircuts were perfect for tucking underneath a stylish cloche hat so nothing but a side curl or two was visible. While young women were the first to engage in the bobbed hair craze, by the end of the decade women of all ages were wearing the convenient and versatile bob.

"Marcel waves" were a tremendously popular feature of the bobbed haircut. In 1872, Marcel Grateau, a French hairstylist, invented a method by which hair could be curled or waved with the use of a curling iron heated on a stove. By the 1920s, more convenient electric curling irons and crimpers became available, making it even easier for women to "marcel" their hair into the deep horizontal waves that were then fashionable. The water wave comb was another implement designed to create wavy hair. Wet hair was set with a series of combs that gently pushed the hair into waves. A scarf or ribbon was then wrapped around the head to keep the combs in place until the hair dried into soft waves and the combs could be removed. Women also created "finger waves" by applying "finger waving lotion" to their damp hair, then combing and pinching their short tresses into waves with their fingers. Until the damp waves

Fashion

were completely dry, women protected their efforts with delicate nets made of real human hair. By the late 1920s, "permanent waves" were also available to women willing to undergo the strong chemical treatments. Although women went to great trouble creating curls and waves, short hair was in general a real timesaver.

While white women tried to make their hair wavy or curly, many African American women worked just as hard trying to make their hair straight. Black newspapers and magazines advertised special pomades, oils, soaps, shampoos, hot irons, and combs that were intended to help relax and straighten curly or kinky hair. Madame C. J. Walker, the nation's first black woman millionaire, developed a revolutionary system to soften and straighten black women's hair around the turn of the century, using a combination of special hair preparations and hot irons. In 1906, she founded the Madame C. J. Walker Manufacturing Company, and later she established a Harlem-based beautician school called the Walker College of Hair Culture, which claimed to teach its hairdressing students how to straighten kinky hair without using curling irons, and promoted a secret formula that supposedly accelerated hair growth. The Walker Manufacturing Company flourished during the 1920s under the leadership of Madame Walker's daughter, A'Lelia Walker, one of the richest and most extravagant residents of Harlem during the Jazz Age. Madame C. J. Walker realized not only that the African American community represented a virtually untapped consumer market, but also that many black women were attracted to products that promised a more "Caucasian" appearance.

WOMEN'S COSMETICS

The cosmetics industry boomed during the 1920s, and thousands of beautician schools and beauty parlors sprang up. Prior to World War I, an American woman who visibly wore makeup, or "paint," as it was often called, was immediately suspected of being immoral—a woman of "easy virtue." But during the 1920s, wearing cosmetics became not just fashionable but respectable. Inspired in part by the glamorous Hollywood movie stars who wore dark red lipstick and heavy black

mascara, women of every age began to apply rouge, powder, lipstick, and eyeliner to their faces. They plucked their eyebrows into dramatic arches and then redrew them using eyebrow pencils. They reddened their lips into the pouty, "bee-stung" look popularized by Clara Bow and Theda Bara. Sales of cosmetics soared from $17 million in 1914 to $141 million in 1925.[2] Both Elizabeth Arden and Helena Rubenstein managed successful cosmetics empires in the 1920s. Following the lead of Coco Chanel and other fashion mavens, American women of the mid-1920s also stopped protecting their skin from the sun and instead gloried in suntans. A winter tan, in particular, became a prestigious status symbol, indicating that the possessor had both the money and the time to vacation in sunny locations such as California, Florida, or even Italy. Those without much disposable income often had to settle for self-tanning liquids and powders that claimed to achieve the effect of a natural suntan.

Not all women, however, desired a dark skin. Some African American women attempted to lighten their skin so it more closely resembled a white complexion. Bleaching lotions and other whitening potions were marketed in beauty shops, drugstores, newspapers, magazines, and mail-order catalogs. Advertisements for products with suggestive names such as "Black-No-More" and "Cocotone Skin Whitener" promised (or at least implied) that, with repeated applications, African American women would achieve pale skin tone. Not surprisingly, the very idea of skin whiteners sparked intense controversies in African American communities. While many African American women bought these ointments, others spurned these products and vehemently rejected the notion that lightening one's skin was either desirable or possible.

WOMEN'S ACCESSORIES

Hats remained a standard component of American women's wardrobes during the 1920s for most social engagements. A ban on feather from exotic birds, coupled with the popular short haircuts of the 1920s, signaled the end of the oversized hat. Around 1923, when the cloche hat (*cloche* means "bell" in French) was imported from Paris, small, trim hats became de rigueur for stylish women. The cloche hat's deep crown and narrow brim fitted snugly over a woman's head and concealed her eyebrows and nearly all of her bobbed hair. Cloches were made of just about every material, including straw, felt, satin, velvet, rayon, and cotton, and could be worn year-round. By 1928, some cloche hats had even been stripped of their small brim, making them look almost like a helmet. Cloches were often decorated with appliqués, ribbons, rhinestones, buckles, beads, small feathers, artificial flowers, or decorative Art Deco hatpins. Most trimmings rested over the ear rather than on the front of the hat.

Although cloches were the dominant style of women's hats during the 1920s, other styles were also popular. During the 1910s, dancer Irene Castle initiated the fashion of wearing decorative bandeaux—headbands that wrapped around the forehead and could be made of anything from ribbons to rhinestones. By the early 1920s, women were wearing these headpieces as a standard part of their evening dress. Women also wore turbans, soft tams and berets, and when Greta Garbo wore a man's slouch hat in the popular film *A Woman of Affairs* (1928), she ignited another craze among American women. *Garbo* soon became a synonym for this style of soft felt hat with a high crown and drooping brim. And women riding in open cars sometimes protected their hair by donning leather aviator helmets resembling those worn by World War I pilots.

The pared-down women's fashions of the 1920s left little room for pockets, so handbags became necessary. While morning appointments generally called for a more casual handbag made of fabric or leather, afternoon and evening engagements required a dressier bag, often constructed of mesh or fancy beadwork. Some bags, called reticules, were pouch-style bags that closed with a drawstring and were made of fabric or, for eveningwear, crocheted out of strands of glass beads. The *pochette,* another popular style of handbag, was a simple, flat, rectangular bag that featured a clasp at the top and a short carrying strap. Metal mesh bags, introduced in the United States in the nineteenth century, also enjoyed tremendous popularity in the 1920s. They could be gold or silver plated, or enameled in Art Deco

patterns resembling flowers, birds, sunbursts, or Egyptian or Oriental motifs. The late 1920s saw a vogue in reptile-skin bags, including those made from the hides of lizards, alligators, and snakes.

During the 1920s, Coco Chanel introduced inexpensive lines of what she called "illusion jewelry," better known as "costume jewelry," and soon the costume jewelry market exploded. Long strands of imitation pearls, faux gems, and opaque glass beads adorned the necks of both wealthy women and struggling shop girls across the nation. A popular, long necklace made of glass beads and ending in a beaded tassel, called a *sautoir,* became known as "flapper beads." Pendant earrings, frequently made of glass, often dangled below a woman's bobbed hair. Bangle bracelets, constructed of celluloid, Bakelite, chrome, or aluminum, were frequently worn several at a time, often on the upper arm left bare by a sleeveless evening dress. The 1922 discovery of King Tutankhamen's tomb initiated a craze for Egyptian-style jewelry, and the popularity of African American nightclub entertainer Josephine Baker sparked a rage for heavy African ivory bracelets. Of course, wealthy women still bought "real" jewelry, but fashion trends favored necklaces made of inexpensive glass, wood, and papier-mâché beads.

MEN'S FASHIONS

Just as women dieted to achieve the lean, boyish figure demanded by Jazz Age fashion, so too did men work to attain the ideal strong, slim body. One proponent of this new muscular male body was strongman Angelo Siciliano who, in 1922, won the title of "Most Perfectly Developed Man" and subsequently renamed himself Charles Atlas. (See "Food of the 1920s.") By the end of the 1920s, advertisements for his bodybuilding regimen appeared regularly in the back of men's true crime and adventure magazines.

While American women turned to Parisian designers for the latest fashions, American men looked to prestigious London designers on Bond Street and Saville Row. The most formal men's suit consisted of a black or midnight-blue worsted swallow-tailed coat ("tails"), trimmed with satin, and a pair of matching trousers, trimmed down the sides with wide braid or satin ribbon. These were worn with a white, waist-length linen or piqué vest over a starched white dress shirt. Dress shirts had buttonholes on both sides of the front opening, but no buttons. Men kept their shirts closed by threading removable buttons, called studs, between each set of corresponding buttonholes. A stiff, detachable collar attached to the shirt with collar buttons, and cufflinks fastened the French-style cuffs. A white bow tie, black silk top hat, white gloves, patent leather oxford shoes, spats, a white silk handkerchief, and a white flower boutonnière completed the outfit. Such a formal outfit, or "full dress," as it was known, would have been appropriate for only the most important occasions, such as balls, large formal dinners,

Man modeling a walking suit, which was generally for the wealthy gentleman, 1925. Prints & Photographs Division, Library of Congress.

evening weddings, and opera performances. Not surprisingly, only wealthier gentlemen could afford such a suit.

A gentleman's semiformal suit, called a tuxedo, was made of black or dark blue worsted material. Unlike a full dress suit, the tuxedo jacket had no tails and the tuxedo pants were trimmed, if at all, in very narrow braid or ribbon. The tuxedo vest could be black or white, but, unlike the obligatory full-dress white tie, tuxedos ties were always black. Men usually completed their tuxedo outfit with all the same accessories as the full-dress suit, except that instead of top hats they would wear dark, dome-shaped hats called bowlers. Tuxedos were appropriate attire at the theater, small dinner parties, entertaining in the home, and dining in a restaurant.

A standard, conservative business suit in the 1920s consisted of a jacket, trousers, and a vest. It came in black and shades of gray, tan, brown, blue, and green. Instead of a bowtie, one would wear an ascot or a "regular" four-in-hand. In the decade's later years, the jackets became longer and roomier, with a less defined waist. Trousers had cuffs, front creases, and button or hook-and-eye flies throughout the 1920s (zippers were not widely used on trouser flies until the 1930s). Professional men wore business suits to work, but also to other daytime occasions, including theater matinees and church services.

During the early 1920s, most men's dress shirts had, instead of a collar, a narrow neckband with a buttonhole in both the front and back. Detachable collars, which came in a variety of styles, were designed to attach easily to the shirts. Men could choose a collar that was stiff, semi-stiff, or soft, with pointed, rounded, or wing-style flaps. Washable collars were made of fabric; others were made of celluloid and could be wiped clean with a damp cloth. By the mid-1920s, however, many men preferred shirts with attached collars, which were softer and more comfortable than rigid, detachable collars.

Men usually wore hats whenever they left the house. Certain hats, such as top hats and bowlers, were reserved for formal occasions. More casual hats included the popular fedora, which was usually made of soft felt and featured a decorative ribbon around the base of the crown and

Advertisement for Arrow Collars and Shirts, approximately 1920. Picture by J. C. Leyendecker. Prints & Photographs Division, Library of Congress.

a distinctive crease that ran from front to back across the top. The fedora's brim usually curled up slightly, but young men often turned the front of the brim down. Another common men's hat was the peaked cap, which was a flat hat with a short front brim, often made of plaid, tweed, or herringbone woolen material, corduroy, or solid-colored poplin.

MEN'S COLLEGIATE STYLES

National celebrities exerted a profound influence on middle-class men's fashion. Sports stars such as golfer Bobby Jones and tennis player Bill Tilden became fashion trendsetters. Well-dressed young men might wear golfing knickers and a sweater or loose, white flannel trousers and V-necked sweater vests over a collared shirt,

whether or not they actually played golf or tennis. Silent film star Rudolph Valentino introduced the image of the suave, sophisticated "sheik" to American men with the release of his 1921 movie *The Sheik*. Young men copied his look by shaving their beards and moustaches and parting their slicked-down hair in the middle or just off to one side. In 1927, after Charles Lindbergh completed his historic transatlantic flight, tens of thousands of men (and some women) bought leather aviation jackets and helmets to wear when riding in open automobiles. American men across imitated every aspect of Edward, Prince of Wales's extensive, impeccable wardrobe, from his stylish tweed plus-fours (baggy knickers worn with knee socks) to his colorful Fair Isle knitted sweaters.

Another British influence on young men's fashion emerged around 1925, when the students at Oxford University in England began to wear extremely loose, baggy trousers that extended all the way down to the tops of their shoes. Supposedly, students wore these "Oxford bags" to cover their knickers, which were considered improper classroom attire. These wide-leg trousers—sometimes measuring as much as 30 inches around the knees—caught on among the fashionable younger set in America. Other, less baggy flannel trousers also became popular on college campuses, and by the end of the decade the slim-fitting pants that had been fashionable in the early 1920s were decidedly passé.

Collegiate men usually wore sports jackets. Some featured a front pocket decorated with a badge or crest. Other jackets were designed in the Norfolk style, with a belt across the waist and box pleats down the sides. College freshmen were frequently required to wear a "dink" or beany—a small felt cap in the school colors—for the first few weeks of classes. The dinks made it easy for upperclassmen to identify the new freshmen and thus contribute to their "hazing" experience. As for outerwear, the bulky, knee-length raccoon overcoat made a strong fashion statement among college men who could afford it during the 1920s, as did the belted trench coat, modeled after British soldiers' apparel in World War I, and the formal knee-length Chesterfield coat, with its distinctive black velvet collar.

MEN'S SHOES, UNDERGARMENTS, AND ACCESSORIES

While formal and semiformal wear required shiny patent-leather shoes, men's casual footwear during the 1920s encompassed a range of styles. The oxford shoe largely replaced old-fashioned tall, lace-up boots. Sport oxfords were made with rubber soles and came mostly in the traditional colors of black, brown, tan, and white. Two-toned oxfords, made of white buckskin and black or brown leather, were also popular. Rubber galoshes with buckles or snaps protected these relatively flimsy shoes in rainy or snowy weather. Men's socks were made of cotton, silk, wool, or rayon. Tall, ribbed socks worn with knickers often featured colorful plaid, striped, or Argyle patterns. Because men's dress socks lacked elasticity, men had to wear adjustable hose garters around their calves to keep their socks from falling down.

During the 1920s, men's undergarments often consisted of the one-piece "union suit," which was a combination of undershirt and underpants. For cold weather, woolen union suits had long sleeves and long pants and featured a convenient "drop seat." For summer, loose one-piece cotton undergarments had short pants and sleeveless tops and buttoned up the front or at the tops of the shoulder straps. Separate undershirts and undershorts for men were also widely available.

Men's wallets were larger in the 1920s than they generally are today, primarily because American paper currency was larger. In 1929, American bills were reduced to their present size ($6\frac{1}{8} \times 2\frac{5}{8}$ inches), but before that, they measured $7\frac{7}{16} \times 3\frac{1}{8}$ inches. These larger wallets were usually folded into thirds and were customarily made of leather, pigskin, or sometimes ostrich skin. Most men carried a timepiece, either a pocket watch on a chain or a wristwatch—a style introduced in the 1920s that soon eclipsed the popularity of pocket watches. Despite National Prohibition, some men (and women) also carried pocket flasks—chrome-plated, monogrammed flasks were particularly trendy.

CHILDREN'S FASHIONS

Ready-to-wear clothing for children was quite popular during the 1920s. Infants, both boys and girls, often wore long dresses with matching bonnets. By the time they were toddlers, children tended to wear more gender-specific clothing. Little girls wore "bloomer dresses," which were short, loose dresses, often of checked or plaid material, coupled with matching panties that peeked out below the bottom of the skirt. In the early 1920s, girls up to about the age of 14 commonly wore loose, feminine dresses that were frequently embellished with lace, ruffles, or artificial flowers and tied with a sash. Also popular were long skirts topped with sailor-style middy blouses made of wool flannel, jean cloth, or serge. These long-sleeved blouses featured a shawl collar, contrasting necktie, and sometimes nautical insignia on the sleeves. Girls also wore thigh-length cardigan sweaters that buttoned up the front and, in some cases, belted around the middle. By the end of the 1920s, young girls had adopted many aspects of flapper fashions—long-waisted and short dresses, simple cloche hats, and bobbed hair. Matching dresses, either big-and-little sister dresses or mother-and-daughter dresses, also became trendy late in the 1920s.

Young boys usually wore shirts that buttoned to short matching pants. Often these two-piece outfits looked like sailor suits, complete with nautical necktie. Boys between five and ten years old frequently wore suits consisting of short pants, a belted jacket, and sometimes a matching vest. Dark stockings and lace-up ankle boots completed the outfit. Late in the 1920s, beltless jackets that more closely resembled adult fashions gradually replaced belted jackets. Young boys usually wore flat, peaked caps made of wool or wool blend fabric, just as their fathers and older brothers did.

Food

of the 1920s

The 1920s saw the emergence of a more homogeneous American cuisine. Prior to World War I, no distinctive American cuisine existed, and diets varied widely according to people's ethnicity, class, income, and region. But during the 1920s, a more standardized diet developed, consisting largely of salads and light, simple meals that frequently included processed food products. The growing popularity of brand-name foods, the influence of scientific nutrition, and the mass marketing of new kitchen appliances, especially gas stoves and electric refrigerators, all contributed to the creation of a national cuisine. So, too, did the widespread use of cookbooks, the rise of mass-circulation women's magazines, and the introduction of radio cooking shows. The number of restaurants dramatically increased, and many immigrant families incorporated American cooking styles and eating habits into their traditional Old World cuisine. All of these national forces and trends resulted in more and more Americans sharing a popular food culture.

DINING IN THE HOME

American Homemakers

Americans continued to eat most of their meals at home during the 1920s. The decade witnessed a trend toward simpler meals that could be prepared comparatively quickly. Several factors accounted for this transformation. First, servants, once common in middle and upper-class homes, began to leave domestic service to take jobs as department store clerks, secretaries, typists, and telephone operators. Thus, middle-class wives who found themselves doing their own grocery shopping and cooking gravitated toward easy-to-prepare dishes. Second, more than three million married women had entered the workforce by the end of the 1920s, and these women had less time to prepare elaborate meals for their families. As a result, they relied on quick recipes and one-dish meals to feed their families.

Many homemakers relied on the dozens of packaged, commercially processed foods that became available during the 1920s. Many of these products, such as quick-cooking rolled oats or dry pancake mixes, were designed to make meal preparation faster and easier. Sales of canned goods and other prepared foods soared during the 1920s, and condensed soups, bottled condiments, and canned fruits and vegetables played an increasingly prominent role in the meals served.

New kitchen technologies and the introduction of electricity into many middle-class American homes also changed the way women prepared

Interior of a model modern kitchen, circa 1926. Frederick Apartments, Columbia, Missouri. Courtesy of Sabra Tull Meyer.

daily meals. Gas and, to a lesser degree, electric ranges replaced wood-and coal-burning stoves in many kitchens, and by 1930, approximately half of all American homes were equipped with gas stoves. During the early 1920s, most electric refrigerators were too expensive for average consumers. However, methods of mass production reduced the price of refrigerators significantly during the last half of the 1920s, and by 1929, more than 800,000 refrigerators were purchased annually.[1] With the advent of widespread electrification, electric pop-up toasters, pressure cookers, coffee percolators, waffle irons, and mixers also became common in middle-class kitchens. Despite the increased use of commercially prepared foods and new labor-saving electrical appliances, urban housewives still devoted an average of 19 hours per week to preparing meals and cleaning up after them during the 1920s, while rural housewives spent almost 24 hours per week on those same chores.

Giant Food Corporations and New Products

By 1920, food processing and manufacturing was one of the largest industries in the United States. Corporations including General Mills, Incorporated (formed in 1928), Standard Brands (1929), and General Foods Corporation (1929),

FOOD HIGHLIGHTS OF THE 1920s

1923 The executive chef at San Francisco's Palace Hotel reportedly invents "Green Goddess" salad dressing in tribute to actor George Arliss and his popular play of the same name. A bottled version by Seven Seas is popular through the 1970s.

1923 The USDA begins a program to grade and certify beef, lamb, pork, veal, and calf for American consumption.

1923 The Genesee Pure Food Company changes its name to Jell-O Company and in the same year markets D-Zerta, the first sugar-free gelatin dessert.

1926 Laura Scudder of Monterey Park, California, launches a food business and is credited with being the first to package potato chips in wax paper to preserve their freshness. She sells her food company in 1957 for $6 million, having rejected higher offers from buyers who couldn't guarantee that her employees would continue to have jobs.

1927 Experimenting with a fruit syrup recipe called Fruit Smack, Edwin Perkins converts it to a powder, packages it in envelopes, and names it Kool-Ade, later changing the spelling to Kool-Aid.

1927 To avoid the tedious chore of hand straining vegetables for her infant daughter, Sally, Dorothy Gerber has her husband do it at the family-owned Fremont Canning Company. By 1928, the Gerbers have developed a line of mass-produced strained baby foods ready for national distribution.

1928 In Minneapolis, Washburn Crosby Company merges with other regional mills to become General Mills.

Food

spent millions of dollars researching and developing better methods of preserving and packaging food. Sugar and flour, once sold in bulk, now came packaged in bags, and milk, once marketed only in glass bottles, now also came in inexpensive cardboard cartons. As more efficient methods of manufacturing tin cans developed, canning became an increasingly economical way to preserve and package foods such as fruits, vegetables, ham, tuna, and even cheese. In 1924, Clarence Birdseye developed a process for flash-freezing fish, and five years later he sold his patents to the Postum Cereal Company (soon to be reorganized as the General Foods Corporation). In 1930, the company sold the first commercially packaged frozen fruits and vegetables under the brand name Birds Eye Frosted Foods, marking the advent of the frozen food industry.

Advertisement for Kellogg's corn flakes and for Camp Fire Girls, showing a Camp Fire Girl in her uniform feeding cereal to a small child, 1929. Prints & Photographs Division, Library of Congress.

These processing and packaging innovations allowed corporations to market many mass-produced foods. Several new breakfast cereals appeared, including Post 40% Bran Flakes (1922), Wheaties (1924), and Kellogg's Rice Krispies (1928). In 1928, the J. L. Kraft & Brothers Company developed a processed cheese food called Velveeta, which came wrapped in a tinfoil package inside a wooden box and did not require refrigeration. Florida orange and grapefruit growers began selling canned pasteurized juice in 1929. Tomato juice, introduced in the mid-1920s, became a popular breakfast drink by 1928. Oscar Mayer & Company began marketing packaged sliced bacon in 1924, and George A. Hormel & Company sold the nation's first canned hams in 1926. Potato chips had been commercially manufactured and sold in bulk since the 1890s, but it wasn't until the development of the continuous fryer and the waxed paper bag in the 1920s that sales of potato chips soared. Other new foods included Wonder Bread (1921, but not sold sliced until 1930), Quick Quaker Oats (1921), Welch's Concord grape jelly (1923), Land O' Lakes butter (1924), Green Giant canned peas (1925), and Peter Pan peanut butter (1928).

Food

Meals

Technological advancements provided a greater abundance and a wider assortment of foods during the decade. Gasoline-powered tractors and improved methods of scientific farming produced larger crop yields. Refrigerated railcars and over-the-road trucks distributed fresh meats, fruits, vegetables, dairy products, and grains across the nation. As a result, homemakers were able to purchase oranges, grapefruits, bananas, lettuce, and broccoli (first commercially grown in the United States in 1923) even during the winter months. Overall, food prices dropped significantly during the 1920s, which allowed even families with modest incomes to eat a wide variety of foods.

During the 1920s, middle-class Americans began to eat relatively light, healthful meals. Earlier generations had eaten breakfasts consisting of large amounts of bread, potatoes, and meats such as steak, chops, sausage, and ham. But during the 1920s, home economists and nutritionists advised homemakers to serve their families breakfasts of citrus juice, dry cereal, eggs, and toast. Common lunches consisted of a sandwich, soup, or salad. Dinners, which changed the least of the three daily meals, typically included a simply prepared meat, potatoes, one or two vegetable side dishes, and dessert. Overall, Americans became more health conscious and as a result consumed smaller amounts of red meats, fats, and starches than they had during previous decades.

Popular dishes during the 1920s included broiled steaks and chops, meatloaf, Swiss steak, and spaghetti and meatballs. One-dish meals and casseroles streamlined food preparation. Several well-known salads were invented during the decade, including the Cobb salad, developed in 1926 by Robert Cobb at his Brown Derby Restaurant in Los Angeles, and the Green Goddess salad, created by Chef Philip Roemer in 1923 at the Grand Palace Hotel Restaurant in San Francisco. The most famous green salad of the decade was the Caesar salad, created by Caesar Cardini, an Italian chef who ran a restaurant in Tijuana, Mexico. In 1924, Cardini concocted his special salad for a group of visiting Hollywood celebrities, and soon the Caesar salad emerged as a favorite dish in the States. Since gas and electric ovens made baking easier, cakes became a common dessert during the 1920s, especially pineapple upside-down cake, devil's food cake, and chiffon cake (invented in 1927). Other dessert favorites included molded Jell-O salads, fruit salads, pineapple fluff, and chocolate mousse.

Cookbooks and Radio Cooking Shows

Cookbooks and promotional recipe booklets helped popularize modern ways of cooking and baking. Cookbooks, many of which were written by famous culinary experts such as Alice Bradley and Ida Bailey Allen, were exceedingly popular with homemakers. One of the standard cookbooks of the 1920s was *The Boston Cooking-School Cook Book,* by Fannie Merritt Farmer, which was first published in 1896. With the aid of

cookbooks and recipes clipped from magazines and newspapers, more adventuresome homemakers dabbled in foreign cooking. Many American cookbooks contained a few Italian and Mexican recipes, but the number of cookbooks devoted exclusively to foreign cuisine, such as *Mexican Cookery for American Homes* (1923), also increased significantly after World War I. Most cookbooks published during the 1920s were written for housewives, but a few targeted other family members, such as *Young People's Cook Book* (1925) or *The Stag Cookbook, Written for Men, by Men* (1922), which included recipes for preparing fresh fish and wild game.

During the 1920s, most major food corporations distributed booklets filled with recipes that listed their brand-name products as necessary ingredients. Kitchen appliance manufacturers and women's magazines also published promotional cookbooks. *Good Housekeeping,* the women's periodical with the largest circulation during the decade, published *Good Housekeeping's Book of Menus, Recipes and Household Discoveries* (1924). The magazine also awarded its "Good Housekeeping Seal of Approval," introduced in 1910, to foods that the Good Housekeeping Institute had tested and approved, and this endorsement served to promote the products of many of the magazine's advertisers.

Homemakers also listened to radio cooking shows for advice about meal planning and cooking. In 1921, the advertising department of the Washburn-Crosby Company created a fictional homemaker spokesperson named Betty Crocker to assist in the promotion of its Gold Medal flour. Three years later, the company began sponsoring the nation's first radio cooking show, *The Betty Crocker School of the Air,* which was later broadcast on the NBC network. Another pioneering radio homemaker program was *Aunt Sammy,* first broadcast in 1926. Sponsored by the U.S. Department of Agriculture, the program could be heard on 50 stations across the nation and led to the publication of a cookbook titled *Aunt Sammy's Radio Recipes* (1927). Cookbook author Ida Bailey Allen, known as "the nation's homemaker," provided cooking lessons and recipes on *The National Radio Home-Makers' Club* (CBS, 1928–1935).

Food

Nutrition and Diet

New ideas about food science and nutrition also helped to transform American cooking and eating habits. A series of breakthroughs in food science in the 1910s and 1920s, including the discovery of vitamins A, B1, B2, C, D, and E made Americans more aware of the importance of proper nutrition. Fruits and vegetables, once considered unnecessary for a well-balanced diet, came to be understood as crucial to maintaining good health. Milk, once viewed as only a children's drink, became popular among adults. Many mothers attempted to feed their children a nutritionally balanced diet to ward off sickness and encourage healthy development. In 1928, the Fremont Canning Company introduced Gerber Baby Food, a line of commercially manufactured strained vegetables for infants, and soon launched a national advertising campaign, featuring the now-familiar Gerber baby, to promote its products.

By 1920, scientists and physicians clearly understood calories and the relationship between obesity and diseases such as diabetes. Many health-conscious Americans began counting calories and dieting, or "reducing." Dieting manuals, along with commercial diet programs, reducing creams, and other weight-loss products, flooded the market. The women's magazines and daily newspapers ran feature articles, advice columns, and weekly menu plans providing readers with hints about how to eat healthfully, count calories, and shed unwanted pounds.

Dieting for beauty's sake also became common among women. By the early 1920s, the curvaceous, hourglass figure of the Gibson Girl had been supplanted by the rail-thin, waistless figure of the flapper. Women dieted in order to conform to the new slimmer ideals of beauty as depicted in advertising and Hollywood motion pictures. New clothing styles also fueled the dieting craze. Many of the fashionable dresses of the 1920s sported hemlines that revealed much of the legs and sleeveless bodices that exposed the arms. (See "Fashion of the 1920s.")

Dozens of doctors and dieting gurus published weight loss books and articles. The most famous proponent of scientific dieting was Dr. Lulu Hunt Peters, a Los Angeles physician, whose *Diet and Health, With Key to the Calories* (1918) remained a national best seller throughout the 1920s. Peters advocated a weight-reduction program that combined calorie counting with the practice of slowly chewing everything—even milk and soup. Also popular was the "Hollywood Eighteen Day Diet," a restrictive, 585-calorie program that recommended eating only "grapefruit, oranges, Melba Toast, green vegetables and hard-boiled eggs."[2] Many medical doctors cautioned that many of these popular diet fads were potentially dangerous, but few heeded their warnings.

GROCERY SHOPPING AND CHAIN GROCERY STORES

Chain grocery stores sparked the beginning of a food merchandising revolution during the 1920s. Chain stores purchased in volume from wholesalers and, as a result, could offer cheaper prices and a wider selection than most independent markets. The nation's leading grocery store chain during the 1920s was the Great Atlantic & Pacific Tea Company, better known as A&P, founded in 1859. By 1929, the A&P was operating more than 15,400 stores across the nation, with combined total sales of more than $1 billion. Other grocery store chains, such as American, Kroger, National, and Safeway, also prospered, and by 1928, some 860 rival chains crowded the highly competitive food retailing business. In 1926, small grocers formed the Independent Grocers Alliance (IGA), a national trade association that made it possible for independent grocery stores to obtain the same wholesale discounts as the large chains and adopt similar merchandising strategies.

Prior to World War I, most food items were located on shelves behind the counter, and store clerks would gather, bag, and often deliver groceries for customers. But in 1916, Clarence Saunders introduced a new self-service shopping format at his Piggly Wiggly grocery store in Memphis, Tennessee. Piggly Wiggly shoppers would select items from the rows of open shelves, place them in baskets, and carry them to the front of the store, where a clerk would ring up their total. By 1920, 515 Piggly Wiggly stores were operating in cities throughout the South and Midwest. The chain

The interior of a neat and tidy Washington, D.C., grocery store, circa 1920. Prints & Photographs Division, Library of Congress.

grew to more than 2,600 stores by 1929. Self-service grocery stores employed fewer clerks, so savings could be passed on to shoppers in the form of lower prices. Self-service stores also allowed shoppers to handle and inspect the products before purchasing them. During the 1920s, most of the nation's grocery stores gradually converted to the self-service format.

DINING OUT

The Growth of Restaurants

During the 1920s, Americans dined out in restaurants and other eating establishments more often than earlier generations did, and the total number of restaurants in the United States tripled between 1919 and 1929.[3] The increasing number of commuters and working women contributed to the popularity of various kinds of eating establishments.

National Prohibition also transformed the American restaurant industry. After 1920, when it became illegal to serve alcohol, many of the nation's first-class restaurants, which had profited from the sale of expensive wines and spirits, went out of business. Prohibition also eliminated saloons as a source of inexpensive lunches for factory workers. Prior to 1920, most working-class saloons had offered "free lunches"—light meals of sausages, hard-boiled eggs, crackers, and cheese—with the purchase of a five-cent glass of beer. These saloons shut their doors in compliance with the Eighteenth Amendment.

Quick-Service Restaurants

During the 1920s, the growing numbers of workers demanded fast, convenient lunches, and thus a whole range of quick-service restaurants, including automats, cafés, lunchrooms, diners, cafeterias, and sandwich shops, sprang up. Automats, which had been operating in the United States since 1902, featured rows of coin-operated vending machines that offered an assortment of both hot and cold prepared foods. For as little as a nickel, a patron could purchase a ham sandwich, a bowl of soup, a dish of ice cream, or a slice of pie.

Lunchrooms, which were usually located on the ground floor of downtown urban office buildings, sported U-shaped counters at which customers could eat cheap meals. Although most lunchrooms remained independently owned, chain lunchrooms made dramatic inroads during the 1910s and 1920s. By 1920, lunchroom chains such as Thompson's Lunchrooms and Baltimore Dairy Lunch were operating more than 100 outlets.

Diners remained popular among working-class Americans. Diners typically occupied free-standing, stainless steel structures that contained a grill, counter, stools, booths, and rest rooms. Diners usually remained open 24 hours a day, although they catered principally to a breakfast and lunch crowd. By 1932, an estimated 4,000 diners were operating across the United States.

Cafeterias allowed customers to assemble their own meals from a wide selection of inexpensive entrees, side dishes, and desserts kept warm on steam tables. This self-service system virtually eliminated the need for a wait staff. Several major cafeteria chains were launched during the 1920s, including Bishop's Cafeteria, Laughner's Cafeteria, Morrison's Cafeteria, and S&W Cafeteria. In 1929, New York City boasted 786 cafeterias, but the greatest concentrations of chain cafeterias were found in the Midwest and South, where regional cuisine, such as fried chicken and biscuits and gravy in the South, dominated the menu.

Tearooms

Affordably priced, mid-range restaurants also grew during the 1920s. One of the most popular formats was the tearoom, many of which were located in urban downtown districts. Most tearooms were owned and operated by women, and they generally catered to a predominantly middle-class female clientele. Tearooms served simple, moderately priced lunches and afternoon tea in warm, charming surroundings. Tearooms hoping to attract male customers sometimes offered hearty fare such as chopped beefsteak or tongue sandwiches. One of the most famous of this style of restaurant was the Russian Tea Room in New York City, opened in 1926 by exiled members of the Russian Imperial Ballet who had fled the Bolshevik Revolution. Although thousands of tearooms continued to operate throughout the 1920s, they declined in popularity as restaurants that offered faster service and lower prices attracted more customers.

Ethnic Restaurants

Partially as a result of National Prohibition, Italian cuisine became popular with Americans during the 1920s. An estimated one-quarter of all the immigrants who entered the United States between 1890 and 1914 were from Italy, and some of them opened pizzerias and ristorantes in the Italian neighborhoods of major American cities. Chefs often adapted traditional southern Italian cuisine to suit American tastes by adding meatballs to spaghetti dishes and expanding their menus to include such traditional fare as steaks and chops. During Prohibition, many Italian entrepreneurs continued illicitly to serve wine, which was central to Italian food culture. Americans who patronized these restaurants for their liquor often developed a fondness for spaghetti and meatballs, fettuccini Alfredo, and other Italian dishes.

Chinese food was another popular ethnic cuisine in the 1920s, and Chinese cooks altered traditional Cantonese, Hunan, and Mandarin cuisine to make them more appealing to American diners. As a result, the menus of many Chinese restaurants contained dishes such as chop suey, chow mein, and stir-fried rice, all of which originated in the United States. Other Americanized dishes featured such non-traditional ingredients as batter-fried meats and pineapple chunks. Other ethnic restaurants that flourished during the 1920s included German beer gardens, Swedish smorgasbords, and Jewish delicatessens. In California and the Southwest, Mexican and Tex-Mex cuisine was popular fare. French cooking declined in popularity during Prohibition because it was difficult to obtain the fine wines often required to prepare and accompany authentic Parisian cuisine.

Roadside Restaurants and Food Stands

During the 1920s, a bustling roadside restaurant industry emerged in the United States. Prior to World War I, when automobiles were less common, travelers had few places to purchase a meal along the road. But as the number of automobiles increased, restaurants catering to motorists sprang up across the country. These restaurants often used flashing neon signs (introduced in 1923), gaudy billboards, and distinctive architecture to attract passing motorists. Roadside restaurants and stands offered fare ranging from quick-service hamburgers, hot dogs, and soft drinks to sit-down meals of steaks, potatoes, and salads. They frequently operated near public beaches, amusement parks, and other local attractions. For example, Howard Johnson opened a handful of ice cream stands near the crowded Boston seashore during the mid-1920s, and he later parlayed these stands into a nationally known franchise of restaurants and hotels. In 1922, Roy W. Allen and Frank Wright opened three walk-up root beer stands in Sacramento, California, under the name of A&W (which combined the first letter of the owners' surnames). Two years later, after acquiring Wright's share of the business, Allen began to sell franchises and built A&W into one of the nation's first chains of franchise roadside restaurants, with 171 outlets across the nation by 1933.

One innovation of the 1920s roadside restaurant industry was curbside service. In 1921, J. G. Kirby and Dr. Reuben W. Jackson opened what is widely considered the nation's first drive-in sandwich restaurant, called the Pig Stand, along a busy highway on the outskirts of Dallas, Texas. A staff of "tray boys" delivered barbecued pork sandwiches and Coca-Colas to customers waiting curbside in their automobiles. By 1930, the Pig Stand Company, Incorporated was operating some 60 franchise roadside eateries across California and the Southwest. Other roadside restaurants soon adopted the drive-in service format.

White Castle and the Rise of Fast-Food Hamburger Chains

In 1921, Walter Anderson and Edgar Waldo "Billy" Ingram opened a hamburger restaurant in Wichita, Kansas, under the name of White Castle. Hamburgers had a reputation of being made from low-grade or spoiled meat scraps, so Anderson and Ingram stressed that their hamburgers were made from specially selected cuts of ground chuck delivered fresh to their restaurants twice daily. They grilled the burgers directly in front of customers, so they could see the sanitary conditions under which their food was being prepared. The first White Castle restaurant served hamburger sandwiches, smothered with cooked onions, for a nickel apiece.

The White Castle System of Eating Houses, as the chain was called, expanded rapidly due in part to its innovative marketing strategies. Originally, the chain catered to a largely working-class clientele, but during the last half of the 1920s it advertised its sandwiches as a convenient carryout food and by urged customers to "Buy 'em by the sack." By 1931, White Castle was operating 115 restaurants across the Midwest and East Coast, all of which featured the same floor plan and distinctive medieval architecture. A host of imitator hamburger chain restaurants sprang up around the nation, including White Tower (1926), White Tavern Shoppes (1929), Toddle House (1929), and Krystal (1932), all of which replicated the original concepts of mass-produced food and standardized service developed by White Castle. By the end of the 1920s, the hamburger had surpassed the hot dog as Americans' favorite fast food.

CANDY BARS AND ICE CREAM

During the 1920s, Americans ate more ice cream and candy bars than previous generations did, in part because technological advancements made them more widely available but also, perhaps, to compensate for the decline in alcohol consumption during Prohibition. Other trends also boosted the popularity of sweets. Chocolate candy bars, long considered primarily a woman's delicacy, did not become widely popular until around World War I. Beginning in 1917, the Hershey Chocolate Company and other American candy manufacturers supplied the U.S. government with chocolate for distribution to American soldiers. After the war, returning veterans helped

A 1929 photo of the first White Castle restaurant, Wichita, Kansas. Copyright © White Castle System, Inc. All Rights Reserved. Reprinted with permission.

spark a boom in chocolate and candy bar sales in the United States.

Technological innovations and rising consumption allowed candy manufacturers to expand and introduce new products. In 1921, the Hershey Chocolate Company manufactured more than eight million pounds of chocolate, with total sales of more than $20 million. By the end of the decade, its yearly sales topped $41 million. The other giant chocolate manufacturer of the 1920s was Mars Candies, founded in 1922 by a former candy wholesaler named Frank Mars. In 1923, Mars introduced his first candy bar, the Milky Way, which racked up sales of almost $800,000 in its first year. By 1929, Mars's Chicago plant was churning out 20 million candy bars a year. In 1920, the Curtiss Company introduced the Baby Ruth, named not for the New York Yankees slugger, as is often assumed, but for President Grover Cleveland's daughter Ruth. By 1925, the Baby Ruth was one of the nation's best-selling candy bars. The Curtiss Company's second candy bar, Butterfinger, first marketed in 1926, also proved to be a hit.

An estimated 30,000 different candy bars, most of them locally produced, were available during the 1920s.[4] Most were made of chocolate with centers of caramel, marshmallow, peanuts, crisped rice, or other ingredients. Other candy bars attempted to cash in on the popularity of national celebrities, fads, or trendy expressions, including candy bars called Bambino and Big Champ (both named for Babe Ruth), the Big Hearted "Al" bar (named for New York Governor Alfred E. Smith, the 1928 Democratic presidential candidate), the Pierce Arrow (named for the luxury automobile), and, after 1927, the Lindy bar and several other candy bars named for aviator Charles Lindbergh. A number of candy bars introduced during the 1920s remain popular today, including Oh Henry! (1920), the Charleston Chew! (1922), Mounds (1922), Reese's Peanut Butter Cup (1923), Bit-O-Honey (1924), and Mr. Goodbar (1925). Candy bars produced during the 1920s usually weighed around 1.25 ounces and sold for a nickel.

Other sweet treats were also introduced during the 1920s. Although Frank H. Fleer, owner of the Fleer Chewing Gum Company, had developed a bubble gum called Blibber Blubber Bubble Gum as early as 1906, it never reached the market. In 1928, an accountant at Fleer's company, Walter E. Diemer, accidentally invented a pink-colored gum that was so elastic that one could actually blow bubbles with it. Within months, the Fleer Company began selling the gum under the name of Dubble Bubble, and it became the nation's first commercially marketed bubble gum. Among other new candies introduced during the decade were Switzer's cherry licorice (1920), Jujyfruits (1920), Chuckles (1921), Dum Dum suckers (1924), Goobers (1925), Sugar Daddy (1925), Milk Duds (1926), Slo Poke suckers (1926), Mike & Ike (1928), Y & S Twizzlers licorice (1928), and Hot Tamales (1928).

With technological advancements and the widespread use of refrigeration, ice cream and other frozen treats became popular during the 1920s. Ice cream cones, first introduced at the St. Louis World's Fair in 1904, enjoyed unprecedented sales during the 1920s, but ice cream also evolved into several new frozen novelty treats. In 1920, Harry Burt, a Youngstown, Ohio ice cream parlor operator, developed a chocolate-coated ice cream bar on a wooden stick that he called the Good Humor Bar. He soon began selling them in nearby neighborhoods using a fleet of trucks, each driven by a Good Humor Man and mounted with bells to alert customers of its approach. In 1921, a Des Moines, Iowa, ice cream plant super-intendent named Russell Stover, in partnership with Christian Nelson, introduced the Eskimo Pie, which sold one million units during its first year on the market. In 1922, William Isaly cre-ated the Klondike Bar. In 1924, Frank Epperson began selling a frozen lemonade bar on a stick to visitors at an Oakland, California amusement park. Originally, he called his frozen treat Epsicles but soon changed the name to Popsicles, which quickly became a nationally popular brand name product.

BEVERAGES

Alcohol during National Prohibition

The onset of National Prohibition in 1920 made beer, wine, and spirits more difficult to obtain, but tens of millions of Americans continued to drink alcohol in defiance of the liquor laws. The cost of alcohol soared during Prohibition, but any-one with enough money could usually purchase whatever liquor he or she desired. One could buy a pint of whiskey from a neighborhood bootleg-ger or persuade a doctor to write a prescription for medicinal alcohol, which could be filled at a local drugstore. During the 1920s, *The New Yorker* published current bootleggers' prices and new cocktail recipes. Speakeasies sprang up across the nation and sold drinks by the glass. Some re-sourceful Americans, especially those of German and Italian ancestry, brewed their own beer, dis-tilled their own spirits, or made their own wines in their cellars and garages. Prohibition drove many Americans to switch from drinking beer, which was difficult to purchase, to drinking more potent alcoholic beverages. In 1919, beer had accounted for 55 percent of all sales of alcoholic beverages in the United States, with spirits accounting for only 37 percent. By 1929, however, liquor and spirits accounted for 75 percent of the overall alcohol consumption in the nation, compared to only 15 percent for beer.[5] Cocktails became especially popular during the 1920s, as drinkers used soft drinks and sweet fruit juices to camouflage the foul taste of inferior whiskey or gin. Hard-core drunks with little money sometimes resorted to drinking cheap, alcohol-based household prod-ucts such as aftershave lotion, hair tonic, and cough syrup. Thousands of unfortunate drinkers purchased adulterated booze that blinded, crip-pled, and occasionally even killed some, most of whom were poor or working-class men.

Coffee, Tea, and Soft Drinks

Coffee, tea, and soft drinks remained popular. The introduction of instant coffee (in 1910) and the marketing of electric coffee percolators for home use also contributed to an increase in cof-fee sales. In 1927 the Postum Cereal Company in-troduced Sanka (a contraction of *sans caffeine,* or "without caffeine"). The popularity of tearooms and tea parties, hosted by women's clubs and or-ganizations, helped to boost tea sales.

For many, soft drinks became the non-alcoholic beverage of choice during the 1920s as a result of both National Prohibition and aggressive adver-tising campaigns and expanding merchandising venues. Between 1920 and 1929, annual sales of soft drinks jumped from 175 million cases of soda to almost 273 million cases, or an average of 53 bottles per person.[6] The Coca-Cola Com-pany, one of the pioneers of modern advertising and the nation's leading soft-drink manufacturer, continued its extensive million-dollar promo-tional campaigns. The firm created a series of ad-vertisements with memorable slogans, including "The Pause That Refreshes," which first appeared in a 1929 ad in *The Saturday Evening Post.*

Expanding merchandising outlets also helped to boost soft drink sales. During the 1920s, most soft drinks came in standard six-or seven-ounce bottles, and usually sold for a nickel. By around 1927, bottled soda accounted for the majority of soft drink sales. Other retail merchandising inno-vations also fueled sales. In 1924, the Coca-Cola Company began selling its product in six-bottle cartons, which gradually caught on throughout the soft drink industry. The Sodamat, one of the earliest coin-operated soft drink vending ma-chines, was introduced in 1925.

Food

The Coca-Cola Company and the Pepsi-Cola Corporation dominated the national soft drink market during the 1920s, but dozens of smaller, regionally produced colas also competed in the expanding soda market, often under highly derivative names. Among them were Celery Cola, Vera-Cola, Afri-Kola, Koca-Nola, and Chero-Cola. Grape-flavored sodas, such as Nu-Grape, Bluebird, and Brandywine, and orange drinks such as Orange Crush, Howdy, and Orange Kist were popular. Many of these soft drink manufacturers went out of business or merged with larger companies before World War II, but several of the brands that have remained popular since the 1920s are Dr. Pepper, A&W Root Beer, and Moxie (which actually outsold Coca-Cola in 1920). Ginger ale was another favorite soft drink. Two of the best-selling ginger ales were Cliquot Club Dry Ginger Ale and Canada Dry Pale Dry Ginger Ale, which billed itself as "the Champagne of Ginger Ale" and sold for 35 cents a bottle—seven times what the average soft drink cost.

Several other soft drinks also appeared on the market during the 1920s. In 1928, the Howdy Company introduced 7-Up, originally called Bib-Label Lithiated Lemon-Lime Soda because it contained lithium, a chemical widely prescribed to treat depression. Fizzier than other soft drinks, 7-Up was advertised as a cure for upset stomach, and it soon became the firm's best-selling product. Yoo-Hoo also appeared on the market during the 1920s, when Natale Olivieri, an Italian immigrant, perfected a process that enabled him to bottle a chocolate drink that would not spoil. In 1927, Edwin Perkins, who ran a mail-order fruit drink syrup business, invented Kool-Aid. Originally, Perkins shipped his syrups in glass bottles through the mail, but the bottles often broke or leaked. Inspired by Jell-O gelatin packaging, Perkins created a powdered form of his fruit drink syrups and began marketing a line of six flavors (cherry, grape, orange, raspberry, lemon-lime, and strawberry) that cost 10 cents per one-ounce package, under the new name of Kool-Ade (soon spelled Kool-Aid).

Food

Music

of the 1920s

The 1920s marked a watershed era in the development of American popular music, both in the ways that music was disseminated and in the ways that music actually sounded. During the 1920s, venues such as commercial radio, phonograph records, Broadway musicals, and sound motion pictures played an increasingly significant role in delivering the latest popular songs to far-flung audiences. The decade also witnessed the emergence of whole new genres of indigenous American music, most notably jazz. Jazz ranked as the nation's most popular music during the 1920s and reflected the expanding African American influence on mainstream culture. During the 1920s, record companies also began to record blues and hillbilly music in an effort to develop new ethnic and regional consumer markets.

AMERICAN POPULAR MUSIC

Tin Pan Alley

Since the 1890s, New York City's Tin Pan Alley had reigned as the undisputed capital of the American popular music industry, and it did so until its demise during the 1950s. By the 1920s, however, "Tin Pan Alley" had emerged as a generic term for the popular songwriting and music publishing industry, as well as a synonym for the commercial music it produced.

Songwriting and music publishing firms produced more new songs during the 1920s than during any other decade in the history of Tin Pan Alley. Many of these songs featured the syncopated rhythms commonly found in jazz and consisted of a series of stanzas, each of which was followed by a chorus, usually of 32 bars with four, eight-bar phrases. Many of these popular songs exemplified the spirit of reckless abandon and frivolity that is commonly associated with the 1920s, such as "Ain't We Got Fun" (1921) and "Yes! We Have No Bananas" (1923). Tin Pan Alley songwriting and music publishing firms were also quick to cash in on—and helped to fuel—the latest musical crazes. Dozens of popular songs, for example, reflected the vogue for jazz and blues, such as "Jazz Me Blues" (1921) and "Wabash Blues" (1921). Other numbers, such as "Charleston" (1923), "The Varsity Drag" (1927), and "Doin' the Raccoon" (1928), emerged as national hits largely because of their association with a particular dance.

FORMS OF MUSIC DISTRIBUTION

Sheet Music

Throughout the 1920s, published sheet music represented one of the most important commercial outlets for disseminating American music, and therefore one of Tin Pan Alley's primary sources of revenue. Typically, sheet music consisted of four or five pages of musical notation scored for voice and piano (and sometimes even ukulele) and wrapped in attractive covers. Sheet music was sold at music stores, 5- and 10-cent chain stores, and through mail-order catalogs, usually for about 25 or 30 cents. However, as radio and phonograph ownership became more widespread, sheet music sales declined, and phonograph recordings routinely began to outsell sheet music.

Phonograph Records

Although phonograph recordings had existed since the 1890s, in the 1920s record sales grew large enough to attract the attention of Tin Pan Alley. By 1920, Victor, Columbia, Edison, and some 200 other independent companies were manufacturing phonographs and phonograph records and cylinders. Most of these recordings were issued on 12-inch, 78 rpm (revolutions per minute) discs that contained one three-minute selection on each side and generally sold for between 35 and 75 cents. In 1922, annual record sales reached 110 million discs (more than four times the number sold in 1914).[1] Beginning in 1920, the entertainment trade daily *Variety* published a Top Ten chart to track the sales of phonograph records. A smash hit record might sell two million or more copies, and by the mid-1920s, the sale of phonograph records had replaced the sale of sheet music as the gauge used to measure the commercial success of a song.

Commercial Radio

Beginning in 1920, popular music broadcasts formed the core of radio programming, and stations generally broadcast live studio performances, as opposed to phonograph records. By 1924, many stations were also airing so-called "remote" broadcasts of musical programs from locations such as opera houses, concert halls, and hotel ballrooms. During the highly experimental era of the early 1920s, radio stations broadcast a wide variety of musical entertainers, and as late as the mid-1920s, radio listeners might hear a pianist, an opera tenor, a classical violinist, an old-time string band, a glee club, a Hawaiian guitarist, and a jazz dance band all on the same day on one station.

With the formation of the National Broadcasting Company (NBC) in 1926 and the Columbia Broadcasting System (CBS) in 1927, the range of popular music heard over the nation's airwaves became narrower and more standardized. Network radio typically featured corporate-sponsored musical programs, such as *The Palmolive Hour, The Goodrich Silvertown Orchestra,* and *The Voice of Firestone,* which originated in the network's main studios in New York City. As affiliated stations across the country began carrying the network's national programs, these network shows crowded out local programming and reduced the radio opportunities of amateur singers and musicians. By 1930, an estimated 51 million listeners tuned in nightly to listen to radio programs, and when they heard a song they liked, they often purchased the phonograph recording, the sheet music, or both.

Radio transformed both home entertainment and how Americans listened to music. Middle-class homemakers listened to the radio during the day while performing household chores, and entire families gathered around their radio sets for an evening of entertainment. Tin Pan Alley quickly seized upon the enormous potential of radio to catapult its latest songs into hits. As early as 1923, music-publishing firms employed "song-pluggers"—professional musicians who would perform a new song on the radio over and over again, hoping that the listening audience would like it enough to buy it. Commercial radio also sparked national crazes for certain songs and sometimes helped to make musicians into overnight celebrities. In 1923, for example, Wendell Hall, a staff musician on Chicago's KYW, sold two million copies of his record "It Ain't Gonna Rain No Mo'" by relentlessly bombarding his radio audience with the song.

Broadway Musicals and Revues

During the 1920s, Broadway theater eclipsed the vaudeville stage as the most important live performance venue for showcasing popular songs. As many as 50 musical shows opened each season on Broadway during the decade, and many of

Music

these shows helped to popularize Tin Pan Alley songs. Among the most commercially successful musicals and musical comedies were *No, No, Nannette* (1925), *A Connecticut Yankee* (1927), *Show Boat* (1927), and *Good News* (1927), all of which featured catchy songs that became major hits. A series of all-black musicals and revues also produced hit songs. Among the best known of these shows were Eubie Blake and Noble Sissle's *Shuffle Along* (1921), which included "I'm Just Wild About Harry," and James P. Johnson and Cecil Mack's *Runnin' Wild* (1923), which introduced the song "Charleston" and the popular dance by that name. Musical revues (shows consisting of a series of unrelated song-and-dance numbers) were also highly celebrated, particularly the annual *Ziegfeld Follies, George White Scandals,* and Earl Carroll's *Vanities.* These revues introduced dozens of hit songs, such as "My Man" (1921), "Three O'Clock in the Morning" (1921), and "My Blue Heaven" (1927). African American revues also spawned hit songs, such as Jimmy McHugh and Dorothy Fields's *Blackbirds of 1928,* which popularized "I Can't Give You Anything But Love," and Andy Razaf and Fats Waller's *Hot Chocolates* (1929), which introduced "Ain't Misbehavin.'"

Hollywood Motion Pictures

Beginning in the mid-1920s, Tin Pan Alley increasingly produced songs and music for motion pictures, including theme songs written expressly for a particular movie. One of the earliest successful movie theme songs was "Charmaine," scored for theater orchestras to accompany the Fox Film Corporation's silent feature *What Price Glory?* (1926). Although songwriters seldom composed music for the silent cinema, the overwhelming success of the first feature-length "talkie," Warner Brothers' *The Jazz Singer* (1927), demonstrated that the movies could provide an important venue for popularizing songs. By 1929, with motion pictures attracting audiences of nearly 100 million moviegoers a week, Hollywood studios began producing lavish, big-budget musicals, such as Metro-Goldwyn-Mayer's *The Broadway Melody* (1929), which was the first musical to win the Academy Award for Best Picture.

POPULAR BANDS AND MUSICIANS

Dance Bands

Given the immense popularity of dancing during the 1920s, it is not surprising that dance bands flourished. Paul Whiteman and His Orchestra reigned as the most popular dance band of the 1920s, and Whiteman became known as "the King of Jazz." His first recording, "Whispering" (1920), which sold more than two million copies, made him a national celebrity. Over the next nine years, his orchestra had 28 number one hits and another 108 top 10 recordings, a record unmatched during the Jazz Age. Whiteman franchised his dance music; by 1930, he was operating 11 official Paul Whiteman bands in New York City and some 57 others across the nation. Other popular dance bands of the 1920s included Isham Jones and His Orchestra, Fred Waring and the Pennsylvanians, and Guy Lombardo and His Royal Canadians, as well as "all-girl" dance orchestras such as Babe Egan's Hollywood Red Heads. Most of these ensembles performed as the regular house bands at nationally renowned hotels and ballrooms in New York, Chicago, Los Angeles, and other major cities. These bands performed a wide range of music, including Tin Pan Alley songs, jazz instrumentals, symphonic compositions, and occasionally waltzes and tangos. They often performed over the radio via "remote" broadcasts, and recorded their most popular songs for major record companies. By 1929, according to *Variety,* more than 700 dance bands were touring throughout the nation, performing in hotels, cafés, vaudeville theaters, and dance halls.

Singing Stars

A number of individual singers also emerged as national celebrities. Most of them had begun on the vaudeville circuit, and then branched into radio, records, and film. The nation's greatest pop star of the 1920s was Al Jolson, a veteran vaudeville singer, dancer, and all-around showman who billed himself as "the World's Greatest Entertainer." Jolson first won national acclaim in 1911 in the Broadway revue *La Belle Paree,* with his dramatic, booming singing style and extraordinary stage presence. During the 1920s, he appeared in a string of musical revues such as *Bombo* (1921) and *Big Boy* (1925), in which he often portrayed a blundering blackface character named Gus. Jolson recorded a dozen number one hits during the decade, including "Swanee" (1920), "Toot, Toot, Tootsie (Goo'bye)" (1922), "Sonny Boy" (1928), and "My Mammy" (1928). He became one of Hollywood's biggest box office attractions as a result of his starring roles in Warner Brothers' pioneering "talkies," *The Jazz Singer* (1927) and *The Singing Fool* (1929).

Eddie Cantor, whose large, expressive eyes earned him the nickname "Banjo Eyes," also ranked among the most popular male singers of the 1920s. Cantor emerged as a major pop idol after starring in a string of producer Florenz Ziegfeld's celebrated *Ziegfeld Follies* (1917–1919, 1923, and 1927) and the Broadway musical comedies *Kid Boots* (1923) and *Whoopee* (1928), in which he introduced "Makin' Whoopee" (1928), a comical song about the shortcomings of marriage. Cantor went on to star in the film versions of *Kid Boots* (1926) and *Whoopee* (1930) and became one of the leading stars of stage and screen during the late 1920s.

HIT SONGS OF THE 1920S

Songs and Performers

"Second Hand Rose" (Fanny Brice)—1921

"I Wish I Could Shimmy Like My Sister Kate" (Jazzbo's Carolina Serenaders)—1922

"Yes, We Have No Bananas" (Billy Jones)—1923

"Charleston" (Paul Whiteman and His Orchestra)—1925

"Do, Do, Do" (Gertrude Lawrence)—1926

"My Mammy" (Al Jolson)—1927

"Blue Yodel No. 1 (T for Texas)" (Jimmie Rodgers)—1928

"Keep On the Sunny Side" (The Carter Family)—1928

"I Want To Be Loved By You" (Helen Kane)—1928

"Nobody Knows You When You're Down And Out" (Bessie Smith)—1929

One of the most celebrated female entertainers of the decade was Sophie Tucker, a vaudeville and Broadway singer known for her racy, sexually suggestive songs and perhaps best remembered for her signature song, "Some of These Days" (1927). Her "I'm the Last of the Red Hot Mamas" (1929), which she introduced in her talking motion picture debut, Warner Brothers' *Honky Tonk* (1929), won her the stage billing, "the Last of the Red Hot Mamas."

Comedian and singer Fanny Brice starred in virtually every one of the annual *Ziegfeld Follies* produced between 1910 and 1923. Later, Brice's life served as the basis for the Broadway musical *Funny Girl* (1964) and the Oscar-winning Hollywood film of that same title (1968), starring Barbra Streisand.

Helen Kane achieved success for her roles in such Broadway musicals as *A Night in Spain* (1927) and *Good Boy* (1928), in which she introduced what became her theme song, "I Wanna Be Loved By You." Known as the "Boop-Boop-A-Doop Girl," Kane is remembered for her distinctive little-girl voice and as the inspiration for Betty Boop, an animated cartoon character introduced by Fleisher Studio in 1930.

Crooners and Torch Singers

Prior to the mid-1920s, most recording artists came out of vaudeville, where they typically sang in a loud, robust style so that their voices could reach the back rows of large theaters, but the introduction of sensitive electric microphones in 1925 led to the development of a more intimate, hushed style of singing known as crooning. Gene Austin recorded one of the biggest hits of the decade, "My Blue Heaven" (1927), which sold more than five million copies and dominated the number one spot on the record charts for 13 weeks. Other prominent crooners included Jack Smith, Nick Lucas, and Rudy Vallee. The rough equivalent for women performers was called torch singing. Torch songs were sad, sentimental songs about heartbreak and failed romance, with the singer still "carrying the torch" for an ex-lover. One of the best-known torch singers of the 1920s was Helen Morgan, star of the Broadway musical *Show Boat* (1927), whose signature song was the self-pitying "Why Was I Born?" (1929). Other acclaimed torch singers of the 1920s included Ruth Etting and Libby Holman, both of whom also starred in several popular Broadway musicals.

JAZZ

Although initially considered a passing musical fad when it was first recorded in 1917, jazz became the most influential form of American popular music during the 1920s. Jazz combined elements of ragtime compositions, brass band marches, minstrel numbers, and, to a lesser degree, blues songs. Ragtime shared many stylistic similarities with jazz, particularly the use of "ragged," or syncopated, rhythms. Classical ragtime was essentially a composed music that stressed the performance of published musical works in precisely the way in which they had been written. Jazz, in contrast, was an unwritten, polyphonic music characterized, at least originally, by blues accents and collective improvisation. Early jazz bands featured cornets, clarinets, trombones, drums, and sometimes banjos, violins, and pianos. By the early 1920s, Chicago had emerged as the nation's jazz center, although bands were also appearing in dance halls, nightclubs, and speakeasies in many East and West Coast cities, and was attracting growing audiences of both black and white listeners.

The popularity of jazz provided new opportunities for African American musicians to make records, occasionally perform on radio, and play for live audiences. Largely as a result of the racism and discriminatory practices of the recording industry, African American musicians did not make any jazz recordings until 1922, when New Orleans Creole trombonist Edward "Kid" Ory and the Creole Orchestra, cut "Ory's Creole Trombone" and "Society Blues." Beginning in 1923, record companies scrambled to record popular jazz bands of both races. During the remaining years of the 1920s, record companies issued thousands of jazz recordings, including those of such legendary African American jazz ensembles as King Oliver and the Creole Jazz Band, Clarence Williams's Blue Five, Louis Armstrong and His Hot Five (and His Hot Seven), Fletcher Henderson and His Orchestra, and Bennie Moten's Kansas

City Orchestra. The rising popularity of radio also helped to disseminate jazz music throughout the United States. As early as 1921, white dance bands such as Vincent Lopez and His Orchestra and the Coon-Sanders Nighthawks, whose repertoires included jazz numbers, were appearing on the radio. But African American musicians were largely excluded from performing on early commercial radio.

Hot Jazz

Beginning in the early 1920s, small African American bands pioneered a dynamic, emotionally charged musical style known as "hot jazz." Hot jazz, which peaked between 1925 and 1929, typically featured fast-paced individual solos and hard-driving, swinging rhythms. King Oliver's Creole Jazz Band ranked as one of the important hot jazz bands of the 1920s. Led by cornetist Joe "King" Oliver, the Creole Jazz Band featured some of the finest New Orleans jazz musicians, including cornetist Louis Armstrong, who joined the band in 1922. In 1923, the Creole Jazz Band made some three dozen recordings that stand out as the most important collection of early recorded jazz, including "Dipper Mouth Blues" and "High Society Rag." Another leading exponent of hot jazz was the flamboyant New Orleans Creole pianist Ferdinand "Jelly Roll" Morton, one of the earliest jazz composers and arrangers, who began playing piano as a teenager in the brothels of Storyville—New Orleans's red-light district. In 1926, Morton moved to New York City. There, between 1926 and 1930, Morton recorded more than 50 selections with his band, the Red Hot Peppers, including "Black Bottom Stomp" (1926) and "Original Jelly Roll Blues" (1926).

In the late 1920s, dozens of talented jazz musicians migrated to New York City, where most of the major recording companies were located. Consequently, New York City replaced Chicago as the nation's premier jazz center. Pianist Fletcher Henderson, who was sometimes billed as "the Colored King of Jazz," led one of the most popular African American jazz bands in Manhattan during the 1920s. Between 1924 and 1934, Henderson and His Orchestra performed as the house band at the prestigious Roseland Ballroom in Times Square. Henderson's Orchestra produced a smooth, sophisticated sound and ranked as one of the most commercially successful black bands of the decade, recording such hit numbers as "Gulf Coast Blues" (1923), "Carolina" (1925), and "Dinah" (1926). In 1928, Henderson began arranging jazz numbers, and he is one of the first arrangers of what became known in the 1930s as swing music.

With the advent of National Prohibition, Harlem nightclubs and cabarets began to attract wealthy white partygoers and tourists who wanted to drink, dance, and hear "exotic" African American music. In 1929, *Variety* listed 11 major nightclubs in Harlem that catered to predominantly white crowds. These swanky nightclubs and cabarets employed hundreds of African American jazz musicians during the late 1920s, including bandleader Edward "Duke" Ellington, a formally trained pianist and the preeminent composer of jazz music. Between 1927 and 1931, Ellington's Orchestra performed as the house band at the Cotton Club, a segregated, white-patrons-only nightclub owned by a syndicate of mobsters and decorated to resemble a lavish antebellum southern plantation. Ellington recorded a series of his own compositions with his orchestra, including "Black and Tan Fantasy" (1927) and "Creole Love Call" (1927). In 1929, Ellington appeared in *Black and Tan,* the first of more than a dozen Hollywood films he would make. Ellington was among the few hot jazz musicians who successfully transitioned to swing music during the 1930s.

By far the greatest jazz musician of the 1920s was Louis Armstrong, a New Orleans-born cornetist and trumpeter whose inventive solos and technical brilliance marked the pinnacle of hot jazz. In 1922, Armstrong moved to Chicago to play with King Oliver's Creole Jazz Band, but in 1924, he joined Fletcher Henderson's Orchestra in New York City. There, during his 13-month stint with the band, he dazzled audiences with his solos and swinging rhythms. Between 1925 and 1928, Armstrong recorded a series of 65 selections for OKeh Records as the leader of his own bands, the Hot Five and the Hot Seven. Among these songs are such classics as "Heebie Jeebies" (1926), "Potato Head Blues" (1927), and "West End Blues" (1928).

A number of white jazz musicians also influenced the development of jazz, including cornet player Bix Beiderbecke, clarinetist Benny Goodman, trombonist Irving "Miff" Mole, soprano saxophonist Milton "Mezz" Mezzrow, guitarist Eddie Lang, violinist Joe Venuti, and trombonist Jack Teagarden.

Sweet Jazz

Although African American musicians were the principal innovators of jazz during the 1920s, most Americans would have heard a diluted, commercial form of the music called "sweet jazz," performed primarily by all-white orchestras. Sweet jazz featured slower tempos and less improvisation and was generally more appealing to the musical tastes of middlebrow white Americans. Paul Whiteman's band performed carefully arranged compositions that, although they included syncopated rhythms and blues accents, remained respectable and genteel. Indeed, Whiteman sought to refine jazz and make it more commercially accessible to mainstream white audiences. Whiteman's Orchestra, which sometimes contained as many as 30 musicians, featured some of the legendary white jazz soloists of the 1920s, including Tommy Dorsey, Frankie Trumbauer, Joe Venuti, Eddie Lang, and Bix Beiderbecke.

BLUES MUSIC

Another form of African American music that rose to prominence during the 1920s was the blues, which emerged around the turn of the twentieth century and evolved from a variety of traditional black musical forms, including field hollers, work songs, ballads, and rags.

Early folk often spoke of work, crime, gambling, alcohol, imprisonment, disasters, and hard times. Above all, the blues commented on the universal themes of troubled love relationships and sexual desire. Although the blues often conveyed a sense of overwhelming melancholy and resignation, many blues songs were high-spirited, rollicking party numbers.

W. C. Handy was one of the earliest composers to write and publish commercial songs inspired by folk blues. His early compositions, notably

"Memphis Blues" (1912) and "St. Louis Blues" (1914), earned him the title "Father of the Blues." In 1926, Handy published his edited collection titled *Blues: An Anthology,* one of the earliest studies to discuss the significant influence of the folk blues tradition on American jazz, popular, and classical music. The book not only celebrated the rich cultural heritage of African American musical traditions but also contributed to the growing interest in the blues and black folk culture.

Vaudeville Blues

Prior to 1920, the recording industry had virtually ignored African American music fans, and those recordings by black singers and musicians that were available consisted largely of racist "coon" songs, comedy monologues, dance num-

The great blues singer Bessie Smith. Courtesy of the Southern Folklife Collection, University of North Carolina at Chapel Hill.

bers, and spirituals. But beginning in the 1920s, companies began to record and market blues music specifically for African American consumers. In 1920, Mamie Smith, accompanied by her band, the Jazz Hounds, recorded "Crazy Blues" for OKeh Records, marking the advent of commercial blues recordings. "Crazy Blues" sold 75,000 copies in its first month, convincing OKeh, Columbia, Paramount, and other white-owned record companies that a lucrative market existed among African Americans for what the industry soon called "race records." Within a few years, most of the great vaudeville blues singers (also known as classic blues singers) had made commercial recordings, including Clara Smith, Ethel Waters, Sara Martin, Bertha "Sippie" Wallace, and Victoria Spivey.

Vaudeville blues singers were almost exclusively women, and as veterans of the vaudeville stage, most of them sang in a light operatic style rather than in the soulful, expressive vocal style commonly associated with authentic blues singing. Small jazz combos usually provided the backup accompaniment, and many of the premier musicians of the 1920s performed on these recordings, including Louis Armstrong, Fletcher Henderson, and Coleman Hawkins.

One of the most influential vaudeville blues singers of the 1920s was Gertrude "Ma" Rainey, who flaunted expensive beaded gowns, a necklace made of $20 gold pieces, and ostentatious diamond earrings and rings. Rainey made her first recordings for Paramount Records in 1923. Billed as "the Mother of the Blues," she recorded more than 100 songs over the next five years. She sang in a raw, expressive style that was deeply influenced by southern folk blues, and she remained one of the preeminent vaudeville blues singers throughout the 1920s.

Rainey's young protégé, Bessie Smith, emerged as an even greater blues star. Smith's first record, "Gulf Coast Blues," coupled with "Downhearted Blues" (1923), sold 780,000 copies in its first six months on the market. Within two years, she became the nation's highest-paid African American entertainer. Billed as "the Empress of the Blues," she went on to record more than 150 songs for Columbia between 1923 and 1931, on which she was often accompanied by the greatest jazz musicians of the age, including Louis Armstrong, who

The Spiritual in Europe

Toward the end of the 1920s, European audiences continued to embrace American musical forms—and became especially enamored of the "Negro spiritual," as it was called at the time. The traditional music of African American workers and worshippers had already developed into such forms as gospel, blues, and jazz, spurring an interest among music fans in London, Paris, Prague, and Berlin, as well as in American concert halls. The form's best-known international performer was Paul Robeson; its expression in movement was championed by the dancer Tamiris.

Robeson, a multi-talented actor, singer, and political activist, launched his first European concert tour in Paris in October, 1927. His imposing figure and sonorous bass voice lent a sense of depth and gravity to his program of spirituals and work songs, which he linked both musically and thematically to folk songs from Russia, Africa, and elsewhere. Robeson's conviction and commitment made a tremendous impression in Europe, and especially in Great Britain, where he went on to make films and now-legendary stage appearances.

The New York-based modern dancer Tamiris aimed to interpret African American musical forms in a program she called "Negro Spirituals." Trained in Russian ballet, Tamiris came to reject such imported and artificial dance techniques. Instead, her choreography evoked athletic moves, such as boxing and football, as well as physical labor and what many saw as the frenetic everyday actions of jazz-age Americans. Her program met with critical raves in Berlin, Salzburg, Paris, and other European capitals in 1928 and 1929, and helped inspire modern dance practitioners to explore their own local movement traditions.

played cornet on her classic rendition of "St. Louis Blues" (1925). In 1929, Smith starred in *St. Louis Blues,* one of the first all-black talking films. With her expressive, soulful phrasing, she remained the biggest blues star of the 1920s, and she is considered by music historians to be the greatest vaudeville blues singer of all time.

Country Blues

In 1924, music companies began to record country blues. Country bluesmen sang and performed in ways that more closely resembled the authentic folk blues than it resembled vaudeville blues. Solo guitarists often employed a call-and-response interaction in which an instrumental riff "answered" the human voice. Unlike vaudeville blues vocalists, country blues singers were almost exclusively men. Most were self-taught musicians who entertained on a semi-professional basis at local dances, barbecues, and other social gatherings.

One of the most influential country bluesmen to record during the 1920s was Blind Lemon Jefferson, a one-time itinerant street musician from Dallas who recording almost 100 songs, including "Black Snake Moan" (1927) and "Matchbox

Blues" (1927). Charlie Patton, "the Father of the Delta Blues," recorded nearly 70 songs for Paramount between 1929 and his death from a heart attack in 1934, including his signature song "Pony Blues" (1929), as well as "Down the Dirt Road Blues" (1929), "Green River Blues" (1929), and "Spoonful Blues" (1929). Other famous country bluesmen of the 1920s include Texas Alexander, Mississippi John Hurt, Blind Willie McTell, Sleepy John Estes, and Blind Blake.

Throughout the late 1920s, as the blues craze intensified, many of the nation's leading record companies, particularly OKeh, Paramount, and Columbia, issued hundreds of race records specifically intended for an African American market. In 1927, African American record buyers purchased an estimated 10 million records. The commercial recording of the blues, like almost all other musical genres, drastically declined after the onset of the Great Depression.

HILLBILLY MUSIC

Another popular sound of the American South was "hillbilly music" (sometimes called "old-time music"), the forerunner of modern country music. First broadcast and recorded in 1922, hillbilly music consisted chiefly of the vernacular music of ordinary white southerners, particularly amateur and semi-professional musicians. These musicians incorporated a wide range of musical influences, including traditional British ballads, fiddle tunes, sentimental pop songs of the 1890s, gospel numbers, blues songs, cowboy songs, and even the latest Tin Pan Alley hits.

Radio Barn Dances

As early as 1922, Atlanta's WSB began airing short live programs of old-time music performed by local fiddlers and string bands. The following year, WBAP, Fort Worth, Texas, launched what is considered the first "barn dance"—a variety program of old-time fiddlers, singing cowboys, and string bands. Other radio stations across the South and Midwest soon began airing their own live barn dances on Saturday nights.

One such popular program was Nashville WSM's *The Grand Ole Opry* (before 1927, *WSM Barn Dance*), which first aired in 1925. To enhance the program's rural image, WSM radio director George D. Hay required his musicians to wear rustic costumes of checkered work shirts, denim overalls, and straw hats for the live studio audiences. By the end of the 1920s, *The Grand Ole Opry* had emerged as a country music institution, and it remains on the air today, making it the longest-running radio show in American broadcasting history.

Hillbilly Recordings

In 1923, an Atlanta musician and radio star nicknamed Fiddlin' John Carson made the first commercially successful hillbilly record, "The Little Old Log Cabin in the Lane." Over the next few years, Columbia, Victor, and other companies began to record similar old-time music. By 1927, record companies were issuing more than a thousand new hillbilly records a year.

Although it often looked nostalgically to the past, many hillbilly recordings chronicled and critiqued significant current events, such as train wrecks, tornados, murders, or social trends. One of the best-known topical songs of the 1920s was

Blind Alfred Reed's "Why Do You Bob Your Hair, Girls?" (1927), which accused fashionable young flappers of being unchristian. The greatest interpreter of topical hillbilly songs was Vernon Dalhart, a light opera singer by training, whose "The Prisoner's Song," paired with "The Wreck of the Old 97," (1924) became the first hillbilly disc to sell one million copies. Dalhart went on to make more than a thousand old-time recordings between 1924 and 1933, many of them songs about highly publicized national events, including "The Death of Floyd Collins" (1925), "The John T. Scopes Trial" (1925), "There's a New Star in Heaven Tonight (Rudolph Valentino)" (1926), and "Lindbergh (The Eagle of the U.S.A.)" (1927).

Hillbilly Stringbands

Originally, most commercial hillbilly musicians were solo artists or duos, but beginning in 1925, string bands emerged as the most commonly recorded ensembles on hillbilly records. String bands usually consisted of a fiddler or two, a guitarist, a banjo player, perhaps a mandolin player, or some combination of these. One of the most influential and commercially successful string bands of the 1920s was Charlie Poole and the North Carolina Ramblers, whose first release—"Don't Let Your Deal Go Down Blues," coupled with "Can I Sleep in Your Barn Tonight, Mister?" (1925)—sold 102,000 copies in an age when hillbilly record sales of 30,000 or more were rare.

The First Stars of Hillbilly Music

The first star of hillbilly music was Jimmie Rodgers, the "Father of Country Music," who sang songs that embodied the rough-and-rowdy ways of hoboes, drifters, and gamblers. A former railroad brakeman, his first hit record "Blue Yodel (T for Texas)" (1927), sold more than one million copies. Over the next five years, he recorded over 100 songs, including "Waiting for a Train" (1928) and "In the Jailhouse Now" (1928), as well as a series of 12 classic "blue yodels." In 1929, he appeared in *The Singing Brakeman* (1929), a film short that showcased his singing abilities. Billed as "The Singing Brakeman" and "America's Blue

Yodeler," Rodgers was largely responsible for transforming old-time music from an instrumentalist genre to one dominated by vocalists. Before he died in 1933 at the age of 35 from tuberculosis, Rodgers sold an estimated six million records, and his tremendous commercial success spawned many imitators, including Gene Autry, Jimmie Davis, and Ernest Tubb.

The other major hillbilly act of the 1920s was the Carter Family, "the First Family of Country Music." The Carters consisted of bass singer A. P. Carter, his wife, Sara, who sang lead and played autoharp (and sometimes second guitar), and her cousin, Maybelle, who played guitar. Between 1927 and 1941, the trio recorded more than 300 songs, including country music classics, such as "Keep on the Sunny Side" (1928), "Wildwood Flower" (1928), and "Wabash Cannonball" (1929). The Carters especially favored late-nineteenth-century sentimental ballads, parlor songs, and traditional mountain folk songs. The group also exerted a significant influence on the musical development of hillbilly music, particularly with their haunting close harmonies and Maybelle's signature guitar style.

HAWAIIAN MUSIC

During the 1920s, a Hawaiian music craze swept the nation. The first widespread exposure that many Americans had to this music came in 1915 at the Panama–Pacific International Exposition held in San Francisco. There, at the Hawaiian Pavilion, mainlanders could hear the lilting tropical melodies of ukuleles and Hawaiian guitars (Hawaiian guitar is an instrumental style in which the guitar is played on the seated performer's lap and is fretted by sliding a knife, steel bar, or other metal object on the strings). Throughout the 1920s, Hawaiian musicians such as steel guitarist Sol Hoopii and ukulele virtuoso Bennie Nawahi toured the continental United States in vaudeville shows and revues, and music companies greatly expanded their catalogs of Hawaiian recordings. Between 1915 and 1929, Tin Pan Alley songwriters wrote hundreds of novelty numbers about the alluring beauty and charms of Hawaiian life, including "Hello, Hawaii, How Are You?" (1915), "Oh, How She Could Yacki Hacki Wicki Wacki

Woo" (1916), "Hula Hula Dream Girl" (1924), and "That Aloha Waltz" (1928).

The Hawaiian music craze inspired many to take up the ukulele. Inexpensive, portable, and relatively easy to play, ukuleles became one of the most popular instruments for home entertaining. Although the instrument was popularized by Hawaiians, its design was originally based on small guitars brought to Hawaii from Portugal in the 1870s. Some ukuleles, such as those produced by the C. F. Martin Company, were finely crafted, professional-quality instruments; most of the instruments manufactured were inexpensive, mass-produced models of varying quality. Correspondence courses and music schools offered lessons in the ukulele and Hawaiian guitar, and amateur musicians formed ukulele and Hawaiian guitar clubs. Music-publishing companies churned out ukulele instructional booklets and song collections. The mania for Hawaiian music and ukuleles waned in the late 1920s.

CLASSICAL MUSIC

The 1920s saw the emergence of several influential American composers, most notably Charles Ives, Aaron Copeland, Virgil Thomson, John Alden Carpenter, and William Grant Still, many of whom experimented with fusing jazz and blues with the art music of European tradition.

Paul Whiteman, bandleader of the most commercially successful dance orchestra of the 1920s, and his arranger, pianist Ferde Grofé, combined elements of modern jazz and classical music to create a synthesis called "symphonic jazz." Whiteman's most celebrated concert, "An Experiment in Modern Music," at New York City's Aeolian Hall in 1924, featured performances of popular songs, jazz instrumentals, and classical selections. This legendary concert included the critically acclaimed premiere of songwriter and pianist George Gershwin's jazz concerto, *Rhapsody in Blue,* which became an immediate sensation. Whiteman staged additional experimental concerts between 1925 and 1938, showcasing selections of popular music, jazz, and classical works. Although best known for his Tin Pan Alley songs and Broadway musical revues, Gershwin composed several

Music

A happy group of young women in bathing suits playing ukuleles, 1926. Prints & Photographs Division, Library of Congress.

other celebrated classical works, including *Concerto in F for Piano and Orchestra* (1925), *Three Preludes for Piano* (1926), *An American in Paris* (1928), and *Porgy and Bess* (1935).

Most ordinary Americans' exposure to the great European classical works came from phonograph recordings and radio broadcasts. Many of the best-selling classical discs of the 1920s appeared on Victor's prestigious Red Seal label,

whose records cost as much as $7 apiece (or almost ten times as much as the company's pop records). During the 1920s, Victor spent millions of dollars advertising its premium-priced classical records and recruited some of the greatest international stars of symphonic music and grand opera to make recordings, including Russian pianist Sergei Rachmaninoff, Italian conductor Arturo Toscanini, and, before his death in 1921,

Italian tenor Enrico Caruso, longtime star of the New York Metropolitan Opera. Classical recordings sold relatively well, primarily to upper and upper-middle-class Americans, some of whom purchased these records more for their cultural prestige than for any appreciation of music. Even as record sales in general declined after the advent of commercial radio, Victor sold more than five million copies of its Red Seal records annually throughout the decade.

Radio networks prominently featured classical music programming and brought the music of nationally distinguished opera companies and symphony orchestras into millions of homes. In 1921, Chicago station KYW inaugurated weekly broadcasts of the Chicago Grand Opera Company, the first such company to have its productions regularly aired on radio. Soon, other stations began to carry operatic programs. Dozens of symphony orchestras, such as the Boston Symphony Orchestra and the New York Philharmonic Orchestra, appeared on network radio during the late 1920s. NBC in particular boasted a strong schedule of classical concert programs, including *General Motors Concerts* and *Mobil Oil Concerts*. Musical education programs such as NBC's *The Music Appreciation Hour,* which premiered in 1928, introduced millions of listeners to classical music. Hosted by Dr. Walter Damrosch, the longtime conductor of the New York Symphony Orchestra, this influential radio show combined classical music performances with down-to-earth explanations in order to foster appreciation for this music.

Music

Sports

and Leisure of the 1920s

In the 1920s, rising numbers of Americans began to enjoy increasing amounts of consumer goods and leisure time. For most members of the middle and working classes, work weeks shortened to an average of 45 hours.[1] Vacations for both white-collar and blue-collar workers became increasingly common. Wages and salaries also rose, sometimes by as much as 30 percent, even as the cost of living remained comparatively steady. These employment-related trends provided ordinary Americans with more leisure time and more disposable income to spend on an ever-expanding variety of recreational activities. Between 1919 and 1929, the amount of money Americans spent on recreation and leisure activities nearly doubled to more than $4 billion a year.[2]

SPORTS

The expansion of commercialized leisure made ordinary people more sedentary. Instead of playing baseball, for example, many attended professional or semi-professional games. During the 1920s, watching and following college and professional sports became, for the first time, a pervasive pastime. Radio broadcasts of the World Series, college bowl games, prizefights, and horse races, as well as newspaper sports columns and daily box scores, boosted the popularity of the

nation's spectator sports and transformed Babe Ruth, Red Grange, and Jack Dempsey into national celebrities. Sports mushroomed into a huge industry as press agents, sports promoters, sportswriters, radio announcers, chambers of commerce, and various media outlets promoted athletic events. For those who did participate in sports and physical exercise, golf and tennis skyrocketed in popularity, as men and women flooded the thousands of newly constructed golf courses and tennis courts. Cities and small towns built municipal athletic complexes. Popular wisdom conceded that exercise was as beneficial for women as it was for men, and so athletics was not limited to males.

During the 1920s, the popularity of sports grew spectacularly, but few professional athletes commanded enormous prestige or whopping salaries. Rather, Americans worshiped amateur athletes who provided admirable models of athletic fitness, moral character, and honorable spirit. Because they seemed to play for the sheer enjoyment and thrill of the sport, rather than for crass monetary reward, amateur athletes such as golfer Bobby Jones, tennis champion Helen Wills, and swimmer Johnny Weismuller became American idols. Over the course of the 1920s, however, hundreds of amateur and college athletes succumbed to the allure of large salaries promised by professional sports clubs. Fans often responded negatively to amateurs who turned professional, believing they had "sold out" and compromised the purity of their sport. Professional baseball, however, never seemed to be troubled by this stigma.

Baseball

Major League Baseball (MLB) rose to prominence as the national pastime during the 1920s, but at the dawn of the decade the sport received a punishing blow, as the "Black Sox scandal" deeply shook Americans' faith in the game. In September 1920, eight members of the Chicago White Sox baseball club—including star outfielder Joe "Shoeless Joe" Jackson, one of the game's greatest hitters—were indicted for conspiring to throw the 1919 World Series against the Cincinnati Reds in exchange for a sizable payoff. During the 1921 trial in Chicago, the signed confessions and other evidence against the teammates mysteriously vanished, thus adding another level of intrigue and corruption to the scandal. The White Sox players were acquitted of intent to defraud, however, the newly installed first commissioner of baseball, Judge Kennesaw Mountain Landis, banned all eight players from the game for life.

Perhaps in part because of Commissioner Landis's fiat, the "Black Sox scandal" dissipated relatively quickly. Baseball soon became more exciting, due primarily to legendary slugger George Herman "Babe" Ruth and the thrill of dramatic home run hitting. In earlier decades, pitching had dominated the game, keeping scores low and strategy confined to singles hitting, bunts, hit-and-run plays, and base stealing. But when Babe Ruth crushed 29 home runs for the Boston Red Sox in 1919 and then followed with an unbelievable 54 home runs for the New York Yankees the next year, baseball fans began to favor these exciting, high-scoring games dominated by power hitters.

Major League Baseball made a number of rule changes that increased the batter's advantage against the pitcher. Beginning in 1920, pitchers were forbidden from scuffing baseballs or altering them with tobacco juice, saliva, mud, grease, or other foreign substances that made a pitched ball move erratically in the air and thus more difficult for batters to hit. In 1920, Cleveland Indian shortstop Roy Chapman was struck in the head and killed by a pitched ball. It was believed that Chapman had trouble seeing the ball because it was so soiled. In the wake of this tragic accident, the league instructed umpires to replace dirty baseballs with clean white ones. This steady rotation of new baseballs made it easier for batters to see, and therefore hit, the ball. The many new baseball stadiums constructed in the 1920s (including Yankee Stadium, completed in 1923, which held 62,000 fans and is still known as "the House that Ruth Built") gave long-ball hitters an edge by enclosing the outfields with fences and bleachers. As a result of this fast-paced, high-scoring style of play, average annual attendance at Major League Baseball games leaped from less than six million during the 1910s to more than nine million during the 1920s. Player salaries also increased, especially for power hitters. While superstars like New York Yankee outfielder Babe Ruth could earn $100,000 or more through salary, bonuses, and product endorsements, average players earned between $4,000 and $10,000 a year—a respectable wage.

Babe Ruth began his career as a pitcher with two remarkable seasons for the Boston Red Sox. After he was traded to the New York Yankees in 1920, he went on an unforgettable streak of record-breaking power hitting, including pounding 60 home runs in 1927—a record that stood until New York Yankee outfielder Roger Maris broke it in 1961. Nicknamed alternately "the Sultan of Swat," "the Bambino," or simply "the Babe," Ruth was one of the highest-paid sports heroes of the decade. Besides his baseball salary, Ruth raked in tremendous sums from his personal appearances and endorsements of sporting equipment, breakfast cereals, candy bars, and even underwear. In 1926, he spent 12 weeks on a nationwide vaudeville tour, earning more than $8,000 a week. He also appeared in several Hollywood films between 1920 and 1931, including *Heading Home, Play Ball with Babe Ruth,* and *How Babe Ruth Hits a Home Run.*

Ruth anchored the lineup of the New York Yankees—the dominant club of the decade. The 1927 team, nicknamed "Murderers' Row," included such stars as first baseman Lou Gehrig, second baseman Tony Lazzeri, and outfielders

Sports

Babe Ruth crossing the plate after making his first home run of the season, 1924. Prints & Photographs Division, Library of Congress.

Sports

Earle Combs and Bob Meusel. Under manager Miller Huggins, the Yankees won six American League pennants and three World Series (1923, 1927, and 1928) during the 1920s. But Ruth and his Yankee teammates were not the only baseball stars. Detroit outfielder Ty Cobb, a ferocious, hard-nosed competitor who had a lifetime batting average of .366, enjoyed a remarkable career that spanned 24 years (1904–1928). Cobb made his mark with clutch singles and smart, aggressive base running. His career record of 892 stolen bases stood until 1977. Other baseball heroes of the 1920s included Cleveland Indians outfielder Tristram "Tris" Speaker, Pittsburgh Pirates third baseman Harold "Pie" Traynor, and St. Louis Cardinals infielder Rogers Hornsby.

Until 1947, strict racial segregation prohibited African Americans from joining professional baseball. In 1920, Andrew "Rube" Foster, the owner and manager of the Chicago American Giants, founded the National Negro Baseball League (NNBL). The NNBL proved to be a remarkable success, despite the difficulties posed by segregated hotels and passenger trains, along with the high fees for the use of white-owned ballparks. The NNLB drew more than 400,000 spectators during the 1923 season. Salaries for African American players compared poorly to those of white MLB players, but the stars of the all-black league, such as pitcher Leroy "Satchel" Paige and catcher Josh Gibson, could earn as much as $1,000 a month.

Boxing

Prior to World War I, boxing was considered to be a disreputable, lowbrow sport that attracted primarily gamblers, drinkers, and rowdies. In 1920, prizefighting was legal only in New York

WORLD SERIES

1920 Cleveland (AL), 5 games; Brooklyn Robins (NL), 2 games

1921 New York Giants (NL), 5 games; New York Yankees (AL), 3 games

1922 New York Giants (NL), 4 games; New York Yankees (AL), 0 games

1923 New York Yankees (AL), 4 games; New York Giants (NL), 2 games

1924 Washington Senators (AL), 4 games; New York Giants (NL), 3 games

1925 Pittsburgh Pirates (NL), 4 games; Washington Senators (AL), 3 games

1926 St. Louis Cardinals (NL), 4 games; New York Yankees (AL), 3 games

1927 New York Yankees (AL), 4 games; Pittsburgh Pirates (NL), 0 games

1928 New York Yankees (AL), 4 games; St. Louis Cardinals (NL), 0 games

1929 Philadelphia Athletics (AL), 4 games; Chicago Cubs (NL), 1 game

and New Jersey, but over the next 10 years, many state legislatures lifted the bans and restrictions on boxing, and state commissioners sought to sanitize this traditionally notorious sport. Boxing promoters such as George "Tex" Rickard publicized big matches to such an extent that gate receipts occasionally topped $1 million and matches began to attract fans from all classes of American society.

The 1920s saw an abundance of boxing champions in virtually every weight class. Lightweight Benny Leonard, welterweight Edward "Mickey" Walker, and middleweights Harry Greb and Theodore "Tiger" Flowers (the first black middleweight champion) are considered by sports historians to be among the finest boxers in history, and they generated a large fan following during the 1920s. Jack Dempsey and Gene Tunney dominated heavyweight boxing in the 1920s. In 1921, Dempsey fought in the first $1 million match against a French war hero named Georges Carpentier, and in 1927, Dempsey's famous bout with Tunney generated a $2 million gate—a record that would stand for half a century. Dempsey held the heavyweight

championship title for seven years (1919–1926), until Tunney finally unseated him in 1926. Tunney retained his title until Jack Sharkey, another great heavyweight of the 1920s, defeated him in 1928.

Football

The popularity of college football rose dramatically as college and university enrollments nearly doubled during the 1920s. Universities built enormous stadiums. Yale University's new stadium held 75,000 spectators, Stanford University's seated more than 86,000, and the University of Michigan's accommodated nearly 102,000. Ticket receipts for college football actually exceeded those for Major League Baseball during much of the 1920s. In 1927, more than 30 million spectators attended college football games.

College football's popularity soared for several reasons. The sport had recently evolved from a strictly running game to a faster, more exciting passing game. Furthermore, the focus of college football had expanded beyond the eastern schools of the Ivy League to include large Midwestern universities such as Notre Dame, Michigan, and Illinois. Famed coach Knute Rockne led his Notre Dame squad to tremendous heights during the decade, including an undefeated 1924 season and a Rose Bowl victory, and he coached superstar halfback George Gipp in 1920 and the phenomenal backfield nicknamed the "Four Horsemen of Notre Dame" (quarterback Harry Stuhldreher, fullback Elmer Layden, and halfbacks Jim Crowley and Don Miller) from 1922 to 1924. These players became national celebrities and further boosted the popularity of the game. The extensive radio broadcasting of college games and the newsreels of game highlights, which were shown in movie theaters nationwide, also contributed to the sport's growing fan base.

Perhaps the best-known college football player of the 1920s and certainly one of the most talented was a halfback named Harold "Red" Grange, whom sportswriter Grantland Rice of the *New York Herald Tribune* dubbed "the Galloping Ghost." At the University of Illinois, where he starred as a three-time All-American (1923–1925), Grange first captured national attention in 1924, when he rushed for 263 yards to score

Sports

The University of North Carolina versus University of Virginia football game, Chapel Hill, North Carolina, 1929. Courtesy of the North Carolina Collection, University of North Carolina at Chapel Hill.

four touchdowns in the first 12 minutes of a game against the University of Michigan. In 1925, he became the first athlete featured on the cover of *Time* magazine. In 1925, the day after playing his final college game, Grange signed a lucrative contract with the professional Chicago Bears football team, guaranteeing him an annual salary of at least $100,000. Many fans felt betrayed by Grange's leap into professional football because they believed he had placed financial gain above the pure love of football. Grange almost single-handedly jumpstarted a stagnant National Football League. He parlayed his gridiron stardom into stardom on the silver screen by appearing in two Hollywood films and a 12-episode movie serial about college football titled *The Galloping Ghost* (1931).

Professional football had existed since the 1890s, but suffered from a lack of organization and fan support. In 1920, the American Professional Football Association (APFA) was founded, in part to provide the nation's fragmented collection of professional teams a stronger sense of organization and leadership. Jim Thorpe, a former Olympic athlete and football star, was elected the association's president, and Stanley Cofall, a former Notre Dame football great, became the vice president. In 1922, this fledgling association was renamed the National Football League (NFL), and several of the original 11 franchises relocated from small towns in Ohio, Illinois, and Indiana to somewhat larger markets in Green Bay, Detroit, Buffalo, and Cincinnati. Nonetheless, professional football continued to limp along until 1925, when Red Grange joined the Chicago Bears. Spurred on by the tremendous exposure generated by Grange, other NFL teams began to recruit more heavily from the pool of talented college players.

Golf

Golf enjoyed a surge in popularity during the 1920s among the middle classes. Fans attended tournaments and followed their favorite golfers in the newspaper. The greatest public acclaim for golfers was for amateurs. In fact, professionals were considered almost a class of servants, whose responsibilities included giving golf lessons, making and repairing clubs, working in the pro shop, and generally serving the needs of country club members. The most prestigious golf tournaments were reserved for amateurs who played merely for the love of the sport.

Three players led American golf during the 1920s: Walter Hagen, Gene Sarazen, and Bobby Jones. In 1922, Walter Hagen became the first American to win the British Open. Hagen, a professional golfer, consistently agitated for including professionals in the major tournaments—a controversial position in the 1920s. Gene Sarazen won the U.S. Open in 1922 as an amateur, before turning professional. He became the first golfer to win all four major tournaments: the U.S. Open (1922), the British Open (1932), the Professional Golfers' Association (PGA) Championship (1922, 1923, and 1933), and the Masters (1935). The most famous and beloved golfer during the 1920s was Bobby Jones, who competed as an amateur throughout his entire career. Between 1923 and 1930, he won 13 of the 21 national championship tournaments he entered. Jones hated to practice and sometimes went several months without ever playing, and he played in only 52 tournaments altogether. In 1930, at the age of 28, Jones became the first player to win the Grand Slam (by winning the British Amateur, the British Open, the U.S. Open, and the U.S. Amateur all in the same year). Later that year, believing that competitive golf held no more challenges for him, Jones retired. In retirement, he designed golf clubs for A. G. Spalding and Company and helped draw up plans for the Augusta National golf course. A member of the World Golf Hall of Fame, Jones is considered by many sports historians to be the greatest golfer of all time.

Tennis

Like golf, tennis enjoyed a tremendous surge in popularity during the 1920s. Middle-class men and women played the game, which had long been seen as the domain of the wealthy. Amateur tennis was seen as more honorable than professional tennis, and many tournaments barred professional players from competing. Both men and women tennis stars captured the public's attention, particularly Bill Tilden and Helen Wills.

Helen Wills, a middle-class Californian, began her tennis career by playing rugged, athletic matches on public dirt courts. She won the U.S. tennis championship in 1924 and 1925. Between 1927 and 1933, Wills was virtually unbeatable. She won eight Wimbledon tournaments, seven U.S. championships, and four French championships, and during those six years she never lost a set in singles competition.

William "Big Bill" Tilden occupied a similarly dominant position in men's tennis. Tilden, the son of a wealthy Philadelphia family, didn't develop a real talent for the game until he was in his 20s. He cultivated a tennis game based on powerful serves and drives as well as on style, finesse, and grace. He became known for his remarkable sportsmanship, and if he believed he had received an undeserved call, he would botch his next shot intentionally to rectify the error. In 1920, Tilden became the first American to win the men's singles title at Wimbledon. He won again in 1921 and 1930. He also won seven U.S. Open Singles Championships, and in 1925 he won 56 consecutive games over two tournaments. Tilden surprised the world in 1930 when he forfeited his amateur status in order to make a series of Hollywood motion pictures. He began playing tennis on the professional circuit the following year and continued to tour until his death in 1953.

Basketball

Although basketball was invented in 1891, its rules still had not been widely codified by the 1920s, so rules were interpreted differently on each court. The same referees generally officiated whenever a team played at home, so visiting teams seldom won. These games generated low scores and even lower fan interest. A handful of eastern colleges, such as New York University and the University of Pennsylvania, were considered strong basketball schools, but nationwide, college basketball was a minor sport. The national championship tournament, which was established at the end

Sports

of the 1920 season, was perhaps the only national recognition that college basketball received.

Professional basketball was somewhat more popular during the 1920s, but it lagged far behind baseball, football, and other professional sports in terms of fans and revenue. Professional basketball was an extremely rough, highly unorganized game. Players signed on with whichever team offered the biggest paychecks per game and often changed teams several times each season. This constant shifting of players effectively prevented the development of real team cohesion or strategy. Basketball's disorganized style of play changed abruptly in 1918, when manager Jim Furey hired a head coach and assembled a roster of players called the "Original Celtics," based in New York City. He required players to sign contracts for the entire season in exchange for a guaranteed annual salary. The team dominated the sport throughout the 1920s. Because they played together for the whole season, the athletes were able to develop plays and strategies that other teams could not match. The Original Celtics often played games every day of the week and two games on Sundays throughout the winter. During the 1922–1923 season, the Original Celtics compiled a 204–11 record; in 1924–1925 they went 134–6, and the following year, 90–12. Their overwhelming success bolstered the national reputation of professional basketball and inspired other managers to sign similar contracts with their players. By the end of the 1920s, basketball had markedly increased in both professionalism and popularity.

Like professional baseball, professional basketball was strictly segregated during the 1920s, but all-black club teams did flourish in large cities. Early all-black club teams with substantial fan support included the Smart Set Athletic Club of Brooklyn, the St. Christopher's Club of New Jersey, and the Loendi Club of Pittsburgh. In 1922, Caribbean native Robert L. Douglass founded the Harlem Renaissance Big 5, a team of talented African American basketball players who took their name from the Renaissance Casino ballroom in Harlem. The "Rens" toured the country during the 1920s and 1930s, playing against black and white teams and usually winning. In 1927, team owner Abe Saperstein changed the name of his Chicago-based black basketball team (the Savoy Big Five) to the Harlem Globetrotters. The Globetrotters combined their considerable basketball skills with astounding tricks and comedy routines, and they played exhibition games and entertained crowds across the nation.

Swimming

Competitive swimming claimed several genuine champions during the 1920s, and their widespread fame led Americans to take up swimming at public beaches and municipal pools. In 1926, 19-year-old Gertrude Ederle became the first woman to swim the English Channel. She completed the 21-mile swim in 14 hours and 31 minutes—besting the men's record by nearly two hours. The feat earned her lasting fame and a ticker-tape parade when she returned to New York City. Ederle also won a gold and two bronze medals at the 1924 Olympics in Paris. Most notable among competitive swimmers was Johnny Weissmuller, who never lost an individual freestyle race throughout his amateur swimming career. In 1921, in his first meet, Weissmuller won the first Amateur Athletic Union (AAU) championship in the 50-yard freestyle. Soon he became known as "the Human Hydroplane" and "the Prince of the Waves." Weissmuller won three gold medals at the 1924 Olympics and two more at the 1928 Olympics in Amsterdam. Overall, Weissmuller won 52 national championships and 67 world championships, and set 51 world records in various swimming categories. After giving up competitive swimming in 1929, he portrayed Tarzan in a dozen different films, beginning, in 1932, with *Tarzan, the Ape Man.*

Horse Racing

Prior to World War I, horse racing did not enjoy widespread popularity in the United States. Considered either a hobby for the privileged elite or a magnet for crooks and gamblers, horse racing was avoided or simply ignored by most middle-class Americans. But between 1919 and 1920, a powerful chestnut thoroughbred named Man o' War attracted the attention and admiration of millions of Americans when he compiled an incredible track record of 20 wins and only one loss (in 1919 to a horse named, appropriately enough, Upset). The beauty, speed, and near invincibility of Man o' War made him such a beloved figure that he is credited with helping to popularize horse racing among the general public. Although his career ended after only two years of competitive racing, in his retirement he sired horses that won dozens of races during the 1920s and 1930s. When, in the late 1920s, network radio began to broadcast major horse races over the airwaves, fans across the country became even more enamored with the Preakness, the Kentucky Derby, the Belmont, and other high-stakes horse races.

Auto Racing

Automobile racing experienced its first surge of widespread popularity during the 1920s, as racecar drivers and their teams invented new ways to soup up their engines and streamline their vehicles. In 1920, Gaston Chevrolet won the Indianapolis 500 with an average speed of just under 89 mph. By the late 1920s, average winning speeds began to approach 100 mph. However, specially built cars designed to break land-speed records dazzled racing fans. In 1927, British driver H.O.D. Seagrave exceeded 200 miles per hour. Despite British dominance in the sport, Americans claimed their own auto racing superstars. In 1921, driver Jimmy Murphy became the first American to win a major European race, the French Grand Prix, driving an American-built Dusenberg automobile. The following year he won the Indianapolis 500 and was the national champion racecar driver in 1922 and 1924, before he was killed in a car crash in late 1924.

Olympics

The 1920 Summer Olympics were held in Antwerp, Belgium, after the cancellation of the 1916 games scheduled for Berlin. Some 29 countries participated in the Antwerp games, with the United States winning 41 gold, 27 silver, and 27 bronze medals, more than any other country. Sweden placed second with 43 total medals, while Great Britain came in third with 43.

View of two-man autos rounding the curve in a race, 1922. Prints & Photographs Division, Library of Congress.

Sports

The first Olympic Winter Games were held in Chamonix, France, in 1924. The new winter festival was held in conjunction with the 1924 Summer Olympics in Paris. The U.S. once again won the most summer medals with 99, while Finland placed second (37), and host nation France in third (38). The 1924 games marked the arrival on the world stage of swimmer Johnny Weissmuller, who won three gold medals. He won two more gold medals at the 1928 games in Amsterdam. As a swimmer, Weissmuller set 67 world records. The athlete parlayed his athletic prowess into a long career as an actor and American icon, with his most famous role being Tarzan.

American athletes won the most medals in the 1928 festival (56), followed by Germany (31), and Finland (25). The 1928 Winter Olympics were held in St. Moritz, Switzerland, the first time as a stand-alone festival. Norway claimed the most medals with 15. The U.S. placed second with six.

TOYS AND GAMES

Although children today seem drawn to the latest high-tech electronic toys and computer games, many of the old-fashioned toys and games that children still enjoy were also favorites during the 1920s. Since 1903, when the first five-cent, eight-crayon box of Crayolas was introduced, coloring with crayons has ranked high on the list of childhood pastimes. Marbles, crayons, jacks, jigsaw puzzles, checkers, dominoes, tiddlywinks, and other traditional games continued to delight children. But by the 1920s, most children's playthings and games were commercially manufactured rather than homemade. By the end of the 1920s, the United States had become the world's leading toy manufacturer, with 539 toy companies in operation and revenues exceeding $90 million a year.

During the 1920s, many American children poured through mail-order catalogs and visited department stores to see the latest toys and games. Many of these toys revealed sharp distinctions between playtime activities of girls and boys. Toys and games designed specifically for girls included Raggedy Ann and Andy dolls, toy sewing machines, sewing baskets, vacuum cleaners, irons and ironing boards, stoves and ovens, and even ringer washtubs and laundry racks. Life-size baby dolls sometimes featured real hair and eyelashes, winking eyes, turning heads and poseable limbs. Concern about children's educational and moral development influenced the toys that were sold during the 1920s, and playing with dolls, sewing machines, and washtubs supposedly prepared girls for their future roles as wives, mothers, and homemakers.

Toys for boys included miniature tool sets, popguns, bows and arrows, train sets, and even fully operational miniature steam engines. Among the most popular playthings for boys were construction toys, including Lincoln Logs, which were invented in 1916 by John Lloyd Wright, the son of architect Frank Lloyd Wright. These sets were named in honor of President Abraham Lincoln, who lived in a log cabin as a child. The Erector set, one of America's oldest continuously produced toys, was introduced at New York's American Toy Fair in 1913 by its inventor, A. C. Gilbert. Tinkertoys, which were introduced at the 1914 American Toy Fair, allowed children to build three-dimensional structures. After sluggish initial sales, Tinkertoys gained enduring popularity.

Wooden, steel, or cast-iron models of trains, cars, trucks, buses, taxicabs, fire engines, tractors, motorcycles, airplanes, zeppelins, and boats remained popular throughout the decade. Charles Lindbergh's historic 1927 flight from New York to Paris boosted sales of toy airplanes, and dozens of new model planes appeared on the market, some of them with wind-up mechanisms that allowed the toy to remain aloft for a few seconds.

Children also enjoyed metal-stamped wagons, such as those manufactured by the Liberty Coaster Manufacturing Company (later Radio Steel and Manufacturing, which built the quintessential Radio Flyer wagons). Two and three-wheeled scooters, and Flexible Flyer and Flying Arrow brand snow sleds appealed to children who desired a speedy way to travel, but nothing could compare to the attraction of a three-wheeled cycles called velocipedes and regular bicycles, complete with headlamp and bell.

Sports

FADS AND CRAZES

During the 1920s, the growing influence of Hollywood motion pictures, commercial radio, modern advertising, and mass-circulation magazines and newspapers generated enthusiasm for new fads. Advertising agencies and publicists often encouraged these fads and crazes to promote a particular product or celebrity. Fads often attracted tens of thousands of adherents because they offered a way for people to conform to the social behavior of others and, at the same time, distinguish themselves from everyone else.

Some people sought to perform feats so bizarre that no one else had ever done them, while others attempted to do something more times than anyone else. For example, an Indiana high school student made headlines by chewing 40 sticks of gum while singing "Home, Sweet Home" and, between stanzas, chugging a gallon of milk. A New Jersey youth, subsisting only on eggs and black coffee, won a $150 contest by staying awake for 155 hours, continuously listening to the radio.[3] Journalists and critics often denigrated these media-hungry record breakers, but during the 1920s, millions of Americans, particularly college students, participated in such fads with great enthusiasm.

Mahjong and crossword puzzles also occupied Americans during the 1920s. The most popular parlor game in the United States during the first half of the decade was Mahjong, a Chinese game of skill usually played by four people using a set of 144 decorated tiles. Introduced to the United States in 1922, mahjong originated in China in the mid to late-nineteenth century. It was marketed in the United States as an ancient Chinese game dating back to the age of Confucius. Parker Brothers and other American game companies began manufacturing sets, complete with simplified rule books based on the original Chinese parlor game. By 1923, an estimated 10 to 15 million Americans were playing the game regularly. Cheap Mahjong sets cost a couple of dollars, but deluxe sets, with beautifully handcrafted, inlaid tiles, could cost $500. The game became so popular that some newspapers published daily Mahjong columns.

CRAZY FOR CROSSWORDS

The first modern crossword puzzle ran in the *New York World* in 1913, and over the next decade the game gained a foothold in U.S. newspapers. In 1924, Richard L. Simon and Max L. Schuster launched their new publishing company by releasing *The Cross Word Puzzle Book,* the first such collection. The book became a national best seller, and sales of dictionaries and thesauruses also soared.

A few months later, the pastime hopped the Atlantic. London's *Sunday Express* ran its first American-style crossword puzzle in November 1924 (it was, in fact, an American puzzle adapted for British English), and in short order the English-language newspapers of Paris ran them too. They were an immediate sensation, and within weeks European puzzle makers were creating versions in their own languages. First out of the gate was *Le Soir* in Brussels, Belgium. The newspaper promoted its crossword with the offer of cash prizes for solvers. More than 6,000 solutions poured in before the authorities shut down the contest, declaring it an illegal lottery. Meanwhile, French newspapers took pains to declare that the crossword was in fact a French invention—that the American puzzle was a mere variation of a "square-word" game created in France in the late 1800s.

In 1923, Eddie Cantor immortalized the game in the song "Since Ma Is Playing Mah Jong."

Dance Crazes

The decade saw a series of dance crazes, including the Charleston, the Black Bottom, the collegiate, the varsity drag, the raccoon, and the tango. A related fad was the dance marathon, which began in March 1923, when Alma Cummings established an international record of 27 hours of nonstop dancing at a contest held in New York City's Audubon Ballroom. Soon, contestants in cities across the country were dancing for days in an effort to break the record. By the end of 1923, the record

Congressman T. S. McMillan of South Carolina shows Misses Sylvia Clavans and Ruth Bennett how to do the Charleston, with the Capitol building in the background, 1926. Prints & Photographs Division, Library of Congress.

for nonstop dancing, set by a Youngstown, Ohio, couple, stood at 182 hours and 8 minutes.

Dance marathons became spectacles, with emcees, orchestras, teams of doctors and nurses, thousands of spectators, and dozens of vendors. By 1924, these contests featured dancing 24 hours a day, usually with hourly 15-minute breaks to allow contestants to rest, eat a snack, and use the rest room. Dance marathons could drag on for weeks, as dancing couples, near exhaustion and suffering from aching feet, shuffled across the floor. Radio broadcasts and tabloid newspaper coverage allowed Americans to follow the day-to-day drama. The most famous dance marathon of the decade occurred in 1928, when Hollywood press agent Milton Crandall staged "the Dance Derby of the Century" at New York's Madison

Square Garden. More than 100 couples competed for the $5,000 first prize, but after a grueling first week, only 13 couples remained. Thousands of spectators paid the $2.20 admission price to watch the spectacle, but the Board of Health stopped the marathon after 428 hours, when one contestant collapsed and had to be hospitalized. Although dance marathons flourished in the 1920s, their popularity soared during the Great Depression, when unemployed Americans competed for badly needed cash prizes.

Flagpole Sitting and Other Endurance Crazes

Endurance contests enthralled the nation. In 1928, for example, sports agent and promoter

C. C. Pyle organized a 3,422-mile transcontinental footrace between Los Angeles and New York City that an inventive sportswriter billed as the "Bunion Derby." A field of nearly 200 runners competed for prizes totaling $48,500. A 19-year-old Oklahoman named Andrew Payne won the first-place prize of $25,000 with a time of 573 hours. Americans competed in rocking-chair derbies, milk-drinking marathons, egg-eating races, gum-chewing contests, marathon eating, and even nonstop talking contests. Children competed in jump-rope contests, ball-bouncing marathons, yo-yoing competitions, and long-distance bicycle races.

Perhaps the most outrageous endurance craze of the 1920s was flagpole sitting, which amounted to perching on top of a flagpole for days and sometimes weeks. The most famous flagpole sitter was Alvin "Shipwreck" Kelly, a Hollywood stuntman who ignited this fad in 1924 when he spent 13 hours, 13 minutes atop a flagpole as part of a publicity stunt for a Hollywood theater. Within weeks, scores of fame seekers across the country attempted to break Kelly's record. Businessmen and promoters hired Kelly to stage flagpole sitting exhibitions at store openings, amusement parks, and county fairs. To ensure his comfort and safety, Kelly perched on a small, cushioned seat, 13 inches in diameter, sometimes outfitted with stirrups for his feet that helped him to maintain his balance. While aloft, he took five-minute catnaps and even shaved and had his hair cut. He didn't eat solid food, drinking broth and water hoisted up to him in buckets; a discreetly concealed tube transported his bodily waste down the flagpole. In 1930, 20,000 spectators watched Kelly shatter his own record after he sat atop a flagpole on the Atlantic City boardwalk for more than 49 days. The flagpole sitting faded from the national scene during the Depression.

Pogo Sticks, Yo Yos, and Miniature Golf

Some crazes of the 1920s evolved out of new children's toys, such as the pogo stick. Wooden pogo sticks had been manufactured in Germany before 1919, but they tended to warp in high

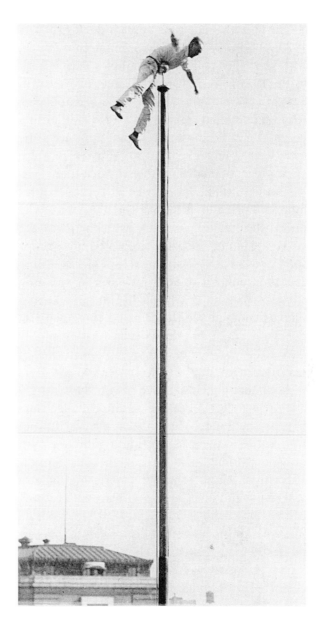

A "human fly" on top of the Times-Herald Building, Washington, D.C., 1924. Prints & Photographs Division, Library of Congress.

humidity. In 1919, George Hansburg patented a pogo stick constructed out of a metal tube with an enclosed spring, which proved to be more practical and durable. Bouncing on pogo sticks became a national craze after the chorus girls of *The Ziegfeld Follies* performed a dance routine performed on pogo sticks. Publicity stunts such as endurance pogo-sticking contests, attempts at world records for most consecutive jumps, and even marriage ceremonies performed on pogo sticks also fueled the fad.

The yo-yo also became popular during the late 1920s. The yo-yo probably originated in China, with the oldest surviving examples dating back to the fifth century B.C. in Greece. However, in Santa Barbara, California, in 1928, Pedro Flores, who remembered playing with a toy similar to a yo-yo as a child in the Philippines, founded the first American company to manufacture these spinning wooden disks. Flores named them "yo-yos" after the Filipino word for "spring." Flores looped a piece of string around the axle of the disk instead of tying it tight, which allowed the yo-yo to spin in place, or "sleep." His first yo-yos soon became a California craze, and Flores further promoted his yo-yos by sponsoring spinning contests. Around 1930, Donald Duncan acquired Flores's company and obtained a trademark on the word *yo-yo*. He, too, began hosting highly publicized yo-yo competitions to boost sales of his Duncan yo-yo.

Miniature golf, also called "Tom Thumb golf" and "pygmy golf," became a national rage during the late 1920s. Most accounts credit Garnet Carter, the owner of a hotel and golf course on Lookout Mountain near Chattanooga, Tennessee, with developing the first American miniature golf course in 1927. Carter originally built his tiny course, which he called "Fairyland," to generate publicity for his resort, but his miniature links attracted so many golfers that he soon began charging his guests to play. By the end of the 1920s, an estimated four million people a day were putting on the nation's nearly 40,000 miniature golf courses—some of them indoor—complete with tiny windmills, clown faces, and medieval castles. Miniature golf became so popular that Hollywood studio executives feared the movie industry would suffer if couples continued to hit the mini-links instead of buying movie tickets.

Body Building and Fitness

The urge for self-improvement sparked health and fitness fads, including dieting and bodybuilding. Weight-conscious Americans, particularly young women, began dieting to maintain proper health and to conform to the new slimmer standards of American beauty embodied by the boyish-figured flapper. Meanwhile, a bodybuild-

ing fad erupted among men and teenage boys. One of the decade's chief promoters of bodybuilding was Bernarr Macfadden, the so-called "Father of Physical Culture," who publicized his gospel of exercise, health, and fitness in his monthly magazine, *Muscle Builder*. The most famous bodybuilding guru of the 1920s was Charles Atlas, an Italian immigrant born Angelo Siciliano, who developed a total-fitness method of muscle building that pitted one muscle against another. Atlas claimed that he had used this program to transform himself from a 97-pound weakling into a muscle-bound he-man. In 1922, Atlas won the title of "Most Perfectly Developed Man" at a Madison Square Garden competition, and two years later, he began marketing mail-order courses of his "Dynamic Tension" program in the back pages of pulp magazines and other male-oriented periodicals. As a result, tens of thousands of American men and boys joined the bodybuilding craze.

Self-improvement impulses also included the psychological. Emile Coué, a French pharmacist turned psychotherapist, made highly publicized lecture tours of the United States in 1923 and again in 1924. The author of the best-selling *Self-Mastery Through Conscious Autosuggestion* (1922), Coué promoted the idea that people could improve their mental health and happiness through a self-hypnosis program that focused on the repetition of an affirmation.[4] The psychosexual theories of Austrian psychoanalyst Sigmund Freud also captivated the nation. Freud's influential *The Interpretation of Dreams* (1900) was widely cited, although seldom read or understood by many Americans during the 1920s. Freudianism became a fad, and such terms as *repression, sublimation,* and *complex* entered people's everyday vocabulary. Conservative critics, however, worried that Freudianism encouraged sexual promiscuity and licentious behavior.

"Exotic" Cultures

An obsession with Egyptian, Asian, and other "exotic" world cultures also produced fleeting fads. In 1922, for example, the spectacular archaeological discovery and excavation of Pharaoh King Tutankhamen's tomb inspired an Egyptian craze in the United States. The iconography influenced not only the styles of American clothing, jewelry, cosmetics, and hairstyles but also architecture, music, and motion pictures. In 1923, the musical team of Billy Jones and Ernest Hare recorded the novelty song "Old King Tut (In Old King Tutankhamen's Day)." The discovery of King Tut's tomb also inspired the architectural design and interior décor of Grauman's Egyptian Theatre, built in Hollywood in 1922, which featured massive Egyptian columns in the fore-court, hieroglyphics, and huge dog-headed Egyptian god statues. Grauman's Chinese Theatre, which opened one block away in 1927, featured ornate architecture resembling a giant red pagoda, complete with sculptures of huge silver dragons on the interior ceilings.

Middle Eastern and Hawaiian culture also enjoyed widespread popularity in the United States during the early to mid-1920s. Tens of thousands of Americans strummed easy-to-play Hawaiian ukuleles and sang Tin Pan Alley ditties about the Hawaiian Islands. (See "Music of the 1920.") Other foreign cultures, particularly those of Turkey and the Middle East, likewise inspired national obsessions. Fraternal organizations, for example, adopted supposedly exotic symbols and motifs, such as fezzes, as part of their initiation ceremonies, official uniforms, and lodge decor. Hollywood silent film heartthrob Rudolph Valentino's 1921 movie *The Sheik* and its 1926 sequel, *The Son of the Sheik,* also helped fuel the American craze for Middle Eastern exoticism.

Sports

Travel

of the 1920s

During the 1920s, Americans were bombarded with advertisements describing wonderful, scenic vacationlands, as well as newer, faster modes of transportation to help them get there. With more leisure time and disposable income, middle-class families traveled farther from their homes to visit seaside resorts, national parks, historic sites, and campgrounds. Railroad and bus lines reached virtually every corner of the United States, and the increasing affordability of automobiles and the nation's expanding network of roads and highways allowed middle-class and even many working-class Americans opportunities to enjoy a Sunday drive, a weekend of auto-camping, or a driving vacation. By the end of the decade, commercial passenger airlines made long-distance travel faster than ever before. As Americans became a mobile society, new businesses—from motels and roadside restaurants to automobile associations and car insurance companies—sprang up to cater to their needs.

MOTOR VEHICLE TRAVEL

Automobiles

Prior to World War I, automobiles were generally unreliable and too expensive for all but the most affluent, but by the 1920s, automobiles were more dependable and, as a result of mass production and new credit plans, more affordable. In 1910, 458,000 passenger cars traversed the nation's roadways. By 1920, that number had soared to eight million, and by 1930, 23 million.[1]

Henry Ford and the Model T

The individual most responsible for putting so many Americans behind the wheel was Henry Ford. (See Travel chapters in 1900s and 1910s.) In 1908, Ford had introduced the sturdy, dependable Model T, a four-cylinder, 20-horsepower automobile that was the first car designed for a mass market. By 1920, half of all cars on the road were Model Ts, and a single car took only an hour and a half to build from start to finish, as opposed to the 14 hours it took in 1913.[2]

Ford's mass production methods revolutionized the automobile industry and transformed his company into the world's largest automobile manufacturer. Ford realized that, by accepting a smaller profit margin on a larger volume of sales, he could reap enormous profits, and through his revolutionary business strategy, he was able to slash the price of his automobiles. In 1909, the Model T sold for $950, but by 1925, a new Model T cost only $290.[3] As a result, middle-class and even many working-class Americans could now purchase their own Model Ts. Consequently, Ford became a national hero and one of the most celebrated men in 1920s America.

The Automobile Industry

As other car companies copied Ford's efficient methods of mass production, automobile manufacturing grew into one of the nation's largest and most important industries. In 1920, slightly more than 100 automobile manufacturing companies crowded the U.S. market, but the so-called Big Three of Ford, General Motors, and Chrysler accounted for more than 70 percent of all of new car sales. Other U.S. manufacturers concentrated on producing more modern, luxurious automobiles that offered an array of newfangled accessories such as self-starters, fuel gauges, and car radios (available as early as 1923). By 1927, General Motors was producing 72 different models of Cadillacs, Buicks, and Chevrolets, each of which could be purchased with an assortment of features and in a wide selection of colors. Smaller companies, such as Packard, Nash, Pierce-Arrow, and Hudson, also commanded a respectable share of the market by providing expensive, high-quality automobiles to wealthier drivers. Although the number of manufacturers had fallen to 44 by 1929, annual automobile production reached 5.3 million in the United States—a figure not surpassed for another 20 years.[4]

Automobile manufacturers generated enormous sales during the 1920s through a marketing strategy of planned obsolescence, sophisticated advertising, and seductive installment plans. Manufacturers unveiled a new line of automobile models each year to encourage consumers to trade in their old cars for newer ones that were faster and incorporated the most modern designs available. The automobile companies spent millions of dollars advertising technical aspects and such intangibles as the pleasures of driving and the freedoms that automobiles offered. Affordable credit plans also encouraged consumers to purchase automobiles, even if they could not pay in cash. Ford and General Motors financed their own car sales, while smaller companies engaged independent finance companies and banks to provide credit to their customers. As a result, 75 percent of all automobile sales by 1925 were purchased on deferred-payment credit plans.

The Ford Motor Company continued to dominate the auto industry during the early 1920s, but its share of the market slipped in the mid-1920s. While General Motors and other companies designed new car models every year, Ford refused to revamp his aging Model T, which had remained virtually unchanged since 1908. Many consumers chose to purchase secondhand Chevrolets, which were more stylish and comfortable, for a few hundred dollars more rather than purchase a new Model T. In 1927, Ford finally introduced a new automobile, the Model A, which proved to be a great success. Nevertheless, General Motors overtook the Ford Motor Company as the leader of the automobile industry in the late 1920s.

Automobiles and American Prosperity

Automobile production helped fuel the nation's booming economy by stimulating the growth and development of related industries, including steel, petroleum, glass, and rubber manufacturing.

Soaring automobile sales also accelerated the expansion and development of America's highways, and government spending on massive road-building projects pumped tens of millions of dollars into the American economy during the 1920s. Since the 1900s, automobile clubs and trucking companies had lobbied federal and state governments to build better roads. In 1921, Congress passed the Federal Highway Act, which provided the states with matching federal funds to finance the construction of a national network of two-lane, hard-surface roads. By 1927, the national highway system totaled more than 96,000 miles, and several transcontinental highways bisected the nation, including U.S. Route 30, which stretched from Atlantic City, New Jersey, to Astoria, Oregon, and U.S. Route 66, known as "the Main Street of America," which ran from Chicago to Santa Monica, California. Automobile travel also stimulated the construction of bridges, tunnels, bypasses, and other structures designed to improve the flow of traffic on the nation's roadways. For example, the Holland Tunnel, which runs under the Hudson River and connects New York and New Jersey, opened in 1927. On its first

Travel

day, more than 51,000 motorists paid the 50-cent toll to pass through what was then the world's longest underwater tunnel.

Meanwhile, an entire roadside service industry of filling stations, garages, camping grounds, motels, and restaurants sprang up across the nation. Between 1921 and 1929, for example, the number of drive-in gas stations ballooned from 12,000 to 143,000.[5] Insurance companies began selling auto insurance policies, and in 1927, Massachusetts became the first state to pass a law requiring all drivers to carry car insurance. Automobile rental companies, which emerged around World War I, catered to traveling salesmen and to those who could not afford to buy their own automobiles. In 1923, John D. Hertz, the owner of a Chicago taxicab company, established the Hertz Drive-Ur-Self Company, the forerunner of Hertz Rent-a-Car.

On the downside, automobiles created numerous problems. Traffic jams, parking problems, and speeding tickets became common. Increased levels of congestion, noise, and air pollution plagued city dwellers. Automobile travel contributed to the destruction of the rural countryside, as motorists tossed trash along the roads, and gaudy billboards and roadway businesses diminished the natural beauty. The rapidly increasing number of cars on the road caused an upsurge in motor vehicle accidents. The death toll from automobile accidents reached 32,900 (most of them pedestrians) in 1930.[6]

Automobiles and American Life

Mass ownership of automobiles spurred the expansion of middle-class suburbs. Many white-collar professionals chose to reside in the suburbs and commute to work. The nation's first suburban shopping center, Country Club Plaza, opened in Kansas City, Missouri, in 1923. Cars enabled farm families to make frequent trips to town, resulting in the closing of many rural crossroad stores, churches, and one-room schoolhouses.

Automobiles created new leisure activities. Cars made it possible to travel long distances relatively easily (by 1925, for example, motorists could cover about 200 miles in an average day), and unlike railroads, automobiles allowed travelers to determine their own departure times, routes, and rates of speed. Family automobile vacations

Travel

A clean and inviting Red Hat gasoline station, Columbia, Missouri. Courtesy of the State Historical Society of Missouri, Columbia.

became common for middle-class Americans. Driving around for the sheer pleasure of it became a popular pastime. Originally, though, driving was strictly a fair-weather pursuit, since most automobiles were open-topped touring cars. But beginning in 1923, when sales of closed cars surpassed those of open-tops, driving became a year-round, though often cold and drafty, activity.

For many, automobiles represented the new freedoms of the modern age, but for others, cars symbolized the nation's crumbling moral standards. Conservative politicians, religious leaders, and social workers condemned the automobile for eroding the cohesion of American families and morally corrupting the nation's youth. Automobiles bred fears about increased rates of premarital sexual activity among young people, and ministers thundered about "the desecration of the Sabbath," as some members of their congregations went out for Sunday drives rather than attend church

THE AUTOMOBILE AND POPULAR CULTURE

Beginning around 1900, automobiles regularly cropped up as the subject of songs, theater shows, motion pictures, magazines, comic strips, joke books, and children's toys. Tin Pan Alley songwriters composed hundreds of novelty numbers about automobiles; more than 60 popular song titles specifically mentioned Henry Ford and his Model T. During the 1910s and 1920s, the Model T inspired a series of joke books that poked fun at Ford's rattletraps. Broadway comedies such as *Six Cylinder Love* (1921) and *Nervous Wreck* (1923) featured plots that revolved around the automobile. Noted illustrator John Held Jr. immortalized flappers and their sporty roadsters in the caricatures he drew for the covers of *Life* and *Judge* magazines. Automobiles featured prominently in Hollywood motion pictures, especially gangster films and slapstick comedies. Mack Sennett's *Keystone Kops* serials, for example, depicted a troupe of bumbling policemen who chased criminals (and narrowly dodged locomotives and pedestrians) in their overloaded Ford patrol wagon. Cast-iron cars, trucks, buses, taxicabs, and fire engines became favorite playthings for boys.

services. Most middle-class Americans, however, had become too attached to their automobiles to be swayed by such condemnation.

PUBLIC TRANSPORTATION

Buses

Long-distance bus companies emerged in the 1910s to meet growing public transportation needs. Originally, bus lines were designed to transport groups of workers over short distances. For example, in 1914, Eric Wickman began shuttling iron miners in his first "bus"—a seven-passenger Hupmobile—between Hibbing and Alice, Minnesota. Wickman soon commissioned the construction of more "buses"—elongated auto bodies welded onto truck frames—and hired additional drivers. In 1915, he and two partners formed the Mesaba Transportation Company in Hibbing, which went through a series of company names before becoming, in 1930, Greyhound Bus Lines. Greyhound was a nickname because of the early bus's appearance: grey and white and considered sleek.[7]

By the mid-1920s, networks of bus lines across the United States carried travelers from city to city. Local bus service also expanded, as passengers and commuters began to take buses across town or back and forth to work. Originally, most of these "buses" were customized automobiles or trucks, but as the demand grew, automobile manufacturers began producing specially designed multi-passenger vehicles for mass transit. By 1925, at least 3,600 different bus companies operated more than 21,000 vehicles across nearly a quarter of a million miles of America's roads.[8] By 1930, an estimated 41,000 buses navigated the nation's roadways. For a one-way fare of $72, passengers in 1928 could travel by bus from Los Angeles to New York, stopping at 132 towns during the five-and-a-half day trip. Although buses proved popular among business travelers, factory workers, and lower-income families who did not own cars, tourists preferred driving their own cars or taking trains. Well-to-do travelers visiting new locales often took scenic bus rides, letting the driver negotiate the unfamiliar terrain while they relaxed and enjoyed the sights.

Travel

Taxicabs

Thousands of independent owners and operators pressed their private autos into makeshift service as cabs during the 1910s and 1920s. By the 1920s, Ford and General Motors operated extensive fleets of taxicabs in major urban centers across the United States. In 1915, Chicago businessmen Walden W. Shaw and John D. Hertz formed the Yellow Cab Company, the nation's largest and oldest taxicab company. This pioneering company operated specially designed taxis that were painted bright yellow in order to make them stand out on busy streets. A Russian immigrant named Morris Markin founded the Checkered Cab Manufacturing Company in Kalamazoo, Michigan in 1922. Soon, his distinctive yellow and black taxis became common in many American cities.

Streetcars

Since the 1890s, urban dwellers had relied heavily on public streetcars for transportation within their cities. In 1917, 80,000 electric trolleys traversed 45,000 miles of track in cities and towns nationwide. Streetcars were an affordable means of mass transit, and low-wage employees depended upon them for their daily commutes. By 1923, however, ridership had begun to dwindle. Most cities failed to give streetcars the right-of-way over private cars, which slowed streetcar service and frustrated passengers. Others abandoned trolleys to ride subways (in major metropolitan areas such

Travel

A woman taxi driver prepares to get into her vehicle. Prints & Photographs Division, Library of Congress.

as New York and Boston) or city buses, which offered more flexible service than trolleys. As the automobile became more affordable and popular, more middle-class Americans drove their own cars, and the popularity of streetcars waned.

VACATIONS

The number of Americans who vacationed rose considerably in the decade. One day excursions to amusements parks, the seashore, or the countryside were common, but vacations of a week or more, spent either at a single location or touring about in an automobile, became increasingly frequent.

Of course, vacationing depended on sufficient time off from work and enough disposable income to spend on travel expenses. In the 1920s, salaried middle-class employees increasingly received short paid vacations. By the end of the decade, an estimated 80 percent of white-collar workers received at least some paid vacation time from their employers. Most took inexpensive trips, such as visiting relatives, fishing, camping, or touring a portion of the country.

Paid vacations were seldom extended to the working classes. In large part, this bias evolved from the notion that industrial workers did not "need" vacations, since only those who worked with their minds, not their muscles, suffered the sort of mental strain and emotional tension that vacations could alleviate. Men employed in automobile factories, textile mills, or meatpacking plants could rest on Sundays and, went this logic, feel refreshed again by Monday morning. Furthermore, blue-collar wage earners seldom worked for a solid year, owing largely to work stoppages or layoffs during slow seasons. Thus, employers believed that their workers already enjoyed plenty of time off (though this was at the employees' expense).

In addition, working-class Americans seldom had the financial resources to take extended vacations. Thus, the working classes spent their leisure hours on more local pursuits. Men joined fraternal organizations, attended prizefights, or watched baseball games. Husbands and wives went to the movies, dance halls, or vaudeville shows, and whole families spend weekend afternoons picnicking or going to an amusement park.

A few progressive business owners did realize that providing paid vacations to their blue-collar employees increased efficiency, promoted loyalty, reduced turnover, and boosted morale. Many of the companies that furnished paid time off guided their employees in choosing the "best" vacations, since employers feared that idle workers with money in their pockets might drink and carouse the whole time and return to work exhausted and in ill health. Thus, many companies actively encouraged camping trips and other low cost, outdoor vacations. Some firms even established their own summer camps, where workers could vacation for little or no money and at the same time be supervised by company employed recreational directors and social workers.

Auto-camping

Since the mid-1910s, "auto-camping" appealed to millions as an enjoyable way to escape the daily pressures of modern life. President Warren G. Harding joined avid outdoorsmen Henry Ford, Thomas A. Edison, and Harvey Firestone on a highly publicized camping trip in 1921. Camping provided outdoor adventure, and, after the initial outlay for a tent and other equipment, it was comparatively inexpensive.

Since the earliest days of auto-camping, motorists had customized their cars and trucks by adding sleeping compartments and other gadgets to outfit them for outdoor living. During the mid-1910s and 1920s, specialized camping trailers appeared on the market, such as the Automobile Telescope Touring Apartment, first manufactured in 1916, which folded out into a bed, kitchen, and shower. Other motorists pulled trailers, or "trailer coaches," introduced in the mid-1920s, which served as both sleeping and cooking quarters. Camping equipment manufacturers, such as Coleman, L. L. Bean, and Eddie Bauer, also produced extensive lines of collapsible beds, portable stoves, folding chairs, ice chests, and other outdoor gear designed to make life on the road more comfortable.

Originally, motorists simply pitched tents and set up campsites along the roadside, often without obtaining the permission of the property owner. But by 1920, cities and towns along well-traveled tourist routes had begun to establish municipal camping grounds to capture tourist dollars and to prevent campers from damaging private property. These campgrounds, which were funded by local taxes, were open to all travelers, and the better ones offered free access to toilets and showers, electric lights, firewood, potable water, and a community kitchen. By 1925, however, many of these municipal campgrounds began to charge entrance and registration fees, as well as to impose stricter regulations and time limits, in order to discourage hoboes and transients from squatting at these campsites.

As the number of free municipal campgrounds dwindled, entrepreneurs began to establish private campgrounds that charged entrance fees, called auto-camps, many of which went by homey, unpretentious names such as "Dew Drop Inn." Cabin camps rented small, sparsely furnished cabins that usually were little more than shacks. Some of the better facilities featured clean, comfortable buildings and the additional amenities of community rest rooms and showers, gasoline stations, grocery stores, lunch counters, and recreation halls. Most of these roadside cabin camps were located in the South and Southwest, where the warm climate made tourism a year round industry. Although hotels continued to accommodate most travelers and tourists, cabin camps attracted tens of thousands of visitors each year who desired something cheaper than a hotel and more comfortable than a campsite.

Motels

Like auto-camps and cabin camps, motels first emerged as a thrifty alternative to hotels. Although motels date to at least the 1910s, the first to use the term was the Milestone Mo-Tel, which opened in San Luis Obispo, California, in 1925. Soon *motel* became a generic term to describe a wide variety of roadside accommodations. As opposed to hotels, which were located in downtown urban centers or at country resorts, motels consisted of a number of small cottages clustered around a main office building. Roadside motels catered to middle-class families who chose affordability and convenience over luxury. Motels did not generally feature a main lobby area, so

road-weary tourists had no fear of looking unpresentable in front of other guests. Motel patrons carried their own bags in from the car, so there was no need to tip a bellboy. And since few motels offered room service, families could eat their picnic meals in their own room or perhaps drive to an affordable roadside eatery. By 1928, there were an estimated 3,000 motels across the nation.[9] One early motel chain, the Alamo Plaza Tourist Court, opened its first outlet in Waco, Texas, in 1929. That same year, the Pierce Petroleum Corporation built a chain of five 40-room hotels in the Midwest along U.S. Route 66.

TRAVEL DESTINATIONS

Resort cities and towns lured millions of vacationers to their hotels, beaches, and boardwalks each year. Resorts offered activities such as swimming, gambling, hunting, fishing, tennis, and viewing the scenery. Racial segregation, anti-Semitism, and other forms of prejudice prevented members of certain minority groups from staying at these desirable resorts. Some African Americans responded to this lack of accessibility by opening their own hotels, boardinghouses, and restaurants in established resort areas and then catering to a black middle-class clientele. Others, unwilling to risk unpleasant confrontations, frequented different vacation destinations. Black seaside resorts sprang up, for example, in Wilmington, North Carolina, Martha's Vineyard, Massachusetts, Sag Harbor, New York, and Highland Beach, Virginia. Jewish vacationers, also unwelcome at many resorts, established their own vacation getaways in the Catskill Mountains of New York and the Poconos of Pennsylvania.

While resorts appealed to vacationers who could afford them, far more Americans chose to "rough it" in the fresh air and scenic beauty of the nation's less-populated areas. For many, this involved a trek to one of the western national parks. In 1916, President Woodrow Wilson signed a bill creating the National Park Service, a division of the Department of the Interior which was charged with conserving the natural resources and beauty of the nation's parks and, at the same time, providing ways for travelers to enjoy these protected public lands. Under this mandate, the Park Service

Travel

authorized the limited construction of roadways and hotel accommodations within the boundaries of national parks. A vigorous publicity campaign encouraged visitors to travel, by car or by train, to such stunning destinations as Yellowstone National Park (Wyoming), Yosemite National Park (California), Grand Canyon National Park (Arizona), and Glacier National Park (Montana). In 1917, approximately 55,000 automobiles entered the national parks, but by 1926 that number had grown to 400,000.[10] Railways carried thousands of guests to the western national parks. For example, between 1921 and 1925, the Yosemite Valley Railroad sold an average of 20,000 tickets annually, and by 1930, five different railroads carried passengers into Yellowstone National Park. Some well-to-do visitors stayed in hotels and inns inside the parks, but the vast majority pitched their tents in designated campgrounds. Conservationists feared the destruction of these protected areas, due to the parks' increasing commercialization and subsequent overuse by hundreds of thousands of tourists, but carefully designed networks of roads and buildings did protect and conserve most of these wild public lands.

Florida's tourist industry successfully touted the state as a tropical playground, despite devastating hurricanes and the infamous Florida land boom and bust of the early 1920s. By 1925, more than a half-million tourists each year motored to Florida, and resorts in Miami Beach, Sarasota, Coral Gables, and Key West attracted visitors from all over the United States.

TRAIN TRAVEL

In 1920, trains were still the preferred means of inter-city passenger travel and, equally important, the primary method of hauling freight. Train travel in the United States peaked in 1920, when a record 1.2 billion passengers purchased rail tickets.

Railroad company advertisements stressed their fine amenities and services. Dining cars allowed travelers to relax, socialize, and watch the scenery, while enjoying an exquisite menu that rivaled those of the nation's best restaurants. Smoking lounges, hair salons, café cars, and observation cars helped passengers to while away the hours.

Sleeper cars, most of which were owned and operated by the Pullman Company, offered guests private quarters attended by porters, but such comforts were reserved for first-class passengers. For coach-class passengers, traveling by train during the 1920s could be hot and dirty, particularly during the summer months, since air-conditioning was nonexistent on parlor cars, and dirt and cinders inevitably blew through open windows. Coach passengers could not always access dining cars, and therefore had to pack their own lunches, eat at depots when the train stopped, or rely on the vendors who walked the train cars selling candy, cigarettes, and sandwiches. Despite the convenience of train travel, it was not comfortable, and a cross-country train trip could take a week or longer.

By 1929, the popularity of automobiles had drastically reduced the number of passengers opting for rail travel; by then, private automobiles carried five times as many passengers as did trains.[11]

Passengers getting off the back of a train, 1927. Prints & Photographs Division, Library of Congress.

OCEAN TRAVEL

For Americans, the only way to reach Europe during the 1920s was by ocean liner. Henry Ford, Charlie Chaplin, F. Scott Fitzgerald, and dozens of other famous millionaires, politicians, and celebrities sailed to Europe in high style and elegance on these grand floating palaces. And for the millions of European immigrants who crowded onto them between the 1890s and the 1920s, these ships represented the opportunity to build better lives in the United States.

After the end of World War I, the demand for transatlantic passenger service grew as the British Isles and continental Europe once again opened to American tourism, despite the tragic losses of life in the sinkings of the *Titanic* in 1912 and the *Lusitania* in 1915. During the 1920s, approximately 80 companies operated dozens of ships that provided weekly express service between New York Harbor and various European ports. Among the great North Atlantic liners of the decade were Cunard Line's *Aquitania,* White Star Line's *Leviathan,* the North German Lloyd Line's *Bremen,* and the French Line's *I^le de France.* These ships sometimes approached 1,000 feet in length and topped 50,000 gross tons. Large ocean liners could carry as many as 3,350 passengers, most of whom were booked in third and fourth-class accommodations. Averaging speeds of around 27 knots, the fastest of these powerful ships could make a transatlantic crossing in four or five days.

The great ocean liners such as the *Aquitania* and the *I^le de France* offered first-class passengers world-class dining, well-appointed staterooms, and quality recreation and entertainment, including golf, ballroom dancing, soaking in the spa, or working out in the gymnasium. Physicians, nurses, activities directors, chefs, waiters, valets, maids, tailors, and shoeshine boys catered to a first-class passenger's every need.

Most steamship passengers purchased far more affordable third and fourth-class tickets, which provided just basic accommodations. These passengers occupied less desirable cabins in the bowels of the ship, and sometimes as many as 2,700 steerage passengers would be crowded into as little as one-fifth of the ship's entire space. During the 1920s, the United States severely restricted immigration, causing a dramatic drop in the number of steerage tickets sold. In response, foreign shipping lines sought to appeal to middle-class American passengers by creating economical "cabin-class" and "tourist-class" rates. Shipping lines recruited some of best graphic artists and illustrators to promote steamship travel through modern, stylish advertising materials. These colorful posters, magazine advertisements, and brochures enticed many well-off Americans to travel to France, Italy, Spain, England, and other European nations. Of course, sailing aboard ocean liners was an experience largely reserved for the upper classes, who could spend several weeks or months touring various destinations. Some middle-class travelers did splurge on a once in-a-lifetime "grand tour" of Europe, but transatlantic travel remained quite uncommon among ordinary Americans.

AIR TRAVEL

The use of planes for combat and reconnaissance during World War I led to rapid development in American aircraft technology. After the war ended, anyone with a few hundred dollars could purchase a surplus military biplane. At the time no airline regulatory system existed—no examinations or licenses for pilots, no safety certificates for the planes. Ex-fighter pilots (and more than a few self-taught fliers) bought these discarded planes, fixed them up, and barnstormed from town to town, thrilling county fairgoers at air shows by offering $5 rides and performing daredevil stunts such as flying upside down and "barrel-rolling" in midair. "Wing-walkers" stood on the wings of a biplane in flight, hit golf balls, turned cartwheels, or parachuted safely to the ground. Self-employed pilots often took odd jobs crop dusting, skywriting, assisting with aerial mapping, ferrying passengers short distances, or even smuggling illegal liquor. Full-fledged commercial airlines, with regular routes, schedules, and employees, did not yet exist.

The earliest commercial passenger airlines used seaplanes, outfitted with pontoon landing gear, to ferry tourists between coastal resort towns. Because seaplanes flew low over the water and could land at any time, they were commonly considered safer than regular planes. Passenger airlines

Travel

The comfortable and formal-looking drawing room of a Handley Page Air Liner, with seven passengers, 1930. Prints & Photographs Division, Library of Congress.

soon inaugurated short-distance service between New York and Atlantic City, Chicago and Detroit, Miami and Nassau, and Key West and Havana. Most of these companies were only seasonal operations, and, since most biplanes could accommodate only one passenger at a time, they failed to be very profitable.

Charles Lindbergh

The commercial aviation industry received an enormous boost from Charles A. Lindbergh's historic 1927 transatlantic flight. In 1919, a French hotelier offered a $25,000 prize to the first pilot or team of pilots who could complete a nonstop transatlantic flight between the United States and France. Several aviators attempted to claim the prize, but each flight ended in disappointment or disaster, including the deaths of at least six pilots. In 1927, former barnstormer and airmail pilot Charles A. Lindbergh made his bid for the prize,

flying solo in his single-engine monoplane, *Spirit of St. Louis.* On Friday, May 20, 1927, he taxied down the runway at Roosevelt Field on Long Island, New York. He landed 33 and a half hours later at Paris's Le Bourget Aerodrome. A shy, introverted Minnesotan who dreaded the glare of the media spotlight, Lindbergh was dismayed to find that his flight had catapulted him to international celebrity. President Calvin Coolidge dispatched the navy cruiser *USS Memphis* to retrieve the nation's newly minted hero, and upon his return, four million fans turned out for a ticker-tape parade in New York City to celebrate his accomplishment. Lindbergh, the unknown pilot, became "Lucky Lindy," the national hero.

More than any other figure of the 1920s, Lindbergh became an object of American hero worship. His celebrity arose from two ideas about what his historic flight meant. First, Lindbergh embodied the courageous individualism and pioneer spirit that many Americans associated

Travel

Charles A. Lindbergh, 1927. Prints & Photographs Division, Library of Congress.

with the founding and settlement of the United States. For them, his feat demonstrated that even in an increasingly bureaucratic and mechanized modern age, the individual human spirit could still triumph. Second, Lindbergh symbolized the wonders and progress of the Machine Age. President Coolidge congratulated Lindbergh for flying a plane constructed of materials and parts produced by more than 100 different companies, acknowledging that the *Spirit of St. Louis* was the result of the research, development, and labor of countless American engineers and workers.

The Rise of Commercial Airlines

After Lindbergh's historic achievement, the possibilities of flight captured the American imagination like never before. The commercial airline industry purchased larger, more powerful planes and expanded their passenger services and routes. In 1926, American aircraft manufacturers, including Boeing, Ryan, Curtiss-Wright, and even Ford, had produced a collective total of only about 1,000 airplanes, but in 1929 that figure reached 6,200. Meanwhile, the number of airline passengers soared from 5,800 in 1926 to 417,000 in 1930.[12] By 1929, airline passengers could travel

Travel

HOW OTHERS SEE US

Paris Does the Lindy

Contrary to expectations, Charles Lindbergh's 1927 solo flight across the Atlantic made him a hero in France, where his 33 and a half hour journey ended on the night of May 21.

Lindbergh's audacious choice to fly solo (not a requirement of the competition) and his flight's New York starting point led some to fear that he would be met with stony silence, or worse, if he landed safely at Le Bourget airfield near Paris.

Instead, the French keenly followed progress reports that ground observers cabled to Paris newspapers as the *Spirit of St. Louis* made its way over Newfoundland, Ireland, and western France. During the final minutes of Lindbergh's flight, excited Parisians scanned the skies for signs of his plane. At least 25,000 cheering Frenchmen thronged Le Bourget to welcome Lindbergh, creating a human wave that overwhelmed the police and military attempting to keep order. At the airfield and in the streets, people celebrated for hours after his landing.

In the week that followed, amid ceremonies and speeches, Paris restaurants named dishes after Lindbergh, people delivered hundreds of congratulatory bouquets to the American embassy, and fashionable women adopted the leather airman's helmet as the latest in hats. The 25-year-old flyer was hailed as "just such a hero as this tired world has been looking for."

After all, as one French soldier commented on joining the airfield celebration, "Il n'est pas Français, mais, après tout, ça se passe a Paris" (loosely, "Okay, he's not French—at least he landed in Paris").

coast-to-coast by flying during the day and riding trains at night (night flight was still deemed unsafe for passenger planes). For around $400, for example, a traveler could purchase a ticket on the transcontinental "Lindbergh Line"—a two-day adventure that required passengers to ride from New York to Ohio aboard a sleeper train, then in the morning board a Ford Tri-Motor monoplane and fly to Oklahoma, then board another overnight train to New Mexico, and then the next day fly to Los Angeles. Dozens of small carriers flew thousands of passengers along shorter routes. Through a series of mergers and acquisitions, American Airways, Eastern Air Lines, United Airlines, and Transcontinental and Western Air (later Trans-World Airlines) dominated long-distance air travel by the end of the 1920s. A fifth, Pan-American, was the only American airline to win contracts for mail routes between the United States and Mexico, Central America, and the Caribbean. By 1930, Pan-Am served 20 countries and ranked as the largest commercial airline in the world.

Air travel in the 1920s was far from luxurious. Airplane engines and propellers were noisy and flights were often bumpy. Cabins were neither pressurized nor heated, so flying at high altitudes meant passengers endured freezing temperatures, and flying too high for too long caused many passengers to faint. Many suffered terrible airsickness, and while some opened the windows and stuck their heads out to vomit into the skies, others simply threw up in the cabin. In fact, the industry's first flight attendants, hired by Boeing Air Transport for its regular passenger routes in 1930, were trained nurses. Since airmail contracts—not passenger tickets—still generated the bulk of commercial airline companies' revenues in the late 1920s, airlines did not yet offer comfortable seats, decent meals, or other amenities.

Travel

Visual Arts

of the 1920s

By the 1920s, American visual arts, especially painting and sculpture, had entered the era of modernism, as evidenced by the 1929 opening of New York's Museum of Modern Art. Although many artists gravitated toward more traditional landscape, portrait, and still-life scenes, some artists created avant-garde works that attempted to capture the realities of the modern world.

MODERNIST MOVEMENTS

A number of European artistic movements in the early twentieth century influenced American modern art during the 1920s. Cubism, perhaps the most influential artistic movement in twentieth century art, began in France in the late 1900s and flourished throughout the 1910s and into the early 1920s. Cubist art emphasized shifting viewpoints, focused on geometric shapes (including cubes), and rendered three-dimensional objects in terms of flat, two-dimensional planes. The Dadaist movement also influenced American art of the 1920s. Rejecting conventional styles of representation, Dadaists sought new ways to express their ideas and shock their audiences. The Philadelphia-born artist and photographer Man Ray is the only American who played a significant role in the evolution of Dadaism, but other American artists absorbed some of Dadaism's unorthodox techniques and philosophies. Surrealism originated in the nihilistic ideas of the Dadaists, but also found inspiration in the psychoanalytic theories of Sigmund Freud and the political ideology of Karl Marx. Surrealist paintings were full of confusing, startling images and unexpected juxtapositions that seem, in some cases, to mirror an irrational, dreamlike reality or the workings of the unconscious mind. Surrealism flourished overseas, but Americans made few important contributions to this movement during the 1920s.

The most important introduction of European modernism to American audiences occurred in 1913, when the International Exhibition of Modern Art, better known as the Armory Show, was held at the 69th Regiment Armory in New York City. (See "Art of the 1910s.") Despite relentless ridicule by critics and near riots by art fans (particularly in Boston), the Armory Show reverberated in American art circles for decades. Modern art had arrived in America.

AMERICAN SCHOOLS OF ART

During the 1920s, many American artists experimented with techniques borrowed from the European modernists. However, new schools of distinctly American art emerged, several of which rejected the notion that Europeans had monopolized new methods of artistic expression. Rather, these American artists found in their native country the inspiration to create powerful and bold artistic styles.

The Ashcan School

Robert Henri, an innovative American painter of the 1920s who had studied art in Europe, founded one of the most important new schools of American art. Henri's New York art school placed him at the center of a group of urban realist painters who called themselves "the Eight." The group consisted of Henri, John Sloan, William J. Glackens, Everett Shinn, George Luks, Arthur B. Davies, Ernest Lawson, and Maurice Prendergast. These painters became known as members of the "Ashcan school," a disparaging term coined by critic Holger Cahill in 1934, because these artists rejected classical themes in

order to paint scenes of ordinary street life and working people.

Two prominent painters closely associated with the Ashcan school were George Bellows and Edward Hopper. Bellows, who studied under Robert Henri, is best remembered for his vivid paintings of boxing matches. In 1923, after boxing had been legalized in New York, the *New York Evening Journal* commissioned Bellows to paint the heavyweight championship bout between Jack Dempsey and Argentinean challenger Luis Firpo. Bellows's famous *Dempsey and Firpo* (1924) depicted the dramatic moment in the first round of their 1923 fight when Firpo knocked Dempsey out of the ring and onto a desk full of sportswriters (Dempsey returned to the ring and retained the heavyweight belt by knocking Firpo out in the second round). Edward Hopper, another of Robert Henri's students, launched his artistic career as an illustrator for magazines such

"Annual parade of the cable-trolley cripple club" by George Luks, a member of the Ashcan school of art. Prints & Photographs Division, Library of Congress.

as *Adventure* and *Scribner's*. His first one-man exhibition as a painter, in 1920, met with little acclaim, but by the mid-1920s, his reputation as an accomplished watercolorist had begun to grow. Hopper's *House by the Railroad* (1925), depicting a solitary house standing starkly alongside the railroad tracks, is considered an American classic, and it was the first painting acquired by the Museum of Modern Art.

American Scene Painting

American Scene painting, another form of American realism rooted in the tradition of the Ashcan school, was exceptionally popular with American audiences during the 1920s and 1930s. American Scene painters captured particular moments in the lives of ordinary Americans; their works often featured rural farm scenes, small-town festivities, or big-city streetscapes. For example, watercolorist Charles Burchfield portrayed commonplace scenes of provincial America in his paintings *House of Mystery* (1924), *Scrap Iron* (1929), and *Rainy Night* (1929–1930). Other important members of this school include Reginald March, Isabel Bishop, and Alexander Brook.

Precisionism

Precisionism, or Cubist Realism, was another American art movement that peaked during the 1920s. *Precisionism,* a term coined in the 1920s, describes a uniquely American painting style that emphasized sharply defined, geometric forms and flat planes. Precisionist painters composed highly structured, somewhat realistic scenes that typically depicted the skyscrapers, bridges, office buildings, and smokestacks of the modern city or the barns, farmhouses, and agricultural machinery of the rural landscape. Three of the most significant members of this school were Charles Sheeler and Georgia O'Keeffe. Sheeler, who also became a well-known photographer, was deeply influenced by the European art movements of Cubism and Dadaism. His Precisionist works of the 1920s, including *New York* (1920), *Offices* (1922), and *Upper Deck* (1929), capture the sharp geometry he saw in the modern metropolitan streetscape. An even more famous exponent of Precisionism was

Thin line drawing shows a jazz singing flapper accompanied by a trombone player on the left and a saxophone player on the right, 1927. Prints & Photographs Division, Library of Congress.

Georgia O'Keeffe, best remembered for her exquisite portraits of enormous flowers and southwestern landscapes. Her large, close-up paintings of flowers, including *Petunia No. 2* (1924) and *White Flower* (1929) emphasized the organic geometry of the blossoms. O'Keeffe also painted cityscapes during the 1920s, including *New York With Moon* (1925), *City Night* (1926), and *The Shelton With Sunspots* (1926). These paintings combined the flat planes and geometric shapes of Precisionism with abstract elements and photographic characteristics. O'Keeffe was well versed in the aesthetics of photography, no doubt due in part to her marriage to famous American photographer Alfred Stieglitz.

ART OF THE HARLEM RENAISSANCE

The Harlem Renaissance, or New Negro Movement, of the 1920s witnessed an outpouring of significant artistic works by African Americans, including sculptors Richard Barthé, Augusta Savage, and May Howard Jackson; photographers Richard S. Roberts and James Van Der Zee; and black painters and illustrators such as Archibald J. Motley Jr., Palmer Hayden, and William E. Braxton. However, the deeply ingrained racism of American culture prevented many of these talented artists from achieving the public recognition received by their white counterparts.

Some museums refused to exhibit the work of black artists, and some art schools declined to consider black applicants for scholarships. In 1923, sculptor Augusta Savage brought this discrimination against black artists to the attention of the American public when, after being rejected for a summer art school in France because of her race, she appealed to the press. Her story appeared in newspapers, and while she never did receive the scholarship, she did focus public scrutiny on the problem. Wealthy white philanthropist William Elmer Harmon tried to rectify this unfortunate situation by establishing the Harmon Foundation in 1922, which gave annual awards and cash prizes for African American achievement in seven categories: literature, fine arts, science, education, industry, religion, and music. In

A painting by Aaron Douglas, 1925. Prints & Photographs Division, Library of Congress.

1928, the Harmon Foundation began to sponsor all-black art exhibits that helped gain more widespread public exposure for the work of African American artists.

Perhaps the best-known African American painter of the Harlem Renaissance was Aaron Douglas. Douglas was a student of the German artist Winold Reiss, who painted African Americans not as crude stereotypes, but as dignified, unique individuals. Reiss encouraged Douglas to incorporate African imagery into his paintings, which he did with great success. His May 1927 cover for the Urban League's magazine *Opportunity,* for example, depicts the proud profile of a long-necked Mangbetu woman with an elaborate African hairstyle. Many of Douglas's works, including this one, feature angular, elongated figures, usually painted in silhouette and often accented by contrasting outlines and radiating circles and waves. Douglas illustrated celebrated novels by Countee Cullen, James Weldon Johnson, and Langston Hughes, and others. In 1928, Douglas became the first president of the Harlem Artists Guild, an organization that helped black artists secure federal funding from the Works Progress Administration during the Great Depression.

PHOTOGRAPHY

During the 1920s, photographs became more common in newspapers, magazines, and illustrated books than ever. However, photography was not generally considered an important art form. Few art museums collected or exhibited photographs, and photography was largely seen as either the pastime of hobbyists or merely an element of journalism and advertising. By the end of the 1920s, several important art museums had begun to include photographs in their displays, including the Metropolitan Museum of Art and the Museum of Modern Art, and the careers of such famous art photographers as Ansel Adams, Imogen Cunningham, Edward Steichen, and Man Ray had been launched.

Art photography constituted only a tiny aspect of the world of photography during the 1920s. Amateur photography was an exceptionally popular pastime during the decade. Around the turn of the century, technological advances helped to

Arts

democratize photography by making cameras much simpler, lighter, and more efficient, and making film developing easier and cheaper. From 1914 through the mid-1920s, Kodak promoted various models of its popular "Autographic Kodak" folding cameras, which allowed users to write on each negative a short sentence identifying the date, place, and subject of the photograph. Kodak advertising convinced consumers that chronicling the lives of their families, particularly their children, was an important endeavor, and sales of photography equipment escalated.

Photography enthusiasts often joined camera clubs, which had flourished since the 1890s. Members gathered to discuss the latest camera technologies and development techniques, though by the 1920s most casual photographers chose to have their film developed in labs rather than doing it themselves. Despite the popularity of amateur photography, professional studios also thrived. By the 1920s, most small towns counted at least one studio photographer among its Main Street businesses.

Photojournalism and Commercial Photography

Newspapers and magazines began to incorporate an increasing number of photographs into their pages during the 1920s, and photography was recognized as an important medium for documenting the political and social realities. The immensely popular tabloid newspapers, such as the *New York Daily News* and the *New York Evening Graphic,* filled their pages with photographs of everything from national celebrities to accused criminals to dramatic images of reenacted or fictional events (called "composographs"). Composographs were collages of photographs juxtaposed in such a way that they portrayed events never actually captured on film. Users of this technique often sacrificed realism for sensationalism. For example, when Rudolph Valentino died in 1926, the *Evening Graphic* published a composograph of the deceased film star meeting his fellow countryman, Italian opera star Enrico Caruso, in heaven. Often the front page of tabloids consisted of nothing but pictures and a single headline. Inside, more photographs—some

authentic, some fabricated—taught readers to rely on images to tell them a story. In 1928, the *New York Daily News* published an illicit photograph of the actual electrocution of Ruth Snyder, a Queens, New York, housewife convicted of murdering her husband. Disobeying the orders of prison officials, a newsman snapped the gruesome image with a hidden camera strapped to his ankle, and when published on the cover of the tabloid, the photograph ignited a storm of controversy. Nonetheless, that edition of the *Daily News* sold an extra half-million copies.[1]

Advertisers were slow to realize the potential of photographs. In 1925, only about six percent of national newspaper ads contained photographs, and advertisers still believed that the best way to attract consumers' attention was through the use of striking artwork and, when possible, bold colors. But by the end of the decade, photography had become increasingly prevalent in newspaper and magazine advertising. Advertising photographers used a variety of artistic techniques, including extreme camera angles, distorting lenses, and artificial backgrounds, to entice consumers into purchasing its product. The fashion industry also began to use photography to showcase the latest stylish outfits. And many commercial photographers experimented with retouching photographs or superimposing multiple photographs onto one another in order to create stunning visual effects.

SCULPTURE

Sculpture remained a rarefied art form that was accessible mostly to urban museumgoers. The general public was exposed, however, to a certain amount of outdoor sculpture, often in the form of large bronze statues of Confederate soldiers, famous generals, or presidents. Tourists in Washington, D.C., could visit the impressive Lincoln Memorial, which opened in 1922 and featured Daniel Chester French's sculpture of a seated President Lincoln. One innovative sculptor of the 1920s, however, set his sights on creating artistic sculpture of a scale never before attempted. Gutzon Borglum's work attracted national headlines as he labored to carve and blast mountains into art.

Arts

Borglum is best remembered for carving South Dakota's Mount Rushmore, but he also created numerous public monuments and outdoor statues, including a dramatic bronze figure of Union General Philip Sheridan on horseback (1924), and an enormous bronze casting of 42 life-size figures, horses, and cannons that memorialized American soldiers and sailors, titled *Wars of America* (1926).

In 1915, the United Daughters of the Confederacy invited Borglum to carve the head of Confederate General Robert E. Lee onto the granite face of Stone Mountain near Atlanta, Georgia. Borglum soon expanded the scope of this project to include the images of Confederate President Jefferson Davis and General Stonewall Jackson, as well as a long procession of Confederate soldiers on foot and on horseback. Stone carving on such a massive scale had never before been attempted, and Borglum had to invent several new techniques to turn the mountainside into art. Using a specially designed projector, he devised a way to project an image onto the side of the mountain so that it could then be outlined in paint. He also worked with engineers to develop techniques for dynamiting out pieces of rock without irreparably damaging the sculpture itself. Drilling began in June 1923, and, seven months later, Borglum unveiled the partially completed sculpture of Lee's head at a dramatic dedication ceremony. In the spring of 1924, however, a rift developed between the sculptor and the Stone Mountain Confederate Memorial Association, formed in 1923 to solicit financial support for the project. Borglum was fired from the unfinished project, and his vision of the enormous mountain sculpture was never fully realized (although, in 1970, the carvings of Lee, Jefferson Davis, and Stonewall Jackson were finally completed). Later in 1924, at the invitation of the South Dakota state historian, Borglum traveled to the Black Hills to begin planning his immense sculpture of four U.S. presidents on Mount Rushmore. Carving began in 1927, and although Borglum died in 1941, before he could put the finishing touches on his great sculpted portraits, he did live long enough to see the gigantic visages of George Washington, Thomas Jefferson, Abraham Lincoln, and Theodore Roosevelt emerge from the stone.

ENDNOTES FOR THE 1920s

OVERVIEW OF THE 1920s

1. Carl Abbott, *Urban America in the Modern Age: 1920 to the Present* (Arlington Heights, IL: Harlan Davidson, 1987), 17.
2. Roderick Nash, *The Nervous Generation: American Thought, 1917–1930* (Chicago: Rand McNally and Company, 1970), 145.
3. Eric Arnesen, *Black Protest and the Great Migration: A Brief History with Documents* (Boston: Bedford/ St. Martin's, 2003), 1.
4. Arthur F. Raper, *The Tragedy of Lynching* (New York: Dover Publications, 1970 [1933]), 25, 27, 481.
5. Robert Grant and Joseph Katz, *The Great Trials of the Twenties: The Watershed Decade in America's Courtrooms* (Rockville Centre, NY: Sarpedon, 1998), 142.
6. Edward Behr, *Prohibition: Thirteen Years That Changed America* (New York: Arcade Publishing, 1996), 87.
7. Robert A. Divine et al., *The American Story* (New York: Longman, 2002), 814.
8. Judith S. Baughman, ed., *American Decades: 1920–1929* (Detroit: Gale Research, 1996), 277.
9. Dorothy M. Brown, *Setting a Course: American Women in the 1920s* (Boston: Twayne Publishers, 1987), 62–63.
10. Winifred D. Wandersee, *Women's Work and Family Values, 1920–1940* (Cambridge, MA: Harvard University Press, 1981), 17.
11. J. Fred MacDonald, *Don't Touch That Dial* (Chicago: Nelson-Hall, 1979), 23.

ADVERTISING OF THE 1920s

1. Editors of Time-Life Books, *This Fabulous Century: Sixty Years of American Life: Volume III, 1920–1930* (New York: Time-Life Books, 1969), 99.
2. Daniel Pope, *The Making of Modern Advertising* (New York: Basic Books, 1983), 26.
3. Baughman, ed., *American Decades: 1920–1929*, 298.
4. Roland Marchand, *Advertising the American Dream: Making Way for Modernity, 1920–1940* (Berkeley: University of California Press, 1985), 81.
5. Marchand, *Advertising the American Dream*, 96–100.
6. Frank Presbrey, *The History and Development of Advertising* (New York: Greenwood Press, 1968 [1929]), 483.

ARCHITECTURE OF THE 1920s

1. Ann Douglas, *Terrible Honesty: Mongrel Manhattan in the 1920s* (New York: Farrar, Straus and Giroux, 1995), 436.

2. David A. Shannon, *Between the Wars: America, 1914–1941,* 2nd ed. (Boston: Houghton Mifflin, 1979), 111.

BOOKS, NEWSPAPERS, MAGAZINES, AND COMICS OF THE 1920s

1. Paul Sann, *Fads, Follies, and Delusions of the American People* (New York: Bonanza Books, 1967), 107.
2. Eric Arnesen, *Black Protest and the Great Migration,* 1.
3. Gilbert Osofsky, *Harlem: The Making of a Ghetto, Negro New York, 1890–1930,* 2nd ed. (New York: Harper and Row, 1971), 128.
4. U.S. Bureau of the Census, *Historical Statistics of the United States: Colonial Times to 1970, Part II* (Washington, DC: U.S. Bureau of the Census, 1975), 809.
5. Ian Gordon, *Comic Strips and Consumer Culture, 1890–1945* (Washington, DC: Smithsonian Institution Press, 1998), 86.

ENTERTAINMENT OF THE 1920s

1. Andre Millard, *America on Record: A History of Recorded Sound* (New York: Cambridge University Press, 1995), 154.
2. Mary Beth Norton et al., *A People and a Nation: A History of the United States,* 5th ed. (Boston: Houghton Mifflin, 1998), 709.
3. Thomas Streissguth, *The Roaring Twenties: An Eyewitness History* (New York: Facts on File, 2001), 126.
4. Geoffrey Perrett, *America in the Twenties: A History* (New York: Simon and Schuster, 1982), 231.
5. Harvey Green, *The Uncertainty of Everyday Life, 1915–1945* (New York: HarperCollins, 1992), 188.
6. Baughman, ed., *American Decades: 1920–1929,* 311.
7. Green, *The Uncertainty of Everyday Life,* 190.

FASHION OF THE 1920s

1. Alan Mirken, ed., *1927 Edition of the Sears, Roebuck Catalogue* (New York: Bounty Books, 1970 [1927]), 92–103, 220–221.
2. Lynn Dumenil, *The Modern Temper: American Culture and Society in the 1920s* (New York: Hill and Wang, 1995), 141.

FOOD OF THE 1920s

1. Richard S. Tedlow, *New and Improved: The Story of Mass Marketing in America* (New York: Basic Books, 1990), 314.
2. Hillel Schwartz, *Never Satisfied: A Cultural History of Diets, Fantasies, and Fat* (New York: Free Press, 1986), 182.
3. Harvey A. Levenstein, *Revolution at the Table: The Transformation of the American Diet* (New York: Oxford University Press, 1988), 185.

4. Ray Broekel, "The Land of the Candy Bar," *American Heritage* 37 (October/November 1986): 75.
5. Andrew Barr, *Drink: A Social History of America* (New York: Carroll and Graf, 1999), 238.
6. John J. Riley, *A History of the American Soft Drink Industry: Bottled Carbonated Beverages, 1807–1957* (Washington, DC: American Bottlers of Carbonated Beverages, 1958), 142.

MUSIC OF THE 1920s

1. Ian Whitcomb, *After the Ball: Pop Music from Rag to Rock* (New York: Simon and Schuster, 1973), 97; Russell Sanjek, *Pennies from Heaven: The American Popular Music Business in the Twentieth Century* (New York: Da Capo Press, 1996), 27.

SPORTS AND LEISURE OF THE 1920s

1. Gary B. Nash et al., *The American People: Creating a Nation and a Society,* 4th ed. (New York: Longman, 2003), 679.
2. Mary Beth Norton et al., *A People and a Nation: A History of the United States,* 5th ed. (Boston: Houghton Mifflin, 1998), 709.
3. Editors of Time-Life Books, *Our American Century: The Jazz Age, the 20s* (Alexandria, VA: Time-Life Books, 1998), 176; "Endurance Contests Sweep on in Cycles," *New York Times,* July 27, 1930.
4. Paul Sann, *Fads, Follies, and Delusions of the American People* (New York: Bonanza Books, 1967), 107.

TRAVEL OF THE 1920s

1. Automobile Manufacturers Association, *Automobiles of America* (Detroit: Wayne State University Press, 1968), 249, 250.
2. Nash et al., *The American People,* 681.
3. Nelson Lichtenstein et al., *Who Built America? Working People and the Nation's Economy, Politics, Culture, and Society,* Vol. 2 (New York: Worth, 2000), 200.
4. John B. Rae, *The American Automobile: A Brief History* (Chicago: University of Chicago Press, 1965), 105.
5. John Margolies, *Pump and Circumstance: The Glory Days of the Gas Station* (Boston: Bullfinch Press, 1993), 44.
6. Stephen W. Sears, *The American Heritage History of the Automobile in America* (New York: American Heritage, 1977), 229.
7. Greyhound Bus Web site. "Historical Timeline." http://www.greyhound.com/home/en/About/Historical Timeline.aspx (accessed August 13, 2008).
8. Margaret Walsh, *Making Connections: The Long-Distance Bus Industry in the USA* (Burlington, VT: Ashgate, 2000), 8.

9. John A. Jakle, Keith A. Sculle, and Jefferson S. Rogers, *The Motel in America* (Baltimore: Johns Hopkins University Press, 1996), 20.

10. John A. Jakle, *The Tourist: Travel in Twentieth-Century North America* (Lincoln: University of Nebraska Press, 1985), 71.

11. G. Freeman Allen, *Railways: Past, Present & Future* (New York: William Morrow and Company, 1982), 185.

12. Allen, *Railways: Past, Present & Future,* 22.

VISUAL ARTS OF THE 1920s

1. Barbara H. Solomon, ed., *Ain't We Got Fun? Essays, Lyrics, and Stories of the Twenties* (New York: New American Library, 1980), 128.

Resource Guide

PRINTED SOURCES

Abrams, Richard M. *The Burdens of Progress, 1900–1929*. Glenview, IL: Scott, Foresman, 1978.

Alexander, Charles C. *Our Game: An American Baseball History*. New York: Henry Holt, 1991.

Allen, Frederick Lewis. *Only Yesterday: An Informal History of the 1920s*. New York: Harper and Row, 1964 [1931].

Aron, Cindy S. *Working at Play: A History of Vacations in the United States*. New York: Oxford University Press, 1999.

Banta, Martha. *Imaging American Women: Ideas and Ideals in Cultural History*. New York: Columbia University Press, 1987.

Barron, Hal. *Mixed Harvest: The Second Great Transformation in the Rural North, 1870–1930*. Chapel Hill: University of North Carolina Press, 1997.

Benson, Susan Porter. *Counter Cultures: Saleswomen, Managers, and Customers in American Department Stores, 1890–1940*. Urbana: University of Illinois Press, 1986.

Berg, A. Scott. *Lindbergh*. New York: Putnam, 1998.

Betts, John R. *America's Sporting Heritage, 1850–1950*. Reading, MA: Addison-Wesley, 1974.

Blackford, Mansel G., and K. Austin Kerr. *Business Enterprise in American History*, 2nd ed. Boston: Houghton Mifflin, 1990.

Blaxter, Kenneth, and Noel Robertson. *From Dearth to Plenty: The Modern Revolution in Food Production*. New York: Cambridge University Press, 1995.

Brands, H. W. *T.R.: The Last Romantic*. New York: Basic, 1997.

Brinkley, Douglas. *Wheels for the World: Henry Ford, His Company, and a Century of Progress, 1903–2003*. New York: Viking, 2003.

Bronner, Simon J. *Grasping Things: Folk Material Culture and Mass Society in America*. Lexington: University Press of Kentucky, 1986.

Brown, Dorothy M. *Setting a Course: Women in the 1920s*. Boston: Twayne, 1987.

Byington, Margaret F. *Homestead: The Households of a Mill Town*. Pittsburgh: University of Pittsburgh Press, 1974.

Carroll, John M. *Red Grange and the Rise of Modern Football*. Urbana: University of Illinois Press, 1999.

Cashman, Sean Dennis. *America in the Age of the Titans: The Progressive Era and World War I*. New York: New York University Press, 1988.

Chafe, William H. *The Paradox of Change: American Women in the 20th Century.* New York: Oxford University Press, 1991.

Chambers, John Whiteclay II. *The Tyranny of Change: America in the Progressive Era, 1890–1920,* 2nd ed. New Brunswick, NJ: Rutgers University Press, 2000.

Chandler, Alfred Jr. *Giant Enterprise: Ford, General Motors, and the Automobile Industry.* New York: Harcourt, Brace and World, 1964.

Chernow, Ron. *Titan: The Life of John D. Rockefeller, Sr.* New York: Random House, 1998.

Clark, Clifford Edward Jr. *The American Family Home, 1800–1960.* Chapel Hill: University of North Carolina Press, 1986.

Cohen, Lizabeth. *Making a New Deal: Industrial Workers in Chicago, 1919–1939.* Cambridge: Cambridge University Press, 1990.

Conn, Peter. *The Divided Mind: Ideology and Imagination in America, 1898–1917.* New York: Cambridge University Press, 1983.

Cooper, John Milton Jr. *The Pivotal Decades: The United States, 1900–1920.* New York: W. W. Norton, 1990.

Cowan, Ruth Schwartz. *More Work for Mother: The Ironies of Household Technologies from the Open Hearth to the Microwave.* New York: Basic Books, 1983.

Cremin, Lawrence A. *American Education: The Metropolitan Experience, 1876–1980.* New York: Harper and Row, 1988.

Crichton, Judy. *America 1900: The Sweeping Story of a Pivotal Year in the Life of the Nation.* New York: Henry Holt, 1998.

Cunliffe, Marcus, ed. *American Literature Since 1900: The New History of Literature.* New York: Peter Bedrick Books, 1987.

Curtis, Susan. *Dancing to a Black Man's Tune: A Life of Scott Joplin.* Columbia, MO: University of Missouri Press, 1994.

Dubofsky, Melvyn. *The State and Labor in Modern America.* Chapel Hill: The University of North Carolina Press, 1994.

Dumenil, Lynn. *The Modern Temper: American Culture and Society in the 1920s.* New York: Hill and Wang, 1995.

DuSablon, Mary Anna. *America's Collectible Cookbooks: The History, the Politics, the Recipes.* Athens: Ohio University Press, 1994.

Dyreson, Mark. *Making the American Team: Sport, Culture, and the Olympic Experience.* Urbana: University of Illinois Press, 1998.

Ely, Melvin Patrick. *The Adventures of Amos 'n' Andy: A Social History of an American Phenomenon.* New York: Free Press, 1991.

Erenberg, Lewis. *Steppin' Out: New York Nightlife and the Transformation of American Culture, 1890–1930.* Chicago: University of Chicago Press, 1981.

Ewen, David. *All the Years of American Popular Music.* Englewood Cliffs, NJ: Prentice-Hall, 1977.

Fass, Paula. *The Damned and the Beautiful: American Youth in the 1920's.* New York: Oxford University Press, 1977.

Faulkner, Harold U. *The Quest for Social Justice, 1898–1914.* Chicago: Quadrangle, 1971.

Feuerlicht, Roberta Strauss. *Justice Crucified: The Story of Sacco and Vanzetti.* New York: McGraw-Hill, 1977.

Finch, Christopher. *The Art of Walt Disney: From Mickey Mouse to the Magic Kingdoms.* New York: Abrams, 1995.

Flink, James J. *The Car Culture.* Cambridge, MA: MIT Press, 1975.

Fox, Stephen. *The Mirror Makers: A History of American Advertising and Its Creators.* New York: William Morrow, 1984.

Fraser, James. *The American Billboard: 100 Years.* New York: Harry N. Abrams, 1991.

Gill, Brendan. *Many Masks: A Life of Frank Lloyd Wright.* New York: G. P. Putnam's Sons, 1987.

Gioia, Ted. *The History of Jazz.* New York: Oxford University Press, 1997.

Goldberg, David J. *Discontented America: The United States in the 1920s.* Baltimore: Johns Hopkins University Press, 1999.

Goodrum, Charles, and Helen Dalrymple. *Advertising in America: The First 200 Years.* New York: Harry N. Abrams, 1990.

Gordon, Ian. *Comic Strips and Consumer Culture, 1890–1945.* Washington, DC: Smithsonian Institution Press, 1998.

Goulart, Ron, ed. *The Encyclopedia of American Comics.* New York: Facts on File, 1990.

Green, Harvey. *The Uncertainty of Everyday Life, 1915–1945.* New York: HarperCollins, 1992.

Haining, Peter. *The Classic Era of American Pulp Magazines.* Chicago: Chicago Review Press, 2001.

Hall, Lee. *Common Threads: A Parade of American Clothing.* Boston: Bulfinch Press/Little Brown, 1992.

Hawes, Joseph M. *Children Between the Wars: American Childhood, 1920–1940.* New York: Twayne, 1997.

Hawley, Ellis W. *The Great War and the Search for Modern Order: A History of the American People and Their Institutions, 1917–1933.* New York: St. Martin's, 1979.

Hays, Samuel P. *The Response to Industrialism, 1885–1914.* Chicago: University of Chicago Press, 1961.

Heinrich, Thomas R. *Ships for the Seven Seas: Philadelphia Shipbuilding in the Age of Industrial Capitalism.* Baltimore: The Johns Hopkins University Press, 1997.

Hill, Daniel Delis. *Advertising to the American Woman, 1900–1990.* Columbus: Ohio State University Press, 2002.

Hiner, N. Ray, and Joseph M. Hawes, eds. *Growing Up in America: Children in Historical Perspective.* Urbana: University of Illinois Press, 1985.

Hofstadter, Richard. *The Age of Reform: From Bryan to F.D.R.* New York: Vintage, 1955.

Hogan, David Gerard. *Selling 'em by the Sack: White Castle and the Creation of American Food.* New York: New York University Press, 1997.

Hold, Hamilton, ed. *The Life Stories of Undistinguished Americans, as Told by Themselves.* New York: Routledge, 1990.

Hooker, Richard. *Food and Drink in America: A History.* New York: Bobbs-Merrill, 1981.

Hughes, Robert. *American Visions: The Epic History of Art in America.* New York: Knopf, 1997.

Isaacs, Neil D. *All the Moves: A History of College Basketball.* New York: Harper and Row, 1984.

Jackson, Kenneth T. *Crabgrass Frontier: The Suburbanization of the United States.* New York: Oxford University Press, 1985.

Jakle, John A. *The Tourist: Travel in Twentieth-Century North America.* Lincoln: University of Nebraska Press, 1985.

Kahn, Roger. *A Flame of Pure Fire: Jack Dempsey and the Roaring '20s.* New York: Harcourt Brace, 1999.

Kennedy, David M. *Over Here: The First World War and American Society.* New York: Oxford University Press, 1980.

Kenney, William Howland. *Recorded Music in American Life: The Phonograph and Popular Memory, 1890–1945.* New York: Oxford University Press, 1999.

Kessler-Harris, Alice. *Out to Work: A History of Wage-Earning Women in the United States.* New York: Oxford University Press, 1982.

Krasner, David. *A Beautiful Pageant: African American Theatre, Drama, and Performance in the Harlem Renaissance, 1910–1927.* New York: Palgrave Macmillan, 2002.

Leach William. *Land of Desire: Merchants, Power, and the Rise of the New American Culture.* New York: Pantheon Books, 1993.

——. *Fables of Abundance: A Cultural History of Advertising in America.* New York: Basic Books, 1995.

Lears, T. J. Jackson. *No Place of Grace: Antimodernism and the Transformation of American Culture, 1880–1920.* Chicago: The University of Chicago Press, 1981.

Levenstein, Harvey. *Paradox of Plenty: A Social History of Eating in Modern America*. New York: Oxford University Press, 1993.

Levine, David O. *The American College and the Culture of Aspiration, 1915–1940*. Ithaca, NY: Cornell University Press, 1986.

Livesay, Harold C. *Andrew Carnegie and the Rise of Big Business*. Boston: Little, Brown and Company, 1975.

Lutz, Tom. *American Nervousness, 1903: An Anecdotal History*. Ithaca, NY: Cornell University Press, 1991.

Lynd, Robert S. and Helen Merrell Lynd. *Middletown: A Study in American Culture*. New York: Harcourt Brace, 1929.

Lynes, Russell. *The Lively Audience: A Social History of the Visual and Performing Arts in America, 1890–1950*. New York: Harper and Row, 1985.

Macleod, David I. *The Age of the Child: Children in America, 1898–1920*. New York: Twayne, 1998.

Marchand, Roland. *Advertising the American Dream: Making Way for Modernity, 1920–1940*. Berkeley: University of California Press, 1985.

May, Lary. *Screening Out the Past: The Birth of Mass Culture and the Motion Picture Industry*. New York: Oxford University Press, 1980.

Meyer, Stephen, III. *The Five-Dollar Day: Labor, Management, and Social Control in the Ford Motor Company, 1908–1921*. Albany: State University of New York Press, 1981.

Montgomery, David. *The Fall of the House of Labor: The Workplace, the State, and American Labor Activism, 1865–1925*. New York: Cambridge University Press, 1987.

Mordden, Ethan. *The American Theater*. New York: Oxford University Press, 1981.

Mowry, George E. *The Era of Theodore Roosevelt and the Birth of Modern America, 1900–1912*. New York: Harper and Row, 1962.

Murdock, Catherine Gilbert. *Domesticating Drink: Women, Men, and Alcohol in America, 1870–1940*. Baltimore: Johns Hopkins University Press, 1998.

Ostrander, Gilam. *America in the First Machine Age, 1890–1940*. New York: Harper and Row, 1970.

Peiss, Kathy. *Cheap Amusements: Working Women and Leisure in Turn-of-the-Century New York*. Philadelphia: Temple University Press, 1986.

———. *Hope in a Jar: The Making of America's Beauty Culture*. New York: Henry Holt, 1998.

Perrett, Geoffrey. *America in the Twenties: A History*. New York: Simon and Schuster, 1982.

Porter, Glenn. *The Rise of Big Business, 1860–1920*, 2nd ed. Arlington Heights, IL: Harlan Davidson, 1992.

Radway, Janice A. *A Feeling for Books: The Book-of-the-Month Club, Literary Taste, and Middle-Class Desire*. Chapel Hill: University of North Carolina Press, 1997.

Riess, Steven. *Sport in Industrial America, 1850–1920*. Wheeling, IL: Harlan Davidson, 1995.

Roosevelt, Theodore. *The Essential Theodore Roosevelt*. Edited by John Gabriel Hunt. New York: Gramercy Books, 1994.

Schlereth, Thomas J. *Victorian America: Transformations in Everyday Life, 1876–1915*. New York: HarperCollins, 1991.

Schneider, Dorothy, and Carl J. Schneider. *American Women in the Progressive Era, 1900–1920*. New York: Facts on File, 1993.

Schwartz, Richard. *Berkeley 1900: Daily Life at the Turn of the Century*. Berkeley: RSB Books, 2000.

Shi, David E. *Facing Facts: Realism in American Thought and Culture, 1850–1920*. New York: Oxford University Press, 1995.

Sklar, Robert. *Movie-Made America: A Cultural History of American Movies*. New York: Vintage, 1975.

Southern, Eileen. *The Music of Black Americans: A History*, 3rd ed. New York: W. W. Norton, 1997.

Toll, Robert C. *On with the Show: The First Century of Show Business in America*. New York: Oxford University Press, 1976.

Wagenknecht, Edward. *American Profile: 1900–1909*. Amherst: University of Massachusetts Press, 1982.

Wainscott, Ronald H. *The Emergence of the Modern American Theater 1914–1929*. New Haven, CT: Yale University Press, 1997.

Watkins, T. H. *The Hungry Years: America in an Age of Crisis, 1929–1939*. New York: Henry Holt, 1999.

West, Elliott. *Growing Up in Twentieth-Century America: A History and Reference Guide*. Westport, CT: Greenwood Press, 1996.

Wiebe, Robert H. *The Search for Order, 1877–1920*. New York: Hill and Wang, 1967.

Wiseman, Carter. *Shaping a Nation: Twentieth-Century American Architecture and Its Makers*. New York: W. W. Norton, 1998.

Zinn, Howard. *A People's History of the United States, 1492–Present*. New York: Harper Perennial, 1995.

MUSEUMS, ORGANIZATIONS, SPECIAL COLLECTIONS, AND USEFUL WEB SITES

"F. Scott Fitzgerald Centenary." University of South Carolina Web site. Available at: http://www.sc.edu/fitzgerald.

Frank Lloyd Wright Preservation Trust. "About Frank Lloyd Wright." Frank Lloyd Wright Preservation Trust Web site. Available at: http://www.gowright.org/flw/flw.html.

Henry Ford. "The Life of Henry Ford." The Henry Ford (museum) Web site. Available at: http://www.hfmgv.org/exhibits/hf.

Library of Congress. "Progressive Era to New Era, 1900–1929." American Memory Web site. Available at: http://lcweb2.loc.gov/ammem/ndlpedu/features/timeline/progress/progress.html.

Masur, Louis P., et al. "The Twenties 1913–1929." A Biography of America Web site. Annenberg Media and WGBH Educational Foundation. Available at: http://www.learner.org/biographyofamerica/prog20/index.html.

National Gallery of Art. "American Impressionism and Realism: The Margaret and Raymond Horowitz Collection." National Gallery of Art Web site. Available at: http://www.nga.gov/exhibitions/horo_intro.htm.

National Portrait Gallery. "Theodore Roosevelt: Icon of the American Century." Exhibit. National Portrait Gallery Web site. Available at: http://www.npg.si.edu/exh/roosevelt/.

U.S. Census Bureau. "Population of the 100 Largest Cities and Other Urban Places in the United States: 1790–1990." U.S. Census Bureau Web site. Available at: http://www.census.gov/population/www/documentation/twps0027/twps0027.html.

U.S. Geological Survey. "The Great 1906 San Francisco Earthquake." USGS Web site. Available at: http://earthquake.usgs.gov/regional/nca/1906/18april/index.php.

Whitley, Peggy. "American Cultural History 1900–1909." Kingwood College Library Web site. Available at: http://kclibrary.nhmccd.edu/decade00.html.

———. "American Cultural History: The Twentieth Century 1910–1919. Kingwood College Library Web site. Available at: http://kclibrary.nhmccd.edu/decade10.html.

———. "American Cultural History 1920–1929." Kingwood College Library Web site. Available at: http://kclibrary.nhmccd.edu/decade20.html.

Woodrow Wilson Presidential Library. Available at: http://www.woodrowwilson.org.

VIDEOS/FILMS

American Experience: America 1900. PBS Home Video, 1998. DVD.

American Experience: Woodrow Wilson. PBS Home Video, 2002. DVD.

The Great San Francisco Earthquake. PBS Home Video, 1987. DVD.

Heaven and Earth: Lindbergh's Journey. ABC Video, 1999. Videocassette.

Jazz. Produced by Ken Burns, Lynn Novick. 10 Discs. PBS Home Video, 2000. DVD. (First three discs cover Beginnings through 1929.)

The Lost Generation. A&E Television Networks, 2001. Videocassette.

Spreading War: America Enters The War. CBS News. FoxVideo, 1994. Videocassette.

Theodore Roosevelt: Roughrider to Rushmore. A&E Home Video, 1995. Videocasette.

Index

About the Editor
and Contributors

SET EDITOR

Bob Batchelor teaches in the School of Mass Communications at the University of South Florida. A noted expert on American popular culture, Bob is the author of: *The 1900s* (Greenwood, 2002); coauthor of *Kotex, Kleenex, and Huggies: Kimberly-Clark and the Consumer Revolution in American Business* (2004); editor of *Basketball in America: From the Playgrounds to Jordan's Game and Beyond* (2005); editor of *Literary Cash: Unauthorized Writings Inspired by the Legendary Johnny Cash* (2006); and coauthor of *The 1980s* (Greenwood, 2007). He serves on the editorial board of *The Journal of Popular Culture.* Visit him on the Internet at his blog (pr-bridge.com) or homepage (www.bobbatchelor.com).

CONSULTING EDITOR

Ray B. Browne is a Distinguished University Professor in Popular Culture, Emeritus, at Bowling Green State University. He cofounded the Popular Culture Association (1970) and the American Culture Association (1975) and served as Secretary-Treasurer of both until 2002. In 1967 he began publishing the *Journal of Popular Culture,* and in 1975 the *Journal of American Culture.* He edited both until 2002. He has written or edited more than 70 books and written numerous articles on all fields in literature and popular culture. He currently serves as Book Review Editor of the *Journal of American Culture.*

CONTRIBUTORS

David Blanke, author of *The 1910s* (Greenwood, 2002), is currently Associate Professor of History at Texas A&M University, Corpus Christi. He is the author of *Hell on Wheels: The Promise and Peril of America's Car Culture, 1900–1940* (2007) and *Sowing the American Dream: How Consumer Culture Took Root in the Rural Midwest* (2000).

Kathleen Drowne, coauthor of *The 1920s* (Greenwood, 2004), is Assistant Professor of English at the University of Missouri, Rolla.

Patrick Huber, coauthor of *The 1920s* (Greenwood, 2004), is Assistant Professor of History at the University of Missouri, Rolla.

Marc Oxoby, PhD, teaches English and Humanities classes for the English Department at the University of Nevada, Reno. He has worked as a disc jockey and as the editor of the small-press literary journal *CRiME CLUb.* A regular contributor to the scholarly journal *Film and History* and *The Journal of Popular Culture,* he has also written for several other periodicals as well as for *The St. James Encyclopedia of Popular Culture, The International Dictionary of Films and Filmmakers,* and *New Paths to Raymond Carver.*

Edward J. Rielly, Professor of English at St. Joseph's College in Maine, has taught on Western film and the history of the west for many years. He is author of several nonfiction books, including *F. Scott Fitzgerald: A Biography* (Greenwood 2005) and *The 1960s* (Greenwood, 2003). He has also published 10 books of poetry.

Kelly Boyer Sagert is a freelance writer who has published biographical material with Gale, Scribner, Oxford, and Harvard University, focusing on athletes and historical figures. She is the author of *Joe Jackson: A Biography* (Greenwood, 2004), *The 1970s* (Greenwood, 2007), and the *Encyclopedia of Extreme Sports* (Greenwood, 2008).

Robert Sickels, author of *The 1940s* (Greenwood Press, 2004), is Assistant Professor at Whitman College, Walla Walla, Washington.

Scott F. Stoddart, coauthor of *The 1980s* (Greenwood, 2006), is the Dean of Academic Affairs at Manhattanville College, New York, where he currently teaches courses in cinema and musical theatre history.

Nancy K. Young, is a researcher and independent scholar. She retired in 2005 after 26 years of a career in management consulting. With her husband, William H. Young, she has cowritten three recent Greenwood titles, *The 1930s* (2002), *The 1950s* (2004), and *Music of the Great Depression* (2005).

William H. Young, author of *The 1930s* (Greenwood, 2002) and coauthor of *The 1950s* (Greenwood, 2004), is a freelance writer and independent scholar. He retired in 2000 after 36 years of teaching American Studies and popular culture at Lynchburg College in Lynchburg, Virginia. Young has published books and articles on various aspects of popular culture, including three Greenwood volumes cowritten with his wife, Nancy K. Young.

ADDITIONAL CONTRIBUTORS

Cindy Williams, independent scholar.

Mary Kay Linge, independent scholar.

Martha Whitt, independent scholar.

Micah L. Issitt, independent scholar.

Josef Benson, University of South Florida.

Ken Zachmann, independent scholar.